Repainting the Little Red Schoolhouse

REPAINTING THE LITTLE RED SCHOOLHOUSE

A HISTORY OF EASTERN GERMAN EDUCATION, 1945–1995

John Rodden

OXFORD
UNIVERSITY PRESS

2002

OXFORD

UNIVERSITY PRESS

Oxford   New York

Athens   Auckland   Bangkok   Bogotá   Buenos Aires   Cape Town
Chennai   Dar es Salaam   Delhi   Florence   Hong Kong   Istanbul   Karachi
Kolkata   Kuala Lumpur   Madrid   Melbourne   Mexico City   Mumbai   Nairobi
Paris   São Paulo   Shanghai   Singapore   Taipei   Tokyo   Toronto   Warsaw

and associated companies in
Berlin   Ibadan

Published by Oxford University Press, Inc.
198 Madison Avenue, New York, New York 10016

Oxford is a registered trademark of Oxford University Press, Inc.

Library of Congress Cataloging-in-Publication Data
Rodden, John.
    Repainting the little red schoolhouse : a history of Eastern
German education, 1945–1995 / John Rodden.
        p.   cm.
    Includes bibliographical references and index.
    ISBN 0-19-511244-X
    1. Education—Germany (East)—History.   2. Communism and
education—Germany (East)   3. Educational change—Germany.
I. Title.
LA772.R56   1999
370'.943'1—dc21   98-30620

9 8 7 6 5 4 3 2 1

Printed in the United States of America
on acid-free paper

For Beth,
a utopian friend,
whose loving support, tender care, and untold contributions
are woven throughout these pages.

The human being can only become human by education.
He is merely what education makes of him.

Immanuel Kant, *Education*

Acknowledgments

Before the fall of the Berlin Wall, few Americans had ever peeked inside the walls of an East German school. Almost all educational institutions were closed to western researchers, except when official approval came down from high-ranking functionaries at the Ministry of Education in East Berlin.

So my trips to eastern German schools, universities, and cultural institutes, which began shortly before reunification occurred in October 1990, often felt like wondrous voyages of discovery. I had read about East Germany for decades and had tried, unsuccessfully, to visit its schools on a previous trip to West Germany. But now the Wall was down, now the frontier was open. Now, in the dying days of the DDR, I could venture at will across the border into that unknown territory that most younger western Germans had never visited—and, as reunification neared, still had little desire to know.

I soon discovered, however, that my first task would be to confront and discard my own stereotypes, both romantic and sinister. An American eastener newly transplanted to Texas, I was much taken by the frontier imagery in the western German media's portrayal of "the wild East," as they called the formerly closed society of the DDR. My own spirited desire to do pioneering research on the frontier of the Cold War was made all the more challenging by the black-hat caricatures of the DDR still alive to my older relatives at home, for whom "East Germany" (crudely symbolized by the impenetrable "Wall") evoked the terrible totalitarian images of "Nazi Germany" and "Communist Germany" combined. Their vaguely uneasy remarks suggesting that my expedition was an ill-fated quest—a sort of "Heart of Darkness" journey destined to end in some kind of "Darkness at Noon" cum "High Noon" showdown—lent my enterprise a touch of the quixotic and utopian.

The actual experience of visiting eastern German schools and interviewing their students and staff proved both more temperate and less alien than my safari fantasies had conjured. Above all, my conversations demystified and humanized the Otherness of the DDR, attuning me to the familiar within the unfamiliar. As I acquired a personal anthropology of everyday eastern German life, I became sensitized not only to how communist and non-communist educational systems foster significantly different societies but also to how the near-universal experience of formal schooling in modern industrialized nations constitutes a common, cross-cultural heritage.

I have returned to eastern Germany for extended periods almost every year since my first trip in 1990. Especially in the early post-reunification years, many of my interviews with eastern Germans were marked by a collision between my stereotypes and their own. Many younger easterners confessed to me their love-hate relationship with "capitalist" America—an ambivalence partly attributable to the fact that they had never before conversed with an American. And many of my interviews were heavily colored by the complicated interaction between my left-liberal, anti-communist cartoon image of DDR society and the natives' powerful, occasionally resentment-laden nostalgia (or, as some commentators have called it, "Ostalgia") for their rapidly vanishing world, the land they voted in 1990 to dissolve, the nation once touted for decades by DDR state propagandists as *das bessere Deutschland*, "the better Germany."

The story of how this book came to be written is an unusual one. Although I have sought to maintain a personal tone throughout this study, I have deleted—with the exception of scattered, brief passages—all autobiographical commentary from the final draft, judging my anterior presence obtrusive to a chronicle of DDR education and its participants. But it seems appropriate in these acknowledgments to mention the book's autobiographical dimension.

Acts of fate and of faith brought this book to life. It was my fate to experience the positive aspects of the socialist ideal—an experience made possible by my German friends' faith in me. Somehow I was fated to encounter what socialism was meant to be (and what it sometimes truly *was* in certain "niches" in East German society), an experience of close fellowship and tight-knit community. And I was vouchsafed this experience through the faith and generosity of spirit shown to me again and again by ordinary eastern Germans.

I began this book a decade ago, after western German friends put me in touch with their eastern German friends and family—who soon became my own friends and extended family. The remarkable, soul-searching, indeed soul-wrenching conversations that I had with my new-found eastern friends—several of whom placed their faith and trust in me with disarming candor—inspired me to undertake this project.

For I never intended in 1990 to write a book about East German education and cultural life; I only wanted to meet other educators, my DDR counterparts—thereby to glimpse eastern life first-hand and see eastern schools from the inside before post-Wall reconstruction effaced all eastern differences with the West. And yet, suspecting that most Americans—like my relatives and like me—knew little more about "East Germany" than the Cold War cartoon, I felt impelled to share my experience of the new federal states with an American audience.

Originally I wrote only the "school portraits" that form Part II of this book. A friend convinced me, however, that these personal histories would come fully to life for an American audience only if I could contextualize them within the history of eastern German education. When thereupon I decided to "sketch the background" for the portraiture, I discovered that no history of eastern German education existed in English, which in turn motivated me to tell the "pre-history" of my subjects' stories in detail and from its beginnings, i.e., to write a comprehensive, albeit selective, history of eastern German education since 1945.

Repainting the Little Red Schoolhouse was written without the aid of any fellowships, foundations, or German university affiliations, but rather exclusively via personal contacts. I moved from household to household, visiting friends of friends and never spending even a single night in an eastern German hotel or rented room. I mention all this to stress that this book could not have been written without the extraordinary magnanimity of my German hosts. They opened their doors and their hearts to me. They fed and housed and even clothed me week after week, year after year. They phoned schools and queried potential interview subjects among their acquaintances and colleagues. Their emotional and financial support for their idiosyncratic American scholar gipsy was staggering in its constancy and beneficence.

And my debts to these friends and benefactors are, in turn, incalculable.

In western Germany, Ilse Kathinka Robaschik contacted eastern friends, adopted me as a house guest, fretted over my dietary oddities with grandmotherly solicitude, and made our regular Monday lunches ("John-Tag") into unforgettable weekly celebrations. Gisela and Hubert Stuchly became my Baucis and Philemon, gracing me with a divine hospitality that received no recompense except my gratitude, as they shared sumptuous vegetarian meals and their colorful life stories with me far into the night. Monika Bassler, Jan Reimers, Heike Schäfer, Holger Schröder, Birte Pampel, Tine Traute, Dorothee Pielow, and Karolin Wyneken represented the best of western German youth for me, teaching the professor far more in our long talks and walks than he taught them, as they introduced me to night hiking, to ballroom dancing, to botanical gardening, and to the wonders of the Black Forest. Rainer and Silvia Imhof, Dietmar Dinklage and Ingrid Koch-Heintzeler, Hildegard Schäfer, Irmgard Bassler, Heinrich von Trott, and Sigrun Hirt taught me the meaning of *Gemütlichkeit*, tutored me in matters of nuanced language and culture, and opened their hearts and homes to me. Three mentors and advisors who have passed away—Ludger Pielow, Thomas Robaschik, and Ignatz Bubis—guided my early steps in this project both by word and example. Rudi and Karin Walter, my editors at Verlag Herder in Freiburg, emboldened me to highlight the utopian journey as a theme in this study and thus to view my unsystematic, serendipitous "research agenda" as a fortuitous pilgrim's progress.

In eastern Germany, Wolfgang Strauss read the original manuscript scrupulously, offered invaluable suggestions, and has generously undertaken the painstaking task of translating it into German for Klett-Cotta Verlag. Bernard Hecker, Karl-Heinz Füssl, Helmut Rook, Monika Schubert, Gert Glaessner, Bernd-Reiner Fischer, Armin Mitter, and Ilko Kowalczuk also furnished encouragement and wise counsel, by either responding to portions of the manuscript or personally discussing my research. Helmut Findeisen corresponded with me and accepted my work on George Orwell and *1984* for publication in his Leipzig journal even before the fall of 1989, invited me to lecture on that topic to his university classes in 1990, and introduced me to numerous colleagues and students. Matthias Pietzonka and Stephan Schwarzkopf represented the cream of eastern German youth, as they lodged me, patiently answered my litanies of questions about their school-days and the DDR's youth organizations, and extended me small kindnesses too numerous to itemize. Christine Lösch and her family introduced me to Weimar, enlightened me about DDR cultural policy, and treated me with royal hospitality. Annaliese Saupe became my eastern Granny and adult-education schoolteacher, lecturing me with upraised forefinger about "vegetarian madness" and proudly instructing me in the history of every sacred kilometer of her beloved Plauen and the surrounding Vogtland.

In Berlin, Karin Hasselblatt, Ulrike Henderson, and Katrin Willmann invigorated me by their unflagging good will and warm regard both for my personal well-being and this book's progress; Birgit Wilke, Ludger Hohmann, Norbert Frye, and Anne Frohn drew upon their vast network of acquaintances and intimate knowledge of the metropolis to make my visits always edifying. For their patience and helpfulness I also thank the staff members at the following archives in Berlin: the Stiftung Archiv der Parteien und Massenorganisationen der DDR (SAPMO), the Deutsches Institut für Internationale Pädagogische Forschung, the Kinder- und Jugendbuchabteilung at the Staatsbibliothek zu Berlin-Preussischer Kulturbesitz, and the Deutsches Historisches Museum.

Friends and colleagues in the United States also helped me, either via correspondence or in conversation, by their kind words of support and knowledgeable observations about European history, German culture, and/or comparative education: Mitchell Ash, Mitch Baranowski, Raf and Jack Bemporad, Beate Blum, John Buettler, Paul Cantor, Erica Carson, Doug Clayton, Thomas Cushman, Pam Daniel, Peter Dougherty, Sonya Forster, Hope Harrison, Volker Kaiser, Eva Knodt, Rob Leventhal, Deanna Matthews, Nancy Maule McNally, Tim Pittman and Susanne Pongratz, Kerry Riley, Edward and Thomas Rodden, Jonathan Rose, Hans Schmitt, Bill and Kim Shanahan, Dieter Schwebs and Monica Schwebs-Schlissel, Margaret Surratt, Mary Triece, Claire Van Ens, and Greg Wegner. Eileen Ridge responded heroically to an SOS and created the index; Kathleen Jamieson intervened at a crucial moment to facilitate my procuring archival photographs from Germany. My sincere appreciation also goes to Oxford's superb editorial staff of Sheldon Meyer, Brandon Trissler, Thomas Le Bien, Susan Ferber, and Will Moore.

I wish to thank those who read the manuscript whole or in part and offered sage advice: Jim Aune, Kit Belgum, Randy Bytewerk, Paul Cantor, Sveta Davé Chakravarty, John Connelly, the late Sterling Fishman, Bruno Forster, Meredith Heiser, Joli Jensen, A. James McAdams, Laurence McFalls, George Panichas, David Pike, Diethelm Prowe, Gerhild Rogers, Christian Söe, and Denise Weeks.

My deepest appreciation goes to Cristen Carson, my *Kameradin*, who not only drew on her years in Germany and the former Soviet Union to provide me with perceptive criticism, but radiated a passionate equanimity and quiet dignity that re-centered me and provided an emotional anchor in my life. Likewise, I extend heartfelt thanks to Kathleen O'Connor, my old running companion and my constant friend, whose enthusiasm for German culture inspired my own; to Walter Sokel, whose exhilarating sense of intellectual adventure in his masterful courses in *Geistesgeschichte* first spurred me to explore German history; and to Paul Rodden, who was unswerving in his support for my unfolding vision for this project, helping me keep faith with it and with myself.

I am equally grateful to my parents, John and Rose Rodden, who accepted this book into their lives and understood its personal significance for me. That tacit affirmation, even more than their countless acts of concrete assistance, sustained me.

Finally, I owe a special debt of gratitude to Beth Macom, who nurtured this project from its infancy, serving as its sensitive midwife and devoted caregiver. I could not have written this book without her. She read every word of it, bestowing it with gifts of inspired creativity that fortified a slowly maturing manuscript through its manifold growing pains and identity crises. Ultimately she became not just an editor but a co-author.

For all these reasons and more, I dedicate this book to Beth.

Austin, Texas   J.G.R.
April 2001

Acknowledgments (?)

Contents

Photo gallery follows page 172

List of Abbreviations

I have sought to minimize use of acronyms in the main text of this book. Still, for purposes of illustration or economy, I have used the following abbreviations throughout the notes and in selected chapters.

German-language acronyms are translated on first citation in the text, but are included here for ease of reference.

ABF   *Arbeiter-und-Bauern-Fakultät*. Worker and Peasant Faculty. Pedagogical division of DDR higher education during early postwar era.

ARD   *Arbeitsgemeinschaft der öffentlichen Rundfunkanstalten der Bundesrepublik Deutschland*. The Joint Association of Public Broadcasting Corporations of the Federal Republic.

BBC   British Broadcasting Corporation.

BDM   *Bund Deutscher Mädchen*. German Girls' League during the Nazi years. The girls' counterpart to the HJ.

BRD   *Bundesrepublik Deutschland*. Federal Republic of Germany. The abbreviated form was used by communist-era officials to refer to West Germany, in order to place West Germany on an equal level with the DDR; avoided by West German officials for this same reason. While the abbreviation "BRD" was generally avoided in West Germany, however, the words were not; there were frequent official and unofficial references to the *Bundesrepublik* or the *Bundesrepublik Deutschland*. Since October 1990, the abbreviation has occasionally been used, both in eastern and western German media, to signify reunified Germany.

CDU   *Christlich-Demokratische Union*. Christian Democratic Union Party, or "Christian Democrats."

COMECON   Council for Mutual Economic Assistance. The mutual economic aid organization of the Communist world. See also RGW.

CPSU   Communist Party of the Soviet Union.

DDR   *Deutsche Demokratische Republik*. German Democratic Republic.

DEFA   *Deutsche Film-Aktiengesellschaft*. DDR state film company.

DKP   *Deutsche Kommunistische Partei*. German Communist Party of West Germany, which was founded in 1968 as a successor organization to the outlawed KPD. The DKP was able to operate legally because West

Germany had, by the late 1960s, become much more relaxed about communism in the post-Stalinist era of détente.

DM   *Deutschmark.* The (West) German mark, or "D-mark."

EC   European Community (formerly known as the EEC, European Economic Community).

EOS   *Erweiterte Oberschule.* The advanced high school of the DDR (11th and 12th grades).

FDJ   *Freie Deutsche Jugend.* Free German Youth. The DDR's mass youth organization for 14- to 25-year-olds.

GATT   General Agreement on Tariffs and Trade.

GST   *Gesellschaft für Sport und Technik.* Society for Sports and Technology. The main DDR athletic association, paramilitary in orientation.

HJ   *Hitler Jugend.* Hitler Youth, the NSDAP mass youth organization.

IM   *Inoffizieller Mitarbeiter.* Unofficial employee. A *Stasi* informant.

JP   *Junge Pioniere.* Young Pioneers, the DDR youth organization for 1st through 3rd grades. The acronym was not in use orally in the DDR, but is frequently found in official DDR publications.

KA   *kapitalistisches Ausland.* Capitalist foreign country.

KPD   *Kommunistische Partei Deutschlands.* Communist Party of Germany, founded in 1919. Refers to the pre–World War II party, which was also among the political parties licensed in occupied Germany in 1945 (including the western zones). The KPD was represented in West Germany's Bundestag between 1949 and 1953—and therefore in a few state parliaments (Bremen, Lower Saxony) before being declared illegal by the Constitutional Court in 1956.

KJVD   *Kommunistische Jugendverband Deutschlands.* Communist Youth League of Germany, a.k.a the Young Sparticists. Pre-war youth organization of the KPD.

LDPD   *Liberaldemokratische Partei Deutschlands.* The Liberal Democratic Party of Germany, a DDR "bloc" party. Founded in 1946 simply as the LPD; it added the extra D shortly after the DDR was founded in 1949.

LPG   *Ländlicher Produktionsgenossenschaft.* Agricultural cooperative.

M-L   *Marxismus-Leninismus.* Marxism-Leninism.

MfS   *Ministerium für Staatssicherheit.* Ministry of State Security of the DDR (also known as SSD and *"Stasi"*).

NATO   North Atlantic Treaty Organization.

NKVD   Ministry of State Security in the USSR, i.e., the Soviet secret police. Term used during Stalinist era. It was superseded by the term MVD in 1946.

NSDAP   *Nationalsozialistische Deutsche Arbeiterpartei.* National Socialist German Workers' Party. The National Socialists, or Nazis.

NVA   *Nationale Volksarmee.* National People's Army.

PDS   *Partei Demokratischen Sozialismus.* Party of Democratic Socialism. The reconstituted, successor party of the SED.

POS   *Polytechnische Oberschule.* The 10-year uniform, general education DDR school.

RGW   *Rat für gegenseitige Wirtschaftshilfe.* Council for Mutual Economic Aid, generally known as COMECON in English. The East bloc equivalent of the Common Market.

RIAS   *Rundfunk im amerikanischen Sektor.* U.S. radio station in West Berlin, administered by the State Department.

SBZ   *Sowjetische Besatzungszone.* Soviet Occupation Zone. The term was used in an adversarial manner by the Springer Press (and other anti-socialist West German media) long after the founding of the DDR in October 1949. (By the 1960s, however, it was more common in the West German press to characterize East Germany dismissively as "the DDR" or "die sogenannte DDR.")

SED   *Sozialistische Einheitspartei Deutschlands.* Socialist Unity Party of Germany. The Communist Party of the DDR. It was founded via a forced merger of the SPD and KPD in 1946, in the mistaken hope of many left-wing Germans in the SBZ that the new "unity party" would avoid the Left's pre-war mistake: the fateful "division of the working class."

SMAD   *Sowjetische Militäradministration in Deutschland.* Soviet Military Administration in Germany. The occupation-era government of the SBZ.

SPD   *Sozialdemokratische Partei Deutschlands.* Social Democratic Party of Germany, or "Social Democrats."

SSD   *Staatssicherheitsdienst.* State Security Service. The "*Stasi,*" or MfS.

TP   *Thälmann Pioniere.* Thälmann Pioneers, the DDR youth organization for 4th through 7th grades. Equivalent of Boy and Girl Scouts. The acronym was used only in West German publications, never in the DDR.

USSR   Union of Soviet Socialist Republics.

VEB   *Volkseigener Betrieb.* People's Own Enterprise.

ZDF   *Zweites Deutsches Fernsehen.* Second German Television (West Germany).

ZK   *Zentralkomitee.* The 170-member Central Committee of the SED.

Prologue

Unlessons, Far and Near

I

An American cartoon from the early postwar era shows a Moscow schoolboy slinking home from class, his shoulders drooping, his head bent. From behind the Party newspaper, whose front page features the usual headlines about Comrade Stalin's heroic exploits, the boy's father puffs stolidly on his pipe and asks:

"Well now! And what have we unlearned today?"

Half a century later, the joke has regained its relevance; ever since the collapse of several East European communist governments in the late 1980s and the breakup of the Soviet Union in 1991, parents in formerly communist nations have asked the question of their own children.

After the fall of the Berlin Wall in 1989, the question possessed a special urgency in the former East Germany—in no small part because its recurrence evoked previous cataclysms of commotion in eastern German schools. In fact, with adjustments to its newspaper headlines, the cartoon could have illustrated German education in the Third Reich or even during the Weimar Republic of the 1920s. Indeed, the practice of rewriting history à la George Orwell's *1984* is one of the few constants in modern German education. From the majesty to the disaster of Prussian monarchy, from the wisdom to the folly of Weimar republican democracy, from the glory to the horror of National Socialism, and from the greatness to the abomination of "Red" communism, German lessons are swiftly learned and "unlearned."

And now the curtain has risen on yet another era.

The following chapters tell the history of this spasmodic process, the more than half a century of successive waves of unlearning and relearning that have swept through eastern German classrooms since 1945. It is a complicated story of repeated attempts to reform an educational system, thereby to foster a new Fatherland. My particular interest lies in the consequences of this renewal process for the newest "New Germany," the region of the former East Germany or DDR (*Deutsche Demokratische Republik*, German Democratic Republic), rechristened after national reunification in October 1990 as "the new federal states" of the *Bundesrepublik* or BRD (Federal Republic of Germany). The "former" DDR, the "new" states: the names alone suggest the dimensions of the identity crisis in the post-reunification decade in eastern Germany, a traumatized land dubbed by one western German "a kind of halfway house for ideologically abused adults."[1]

To speak of the frenzied, headlong changes that have occurred in the eastern educational system as "reform" is to choose a prosaic characterization, but the breadth of the term suggestively embraces the range of controversy involved in the region's turbulent transition from communism to capitalism. Outraged, resigned, assertive, and confident voices have variously called the current transition a *Wessi* (western German) occupation-style reconstruction, a conservative restoration or even retrogression, a Teutonic regeneration, or a democratic renewal. Whatever their views, however, few *Ossi* (eastern German) families have been untouched by the most recent *Wende* (turn), especially as it has transformed the educational system, which mutated overnight from a centralized bureaucracy within a communist state into a federalized bureaucracy within a capitalist one.

Americans and others in the West have followed with interest the dramatic economic and political upheavals since 1989/90 in the former DDR: its severe unemployment, its deeply ingrained *Ausländerfeindlichkeit* (hostility toward foreigners), its serious neo-Nazi violence. But we have scarcely noticed the sea change in its educational system; indeed, no comprehensive English-language study of the history of the DDR educational system has ever appeared, either before or after the latest *Wende*.[2] Most Germans, however, consider educational reform one of the long-term issues facing eastern Germany, perhaps even a key both for coping with the region's social crises and for shaping the future of united Germany in the twenty-first century.

II

So once again, eastern Germany has undergone a round of re-education. Rapidly and inexorably, the little Red schoolhouse has been freshly repainted. Then again—depending on your perspective—perhaps it's been razed and completely rebuilt, this time incorporating all the structural flaws of western, "imperialist" social problems. Or maybe neither: Numerous eastern Germans victimized under the ancien régime claim that high Communist Party officials and *Stasi* (secret police) informers have managed to retain their responsible positions in the educational bureaucracy, hardly punished under Federal Republic law. Antagonized by what they consider a new politics of injustice, these vocal critics see Comrade Wessi as little better than Comrade Stalin; indeed it seems like the communist epoch all over again. Big Brother, *noch einmal:* Eastern schools haven't been repainted, let alone stripped for a new coat—just whitewashed.

So if eastern German schools are indeed helping to foster a new Fatherland, the unquiet doubts still resound: How new? And of what sort? A decade after the fall of the Wall, what clues from the past do we have about the future of the "New Germany"? Is reunified Germany the precursor of a Fourth Reich? Or a throwback to the last united German republic—the struggling, unstable, prewar state of the Weimar era? Or an affluent, powerful, and peaceful member of the European Union? Or something else entirely?

Many commentators look to the German past for the answers—and specifically to Germany's last encounter with "re-education." For talk of eastern German "educational reform" has often been euphemistic for "political re-education"—itself a deliberate euphemism for the Allied policy of denazification and democratization during the 1945–49 occupation. That program applied to peacetime conditions what Allied intelligence had otherwise called "psychological warfare." In a word: propaganda. For occupation authorities judged that the punitive measures dictated to the Germans after World War I, as defined by the 1918 Treaty of Versailles, had failed disastrously. In the three western zones, as well as in the Soviet zone in the east, the Allies decided to embark upon a different strategy this second time: to win German hearts and minds.[3]

The onset of the Cold War in 1947 cut short re-education programs in the western zones, which united to become the *Bundesrepublik* in May 1949. But anti-Nazi re-education in the schools of the Soviet zone was thoroughgoing—if also thoroughly pro-Soviet.

Whatever their view of events since 1989, easterners have agreed the similarities between Allied "re-education" of the 1940s and western "re-education" in the 1990s were uncanny. Eastern Germans witnessed more than educational "reform" or partial "de-communization"; they experienced political re-education in its classic form. Their hearts and minds—first and foremost through the schools but also through advertising, the media, and other institutions—were wooed to western democracy, capitalism, and consumerism. Throughout the 1990s, as well as a half-century ago, it was fitting to speak not just of *Umerziehung* (re-education) but what could be termed in Orwellian language *Un-erziehung* (un-education)—or more familiarly, *Verlernen* (unlearning).

Is "re-education" even possible? Or is it inevitably just propagandizing in a new direction—e.g., from Nazism to communism, from communism to capitalism? Eastern Germans have been unlearning socialism and communism. They have been unlearning the virtues of centralized planning and the vices of world capitalism, and learning the wonders of the marketplace and the joys of competitiveness. Among the "young revolutionaries" turned young consumers, socialist faith has proven just as obsolete as DDR products; today, it has become D-marks *über* Karl Marx.

"All history," wrote George Orwell in *1984*, "was a palimpsest, scraped clean and reinscribed exactly as often as was necessary." The rewriting of history: in Germany, it has been the Orwellian "mutability of the past" all over again. Like Winston Smith, "tutored" in Room 101 by the schoolmasterly re-educator O'Brien, another generation of eastern Germans has been, once again, unlearning—or re-learning?—that 2 + 2 = 5.

III

German history and *1984* share more than a casual relationship; indeed the association is bizarre and schizophrenic. In West Germany, Orwell stood for years as an English prose model for older *Gymnasium* pupils and as an intellectual hero for liberal writers such as Heinrich Boll and Günter Grass. But even as *1984* topped *Der Spiegel*'s best-seller list for almost two years running during 1982–84, Klaus Höpcke, DDR Deputy Culture Minister, was declaring in the Party's leading theoretical organ that *1984* addressed "the characteristic features of capitalist reality," "the multinational firms and their bloodhounds." Höpcke's reading of the novel—which had been banned with the rest of Orwell's oeuvre since the DDR's inception—put Party functionaries in the curious position, much like Winston Smith, of falsifying history even as they discussed a book about the falsification of history—indeed, as they discussed an officially banned book that DDR citizens could not admit they had read.[4]

Within a few years, however, the situation was almost reversed—ironically, not so much because of the passing of 1984 as of the arrival of 1989. Even as the toppling of neo-Stalinist regimes and the discrediting of totalitarian ideologies threatened to render Orwell's novel of the future an historical curio for western readers, the reading of Orwell—persona non grata throughout the existence of the DDR—became part of the much-discussed eastern German *Nachholbedarf* (need to catch up)—and easterners, especially students, began reading *1984* voraciously.[5]

Written in the wake of World War II and published in 1949, *1984* depicts a world of three totalitarian superpowers that have arisen in the aftermath of an atomic war, a scenario roughly corresponding to the western "free" world, the communist world, and the Third World (led by communist China). During the early postwar era, when the separate states of partitioned Germany came to embody the opposing ideological divisions between the capitalist West and communist East along with their opposing ideologies, Germany occupied the front line of the bipolar Cold War. Attacked in East Germany as anti-Stalinist propaganda, and promoted in West Germany as anti-Stalinist warning, *1984* came to represent for many Germans a horrifying prophecy not only of what the Reich might have been—but of what the DDR, as a Soviet satellite, had actually become.

It was in this context of what one historian has called the Germans' "fascination" with *1984* that I began to explore German history.[6] My encounter with Orwell's work a quarter-century ago had established my first visceral connection to postwar socialism, anti-totalitarianism, and European cultural politics.[7] Indeed, it was precisely the convergences between the worlds of *1984* and divided Germany, and most especially the Orwellian flavor of DDR life—with its Newspeak, its Party-line rectifications, its ideology of "All animals are equal, but some [Party] animals are more equal than others," and above all its mutable past belched from versificators and sucked down memory holes—that originally drew me to study Germany's cultural politics. I devoted the 1980s—*Orwells Jahrzehnt* (Orwell's decade), in Günter Grass's phrase—to writing a scholarly book on the checkered afterlife of the socialist Orwell, the most influential English-language anti-communist writer. One chapter in that book dealt with the postwar West German reception of *1984*—where Orwell is the best-selling English-language writer of the century. I also wrote a piece on *1984* as "prophecy and warning" for a Leipzig journal (courageously accepted, the editor proudly reminded me on our first meeting, even before the fall of the Wall).[8]

In the course of my research during the 1980s, I became electrified by my conversations with several middle-aged eastern Europeans and East Germans, who told me how they had procured copies of *1984* in the 1960s—in *samizdat*, since reading the novel was strictly illegal. Devouring the book overnight, they passed it on through the dissident underground—knowing they faced imprisonment if caught with it.[9] The East Germans described the eerie experience of already having known Orwell's catch phrases—e.g., *der Grosse Bruder, Zweidenken* and *Doppelzüngigkeit* (doublethink), *die Gedankenpolizei* (Thought Police), *Gedankenverbrechen* (thoughtcrime), *Neusprech* (Newspeak), *Krieg ist Friede, Freiheit bedeutet Sklaverei, Unwissenheit ist Stärke* (War is Peace, Freedom is Slavery, Ignorance is Strength)—through western as well as DDR news sources.[10] They recalled their astonishment that an Englishman who had never lived under a dictatorship could describe with such accuracy the regime of terror that they had experienced as young people in rebellion against the state. For them, *1984* crossed the line from dystopian fiction to living nightmare.

By 1990, it was no longer enough for me just to read about the DDR's Communist Party, the SED (*Sozialistische Einheitspartei*, Socialist Unity Party). I wanted to experience it—or at least its demise—firsthand. The Orwell connection led me to spend 20 months during 1990–95 in the "New Germany" and to visit eastern Germany's schools, universities, and cultural institutions. And to ask: What did East German students learn? What are they now unlearning? For some aspects of their *Umerziehung*, or *Un-erziehung*, strike me as special forms of doublethink, which entails "holding two contradictory beliefs in one's mind simultaneously, and accepting both of them." The Party hack—a.k.a. the "doubleplusgood duckspeaker"—knows in which direction the Party wishes his or her views to be altered, writes Orwell, and thus "knows he is playing tricks with reality." Yet, Orwell adds, "by exercise of doublethink he also satisfies himself that reality is not violated."

So I wanted to know: How Orwellian was—and is—eastern German life? How are eastern Germans confronting the waves of new revelations about their own Nazi and Stalinist collaborations? And is the ongoing political re-education of eastern Germans—into (among other transformations) good consumers—just another form of thought control?

Again and again in our interviews, my East German dissident acquaintances had given me a starting point for the answers: All of them affirmed that the communist campaign to win minds began on the "cultural front" with my own profession of teaching. The offensive commenced in the schools. Youth and education formed the two pillars of the DDR utopia. As the old SED slogans trumpeted:

WER DIE JUGEND HAT, HAT DIE ZUKUNFT!
[Who has the youth, has the future!]

MAN MUSS DIE MENSCHEN NUR GEBÜHREND SCHULEN—DANN WERDEN SIE SCHON RICHTIG LEBEN!
[You need only to school people properly—then they'll live right!]

Some of my East German acquaintances re-enacted, often with mock-serious voices and gestures, the ceaseless, ritualistic SED sloganeering; their descriptions of their own DDR school days—especially when leavened with vivid accounts of Nazi catchwords and youth activities—eerily evoked for me the climate of *1984*. Indeed SED Newspeak—or Ostspeak—was ubiquitous in the former DDR. The

Party had a slogan for everything, because so-called DIAMAT (dialectical materialism) claimed to be a comprehensive Marxist-Leninist *Weltanschauung* that explained everything—a claim promoted by the title of a standard book gift for youth of the 1950s, *Weltall, Erde, Mensch* (*Cosmos, Earth, Human Being*).

Indeed, for East German youth above all, SED Ostspeak became the public mother tongue. In school and through the national media, the SED droned and drummed and dinned Party duckspeak into schoolchildren and even preschoolers. Following Stalin, SED leaders built their collectivist chimera on an ideological campaign based on thought control: in education and of youth. "*Sturmt die Festung Wissenschaft!*" ran the old Party slogan. "Storm the citadel of learning!" Marshal Stalin himself had issued the marching orders, declaring educational institutions "the citadel of learning" that "we must capture at any price. This citadel must be taken by our youth, if they wish to take the place of the old guard."[11] The Soviets called the campaign *vospitanie* (moral-social development); the East Germans termed it *weltanschauliche Erziehung* (education for a world outlook). Whatever the name, the intent was the same: creating the new socialist *Mensch*. Ideology and character-building were the content, civic training was the method.

It was too late to convert most of the old-timers, the SED agreed. But certainly the youth could be persuaded of the validity and inevitability of communism, even if demonstration of its superiority entailed a dialectical sleight-of-hand, what Orwell in *The Road to Wigan Pier* called "that pea-and-thimble trick with those three mysterious entities, thesis, antithesis, synthesis." The Kremlin had long known how to play DIAMAT. "Marxism is omnipotent," Lenin proclaimed, "because it is true!" Stalin advanced the corollary: "Marxism is true, because it is omnipotent!" Countless SED leaders, quacking DIAMAT logic, affirmed both propositions, and bannered the triumphant conclusion in DDR schools for decades: "*Der Sozialismus siegt!*" "Socialism is winning!"

The children could be "persuaded." Stalin himself, lionized in SED meetings as "the world's greatest teacher and scholar," had promised: "Give me four years to teach the children, and the seed I have planted will never be uprooted!" Comrade Josef Vissarionovich, of course, was himself extirpated from Soviet and DDR life soon after Khrushchev denounced his big brotherly "cult of personality" at the Twentieth Congress of the Communist Party of the USSR in 1956. But Stalin's seed found fertile soil in the progeny of Party pedagogues. Through school and youth programs, post-Stalinist DDR and Soviet bureaucrats tirelessly propagandized—or re-educated—the young. For to remake humanity, to form the "new socialist human being," demanded seizure of the "citadel of learning."

IV

There are two citadels to be captured, however, just as there are two sorts of eastern German un-learning. The first fortress is the citadel of the knowable and ascertainable. Its seizure entails the unlearning of facts and dates, of sacrosanct dogmas and doctrines, the knowledge of what was and what is. This is unlearning as faith-stealing. Reality becomes an ideological shell game whereby State propagandists replace one citadel with another, so that only a spectral citadel remains:

the Ministry of Truth. Now the command economy of the mind prevails: You unlearn and relearn to hold two contradictory ideas in mind at once. And believe both—on command. Classic Orwellian doublethink: 2 + 2 = 5.

IGNORANCE IS STRENGTH!

But there is also unlearning to dream, to wonder about what yet might be. This second fortress of the self is the citadel of the imaginable. You unlearn to hope, to aspire to a different and radically better future. You undergo the de-illusioning that spirals downward into disillusion—and ultimately into cynicism or nihilism.

How Orwellian was—and is—eastern German life? The Orwellian dimension of eastern German life since 1989 has consisted not just in the incessant, relentless, systematic unlearning of Party lies and the "rectification" of historical falsehoods, but in dream killing, in the unlearning of utopian possibilities. As one elderly woman in Weimar, daughter of an SS soldier and herself an SED member, cried to me at the close of a six-hour conversation in 1990:

"Now? Now I believe in nothing! Nothing and nobody! Except my family. Church, state, Party, nation—they've no meaning for me. . . . They [the Nazis and SED] robbed me of my innocence, cheated me of my youth, duped me of my ideals."[12]

We in capitalist America have never had to unlearn our ideals, the ideals of liberal democracy, in so radical a fashion. So we sometimes forget that, for hundreds of millions of people, communism once was—and, for many millions still remains—a dream of justice and equality. "A spectre is haunting Europe—the spectre of Communism," wrote Marx and Engels in *The Communist Manifesto*, and for postwar Americans that apparition became the totalitarian terror of *1984*. "Better dead than Red," we told ourselves through wave after wave of the "Red Scare." Witness the terms "Iron Curtain," "the Wall," "the Evil Empire": decade after decade, "communism" has meant to us the abolition of freedoms, confiscation of property, overthrow of governments, and revolutionary violence. We often fail to appreciate that, for the citizens of many countries, "communism" has long signified a utopian dream, not a hellish nightmare:

> . . . [I]t was a dream that gave it birth
> Not a dream that will dissolve in mist by day
> But one that was also Lenin's:
> "Thunder! Strike! But also dream!"
>
> Our songs are quaked from anger
> From beautiful words, careful tones . . .
> We have lived every syllable
> Every note is written with blood. . . . [13]

Today, most younger eastern Germans have learned to "think like westerners," especially Americans, and to equate Leninist dreams with Orwellian nightmares. Several older generations of eastern Germans—and their counterparts throughout the European continent—share the existential despair of my acquaintance from Weimar, a melancholy not limited to a handful of disaffected intellectuals, but rather a mass phenomenon.

This mass experience, especially as it relates to the imagined world of *1984*, is a theme of a university course I once regularly taught in the history of utopian thinking. Titled "The Quest for Community," it traces a dream—or chimera?— whose pursuit has cast a long shadow across the twentieth century. Now, as did their parents a half-century ago in the wake of the collapsed Nazi "utopia," a new generation of Germans is mercilessly unlearning to dream about the best of all possible worlds, and even to trust in ideals at all.

In 1991, I lectured at Leipzig University on Orwell and *1984*. The parallels between *1984* and the police states of Nazi Germany and Stalinist Russia are obvious and well-known, and I myself had already written about them. But in a post-lecture discussion, I listened as Leipzig students—not all of whom had read *1984*—immediately drew detailed analogies between Orwell's Oceania and the DDR. "Big Brother's little twin!" one student called the former DDR. Indeed the DDR and *1984* entered the world together in 1949, another noted; several remarked, contemptuously, that the closest approximation to stultifying Oceania in Eastern Europe turned out to be their own tiny land located on the Elbe. Warming to their task, they elaborated: the Party in *1984* was the SED; the Thought Police was the *Stasi*; Goldstein and his Brotherhood were the DDR dissidents; the child Spies (*Späher*, "scouts") were the JP (*Junge Pioniere*, Young Pioneers) and FDJ (*Freie Deutsche Jugend*, Free German Youth); and Newspeak was the Party mumbo-jumbo (*Parteirotwelsch*) at SED meetings. Even Orwell's Two-Minute Hates and Hate Week had their analogues in Party slogans, youth rallies, and school programs. "*Tragt den Hass in jedes Herz!*" ("Carry Hatred in Your Heart!") ran one slogan, which could often be heard during the DDR's mandatory "anti-fascist" "defense education" sessions, including school rifle practice and military drills for 15-year-olds. And on and on and on.[14]

As in 1945, so too in the 1990s in eastern Germany: the promise of collectivist utopia gave way to the fear of Orwellian anti-utopia. Ideals can be perverted, idealists can go too far. Idealism is the utopiate of the apparatchik. The Stalinist reaction to the horrific Nazi utopia led to a communist police state itself not so different from the empire of Oceania in *1984*. And the lessons of anti-utopian thinking have penetrated deeply into eastern German minds. Today, capitalism seems to be teaching *Ossis*, however belatedly, that you must reject utopianism in toto as dangerous and deluded idealism. You must face the hard limits of what human nature and the here-and-now make possible. You must make the best of the actual choices presented by reality, rather than pursue a communitarian dream.

V

The unlearning proceeds apace. Not that most DDR adults had grand illusions, at least by the late 1980s, about the virtues of the much-heralded *Erste Deutsche Arbeiter-und-Bauernstaat* (First German Workers' and Peasants' State). But many of the children did—and so did some of the educators themselves, who created and distributed the propaganda in which they partly believed. Moreover, as one Party functionary in Leipzig told me, even the skeptics had believed more than they had thought they had: "Sure, I knew that not much work got done. And I knew the estimates of DDR emigration. But I had no idea that the Party was so corrupt, and that the system was so moribund and decrepit. I had only a vague idea of the yawning gap between the propaganda and the truth."

No generation of Germans in this century has possessed more opportunities than the present one of the new millennium: no war from which to recover, no dictatorship to endure, no hyper-inflation. Yet many eastern Germans have felt less like proud victors in a peaceful revolution—free at last to rejoin their long-lost family members in the West—than gullible victims and war-weary losers faced with occupation by a smug, alien power. For many eastern Germans have felt deprived of everything they knew. Now, it is *all* untrue; now they're radical skeptics or revolutionary nihilists. As one teenage FDJ member in Berlin, in his final year of high school, told me in 1990: "Everything we learned was a lie! And now— now?!—we're going to get the TRUTH?! C'mon! Gimme a break!"

"*Die Partei, die Partei! Die hat immer recht!*" went the old song: "The Party, the Party! It's always right!"

> It gave us everything
> Sun and wind
> And was never miserly.
> And what it was
> Was Life
> And what we are
> We are through it.
>
> It never abandoned us.
> When the world almost froze over
> We stayed warm.
> This Mother of the Masses
> Fed us and cradled us
> In her mighty arm.
>
> The Party, the Party,
> It's always right!

When "it"—Life itself—no longer *is*, what then? When the Mother of the Masses ups and leaves? When the world does in fact freeze over?

What happens when it comes to this? The notion that you can know *anything* is undermined, that you can trust in *anything* is subverted, that you can believe in or hope for *anything* is crushed. At that moment of shattering revelation, Orwellian unpersonhood and Nietzschean nihilism pass into Kafkaesque despair.

Until something or someone comes along to fill the vacuum. Then $2 + 2 = 5$, if Big Brother says so.

VI

A battle of re-education versus reaction has been scourging eastern Germans' souls. This book tells part of the story of their struggle, portraying chiefly an educational system that was and is no more, giving an account of the rise and fall of DDR education. These chapters do not present the complete story; rather, they depict some crucial scenes and dramatis personae. The focus throughout is not merely on education in the narrow sense—not exclusively on schools and universities—but also on re-education, i.e., on *weltanschauliche Erziehung* as the re-formation of national identity, as the historical-cultural process of a people repeatedly re-conceiving themselves. Perhaps a better term is that far-reaching German concept *Bildung* (education, culture, self-development)—by which I also mean to include the extracurricular educational/cultural institutions and the general ideological climate in which DDR youth were "bred" to be "young revolutionaries." Accordingly, the book discusses "education" variously as schooling, acculturation, and agitprop. Among my key concerns are the relationships between DDR youth culture and western popular culture, especially the roles of music, sport, national heroes, and the Party youth organizations in DDR *Bildung*. Indeed, I could have alternately subtitled this book: "A History of Eastern German Education and Re-Education." That seemed to me a bit unwieldy, but the added phrase underscores that a history of eastern German education is necessarily also a history of eastern German re-education.

Mine is admittedly an eastern Germany seen through American eyes, indeed through American academic eyes. And so these pages also mirror back, however intermittently, an American academy refracted through eastern German eyes. I went to the eastern German schools to grasp more fully how ordinary people participate in epoch-making History, how it bears on and unfolds in their lives, how they assimilate and incorporate it into their self-images. I traveled there to comprehend more clearly how a people copes with a failed revolutionary dream—indeed, with two dashed dreams: socialism and fascism both. And I emerged with dual insight: first, and primarily, into that uniquely eastern German burden. But secondly, and unexpectedly, my intimate encounter with the extreme example of an educational system run on ideology has sensitized me to the subtler case of its American counterpart. My extensive contact with eastern Germany has vouchsafed me a more concrete and nuanced understanding of my own immediate world—of the ideological character of American schooling, of the dangers of excessively politicizing the American academy, and of the tradeoffs between excellence and equality—or between elitism and egalitarianism—inherent in the American educational experiment.

The present work is not, therefore, the straightforward, full-scale institutional history of DDR education that it might have been, but rather an unconventional and occasionally idiosyncratic study in comparative education and in the social psychology of re-education. I found that I could make sense of the communist experience generally and the DDR educational and cultural apparatus in particular only by acknowledging my own—quite unscholarly—urge to share my personal meeting of East and West. And so these pages testify also to a profound personal education—and to my own unlessons. From a process of back-and-forth movement between two radically different educational systems, I unlearned lessons about utopianism, the state, and education: lessons not easily relinquished, lessons that I could not have unlearned in any other way.

And to unlearn can be more than a loss; it can also be to learn something invaluable.

Repainting the Little Red Schoolhouse

"Who Has the Youth, Has the Future"

All fixed, fast-frozen relations, with their train of ancient and venerable prejudices and opinions, are swept away. . . . All that is solid melts into air, all that is holy is profaned, and men at last are forced to face . . . the real conditions of their lives and their relations with their fellow men.

Marx and Engels, *The Communist Manifesto* (1848)

"Like the school, like the state" goes an ideological proverb. "Like the state, like the school." This would be the genuine translation and transposition in the sense of Realpolitik. The school is the mightiest instrument for liberation, and the school is the mightiest instrument for enslavement, depending on the nature and the purpose of the state. In the free state, it is a means for liberation; in the unfree state, the school is a means of enslavement. *Bildung macht frei*—education makes you free. To expect the unfree state to educate its people would be equivalent to expecting it to commit suicide.

Wilhelm Liebknecht, "Wissen ist Macht, Macht ist Wissen" ("Knowledge Is Power, Power Is Knowledge") (1872)

If you shut up the truth and bury it under ground, it will but grow, and gather to itself such explosive power that, on the day it bursts through, it will blow up everything in its way.

Zola, *J'Accuse!* (1898)

The Banana Revolution?

Experiencing everyday life in another culture places your own in stark relief. Assumptions stand revealed, often by utterly minor objects and events.

Consider, for instance, bananas. Bananas? We Americans take them for granted, we even trivialize them—playing second banana, being driven bananas, going bananas, and on and on.

But not so in Germany. To Germans, bananas are not such a light-hearted matter. As one well-known Cologne artist who has stenciled his Andy Warhol–style, Day-Glo bananas on the outer walls of hundreds of art galleries has proclaimed: "Bananas are almost a holy object in Germany."[1] Banana-crazed Germans, joked *Der Stern* in 1992, are "the apes of the EC."[2]

3

These exaggerations warrant our attention. For bananas are an impossibly over-determined symbol in Germany, signifying justice, national self-determination, cultural pride, deprivation, prosperity, communist tyranny, capitalist luxury, unity, and economic and even sexual freedom. The banana occupies a special place in Germany's national psyche and in the history of German re-education, given its role in both early postwar reconstruction and recent reunification. Let us therefore examine that role at some length here, for it turns out that "banana politics" bears revealingly, if unexpectedly and often amusingly, on the issues of German identity and German re-education—and reflects Teutonic tensions both within and outside reunited Germany.[3]

Ever since hunger overtook war-torn, occupied Germany in the mid-1940s, when even basic foodstuffs were unobtainable, bananas have symbolized Plenty to both western and eastern Germans—the plenty western Germans eventually obtained, the plenty eastern Germans always lacked.

In West Germany, the early postwar generation endured rationing and shortages until mid-century. As children, many of them knew of bananas only through the reminiscences of their elders. For them the fruit still evokes childhood memories of humiliation, dispossession, and hunger.

All this began to change in West Germany with the *Wirtschaftswunder* (economic miracle) of the 1950s. West German parents delightedly weaned their infants on "Banana Salad" baby food, the leading seller of Hipp, the Gerber's of West Germany. Older western Germans still recall with pride the dramatic speech of Chancellor Konrad Adenauer in July 1957, when he brandished a banana at the Bundestag podium, hailing the fruit as "paradisiacal manna": "It represents the hope of many of us and a necessity for us all!" Adenauer had just returned in triumph from a four-day filibuster in Rome, having finally gotten "Protocol Number 10"—which guaranteed West Germans tariff-free bananas in unlimited quantities—written into the founding Treaty of the European Economic Community (EEC).[4]

Until the mid-1990s, the single major policy issue concerning tariffs in the (renamed) European Community (EC) involved reunified Germany's obsession with bananas.[5] (The EC was renamed the European Union [EU] in November 1993.) Germans, who consume twice as many bananas as do citizens of any other EU nation, insisted on continuance of the special duty-free treatment for German banana imports, consistent with the 1957 EEC protocol and contrary to the general guidelines of the 1992 Treaty of Maastrich. Germans favor the longer Latin American "Dollar" bananas; when the EC voted in February 1993 to impose quotas and a high tariff on non-EC bananas, outraged Germans protested. Stickers in car windshields and shop windows in Gothic script urged patriotic Germans: *"Esst deutsche Bananen!"* ("Eat German bananas!"). "I have never seen the chancellor with a banana, but he has always been angry about this issue," said Helmut Kohl's press spokesman.[6] "Why should Germans enthuse about the EC, when we see what the Community is doing to our bananas?" objected a disgruntled German EC representative.[7]

The "EC banana split," as journalists quickly tagged the controversy, exposed the sharp political tensions underlying the move toward a single, borderless European market. German trade officials attacked France and Spain, whose banana-growing former island colonies were the chief beneficiary of the new ruling, and warned that the new tariff would not only double banana prices and reduce German banana imports by more than 50 percent, but also cause "low-income Germans to lose a particularly important source of nourishment."[8] *Bild* reported that tennis star Boris Becker faithfully ate two bananas per day, and stressed the preventive medicinal powers of bananas (given their magnesium and Vitamin B6) against everything from heart attacks to mild immunology deficiencies. The German Interior Ministry predicted that the EC measure would ultimately cause a flood of cheap cocaine into Europe, because Latin American banana farmers would switch to growing coca to survive. As the new regulations took effect in July 1993, the German Association of Fruit Companies appealed the ruling to the European Court of Justice in Luxembourg—and lost.[9]

For eastern Germans, the timing of the ruling from Brussels came at a particularly cruel moment. Denied bananas and other tropical fruits throughout 40 years of communism, easterners were, by 1992, consuming nearly twice as many bananas per year as westerners (27 to 14 kg)—more than a banana per person per day. After the war, bananas had been simply absent from East German life. "Capitalist" bananas came to be regarded as a western delicacy; only at Christmas time (a holiday never officially recognized in the atheistic DDR) were they available, as a special treat, courtesy of the SED and Party chief Erich Honecker. For DDR citizens, that absence came to symbolize communism's failure to provide simple pleasures taken for granted in the West.[10] Even through the 1980s, bananas were virtually unavailable to ordinary DDR citizens. Indeed, before the Wall fell, bananas were a coveted house gift when West Germans visited their East German relatives. East Germans would devour the western manna in private; even in 1988, children who brought bananas to school would be harassed or beaten up by their classmates.[11] When the Wall crumbled, the banana became an unofficial emblem of German unity in the east. Jubilant East Germans sported bumper stickers featuring two bananas forming the letter "D" (for *Deutschland*), or hung Dollar Bananas on the windshields of their little two-cylinder Trabant cars, under the words: "German Banana Republic, R.I.P." It all seemed a sign of better days to come. Even amid their post-reunification disappointments and anger of the early 1990s most eastern Germans considered the advent of cheap bananas as one of the few aspects of daily life that had indisputably changed for the better since that fateful final November of 1989.[12]

Imprinted in my memory are a few ironic scenes from life in eastern Germany, from the days and months immediately following November 9, 1989, marking the passage from old to new.

November 11. A TV shot near Checkpoint Charlie. A young East German schoolboy has clambered up on the Wall. Like an Old World conquistador, he gazes with pride and wonder at the New World spread before him. Suddenly a West German well-wisher tosses him a banana. The boy catches it and caresses it, enthralled and puzzled. He glances from banana to benefactor and back again, then grins bashfully as he raises the banana self-consciously to his lips. The West German laughs good-naturedly; gesturing demonstratively, he calls to the boy: *"Du musst sie erst schälen!"* "You have to peel it first!"

March 1990. A Leipzig newspaper reports that West German politicians visiting the soon-to-be defunct DDR to lend support to the election campaigns of East German politicians are attracting crowds by handing out bananas—free of charge— but only to those of voting age. An unaccompanied child was told that he could have a banana only if his parents were present. Most of the West German politicians were from the CDU (*Christlich-Demokratische Union*, Christian Democratic Union), whose DDR counterpart captured almost 50 percent of the vote in a multiparty election. A dejected leader of the New Forum party, whose members had formed the most prominent opposition group in autumn 1989 and had mobilized thousands of protesters—yet received only 2.8 percent in the March election— declares: "The mass of people voted for the banana—not for the ideas and the struggle and the contribution we made." East Germany's U.S. ambassador angrily attacks Chancellor Kohl for interfering in the DDR elections, attributing the CDU victory to "two months of banana policy."[13]

July 1990. An East German newspaper illustration portrays a young man's outstretched arm, muscles rippling, raised skyward: the athletic champion's familiar gesture of sweet victory. Clasping itself firmly, the hand forms a tight fist around the hard-won trophy: a large yellow banana. A relaxed moment, when proud East Germans, now possessing D-marks as a result of the recent currency reunion, can gently poke fun at themselves. Hints of the new East German Olympian as World-Class Consumer. But the unintended allusion also resonates: Imperialist too? In the background of the illustration unfurls a map of eastern Europe. Through its center runs the blazoned words, á la Marie Antoinette: *"Dann sollen sie Bananen essen"* ("Let them eat bananas!").

Now, more than a decade later, it is clear that the golden fruit of autumn 1989 has ripened—and spoiled. And, finally, rotted and decomposed.

Yes, the extravagant dreams of effortless family unity and eager sharing of the fruits of prosperity proved short-lived.

"Es wird keinem schlechter gehen!" ("No one will be worse off!"). The immortal "read my lips" campaign promise of Chancellor Kohl, quoted derisively millions of times by outraged, depressed East Germans after he delivered it during the election campaign of 1990, was still on people's lips years later. "Tell that to my unemployed father!" one teenager shouted at me in 1992, spitting as he recalled Kohl's electioneering. In the east, negative feelings were strong: frustration, rage, bitter betrayal. "In five years, the countryside will be blooming!" Chancellor Kohl promised eastern Germans in 1990. By 1994, eastern living standards were 50 percent higher than in 1989 and the region was growing at a healthy rate of 8 percent. But the east was still living mostly off western transfer payments—$115 billion per year. Moreover, though the official figures for unemployment in the east were bad enough at 17 percent, the unofficial rate (excluding government pay-for-no-work schemes) remained an intolerable 31 percent—indeed up to 45 percent if those forced into early retirement or obliged to work in the West were included. Given the dismal employment situation at home, more than a tenth of eastern German youth were still leaving each month for the West.[14]

"Don't you forget," a retired 80-year-old schoolteacher admonished me, wagging her forefinger, "there's been no democracy here since 1933! Even we old ones don't know what it is!" Never having experienced anything like a free election in 57 years, many East Germans had naïvely believed Kohl's 1990 campaign promises. Their disillusion was the bitterest of all. *"Nur Kohl bringt die Kohle!"* they believed ("Only Kohl will deliver the cabbage [cash]!"). The elderly schoolteacher sighs. *"Tja, das war ein Märchen!"* "It was a fairy tale." Buying the fable that only Kohl could awaken them from their decades-long torpor, many easterners seemed to expect a happily-ever-after ending to the 45-year forced separation. But the envisioned storybook reunification left, instead, feelings of betrayal and bitter disillusion.

A 1993 poll: 95 percent of eastern Germans identify "many good sides" to the former communist regime: guaranteed employment, low taxes, free child care, slower pace of work, rent control. And 25 percent would "prefer to have the Wall back." An October 1996 poll: 29 percent of western Germans and 57 percent of eastern Germans said they felt "more alienated from each other" than six years earlier.[15] Easterners once derided West Germans as *"Bundis"* and joked about themselves as *"Zonis"* (residents of the *SBZ, Sowjetische Besatzungszone,* Soviet Occupation Zone). But now the *Ossis* are *Bundis* too—albeit "second-class *Bundis,"* as many insist resentfully. The poll results remind me of a retiree's comment to me: "Bonn doesn't care about us. I feel more an *Ossi* than ever. I'll never be a *Bundesbürger* [citizen of the Federal Republic]."

It wasn't supposed to turn out this way.

Without reflection, I regale an eastern German acquaintance in Leipzig with my banana vignettes, joking about "the banana revolution" of the DDR.

Manfred, born in 1949, the same year as the founding of the DDR—the members of his class year were known in the DDR as "children of the Republic"—is not amused. A history teacher, he chides me for my insensitivity. Do I not appreciate how scarce a commodity bananas were in the DDR?

"A strict vegetarian like you would have starved to death within weeks."

In the DDR, I would have been regarded as a snob and an elitist, unwilling to accept the standard diet of meat and animal products, Manfred says. He pauses. Then he deadpans: *"Nun ja, die DDR war doch keine Bananenrepublik."* "After all, the DDR was no banana republic."

A tense silence hangs in the air, then dissipates as we chuckle together uneasily. Turning adversity to necessity, Manfred explains, the DDR had even—in another display of dialectical virtuosity—argued that the absent banana was a positive, inspirational symbol, testifying to the nation's heroic resistance against the imperialist, materialist, consumerist West, which "had everything."

The moment of shared bemusement, however, does not delude. An historical abyss of unshared experience lies between us. Manfred pauses. He understands the boy atop the Wall, he says. I wait for Manfred to elaborate. But nothing follows. My stories, I begin to suspect, are humiliating to him. Bananas: Manfred, too, *ought* to have known what they were, *ought* to have known to peel them, *ought* to have had the casual pleasure of eating them. . . .

And only then do I perceive the decades of dream worlds dividing us in the 1990s, the divergence between my taken-for-granted, variegated consumerist cornucopia and his stern, black-and-white socialist realism: that infinitude of difference signified best not by the dead metaphor of a towering concrete Wall but by the everyday, almost comical image of a ripe banana. Yes, that's it exactly: What marks our mutual wariness are the Walls of Smugness and Shame symbolized by the forbidden fruit that rested casually in westerners' hands, so near to his TV screen that he could have tasted it and yet apparently forever beyond his reach.

"If they had only let us travel," Manfred says. A long sigh. "We would have come back. . . . I have my home, my job, I have all my family and friends here. I would have come back. We just wanted to see what it was like elsewhere. . . . But they were afraid. They were afraid of people."

And now, spinning out my own web of associations, I can't get my version of that silly American tune out of my head: *Yes, he had no bananas!*—a 1920s hit that also became a popular song in German in the late 1940s. Bananas: a metaphor for that imagined paradise of Plenty—the western sitcoms and sports cars, the home telephones, the computers, the rock music, the comic books, the sneakers, the jeans, the books, the plane flights, the bubble gum, the chocolates, the burgers, the hot dogs, the Cokes—the Sears *cum* snack-bar utopia—that Manfred, like that boy atop the Wall, never knew. Bananas: a universal metaphor for East Germany past and present—a metaphor for a lifetime of playing second banana, of being driven bananas by the comparisons, of going bananas in the race to catch up, of being, yes, the German Banana Republic.

"It was something we didn't talk about when they visited," he says. "They" are the few West German cousins of his father's family who every three or four years would spend a week in Leipzig. Manfred confesses: "We were torn between being ashamed of hosting them in 'our poor home' and being angry with ourselves for exaggeratedly feigning gratitude when they gave us 'special Western' gifts. . . . It was hopeless."

I'm still in the present, as Manfred muses on that unsharable past. OK: Yesterday they had no bananas. But what about *today*, I want to ask. Now Manfred *can* have them! Bunches and bunches of them! But, again, I say nothing. Now that Manfred can have them, I realize, they seem not so much to matter to him any more.

As I look back on that revelatory conversation, it strikes me that my "amusing" vignettes represent three eastern Germanies—of the past, present, and future. And, even more so, three snapshots of eastern re-education, three images of eastern German youth unlearning and learning their lessons: scenes of East meeting West, of awestruck discovery, impatient expectancy, exultant exertion. The vanished dawn of the boy cradling the banana captured an eternal moment of prelapsarian innocence—or of virtuous ignorance borne of deprivation. It portrayed East German life before the razing of the Wall, a child's existence in the controlled, anti-western, schoolmarmish environment of the former DDR.

Within weeks, however, even before 1989 was out, this image had altered in the German media, as if anticipating the banana electioneering soon to come.[16] The "bananas for votes" psychology of the second tableau disclosed the hunger of many eastern Germans for western goods. It reflected the widely publicized East German *Nachholbedarf*, felt most keenly by the youth, the "need to make up" for lost time and opportunities. And, finally, the banana-as-trophy illustration evoked the spectacle of a reunified Germany as economic powerhouse. It depicted Germany as the exhausted but elated Olympian, conqueror of eastern European markets, Autocrat of the continental breakfast table. But for anxious observers, in- and outside Germany, that clenched fist provoked darker visions—memories of the last time a united Germany hosted the Olympics. For them, the spectre haunting Europe was the spectre of German capitalism—and soon perhaps fascism. For them, the third scene completed what the second began: the imperialistic triumph of marks *über* Marx.

Education and Youth—and Re-Education

The SED immortalized it: *"Wer die Jugend hat, hat die Zukunft!"* ("Who has the youth, has the future!").

But the line is sometimes attributed to Martin Luther, and it gained fame in German socialist circles due to a celebrated 1872 speech, "Knowledge Is Power, Power Is Knowledge," delivered by Marx's old colleague, Wilhelm Liebknecht, the nineteenth-century socialist theorist and agitator.[17] At the turn of the century, in late Imperial Germany, the statement served as a battle cry for radicals seeking to win young workers to their banner; decades later the SED adopted it, even altering it during the repressive Stalinist era of the late 1940s and early 1950s (when the Party was storming the "citadel of learning" most aggressively and imposing its own choice of professors on the universities) to *"Wer die Kader hat, hat die Zukunft!"* ("Who has the Cadres, has the Future!").[18] Both slogans became not just official mottoes of the DDR's youth organizations, but were treated by the Party as touchstones for policymaking. And with good reason: Liebknecht was right. As the communists knew, the fate of a nation depends upon the education of its people.

"Das neue Leben muss anders werden!" schoolchildren in the JP used to sing: "Our new life must be different!"

By 1990 it was different indeed. One of the first things I noticed during my initial tour of East German schools in the fall of 1990 was a Leipzig first-grader with a banana in his lunch box. The stuff of dreams just a year earlier.

Education and youth.

"If you want to understand us, go to the schools," a retired East German teacher in Erfurt had written me. "Nowhere will the rise and fall of the DDR be more sharply and poignantly revealed to you than in the relation between the school and the state." Or as Freya Klier wrote in her study of East German education, *Lug Vaterland*: "The key to understanding West Germany since the 1950s, *das deutsche Wirtschaftswunder* [the German economic miracle], lies in comprehending their business and industrial development. But the key to understanding the DDR lies in grasping the functioning of the educational system. No area of East German society more decisively formed the 'socialist citizen' than education."[19]

Both the teacher and the author were right. But I learned from my travels in eastern Germany during the 1990s that more than the contents of lunch boxes had changed in eastern schools and universities since November 1989. Long gone, of course, were the busts of Walter Ulbricht and Erich Honecker, who between them had presided over the SED since 1945. Gone too were the literature classes featuring paeans to intrepid proletarians such as young Pavel in *How Steel Is Made Hard* or the adventures of Bolshevik boy scouts such as Timur in A. Garzin's *Timur and His Troop.*

During the annus mirabilis of 1989/90, however, the coveted models in eastern Germany were saints, not socialists. One teacher in Berlin told me that book collectors were paying top prices for volumes of *The Collected Works of Marx and Engels*—and not for reasons of sentiment or nostalgia. Printers who were publishing expensive new editions of bibles and prayer books valued the old-fashioned cloth bindings, which tended to be in mint condition since the volumes had never been read. His colleague added that, in Catholic towns, illustrators were buying and "touching up" portraits that once hung in East German schools depicting glorious scenes of a bushy-bearded Marx laboring among the workers. With only small modifications Marx could be refurbished (or "rehabilitated") into St. Joseph, the patron saint of the worker.

Unfortunately, hot on the heels of the bananas and bibles also came a fusillade of drugs, pornography, dropout cases, discipline problems, and neo-Nazi graffiti—none of which had been much seen, let alone highly visible, in DDR schools. Not to mention the traffic jams, homelessness, prostitution, and violence outside the schools. After the triumph of marks over Marx—money over ideology, consumer society over the planned economy, capitalism over socialism, *das Kapital* over *Das Kapital*—come the surcharges. For capitalist freedom is not just the freedom to consume, but the license to consume *to excess*—and eastern Germans are learning how difficult it is both to consume freely and to hold fast to socialist principles and Lutheran values—how *un*fixed and sometimes unfavorable is the exchange rate of Marx for marks.

Modern history has not witnessed a similar experiment. German reunification: two states, with utterly opposing economic and political systems, one of 60 million citizens and another of 16 million, voluntarily and mutually agreeing to become one nation, with the larger state aiding and modernizing (or, arguably, swallowing or exploiting) the smaller one.

The unsurprising result for eastern German schools has been a mix of jarring oddities and ironies, the legacy of this frenzied transition from communism to consumerism. Or as one teacher joked to me in 1990: "It used to be all Marx; now it's all *murks* [bungling]." While the final report card isn't yet in, this much is clear: eastern German schooldays aren't what they used to be. Cases in point during 1989/90:

In the Carl Ossietzky School in East Berlin, Lenin in marble miniature surveys a history class, eyeing with impassive disdain students' Walkmans with their cassette tapes of Madonna and 2 Live Crew. Students entering and exiting the building seem blasé about the graffiti—scrawled in colloquial English—on the schoolyard wall: "Fuck Off, GERMONEY!"

At the Rosa Luxemburg School in Leipzig, a neo-Nazi slogan—"*Ausländer Raus!*" ("Foreigners Out!")—defaces the side wall of the main building, even as a large mural of Marx and Engels, walking with a dozen bright-eyed socialist children, still greets visitors in the front hallway.

In the foyer of the Humboldt University in East Berlin, several skinheads swagger up the main steps, oblivious to the quotation engraved on the wall, a line from the university's erstwhile prize alumnus, the bushy-bearded revolutionary whose Falstaffian countenance once graced the DDR's highest banknote: "Philosophers have heretofore only interpreted the world; the point, however, is to change it."

In 1989/90, East Germans took Marx's point doubtless further than he intended—and rid themselves of Marxism itself—perhaps taking their cue from the worldly wisdom of Frau Henriette Marx, Karl's mother, who busied herself with everyday undialectical materialism and once remarked: "If Karl, instead of writing a lot about capital, had *made* a lot of capital, it would all have been much better."

WHO HAS THE YOUTH, HAS THE FUTURE!

Today consumerism has the youth, and the future of Germany seems solidly bourgeois. And doubtless many former DDR citizens would nod their heads in agreement with the good business sense of Frau Marx, who probably passed away with the binding of her own copy of *Das Kapital* in mint condition.

But while the D-mark may be firmly established as the coin of the German realm, the minds of eastern Germans are still operating on separate, older currencies.

"*Vorher*," one eastern German family in the town of Apolda in Saxony kept repeating to me, with a backward wave of the hand, during our interview in 1992: "Before." They meant the days of the DDR, before November 1989 and before reunification. Their intonation pattern rose and fell, the second syllable released with a sigh as they pronounce the word. "*Vorher*" was suffused with their nostalgia for more secure and happier days. Emotionally and spiritually, the two Germanies were still divided. But now by a Wall of time, not place. Now the division was "before" and "after." As in "before November 9" and "after the Wall."

East and West Germans used to say "*drüben*" ("over there"). For me the word evokes the refrain of the old U.S. battle song from World War I. But to Germans it simply meant "the Other Germany." In both Germanies, people spoke in terms of "here" and "over there." And as the years of division lengthened into decades, the Other became an abstraction for new generations of both states. Only with difficulty—and for most DDR citizens the restrictions were draconian—did you ever get from "here" to "there." Today, though both eastern and western Germans can freely travel, opening borders does not automatically open minds. Geography is one matter, history another.[20]

The old nations of West Germany and the DDR may be gone. Still, while there is a Germoney, there is not quite yet a Germany.

Schooling Society and Taming Minds

Any serious attempt to understand the "New Germany" struggling into being in post-totalitarian Europe cannot avoid examining the history and legacy of DDR education. Indeed DDR education sheds distinctive light both upon pre- and post-1989 Germany and upon postwar communism. Certainly no institution offers a more penetrating glimpse of DDR life and of the fundamentals of communist agitation and propaganda than the educational system. And no nation better illuminates the interplay between the theory and praxis of communism, especially in cultural policy, than the former East Germany. For SED leaders pursued a more orthodox, "purer" communism than their socialist *Brüderländer* (brother nations), a neo-Stalinism whose rigidity in the post-Stalinist era exceeded even that of the Kremlin.

The strictness was variously attributed. Some observers ascribed it to the militaristic Prussian character (some of the *Brüderländer* contemptuously nicknamed Walter Ulbricht "the little Saxon corporal," an unsubtle allusion to the insulting diminutive applied to Hitler, "the little Austrian corporal"). Others imputed it to the SED's paranoiac drive to stamp out every last vestige of Nazism and guard against the ever-present ideological danger from "revanchist" "Nazi" West Germany.

This book is first a study of DDR education and its aftermath. But the central place of education in DDR and communist state policy, as well as the central place of the DDR for grasping communist ideology, furnish invaluable opportunities for insight into issues of much wider scope. Situated at the crossroads of modern Europe, where nation-building and state pedagogy meet, the fate of DDR education touches the fates of (eastern) Germany and of communism—and the prospects of the "New Germany" and the New Europe as a new millennium dawns.

Repainting the Little Red Schoolhouse is thus about the role of education in the DDR and in eastern Germany—and also about those oddities and ironies characteristic of a nation and *Weltanschauung* that indoctrinated millions of banana-less boys and girls to interpret their deprivation as a beneficent Law of History. My title is an Americanism—neither the Federal Republic nor the DDR ever referred to the DDR one-room schoolhouse or *Dorfschule* (village school) in this way— whereby I wish to stress that mine is an American perspective. But such a quaint Americanism also raises explicitly the issue of what the DDR called *Aneignung* (appropriation). How do you bring the alien home? How do you participate without utterly assimilating? How do you translate without domesticating? How do you import the foreign? And through these questions I explore the problem of German identity and Germany's educational challenges from the standpoint of my own.

For betwixt and between all the confusion over Germany's upheaval in the 1990s was the never-settled question of German identity. "And *now* who are we?" the Manfreds of every generation wondered aloud throughout my conversations with them. "And who will we become?" Because now there was no DDR, indeed not even an "East Germany" officially—just "eastern" Germany, or "the five new federal states." "What's happening to us?" easterners asked. "Was there in fact a 'revolution' in 1989?"—if, perhaps, only a banana revolution? Or was it "just a *Wende*," the word commonly employed to characterize the "turn" of events in 1989/90?

No agreement exists on the answers. Nevertheless, after interviewing dozens of educators, cultural officials, students, former students, and parents of students in eastern Germany, I have learned that the deepest roots of DDR society were indeed located in the institution that molded the youth of its citizens, and that some of the most searching questions about East German identity and the repression of the political past are in fact to be found there: eastern educators have been one of the largest, most articulate, most traumatized segments of the population affected by events since 1989.

For education was a DDR ministry tightly controlled by the Party, anointed with the sacred task of socializing East German children. The regime of fear began in the schools, which served as an important mechanism for upholding the German communist state. SED educators, of course, held that their policies merely realized their forefathers' great revolutionary socialist vision: "And your education!" wrote Marx and Engels in *The Communist Manifesto*. "Is not that also social, and determined by the social conditions under which you educate; by the intervention, direct or indirect, of society, by means of the schools?"

Indeed it was. In a society in which all able-bodied men and 95 percent of women under 50 worked full-time and virtually no recreational activities existed outside of Party sponsorship, it is no exaggeration to say: the socialist state, via the teachers, reared the children.

And, for a time at least, it seemed to work. Western observers long held that the DDR's single greatest success story was in education. The price paid by young "anti-revolutionaries" and the limitations on bourgeois notions such as free speech were lamentable, westerners agreed, but the educational system was widely praised by western liberals and radicals, since a greater percentage of DDR youths completed high school than that in West Germany. After the 1965 "Law on the Unified Socialist Educational System," almost 100 percent of DDR students completed 10 years of education, "visible proof of the deeply humanistic character of socialism and of its superiority to capitalism," in Erich Honecker's words.[21] Moreover, the DDR student/teacher ratio was 70 percent lower than in the *Bundesrepublik;* DDR class size was 33 percent smaller. Before the BRD reformed its educational system in the early 1970s, the liberal West German weekly *Die Zeit* raved that DDR education was "an entire epoch ahead of the Federal Republic."[22] Even in the 1980s, *Die Zeit* lauded the DDR for "an exceptional educational system" that had created "a skilled work force . . . [driven by] ideological purity."[23] The DDR's polytechnical emphasis and its special sports schools were credited with having brought modest economic prosperity and Olympic success. A little nation of 16 million people—the size and population of Ohio, with roughly the same climate—was hailed as the most affluent country in the Communist world and "the 10th-ranking industrial power of the globe" (a statistic that said more about the unequal distribution of global economic power than about the economic might of the DDR). Still, East Germany's athletic success couldn't be denied: DDR Olympians sometimes won more gold medals than even the United States or USSR. (Reports throughout the 1990s, however, which confirmed charges that many DDR Olympic medalists used steroids, have tainted the achievement.)

Moreover, the DDR mania for education was not restricted to an elite. Thousands of youngsters "trained" for the Mathematics Olympiad. Anticipating the Russian Olympiad made even Russian grammar palatable for many children. DDR adults were equally obsessed with learning—it always seemed to outsiders as if half the country were going to night school, taking extension courses, and/or obtaining advanced degrees. To an extent, the perception was accurate; DDR citizens did value learning highly. Under the circumstances, however, erudition meant chiefly technical competence and book knowledge from a tightly circumscribed library. East Germans turned to the accumulation of degrees and knowledge largely because a near-total ban on foreign travel prevailed; the DDR vied with Albania for the title of most provincial Soviet satellite. Restrictions even within Eastern Europe were stringent; as a consequence, many East Germans traversed only the world of books and culture—a voyage comparable to the "inner emigration" of educated, nonpolitical Germans during the Nazi era.

And what were DDR citizens taught? "Our new life must be different!" The Party, through the education system, made every effort to convert young minds to communism. Education as re-education constituted an unremitting ideological offensive—day in, day out, all day long. A boy whose imagination ran wild, who drew flying horses in art class, would be reprimanded by his teacher for violating the canons of socialist realism—and mocked by his classmates for his lack of a "scientific" consciousness. A girl who wrote an essay saying that she "values solitude" would be censured by her civics teacher as an example of individualistic, anti-social thinking. And when school let out, the lessons continued. Even after regular school hours, most children under 10 remained in the after-school day nursery until 5 or 6 P.M. Singing "Tractor Thomas" or "We Are the Young Pioneers." Writing "friendship letters" to the Lenin Pioneers of the USSR. Listening to elderly communist visitors tell of their breathtaking underground exploits in the darkest days of the Third Reich.[24] From dawn to dusk, DDR schoolchildren guzzled collectivist ideology and gulped down stories of the heroic socialist Fatherland. Home *was* the little Red schoolhouse.

That era of rosy socialist realism is, certainly, passed—but the past lives on in the present. For educators and students of today the uneasy questions still loom: What remains of the DDR educational experiment? What remains of four decades of socialist education—or propaganda? And what remains of the DDR socialist ethos in the lives of its 16 million citizens? Or as Christa Wolf—one of the leading writers of the former DDR, who lived during 1992/93 in uneasy exile at a corporate American think tank, the Getty Center in sunny Santa Monica—summed it up in the title of her controversial 1990 memoir about life in the DDR, the question is: *Was bleibt?* Indeed: What's left?

Not much, it seems—especially in education. Socialist teachers have undergone political re-education and professional retraining (especially in ideologically sensitive subjects such as civics and history). Widely regarded throughout East Germany as members of the DDR's "cultural front," educators were among the most loyal and ideologically orthodox Party members. The major qualification for teachers of German and history, for example, was not special knowledge or teaching skills but rather the proper "class perspective." After reunification, teachers in particular suffered the scrutiny and wrath of eastern German parents. Much of the anger was a reaction against the idealized "socialist school," a favorite child of Politburo heads Ulbricht and Honecker (whose wife Margot Honecker ran the education ministry with authoritarian firmness for the last quarter century of the DDR's life). Originally one of the most unruly and resistant groups in the early postwar days of the DDR, university professors, schoolteachers, and students were harshly disciplined by the Party for wayward behavior. By the 1960s, as a result, the DDR's educational system was regarded as among the most repressive in Eastern Europe.

Thus did the critique of capitalist education by Marx, Engels, Liebknecht, and Rosa Luxemburg turn out, ironically, to be nowhere truer than in the DDR: the schools served as the prime means of social control by a ruling elite. *"Gleichheit für Alle!"* ("Equality for all!") was the Party motto: the DDR proclaimed its uniform system of primary and secondary education as a symbol of socialist equality. No private schools, no religious or sectarian schools, all children (except those gifted in sport or music and willing to represent the state in international competitions) enrolled in 10-year polytechnical *Einheitsschulen* (uniform schools). Endlessly the SED proclaimed that the teachings of Marx inspired its schools, citing Marx's passing comment in volume I of *Das Kapital* that schooling combining instruction and productive labor was "the only method for producing fully developed human beings." Unceasingly, the SED touted DDR education, especially the uniform polytechnical school, as its "greatest achievement."[25]

The little Red schoolhouse of the DDR faithfully inculcated the traditional Prussian values of order, cleanliness, and punctuality. And yet, behind the scrubbed schoolhouse door crouched a faceless, hulking, centralized bureaucracy. Mired in inefficiency and incompetence, it formed teacher and student outlooks that combined cultural provincialism with dependence on the state, cravenness to authority, and self-forgetfulness.

THE PARTY, THE PARTY! / IT'S ALWAYS RIGHT!

"Parteilichkeit" (party-mindedness, partisanship) governed every sphere of DDR education. "How does this drawing, this essay contribute to 'the struggle'?" asked the teacher. Just knowing that question lurked behind every assignment served to vaporize, Orwellian-style, any pictures of flying horses and or paragraphs on solitude. DDR education indoctrinated a preference for groupthink rather than a love of learning or a capacity for individual expression, devoting itself not to enlightenment but to social control.

For East German education existed primarily to legitimize socialism as a worldwide movement and validate its historical destiny to replace capitalism. It instilled absolute loyalty to the Communist Party, to the socialist Fatherland, and to the Great Soviet Brotherland—the land of "The Big Red Schoolhouse," as one American journalist dubbed the USSR in the 1950s.[26]

Many DDR university students received advanced degrees primarily on account of faithful Party service. And many DDR citizens regarded their educational system as a proud achievement. Via cultural distinctions, economic incentives, and constitutional decrees, the SED fortified Stalin's "citadel of learning." The DDR's *Jugendgesetz* (youth law) of 1964, which formally made the state and socialist youth organizations responsible for rearing DDR children, ordained the development of the "socialist personality" as educators' "principal task," the fulfillment of which would lead to the creation of the "new socialist human being." Nowhere is an official statement of DDR educational philosophy better expounded:

The task of every young citizen is to work, to learn and live in a socialist way, selflessly and with determination for the benefit of the socialist Fatherland of the DDR. He should act in such a way as to strengthen the bond of friendship with the Brotherland of the Soviet Union and to promote the thoroughgoing cooperation of the socialist international community. It is the honored duty of youth to respect and defend the revolutionary traditions of the working class and the achievements of socialism, to campaign for peace and friendship among peoples, and to practice anti-imperialist solidarity. All young people should distinguish themselves through socialist work attitudes, practical knowledge, and skills; make high moral and cultural values their own; and participate actively in social and political life and in leadership roles in the state and society. Their efforts to acquire Marxism-Leninism, the scientific world view of the working class, and to go on the offensive against imperialistic ideology, are in every way promoted. Young people should distinguish themselves through qualities such as a feeling of responsibility for themselves and others, a consciousness of the collective good, a readiness of help, determination and goal-orientation, honesty and modesty, courage and persistence, endurance and discipline, respect for their elders and their achievements and merits, along with responsible behavior toward the opposite sex. They should keep themselves healthy and capable of performing well in life.[27]

The *Jugendgesetz*, which was stringently enforced, turned the schools and youth programs into boot camps for martial Boy and Girl Scouts—ultimately including mandatory training in weapons use for boys and first aid for girls. And such results encapsulate the darker side of the DDR educational experience.

By the 1970s, the DDR was among the most restrictive of all communist countries, both culturally and pedagogically. The German socialist Fatherland was a martinet and disciplinarian, its child-citizens docile and compliant. After Gorbachev introduced *perestroika* into the USSR in 1985, the DDR and its schools stood out as antiquated Stalinist models of ideological obduracy whose Prussian rigor astounded even Soviet hard-liners. Indeed, what Liebknecht declared of German schools in 1872 under Bismarckian imperialism was fully applicable to DDR schools a century later:

The very essence of the modern class state requires lack of freedom. The school as it is versus the school as it should be: the relation is exactly the same as that between the state as it is versus the state as it should be. The state as it is, i.e., the class state, debases the school into an instrument of class rule. The class state has no use for free persons, only obedient subjects; not persons of character, only the souls of servants and slaves. . . . Thus the school becomes an institution for breaking in animals, rather than an educational institution.[28]

Or as another Party motto had it: *"Vertrauen ist gut, aber Kontrolle ist besser!"* ("Trust is good, but control is better!"). To tame minds as it trained minds: the little Red schoolhouse did its homework well.

DDR schooling was one of the most far-reaching educational experiments in history. DDR schools demanded total conformity to neo-Stalinist precepts—or silence. Confronted with the enormity of overcoming Nazi racial doctrine, national and class dogmas, leader worship, and anti-communist propaganda, their revolutionary assignment was nothing less than to help invert—overnight and by repressive means—a nation's view of the world and of life itself.

Reality being notoriously recalcitrant, however, the result was that DDR citizens voted with their feet for the Good Life *drüben*: the DDR was the only country in the world to lose population steadily during its entire existence, with low birthrates and liberal abortion laws helping to depress population growth after the Berlin Wall ended wide-scale emigration in 1961. The region lost more than four million people between 1945–89, i.e., a quarter of its population. So-called *Zonis*—DDR citizens—interviewed in West German refugee camps of the 1950s and early '60s cited ideological indoctrination of children as their number-one reason for emigration.[29]

The old joke was that the one constant about the DDR was that everyone wanted to get out of it. Indeed the erection of the Wall was Ulbricht's confession of defeat in the competition with West Germany. The regime's officially termed *antifaschistischer Schutzwall* (anti-fascist wall of protection) was built chiefly to keep East Germans in—not "fascist" foreigners out. It aimed to dam the westward flow of DDR citizens that had risen to a flood tide by the mid-1950s, when it was not unusual for 200–300,000 people to flee to the West per year—approximately the population of Nevada. The German equivalent of "Go west, young *Zoni!*" became a headline in early postwar West German newspapers and a dream of manifest destiny for East German youth. Despite trigger-ready border guards and lengthy jail sentences to deter illegal emigrants, and notwithstanding years of waiting for official permission (and kilometers of Red tape) in order to discourage legal emigrants, thousands of DDR citizens crept, crawled, swam, stowed away, bribed, and bought their way to freedom.

And after mid-1989, eastern Germans also voted with their feet. In 1989/90 alone, more than 600,000 crossed to the West. Westward migration has, of course, long had a crippling effect on the eastern German economy. Since more than half the emigrants have been under 25, the exodus has been, above all, a youth problem. No region can prosper if it continues to lose its youth. That simple fact represents, as it were, a sobering corollary to the SED motto:

Who loses the youth, loses the future.[30]

Born Unfree

The imperative mood was well-chosen by the SED: "Our new life *must* be different." A climate of obligation, necessity, and compulsion enveloped the training maneuvers drilled in its citadels of learning. It was an environment that provoked Martin Buber to declare:

> The real struggle is not between East and West, or communism and capitalism, but between education and propaganda. Education means teaching people to see the reality around them, to understand it for themselves. Propaganda is

exactly the opposite. It tells the people: "You will think like this, as we want you to think."

Especially in its early years, the DDR's Party propaganda was ubiquitous and ceaseless, as if agitprop functionaries were self-consciously modeling their work on the blaring slogans of Orwell's *1984*.

YOU ONLY NEED TO EDUCATE PEOPLE PROPERLY—THEN THEY'LL LIVE RIGHT!
TRUST IS GOOD, BUT CONTROL IS BETTER!
THE PARTY, THE PARTY! / IT'S ALWAYS RIGHT!

"Give me four years to teach the children," said Stalin, in a line already quoted, "and the seed I have sown will never be uprooted." Thus did Stalin, echoing the behaviorist Ivan Pavlov, one of the forefathers of Marxist-Leninist educational psychology, announce his pedagogical equivalent of a Five-Year Plan. To Stalin, writers were "the engineers of human souls," teachers were the mechanics, and children were the raw material to be molded in the image and likeness of scientific socialism. You made socialists like you made steel: hard.

The DDR, of course, gave Stalin 40 years. But the "children of the Republic" finally came in from the desert to quench their thirst for Liberty. Still, SED-style Stalinism—or DDR "*Stasi*nism," as a few western observers called it—did indeed sink deep roots into DDR hearts and minds.[31] Its hold validated the Stalinist conviction that the "citadel of learning" was worthy of "capture at any price."

And the price turned out to be very high indeed for the DDR. Stalin operated by two old Russian proverbs about the German: "A good fellow maybe, but better kept under foot," and "Much may be made of the German if he be caught young." The citadels of learning became citadels of political re-education. The DDR school spewed propaganda perpetually, equating resistance to communism with unreconstructed Nazism and thereby setting young against old in every family.

How could this not have imprinted itself deeply on the generations of East Germans to pass through DDR schools since 1945? Just as high school is closer to the core of the American experience than anything else in our national life, so too did the same hold true for the DDR. Only more so, since there was practically nothing outside school for young people, apart from Party-sponsored youth organizations affiliated with school, e.g., the FDJ. And as I discovered in a 1990 conversation with an eleventh-grade student at the Friedrich Schiller EOS (*Erweiterte Oberschule*, advanced high school) in Weimar, that organization's name—Freie Deutsche Jugend (Free German Youth)—was another piece of pure Ostspeak:

"What percentage of your classmates belonged to the FDJ?"

"Everybody in the class. . . . You pretty much had to join. You had no choice."

"What happened if you didn't join?"

"Hard to predict. I always figured it was better to be safe. Why take the risk? You could lose the chance to go to university, or to study your chosen subject, or to get a good apprenticeship. Your parents might get in trouble, or you'd get a bad assignment in the People's Army, or a host of other things. . . ."

Education, and especially participation in the communist youth organizations, was the path to a good career in the DDR. Every SED elder knew that Erich Ho-

necker himself served as the first head of the FDJ (1946–55). And that, on succeeding Walter Ulbricht as Politburo head in 1971, Honecker had brought dozens
of old FDJ cronies into powerful government positions. And that he now supervised his old beat closely with his wife Margot, Minister of People's Education
since 1963, and had chosen Egon Krenz, his successor at the FDJ, as his heir
apparent. The central role of education in the DDR could not be clearer: virtually
from the creation of the SBZ to the DDR's demise, Erich, Margot, and their ward
Egon personally attended to the running of the youth organizations and the
schools. Nothing in the education system would be left to chance; it was a family-
run operation.

That lesson too was communicated clearly to me during my visit to the Friedrich
Schiller EOS. A history teacher handed me an official manual from Panorama, the
DDR press office. The title alone implied a confident answer to its question: "Stu-
dents and Studies in the DDR: How Does the DDR Solve the Problems of Higher
Education?" The teacher flipped past the chapters headed "Universities of the
People" and "Students Without Worries," stopping at page 26, "How Free Are
Students in the DDR?"

> The freedom of DDR students is inherent in their complete certainty that they
> will not be made use of for the profit and power interests of big capital. It is
> inherent in the fact that they need have no fear of unemployment. It is in-
> herent in the fact that they have unlimited opportunities to gain scientific
> knowledge, to make the Socialist mode of thinking and acting their own in
> the shortest possible time. And all of this, not as a goal in itself, but in order
> that the students can thus fully participate in the shaping of the Socialist
> social order. . . .

After this reminder of the revolutionary forbearance "inherent" in the Socialist
faith, the section closes with a quotation from Engels, which my acquaintance
read aloud: *"Freiheit ist die Einsicht in die Notwendigkeit"* ("Freedom is the recognition of necessity").

"Freedom is Slavery!" I thought. But the teacher drew the moral himself:

"That sums it up," he told me. "You want to know about my *Freiraum* [free
space] in teaching? There was no such 'freedom.' What was 'freedom' to us? A
word. The Free German Youth were not free. The German Democratic Republic
was not democratic. The People's Ministry for Education, the People's Police—
and a thousand other 'People's' agencies—never served the People."

He pulled another official booklet from what he jokingly called his *Giftschrank*
(poison shelf), the word formerly used in the DDR for those library stacks holding
proscribed books. "Education in a Socialist Country: The DDR's Education Policy."
We turned to page 36:

> The aim of our education is a self-confident socialist personality committed
> to socialism and creatively active in many fields together with fellow citizens.
> This aim determines instruction in all subjects and school activities, but can
> only be accomplished if school and life form an entity.

The booklet gives a running list of postwar examples of the perfect dialectical unity practiced by the socialist school and the youth organizations:

> Great events of international importance always set off activities on the part of pupils in the DDR. . . . Young Pioneers and members of the FDJ supported the struggle of the Algerian people against French colonialism by collecting exercise books, pencils, and toys. They expressed their solidarity with the brave people of Vietnam in their struggle against U.S. imperialism by collecting money and signatures. . . . The DDR's young people extend their solidarity to the people of Chile. . . .

The booklet concludes with the ringing words:

> Educators will look for even better ways to implement our programs, to constantly improve conditions of instruction, and to realize ever better the available potential for the all-around development of socialist personalities. The communist future will make itself felt more strongly in present-day educational developments, because, as Margot Honecker stated in her contribution to the discussion of the Ninth Party Congress, "We have always looked on education as the preparation of young people for their active participation in shaping the new society."

OUR NEW LIFE *MUST* BE DIFFERENT!

You were free in the DDR to conform, to obey, to yield. You had liberty so long as you took no liberties. DDR pedagogy meant inculcation of ideology and information, not the development of persons. Education was not an existential, I-Thou relationship, as Buber had urged. Education was not cultivation but implantation. Rearing little Party members, it was "a pedagogy absent a pupil."[32] Not just that it wasn't "child-centered"; it was *child-absent*. Or as the old German aphorism has it: *"Freiheit ist von Gott, Freiheiten vom Teufel"* ("Liberty is from God, liberties from the Devil"). The pupils at the Friedrich Schiller EOS would have done far better to heed the words of Schiller himself: *"Das Gesetz hat noch keinen grossen Mann gebildet, aber die Freiheit brutet Kolosse und Extremitaten aus"* ("Never yet has law formed a great man; 'tis liberty that forges giants and heroes").

Freedom is the room to expand—but that wasn't possible in the DDR, "that fenced-in playground that was my land," as the novelist Christoph Hein once wrote. Few DDR citizens took liberties beyond the playground square. Their emancipation was a state proclamation, not a fact.

Such a state of affairs was defensible in the dialectical wonderland of Marxist-Leninist theory, for freedom had always been suspect in revolutionary catechesis. Lenin himself called liberty "a bourgeois dream." "It is true," he said cynically, "that liberty is precious—so precious that it must be rationed." In *State and Revolution* (1918), directed against the "opportunism" of Marxist opponents such as Luxemburg and Karl Kautsky, Lenin developed his doctrine of "democratic centralism," according to which the "social" liberty of the individual was identified with party-mindedness and state collectivism. Under this formula, bourgeois "individualism" was a form of social pathology—"Freedom is Slavery!" In SED Ostspeak, to be "for society" was to be "for oneself." "While the state exists," wrote Lenin in *State and Revolution*, "there can be no [traditional concept of] freedom. Where there is freedom, there will be no state." It is yet another delicious irony that, in the fullness of revolutionary History, the DDR fulfilled Lenin's prediction to the letter. So long as the DDR existed, there was no freedom; almost as soon as truth burst out—as if with an apocalyptic Zolaesque cry of *"J'Accuse!"*—the state "withered away." The DDR had reached, as it were, Lenin's "higher" phase of communism. For Lenin had argued that, as long as reward is proportional to worker output, a "lower" form of communism prevails, in which the state is still needed. When reward becomes proportional to worker *need*, the state will dissolve naturally.

After 44 years of communist rationing, *das Volk* "needed" Liberty. The avenging dialectic finally turned on the SED itself; 1989 became the year of Marxism in the streets. East Germans heeded at last the words of Lenin's most outspoken German antagonist, their own Rosa Luxemburg, who wrote in her 1919 study of the Russian Revolution: *"Freiheit ist immer nur Freiheit des anders Denkenden"* ("Freedom is freedom only if it also applies for the one who thinks differently").

For decades, citing that passage in SED meetings was forbidden. Honoring her in the breach, the SED had instead named dozens of schools and streets after Rosa Luxemburg.

Her name had become—like freedom—only a word.

Fostering a New Fatherland?

"After the Wall." The usage recurs in conversations about present-day Germany, and it is likely to be current for a long time to come. For neither Germany's transition from communism to capitalism nor eastern Germans' embattled striving to cope with four decades of socialism is near completion.

Because it also addresses this period of upheaval in the years since the fall of the Wall, especially in the new schoolrooms of eastern Germany, this book has furnished me with an unusual opportunity: to investigate what "turning capitalist" means to eastern Germans, and to identify those features of eastern German life likely in the long run to prove constant, ephemeral, or dominant. For young people are not just the abstract "future" of Germany. Alienated German youth—both western and eastern—already constitute the core of the problems of German unemployment, neo-Nazism, and anti-foreigner violence. They are the primary cause of social unrest in the new Federal Republic—and behind fears of a German Fourth Reich among many European neighbors. And as my Erfurt correspondent made clear, some institutions, as the SED knew, are more equal than others. The schools must play an active role, she emphasized, in fostering a new, peace-loving Fatherland. They must help eastern students to face up to decades during which their elders largely denied responsibility for Nazism and the Holocaust, decades of provincialism enforced by travel restrictions and underlying the fear of foreigners, decades of dialectical doublethink whereby the negation of freedom equaled a higher, "socialist" freedom.

"The schools undergirded the system," she wrote me. "And all the problems now facing us—the economy, the influx of foreigners, the neo-Nazi violence—are tied to education. If we don't succeed in renewing our educational system, which also means confronting and exorcising the ghosts of the Nazi and Communist past, all our other problems will only intensify."

Whereupon another, utterly un-peaceful explosion may erupt. . . .

"Drugs, porn, violence, and homelessness—that's what's coming to our schools and streets, mark my words," a German teacher in the Friedrich Schiller EOS warned me during my 1990 visit. Has time already borne him out? We argued together, cordially, about the pluses and minuses of reunification for the next generation. Unlike his colleague, the history teacher, he did not rush to condemn the SED. Like many teachers, he had been a "convinced communist" in earlier days. From the *Giftschrank* in the storage room next to the teachers' lounge he fetched yet another official booklet, "General Education in the DDR." We turned to the question-and-answer section on page 23. The question was the same one I had just posed to the history teacher, to which the booklet brightly answers:

Q: Can one say that "youth problems" do not exist in the DDR?

A: Yes, with certain reservations one can say that, because in the DDR such grave problems as unemployment, with all its detrimental consequences to the harmonious development of young people, do not exist. Youth in this country does not know the merciless competition for apprenticeships, study places and jobs, which young people in many other countries confront. There is no "drug scene" here and juvenile delinquency is at an extremely low level compared to Western countries. . . . The overwhelming majority of young people feel really at home in socialist society.

"False—" said the German teacher, as if it were a true/false test, pressing his finger to the final sentence and then waving the booklet at me remonstratively, "—but not altogether false, not by a long shot."

Drugs, porn, violence, homelessness. Yes, they have become highly visible in eastern states. The eastern passage to capitalism is turning out to be neither so smooth nor so programmatic as implied by a 1990 two-panel cartoon ad promoting *Business Week*, which contrasted the forbidding "before" picture of a portly, un-kempt Marx as radical agitator with the smiling "after" visage of slimmed-down, clean-shaven, three-piece-suited Karl as networking entrepreneur.

Rather than engage in cultural forecasting, however, the succeeding chapters of this book raise, from the angle of curricular and extracurricular life, immediate issues of wide scope about eastern German life "after the Wall": the special problem of German identity, the tensions between *Wessis* and *Ossis*, the idea of utopia, the hunger for and danger of national heroes, the dim though flickering flame of German socialism, the haunting if still-repressed ghost of Nazism, the lengthening shadow of the Holocaust, the resurgent neo-Nazi movement, the uneasy prospect of a German-dominated European Union, and especially the relation between education and the state.

Repainting the Little Red Schoolhouse is divided into two parts. Part I focuses on the rise and fall of the educational system in eastern Germany between 1945–89. Each chapter opens with a pair of vivid, contrasting scenes that impinge on the fate of DDR students and youth, or show DDR youth playing a vital role, or capture a crucial moment in the state's campaign to foster socialist personalities. Chapter 1 portrays the first university semester in fall 1945 and Ulbricht's arrival in Berlin a few months earlier; chapter 2 sketches the August 1951 World Festival of Youth and Students for Peace and the workers' uprising of June 1953; and chapter 3 depicts the erection of the Berlin Wall in August 1961 and the triumphs in the Olympic Games in 1972. These and other scenes—e.g., the portraits of Wolf Biermann and Robert Havemann, and the sketch of the 1973 World Youth Festival in East Berlin—aim to give the reader not just the running narrative of the educational and cultural history, but a sense of the twists and turns of events, their political context, the odd and often unexpected interconnections among them, and the contributions of great and small personalities to the unfolding story. Periodically I also discuss how DDR schools, via their curricula and educational philosophy, bred what might be termed "Textbook Reds." Because I am interested throughout in the language and imagery that formed the minds of DDR youth, classroom and youth organization materials, as well as popular music lyrics and Party slogans (and anti-Party street chants), receive attention in this study. Many of these materials, given their simplified world view, are also highly revealing about the popular consciousness of the former DDR. Most of all, I have found these materials invaluable for reconstructing both the history of the DDR educational system and the socialization process undergone in its schools.

Part II takes the story of eastern education and youth culture up to 1995, the full half-century mark. It features nine "school portraits"—including "extracurricular" activities in eastern cultural life—narratives which, even as they dwell on the past, gesture anxiously toward what expectant voices call "the unfinished revolution." Each portrait acts as a frame through which to observe larger, turbulent social currents, such as the destinies of Germany or communism or the dream and nightmare of utopia. Each constitutes a personalizing of the historical and an historicizing of the personal, an effort to capture the human meaning in the mural of world-historical events and to spot the broader, sociopolitical brushstrokes that sweep across the physiognomy of private lives. Each is a profile of an historical moment, capturing the dilemma that arises when all that is solid melts into air. Though I have selected them for their wider significance, my East German interlocutors are not in any sense Emersonian representative men and women. Rather, they are voices in a post-revolutionary wilderness, speaking within scenes aspiring to form a selective anthropology of eastern life. As such, the portraits constitute ethnographic attempts to lend public events a personal voice and to make public a texture of experience common to non-easterners too.

Based on my travels in eastern Germany, then, here in Part II are the stories of a handful of winners and losers, agitators and functionaries, dissidents and apparatchiks, beneficiaries and victims—presented by an American visitor struggling to make sense of them all amid the maelstrom of events. We move back and forth from Leipzig, the so-called City of Heroes, where the legendary Monday demon-strations inspired the peaceful revolution of 1989, to the small provincial city of Plauen, to the metropolis of (east) Berlin, former DDR capital, to the cultural center of Weimar.

What did it mean to live under communism—and, before that, Nazism? What was it like to imagine *drüben*, the other side, the West—as close as that TV screen, as real as that banana from Uncle Ludwig's visit—and yet never grasp it? How did it feel to live through "the revolution"? What is it like to live without—yet still with—the Wall?

Wherever possible, I have let my German interlocutors tell their versions of these stories in their own voices. For the most part, rather than interview top government and school administration officials, I sought out faces in the crowd—rank-and-file teachers and students whom I met through friends and acquain-tances. Nineteen eighty-nine was a season of history in East Germany such as one rarely encounters in a lifetime, and I have striven to capture some sense of the drama of history from below, of *erlebte Geschichte* (lived history)—not, therefore, to produce a top-down explanation from former Communist Party bureaucrats or new administration officials, but rather to furnish a glimpse as to how historic events often touch the lives of ordinary citizens—often in extraordinary ways.

For 1989 proved Winston Smith in Orwell's *1984* right after all: "If there is hope, it lies in the proles."

It was the common people of the DDR, marching calmly in the streets by the tens and hundreds and thousands, who overthrew the SED dictatorship. Granted, some eastern Germans later came to feel less like the courageous architects of a great and peaceful revolution, and more like hapless dupes wriggling under a foreign occupying power, the arrogant so-called *Besserwessi* (West German know-it-all). But that does not negate the extraordinary events of 1989/90: *"Wir sind das Volk"* ("*We* are the people"). Hope *did* lie in the proles.

And as I talked with hundreds of ordinary eastern Germans, I realized that the common people continued to embody the hope of eastern Germany. Their hope commingled with confusion and despair. But hope *still* lay in the proles.

And so, though there are a couple of publicly recognizable names among them, Part II introduces mostly low-level Party functionaries, rank-and-file teachers, and students from in- and outside the former education and youth bureaucracy. The fact is that most well-known people tend to be somewhat removed from ordinary life; this book aspires precisely to draw readers into lives not too unlike their own, so that they might have cause to ponder both the similarities and differences of the American educational experience.

Among those featured are Jürgen, a 34-year-old instructor at the university, sud-denly without a Party career and a university job; Annaliese, 81, a retired school-teacher and quixotic dissident, who unexpectedly became a heroine for a few weeks in October/November 1989; Wolfgang, 41, a West Berlin instructor suddenly aware of his special relationship to East Germans; Holger, 36, a talented historian at the Humboldt University soon facing unemployment; Heike, 44, a disillusioned middle-aged Russian and Slavic scholar; Gerhard, 25, a still passionately loyal socialist student; Ute, 23, a Leipzig student still recovering from her painful brush

with the *Stasi;* Hedwig, 38, a non-Party member of the former DDR cultural establishment nevertheless made uneasy by memories of her role as a representative of
"socialist culture"; Ulla, 33, a former teacher in an elite POS, now teaching in
Germany's sole Jewish *Gymnasium* and coping with her family's burdensome past;
Bärbel Hintze, a *Gymnasium* teacher in her mid-50s experiencing the challenges
of adjusting to western "critical thinking"; and the late Wolfgang Harich, then 72,
a DDR philosopher still grappling with the aftermath of his eight years in solitary
confinement in a DDR jail, his punishment for challenging the Ulbricht regime to
reform.

The question, "Is there life 'after the Wall?' " is not one that all my interview
subjects answered unequivocally in the affirmative.

In the epilogue to this book, I return to the question of German and eastern
German identity, placing issues of German education and re-education within the
context of ongoing debates in Germany about the nation's unmastered and perhaps
unusable past.

Repainting the Little Red Schoolhouse thus aspires to serve as a sharply focused
history of DDR education and youth culture, and also to be a short history of post-
1989 education and youth life in the east, enriched by portraits of selected lives
since the *Wende.*

Eastern Germany's little Red schoolhouse: What did it mean? What might it—
and what might the next German generation—become? For western and eastern
Germany alike, those questions are writ large since 1989 on the national black-
board. If history is any guide, the answers will possess significance not only for
the future of Germany but also that of Europe and the world. For however exploitative and ruthlessly applied the Party slogan, it contained not just a Party
truth but testified rather to an historical fact:

WHO HAS THE YOUTH, HAS THE FUTURE!

And to appreciate the application of that fact in German history, we turn now
to the capture and conquest of "the citadel of learning," and to the leading role it
played in the making and unmaking of the German communist.

PART I

"THE CITADEL OF LEARNING"

The Making and Unmaking of the German Communist, 1945–89

Gray, dear friend, is all Theory
And green is the golden tree of Life.

Mephistopheles, "Schoolroom Scene,"
Goethe's *Faust I*, verse 2038

1

From Brown to Red

The Fall and Rise of an Educational System, 1945–51

The future smells of Russian leather, blood, godlessness, and many whippings, and
I should advise our grandchildren to be born with many thick skins on their backs.

Heinrich Heine,

Lutetia (1842)

Should the German people lay down arms, the Soviets . . . would occupy all eastern
and southeastern Europe, together with the greater part of the Reich. Over all this
territory, which with the Soviet Union included would be of enormous extent, an iron
curtain [*ein eiserner Vorhang*] would at once descend.

Joseph Goebbels,

Das Reich, February 23, 1945

We have a saying that the sun always rises from the East. . . . I am pleased that I
have been to the country from which the sun rises. May it shine bright and brighter.

Otto Grotewohl, toasting Soviet leaders

during his March 1948 visit to Moscow

Sunrise in the East

October 1945. It is a testament to the determination of Soviet and German education officials that the schools and universities east of the Elbe have opened at
all this fall. Just as in the western occupation zones of the Americans, French, and
British, school staff in the SBZ labor under appalling conditions. Although the
SBZ is better off in some ways than the western zones—it has more food, coal,
newsprint—its major cities, such as Dresden and Leipzig, sustained greater physical damage during the war. And now the eastern zone is suffering massive Soviet
dismantling of its factories and railroads.[1] In several cities, devastated by heavy
bombing, some school buildings are partially or totally destroyed. Only 20 of Leipzig's 105 schools have been spared; 95 percent of the school buildings in Frankfurt
an der Oder are in ruins. Even in the undamaged schools, central heating is impossible: there is no fuel.[2]

And virtually no books, no pencils, no crayons, no paper. But there are children
everywhere, 100 or more per classroom in some urban school districts, huddled
together on the floor for warmth. For while there are many fewer schools open,
there are many more children to educate. The SBZ is overflowing with more than

three million refugees who have fled before the advances of the Red Army or have been forcibly expelled from German-speaking areas of eastern Europe. Month after month for the last year the DPs (Displaced Persons) have been pouring into the SBZ. And still they come: the SBZ contains 500,0000 more children in 1945 than in 1939; an additional 319,000 will come in 1946.[3] Far worse, hundreds of thousands of children are orphaned and literally starving. In Berlin alone, the emergency relief program Rescue the Children will distribute food, clothing, shoes, and other articles to 364,000 children in the coming harsh winter of 1945/ 46.[4]

The University of Jena is also open, and the other five universities of the SBZ— in Berlin, Leipzig, Halle, Greifswald, and Rostock—will reopen in the winter. University students take lecture notes across their knees; the desks have been burned as fuel. Due to the paper shortage, few books and journals can be purchased. And Nazi book-burnings, Anglo-American bombs, and Soviet proscriptions of fascist literature have combined to decimate libraries; the circulating library at Leipzig University fills only a single small basement room.

As the days grow colder, students wear dyed *Wehrmacht* overcoats to lectures, but basic articles of clothing are hard to come by; student government leaders set up makeshift shoe repair and textile workshops on university grounds.[5] Chilling winds whistle through holes in bombed-out walls. Broken windows are patched over with "Hitler glass," as students call the thin cellophane that covers the shattered panes. "Yet another glorious gift from the *Führer!*" a few students jeer, indulging in a bit of black humor. Outside the windows, *Trümmerfrauen* (rubble women) scrounge for wood and students sift through mountains of debris for scraps of laboratory equipment and other usable supplies; all able-bodied male students must volunteer several days per semester to clear away rubble. But many are not able-bodied—most male students are war veterans, some of them suffering from tuberculosis; 20 percent are disabled or amputees.[6] Rows of seats up front are reserved for them. With their mothers or sweethearts carrying their notes and lunches, they limp to their places, faces contorted with pain. Given the shortage of seating, other students carry chairs from class to class. Or at least the lucky ones do; the remainder squeeze together atop window sills or crouch on the floor of the soot-and-ash-covered aisles. The cold air reeks of decay. But the students are grateful simply to be students.

It's 1945, and both the comforts and the venerable traditions of German university student life are no more than memories. In occupied Germany, west and east, all German traditions are suspect; the dueling fraternities of earlier eras are outlawed. But this first generation of postwar students is ravenous to make up for lost opportunities, driven by a fierce *Nachholbedarf* to compensate for the deprivations of the Nazi era: a foretaste of the feeding frenzy that will seize their intellectually starved grandchildren 45 years later with the fall of communism.

Mass devastation, fiscal anarchy, and famine-stricken, incapacitated students face educators in all four occupied zones. The SBZ, however, has an additional, long-term problem: teachers. Most of those who taught last year have been or will be fired, relegated to manual labor jobs in factories or on farms. Soviet authorities are determined to stamp out all vestiges of fascism; the USSR has suffered far more than the combined losses of the western Allies: 28 million dead, 20 million wounded, whole regions ravaged by Nazi advances and scorched-earth retreats. To the Soviets, virtually all non-leftist Germans are suspect as Nazis.

The execution of educational policy is in the hands of the education officers of SMAD (*Sowjetische Militäradministration in Deutschland*, Soviet Military Administration of Germany), the occupation government in the SBZ until 1949 and the executor of Moscow's orders in the zone. They believe that no profession is more important to cleanse of Nazi ideology than education. Seventy-two percent of the teachers in the SBZ were Nazi Party members, and the percentage of professors was even higher; all faculty in Germany were civil servants and took an oath of allegiance to the state. Like most German civil servants, faculty had traditionally opposed socialism and democracy. And whereas the western Allies are screening the political backgrounds of teachers individually and will retain or eventually rehire the majority of them, SBZ educational officials have already discharged most teachers with Nazi affiliations, keeping only those in scientific-technical subjects whose expertise is deemed indispensable.

As part of its *Entnazifizierung* (denazification) program, therefore, SMAD has or will dismiss on ideological grounds practically all teachers who had been hired during the Nazi era: 75 percent of SBZ teachers in 1945 (28,000 out of a total of 39,000) and an additional 5 percent in 1946. This leaves a staff largely consisting of the older Weimar- and Wilhelmine-era teachers, so that the mean age of the remaining staff is 52.5 (59 in Berlin), with 22 percent of teachers more than 60 years old. (At the universities, all Nazi Party faculty members have been fired, and politically persecuted or dismissed faculty have been reinstated, leaving the majority of remaining professors older than 70.)[7] Overnight, given the increased student population, the SBZ needs 40,000 new teachers.[8]

To meet the crisis, SMAD is setting up slapdash three- and four-week "crash courses" for *Neulehrer* (new teachers) and *Schulhelfer* (teachers' aides) in the summer and fall of 1945; in 1946 the course will be extended to eight months and in 1947 to one year. Sons and daughters of workers and peasants are the preferred students; they become known as the generation of *Neulehrer*. Selection criteria are ideological rather than pedagogical: "Their level of education is an indifferent matter," announce education authorities. "Elementary school education is sufficient, if the applicant is a mentally alert person and has attempted to further his own education."[9] And so numerous regions wind up with elementary schools in which 90 percent of the staff are *Neulehrer;*[10] and in the state of Mecklenburg-Vorpommern, the education minister himself has only an elementary school education.[11]

It's 1945, and educators face a formidable, even overwhelming task. And yet, a feeling of expectancy, even excitement, prevails among numerous faculty and students of anti-fascist conviction, especially those supportive of or sympathetic to communism. And no wonder: Educators have already made amazing strides in the few short months since the end of the war. . . .

April 30, 1945. In another of those strange synchronicities that seem to haunt German history, the past and future turn to face each other. On the very day that

Adolf Hitler commits suicide, and as the fires still flicker after the Battle of Berlin, two transport planes touch down in Calau, east of the Oder River. Bearing the Red star, the planes also bear the select group of German exiles who are communist Germany's future, some of them in their 30s or even 20s—an early sign of the prominent role that youth and youth policy will play in eastern Germany.

As Red Army soldiers hoist the Soviet flag atop the Reichstag on this warm spring day, Walter Ulbricht prepares with Soviet authorities to assume control of the SBZ. Like his German comrades, some of whom are returning after more than a decade in exile, Ulbricht has been waiting a long time for this day.[12] Son of a tailor, Ulbricht had become a leader of the local KPD (*Kommunistische Partei Deutschlands*, Communist Party of Germany) and a Reichstag representative during the 1920s. Known as *"Genosse Zelle"* ("Comrade Cell") for his skills in political organization—the KPD's chief activity was to establish communist cells in every factory—Ulbricht succeeded Wilhelm Pieck in 1929 to become the top official in the Berlin Party organization. When Hitler was appointed chancellor in 1933, the 40-year-old Ulbricht went underground; in 1934 he fled to Prague and then Paris. In 1938, Ulbricht was summoned to Moscow. Amid a decade of mass purges of both Russian and foreign comrades, Ulbricht assiduously worked his way up through the Moscow-based Party hierarchy, partly by following every twist and turn in Stalin's line (including a vigorous defense of the 1936–38 Moscow show trials and the 1939 Molotov-Ribbentrop Nonaggression Pact), and partly by outmaneuvering less adroit rivals. (More than 70 percent of KPD members in Russia during 1936–38—a total of 841—were arrested; only 8 were eventually released.)[13] When many foreign comrades who had spent the war years in the USSR were later asked what they'd done, they replied with dark humor: "I survived."

But by April 1945, Ulbricht has done far more than survive. Supported by Stalin and other Soviet officials, he has risen to become KPD deputy chairman; he and the 69-year-old Pieck, titular leader of the Party and future president of the DDR, are returning to Germany victorious. Prominently absent from the roll call of the KPD's top echelon is Ernst Thälmann, who was murdered in Buchenwald on direct orders from Hitler in August 1944. The leading German communist for two decades, Thälmann's arrest by the Gestapo in March 1933, imprisonment by the Nazis, and execution in Buchenwald is a story that will soon transform him into a permanent martyr of German communism.

While instructions for regulating political and cultural life in the SBZ will be issued by SMAD, German communists will administer the task of reconstruction and, at times, influence the formation of SBZ policy. The task is overwhelming: The scale of destruction that Ulbricht and the other KPD exiles witness in Berlin alone is mind-boggling: 1.1 of the 1.5 million dwellings damaged, the transportation system shattered, the food and health situation critical.[14]

Faint rays of hope, however, glimmer through the wreckage. The Dozen Year Reich is at an end. It is a moment that some older eastern Germans would later remember (or romanticize) as *"Sonnenaufgang im Osten"* (sunrise in the east), the *Stunde Null* (zero hour).[15] Despite physical ruin and human misery unmatched in Germany since the close of the Thirty Years War in 1648, the future beckons, and with it the chance to break with Germany's imperialist past.

The educational plans of the KPD have been a long time in the making. As early as the formation in July 1943 of the Moscow-based National Committee for a Free Germany, headed by Ulbricht and Pieck, the KPD had begun to grapple with the question of German educational reconstruction. In early 1944, the KPD Politburo set up a 20-member commission to determine "how the entire curriculum should be changed to liberate German youth from all fascist and imperialist influences."[16] With the Nazi regime furnishing an unforgettable illustration of how the schools could serve as an effective agency of social control, Stalin and the KPD made plans to cultivate the political advantages of direct regulation of the SBZ educational bureaucracy.

Now, in 1945, with their plans come to fruition, education and youth affairs are regarded as so important that administrative responsibility for them is assumed solely by the KPD cadre that has spent the war years in Moscow. For instance, on entering Germany in May, Anton Ackermann, one of the three leading KPD functionaries, is made responsible for "People's Education." In July, Paul Wandel, who soon serves as the first DDR Minister of Education, will take over for Ackermann and oversee faculty *Entnazifizierung* and curriculum revision as head of the newly created Educational Administration. Wilhelm Pieck's portfolio of responsibilities includes supervising KPD youth policy. Otto Winzer, later a DDR Foreign Minister, will also soon take a top post in the education ministry in Berlin's City Council. And when SMAD, usually after consultation with Ulbricht's men, appoints the education ministers for the *Länder* in a few months, all of them will be reliable communists, without exception. To an extent rivaled only by the police and security forces, all key positions in education will be occupied by top communist functionaries, and then their goal will be, as Anton Ackermann phrased it, to carry out "the political *perestroika* of the school."[17]

They will create not a "dictatorship of the proletariat," but rather an "anti-fascist democratic republic": that is the motto by which the KPD identifies its program in 1945. Or as an American historian of the DDR later put it: "To use the analogy of Russia in 1917, Germany in 1945 was experiencing its February Revolution; the October Revolution which would usher in socialism would follow later."[18]

Or, to apply the Russian comparison directly to education: This brief period in the SBZ is like the halcyon decade of creative experiment in pedagogy during the 1920s, when Lenin's wife Nadesha Krupskaya and Anatoly Lunacharsky, the first Soviet People's Minister of Education, introduced sweeping educational reforms that were themselves to be swept away by the final Stalinist crackdown in 1931.

The analogy merits consideration. For the 1930s and '40s, a period of iron-handed, tyrannical Stalinist orthodoxy in the USSR, were precisely the years that Ulbricht and the KPD exiles spent in Moscow. Toeing Stalin's shifting lines, the exiles learned to repudiate the preceding era of intellectual ferment as merely "reformist" and anarchist, an attitude that set the stage for the Stalinization of East German education. But in the summer of 1945, the climate in the SBZ is still liberal—for tactical reasons deemed necessary by the Soviets. The "iron curtain," about which Goebbels warned more than a year before Churchill's use of the phrase in his famous speech in Fulton, Missouri, has not yet descended. The Russian bear is still hibernating: Stalin has not yet been raised to the rank of "the greatest scholar of all time"; the long winter night of terror against "cosmopolitanism" and "objectivism" has not yet fallen over the SBZ. And yet: the Orwellian chants portended that a new German dictatorship is about to replace the old one.

WHO HAS THE YOUTH, HAS THE FUTURE!

KNOWLEDGE IS POWER! / POWER IS KNOWLEDGE!

OUR NEW LIFE MUST BE DIFFERENT!

That summer and fall of 1945 witness the fall and rise of an educational system, and the fall and rise of two radically opposed ways of life in eastern Germany: the beginning of the excruciating, albeit inexorable forced march from National Socialism to German "democratic" socialism.

This is the opening scene of education's role in that transition and in the drama of postwar German reconstruction that follows, the story of the function of the educational system in East German life—from Hitler to Ulbricht to Honecker, from the Reich in rubble to "sunrise in the East" to ultimate disillusion with communism. As we shall see, the making and unmaking of the German communist bore notable similarities to the making and unmaking of the German Nazi.

And in both cases, education—the "citadel of learning"—was of paramount importance. "Let the children come unto me," declaimed Hitler, "for they are mine unto death!" Declared Stalin: "Education is a weapon, and its effect depends on who holds it in his hands and at whom it is aimed."

Given its abrupt metamorphosis from Nazism to Stalinism, no nation furnishes the historian with a better opportunity to study the interaction between ideological politics and educational policy than the former East Germany. For nowhere was the trench campaign to win minds more fierce than in divided Germany—particularly in East Germany, with the West's so-called Isle of Freedom, West Berlin, encamped at its very heart. Until 1961, educators and propagandists of both Germanies were constantly confronted with the success or failure of their efforts: Germans east and west could vote with their feet and easily resettle *drüben*. Even after the borders were closed, DDR citizens were deluged by western TV, music and ideas. East German education necessarily, therefore, became more overtly ideological than elsewhere in Eastern Europe. It needed to wipe out tendencies toward both capitalism and Nazism—while implying, meanwhile, that nobody left in "*das bessere Deutschland*" ("the better Germany") had a Nazi past. It also had to distinguish itself in extreme form from West Germany: aside from ideological differences—the DDR's claim to be the better, "socialist" Germany—there was simply no compelling reason for the tiny DDR to exist at all. Unlike other Eastern European countries, the five states of the DDR had never previously been an administrative unit. Without a common history or common traditions, their linkage was purely a creation of World War II and Stalin himself. No other communist state faced a comparable problem of legitimacy and identity—and risked losing millions of its citizens to a rival neighbor. So East German educators needed to promote Marxism-Leninism more aggressively than communists elsewhere—and they did so by mid-century, after the Soviets largely abandoned their democratic tactics (and their hopes of a neutral reunited Germany) and began to sovietize the SBZ relentlessly.

Today we know the disastrous dénouement of the DDR's failed campaign. But few Americans know this dramatic, complicated history and its relevance to us. The repeated ballyhoos over "anti-fascist democratic" reforms in the 1940s, the Stalinization and militarization of the system in the late 1940s and 1950s, the shift to polytechnical education in the 1960s, the emergence of an educational elite in the 1970s, the losing race in the 1980s to adapt education to the economic realities posed by the "technical-scientific revolution": education occupied the front lines of East Germany's vain struggle to keep pace with capitalism. As we shall see, a sketch of its vicissitudes offers a sharply focused history—from the communist side—of the role of state cultural policy in education and of the postwar propaganda battle between East and West.

From Brown to Blue?

In Germany you cannot have a revolution because you would have to step on the lawns.

Lenin

The communist phoenix ascended from the Nazi ashes. But was its own pitiful end 44 years later inevitable from its beginning? It is clear alone that the postwar course of development of the region that became the SBZ, and then the DDR, would have taken an entirely different course if administered by the western Allies or occupied in common by all four countries.

And indeed it began quite differently: much of the area that became the SBZ had been occupied by the American and British armies in the spring of 1945. But because the Yalta Conference of February 1945 had specified that the Soviet Union would administer the German *Länder* east of the Elbe, Anglo-American troops departed once the Red Army arrived. That wartime agreement determined the fate of Germans along the Elbe for decades: "eastern" Germany—which most Germans continued to call *Mitteldeutschland* (middle Germany), even though the further-most eastern territory of Greater Germany had been parceled out to Poland and the USSR in 1945—became the SBZ.[19]

But "eastern" Germany might not have remained the SBZ—after all, the Allied powers had also occupied, and split up, Austria, nevertheless agreeing to its re-unification on the condition that it remain politically neutral. But Yalta was followed by the Potsdam Conference in July/August 1945, at which the Allied consensus emerged that the special case of Germany warranted special treatment. Germany was different: Not only the aggressor in the war, it was also the key nation on the continent. As Lenin once said, "Who controls Germany, controls Europe." And so the four Allies formulated their postwar aims of German occupation as the 4 Ds: demilitarization, deindustrialization, denazification, and democratization.[20]

Umerziehung or "re-education" was chosen as the means for achieving the latter pair, a psychopolitical strategy aimed at altering the authoritarian, militaristic foundations on which earlier German regimes had been based.[21] Germans would be re-educated to embrace liberalism and the rule of law rather than Hegelian statism and the ideology of power politics.

To all four Allies, re-education meant inculcating the principles of "democratic" thought and practice according to their own national ideals. And so it was, in each of the four Allied zones, that occupation authorities attempted to reform German institutions—through Leninist "democratic centralism," in SMAD's version.[22]

Nor were the Soviets the only occupying power to focus upon the educational system. The western Allies had high hopes for their own programs of democratic re-education, believing that the schools were the key to re-education. "In no field," one American report concluded, "is complete denazification so important."[23] Or as one British wartime policymaker bluntly put it, education was the crucial institution for "stamp[ing] out the whole tradition on which the German nation has been built."[24]

By late 1946, however, the western Allies had all but forsaken any systematic attempt to achieve such ambitions, abandoning the original grandiose plans of Potsdam, whereby re-education would revolutionize and democratize the allegedly "authoritarian personality" of the Germans.[25] In the western zones, re-education efforts were largely thwarted by the local population, by "a clear majority who, while they accepted the desirability of sweeping away Nazi innovations, were inclined to regard the approach to education enshrined in pre-1933 institutions as essentially sound."[26] In contrast to the western disinclination toward rigorous *Umerziehung*, the Soviets executed the policy ruthlessly, from teacher denazification to curricular and syllabus reform. Aside from their determination to extirpate anti-fascism, however, this is not to say that Soviet re-education policymakers executed a carefully worked-out vision for the SBZ's future. Indeed, it is fair to say that "SBZ re-education was characterized by the unplanned destruction of everything nonconformist."[27]

Reasoning that the 19 million Germans of the Soviet zone were, aside from a small minority, Nazis who had forfeited the right to voice any opinion about their future, Soviet officials did not seek the close cooperation of the SBZ populace, though they often consulted with Ulbricht's men on execution of policy. Thus, for instance, in its very first week, SMAD simply ordered the permanent closure of all religious schools, reopening them as public institutions in which religious instruction was permitted, provisionally, on a voluntary basis. Even more so than in the case of the western Allies, the Soviet relationship to Germans was more that of victor to vanquished.

And yet anti-democratic tendencies would survive both approaches to education. In the western zones, because of the increasing western concern with combating communism rather than Nazism, serious educational reform was stymied; it did not begin in West Germany until the late 1960s. "No experiments" in education was the rule, since experimentation evoked fears of left-wing schemes. As a result, the West German school system remained essentially in its nineteenth-century condition, largely untouched by the reforms that had occurred throughout the remainder of postwar Europe, until the worldwide student unrest of 1968. Well into the 1970s, the BRD was among the most educationally backward of northern

European countries, an unreconstructed exception among the increasingly egalitarian school systems of Europe. Meanwhile, East-West tensions also made SMAD anti-fascist education policy, and indeed the entire DDR educational system, all the more rigid and imperious, so that much of the Prussian tradition that had inspired and nurtured National Socialism survived in the east too. Thus the Cold War cut short *Entnazifizierung* in western education, and by combining it with Stalinist indoctrination, transformed and intensified it in eastern education. Indeed, some historians argue that re-education failed in the west because occupation authorities heeded the Germans too much—and in the east because they consulted them too little.[28]

But that wasn't how the majority of the million rank-and-file members of the German Left in the SBZ felt in 1945. Their sense of promise was celebrated in the East German national anthem, written by the regime's leading writer Johannes Becher and set to melody by national award-winning composer Hanns Eisler when the SBZ became the DDR in 1949:

> Arisen from ruins
> and gazing on the future,
> let us serve the Good,
> Germany, united Fatherland.
> Ancient hopes impel us,
> and united we urge the prospect on.
> It will yet pass
> that the sun, more beautiful than ever,
> shines over Germany,
> shines over Germany.

The national anthem gave pride of place to the forthcoming generation of German youth. As the final stanza declared:

> Let us plow, let us farm,
> learn and create as never before,
> and if we trust to our capacities,
> a free race will arise.
> German youth! The best hope
> of our people is embodied in you.
> You will become Germany's new life
> and the sun, more beautiful than ever,
> will shine over Germany,
> will shine over Germany.

Indeed, much of the widespread hope about the SBZ in those early postwar years had to do with educational reconstruction and progressive youth programs. Whereas the *Länder* in the western zones were returning to versions of the elitist Weimar educational system, educators in the SBZ rhapsodized about their introduction of *die neue schule* (the new school).

"die neue schule."

With the noun deliberately dethroned to the lower case to symbolize the populist character of the democratic school, communist educators announced their program in a phrase that resounded in Party meetings and schoolrooms throughout the late 1940s. Arisen from ruins, proclaimed the politicians, eastern Germany was launching one of the most far-reaching experiments in educational history: the radical transformation of an advanced nation's view of the world, its history, and reality itself. To most lower-echelon left-wing politicians and educators, *die neue schule* promised an egalitarian future. It would enable German youth to "learn and create as never before." *"Der neue sozialistische Mensch"* ("the new socialist human being") of democratic Germany would be its handiwork: "German youth! The best hope / of our people is embodied in you."

In this spirit, the *Tägliche Rundschau*, the official organ of SMAD, greeted children on the opening day of school:

> The young people that are streaming on this day into school will not—from the outside—exactly see an ideal state of affairs. And yet, one must emphasize that this school year is the happiest ever for German youth.[29]

But anyone who could see—and hear—beyond the rhetoric might have discerned that communist machinations were already under way in the SBZ to transform the new school into an institution not so different from its immediate predecessor.

OUR NEW LIFE MUST BE DIFFERENT!

SMAD and the KPD did not show their true colors all at once. The progress from brown to red was a camouflaged process, the meanings of the shifting tints and tones of KPD proclamations and SMAD policies obscure to the uninitiated. Indeed, despite the extraordinary hardships of postwar rebuilding, the outlook for the SBZ educational system did seem auspicious during its first stage of development (1945–47). To unsuspecting eyes, a democratic spring appeared ready to bloom. *Pace* Lenin, eastern Germany's trampled lawn had been replanted as a botanical garden.

Or so it seemed.

Only Ulbricht's inner circle knew that his operative strategy was what some German historians subsequently termed *Scheindemokratie* (seeming-democracy).[30] "It must look democratic," Ulbricht told his lieutenants. "But we must keep everything in our hands."[31] Following Stalinist practice and guided by SMAD's aims, he opposed all individual initiative on political matters. The multitude of tiny anti-Nazi groups that had sprung up spontaneously in the last months of the war were forced to disband, their members told to work for SMAD or retire from politics. The "anti-fascist democratic revolution" was to be administered from above.

Thus, even as KPD politicians were heralding the birth of a democratic age in German history, the KPD was maneuvering to gain control of key institutions through the subterfuge of *Scheindemokratie*, which made a policy out of Lenin's famous slogan, "One step backwards—two steps forwards": First pursue the class struggle via liberal bourgeois policies, counseled Lenin; then, striking from within, vitiate the policies and subvert their reformist supporters; finally, execute the revolutionary communist program. In education, the strategy ensured the safe passage from "the new democratic school" to the little Red schoolhouse.

And so the fate of eastern Germany and its schools *was* decided in those early months in 1945 after all, even if the precise direction of SBZ/DDR policy may have remained unclear to Stalin himself. With the accident of Soviet occupation came the inevitability of Soviet domination, though the extent of the control was at first concealed, especially within the educational system. Whatever their official pronouncements, however, genuine "pedagogical reform never entered the calculations of communist education" policymakers.[32]

Still, it wasn't yet obvious in 1945, as apparently democratic institutions sprouted in the SBZ, that SMAD would operate in a rigidly authoritarian manner or that the Soviets were little committed to notions such as forming "the socialist human being," but rather to advancing their own geopolitical interests. In hindsight, however, it is clear that SMAD's central goal was always to further Moscow's two long-term strategic options: first, to transform the SBZ into a Marxist-Leninist state; or second—and even better if possible—cloak its development as democratic in order ultimately to win over a reunited Germany to Marxism-Leninism (or, at minimum, to political neutrality). In the early postwar years, Moscow pursued the latter option; when its prospects for success darkened in the Cold War climate of the late 1940s and early 1950s, it settled for the former.

Understandably, after the trauma of Nazi tyranny, it was, at first, easy for even the East German bourgeoisie to identify with the progressive SMAD/KPD program; the SBZ would very likely have voted socialist or social democratic in 1945 had SMAD permitted free elections. Moreover, SMAD and the KPD took pains to allay widespread (and, in hindsight, thoroughly justified) German fears that the USSR's ambition in the SBZ was merely to replace a right-wing dictatorship with a left-wing one: to substitute Soviet rule for Nazi rule. Because most Germans harbored a strong antipathy toward the Russians, KPD leaders publicly dissociated the KPD from the USSR to dispel the (correct) impression that the KPD was "the Russians' party." In its opening proclamation of June 11, 1945—delivered just two days after SMAD itself was formally instituted—the KPD assured Germans that it considered the Soviet Union an inappropriate model for the future of the SBZ:

> We believe that to coerce Germany to adopt the Soviet system is a false course. For such a course does not correspond to the present conditions of development in Germany. Rather, we believe that the interests of the German people necessitate another course: the construction of an anti-fascist, democratic republic, with full democratic rights and freedoms for the people.[33]

This statement was immediately applied to educational reconstruction; it anticipated perfectly the spirit of Point 7 of the Potsdam Agreement of August 1945: "German education shall be so controlled as to eliminate Nazi and militarist doctrines and to make possible the successful development of democratic ideas."[34] In addition to the "new democratic school," the KPD publicly supported free trade, private business initiative on the basis of respect for private property, and the formation of a parliamentary, democratic republic.

And there seemed to be free public argument about the nature of the socialist future for the SBZ—indeed, a number of prominent German non-communist radicals and Social Democrats disagreed vocally with Ulbricht's hard-line, pro-Soviet policy. There even seemed to be opposing public viewpoints within the KPD. Arguing that communism could not ignore particular national developments, some German communists supported instead a separate "German road to socialism," the phrase of Anton Ackermann's much-discussed February 1946 article in *Einheit*, the KPD's theoretical journal. Titled "Is There a Special German Road to Socialism?" the article is now considered by most historians to have been part of *Scheindemokratie*, designed in particular to allay widespread fears among non-communist leftists that the KPD aimed to abandon the German socialist tradition, thus consigning the SBZ to the fate of becoming Stalin's puppet.[35]

That, of course, is precisely what did happen, in line with the SMAD/KPD blueprint. And whatever Ackermann's own intentions, *Scheindemokratie* served to deceive the East German public about their leaders' long-range plans.

Scheindemokratie thus operated as an attractive, if clandestine, policy choice for SMAD and the KPD, the ideological outcome of which was that the KPD revived the Communist International's prewar Popular Front policy. This strategy was designed, as in the 1930s, to broaden the communists' base of support among social democrats and centrists. The word *Scheindemokratie* sums up the complicated strategy well: the use of apparently democratic (albeit undemocratic in fact) means to secure "democratic"—i.e., democratic *centralist*, a.k.a. Marxist-Leninist—ends. Dictatorial methods would be used to achieve the dictatorship of the "proletariat"—i.e., of the Party leadership.

Once again: the Russians and the German communists did not conduct these political maneuvers openly. Rather, Ulbricht and his circle worked to create the appearance of commitment to building a bourgeois, anti-fascist order, reasoning it was more to their long-term benefit to make it seem as if the Germans' embrace of communism arose as a popular initiative from below.

This approach applied especially to education. The declarations of Ulbricht's cadre during 1945–47 made no explicit mention of "socialist education" or "Marxist" approaches to school reform. The bywords were "anti-fascism," "anti-militarism," "peace," "freedom," "democracy," and "humanism." Speaking the language of the Weimar educational reformers, the Ulbricht circle limited public discussion to those liberal and radical proposals that had won broad support on the Left during the Weimar era: the abolition of educational privilege, the firm separation of church and school, and the creation of the uniform, comprehensive school.

And yet: though SMAD and the KPD moved quickly to capture "the citadel of learning," their careful campaign might never have succeeded without crucial support from another socialist ally: the SPD (*Sozialdemokratische Partei Deutschlands*, Social Democratic Party of Germany).

Historically, the KPD and SPD had vied with each other for leadership on the Left since the founding of the KPD in the wake of the Russian Revolution and the failed November Revolution of 1918/19 in Germany. As the older party, however, the SPD had remained the larger of the two, always committed to a gradualist reform program and parliamentary methods. In the 1930s, attempting to win workers away from its more moderate rival, the KPD castigated the SPD, arguing that the Social Democrats, by undermining the revolutionary workers' movement led by the communists, were—"objectively," in Marxist-Leninist jargon—"social fascists." The mutual hostility arising from that struggle had split the Left and eventually facilitated Hitler's rise to power. Hitler soon declared both parties illegal; their leaders were jailed, went underground, or fled the country.

In June 1945, mindful of this history, the renascent SPD proposed that the two parties reunite and thereby ensure that socialist forces would dominate political life in the SBZ. Still the bigger party (SPD: 680,000; KPD: 620,000), the SPD reasoned that it would be the senior partner in any union. But, adhering to his strategy of *Scheindemokratie* and seeking with SMAD's help to build up the KPD, Ulbricht opposed what he termed "premature" fusion, claiming that the parties were not yet "ready" to merge. Less than a year later, however, worried because communists in Austria and Hungary had fared poorly in recent elections there, and hoping to avoid a competitive election campaign that would expose his party's own weaknesses, Ulbricht reversed his position and advocated immediate union.[36] But by then the SPD was reluctant, suspecting the KPD's *Scheindemokratie* strategy.

After enormous pressure from SMAD and the KPD, who worked together to license other political parties and then coopt them, the SPD hesitantly agreed to form a left-wing "unity party" with the KPD.[37] The result was the founding of the SED (*Sozialistische Einheitspartei*, Socialist Unity Party).

That step of April 22, 1946—significantly, the anniversary of Lenin's birthday—constituted a major triumph for Soviet policy, determining the course of East German politics for the next four decades. It followed by several months an equally important step, the formation of an "anti-fascist democratic bloc" party system, into which the CDU (*Christlich-Demokratische Union*, Christian Democratic Union) and the LDP (*Liberaldemokratische Partei*, the Liberal Democratic Party) entered. These parties, versions of which had also been outlawed under Hitler, were beginning to reconstitute themselves even before this political bloc system developed. The new bloc, however, proved with time to be little more than a front for the SED, which in turn was ruled by the KPD old guard. The inexorable rise of the SED, as one western Sovietologist observed, showed that Stalin had learned from Hitler the "technique of the 'legal' seizure of the state machine."[38]

Nevertheless, in the autumn of 1945 the KPD and SPD were still operating independently, cooperating especially closely in the area in which they shared much common ground: education. Above all, the KPD and SPD could agree here on what they opposed: fascism.

In their first major joint declaration that October, the KPD/SPD gave priority to education and youth policy. A broad coalition of left, center, and even conservative SBZ Germans found little to dispute in their democratic rhetoric:

With an inhumanity that is hardly comparable in all of history, [the Nazis] extinguished the moral and physical energies of our youth and subverted their education. Our youth's course of development was undermined by forced participation in hollow organizations; they were sacrificed in a criminal war just as they were on the brink of their mature years, before they could realize the potential of their lives. . . . It was also part of the evil heritage of the German school that children were educated to be passive subjects rather than independent thinkers. Nazi rule deformed the school into a drilling institution, in order to prepare youth for its predatory war. The result was that our own children were ultimately fed to the canons too.[39]

Today that statement, in the historical aftermath of decades of the SED dictatorship, rings ironically. The KPD, with the unwitting support of the SPD, renewed rather than overcame the "evil heritage of the German school" through *Scheindemokratie*, which it pursued single-mindedly during 1945–47. A significant example was the reorganization of extracurricular youth activities, which were declared "liberated" from the influence of the political parties.

Here too a democratic ray of hope seemed to shine. Behind the scenes, however, SMAD and the KPD pursued their mutual agenda. After SMAD licensed the formation of youth committees in June 1945, Ulbricht announced, in an apparent show of tolerance, that the KPD did not seek to organize a specifically communist youth committee. Rather, it supported the creation of a nonpartisan, anti-fascist, common "free youth movement."

The affiliation of youth organizations with major political parties had long been a German tradition. In the Weimar era, each party had its youth organization. One of the Nazis' first political moves in 1933 had been to disband all non-Nazi youth organizations; in 1938, the Third Reich required that all Aryan boys and girls, at the age of 10, join the junior affiliates of the HJ (*Hitler Jugend*, Hitler Youth) and BDM (*Bund Deutscher Mädchen*, German Girls League), where they were told that their lives were to be dedicated to the state. In the HJ, young boys donned uniforms and received daggers to wear in their belts; chanting marching tunes, they carried flags as they paraded down the street to the *"hurra!"* of their neighbors, "just like big soldiers." In the BDM, young girls were taught to dream of mothering golden-haired, blue-eyed Aryan children, perhaps even becoming "Hitler brides." Some girls signed papers avowing their willingness to bear children for the state from "Germany's noblest manhood"—an SS soldier. In strong pro-Nazi circles, such an illegitimate pregnancy usually brought no shame upon them; to the contrary, if a girl were "carrying the *Führer*'s baby," she was a heroine.[40]

At first glance, the KPD's break with such exploitative practices, which had turned German youth organizations into blatant instruments of Nazi ideology, seemed consistent with its rejection of fascism and call for a fresh start. In time, however, the real reason became clear: the KPD wanted an unaffiliated, unified movement that it could, in turn, then dominate. It agreed with SMAD about the abolition of all denominational schools and the establishment of a single, compulsory school system for the same tactical reason: to prevent sectarianism and to work instead on delivering control of one organization into communist hands.

The strategy soon proved successful. In March 1946, SMAD recognized the founding of the FDJ (*Freie Deutsche Jugend*, Free German Youth). "The new organization may on no account support military or fascist tendencies," said SMAD. "It must serve the friendship of peoples."[41] Not a word about support for socialism or communism. Indeed, to avoid any appearance of its being communist-dominated, the KPD urged that the FDJ flag *not* be red. To give the impression of a politically and spiritually ecumenical youth organization, the KPD welcomed the FDJ's choice of blue,[42] traditionally associated with innocence and purity— "the color of youth," as KPD leaders put it. In the flag's center, against a sky blue background, blazed a bright yellow, rising sun.[43]

In December 1946, 34-year-old Erich Honecker was elected chairman of the Central Council of the FDJ. Following his father, who was a miner, a trade union activist, and a KPD activist, young Erich had already, by the age of 10, joined the KJVD (*Kommunistische Jugendverband Deutschlands*, Communist Youth League of Germany, a.k.a. the Young Spartacists). At 17, working as an apprentice roofer, Erich became a full KPD member. The next year, he was chosen to attend a special cadre school of the Communist Youth International in Moscow. After 1933, he operated as the underground agitprop leader of the KJVD in his native Saar, headed the Berlin KJVD, and was elected a member of the KJVD Central Committee. In December 1935, he was arrested for high treason and sentenced to 10 years' hard labor in Brandenburg-Görlitz prison. There he befriended many elder communist inmates and established contacts that would later prove useful to his Party career. During the closing weeks of the war, he escaped from prison, but secretly returned amid the chaos of the Battle of Berlin, fearful that roving bands of Allied troops might mistake him for a Nazi. Finally liberated from prison by the Red Army, he returned to KPD activism in May 1945, becoming the youth secretary of the KPD Central Committee; given his experience with the KJVD, he was regarded as well-qualified to head the FDJ. As FDJ president, a position invested with considerable patronage powers, Honecker worked with his superiors to choose the members of what would become the FDJ Central Committee. Eighty of its 100 seats were given to members of the SED; within a year, all non-SED members were expelled.

WHO HAS THE YOUTH, HAS THE FUTURE!

FDJ "Blueshirts," appearances notwithstanding, were to be good Reds. Parallels with the Hitler Youth and the Brownshirts went unremarked in the SBZ—at least publicly.

The evolution of the FDJ exemplifies the lightning pace of events in early post-war SBZ education. Such developments in youth and education policy mirrored the rapidly changing political situation in the SBZ during its first two years, as tensions between the Soviets and western Allies mounted. The four Allies re-mained uneasily united by virtue of their anti-fascism, but a period of pre–Cold War shadow-boxing ensued, with the West and the USSR each competing to win German public opinion in and outside their occupation zones.

Nevertheless, still laboring under the guise of *Scheindemokratie*, SMAD took no chances when it came to education, especially with the landmark legislative event of the early postwar era in education: the 1946 "Law on the Democratization of the Schools." SMAD simply decreed the law on June 12, 1946—the date was celebrated from 1951 on as Teachers' Day—and the provisional administrations of the *Länder* ratified it before the local and *Land* elections in October 1946. These were the first and last elections in eastern Germany in which a political choice was open to voters; from that time forward in the SBZ and DDR, there were only single lists of candidates. Thus, in sharp contrast to the western zones, where educational policy was endlessly debated and changes were strongly resisted by the local population, education in the SBZ did not become an issue on which public opinion in the SBZ was directly consulted: SMAD and the KPD/SED judged the risk of opposition too great. As a DDR historian later explained:

> To renounce public discussion of the crafting of the Education Act aimed to hinder the reactionaries, who by pseudo-democratic methods would have frustrated a true democratization of the education system. The approach corresponded fully to the task of the revolutionary workers and peasants. It was in the interest of the overwhelming majority of the people to apply dictatorial methods toward the imperialistic bourgeoisie and their political followers.[44]

The Education Act was—on paper—a model of democratic legislation. It established that

1. all children were to have equal rights to education regardless of property, religion, or ethnic heritage;
2. education was the responsibility of the state;
3. private schools were forbidden;[45] and
4. the former hierarchical, undemocratic system of primary and secondary schools was to be replaced by a uniform, compulsory eight-year school.

State-administered common schooling, the SED held, guaranteed social justice: upper-class children would lose their traditional advantages afforded by the *Gymnasium;* working-class children would have a fair chance of gaining entry to secondary and higher education. The Act thus eliminated two long-standing features of German education: decentralized administration and elite schooling. Although the populace was not consulted, most of the changes—with the exception of the abolition of religious schools and of the traditional *Gymnasium*—were widely welcomed as a return to pre-Nazi educational values and the enactment of the best features of the Weimar-era *Reformpädagogik* (pedagogical reform) movement—support for which had, by chance, been strongest in the region of the SBZ.[46]

The 1946 Act did not mention socialism or communism. Instead it simply hailed *die neue schule* as a break with imperialism and the fulfillment of the German humanistic tradition:

> The new democratic school must be free from all tendencies toward militarism, imperialism, popular agitation, and racial hatred. It must be developed so that all youths, boys and girls, urban and rural children, without distinction according to the wealth of their parents, are guaranteed the same right to education and the realization of their abilities and potentials. . . .

As the transmitter of culture, the school has the task of liberating the youth from nazi and militaristic ideas and educating them toward a belief in the peaceful and friendly communion of peoples and the spirit of true democracy and genuine humanity. Without regard for their possessions, religious beliefs, or ethnic heritage, the school must provide, according to social need, full training of their abilities. . . . [47]

"It wasn't a school reform," wrote a DDR historian of that first year. "It was a revolution."[48]

And the revolutionary fervor swept the universities too.

Here too, from the outside, everything seemed democratic. *"Erziehung zum wahrhaft fortschrittlichen Humanismus!"* was the slogan proclaimed by SED education officials: "Education toward truly progressive humanism!" The revival of the hallowed German tradition of *Lehrfreiheit und Lernfreiheit* (professorial and student freedom) was announced, along with the principle of nonpolitical criteria for student admissions, the free choice of academic courses, and the independence of university administrators from state interference. SMAD "summoned the Herren Professoren to execute the work of *Umerziehung* toward democracy of the German *Volk*."[49] In addition to the dismissal of all Nazi faculty, the work included rehabilitation and reinstatement of all politically persecuted or dismissed professors and the development of special admissions criteria for students disadvantaged or disqualified from study by the Third Reich. Anti-fascist professors like Eduard Spranger in Berlin and Hans Georg Gadamer in Leipzig assumed leading administrative positions; refugee scholars flocked back to the SBZ to occupy the vacant academic chairs, joining scores of prominent anti-fascist German artists and writers—among them Alexander Abusch, Bertolt Brecht, Willi Bredel, Stephan Hermlin, Stefan Heym, Theodor Plievier, Anna Seghers, Bodo Uhse, Erich Weinert, Friedrich Wolf, and Arnold Zweig—who were coming to the SBZ because they identified strongly with the German progressive tradition and wanted to place their talents at the service of the reconstruction effort. Many of the returning professors and artists were "bourgeois humanists" rather than Marxist-Leninists; roughly half of the aforementioned figures were long-standing KPD (and later SED) members. Surely the universities would lead the SBZ in its quest to become the first stable, enduring democracy on German soil.[50]

And yet, an observer with an eye for detail might have caught a hint of magenta in the FDJ's blue shirts even at the start. The future could already be glimpsed in December 1945 when the University of Jena was closed, just two months after it opened, because SMAD discovered "fascist elements." A SMAD representative had delivered a lecture in which he had stressed the extraordinarily high living standard of Russian workers. His claim had met with skepticism on the part of many Jena students. Such freethinking rendered the entire student body suspect as fascists, and all students had to undergo yet another political screening. The incident was not reported in the SMAD-licensed press; the German public remained largely unaware of it.[51]

And indeed the universities proved difficult for the SED to bring under control. Although 90 percent of the faculty had been fired as "Nazi-compromised" at some universities, and 54 percent of newly hired faculty belonged to the SED by late 1946, most professors and students still did not toe a party line. For this brief moment, faculty hiring and student admissions criteria still focused on merit rather than political orthodoxy. And in the student government elections of spring 1946, SED candidates did not dominate the newly formed "anti-fascist student boards," receiving no more than 10 to 45 percent of the vote. All this would change, but it would take more than a decade to bring the universities to heel.[52]

In 1946/47, however, the SED still hoped that strong-arm tactics wouldn't be necessary to transform their ideals into reality. Committed both to social justice and to developing every individual's capacities fully, educators swung open the doors of the university to all student applicants, even former military officers and members of the NSDAP (*Nationalsozialistische Deutsche Arbeiterpartei*, National Socialist German Workers' Party; the Nazis). Only SS members or high NSDAP officials were excluded.

Even in higher education, insisted SED officials, the SBZ could become an equal opportunity educator; they dreamed not just of building a true, egalitarian *Volksschule* (people's school) but of creating a *Volksuniversität* (people's university). Traditionally, only about 4 percent of German university students had been from working-class and peasant families, whose children commonly left school at the age of 14. To diversify the student body and provide future access to lower-class children, education authorities introduced special preparatory courses to accelerate their progress toward the *Abitur* (high school diploma) and university—an idea anticipating American remedial and affirmative action programs. This new initiative took root. Soon officials formalized it into a pedagogical division of the universities, the ABF (*Arbeiter-und-Bauern-Fakultät*, Worker and Peasant Faculty). All universities also founded institutes of teacher training, reflecting the new priority in the arts and humanities of teaching over research. Such measures boosted the proportion of students from worker and peasant families attending secondary schools (from 19 percent in 1946 to 36.2 percent in 1949) and improved the quality of teaching in the schools.[53]

For years afterward, leaders of the self-proclaimed "First German Workers' and Peasants' State" would proclaim the educational revolution of 1945–47 as one of East Germany's greatest achievements, the realization of Marx's hopes voiced in *The Communist Manifesto*. SED officials exalted its centerpiece, *die neue schule*, as the culmination of a distinguished line of progressive educational experiments, and the fulfillment of the egalitarian dreams of political leaders and educational reformers on the Left—hallowed names stretching from the Renaissance to the Second Reich and the Weimar Republic, from Comenius to Marx, Wilhelm Liebknecht, Clara Zetkin, and Georg Kerschensteiner.[54] "A struggle that has persisted for a century," proclaimed the mayor of Leipzig about the Education Act, "has finally reached its successful end."[55]

Not quite yet it hadn't.

Nor, we now know, would it ever.

The Democratic Experiment is *zu Ende*

Wherever Stalin walks, the grass grows no more.

German proverb

And what do I tell the people now? That we fought against one tyranny, only to replace it with another?

Stefan Heym,
The Papers of Andreas Lenz (1964)

Had the SED actually followed through on the 1946 Education Act, had its vaunted reforms been more than merely the facade of *Scheindemokratie*, the speech of the mayor of Leipzig would have been merely hyperbolic: SBZ education *would* have led the next generation, if not to a conclusive success story, at least to a promising new beginning. Even education officers in the American occupation zone expressed grudging admiration for the radical reforms begun in the SBZ.[56] Moreover, though SMAD did not seek public approval for its educational policy, many eastern Germans—at least until 1947—apparently believed and supported the SED statutes and proclamations. They believed, that is, that blue meant blue: that their leaders' democratic aspirations were genuine.

And indeed, the opening phase of East German education appeared democratic in design *and* execution. The uniform school, the abolition of educational privilege, the guarantee of a free elementary schooling: these *were* democratic reforms. In July 1947, continuing in the spirit of *Reformpädagogik*, the KPD and SPD issued a joint declaration as one of their final acts as distinctive parties within the SED. Titled "The Educational Principles of the Democratic School," the declaration proclaimed five essential precepts: equal educational opportunity for all, a uniform school system, the development of civic responsibility in students, the inculcation of a democratic *Weltanschauung*, and respect for all nations and races.[57] But in the next two decades, the SED would betray every one of these principles: children of SED members would receive numerous educational advantages, special schools for the gifted would be introduced, mass youth organizations run by the state (e.g., the FDJ) would wrest all personal initiative from the youth, Leninist bureaucratic centralism would be enshrined as official doctrine, and ideological intolerance and even hatred would be inculcated toward non-communists. Indeed, already by the end of the second phase of its educational history (1947–51), the SBZ/DDR had effectively abandoned all attempts to live up to "The Educational Principles of the Democratic School." Or as one scholar of DDR education has noted, by mid-century "the transformation from a pedagogy without a people to a pedagogy against the People was nearing its end."[58]

In fact, as early as 1947, Stalin's boot prints were becoming visible across the landscape of Soviet zone education: the unmistakable sign that the transplanted garden of democracy would never take root in the SBZ. That year the SED began selectively excluding from the so-called People's Universities qualified applicants who had bourgeois backgrounds or whose families had any Nazi connections whatsoever.[59] Educational opportunity became the explicit instrument for radically restructuring the social system. Now class background, rather than academic achievement or family income, served as the sole criterion for financial aid; 75 percent of scholarship assistance was reserved for workers and peasants. Where once it had been hard for a worker's child to go to university, now it became difficult in the self-proclaimed First German Workers' and Peasants' State for a bourgeois son or daughter to do so.[60]

SMAD's original concerns during 1945/46 about the narcotic of fascist ideology surviving in the schools had been legitimate.[61] But now, once enrolled in the People's University, the SBZ student received large doses of SMAD's own opiate: Marxist-Leninist ideology. By 1947, universities began to require courses such as Philosophy of Marxism-Leninism, Dialectical and Historical Materialism, Political Economy, Introduction to Social Studies, and the History of the Soviet Union. The fields of political science, economics, and history became Marxist-Leninist training centers: 95 percent of students pursuing degrees in the social sciences were SED members. In 1948/49, the universities instituted additional requirements in the History of the Labor Movement, Political and Social Problems of Today, and German History.[62] The transformation of the SBZ into the DDR in October 1949 had little effect on educational policy; the SED's ideological campaign proceeded apace. In 1949/50, the schools officially adopted the new curricula too: *Gegenwartskunde* (Marxist-Leninist current events) laid down the Party line on topical issues and featured weekly themes such as "Stalin, leader of the world peace front."[63]

"Communism," Stalin had told the wartime Polish leader Stanislav Mikolajczyk, "fits the Germans as well as a saddle fits a cow." By mid-century, Ulbricht appeared to have saddled the cow. Now came the time to milk it.[64]

So now the real horror stories of Stalinist terror commenced—or, for some unfortunates who had also suffered under the Third Reich, resumed once again. The economics student at Halle who admitted in an interview that he had read several pages by Adam Smith; the English teacher in Leipzig who had used an old copy of *National Geographic*: both were forced to engage in public self-criticism, guilty of the sins of "cosmopolitanism" and "objectivism," i.e., maintaining openness toward or sympathy for "western" ideas.[65]

But they were lucky. In 1950, 19 high school students from Zwickau were arrested for protesting against the election to the People's Parliament that October, the first election in the infant DDR. "Vote 'No' Against Stalin's Pathetic Toadies!" they chanted. "Vote Against the SED-Bigwigs and for Freedom from Fear and Need!" "Rise Up Against the Soviet Dictatorship!" The bill of particulars against them read:

- incitement to boycott against democratic institutions and organizations;
- hatred of the People;
- incitement to war;
- propaganda for National Socialism;

- the invention and spreading of tendentious rumors that endanger the freedom of the German people and the peace of the world.[66]

The pupils were sentenced to an aggregate of 130 years in prison. The DDR election ended with a result of 99.71 percent "yes" votes, exceeding even Hitler's record of 98.81 percent in 1936. By all accounts, DDR pedagogues had heeded the Party's slogan of the season: "Every teacher and educator an agitator for the elections!"[67]

An even more sobering story about the October 1950 election charade concerned Hermann Josef Flade, a 17-year-old high school student.[68] One evening before the election, Flade was attacked by dogs from the *Vopos* (People's Police) while pasting his homemade protest leaflets on neighbors' doors. He resisted arrest and gashed a *Vopo* with his penknife during the ensuing scuffle. (The policeman was not seriously injured.) But his real offense was the leaflets, which allegedly contained seditious statements: "The fight of the Americans in Korea is a righteous war"; SED control of East Germany "is inhuman."

Four months later, the election safely "won," Flade stood before the Dresden Criminal Court. Intent on making a public example of Flade and confident that he would admit his guilt and beg forgiveness as a repentant traitor, prosecutors arranged for the trial to be conducted on the floodlit stage of a Dresden ballroom, carried by loudspeakers, and broadcast throughout the DDR. The accusations were read aloud: Flade was guilty of endangering the peace, reviving Nazism, engaging in Anglo-American espionage, and attempting first-degree murder.

"What have you got to say in your defense?" the judge demanded. Everyone expected that the boy would pour out a woebegone admission of his villainy, plead for mercy, and denounce the adults who had corrupted him. Instead, with a clear, firm voice, he declared:

"Marxism-Leninism is not the truth. God is the truth."

The loudspeakers fell silent; the transmission was broken. The rest of the trial was held behind closed doors. But a transcription of the trial was smuggled out of the DDR and publicized in the West. And so we know how it continued. Quietly and deliberately, the young man explained why he distributed his leaflets:

"I took the decision by myself. I was aware that it might lead to a very heavy punishment. I was convinced that it was right and just to resist the acts of the Soviet government. It took me five years to arrive at the decision that we have to resist the communists actively and passively."

The judge pronounced the sentence: death by guillotine. As Flade was led away, he cried out in the courtroom:

"Die Freiheit ist mir mehr wert als das Leben!" ("Freedom is worth more to me than life itself!").

That sentence echoed in living rooms throughout Germany, turning Flade into a national hero among anti-communists in both the DDR and BRD—and even among many SED sympathizers, especially given that beheading had been officially outlawed in the DDR. Many Germans compared Flade to Hans and Sophie Scholl, the anti-Nazi student martyrs who had led the tiny, doomed White Rose protest circle at Munich University, and had been executed in 1943 for distributing anti-Hitler leaflets. The public outcry against Flade's imminent execution—which included two weeks of student rallies and mass meetings in West Berlin, telegrams from international peace organizations, and official protests lodged by the Allied occupation authorities—eventually induced his judges to commute the sentence to 15 years' imprisonment.[69] But neither Flade's heroism nor the storm of protest slowed the progress of the ideological crackdowns.

Nor were the cases of the Zwickau students and Hermann Josef Flade isolated examples. During 1948–51, some 300 high school and university students were arrested for political reasons and sentenced to hard labor, with terms averaging 25 years. In Jena, 68 young boys were sentenced to 10-year terms at hard labor for throwing stink bombs at officials during their school festival celebrating the birthday of President Wilhelm Pieck. In Mecklenburg, eight teenagers caught by the People's Police with "traitorous" handbills—"We want free elections in Germany!"—received prison terms ranging from 10 to 15 years. In Rostock and Berlin each, two students received death sentences for distributing western magazines; just for passing on a western newspaper, the minimum punishment was five years of hard labor.[70] In 1950/51, near the height of what Wolfgang Harich later termed "the terror," the "worst" period in DDR history, 6,000 youths under 18 received jail terms for political causes. Indeed, DDR concentration camps at mid-century held 800 boys and girls under 17 who had distributed allegedly seditious leaflets, secretly scrawled "F" (for *Freiheit*, Freedom) on city walls at night, or "grimaced" during a paean to Stalin.[71]

TRUST IS GOOD, BUT CONTROL IS BETTER!

YOU NEED ONLY TO SCHOOL PEOPLE PROPERLY—THEN THEY'LL LIVE RIGHT!

OUR NEW LIFE MUST BE DIFFERENT!

How different? Revealingly and chillingly, in his speech at the conference of regional FDJ chairmen in November 1948, Erich Honecker declared, without apparent concern (or awareness) about his use of a notorious Nazi concept: "The moment of *Gleichschaltung* [coordinating the gears] has not yet arrived. Our development is not yet sufficiently and widely advanced for that."[72]

But the nakedly public moment was fast approaching.

Meanwhile, the flight of the teachers—an exodus that continued until the 1960s—accelerated. Teacher turnover rates skyrocketed. Aggravated by the inexperience (and incompetence) of the *Neulehrer*, classes often became a shambles of disorganization.[73] In 1949/50, 7,000 of the approximately 65,000 teachers quit. In 1950/51, 10,000 more.[74] In December 1950, the Ministry of People's Education estimated that fully 20 percent of the teaching staff had resigned that year, leading one West German educator to dub 1950 "the year of the great teacher emigration" in the DDR. Many departing teachers were *Neulehrer*, who decided that they were unsuitable for teaching and went back to their old jobs in factories or on farms.[75] Other *Neulehrer* sought better-paying positions: they headed West. Still others, along with many experienced teachers, writhed within the ideological straitjacket, ambivalent about the SED's "call to carry the class struggle into the villages."[76] They acquiesced in the Party's program to turn the little Red schoolhouse into the chief means for producing generations of young "socialist personalities."

The democratic "blue period" of the SBZ was fading. The "moment" of *Gleich-schaltung* seemed near. Power had passed from the Third Reich to the apparently democratic SMAD; now it would be transferred to Ulbricht and the openly Stalinist SED. The swastika would be supplanted by the hammer and sickle, the *Heil Hitler!* by the clenched fist. Now the pendulum was swinging left, far left: the vengeful turn of "dialectical"-historical materialism. And with it goose-stepped a jackboot across the color spectrum of coercion: beyond blue and magenta and even red. As the SBZ became the DDR, magenta gave way to maroon: the dawn of Red Fascism.

Red Fascism: the Orwellian nightmare of Stalinism and Nazism rolled into one. In the western (and especially the American) imagination, nowhere did this model of totalitarianism seem more horrifyingly realized than in East Germany.[77] Surrounded by barbed wire by the early 1950s, the DDR was, to mainstream western policy-makers, a police state combining Prussian technical efficiency and Russian brute manpower. Red Fascism: a new form of bureaucratic state collectivism. Its method was a pro-Soviet, anti-western, anti-American campaign branding "bourgeois democracy" reactionary, and it aimed through national appeals to build domestic unity and "real democracy" across class divisions. The mixture was well-expressed by a DDR youth leader who, in a slip of the tongue, exhorted his listeners to fight the imperialists "according to the principles of Nazism-Leninism-Stalinism."[78]

Red Fascism: The phrase is often taken as a McCarthyite smear of Communism. And indeed it was often used as an American "Red scare" headline around mid-century. "Commies Brainwash John Q. Public into Backing Fluoridation!" "Reds Plot to Conquer Solar System by Year 2000!" Such far-fetched headlines represented hysterical American anti-communist propaganda; those pertaining to the "Red Reich" of the DDR often made sweeping (and false) claims of equivalence between the Third Reich and the DDR.

But the more moderate claim that the early, prewar years of the Third Reich and the Stalinist era of the DDR bore striking resemblance *is* reasonable. It is beyond the scope of this book to compare the regimes of the Third Reich and the DDR, except to note that simplistic equations of Nazism and Stalinism (or communism)—especially given that the latter changed significantly over time—are untenable. Still, while stressing this fact, it also bears emphasis that the parallels between the DDR's so-called "democratic" socialism of the 1950s and German National Socialism of the 1930s extended beyond punishment for public protest: Almost every sphere of DDR life, from industrial production to art and culture, once again came under tight state control.[79]

None of this means equating Hitler with Ulbricht (let alone with Honecker). Rather, it entails the recognition of notable continuities between these two German dictatorships, despite their significant differences. In education and youth policy, as one scholar has written, DDR children "already had the experience of nationalist socialist mass meetings, which gave them a fascination with the totalitarian state and made the indoctrination of communist ideology something that they experienced as an everyday normality."[80] Indeed, although the DDR youth organizations were obviously modeled on the Soviet *Komsomol*, DDR youth policy eerily began to mirror that of the early Nazi era: Soviet-derived or not, the organizational structure, the uniforms, the sloganeering and marching, and the militant songs of the DDR youth organizations immediately evoked the Hitler era. (Even the FDJ emblem—the rising sun, blazing against the blue sky—evoked, however inadvertently, memories of the Nazi warrior's symbols of the fire and sun, whose control by him exemplified his heroic command over Nature.) Moreover, just as the Nazis had built a school system within the Party, so too now did the SED begin to do the same. The Third Reich concepts of *Ordensburgen* and Party schools were resurrected in the organization of SED leadership schools throughout the DDR. Just as the Nazis had set up the elite Adolf Hitler Schools and required courses in Nazi history and biology, the SED instituted in 1946 the Karl Marx Party School in Teltow (near Berlin), which gave intensive university-level courses to leading SED functionaries, and systematically established Marxist-Leninist curricula in the schools and universities.[81]

"Education must be so arranged," Hitler had declared in *Mein Kampf*, "that the young person leaving school is not half pacifist, democrat, or what you will, but a complete German." Substitute "communist" as the last word of that sentence: by mid-century, the statement applied to the DDR. "The task of our century," wrote Alfred Rosenberg, the Nazis' leading philosopher, "is to create the new human type. . . ." Like the Nazis, DDR youth policymakers proceeded to ban Hollywood films, "hot" American jazz, "poisonous" western dances like the samba and rhumba,[82] "decadent" snack items like Coca-Cola and chewing gum—not to mention anti-communist or subversive books such as Koestler's *Darkness at Noon* and Orwell's *1984*. "A democracy of higher rank," the DDR propaganda chief characterized the East German political order in 1950: inadvertently the same phrase that Goebbels had once used in 1934 to describe National Socialist rule. Indeed the title of one DDR anti-western magazine would have made Goebbels smile: *Der Neue Stürmer*.[83]

These developments in East German education and youth policy played themselves out against the background of negotiations for German reunification and the rise of the Cold War. Nineteen forty-seven began with the American and British decision in January to create the Bi-zone, a development widely interpreted as signaling diminishing expectations of future cooperation with the USSR. Allied foreign ministers meeting in Moscow in April then failed to reach any consensus on a timetable for German reunification; without Soviet cooperation, the Americans, British, and French began the enormous reconstruction project of the Marshall Plan in the western zones that summer. In January 1948 all three western zones merged; in March, trade was cut off between east and west; on June 20, the western Allies introduced a currency reform, which left the western and Soviet zones with different currencies, effectively turning them into separate countries.

The Soviets were outraged by the currency reform, which the western Allies extended to West Berlin; on June 24, 1948, SMAD blockaded the land routes used by the western Allies to reach Berlin. Two days later, an Anglo-American airlift began, carrying crucial foodstuffs and medical supplies to the more than two million West Berliners suddenly cut off from the West. (The Berlin Airlift—which was code-named "Operation Vittles" by the Americans—would continue for almost a year until Stalin called off the blockade.) By the end of that June, the western Allies had announced the planned formation of a West German republic. Little more than a year later, in the fall of 1949, the BRD and the DDR became separate, independent states. The Cold War was fully under way.

By now, partitioned Germany occupied the front line of the bipolar Cold War and mirrored in heightened form the opposing ideologies of the two postwar superpowers; it became a microcosm of the world struggle between capitalism and communism. The Soviet-sponsored communist coup in Czechoslovakia in February 1948, Mao Zedong's communist victory in China in February 1949, the formation of the North Atlantic Treaty Organization (NATO) in April 1949, the wave of show trials of purported spies throughout Eastern Europe in 1949/50, the invasion of South Korea in June 1950, the Soviet "Hate America" campaign of January 1951, and the rising anti-Communist hysteria in the U.S. provoked by Wisconsin Senator Joseph McCarthy: escalating American-Soviet hostilities resulting from these events also exacerbated tensions between East and West Germany. With the outbreak of the Korean War, both Germanies began to rearm. Under such circumstances, it is hardly surprising that, during this second period of educational history in Soviet Germany, the *Schein* fell from the *Demokratie*. Alas, that did not herald the advent of "real" democracy: the *Schein* proved to be all there had ever been.

June 1948 turned out to be the watershed moment in postwar East German affairs. On June 29, only days into the Berlin crisis, Tito defied Stalin, adopted a conciliatory stance toward the West, and took Yugoslavia on its own "special road" to socialism. "I will shake my little finger—and there will be no more Tito!" Stalin had thundered in the spring of 1948.[84] But Tito prevailed and launched an independent course outside Stalin's orbit.

And so the questions loomed: Which way would the SBZ go? West or East? And if to the east, toward the model of Yugoslavia or the USSR? Given that Stalin had 500,000 troops in the SBZ, the answer was never really in doubt. Nevertheless, envisioning dangers to the SBZ's development in both directions—West German cosmopolitanism and Yugoslavian separatism—the Soviets were panicked into restricting political freedom in the SBZ, tolerating little deviation.

The economic blockade of Berlin and the Stalin-Tito split were the triggering events for a policy shift by the SED, crises that set the Party on a course it would follow for the next four decades. No longer hopeful, by 1948, about a reunified socialist Germany or about winning over the western zones to communism, the SED dropped its democratic mask. Proclaiming itself (after Lenin's phrase) a *"Partei neuen typus"* ("party of the new type")—a so-called Marxist-Leninist vanguard party—the SED jettisoned its Popular Front rhetoric and became outspokenly Stalinist. It discarded the pretense of "a special German road" to socialism and instead embraced an "internationalist" course under the aegis of the USSR.

In reality, the "new type" SED was simply the old KPD reverting to type. Restyling itself a cadre party committed to ideological purity, the SED now sought orthodox believers, abandoned its guise of being a "socialist unity" party interested in building a mass membership, and openly practiced one-party "democracy." A severe purge beginning in 1948/49—officially termed "the investigation and exchange of party membership cards" in SED Newspeak—sliced Party rolls by a third; only active, unquestioningly loyal comrades survived, and they were required to participate more fully in Party activities and enroll in special schools for political indoctrination.[85] "Separatists" who continued to push for a "special German road" toward socialism were condemned.

The SED justified its policy shifts as part of an historical transition. Socialism in the SBZ had to develop in two phases, explained Party spokesmen. The first task had been to finish the failed "bourgeois revolution of 1848"; now, a century later, that stage was deemed complete. So the need for liberal methods—a.k.a. *Scheindemokratie*—had ended. Having achieved "socialism," the SED announced, it could now move on to the second, communist phase of its revolutionary program. Speaking of the climate of events in 1948, Wolfgang Leonhard, a member of Ulbricht's inner circle at this time and formerly a department head for educational materials, revealed after escaping to Yugoslavia and then to the West how *Scheindemokratie* had paved the way for a more aggressive SED strategy:

> Ulbricht spoke of things that, six months later, did become official. The most important statements were the following: in the period from 1945–47 many questions wouldn't be openly stated. The SED had to proceed step by step, both on account of the backwardness of the Party and on foreign policy grounds. Until 1947 we had to establish the foundation of an anti-fascist democratic order. [According to Ulbricht], now that 40 percent of industry is in state hands—in the spring of 1948—and that capitalism has become decisively weaker, we can regard this period as over. Now we have the possibility to realize our demands with the help of the Soviet state apparatus.[86]

The chief values that had dominated debate in 1945/46 were democracy and anti-fascism. Now the talk was of socialism and internationalism (i.e., the USSR line). As time passed, the basic negative value—anti-fascism—faded into a misty abstraction linked to the receding Nazi period and was romanticized by SED propaganda implying that heroic communists had fought Hitler single-handedly in the 1920s and '30s. The positive goal of a democratic order was redefined in terms of Leninist democratic centralism.

What were the consequences for education? "Anti-fascist democratic" reforms gave way to hard-line SED commands to politicize (i.e., "sovietize") the curriculum and youth organizations: shades of the Prussian and Nazi pasts. Educational policy turned from building the democratic "new school" to fortifying a Marxist-Leninist ideological bulwark.[87]

That was the crucial change during 1947–51: Democratization metastasized into "sovietization." Sloganeering for "progressive humanism" gave way to militant calls. *"Für eine kämpferische Demokratie!"* ("For a fighting democracy!"). And, of course, Stalin's famous summons: *"Stürmt die Festung Wissenschaft!"* ("Storm the citadel of learning!"). In other words, East German education was now to become, in Lenin's phrase, a "transmission belt" for conveying communist policies.[88]

The first official sign of the shift was inconspicuous. The SED merely legislated an element of its surreptitious policy. The traditional German ideal of classical humanist education, enshrined in the constitution, was quietly replaced in early 1947 by a paragraph in the bylaws referring to "socialist humanism."[89]

But this small change was a portent of further "revisions" soon to come.[90] Now politicians spoke less about "education toward anti-fascism" than "education toward socialist humanism." SED educators made it clear that the "individualistic" humanism of the past was to be replaced by a collectivist ethic in which each person served society, i.e., the State. To the SED, this meant injecting humanism with a strong dose of socialist activism.[91] "The school must stimulate youthful enthusiasm for such an idea, so that our youth is always ready to defend the State, which stands for these ideals," announced one SED politician. "Schools should implant in the heart of every human being how great a task it is to serve the State and humanity."[92] Other SED officials declaimed about "education for democratic patriotism."

In pedagogical practice this change meant the rejection of German pedagogy and the acceptance of Soviet dogma in all things. Wilhelm von Humboldt, who had revived classical education in Germany and virtually created the modern *Gymnasium*, was condemned as elitist; Georg Kerschensteiner, who pioneered field work in nature study, counterbalancing what he termed the over-intellectualized German *Buchschule* (book school) by introducing vocational education into his *Arbeitsschule* (activity school), was attacked as reformist; Friedrich Froebel, the advocate of student self-expression and champion of humanistic pre-school and primary education, was dismissed as unscientific. Thus did the great German tradition of educational philosophy represented by these thinkers, as well as by Herder, Fichte, and Johann Friedrich Herbart—a tradition that had inspired socialists such as Wilhelm Liebknecht, Karl Liebknecht, Rosa Luxemburg, Clara Zetkin and August Bebel—give way, along with the Weimar tradition of *Reformpädagogik*, to the wholesale importation of Marxist-Leninist formulae and methods.

What followed was a pathetic cult of Soviet worship, ranging from the required teaching of Russian, to the highlighting of the October Revolution in history courses,[93] to rote memorization of the theories of behaviorist Ivan Pavlov and the charlatan geneticist T. D. Lysenko. Above all, teacher trainers practiced slavish reverence toward the pedagogical theories of Anton Makarenko. Indeed the period of East German pedagogy at mid-century, one West German historian has written, was "probably the most miserable in the history of any perverted teacher training."[94]

It was just at this moment in the late 1940s that the DDR began recapitulating the USSR's retreat from innovation toward orthodoxy almost two decades earlier.[95] Whereas 1945–47 was an era of experimentation in light of German traditions, the next period was characterized by Party-determined conformity according to the Soviet model. The slogan became: "Study, Study, Study—and Once Again, Study!" The year 1948 in the DDR mirrored the year 1931 in the USSR—the advents of the DDR's first Two-Year Plan and the USSR's first Five-Year Plan, respectively—and set the DDR on Big Brother's path. In education, it began to copy slavishly the big Red schoolhouse.

It is at this point that we might pause to examine the experience of Soviet educators under Stalin, a tragedy that sheds much light on the course of events that DDR educational history will soon take. The DDR's drive to revolutionize education cannot be understood apart from the context of the Two-Year Plan. What applied to industry, Soviet leaders held, applied for education. What worked in the factory worked also in the classroom. Learning was production; the student was a product. The aim, as western critics put it, was to manufacture *Planmenschen* (planned human beings),[96] a vitriolic term yet not at all far-fetched, since SED cultural functionaries did, in fact, speak of the "cultural two-year plan" for 1949–50.[97]

Stalin's own "production targets" in education and culture entailed rejecting the USSR's experience in the 1920s. Influenced heavily by Tolstoy and John Dewey, Soviet pedagogy under Krupskaya and Lunacharsky had embarked on a heady, romantic period of free experimentation in which it sought to reconcile the individual and the collective, to unite high respect for the single personality with an ideological doctrine glorifying the revolutionary, historic mission of the proletarian mass.

With Stalin's defeat of Trotsky in 1928, however, a new epoch began, characterized by hostility toward novelty and originality and a return to more rigid, formal, even pre-revolutionary practices. Even before this, a Soviet law had decreed that "difficult personalities" (i.e., critics of the regime) and children of Gulag inmates would be excluded from higher education, and that children of Party members would receive educational privileges. In 1931, when Andrei Bubnov replaced Lunarcharsky as People's Commissar for Education, the discriminatory, exclusivist trends accelerated. Bubnov, a former general, used the model of military discipline to expedite education toward his goals of raising the level of technical proficiency and contribution to the industrial economy. The Russian miner Alexei Stakhanov, who on one shift in 1933 had overfulfilled his work norm by 1450 percent, was elevated into an example of the heroic worker.

In 1936 a new movement for worker productivity, the Stakhanovite Movement, was created, and it soon spread to education. Stalin's new slogan became the reigning gospel: "Cadres decide everything!" As the USSR turned to more systematized teaching, emphasizing ever more the idea that the individual labored for the common good, small work cadres became the model for learning—precisely the method that Makarenko, toiling away in obscurity, had already worked out in the 1920s.[98]

Now Makarenko became Stalin's favorite. In effect, Makarenko's practices represented Stakhanovism applied to education. As director of the Gorky Colony and the Dzerzhinsky Commune, two labor reformatories for juvenile criminals, Makarenko had supervised abandoned and delinquent youths. In *The Road to Life*, he explained how he organized them into work cadres and achieved remarkable results, producing obedient, model citizens. Makarenko promoted what he termed "communist morality," which emphasized the social importance of honesty, trust, and purity of moral character. The child's first lesson was to learn to accept the traditions of the collective—first the family, then the school, and finally the commune—as his or her own.[99]

Makarenko's educational "commune" was a controlled environment. It operated under a daily routine, precise rules of conduct, and military customs, e.g., reveille at 6 a.m. Personal hygiene, table manners, tidiness, and punctuality became the essence of the individual's and the collective's own sense of worth. A follower of Pavlov, Makarenko spoke metaphorically of molding human behavior through dies, as if he were cutting and engraving designs upon soft material as does a stamp or coin machinist; such analogies led critics to accuse him of indoctrinating children into blind obedience through a system of conditioning. Indeed Makarenko's language did echo Stalin's phrase that writers were to be "the engineers of human souls" and Makarenko himself noted ruefully that he had produced no artists among his students.

Makarenko limited the freedom of his pupils and oriented them strictly toward work, winning few admirers among the experimentalists. But he achieved exactly what the innovators hadn't: higher worker productivity. Having accomplished this exclusively through the socialization of problem children and orphans, Makarenko expected that his methods would succeed even better in mainstream Soviet society. His commune slogan became "All Energies for the Buildup of Socialism!" By the time he died in 1939 at the age of 51, his name rang through Soviet teachers' meetings. Already, however, his doctrines were serving Stalin not as a child's road to life but as yet another road to Stalin's own power. However fruitful Makarenko's experiments in moral cultivation, the harvest under Stalin was merely a militaristic, collectivist husk.[100]

Nearly two decades later, East Germany inexorably followed this Soviet road. Keen to ape Moscow, SED educators bypassed the enlightened era of Soviet pedagogical experiment and eagerly adopted a simplified Stalinist view of Makarenko. To them, his writings confirmed the status of education as the key institution in identity formation. His work seemed a model of *Umerziehung*, an example of re-education under the most difficult circumstances. Just as Makarenko had confessed "an infinite, reckless and unhesitating belief in the power of educational work," SED educators professed a similar faith in the messianic potential of Soviet *Umerziehung*.[101]

"The new socialist human being," declared Ulbricht, "should think like Lenin, act like Stalin, and work like Stakhanov"—all three names by now intimately (if not nauseatingly) familiar to East Germans. And soon the DDR had a Stakhanov of its own. His name was Adolf Hennecke. On October 13, 1948, Hennecke, also a miner, performed a special shift in which he topped his daily quota by 287 percent—no match for the great Stakhanov, ran the joke, but Alexei was, after all, a Russian. (October 13 was preserved for several years in the DDR as a commemoration day of Hennecke's pioneering feat.) The Zwickau miner's performance was turned into a springboard for a general call for increased efficiency at work.[102] A Hennecke movement was engineered, accompanied by a surge of rallies, placards, speeches, and even poems.[103]

Special appeals went out to young people and students. Become a "Hero of Labor" or "Distinguished Worker"! Exceed the work norm on your next "Hennecke shift"! Be a "Hennecke Activist"! Inspired by Hennecke, schoolchildren mastered exercises with lightning speed in Hennecke academic competitions. Honored "Best Students" completed their programs of university study in record time. "Distinguished Teachers of the People" covered material brilliantly and far ahead of their lesson plan schedules. Old and young workers imitated the master and even launched their own movements; by 1949, there were an estimated 60,000 Hennecke activists.[104] For example, a 17-year-old girl sorted 20,000 cigarettes in a single day, surpassing the previous record of 14,000. A 16-year-old boy installed 20 radio tubes per hour.[105] A Leipzig train conductor spearheaded the "500 Movement," whereby every locomotive had to be driven 500 kilometers per day. A truck supervisor outdid that: he launched the "100,000 Movement," whereby his truck drivers would travel 100,000 kilometers without repair. Not to be left out, a "4,000 Liter Movement" enlisted Hero of Labor cows to contribute 4,000 liters of milk annually.[106]

Ulbricht had not just saddled the cow but was milking it for all it was worth—despite, at times, the protests of leading educators.[107]

OUR NEW LIFE MUST BE DIFFERENT!

A chief aim of the Hennecke movement was to revolutionize education for the planned economy. The goal was to increase economic productivity and salvage the fledgling Two-Year Plan, which was floundering under the constraints of the western Allies' trade cutoff.

Thus, economic priorities also supported the pedagogical turn away from the German intellectual tradition and toward Makarenko and Soviet dogma. Russified "scientific cadres" and "collectives" replaced bourgeois individual scholarship. Feeling pressure to raise industrial output and ingratiate themselves with the USSR after Tito's insubordination, SED officials ordered that the newly founded Pedagogical Faculties at the universities institute centralized, strictly "scientific" (i.e., Marxist-Leninist) teaching training. *Reformpädagogik*, they decreed, which focused on humanism and general knowledge rather than specialized and technical training, was ideologically flaccid and did not contribute sufficiently to building an industrial economy. "Students of the new type," proclaimed the SED, did not require comprehensive general knowledge, but rather needed specialized skills. A broad liberal education was replaced by a foundation in Marxist-Leninism.[108]

Until 1948/49, many teachers had resisted the Russian revolution in pedagogy. Many German communists and Social Democrats returning to the SBZ believed that the German progressive educational tradition was retrievable. Liberated from the legal and spiritual chains of the Nazis, they imagined that they were free to build on the tradition that they themselves had developed. With its emphasis on independent activity and personal initiative, *Reformpädagogik* seemed to many teachers an effective antidote to the authoritarian legacy of the Third Reich. In the 1946 Weimar Manifesto, SBZ teachers had agreed to combine practical school experience and traditional perspectives with new progressive innovations. The manifesto urged the promotion of respect for the child's autonomy and individual character. Teachers embraced Clara Zetkin's "Mannheim Principles" on humanistic education, Otto Ruhle's insistence on the uniqueness of each individual child, and Kerschensteiner's experimental, open-ended *Arbeitsschule*.[109] Indeed the very first *Neulehrer* of 1945/46 were trained in this German tradition, using whatever progressive pre-1933 German pedagogical literature could be found (which was the only anti-fascist literature available); Soviet translations did not as yet even exist. But by 1948/49, translations of Soviet pedagogy books were fast supplanting the German texts; SED educators, demanding didacticism and opposed to "western" pedagogy, learned their lessons and branded the Weimar Manifesto a reactionary bourgeois document. Indeed, especially after the purge of SED membership rolls began in 1948/49, antagonism toward the West became a key litmus test for teachers. As one high education official told delegates at the Fourth Pedagogical Conference in 1949:

> The Anglo-American generals and their [West] German subordinates believe that, just because American and English education has been made fascist according to the model of Schirach [former head of the HJ], Goebbels, and Himmler, that the same model can be transferred to Germany once again. They behave arrogantly, already according to the motto: As the lords are, so will be the slaves. . . . How completely different behaves the Soviet Union, that socialist land of peace, toward the German Volk, toward its children and its youth! . . . The Soviet Union is an example of the generosity and readiness to help socialist human beings, for which we should constantly be thankful.[110]

To be in the Party meant to be an *Aktivist*, a "good functionary of the democratic parties or mass organizations." Now teachers would head the revolutionary avant garde; the call went out to fulfill Lenin's summons from 1918: "The People's Teacher should have a leading role in society such as he never before has occupied, a role that he does not at present yet have, that in bourgeois society he can never have."[111]

And with Party discipline of teachers increasing, formal administrative control also tightened. Central administration of education from Berlin raised still another maroon flag for independent-minded teachers, eerily evoking Nazi policy. For no central educational authority had ever existed in Germany until after World War I, when in 1919 an educational office was set up in the Ministry of the Interior. Not until the Third Reich did a full-fledged Ministry of Education exist, with Berlin rather than the *Länder* determining educational policy. Nazi educators created a central ministry to impose uniformity, politicize the curriculum, and pressure recalcitrant teachers to adopt or acquiesce to Party ideology.

Now, to numerous social democratic teachers, SED educators seemed to be doing the same: in 1951 the *Länder* parliaments were formally dissolved, marking the final stage of school policy centralization in Berlin. Not the least of the tragic ironies of these years was how many courageous anti-Nazi teachers in the SBZ— fired from their teaching positions during the Third Reich, imprisoned, beaten, tortured—were now dismissed or jailed by the SED because they were not good Stalinists. Some even found themselves reliving the nightmares of their recent pasts, sent back for their defiance of Stalinism to concentration camps in which they had spent the Nazi years.[112]

Step by step, the SPD's declining influence during 1947–51 within the SED tolled the death knell of social democratic ideas in education. Through it all, however, the official pretense of "socialist unity" remained. Even through the 1980s, the SED trademark, the brotherly handshake, adorned the pages of all East

German schoolbooks in the DDR. It commemorated that fabled day of March 21, 1946, when the KPD's Wilhelm Pieck and the SPD's Otto Grotewohl shook hands in the Admiralspalast in East Berlin—the former coming, symbolically, from the left and the latter from the right side of the stage, dramatizing their mutual willingness to compromise in the new SED. And yet, within two years, the real story was clear: the "unity" handshake had actually been a death grip that would crush the SPD forever. In education, the "sovietization" of the schools was near-complete by mid-century.

The universities were a different story—temporarily. "The university must be sovietized," a SMAD education officer decreed in 1947.[113] But that decree was hard to execute. The prestige of the German university, the traditions of *Lehrfreiheit und Lernfreiheit*, the public commitment in 1945 to nonpolitical admissions criteria and to the independence of the academic administration: all of this made the SED hesitant to interfere in academic affairs and empowered the university community. The citadel of higher learning continued to elude capture—for a while.

Indeed, at first, many of the 22,000 students boycotted the newly introduced "M-L" (Marxist-Leninist) courses, also known as DIAMAT (dialectical materialism). When philosophy and history courses finally returned to universities in 1946/47, large numbers of students skipped M-L lectures. They mocked the Soviet worshippers who espoused Lysenko's biology, Ivan Pavlov's psychology, N. Marr's linguistics, A. Mitchurin's materialist genetics, or Russian "dialectical-historical" physics. Contemptuous of crude *Umerziehung*, they criticized Party-line professors in student government open forums.[114] They put up posters castigating restrictive SED policies. They even protested examination materials. For instance, at Rostock University, law students refused to write an exam on the topic, "The Justified Basis of the People's Ownership of Property"—branding it a "lie"—and marched out of the auditorium en masse.[115]

Professors resisted the new ideological turn too. Most of the 1,500 faculty in the SBZ's twenty institutions of higher education initially refused to join the SED.[116] They also defied, or sought to circumvent, new policies aimed at controlling them politically. For instance, beginning in 1946/47, every professor had to write lesson plans accounting for every classroom hour and explaining the topic's "re-education value." SMAD devoted most attention to philosophy and history, which it regarded as the key subjects for *Umerziehung*.[117] Faculty in philosophy had to write 100-page essays on "My *Weltanschauung*." The results of these initial attempts at intellectual intimidation were sometimes comically Kafkaesque. Although many professors submitted, others sought to outwit their examiners through stealth and cunning. To frustrate the Thought Police—many of whom were half-educated Party ideologues and SMAD education officers who spoke little German—these professors "summarized" their lectures in 500-page treatises, pontificating exhaustively on arcane issues. Or they explicated their *Weltanschauungen* in hopelessly technical jargon that only fellow experts could hope to decipher.[118]

Nevertheless, the documents gave SMAD officials a useful list of suspect names and themes. SMAD forbade professors to diverge from their approved lesson plans;

SMAD representatives would, unexpectedly, audit classes or assign students to take and hand over careful notes. These notes would be quoted, sometimes years later, if accusations arose against a professor's political stance.[119]

Despite, or perhaps because of, faculty recalcitrance, ideological screening procedures tightened—and penalties increased. In 1947, SMAD sought to finish off *Entnazifizierung* at Greifswald University by firing en masse faculty with former NSDAP affiliations. The Greifswald rector refused, demanding individual evaluations instead. He received 25 years at hard labor. The institution of mandatory Marxist-Leninist curricula throughout the SBZ/DDR followed in the next two years. In 1950, the SED stepped up its offensive further, launching two campaigns promoting "the most advanced science" of Marxist-Leninism: "The Battle Against Objectivism and Cosmopolitanism" and "Partisanship in Scholarship."[120] Given its traditionally central role in the German curriculum, philosophy received especially close scrutiny. SMAD distributed a detailed questionnaire on ideological stance to every philosophy professor, which each professor was required to answer, point by point. Recalling the interrogation of suspected heretics during the Inquisition, this procedure allowed for no tricks or evasions.[121] Indeed, the Institute for Dialectical Materialism at Jena—whose director had recently received his doctorate through SED machinations[122]—became the Vatican of the DDR by midcentury. It was explicitly authorized to "answer" all "theoretical issues that cannot be resolved."[123]

"Philosophy," wrote one professor in 1950 who had escaped to the West, "is dying out in the DDR." The choice finally exercised by most independent-minded faculty of world renown was a secret *Republikflucht* (flight from the Republic)— a crime whose attempt was punishable by a long prison sentence. Often at the cost of leaving behind his or her books, manuscripts, furniture, and even family— anything more than the clothes on one's back might attract the notice of authorities—a professor would disappear, without telling a soul, and re-emerge days later across the border.[124]

Nor did the students' defiance of the SED long endure. The first wave of student arrests on political grounds began in 1947 with the dissident Henschel group at the University of Jena, a cluster of independent anti-fascist students who had refused FDJ membership.[125] That year also witnessed the first round of political kidnappings, when several dozen outspoken student critics of the SED at the University of Berlin disappeared—vaporized, Orwellian-style.[126] The SED now moved to ensure that only "students of the new type" would matriculate. In 1948, political courses became university requirements regardless of one's area of study. To assure attendance in political courses, two unexcused absences were made grounds for dismissal from university; to guarantee attention, universities introduced comprehensive examinations every other semester.[127] Students who did well in these examinations received the FDJ medal "For Good Knowledge," coined in gold, silver, and bronze. Those who received scholarships saw their funding calculated on an ideological scale, "like Stakhanovite wages, according to their political enthusiasm."[128]

But the changes did not stop with the new required curriculum. It was not enough to command the citadel from the inside; now the SED began to exert pressures on youth *outside* the school—or to turn all youth activity into "educational" activity.

The main vehicles were the FDJ and its junior branch, the JP, which was founded in 1948 for children under the age of 14. Now students were pressured to join the "new type" FDJ and JP.[129] And with their full-scale transformation into an arm of the Party, we enter the inner chamber of the so-called Red Reich at mid-century. Indeed the "new type" FDJ and JP became very much like the Child Spies of *1984*. (In fact, a Party-promoted bestseller in the early DDR days was Alexander Fadayev's *Young Guard*, which features an heroic little Lenin Pioneer in Moscow who informs on his parents to the NKVD.)

Today, five decades later, this Orwellian world is incomprehensible to most Americans. How can present-day Americans even begin to conceive the climate of these East German schools at mid-century?

Imagine that the Cub Scouts and Brownies literally trained preschoolers to spot suspicious aliens and build miniature watchtowers, that the Boy and Girl Scouts were dominated and completely politicized by the hard Left or the extreme Right, that membership in the Scouts was the prime criterion of university acceptance, that Scout leaders interviewed you for admission, that in every class Scout members monitored your attendance and informed FBI and CIA authorities about your personal behavior and offhand comments, that 40-year-old "Scouts" sat on university examination committees, that young and middle-aged Scouts participated in faculty meetings, that. . . . [130]

And that only begins to suggest the power and the terror of the "new type" FDJ.

Nineteen forty-nine—the publication date of *1984*—proved, all too fittingly, the decisive date of no return. Operating under a freshly drafted constitution that subordinated it directly to the SED and ended all heterodoxy among members, including toleration of Christian youth members, the "new type" FDJ received its appointed tasks: screening university applicants, taking attendance at lectures, and so forth.[131] In 1949 the FDJ also ceased to be merely extracurricular; its activities were coordinated with school plans and it became the only legal organized expression of student interests. That year witnessed too the abolition of secret FDJ elections and secret student government elections in school and university. The Party leadership made all selections. Now there was a simple list of candidates determined from on high; a year later, FDJ membership was declared mandatory for all DDR university students in vocational and professional programs, and the FDJ slogan for 1950 trumpeted: *"Der beste FDJler—der beste Student!"*[132]

Now the blue shirts were stained dark maroon.

The dawn of Red Fascism: shades of brown shirts past.

The democratic experiment was over. The age of the "new type" of German, the *Planmensch*, was indeed at hand.

And now the hour had come to unveil and parade this creation before the world.

Marooned in the Workers' Paradise

Cold War Catechetics, 1951–61

It is not the neutrals or the lukewarm who make history.

Adolf Hitler, April 23, 1933

Hitlers come and go, but the German people and the German state remain.

Josef Stalin, February 1942

Power is not a means, it is an end. One does not establish a dictatorship in order to safeguard a revolution; one makes the revolution in order to establish the dictatorship.

George Orwell, *1984* (1949)

Of Carnivals and Graveyards

August 12, 1951. It's a brilliant Sunday afternoon in the eastern sector of Berlin, the DDR's capital, now an urban showplace of 1.7 million residents and proudly known on road signs as *Berlin, Hauptstadt der DDR*—a simple declaration of the SED's ongoing claim to the entire city as DDR territory. The boulevards are clean and neat in Alexanderplatz, the downtown area of East Berlin. Windows are be-decked with flowers, and flags from every nation of the globe festoon the buildings, which are draped with tapestries displaying the goal of world socialism in dozens of languages: *Friede, Pokoj, Paix, Beke, Pax, Pace, Peace.*

But a walk off the main drag casts doubt on whether there is much cause to preen: six years after the war's close, block after block of row houses are still gutted. The decrepit trolley cars are slow-moving war survivors; postwar auto-mobiles are nowhere to be seen, except for a few "official" vehicles of the govern-ment and People's Police. Rubble lines every side street. The National Reconstruc-tion Program, a much-publicized campaign to repair the DDR's war-scarred cities, is not slated to begin until late fall. Economic reconstruction is barely under way.

But ideological reconstruction is well advanced. Waves of Blueshirts, 100 abreast, pass at the rate of 30 ranks per minute in the gala marking the climax of the two-week World Festival of Youth and Students for Peace. Sponsored by the international Communist Youth Organization, this year's festival dwarfs its pred-ecessors in Prague (1947) and Budapest (1949), as well as the "Storm Berlin" *Deutschlandtreffen* (German rally) of 500,000 youth in May 1950. The theme for the 1951 festival is "Stalin's Call to Arms for Peace." The vast majority of the participants belong to the FDJ and JP, which together boast almost three million members.[1]

Down the treeless center parkway of Unter den Linden—the lime trees were cut down years ago—and from the side streets filled with debris sweep one million East Germans, along with 26,000 foreign guests from 104 countries. They advance past the sooty gray Brandenburg Gate, on toward Marx-Engels Platz, in the center of Berlin. Like "a carnival in a graveyard,"[2] 500,000 shields of blue, each affixed with a yellow rising sun, rise to greet the day. From every vantage point, big brotherly portraits of Stalin, Lenin, and East Germany's own President Pieck survey the spectacle. Stepping out of the parade lines, little JP girls fling flowers at the patriarchs' 10-foot faces and scream *"Friede! Friede!"* ("Peace! Peace!"). Above the din of the drum and fife corps and the military songs broadcast by loudspeakers rise the battle cries of the marchers: *"Freundschaft! Freundschaft!"* ("Friendship! Friendship!"). *"Immer bereit! Immer bereit!"* ("Always prepared! Always prepared!") And then the 1951 FDJ motto: *"Von der Sowjetunion lernen / Heisst siegen lernen!"* (To Learn from the Soviet Union / Means Learning to Triumph!").[3]

The acre-wide stripe of blue rumbles on, past the newly built Walter Ulbricht Stadium, past the Ernst Thälmann Platz and Stalinallee. Clapping their hands over their heads to keep rhythm, the marchers chant FDJ hymns ("We are the Children of the New Era!" "We must be strong, comrades / We must fight for peace!"). They sing "The March of the Soviet Youth," the prize-winning festival entry in People's Songwriting:

> Stalin's words ring in our hearts
> Everyone sings along
> Stalin leads and our work succeeds
> We keep pace
> Stalin leads and our work succeeds
> Because it brings peace to all peoples.
>
> Peace to the world!
> We youth of the earth swear
> Peace to the world!
> Our seed will destroy nothing
> Peace to the world!
> The flags and choruses rejoice
> And young people radiate
> And they sing out and bloom
> And the youth march ahead.[4]

Then they hurl staccato slogans ("Amis go home!" "Hands Off Korea!") calling for the western powers to cease rearmament and withdraw troops from Germany and Korea. The Cold War is at its height. The atom bomb, germ warfare, German remilitarization, McCarthy's anti-communist witch hunt, and the executions in New York of Julius and Ethel Rosenberg for peacetime espionage dominate East German headlines; the festival itself is part of the stepped-up anti-American campaign that the SED has pursued since the outbreak of the Korean War in June

1950. The "Amis" are the chief enemy of peace, global warmongers and "air gangsters" whose bombs are responsible for the devastation of the German capital and whose nuclear weapons threaten to trigger World War III and annihilate the planet.

FDJ banners underscore that the peace offensive halts at enemy borders; *Freundschaft* cannot be extended to those of opposing views: "Death to the Anglo-American Criminals!" "Death to the German Imperialists!" FDJ youth carry an "Amis" vs. "DDR" diptych of patriotic femininity: Two aggressive American mud wrestlers pictured opposite a pair of graceful FDJ athletes. Western cutthroat competition posed against the beauty of socialist Friendship and Peace! Another placard: Uncle Sam, his hands dripping with blood, greedily caressing a pile of dollar bills as he leers at his missiles. Mother Courage never said it better.

Past the Parliament of the DDR (once Hermann Goering's Air Ministry headquarters) they advance, on toward the reviewing stand of East German leaders. The loudspeakers blast *"Hoch! Hoch! Hoch!"* as the cheers go up: *"Hurra* for our great leader and our friend Stalin!" *"Hurra* for the brave heroes who are helping to defend Korea!" *"Hurra* for the invincible Soviet Union!"

Today, just as on yesterday's Day of the Young German Fighters for Peace and Thursday's Solidarity Day Among Young Girls, DDR leaders receive a public statement from their nation's youth. This time it is a peace petition, the result of a signature campaign for a message of greetings and gratitude to "the great Leader of the world's peace camp," for the man whom President Pieck hailed, in his opening address, as "the great *Führer* who gives the foremost example in the world fight. . . ." The petition concludes: "Millions of Germans have shown their love for you, dear Josef Vissarionovich Stalin, and thus for the great Socialist Soviet Union." Circulated for months by FDJ leaders, from schoolrooms to factories, the petition has received 4,145,839 signatures, almost a quarter of the total population of the DDR. President Pieck, "Father of the Nation," accepts the petition with a word of thanks. And then the loudspeakers roar:

> *Stalin, auf Dich schauen wir voll Vertrauen,*
> *Dir sei unsere ganze Kraft geweiht!*
> [Stalin, we trust in you completely
> All our energies are devoted to you!]

Whereupon a final cry goes up from the million marchers:

> *Der Sozialismus Siegt!*
> [Socialism is winning!]

They wear blue shirts, not brown; they shout *"Friede!"* and *"Freundschaft!"* not *"Sieg Heil!"* But for those old enough to remember the Reich before the rubble, the parallels are unmistakable. Marooned in their new cult, already cut off from almost all contact with the West except through Berlin, the young East German "peace fighters" of 1951 eerily evoke the goose-stepping German youth of less than a decade before.

"It is history repeating itself," editorializes the *New York Times*, "but a mad and vicious history."[5] Or as some old Berliners whisper: "If we must have a *Führer*, let it be Hitler. At least he was our own."

Can a passion be overcome only by a new passion? Must a people shorn of one false god embrace another?

"Hitlers come and go. . . ."

Shades of Brownshirts past.

Numerous columnists in the West view the festival as proving the wisdom of the Soviet policy of concentrating energies on winning over German youth to communism. They believe that the rally is convincing many Germans and East Europeans that Stalin's satellites are workers' states. Stalin's power, they warn, keeps growing in the east.

From the communist standpoint, the single blemish on the success of the occasion is that almost half a million young people from all over the DDR slip over to West Berlin for a visit during the rally and are reportedly astounded by the stores, the streets, and the friendliness of most West Germans; 2,000 receive official asylum, though many more are discouraged from remaining in West Berlin by the authorities on the grounds that they are not proven victims of political persecution.

Is socialism winning in the DDR? Is the populace ready to embrace communism wholeheartedly?

Where will it all lead?

June 17, 1953. "*Ivan muss weg! Ivan muss weg!*" ring the shouts through the streets: "Ivan must go! Ivan must go!"[6]

An unexpected answer. East Berlin streets are once again filled with marchers, but this improvised Wednesday demonstration, bubbling up less than two years after the 1951 World Festival—indeed, just three months after Stalin's death—does not express *Freundschaft* toward SED leaders, the Soviet Union, and world communism. On the contrary: it is directed against the East German government, against the USSR, against the communist system.

Seven A.M. Hundreds of workers from building site 40 are arguing in the Stalinallee—the newly constructed DDR showcase, an area of apartments built with great fanfare as part of the National Reconstruction Program and as a 1952 birthday present to the great Stalin. Employing it as a stage for Party spectacles and Politburo photo opportunities, DDR policymakers have decided to concentrate East Berlin's reconstruction in this single planned area.

Now, however, the curtain is about to rise on a drama of bloody socialist realism—featuring real workers' heroes—that the planners haven't planned.

In the gray morning rain, the construction workers end their debate and lay down their tools. The "men of Block 40" will walk. Their destination: Marx-Engels Platz, where they will present their grievances to the government. Immediately, other workers from the Stalinallee join them, and a corps of 10,000 workers—masons in white overalls, carpenters in black corduroy smocks, factory hands in worn boots and tattered suits—fall into an uneven beat.

"We want butter!" a call goes up. At once, 10,000 voices echo it. Another shout: "Down with the People's Army!" It too is answered in turn. "Freedom! Freedom!"

cries a third. *"Wir fordern freie Wahlen!"* ("We demand free elections!"). *"Wir wollen Butter statt Nationalarmeen / Und endlich unsere Freiheit sehn!"* ("We want butter instead of the army / and at long last our freedom!").

Suddenly the parade halts: at the end of the street stands a wall of *Vopos*, their gray raincoats flapping in the gusting wind, their arms locked elbow to elbow, their weapons visible. The crowd wavers, then drives ahead, disregarding thudding truncheons. The police barricade collapses, and with a roar the motley torrent surges forward.

Ten A.M. On East Berlin streets, in parks and vacant lots heaped with war rubble, astonished bystanders gape at the spectacle. The elated strikers stream along Unter den Linden, their chants peacefully reverberating through the air:

> Berliner, reiht euch ein,
> Wir wollen freie Menschen sein!
> [Berliners, join the ranks,
> We want to be free people!]

Thousands more fall in. At the State Opera House, 500 workmen climb down their scaffolds and swell the tide, their FDJ members shrugging off their blue shirts and marching in step. At Humboldt University, dozens of male and female students spill into the procession; and so, incredibly, do 250 employees of the Friedrichshain office of the Inspector of Taxes.

Now the throng has swollen to 100,000, many of whose younger members had paraded in the 1951 World Festival of Youth and Students. Today East Berlin is witnessing primarily a workers' march, not a student demonstration; but it is also, in part, a youth protest. At the head of almost every column are men under the age of 25, who have been hurriedly chosen as the informal leaders of their workplaces' strike committees.

Past the ubiquitous posters of Stalin and Pieck the horde gushes, past the red streamers that proclaim: "German Youth United for Peace!" "The German Democratic Republic is the Unshakable Bastion of World Peace!" "Only the Imperialists Stand Between You and a Happy Life!" Laughing bitterly, the protesters spit on the propaganda. Several house painters, brushes in hand, cover the posters with *"Nieder mit Ulbricht!"* ("Down with Ulbricht!"). They edit Party slogans, completing "Peace and Freedom" with "Through Free Elections" and changing "Solidarity with the USSR!" to "Solidarity with the German Working Class!"

Now the crowd reaches the new Soviet embassy on Unter den Linden. A pair of Soviet reconnaissance cars wheel to face the multitude; soldiers swing their machine guns to aim at, if above, the heads of the marchers. And yet, the atmosphere remains almost gay. For the marchers know that an unheard-of thing is happening: a demonstration against the government—indeed the makings of a general strike—is under way.

In the steady rain, the flood of sodden marchers rolls on. Along with 8,000 *Vopos*, hundreds of Soviet infantrymen and six Soviet mobile anti-aircraft trucks monitor its progress, weaving in and out of the swirling mass to contain and direct its flow.

11:30 A.M. Now the parade reaches the corner of Leipzigerstrasse and Friedrich-strasse, rapidly filling the Karl Liebknecht Platz, site of several of the SED government buildings. A sea of feisty marchers surrounds the House of Unity, where SED Central Committee members sit in their third-floor offices.

"*Freiheit!*" the demonstrators chant. "We demand the overthrow of the government!" "*Wir wollen keine Sklaven mehr sein!*" ("We won't be slaves anymore!"). "*Wir sind so sehr verbittert, / Dass uns der Regen nicht erschüttert!*" ("We're so outraged / That a little rain won't unsettle us!").

The strikers call for the government leaders to come out and speak with them. No response. Taunts aimed at the government's trio of leaders continue:

> *Ulbricht, Pieck, und Grotewohl*
> *Wir haben von euch die Schnauze voll!*
> [Ulbricht, Pieck, and Grotewohl
> We're sick and tired of you!]

The government sends out a few minor officials to explain its policy, but their Marxist-Leninist jargon—*Partei chinesisch* (Party Chinese), in the workers' contemptuous phrase—only aggravates the crowd. For 10 minutes, the marchers chant for the Party's top leaders, the bearded Ulbricht and the bespectacled Grotewohl, and sometimes also for the paunchy Pieck, to appear:

> *Wir wollen den Spitzbart! Wir wollen die Brille!*
> [We want Goatee! We want Four-Eyes!]

> *Spitzbart, Bauch, und Brille / Sind nicht des Volkes Wille!*
> [Goatee, Fatso, and Four-Eyes / Are not the will of the People!]

> *Grotewohl und Ulbricht raus, / Dann ist dieser Streik hier aus!*
> [Get rid of Grotewohl and Ulbricht / Then this strike will be over!]

> *Es hat keinen Zweck / der Spitzbart muss weg!*
> [It's hopeless / Goatee must go!][7]

To the amusement of the crowd, demonstrators hold up large posters of the SED triumvirate, their names blacked out except for the surname initials, so that the letters spell out "G.P.U.": the Soviet secret police.

But watchful Soviet officers are not amused. And as Soviet soldiers take up position near the House of Unity, the crowd starts to taunt them too, inverting anti-American slogans (*"Russkij Ivan—go home!"*), and even breaking out into the forbidden former national anthem, the *Deutschlandlied*:

> *Deutschland, Deutschland über alles*
> *Über alles in der Welt.*
> [Germany, Germany above everything
> Above everything in the world.]

And then a long-suppressed undercurrent of anger surges to the surface, and cries of frustration pour forth from the drenched and restless crowd.

Wir wollen Freiheit, wir wollen Brot
Wir treten den Kommunismus tot.
[We want freedom, we want bread
We will crush communism dead.]

Nieder mit der Hungerregierung!
[Down with the hunger government!]

The first brick breaks a government window.
"Ivan muss weg!" "Der Spitzbart muss weg!"
Now sticks and stones cascade off the walls.

Maintaining their position between the protesters and the government building, the *Vopos* and Soviet security forces glare menacingly, but do not interfere. Checked, though unappeased, thousands of demonstrators simply move down the street, enter the big state-run department store, and begin to loot it. Two blocks from the House of Unity, on the Soviet side of Potsdamer Platz, and in full view of a lunch-time crowd of West Berliners, a group of marchers manages to light a bonfire, feeding it with portraits of Ulbricht and with SED banners ("Forward to the Building Up of Socialism!").

12:30 P.M. Above the cacophony of confusion comes a new sound: the leaden rattle of tank treads on cobblestones. "The *Panzer* are coming!" thousands shriek.

And as a dozen Soviet tanks turn onto the Leipzigerstrasse, and release their first rounds, History too seems to turn a corner, as the last flickering embers of the humanist tradition of German socialism are buried alive under the weight of Soviet aggression. That the Politburo leaders in the House of Unity in Karl Liebknecht Platz have called in Russian tanks to crush a German workers' uprising must have left Karl Liebknecht and Rosa Luxemburg writhing in their graves. And now it is clear, for all the world to see, that the Socialist Unity Party derives its authority from the Russian whip, not from the will of the East German people. In the show-window city of Soviet Europe, East Berlin, a bloodbath ensues that the West is able to watch from—quite literally—across the street.

Along Friedrichstrasse and other major streets roll 200 field-green Soviet T-34 medium tanks, emblazoned with the Red star and featuring 85-mm guns. Suddenly machine and submachine guns erupt everywhere; thousands of *Vopos* have just arrived to reinforce the Red Army. Horrified witnesses watching from West Berlin later report that while the Soviet soldiers seemed to aim above the crowd, the *Vopos* fired point-blank at their countrymen.

2:30 P.M. Both the rain and the shooting have subsided. Dozens lie dead or injured in the streets. An additional 25,000 Soviet troops and 300 tanks—two entire armored divisions—are on the scene, along with thousands of *Vopo* reinforcements.

The revolutionary "First German Workers' and Peasants' State" is saved!

Meanwhile, dank figures dart through the scorched and sodden streets, desperately seeking safety. Word spreads that all passages to West Berlin are being sealed off by the *Vopos* and Soviet troops: no escape, no asylum.

Evening. As the western media honor—and mourn—the "rebellion in the rain" of June 17, the reprisals commence in the east. Suspects are rounded up; now, a "parade of the new type" begins: at dawn, the first group of "traitors" is marched to a little field near the Brandenburg Gate and, without a trial, set before a Soviet firing squad. Signs labeled "Hitlerite murderer" and "American spy" are hung around the necks of the executed. DDR radio terms the revolt *"Tag X"* (Day X), a second "D-Day invasion" to "overthrow the Workers' and Peasants' State," lamely attributing it to the "hireling-provocateurs of war and instigators of excesses from the three powers in West Berlin."[8]

The final casualty total in Berlin: up to 300 dead, thousands injured.[9]

TRUST IS GOOD, BUT CONTROL IS BETTER!

THE PARTY, THE PARTY! / IT'S ALWAYS RIGHT!

TO LEARN FROM THE SOVIET UNION / MEANS LEARNING TO TRIUMPH!

Der 17. Juni. "Bloody Wednesday," when Soviet tanks painted the town red, as the western media proclaim. A deliberate allusion to "Bloody Sunday" in 1905, when Russian workers were butchered by the troops of the Czar. Young East Germans have learned in their school history classes since World War II about that popular revolt; they know that June 17 was a textbook re-enactment of Bolshevik prescriptions about workers' revolutions. Indeed, the events of June 17 form the outline of a classic Marxist story: The People, oppressed by a hated government, rise up, confront it, and. . . . [10]

Yes; but this uprising was not made by the Communists; it was made against them. The despised troops were not those of some "capitalist" or "feudalist" state oppressor, but of the Red Army; the demonstrating workers were not chanting the slogans of communism, but for free elections, the battle cry of the western democracies.

Der 17. Juni. In West Berlin, the Charlottenburger Chaussee, an avenue running up to the Brandenburg Gate, is renamed *Strasse des 17. Juni;* a cross is raised there to the memory of the fallen. In Bonn, the Bundestag declares June 17 a legal holiday, naming it the Day of National Unity.

Berlin, divided city in a polarized world. From "Dear Josef Vissarionovitch" to *"Ivan muss weg"*; from the cries of *"Freundschaft!"* and *"Friede!"* to the shrieks of "The *Panzer* are coming!"; from the roaring loudspeakers of the carnival to the silence of the graveyard: in 20 short months, how did it come to this?

How, in the "workers' paradise," did it happen? And what were the immediate and long-term consequences for DDR youth?

To answer these questions, let us situate these two defining historical moments—East Berlin's triumphant carnival of 1951 and its mass graveyard of 1953—in wider context. For in hindsight, they marked for DDR pupils and young workers a seismic shift from political illusions to disillusions, thereby symbolizing the end of one era and the beginning of another.

For most June 17 protesters, the chief issue was economic. The hoopla of the 1951 World Festival of Youth and Students had its counterpart in the SED's heralded announcement of the 1951–55 Five-Year Plan. Emphasizing heavy industry, the first Five-Year Plan was symbolically inaugurated on January 1, 1951, when the foundation stone for the first blast furnace of the Ost steel mill, the key project of the Plan, was laid near Furstenberg an der Oder. The USSR supplied the technological data, the specialist technicians, and the ore for the new foundry; Poland provided the coal. In June, the SED Central Committee mandated the formation of production cadres on the Soviet model in all state-owned firms, which replaced capitalist methods of factory management and shop floor organization. In September, the DDR signed its first long-term trade agreement with the Soviet Union, followed by similar accords with Poland and Czechoslovakia. By year's end, socialist nations accounted for 74 percent of the DDR's foreign trade. A new socialist Germany, a leader on the international scene, was assuming its place in the brotherhood of socialist nations.

With the beginning of the first Five-Year Plan, "sovietization" became more aggressive, escalating into Stalinization. In every sphere of DDR life, "anti-fascist democratic reform" now officially gave way to the "socialist revolution." But it was ever more a revolution from above: a dictatorship not of the proletariat but of the Party. The Central Committee of the SED, not the workers or peasants, ruled the land.

In 1952, the SED inaugurated its "Build Socialism" campaign, designed to implement the Five-Year Plan and aggressively promote DDR heavy industry, but having the major effect of draining away manpower—chiefly young people under the age of 25—at the rate of more than 20,000 workers per month. By 1953, East German citizens were facing hunger comparable only to the "starvation winter" of 1945/46,[11] chiefly because of colossal agricultural mismanagement—in a region that was once the breadbasket of all Germany—as well as the relentless concentration on heavy industry at the expense of consumer goods desperately needed by East Germans. The standard of living in the DDR was at least 40 percent below that of West Germany, which itself was just beginning to ascend from the depths of World War II.

Stalin's death in March 1953, however, ushered in a liberalized "Thaw" in the USSR. The DDR, under Soviet prodding, introduced an equivalent policy that abandoned the accelerated program to "build socialism" in favor of a so-called New Course of greater emphasis on consumer goods, raised living standards, greater cultural freedom, and conciliation toward dissident groups. And so, on June 10, 1953, the SED promised numerous concessions, among them a lowering of high crop quotas, a return of confiscated property to homecoming refugees, an easing of curbs on travel, and amnesty for some political prisoners.

One concession Ulbricht did not make, however, angered East German workers. A recently instituted and much-hated item in the "Build Socialism" program had been raised work norms for construction workers, which amounted to a 10 percent increase in hours for the same pay. That was bad enough. But on June 15, when the Block 40 construction workers in the Stalinallee housing project received their pay, the wage stubs showed that, though the workers were doing more work, they were actually receiving up to a third *less* pay. Chronic dissatisfaction turned to outrage, and some of the workers decided, then and there, to march the following day to the Leipzigerstrasse and protest directly to the government. At one P.M. on June 16—with the last-minute tacit approval of the SED, which wanted to show the West that it could accept and heed workers' criticisms—a band of 70 men began to march. But a few blocks later, other workers fell in, up to 3,000 of them—

word of the Block 40 protest had gotten around. That wasn't part of the SED "plan" either.

The *Vopos* radioed for instructions; they were ordered to let the demonstration proceed without interference. That afternoon, *Vopo* loudspeaker vans rode through the city, announcing the cancellation of the norm increases.

The Party's contribution to the strike "planning" ended on June 16, but the easily won concession didn't satisfy the workers. On the contrary. Smelling Ulbricht's weakness amid the uncertainty of the post-Stalinist transition, the Stalinallee workers felt ready to take on the government. Emboldened, they decided that evening to march the next day and express their *political* grievances.

And they were not alone, for June 17 would be a day of revolt in more than East Berlin. On the night of June 16, citizens throughout the DDR listened to West Berlin radio reports about the Stalinallee strikers and their victory; it was well known that these men were *Aktivisten*, elite workers hand-picked for their loyalty and efficiency. The conclusion was inescapable: If even the Stalinallee workers are discontented, things are bad indeed; if they can win concessions through protest against the regime, so can we. Spontaneously, workers across the land employed in the state-owned firms, known as SAGs (*Sowjetische Aktiengesellschaften*, Soviet Joint-Stock Companies), decided overnight to strike.

And so, as the day of June 17 dawned, the SED had more to cope with than just a few thousand disgruntled construction workers in East Berlin. At Merseburg, the 28,000 workers in the Walter Ulbricht Leuna Works, the DDR's largest chemical plant, went out on strike. At Halle, 18,000 workers set fire to the synthetic petroleum plant and struck. At Aue, 100,000 workers in the uranium mines walked away from work after destroying the shafts and flooding the mines. In many towns, strikers marched to the jails and freed any remaining political prisoners.

In all, according to western figures, 372,000 workers and several thousand pupils demonstrated on June 17 against the government in 274 cities and towns throughout the DDR.[12] Only a few schoolchildren protested. Pictures of Party leaders were ripped from some classroom walls; teachers and pupils marched together against the government. In one school, students formed a committee and issued demands: dismiss two SED loyalist teachers immediately, exclude the FDJ and JP from all participation in academic affairs, free history teaching from communist ideology, and drop Russian as a compulsory subject. On June 18, police arrested five of the student committee members. Released a few days later, they fled immediately to West Berlin. But most DDR youths remained loyal to the government. Indeed, in the aftermath of June 17, 44 youths throughout the DDR received the highest JP medal—for informing on demonstrators—like the Child Spies in *1984*.[13]

June 17, 1953. On this day East German workers rose like Spartacus and his gladiators, unleashing their contempt for the Kremlin's puppet rulers with a fury that made a mockery of the trumped-up petitions signed by millions of FDJ youth in 1951.

By week's end, 30 East Germans had been executed; at least 10,000 "provocateurs" had been jailed. The universities, which had largely remained "quiet" on June 17—most professors had remained "loyal to the regime" and had not participated in any strikes or demonstrations—now delivered declarations of support. The rector of Berlin University expressed the professoriat's "fervent wish to help" the regime. Scattered professors evidently voiced reservations: e.g., at the Technical College in Dresden, a few faculty gave only "a weak declaration" of faith in the DDR government; the dean of the theological school of the Martin Luther University in Halle withdrew his signature from a university-wide, pro-Ulbricht statement.[14]

Similarly, a few isolated exceptions to the general quietude occurred among the students. A university student in Halle was a member of the strike committee in one factory; four students joined the strike committee at the Martin Luther University in Halle, and one university instructor in the Agriculture department was executed for his support of the agitators. In Rostock, 100 students participated in anti-Soviet activities.[15] By and large, however, students in both the universities and the schools remained docile; their moderate response on June 17 showed how far the SED had come in getting DDR education under its control.

Ulbricht recognized that the political situation was unstable, especially outside education. Again proceeding by the Leninist tactic of "one step backward, two steps forward," he attempted to appease the nation by increasing food rations temporarily; then he set out to punish the rioters and discipline "soft" SED members. The SED's New Course of liberalization and conciliation was, at least unofficially, finished in the DDR. In the next four months, production norms were restored to their former levels and the secret police reinforced. As Soviet tanks continued to patrol the streets, 422 people would be sentenced to death or to long prison terms at hard labor; more than 7,000 disappeared without a trial.[16] The 145,000 *Vopos* were soon purged of those who had been reluctant to shoot unarmed protesters; Party rolls were slashed by 150,000, and even top government officials, including leading Politburo members, were fired.

Brecht, the hard-nosed exponent of *Realpolitik* and Party discipline, had ambivalently supported Ulbricht in a sharply worded letter;[17] later he wrote, in "The Solution," a sardonic epitaph on June 17 and the regime's legitimacy:

> . . . the People
> Had lost the government's trust,
> And . . . it could be restored
> Only by redoubled work.
> Would it not have been simpler
> If the government had dissolved the People
> And elected another?

"Der Ivan geht nie weg," resigned East Germans now whispered: "Ivan will never go away."

So instead, millions of East Germans did. Although two million eastern Germans had already fled since 1945, the exodus now assumed the urgency of a mass evacuation: 331,390 left in 1953, almost as many as in the previous two years combined. And still the flight continued: 184,198 in 1954; 252,870 in 1955; 279,189 in 1956; 261,622 in 1957; 204,092 in 1958; 143,917 in 1959; and 199,218 in 1960, the final year of relatively open access to West Berlin.[18] Throughout the 1950s, DDR citizens, especially East German youth, continued to flee the country—at a cost to the DDR of $1–2 billion annually. One of every two exiting East Germans was under 25 years old.[19]

Young people could more easily leave everyone and everything behind; they chose to flee rather than stay in the DDR, even though they faced weeks and months in refugee shelters, and an uncertain future afterwards. By 1952, the DDR was surrounded on all sides by barbed wire and watchtowers; only the escape hatch of West Berlin, still formally occupied by the three western Allied powers, remained. No barrier or blockade impeded a trip to the western sectors of the city, where 2.5 million Berliners resided: Though a departing East German wouldn't carry a suitcase, out of fear of being stopped by *Vopos*, he or she could probably smuggle through some precious small belongings inconspicuously by making a few preliminary trips with shopping bags. More than 250,000 East Berliners traveled west to shop or visit relatives every day; indeed, 40,000 East Berliners, and 26,000 West Berliners were official *Grenzgänger* (border-crossers), shuttling across town daily to work. For 20 *Pfennig* (= a nickel) on the subway—or simply on your own two feet—you could still, in 1953, cross the dividing line between East and West without a visa or passport. All it took to leave forever was courage—or desperation.

One might have assumed that the leading cause of the emigration stampede was economic or political. But the East Germans reporting to West German refugee camps cited "political pressure" as only the third-ranking reason. Their second motive was "lack of opportunity to travel abroad." The chief factor, as we have already noted, was "unsatisfactory or insufficient education of children." But the migrants did not cite mainly the discrimination against bourgeois children or the ineptitude of *Neulehrer;* their outrage was simply with ideological indoctrination and the religious and generational tensions it created within the family: they just did not want their children brainwashed into becoming communists.[20]

Nevertheless, despite the raging, nationwide discontent and the constant manpower drain imposed by its ideological campaign, DDR educators followed their hard-line course throughout the 1950s. Indeed, above all in DDR education, the decade following the 1951 World Festival of Youth and Students, especially the months before Stalin's death, witnessed the DDR plunge into its deepest freeze of the Cold War. After *der 17. Juni*, the short thaw turned to frost; DDR leaders gripped the reins of power ever tighter. (Unlike in 1950, when student protesters like Hermann Josef Flade marred the show, the 1954 elections went off smoothly and the returns were better than ever: a record 99.3 percent "yes" vote.)

History was still on their side, the SED leadership erroneously believed; it was all just a matter of time—and "re-education." Yes, "Stalins come and go . . . ," but the Cold War catechetics of Soviet rule remained. By the mid-1950s, the FDJ and JP had grown to four million members. SED leaders failed to grasp that the uprising of June 17 and the unceasing youth exodus portended the definitive passing of communism's ideological appeal to new DDR generations and thus also of its viable historical moment. Instead they redoubled their efforts to rear model young communists: their campaign to "Stalinize" the schools and youth organizations

grew ever more systematic. Stalin or no Stalin, and the vicissitudes of DDR industrial and foreign policy notwithstanding: the Stalinization of East German education—and the production of sovietized German *Planmenschen*—advanced.
And it is to the story of that progress that this chapter now turns.

Stalinizing the Schools

The Pope?! And how many divisions has he got?

Stalin[21]

In the years that witnessed the DDR's first Five-Year Plan of 1951–55, educators
too were following to the letter the motto: "To Learn from the Soviet Union /
Means Learning to Triumph!" More closely than ever before, the ideological campaign was geared to economic imperatives: whereas industrial policymakers
aimed to complete the transition from capitalism to communism, agitprop leaders
strove to overcome bourgeois attitudes and forge a new socialist consciousness.
And the school system was crucial: "The main task during this period of the Five-
Year Plan," Ulbricht announced, "is to raise the scientific [Marxist-Leninist] level
of our entire educational system."[22]

And so DDR education entered its third, most ideologically feverish stage (1951–
56), largely unaffected by Stalin's death, June 17, the Thaw in Moscow, and the
New Course (which effectively ended shortly after the February 1955 purge of
Malenkov, the Kremlin's leading proponent of liberalization after Stalin's death.)

Throughout the period, and in the service of the Five-Year Plan, the Ministry of
People's Education stepped up its own production pace. The ABF programs, designed to prepare lower-class children for higher education and viewed as the
"nurseries" of the future socialist intelligentsia, quickly multiplied. In February
1951, with the founding of the Central Secretariat for Higher Education, the universities were formally brought under Party control; in a related move, the Institute
for Social Sciences, attached to the SED Central Committee, was founded to train
Marxist-Leninist cadres for the management of the state and economy. Meanwhile,
school education took another step toward streamlined ideological orthodoxy that
fall, when the first SED-sponsored parent-teacher collectives and the first textbooks
systematically written according to Marxism-Leninism were introduced. These
changes were significant: a 1951 report of the western Allies concluded that the
SED reorganization of the educational system posed, along with the growing dominance of the FDJ in youth life, the single most serious barrier to reunification with
West Germany.[23]

And such educational changes were in lock-step with the SED's economic program. In July 1952, at its Second Party Conference, the SED announced plans to
accelerate industrial development. Echoing Makarenko, the Party would henceforth direct "all energies toward the buildup of socialism."

The coordination of education with the SED campaign to "build socialism"
turned education and youth policy into a mechanism for producing *Planmenschen*
by glorifying labor and the collectivist work ethic.[24] That aim too fit with the
directive of the Second Party Conference, which launched yet another new slogan

in that spirit, derived from the lyrics of Louis Fürnberg's *Die Partei* (a.k.a. "The Party Is Always Right"):[25]

> *Aus leninischem Geist, von Stalin geschweisst!*
> [From Lenin's spirit, and welded together by Stalin!]

Indeed, after his 70th birthday in December 1949, the figure of Stalin—even more so than Lenin—became ubiquitous and almost godlike in East German as well as Soviet schools. Now there was no end to the obsequious, unctuous sloganeering in worship of his name. *"Von Stalin, dem weisen Lehrer aller Völker und grössten Freund des deutschen Volkes, lernen!"* proclaimed SED educators: "Learn from Stalin, the wise teacher of all peoples and the greatest friend of the German people!" Along with hundreds of other educators, SED propaganda chief Kurt Hager lionized Stalin as "the greatest scholar of all time."[26]

DDR textbooks of the early 1950s conspicuously reflected this same spirit of unqualified homage of Stalin. The 1953 edition of the 8th-grade history text, which treats world events since 1917, opens with full-page portraits of Lenin and Stalin, and continues with sections such as "Stalin's glorious deeds in the civil war" and "The Stalinist Constitution [of 1936]—the most democratic constitution of the world."[27] Similarly, the 1953 and 1956 editions of the 10th-grade textbook, which covers the twelfth through eighteenth centuries, cites authoritative scholarly works such as Stalin's *Marxism and the National and Colonial Question* and his *Dialectical and Historical Materialism*.[28]

Thus, even after Stalin's death[29]—and especially during 1953–56, when Malenkov, Molotov, Beria, and Khrushchev vied with one another to fill the sudden power vacuum in the USSR—Stalin's "cult of personality" flourished in East Germany. The lionizing of Stalin as "the great *Führer*" exemplified well the metamorphosis of Bolshevism into Red Fascism in the DDR, and the idolatry declined only in 1956 with Khrushchev's "Secret Speech" at the Twentieth Party Congress of the Communist Party of the Soviet Union (CPSU) and subsequent, definitive triumph over his Party rivals.

Although nothing could have more contradicted Marx's vision of a classless society and Lenin's principle of collective leadership than such leader worship of Stalin, his exalted status was reaffirmed repeatedly in DDR youth literature of the period, just as in other spheres of DDR life and elsewhere in the communist world. And the Stalin cult did serve the SED's purposes: "Stalin" became a flesh-and-blood symbol for "socialism." Story after story in DDR school readers and children's magazines exalted a young Josef who studies diligently, works hard, and practices "communist morality" scrupulously—the ideal of the Stakhanovite worker. Building up Stalin, therefore, helped "build socialism" by elevating those values that would strengthen the collectivist work ethic. The Stalin cult thus fulfilled the directive of the DDR state publishing house for children, which insisted in 1951: "Our literature—from literature for the smallest ones to literature for the greatest ones—can only be viewed according to one single criterion: How does this literature help us to achieve communism and build socialism?"[30]

A representative 1951 story in a 4th-grade reader, titled "Stalin's Schooldays," illustrates how the Stalin cult contributed to the industrialization campaign. Stalin is depicted as a model boy, diligent and successful in everything he undertakes. He is to be emulated in all things:

His mother took care that her son was always dressed cleanly. He wore a blue coat and high boots. His lively dark eyes looked cheerfully on the world; he wore grey gloves and a red scarf.

His comrades recognized him by his scarf.

"Here comes our Josef!" they called and hurried toward him. Everyone in the school loved him, because he was so lively and strong. He was an excellent ballplayer, knew well how to select his teammates, and his team was almost always the victor.

Besides his school book Josef always had another book in his school bag. He read during every free minute. How many books he already had read! In the school library there was hardly a book he hadn't already read. Therefore he bought new books in the book shop.

Everything that he read he remembered. He could talk about many interesting things. Even the adults liked to listen to the boy, and often the old people asked him to tell them something about what he had read.

Josef knew more than the other children. He was the best student in the class. But his schoolmates never felt any sign of superiority from him. He was a good comrade, always prepared [*immer bereit*] to help the weaker comrades. He helped them with homework and with drawing. For Josef was a good drawer, even though there wasn't yet any drawing class in schools. At 15 he ended his school years and received a certificate of honor.[31]

This example shows how the cult of personality is communicated to a 9 year old. Stalin is a child hero: the best ballplayer, the most voracious reader, the most intelligent student, the best artist in the class—but also helpful to everyone and possessed of superior modesty. He embodies all the virtues of communist morality: cleanliness, physical dexterity, perseverance, intelligence, generosity, simplicity, humility.

Another tribute was "Gisela's Gift to Stalin," a narrative poem presented as if written by a child, which appeared in the *ABC Zeitung*, a magazine read by 1st through 4th graders. "Gisela" represents the DDR citizenry, who should be happy to contribute (i.e., give war reparations) to "the *Heimat* of peace" and the lovable Stalin. The story shows how, as if Stalin were Christianity's God-the-Father, ordinary people can have a special, warm, personal relationship with him. Stalin is the deliverer of peace, the friend of all children. When one thinks of the millions of people that Stalin ordered to be murdered—indeed the hundreds of thousands of his victims, including German POWs, still in the Gulag in the early 1950s—this poem exploits children's innocence with excruciating cruelty.

In the east, where the sun rises
where the wind blows so cold

there lies a great, beautiful land
far beyond our forest.

Even before you are in school
it's probably familiar to you
because it is the *Heimat* of peace
that's what you've named it.

That land is the Soviet Union
you love it, for you know
for many years already
a man lives there called Stalin.

He liberated human beings
he taught the whole world
how one guards freedom
and maintains true friendship.

That's why children love him so,
for only in peace
can everyone learn and
be cheerful and always happy.

Gisela wants to give Stalin a birthday present.

I thought of gloves
because it's so cold and raw there;
I've brought a design with me
I made it myself—Look!

That he perhaps already has a pair
is not a waste
In the big city
he'll like to wear another pair.

The spinning wheel turns quickly
Grandmother sings along
and outside the window
the wind rustles without pause through the leaves.

When Gisela took the needle
it went one, two, three,
only when she came to her thumb
did Grandma help her.

The beautiful work was soon completed
made of fine, soft wool
Mama packed it
and brought it immediately to the post office.

So it was sent off
to that distant, beautiful land
"From Gisela" and "knitted by myself"
were written inside.

> And Gisela, with cheerful temper,
> thought often about it
> "If Stalin travels today into Moscow,
> he's wearing the gloves."[32]

While the cult of personality around Stalin illustrates graphically the acceleration from "sovietization" to Stalinization in the DDR, it was merely one aspect of a comprehensive educational campaign, known as Education for Socialist Patriotism, instituted in 1952. Indeed it was merely the positive side of that offensive, better known in the West as *Erziehung zum Hass* (Education for Hatred), the phrase that the DDR used for its program of school paramilitary training, exercises that included training in archery and the use of air guns. FDJ chief Erich Honecker's contempt for *Nursportler* (pure athletes) signaled the program's priorities: "Sports have no purpose in themselves; they are a means to an end. . . . [T]o engage in sports, youths must be anti-fascist and oppose the American imperialists."[33]

Education for Hatred—the very name evokes Hate Week and the Two-Minute Hate sessions in Orwell's *1984*—was a stepchild of the 1951 "Hate America" offensive launched by the USSR. Like the USSR, the DDR—in both its general education and special paramilitary programs—exalted the "socialist peace camp" and castigated variously the western "imperialistic warmonger camp," the bourgeois German past, capitalism, and "Americanism."[34]

The SED hate campaign emerged from and owed much to the escalation from sovietization to Stalinization, an advance on the 1949 educational initiative, Education for Democratic Patriotism, which had emphasized love of country (though it too had embraced "hatred of the enemy" and of all "opponents of progress"). On balance, "democratic patriotism" had amounted to wary, if peaceful, coexistence with capitalists, generating courses on such topics as *Deutschkunde* (geography of Germany), which promoted patriotism and the defense of the homeland. One DDR historian later explained the difference between the two programs: "[A]fter 1952, Education for Democratic Patriotism had an explicitly socialist content; it led students to a declaration of faith in socialism. . . . At the same time, Education for Hatred against the enemies of peace, socialism, and the DDR became more and more an essential part of patriotic education." The significance of *Deutschkunde* reflected the change: between 1951 and 1956, the number of school hours devoted to it rose by a third.[35]

The transition beyond strident calls for anti-fascist democracy to a bellicose, negative "socialist patriotism" was marked by a directive of the Ministry of People's Education, issued in 1951, which anticipated the Party's 1952 announcement to "build socialism":[36]

> In light of the growing danger of war as a result of the direct war preparations of American imperialism and in view of the revival of German imperialism [West German rearmament and U.S. military aid] as America's major ally in Europe, the DDR must serve as a bulwark in the battle to maintain peace against the aggressive politics of the American and West German imperialists.[37]

In language that echoed the proclamations of the Third Reich, the directive continued:

> The education of our youth to become active promoters of a united, peace-loving, democratic Germany and burning partisans who will defend the Fatherland and the achievements of its democratic reconstruction till the end, is the holy duty of every German teacher.[38]

And some teachers embraced their duty with the fervency of HJ and BDM leaders. One example here may suffice. A kindergarten teacher explained in 1951 in *Neue Erziehung*, the journal of the German Institute for Kindergarten and Boarding School Education, how she promoted hatred toward "the enemies of goodness and progress":

> See, children, I say, many schools were totally destroyed in the war. Then the children themselves mention a number of examples. I explain how teachers and children worked together on the building of the new school, how we strove with all our might, and now that it's here, how evil people are trying to destroy it again.
>
> "They are the war-makers," the children interrupt me. "Adenauer himself has a factory, where he produces war materiel, that's why he wants war!" Karla informs us. "We must put these war-makers behind bars," demand the children. Yes, some of the children go even further in their hatred toward these evil people who want to destroy what we've built: "We must kill them," they demand.
>
> Now the class is filled with outrage. Small fists are rolled into a ball. Passionately, Wolfgang demands that we beat the evil people to death.

The kindergarten teacher concluded:

> This experiment showed me that we can interest and win over our children—if we proceed in a fashion appropriate to their stage of development—on all questions of life. Children should indeed have a childhood without grave worries, but they should never be isolated from real life. Their future should be bright and happy, and therefore it is necessary that they participate, beginning in their early years, in the life we are building. We must not underestimate how deeply the roots of what we plant go into our children. Our effort will bear fruit—it will prevent them from ever tolerating, overlooking, or supporting the enemies of goodness and progress.[39]

This message was itself unmistakable. What the story planted, of course, was hatred: hatred against nonconformists, hatred against critics of the DDR, hatred against the West. It was Hate Week to last a lifetime: to love your *Heimat*, you must hate your adversaries.

And it was never too early to begin. Addressing this theme, an official of preschool education in the Ministry of People's Education in Thuringia seconded the kindergarten teacher:

Even our little ones in kindergarten participate in the political events of our time, insofar as their powers of comprehension permit. Love of our people, love for our German Democratic Republic is sowed in their hearts. But also hatred toward all enemies, who aim to disturb our peaceful construction [of socialism].[40]

To "sow" these lessons thoroughly, some kindergartens even included shooting practice for tots, in which the targets were likenesses of Adenauer and Uncle Sam.[41]

"Learning from the Soviet Union," therefore, had both its tender-hearted and tough-minded sides.[42] The major goal, however—whether it involved fostering a cult of personality or exploiting emotions such as love and hate—was usually to "build socialism." Whether workers or students, DDR citizens would be "welded" into model socialist laborers. Or as Gorky once laid down the line for Party writers: "The true hero of our books should be labor, that is, man organized by the process of labor."

It sounds ominous, but the results often struck westerners as ridiculous rather than threatening. Take, for instance, this progressive poem in a 1951 4th-grade reader:

> My brother is an *Aktivist*
> In a village in Saxony
> He does whatever is necessary
> To make the corn stalks grow.
> He clatters in his tractor
> Over all the fields he plows
> And however hard the work is
> It brings him only pleasure.[43]

Or consider the much-publicized 1952 JP contest, "My Friend—The Plan," in which children vied to create pictures, assemble plastic models, and tell stories about "the happy future of the workers" and how the Five-Year Plan was changing everyone's lives for the better.[44]

Similar themes were highlighted in the hymns to socialist labor learned by the FDJ and JP during the early 1950s. During and after school, at FDJ and JP meetings, at summer youth camps, DDR youth sung countless tunes—songs like "You Have a Norm in Front of You" and "A Thousand Tractors"—that sounded as if they had been belched out of an Orwellian versificator.[45] There was the "Song of the Young Coal Miners," "The Railwayman's Song," and "The Song of the Agricultural Brigade." Typical was "Departure for the Depot":

> I sing, I sing, I sing;
> The work bids me adieu,
> I take my gun and go on guard
> For you, my lathe, for you![46]

Or take "The Ladder Has Rungs":

> The ladder has rungs and the monument has eight corners
> And all must first build
> If they want to attend the celebration.
> And all must first build
> If they want to attend the celebration.
>
> That's why everyone runs to work,
> To show what he can do
> And the laughing, free youth advance in the work.
> And the laughing, free youth advance in the work.
>
> And the young ones and the old ones
> Team up together
> But what use would all the work be
> If we didn't have a Plan?
>
> Our Plan teaches us to build
> To renew our capital
> And as we sing, we march along
> To the youth celebration party.[47]

FDJ lyricists did not hesitate to draft tenderness in service of the state, as in the love songs about heavy machinery operators, tunes like "Fritz the Tractorist":

> Who is the best of all everywhere?
> That's Fritz the tractorist!
> Whether it's in sowing or reaping, or in learning.
> He always sings the best song in the fields during work
> And Gretel hums along softly,
> Because her heart is burning with desire
> For Fritz with his tractor,
> For Fritz, yes!
> Fritz, Fritz, Fritz
> The tractorist.

Or "When my Heinz Comes Home for the Holidays":

> My Heinz, he was a tractorist
> He plowed the land for us
> But one night, when he came home for the holidays
> He took me by the hand
> "I am protecting our harvest,"
> He said with a happy look
> So that it can bloom and grow,
> Just like our Republic.
>
> Yes, when my Heinz,
> When my Heinz now comes home for the holidays
> Ach, how nice that'll be
> Then we'll take a walk through the village to the fields,

Just the two of us,
Just the two of us, completely alone.
Ach, how happy and proud I'll be of my Heinz,
The Coast Guard Policeman.

I'm fine, I've written to him at the seaside
I'm so proud of you, my Heinz
And I've been faithful to you.
As far as your tractor is concerned—
I wrote to him at the seaside—
It's oiled and hasn't had a glitch
Because now I'm sitting on it![48]

Such catchy ditties were widely (and often sincerely) sung—and listened to on the radio; indeed, there was nothing else to listen to, except on West Berlin stations. Whether such tunes, however, really helped "build socialism" or transform FDJ youth into convinced communists is questionable: an informal 1952 survey of East German youth, conducted by an American academic, estimated that only 16 percent were, as of yet, "believers."[49] And a study undertaken during the previous August by staff members of the American High Commission in West Berlin, who interviewed FDJ members crossing the border from the World Festival of Students and Youth for Peace, concluded that less than 14 percent were "believers" and that 60 percent held that their teachers "were communicating a false picture" of the East-West situation to them. Further, 55 percent "blamed the Soviets" for the hostile climate and only 7 percent judged the United States responsible.[50]

Aware of the formidable task still before them of winning youth to communist morality, SED educators—just two weeks after the Party's proclamation of July 1952 to "build socialism"—threw into higher gear their engines of agitprop. They would weld young hearts and minds into "*allseitig entwickelte Persönlichkeiten*" (fully rounded personalities)—Marx's famous phrase in *Das Kapital*—"able and ready to build up socialism and defend the achievements of the workers to the utmost."[51]

In practice, "defense" meant military training. And that was the key to the Stalinization of education in the DDR: Stalinization meant, finally, militarization.[52] Mussolini had proclaimed three fascist virtues: "Believe, obey, fight." Now SED educators systematically addressed that triad. As the FDJ's performance at the 1951 World Festival had demonstrated, a rudimentary foundation had already been laid.

DDR youth could and would obey, and at least a strong sixth did believe. But that, of course, was not enough for SED educators. They set out first to enflame belief, to inculcate a passionate, tenaciously held faith; and then to achieve total submission of the will and immediate readiness for combat (*Immer bereit!*). That was the Stalinist pedagogical line: First establish militantly communist conviction, then—as the World Festival of Youth and Students had phrased it—preparedness to act on "Stalin's call to arms for peace."

And so, the new teacher training programs of 1951/52 aimed to broaden and deepen communist conviction. Whereas Makarenko, until mid-century, had been introduced piecemeal and selectively into DDR pedagogy, he was now systematically promoted. Pockets of resistance to Soviet didactics had heretofore existed in many school districts; now the last vestiges of *Reformpädagogik* were rooted out. For books in the DDR had to be, as Premier Otto Grotewohl proclaimed, "weapons—revolutionary weapons!"[53]

In the martial spirit of Makarenko, DDR teacher methodology sessions now consisted of exhaustive, inflexible instructions on how to use the new Stalinized weapons, including precise directions on how to teach and evaluate students. The new honor of "Distinguished Teacher of the People" was awarded strictly on the basis of political conviction. In 1951, all teachers began an intensive course of study in the fundamentals of M-L pedagogy, culminating in special examinations. The courses gave no attention to German or even European pedagogical theory, but rather concentrated exclusively on the work of Soviet scholars, sometimes featuring Stalin's own works. The titles evince the relentless one-note theme of the transition from anti-fascism to sovietization and Stalinization:

- *February*: "Soviet Pedagogy—the Most Advanced Pedagogy"
- *March*: "Dialectical Materialism, the *Weltanschauung* of the Working Class, and the Marxist-Leninist Party as the Foundation of All Scholarship"
- *April*: "The Four Bases of Dialectics"
- *May*: "The Basic Characteristics of Marxist Materialism"
- *June-July*: "Dialectical Materialism and Soviet Pedagogy"
- *September*: "The Marxist Dialectic as Methodological Foundation of Soviet Pedagogy"
- *October*: "The Bolshevik Party of Lenin and Stalin and Its Leadership in the Field of Pedagogy"
- *November*: "The Party as Productive Guide for the Theory and Practice of the Soviet School"
- *December*: "School and Youth Organizations in the USSR"[54]

The new M-L pedagogical content mandated the "unity of theory and praxis." To achieve such unity, declared Marxist-Leninist educators, pedagogy must conform utterly to politics, just as the individual must unprotestingly sacrifice himself or herself to Society, i.e., the Party-determined course. Because the campaign to "build socialism" entailed, according to Stalin's blindly quoted dogma, a constant intensification of the class struggle, the current phase of DDR education necessitated a rigorously "scientific" pedagogy, i.e., Party-directed and class-conscious.

So teachers were now trained to be unvarnished party propagandists. They were "assisted" by the FDJ, which appointed "class leaders" to share responsibility with teachers for shaping socialist consciousness in each class. This meant crudely enforcing the principles of a debased Makarenko to the letter. Such a Stalinist pedagogy effectively denied the concepts of childhood and adolescence. "Childhood" was branded an idealistic, reactionary notion of "pedagogical liberalism" and of the old, bourgeois order. Going a step even beyond Makarenko at his most militant, SED educators treated the child as a small adult; school lessons paid no attention to developmental psychology, only to national political and economic goals. "Unity of theory and praxis" also mandated "harmony" between school lesson and the student, i.e., the child was to serve the lesson, or to be an "inner unit" of the lesson; the teacher was to direct the child toward the highest possible achievement, as exemplified by the lesson, which itself typically taught allegiance to the collective and the state. Teachers were to discourage children from following their own inclinations, thereby to avoid any "deviation" from the SED line.[55]

These Party orthodoxies led to catastrophic student failure rates, up to 30 percent around mid-century.[56] And they provoked yet another exodus of experienced, qualified teachers; conformists and Party careerists replaced older teachers who had distinguished themselves in the 1930s and '40s as anti-fascist resisters. Meanwhile the *Neulehrer* came and went; annual turnover rates ranged between 25 and 45 percent.[57] Constant instability was the most immediately apparent price the DDR paid for swallowing a martial Makarenko and abandoning its own tradition of German humanism. (In 1952 the SED forbade further official use of the term *Neulehrer* because the public associated it with "unqualified."[58] Now all schoolteachers were simply called *Lehrer*.)

SED educators' opposition to the West became absolute. As the arms race with the West accelerated—the USSR exploded its first atomic bomb in 1949 and first hydrogen bomb in 1953—educators' belligerent rhetoric escalated too. "The victory of one side demands the annihilation of the other," thundered *Pädagogik*, the journal of the Academy of Pedagogical Sciences, since the differences between Marxist and bourgeois pedagogy were "irreconcilable":

- consistent scientific levels vs. mysticism and idealism;
- freedom to learn and develop, and happiness in learning vs. educational privileges and hostility toward learning;
- peace and satisfaction with learning vs. militarism and competitive struggles against everyone;
- international respect vs. chauvinism and racial hatred;
- reconciliation between intellectual and physical work vs. tension between them;
- social justice and prosperity vs. the gap between rich and poor;
- steady development vs. economic crisis;
- morality vs. ethical hypocrisy;
- genuine humanity vs. the breeding of human beasts.[59]

The bellicose Stalinization campaign in education manifested itself most obviously in the decision in 1952/53 to introduce paramilitary training in the schools. Now youth would be educated to become patriots wielding real weapons.

The paramilitary training was coordinated with the founding in 1952 of the GST (*Gesellschaft für Sport und Technologie*, Society for Sport and Technology), an athletic association founded on the Soviet model that specialized in military-oriented activities (e.g., marksmanship, riding, skydiving, scuba diving). That fall the People's Police was also unofficially converted into a full-fledged People's Army,[60] and an ordinance of the Ministry of People's Education ordered that one class period per day was to be devoted in every grade to military education.[61] Girls as well as boys from the ages of 12 to 14 were required to take shooting lessons in firing small-bore rifles; those over 14 fired army rifles and revolvers. At 15, all children were also instructed for two hours per week in the commando techniques of street fighting, hand-to-hand combat, and sniping.[62]

The universities also introduced military education, in order to transform institutions of higher education, as the Associate State Secretary of Higher Education proudly phrased it, into "military academies of the class war."[63] Girls were "excused" from this further indoctrination, but the privilege of a university education for boys now depended not only on the proper class attitude but also partly on their willingness to enter the military. Many universities mandated marksmanship training: medical students at Humboldt University were admitted for their final examinations only after scoring passing marks on the rifle range; selected nurse trainees had shooting practice for two hours per week as well.[64] Thus did the same young men and women, who in 1945 as shivering, half-starved schoolchildren stood amid the rubble holding anti-war signs ("Never Again German Soldiers!"), now find themselves taking target practice between classes.

Indeed the universities were becoming less centers of higher learning than communist trade schools and "military academies of the class war." The new slogan now on SED educators' lips, a variation on Liebknecht's motto, reflected the change: *"Wer die Kader hat, hat die Zukunft!"* ("Who has the Cadres, has the Future!").[65] FDJ student activists now spent little time on their studies; like top American student-athletes, such "students of the new type" could scarcely be called students at all.

To weld students into patriotic, socialist *Planmenschen*, the planners adopted a simple tactic: pile requirement upon requirement, so that they would have no time whatsoever for anything outside their classes and mandatory political meetings. "Keep them on the move and they'll never have time to think, let alone protest," ran the logic. Required classes took up 25 hours per week, not counting electives; required political meetings consumed another 10 or 20, with "homework" now including an evening spent proselytizing non-Marxists. Regardless of his or her subject of study, every student took a mind-boggling 16 hours per week of political courses, including courses in the History of the Communist Party of the USSR, the Theory of Marxism-Leninism-Stalinism, Social Studies,[66] and Applied Marxist-Leninist-Stalinist Theory[67]—not counting their paramilitary courses. Some *Aktivisten* reported that they were devoting 60 or even 70 hours per week to class and FDJ activities, with no time left except on Sundays for reading and writing assignments.[68]

As if that weren't enough, the SED also lengthened the semester and instituted the "10-month school year" in 1952/53. (The traditional German semester system totaled less than eight months.) This was an attempt to impose factory-like norms on "intellectual workers" similar to those for industrial workers. Summer "vacation" was taken up mostly by a six-week industrial or agricultural "internship" in the coal mines or the harvest fields. Now the academic year ran from September 6 to May 6, followed by examinations and "internships," which lasted until July 10—reducing the summer break to little more than a month. So students received little study or leisure time between semesters either.[69]

One ostensible achievement of the higher education reforms was that, by 1954/55, 55 percent of the students were of working-class origin.[70] But even this was deceptive—and led to new abuses that betrayed not just the DDR's former commitment to equal-opportunity education,[71] but made a mockery of the very idea of a special "working-class consciousness." Because middle-class students received no state aid, they took jobs in steel mills and restaurants to pay for their educations. Given the number of hours of required classes, some of them were often sick from sheer exhaustion. Often such students of "bourgeois" origin finally decided to "work off" their heritage: they devoted two years to the state, laboring in mines or factories. Thereafter they were categorized "working class" and eligible for stipends. (By 1956, extra service time in the newly founded NVA [*Nationale Volksarmee*, National People's Army] earned similar dispensations.)

Now the SED was finally getting the last stronghold of the citadel of learning, the universities, "completely in hand," as Ulbricht put it.[72] But two factors still impeded the Party: first, the fear of driving away too many useful scientists and gifted students into the BRD; and second, the authoritative presence of a few great, outspoken humanist professors—such as Ernst Bloch and Hans Mayer—whose intellectual aura and personal integrity cowed Party ideologues, making it impossible to snuff out utterly the flame of freethinking and disinterested scholarship.

So Party leaders worked through the youth organizations, regularly whipping up hysteria about foreign agents in the student body. In February 1955, FDJ students officially became something very close to student Thought Police agents, now formally required to report on the activities and conversations of fellow students and professors. And, Orwell might have said, Intolerance was Strength: The dean of student affairs at the University of Halle condemned the "destructive tolerance" of his students; an FDJ conference concluded that "tolerance is the ground in which unscientific and oppositional ideas grow."[73]

The few remaining student resisters were handled with dispatch. The biggest show of SED Intolerance as Strength occurred in September 1955, when 200 Greifswald University medical students refused to attend lectures after the SED announced that the medical school was being transformed into a military school of medicine under *Vopo* supervision. The SSD (*Staatssicherheitsdienst*, State Security Service or secret police) arrested them immediately; five students received jail terms.[74]

Because Stalinization and militarization were linked to an anti-pacifist, pro-atheist campaign, the most severe persecution was of Christians. Already in 1945, over the objections of the churches, SMAD had outlawed all denominational schools; in 1952 the SED restricted freedom of religion and speech even further. As of 1952, however, the DDR was still a Christian country: 83 percent Protestant—primarily Lutheran—and 13 percent Catholic. The stage was thus set for a no-holds-barred battle between the communists and the churches for the nation's youth, and the "Build Socialism" campaign of 1952 furnished the occasion.

Beginning in January 1953, the FDJ launched an aggressive atheism campaign that featured fierce castigation of the *Junge Gemeinden* (Youth Congregations), the youth groups sponsored by Protestant churches; soon the SED banned *Petrusblatt*, the Catholic newspaper of Berlin, and lashed out at Catholic youth leaders. FDJ leaders accused *Junge Gemeinde* leaders of "espionage, sabotage, and terroristic acts committed on American orders." Aiming to establish itself as the only youth group in the DDR, the FDJ subjected church youth to public inquisitions, during which individuals were interrogated before school assemblies by FDJ leaders. Some church youth, intimidated, signed a declaration that read, in part: "Diversionist organizations are organizations of the Catholic and Protestant churches, particularly the *Junge Gemeinden*. As responsible German youth, we must fight these organizations. The SED is the educator of youth. I promise always to recognize the tenets of the Party."[75]

Unexpectedly, however, the great majority of church youth and their leaders stood their ground. By March, 3,000 students had refused to sign; they would not renounce their memberships in the youth groups and thus were expelled from school and barred from further education. For continuing to sponsor church youth activities, 50 Protestant and Catholic church officials and lay workers received prison terms of up to 12 years. In April, the *Junge Gemeinden* were ruled illegal. "Under the cloak of religion," announced the SED, they had promoted "pacifism and Western ideas."[76]

At that very moment, however, warmer breezes from the Thaw in Moscow reached East Berlin, persuading Ulbricht that he should reach a timely compromise with church leaders, which in turn led to the June 10 concessions whereby the SED pledged to cease harassing the churches if the churches promised not to interfere in DDR political life. Ulbricht readmitted expelled students to class, rehired purged Christian teachers, voided the jail terms of 20 pastors, returned confiscated church property, and restored voluntary religious lessons in school. In practical terms, the churches had won.

But not for long. Cognizant of the significant, if often overlooked, role that Protestant church youth groups had played in the weeks leading up to the June 17 revolt, and in full awareness of the danger that the churches posed to the Party's hold on power, the SED again cracked down on the churches in 1954/55. With the formation of the Society for the Promotion of Scientific Knowledge in June 1954, headed by Johannes Becher in his official role as Minister of Culture, plans were made to replace Christian confirmation with a communist ceremony. This was called the *Jugendweihe* (youth consecration), a communist confirmation rite administered to DDR youth at the age of 14, in the spring of their year of graduation from school. Such secular youth-pledging ceremonies were first developed by German socialists during the Weimar era and later adopted by the Nazis. Traditionally, the *Jugendweihe* was voluntary, marking a rite of passage: a celebration for Party youth of the beginning of their glorious life of labor and full contribution to the Party. But the SED sought to make the *Jugendweihe* mandatory for all children and turn it into a ceremony dedicating oneself to the socialist state.

Like Christian confirmation in Germany, the *Jugendweihe* was held on Sundays during the Easter season and consisted of a 10-week course of instruction known as "Youth Lessons." Of course, these classes were in Communist theory and dialectical materialism, concluding with an oath on the big Sunday to devote one's life to "the peace camp."[77] Both the Protestant and Catholic churches viewed the *Jugendweihe*, accurately, as an initial communist attempt to inculcate a mild form of atheism, a first step toward the ultimate goal of displacing Christian confirmation altogether and instituting atheism and dialectical materialism as the DDR state religion. Protestant leaders fought back by declaring that those who entered the *Jugendweihe* could not receive any sacraments (even matrimony); the Catholic bishops did likewise, and formally announced that participation was a sin.[78] Although children were pressured by classmates and teachers to participate, by 1955 only 17.7 percent did so; 23.7 percent in 1956.[79] (By 1989, however, the percentage had risen to 98 percent.)

In 1955, reviling DDR Christians as anti-socialists, pacifists and pro-western sympathizers, Ulbricht banned all church groups from using university premises for their meetings and barred most children of ministers from higher education.[80] That fall, the SED also began using blatantly anti-religious slogans to promote youth enthusiasm for the crop harvest. One example of a slogan displayed prominently on the main streets of villages and in state-operated tractor-lending stations: "Without God and even without sunshine, we are bringing in the harvest."[81]

And so was the SED. After a weary decade of planting orthodoxy and sowing groupthink, the Party was reaping "students of the new type" at last. Or as Kurt Hager, then-Secretary for Higher Education, put it: "The university has transformed itself into a university of the People."[82]

So now the citadel of learning seemed firmly in SED hands. Only a final "cleanup," as the Party called it, remained. And then suddenly—just as the SED was unveiling both its Second Five-Year Plan and the NVA in January 1956, and was re-establishing its anti-Christian campaign on a successful new footing—a shocking blow sideswiped its own secular religion. Not from the churches or DDR workers, or even the hateful "Amis," but from the holy of holies in the Promised Land: the Kremlin itself. The effect among DDR educators of Khrushchev's denunciation of Stalin's cult of personality in February 1956 was electric. For another brief moment, the cringing subservience to Party dogma among educators ceased—in the year of the DDR intellectuals' revolt, the annus mirabilis of 1956 throughout East Europe, when warm zephyrs carried a democratic Indian summer to East German education.

Alas, this final East German summer would soon, all too soon, give way to another deep chill—a winter from which the DDR would not wake for decades to come. Ulbricht would exploit yet another convulsive crisis and consolidate, this time once and for all, his control of the Party and government. Minor tremors would follow in the DDR; but after 1956, his power—i.e., his role as Khrushchev's master puppeteer—was secure.

And East Germans would be heard to whisper: *"Der Spitzbart geht nie weg."*

Ulbricht *über allen*

The revolution devours its own children.

Georg Büchner, *Danton's Death*

Nineteen fifty-three was the year for a failed uprising by the workers; 1956 would be the educators' turn. Only this time the "revolt" was laid waste by the SED before it ever took root, trampled once again by Stalin's jackboots. Once again, Ulbricht would face off against his critics, but this time he would defeat them directly, in an intra-Party dispute between Party loyalists and dissidents that would never become a popular, or even workers' uprising—let alone a nationwide student revolt. This confrontation would feature Ulbricht against the intellectuals, his elitist, neo-Stalinized oligarchical collectivism against a "revisionist," humanistic socialism indebted to Marx and the German Enlightenment. "The intellectuals need a good kick in the groin," Ulbricht remarked during the crisis,[83] a statement that would become his slogan—and words that his true Blueshirts would turn into deeds.

The events of 1956 would prove to be the independent-minded intellectuals' major last stand; in hindsight, it is clear that they never really had a chance. But the spring of 1956 didn't begin that way. An extraordinary, initially hopeful ferment within the Party was triggered unexpectedly by Khrushchev's so-called Secret Speech at the Twentieth Congress of the CPSU on February 25. Although the 75-page speech was never formally published in the USSR or its satellites, parts of it were read aloud at CPSU meetings to the rank-and-file, and word of it spread like wildfire, as Khrushchev had obviously intended. In the speech, Khrushchev castigated Stalin's "violation of the principle of collective leadership" and his personality "cult, which became the source of a whole series of exceedingly serious and grave perversions of party principles, of party democracy, of revolutionary legality. . . . Such a man supposedly knows everything, sees everything, thinks for everyone, can do anything, is infallible in his behavior." The indictment continued:

> [Stalin] practiced brutal violence, not only toward everything which opposed him, but also toward that which seemed, to his capricious and despotic character, contrary to his concepts. . . . [M]any prominent party leaders and rank-and-file Party workers, honest and dedicated to the cause of communism, fell victim to Stalin's despotism. . . . [H]e often chose the path of repression and physical annihilation, not only against actual enemies, but also against individuals who had not committed any crimes against the Party and the Soviet government. . . . [This included] the fabrication of cases against communists, false accusations, glaring abuses of socialist legality, which resulted in the death of innocent people. . . . [84]

The shock waves generated by these accusations proved seismographic, soon spreading through the entire Soviet empire, even though Khrushchev confined his criticism to Stalin's "terroristic methods" after the Kirov murder of 1934 and against fellow Party members. In a three-hour speech, Khrushchev did not mention Stalin's ruthless extermination of the common people and peasantry in the 1930s. (Most estimates range from 20–25 million deaths, though some distinguished commentators, such as Russian historian Roy Medvedev, have placed the total as high as 60 million.)

Of course, tales of the enormity of Stalin's misdeeds were already well-known, in the East as well as the West, to anyone who had ears to listen. But never before had the CPSU acknowledged *any* of Stalin's crimes.[85] For to do so would have meant acknowledging its own complicity in those crimes. Khrushchev's virtuosity was to excoriate Stalin's "cult of personality" precisely to deflect criticism from the Soviet system to a single individual.

Khrushchev's speech took the SED leadership by surprise; how little Ulbricht was in the confidence of Kremlin leaders can be gauged from his DDR message of advance greetings to the congress, which ended with the words: "Long live the invincible teachings of Marx, Engels, Lenin, and Stalin." Delivering the message in person two days after Khrushchev's speech, Ulbricht amended the ending to "Long live Marxism-Leninism."[86]

The emendations continued on Ulbricht's return to East Berlin. In early March, Ulbricht wrote in *Neues Deutschland* that Stalin could no longer be considered one of the "classical thinkers" of Marxism-Leninism: "He caused the CPSU and the Soviet Union considerable damage when he placed himself above the Party and engaged in a cult of the personality." This cult had duped the young, who "know more about Stalin's biography than the entire Politburo does," though Party leaders like himself had never been deceived into overestimating Stalin. Ulbricht, who now criticized Stalin's interpretations of Marxism and his leadership of the USSR during World War II, did not mention that he himself had hailed Stalin as "the greatest scientist of the present epoch" and "a military genius."[87]

In the course of a six-hour, 200-page address at the Third SED Conference in late March, Ulbricht did not mention Stalin by name even once. Of course, that omission—from Stalin's most faithful protegee—was itself deafening. The message was unmistakable: Stalin was out. But if East Germans thought that Khrushchev's consolidation of power would bring a loosening of Moscow's grip, they were to be disappointed; Khrushchev's admissions of Stalin's "errors" stopped well short of legitimizing criticism of the Party itself or former colleagues of Stalin now in the CPSU Politburo. And Ulbricht himself made it clear to East Germans that Stalin's dethronement did not taint the CPSU: its authority was to remain beyond question.[88]

In May, Ulbricht included a harsh censure of Stalin in a message to the SED. It was now time, he urged, to return to the genius of Lenin. Ulbricht publicly embraced the wisdom of Lenin's dictum of the different roads possible for reaching socialism—formerly touted in the liberal *Scheindemokratie* era a decade earlier, and officially dropped in 1948 in the rush to "sovietize" the SBZ[89]—and proclaimed that there was indeed a separate (and special) German road. In fact, Ulbricht claimed, because SMAD's officials had actually been Leninists all along, the German "separate road" had *never* been abandoned; he did concede, however, that "many people did not know it."[90] And so, QED: because "Stalinism" and the "cult of personality" had *never* flourished in the SBZ/DDR, there was obviously no need for "de-Stalinization."

Ulbricht's apparent about-face was, as ever, on orders from Moscow; as before, the new policy of separate national roads to socialism was mere *Schein*, designed by Khrushchev himself both as an olive branch to facilitate reconciliation with the still wayward Marshal Tito and as a sop to assuage the East European satellites' general outrage at the sudden revelations about "the invincible Stalin." But if

Khrushchev was merely assuming a pragmatic stance in the post-Stalinist period of uncertainty, many Eastern European party leaders nevertheless took the new CPSU line about the possibility of various national communisms seriously.

In the SED, Khrushchev's speech exploded like a bombshell: How could Stalinism and the cult of personality have arisen in the workers' paradise ruled by a party acting on the scientific principles of Marxism-Leninism? Because Marxism-Leninism had founded itself on doctrines worked out by Party ideologues and philosophers, a crisis in politics, especially if it involved the discrediting of the presiding "genius" of Marxism, must inevitably have grave intellectual consequences. And so, educators, especially university professors, would play a central role in the soul-searching that would follow.

The struggle that emerged between Party loyalists and dissidents or "revisionists" would dominate this fourth stage of DDR educational history (1956–61), beginning in May 1956 and intensifying over the next two years. "Revisionism" was a reaction against Stalinism, a response to the ferment in Hungary and Poland, and a protest against the DDR's restrictions on personal freedom. And ultimately, it was a war of Party *apparatchiki* and *Realpolitiker* against utopian educators and students, of bureaucrats against idealists—of two contending views of socialism, the Leninist against the humanist. Would "democratic centralism" or representative democracy prevail? The showdown of socialisms starkly divided camps with divergent views on the near vs. the far, on opportunism vs. principle, on Party discipline vs. individual conscience, on means vs. ends: socialism as a here-and-now strategy for attaining and maintaining power vs. socialism as a vision of great-souled possibilities, of a world that might yet be.

MARXISM IS ALL-POWERFUL, BECAUSE IT IS TRUE!

YOU NEED ONLY TO SCHOOL PEOPLE PROPERLY—THEN THEY'LL LIVE RIGHT!

OUR NEW LIFE MUST BE DIFFERENT!

By the spring of 1956, three years after Stalin's death and June 17, the grass seemed to be growing again in the DDR. Khrushchev's speech had ushered in a liberal climate throughout Eastern Europe and Ulbricht's turnabout had raised expectations of a truly democratic DDR. Confident about its hold on power, the Party had already reduced the severity of state punishments for dissent. Since June 17, the SSD no longer pursued obscure, individual critics like Hermann Josef Flade; it focused instead on cases of organized opposition. In contrast to the early 1950s, a few critical words about Pieck or Ulbricht did not usually land one in jail. Life in the DDR was settling into a kind of normalcy, and citizens' fears were more mundane: losing their jobs, being expelled from the university, or being stigmatized by the Party and therefore blocked in their own or their children's or relatives' career advancement. For the first time in almost a decade, critical voices were emerging within the SED.

Public criticism was, however, advanced solely by the intellectuals and professors; the workers had not forgotten the lesson of June 17. Leading writers and artists in the 180,000 member *Kulturbund* (Cultural League) leveled open assaults on Stalin and implied criticisms of the toadying allegiance of his hand-picked henchman, almost universally regarded as a Russified satrap (right down to his

Lenin goatee) and as a pure political animal, the most *unsympathisch* (dislikable) figure in the DDR.

Even more influential were the reproofs from prominent Marxist-Leninist philosophers (Ernst Bloch, Wolfgang Harich, Günther Zehm), historians (Jürgen Kuczynski, Joachim Streisand), economists and agronomists (Alfred Lemnitz, Fritz Behrens, Kurt Vieweg, Arne Benary), and physical scientists (Robert Havemann, Martin Strauss, Friedrich Herneck).[91] These professors, all of whom considered themselves "good Marxists," promoted greater political pluralism, workers' self-management, and various private enterprise initiatives and free market mechanisms. Condemning "Stalinism" as a degeneration of the workers' movement, they attributed its emergence to factors particular to Russia and foreign to Germany. Given the political backwardness of Czarist Russia, they argued, progressive, democratic forces in Moscow were forced to resort to undemocratic methods, deforming the dictatorship of the proletariat into the dictatorship of a single party—indeed of a single man. So far they were on safe grounds, echoing Khrushchev's and Ulbricht's own criticisms. They earned the enmity of Ulbricht, however, when they began to lash out at SED "citationism" in particular, i.e., the doctrine that only Stalin could discover new Marxist-Leninist truths and was worth quoting at all—a thinly veiled attack on Ulbricht himself.

The most visible critics were Bloch and Harich, philosophy professors and co-editors of the prestigious *Deutsche Zeitschrift für Philosophie*, which wielded notable influence within the DDR intelligentsia, since philosophy effectively meant Marxism and Marxist philosophy undergirded SED ideology. Between them, Bloch and Harich represented the best of the elder and younger generations of independent-minded DDR intellectuals.

A chaired professor at Leipzig, Ernst Bloch was widely regarded as the intellectual elder statesman of the DDR. Son of a Jewish official and already a KPD member in the 1920s, he had taught at various German universities and worked with members of the famed Institute for Social Research in the 1930s, only to flee Germany when Hitler came to power and settle eventually in the United States. Fiercely critical of capitalism and loyal to the USSR throughout his American exile—e.g., he supported Stalin loudly through the Moscow Trials and the purges[92]—Bloch had returned, with great official fanfare, to a chaired professorship in Leipzig to help found the DDR in 1949.

But Bloch was never an orthodox Marxist or Party mouthpiece. Known for his crafty *Sklavensprache* (slaves' language) during lectures, Bloch perfected a humorous, defiant, and indirect criticism "from below" against the regime. One day he quoted Lenin, who said, "We must bring things to the point that a cook can rule the state." After a well-timed pause, the professor concluded: "Well, ladies and gentlemen, we in the German Democratic Republic have already succeeded, haven't we!" Publicly asked by his students for his opinion of Ulbricht, whom Bloch did not especially like, the professor sighed, "*Ach*, unfortunately the man just has no sex appeal."[93]

Bloch had sympathized with the workers on June 17, but a mixture of careerism, old Leninist discipline, and loyalty to the regime stayed his tongue. Still, though he did not criticize the SED publicly, June 17 was a decisive event for Bloch, after which he became increasingly outspoken.[94] Nevertheless, he managed for the most part to balance support and Party criticism; the SED officially sponsored his books and hundreds of students flocked to his lectures in Auditorium #40. Regarded as the most distinguished professor in the entire DDR, and along with Heidegger and Jaspers, one of the three great philosophers of early postwar Germany, Bloch was canonized as virtually a state philosopher. "The flag of reason," he put in a much-quoted line of 1951, "is red."[95] In the year of his 70th birthday in 1955, in the immediate aftermath of the publication of the first volume of his masterwork, *Das Prinzip Hoffnung* (*The Principle of Hope*) (1954), he was awarded the National Prize and the Order of the Fatherland, the DDR's highest civilian honors. A thinker with his own elaborate system—a complicated Romantic synthesis of Schelling and Marx, of *Naturphilosophie* and *Ideologiekritik* (a "marxified Schelling," Habermas once called him[96])—Bloch developed his own liberatory *Hoffnungsphilosophie* (philosophy of hope); his ambitions and status recalled the great German intellectual figures of earlier centuries. And he remained a Leninist and an apologist for Stalin, faithful to his famous line in the conclusion of *Das Prinzip Hoffnung*: "*Ubi* Lenin, *ibi* Jerusalem." ("Where the true Marxism reigns, there flourishes the Promised Land").

Wolfgang Harich, on the other hand, was in the fall of 1956 a 32-year-old professor in Historical Materialism at Humboldt University in Berlin, widely regarded as "the most brilliant head in the SED," "an intellect on two legs," "towering like a skyscraper over the rest of the younger East intellectuals."[97] Self-transformation was the governing principle of his being. Born into an upper-class literary family, he had studied philosophy during the war at Berlin (later Humboldt) University. He was drafted as a *Wehrmacht* soldier in 1943 and deserted in 1944, joining an anti-Nazi underground group. A pacifist despite his war service, he had become interested in Buddhism under the influence of Japanese friends; later he flirted with Roman Catholicism. Now a convinced communist, he remained a peacemaker and a utopian. By 1946 he was making a name for himself as a journalist for the French-licensed daily *Der Kurier* and the Soviet *Tägliche Rundschau*; by his mid-20s he was also known as one of Berlin's best theater critics. In 1946, he resumed his work in philosophy and *Germanistik* at Humboldt University, studying with Nicolai Hartmann. After a semester at an SED Party college in 1948, he started teaching at Humboldt in 1949 and became a Humboldt professor of philosophy in 1952. In 1953, he assumed the co-editorship of the *Deutsche Zeitschrift für Philosophie* (its first number opened—in a gesture that later would demonstrate how far both editors had traveled politically by 1956—with an lavish eulogy to Stalin) and became an editor at Aufbau Verlag, the leading publishing house in the DDR. That same year, at Brecht's behest, Harich received the prestigious Heinrich Mann Prize for editing and journalism, conferred by the DDR Academy of Fine Arts. At 29, he stood formally anointed as one of the leading young intellectuals in the communist world.

Harich was a doctrinaire Stalinist until the early 1950s; in one memoir, he recalled crying an ocean of tears over Stalin's death.[98] But June 17 also became the turning point for him, after which he had increasingly employed the journal as a sounding board for attacks on Marxist orthodoxy. Chiefly interested in Marxist aesthetics, Harich had edited a Gottfried Keller volume and a six-volume Heine edition for Aufbau Verlag, and established himself as not just the chief disciple but the self-proclaimed "prophet in the DDR"[99] of Hungary's stellar philosopher and literary theorist, 68-year-old Georg Lukács of the University of Budapest.

Lukács had long exerted tremendous influence in the DDR. A Marxist who read Marx from the vantage point of his debt to Hegel's views of history, consciousness, and dialectical reason, Lukács published all his work first in German, often in the *Deutsche Zeitschrift für Philosophie*, and regularly lectured in Leipzig and Berlin. Anticipating the Czech call for "socialism with a human face" in the 1960s, Lukács was the first to speak, in 1956, of creating a "humanistic socialism":

> The more humane we make socialism, the more we contribute to the ultimate triumph of socialism internationally. . . . If we can succeed in making socialism attractive, then it won't be a ghostly monster for the masses any longer.
>
> I'm not thinking of the small group of imperialistic capitalists; for them, expropriation will always be a horror. But let's be honest: There are countless workers in the West who recoil from socialism in its current form, to say nothing of the attitudes of the great mass of farmers and the intelligentsia, whose repudiation, whose terrified reaction could be overcome by the correct explanation of and propaganda for genuine Marxism.[100]

Like Bloch, Lukács had been a loyal Stalinist through the early 1950s and an even stronger supporter of Party discipline (he had repudiated several of his own major works, including *History and Class Consciousness*, as "idealist" heresy); but he embraced Khrushchev's criticism of Stalin with enthusiasm. Bloch and Harich both agreed with Lukács on the need, however belatedly, to criticize Stalinism and renew Marxism from a humanist/naturalist standpoint, and they made plans together to take their journal in that direction in mid-1956. But Bloch remained largely above the political and polemical fray—Harich said Bloch had no exact political program except to "get rid of Ulbricht." Bloch provided rather the intellectual framework for criticism and gave the go-ahead by indirection. Harich, on the other hand, polemicized and visited friends and opponents alike. Initially unknown to the wider public, Harich ultimately came to play the central role in the events of 1956.

Harich's own *politics* of hope dreamed of a "third way" between Stalinism and capitalism, of the possibility of a "humanistic socialism" in a reunified Germany. Harich always regarded the DDR as a *Notlösung*—a necessary (and temporary) stopgap forced on Germany by History (and the Allied occupiers)—and dreamed of the day that Germany would be united again. He was a friend of poet (and, by 1954, Minister of Culture) Johannes Becher and took Becher's lyrics in the national anthem (*Deutschland einig Vaterland*) most seriously.

So whereas Ulbricht was still engaging in the rhetoric of the "special road" merely as an expedient for holding onto power, Harich actually believed it might lead to the realization of his vision of a reunited, socialist Germany. Harich hoped to create a reformed DDR socialism that would also be acceptable to the BRD.

Establishing unofficial contact with Social Democrats in West Germany, he argued among confidants that the DDR should assume the initiative in making reforms that would pave the way for reuniting Germany.

Although both friends and enemies regarded Harich as voluble and even loose with his tongue (his parlor burlesques of *Der Spitzbart*'s Saxon dialect were party favorites), nobody in his wide circle of acquaintances considered him a conspirator, let alone an "enemy of the people"; indeed he even presented his ideas in October-November 1956 both to G. M. Pushkin, the Soviet ambassador, and to Ulbricht himself. Possessing no apparent political ambitions for himself, Harich did, however, want to influence the intellectuals in the Party to campaign for Ulbricht's replacement as SED chief; evidently, Harich saw such a move as consistent with the newly open spirit of the anti-Stalinist, "back to Lenin" climate.

Harich was not the only dissident calling for reform in 1956; nor was East Germany the only Eastern European country undergoing turmoil. Even more aggressive demands for separate roads of national communism were shaking Poland and Hungary. In June, strikes erupted in Poznan; a workers' revolt in Poland was only avoided when Wladyslaw Gomulka, a victim of the Stalinist purges, was freed from prison and elected first secretary of the governing United Workers' Party. On October 20, Gomulka assumed power and introduced (albeit only temporarily) significant reforms that went far beyond the "deviations" in Yugoslavia. Three days later, he was able to convince a Khrushchev-led delegation in Warsaw that Poland would continue to be a firm ally of the USSR, thereby narrowly averting a Soviet crackdown.

On the same day in Hungary, where Moscow's policy flip-flops between Stalin's "Build Socialism" campaign and the post-Stalinist New Course had generated economic suffering even more severe than in Poland and the DDR, a new regime under Communist reformer Imre Nagy took power and announced plans for Hungary to take its own special road. A popular revolt against the Soviet presence broke out, and Nagy demanded that the USSR withdraw its troops. At first irresolute, Moscow secured the support of China, Yugoslavia, and the other East bloc countries for an invasion. On November 4, Soviet tanks, with DDR forces from the newly established NVA at their side, rolled into Budapest and crushed the uprising. A puppet regime replaced Premier Nagy's reformist government. The SED explained to an increasingly skeptical East German populace that anti-socialists and fascists, supported by the "imperialist secret services" of the West, had staged "a counterrevolutionary putsch" in "the Hungarian People's Republic," defeated with the help of "the working people of the DDR," who "extended solidarity to their Hungarian class brothers. . . ."[101] Soviet and DDR troops had once again—as in June 1953—restored "order" in Eastern Europe.

Many DDR students were outraged. June 17 had largely bypassed the universities, and despite the shattering news of Stalin's barbarism in February, student criticisms had remained muted. The image of the USSR as "the first socialist state" was still intact for most DDR students through the summer and early fall of 1956. With the news from Budapest in November, however, the idol—and the idyll—collapsed with a resounding crash. In an attempt at damage control, *Neues Deutschland* began, in mid-November, to admit that the Hungarian workers had not been entirely opposed to the "counterrevolution." Rather, they were "embittered by mistakes and grave defects"; only the lack of strong Party leadership in Hungary made the intervention of the Soviet army necessary.[102] But DDR students were not appeased.

Entire lecture audiences stood in silent tribute to the Hungarian heroes; anti-Hungarian propaganda speeches by SED and FDJ officials were boycotted or received in silence. And in one university after another, students presented demands for reforms: less Russian, more western languages; less Marxism-Leninism, more natural sciences and social studies; reduced army service requirements; no restrictions on the student press; the founding of a new student organization independent of the FDJ; and full and accurate reporting of the events in Poland and Hungary. The medical, veterinary, and agriculture students—most of whom came from middle-class families and who regarded DIAMAT as having little relevance to their studies—protested loudest of all.[103]

Perhaps the climactic event of the November demonstrations was a seven-hour open student forum, sponsored by the FDJ at Humboldt University in East Berlin—next door to the mammoth new Soviet embassy—during which 500 students, most of them from the sciences, demanded that the DDR press publish the truth about Hungary and that other student organizations besides the "untrustworthy FDJ" be formed. While the students criticized the Party leadership, subversive leaflets floated down from the rooftops. "We Demand More Thorough Training within the Society for Sport and Technology," proclaimed their headline, urging more intensive pre-military training for students. Underneath, in small italics, was the ironic—and threatening—tag line: *"Because the example of Hungary shows that we can use it!"*[104] When FDJ leaders moved to close the meeting with a chorus of the FDJ student anthem, the "Song of the World's Youth," all but 50 students got up and walked out.[105]

Even high school students protested. At an SED meeting in Dresden in mid-November, pupils protested that the Hungarian rebellion "had not broken out without cause." The official Dresden newspaper reported this comment, only to dismiss as "absurd" the notion that "the system of socialism is not in order." *Junge Welt*, the FDJ newspaper, sprang into action to deflect any analogies between Hungary and the DDR: "Often youths ask whether the presence of Soviet troops on the territory of the German Democratic Republic is necessary at all, and whether that does not restrict the sovereignty of our state." It answered that Soviet troops were only present to serve "the interest of the German people."[106]

It was within this volatile situation that Harich wrote a bold (and as-yet unpublished) manifesto calling for sweeping reforms and across-the-board liberalization in the DDR:

We have been inspired by the resolutions of the Soviet Twentieth Party Congress and by contact with comrades abroad. Personal discussions with Polish, Hungarian, and Yugoslav comrades have confirmed us in our conclusions. Our ideological development owes most to Comrade Georg Lukács. . . . After the Twentieth Party Congress, we worked out a program outlining the special German road to socialism for internal party discussion. We tried to acquaint the party leaders with this program, but found them unapproachable. Hence we felt compelled to hand it to the Soviet Ambassador, Comrade Pushkin, in order to reach our party leaders through his good offices.

The program was designed to serve as a basis for internal discussion on reforming the party. It is not our intention to break with the party and to become renegades . . . We intend not to repudiate Marxism-Leninism, but to liberate it from Stalinism and dogmatism and to restore its basis in humanist thought. . . . The USSR is the first Socialist state in the world; not even Stalinism can change this fact. But the Soviet pattern of socialism cannot be a model for every other country. . . . [107]

Harich thus drew the conclusion from the lesson of Stalinism in the USSR: DDR socialists could and should go their "special way" and no longer be beholden to Moscow. His proposals included ending Ulbricht's dominance of the SED and democratizing the government and Party; holding elections with genuine choices, and ultimately multiple parties; abolishing the secret police and secret trials of dissidents; and guaranteeing freedom of speech for educators, churchmen, and artists.[108] Ultimately, Harich hoped that German reunification would see the SPD come to power and the main achievements of the DDR affirmed: nationalization of industry, land and education reform, the removal of formerly prominent Nazis in government.

If ever Ulbricht might have entertained these proposals, this was not the time. A harsh season of neo-Stalinization now commenced. Ulbricht's strategy was to nip in the bud any emergent solidarity between the intelligentsia and the working class, as had occurred in Poland and, especially, in Hungary, where the Petofi Circle, consisting mostly of dissident intellectuals from the Hungarian Youth Group, first raised the banner of liberal revolt against the Party leadership. Ulbricht's real fear was of the workers; among Harich's proposals were calls for the workers to direct their ownership of the means of production via their own factory councils, as in Poland (thereby following Lenin's wartime slogan, "All power to the councils [soviets]!").[109] Sensing that another June 17, or even Hungary, might be in the air, and seeking to prevent the emergence of another Gomulka or Nagy, Ulbricht incited workers' antagonisms toward the intelligentsia. Thus Ulbricht was able to isolate the intellectuals from the public, which never came to view the dissidents as their spokesmen, thereby dooming the intellectuals' revolt to mere campus protests.

Mass reprisals were out of the question, Ulbricht realized; Harich would serve as the chief scapegoat. Harich's clandestine meetings with the SPD bureau in West Berlin and his now-suspect foreign associations alone were enough. The writings of Lukács, recently condemned by the SED as "an agent of Idealism," had formed the spiritual background of the Hungarian uprising. Lukács had accepted the post of Minister of Culture in Nagy's one-week government, and was now under house arrest in Budapest. And even now, Harich was in Hamburg, discussing his manifesto with the editors of *Der Spiegel*, unaware that the SSD planned to arrest him as soon as he set foot again in the DDR.

Ulbricht specifically singled out Harich's circle as the "great inner danger of socialism," the infection of a "bourgeois ideology in the workers' movement."[110]

On November 29, on the morning of his return from his Hamburg visit, Harich was arrested, branded a "revisionist," and indicted with "formation of an enemy group" on behalf of the West German SPD and with connections to the "reactionary Petofi Circle." The SED charged Harich with "counterrevolutionary plotting"; he had spearheaded a group "estranged from socialism and the workers' movement [which had] the goal of restoring the capitalist order in the German Democratic Republic." *Der Spiegel* devoted its December 19 cover story to Harich, saying that West German intellectuals regarded him, "despite his youth, probably the only [DDR] intellectual capable of calling into question the current foundation of the communistic state, the doctrine of ice-hard Stalinism."[111]

But it was not to be: After a show trial much like those he had condemned, Harich would be sentenced in March 1957 to 10 years in jail; in excerpts from the tape-recorded trial played on DDR radio, a chastened Harich would confess: "I wish to deliver my thanks to the SSD. . . . I've found that they are correct and decent. . . . I had gotten completely out of control. . . . I was a runaway horse, which no call could have stopped . . . If I hadn't been taken into custody, I wouldn't today be ready for 10 years, which the Herr Prosecutor has recommended, but only for the hangman, and therefore I thank the SSD for their alertness."[112]

And what of Bloch? Ulbricht personally countermanded an order to arrest him, believing that it would be tactically wiser to silence him and condemn his writings, rather than risk making a martyr out of a 72-year-old prisoner. But Ulbricht had clearly run out of patience with Bloch, too. As *Der Spiegel* pointed out, for a *Realpolitiker* like Ulbricht, it was a forgivable irrelevance for professors to dissertate in little seminars about the need to appreciate the young Marx's debt to Hegel and German idealism, but quite another thing once they stumbled upon the transfiguring insight of their young Hegelian: "The philosophers have only heretofore interpreted the world; the point, however, is to change it." And so Bloch was forcibly retired, lamented by the leadership as a misguided Socrates, a tempter of youth who "contaminated hundreds of students," as the SED Central Committee put it.[113]

Another round of the soul murder of East Germans was over. Over was the Indian summer that thought it could be spring.

Hereafter, for most members of the founding generation of the DDR, there would be no more agonizing "years taken up with doubts and recantations, and pangs of conscience and fabricated theories to set the conscience at rest," as Wolfgang Leonhard put it in *Die Revolution entlässt ihre Kinder* (*The Revolution Discharges Its Children*).[114] The dialecticians would become doublethinkers, the dissidents would depart. The revolution had discharged—and then devoured—its own children. Or as 58-year-old Alfred Kantorowicz, one of the great intellectual figures of the older generation—Spanish civil war veteran, chaired professor of *Germanistik* at Humboldt University, director of the Heinrich Mann Institute—looked back in anguish after his 1957 escape:

Can't one understand how I postponed my radical decision for years and years in the desperate hope that the rawness, stupidity, violence, lawlessness, the oozing mire of lies, the strangulation of intellectual liberty—that all this was only a transitional convulsion, and that out of these awful labor-pains a new society would still issue forth, a society in which social justice and personal freedom would be beautifully balanced?

Twenty-six years long . . . [in] the Communist Party, I held fast to a dream. From the events of June 17 to the heart-breaking and nerve-wracking (for so many of us, especially old communists) Hungarian tragedy and the reign of terror against the intellectuals, I have finally had to give up the last hope— what am I saying? to give up the last illusion—that out of such dregs a new and better world could ever be born.

And now I cannot conceal even to myself that feeling, which always came forward and was always painfully repressed, of the tragic tiny part that I contributed to build up exactly what I had wanted to stand against: I mean lawlessness, exploitation of the workers, the intellectual enslavement of the People, the arbitrary rule of an unworthy clique that disgraced the name of Socialism in the very way in which the Nazis disgraced its name. . . . No, I could no longer close my eyes. . . .

What weighs heavier than everything else is the knowledge of what I have put behind me, which made it so difficult for years just to breathe: the knowledge of this injustice, these lies, these acts of violence, about which, given the danger to my freedom and my life, I felt I had to keep silent. And more: through my presence, through my public action as a university teacher and writer—even though for years I published only scholarly or literary works— I served as a witness for the shameless regime of violence of the Ulbricht-Clique. No, I couldn't any more. . . . [115]

For those who stayed, however, the fate of the "Harich group" was a warning, and it was taken to heart: The System has no place for people who think. On December 3, the *Kulturbund* pledged its loyalty to Ulbricht. On December 6, Politburo member Karl Schirdewan lectured leading FDJ and *Kulturbund* functionaries: "Harich thought he had permission to found a new Marxist philosophy. A philosophy stirred with the ideology of the capitalist brothers' soup of the imperialist camp. But Marxism isn't a dung field on which anyone can just heap a lot of muck."[116] DDR intellectuals got the message: recant your heresies and toe the Party line.[117] By early December, the push for de-Stalinization by the DDR intelligentsia was over: the young German Danton was himself in the Bastille; his truculent followers were left clutching their groins.

The revolution had indeed devoured its most brilliant children.

But not the youngest of them—at least not yet. Thousands of DDR students still refused to back down. As punishment for observing a minute of silence as a sign of mourning for the defeated Hungarian revolutionaries, 20 dissenting chemistry students were forced in mid-December to leave the Technical University in Dresden. In retaliation for similar gestures, students at other universities lost their stipends, effectively compelling them to resign. In late December, seven 18- to 20-year-olds were jailed for a pro-Hungary sympathy strike and received one- to three-year prison terms.[118] Through *Forum*, the DDR university student newspaper, Ulbricht warned in mid-December against such "troublemakers," who were "confused by demagogic slogans." "Only those who are loyal to the workers and students can study at our universities and academies. . . . Anyone who tries to preserve or restore capitalism, even if he conceals it with hypocritical or pseudo-revolutionary phrases, attempts to turn back the wheel of History and will be shattered [upon it]."[119]

To bind DDR students more tightly to the wheel, Ulbricht called upon the FDJ to pilot a re-education campaign. A mass meeting of 1,500 Leipzig students organized by the FDJ in late December ended with the following "unanimous" resolution against the Petofi circle: "We are decidedly against such people, who are trying here by the same slogans to destroy the unity of the progressive powers and thus help international counterrevolution." The FDJ also denounced the Polish student newspaper *Po Prostu* for having urged reforms, which would only produce "anarchy" in the Party.[120]

The education of the current student generation "to be loyal to the workers' and peasants' state" had been sorely "neglected," Ulbricht sternly lectured, which "facilitated the invasion of hostile ideology into the heads of many students." "Petit-bourgeois tendencies" were still observable among students, he warned, even in Party functionaries, who would often skip mass organizational activities after their eight-hour work days.[121]

Ulbricht now pronounced that any retreat to national communism on the Polish and Yugoslav pattern was unacceptable. Hungary had proven that "there is no third way between communism and capitalism," Ulbricht said. The West Germans and Americans, he maintained, having ascertained that Hungary was a weak point in the communist bloc, had helped prepare an armed revolution there. "The major lesson of Hungary is that communists, to stay in power, must keep unity. . . . There can be differences of opinion, but after an exchange of views, a resolution will be adopted that will be binding for all. . . ."[122]

That was Ulbricht's final notice: the formal "democratic" exchange of views had now occurred; he would entertain differences of opinion no longer. The universities had always been his "neuralgic wound," as one West German scholar observed;[123] henceforth, Ulbricht made clear, any pains in the neck would be suffered by his critics:

There are "elements" among the students who direct all their attention to the past. How should one handle such students? I agree with the worker who said: "They require a sharp blow in the neck."[124]

The word went out: acquiescence or arrest. Now the cold winds from Moscow were blowing hard; the last season of DDR freethinking was definitively over.

TRUST IS GOOD, BUT CONTROL IS BETTER!
THE PARTY, THE PARTY! / IT'S ALWAYS RIGHT!
OUR NEW LIFE MUST BE DIFFERENT!

In a final gesture of *Scheindemokratie*, however—yet another go-round in the Leninist masquerade dance of one step backward, two steps forward—Ulbricht met with student leaders and yielded to a few student demands, e.g., allowing students to wear cowboy shirts and play "decadent" boogie-woogie. But the new concessions lasted less than a month. Then, not only were they withdrawn, but student protest leaders were expelled as "troublemakers" or drafted for terms of service into the DDR's undermanned lignite and uranium mines as virtual slave labor. The regime fired suspect dissident lecturers and shifted large numbers of students from university to university, aiming to break up groups of friends who might conspire.[125] The JP was also split into two age groups, in order to tighten ideological control: now the JP would consist only of 8- to 14-year-olds; younger children would belong to the *Thälmann Pioniere* (Thälmann Pioneers), named after the late KPD leader Ernst Thälmann.

At the Thirtieth Meeting of the Central Committee of the SED in January 1957, the official campaign against revisionism began. Bloch and Harich were condemned as "deviationists" and "revisionists" in philosophy; and Havemann, a well-known physicist at Humboldt, was targeted in the natural sciences. All three men were guilty—in the Party jargon of the day—of objectivism, cosmopolitanism, and social democratism. Ulbricht delegated sponsorship of the DDR's leading philosophy conferences to the Institute of Social Sciences, which reported directly to the Central Committee; and it ordered that the philosophy list of Aufbau Verlag be altered for 1957/58, effectively reducing philosophy to agitprop. Study of Bloch's and Lukács' writings was proscribed. Aufbau Verlag put their works in its basement; librarians relegated their titles to the *Giftschrank*.

When Gomulka had announced his program of an independent national communism for Poland in June 1956, many DDR intellectuals had believed that the days of Ulbricht's rule were numbered, a belief strengthened by the success of SED moderates on the Central Committee who managed to push through rehabilitations of several Politburo members ousted in 1953.[126] But the Hungarian revolt induced Moscow to agree with Ulbricht that liberalization would lead the DDR toward Hungary rather than Poland, and that any alternative to his own leadership was less a special road to German socialism than a detour toward fascism and capitalism. The example of Hungary—unlike Poland, Nazi Hungary had fought against the USSR during World War II—proved what could happen when the Party loosened the reins; it thus provided Ulbricht with the Soviet-sanctioned pretext to strike back hard at his detractors. And so, ironically, as with June 17, Ulbricht was *saved*, rather than undermined, by the calamity on his watch: the Kremlin decided that to purge Ulbricht would signify surrender to the protesters' demands, "a concession from weakness, leading in turn to new disturbances with even more far-reaching demands."[127]

And so, as in 1953, Ulbricht again used the crisis within the Party to outmaneuver his rivals in the SED leadership, counting on the fact that Khrushchev, who had in June 1957 defeated his own Politburo enemies, the "anti-Party group" led by Molotov and Malenkov, would identify with and back his efforts to extirpate Party "factionalism." The SED Central Committee purges of October 1957 and February 1958—the key administrative aspects of which Ulbricht delegated to his new lieutenant, Erich Honecker—focused on moderates supportive of de-Stalinization, including Deputy Prime Minister Fred Olssner, SSD chief Ernst Wollweber, chief ideologist (and former heir apparent) Karl Schirdewan, and Culture and Education minister Paul Wandel.

Now, more than ever, Ulbricht reigned supreme; it was Ulbricht *über allen*. In years to come, especially after President Pieck's death in 1960, when Ulbricht took over his offices and became head of both the Party and the state, an Ulbricht "cult of personality" would develop, a case of neo-Stalinist leader worship found nowhere else in Eastern Europe.[128]

And now, more than ever, dogmatism and party-mindedness in the DDR became the order of the day.

But the intellectuals' and students' revolt had shown that the Party had been premature in supposing that it controlled higher education. It was now clear that discontent was widespread, though it did not lead to campus-wide protest at all DDR universities, let alone turn into a nationwide uprising as in Poland and Hungary.

And why not? In the end, two factors accounted for the failure of the student revolt to spark a popular uprising in the DDR, illuminating why indeed a strong dissident movement *never* emerged in East Germany: the deterrent lesson of June 17 and the escape route of West Berlin. Unlike citizens of other East European nations, East Germans fed up with the regime didn't join opposition groups; they left for the West. "Troublemakers" always had an escape hatch (though, after the Berlin Wall's erection, it narrowed drastically), and potential dissident leaders generally chose to head west, rather than lead a movement for change. And so, by mid-1957, few "troublemakers" remained; they had acquiesced, were in jail, or had fled west.[129]

With the Harich circle in jail, Bloch retired, and the Party solidly in hand, another "special road" was now clear: the way beckoned for Ulbricht's views on common schooling, on polytechnical education, and on socialist morality to be implemented. The visionaries had proven themselves myopic; the organization men had been clear-sighted. Or, as one British observer put it: "The philosophers had failed to change the world. It was now up to the technocrats."[130]

So now, by 1958/59, with the first three stages of DDR education fully completed, the final, transformative step in the forced educational march—from liberalization to sovietization to Stalinization, from the "new democratic school" to Stakhanovism to militarism—could be taken at last: "the socialist school."

Now "*die neue schule*" meant something different than it had a decade before. It meant "the socialist school," which would engender that new being, the polytechnical *Mensch*, who would at last "build socialism." Ulbricht laid the New Course, begun—and de facto ended—in June 1953, officially aside. Once again, Lenin's theory of stages in the revolution was cited: the anti-fascist democratic phase was complete; now it was time for full-scale communism. And so Ulbricht resumed the accelerated campaign to "build socialism,"[131] within which education would play a key role: "The building of socialism," Ulbricht declared in October 1957, "is first and foremost the education of human beings."[132]

Polytechnical education, first touted by Marx, sought to combine general education and productive labor. Khrushchev believed that postwar socialist youth were losing respect for manual labor; polytechnical education, within the framework of the common "socialist school," was his remedy. Until now, the idea had received little attention in the DDR; Party theorists had held that only under "fully developed socialism" would such a transformation be possible. But because the "advanced socialist" USSR was preparing to introduce polytechnical education in all schools in 1958, with one-third of the curriculum in the last four school years devoted to practical problems of industry and agriculture, Ulbricht waved the Leninist dogma of revolutionary stages aside and leaped to follow suit.

Thus, just as had occurred in Ulbricht's dealings with Stalin, Khrushchev's wish became Ulbricht's command; Ulbricht's eager adoption of Khrushchev's pet project in education helped ensure that the Kremlin would retain him in the aftermath of the 1956 unrest. Ulbricht in fact pursued polytechnical schooling so fervently that Khrushchev insisted—basing his argument on the East German example—that the other Eastern European satellites adopt it too.

So Soviet pedagogy once more became an issue for DDR educators. The choice was no longer German *Reformpädagogik* vs. Makarenko and Stakhanovism; now it was the tradition of German *Allgemeinbildung* (general education) vs. the polytechnical panacea—and the SED applied the "revisionist" smear to any teacher resistant to the latter.

All this meant that differentiation, tracking, and freedom of choice in course selection in DDR schools were to be abolished—all over the protests of many experienced, humanistically oriented teachers, most of whom were intimidated into silence by the charge of revisionism. In addition, the SED added two required years of schooling, so that all students now attended a new 10-year polytechnical school, which featured work-study programs in industry or agriculture. The larger idea was to link education and Life; in practice, academics gave way to ideology and vocational education. Syllabuses were designed for new courses in socialist citizenship and for the two polytechnical subjects, Introduction to Socialist Production and UTP (*Unterrichtstag in der Produktion*, class day in production), a co-op course in industry or agriculture. Some educators voiced concern that the "socialist school" and polytechnical curriculum would accelerate the youth migration;[133] predictably, such desires to preserve some educational differentiation and even a few components of the humanistic curriculum were also branded "revisionism."

Polytechnical education had a hidden advantage, more valuable to the DDR than to other Soviet bloc nations. Although it accelerated emigration, it more than offset the outflow, because it amounted to a form of free child labor. Thus it was especially useful because of the emigré problem, which created a tremendous shortage of able-boded workers. Indeed, although the introduction of the 10-year school and polytechnical education occurred at the end of a fierce ideological struggle, their promotion by the SED reflected economic priorities as well as political concerns. More years of common, required schooling and polytechnical education were viewed as another means for producing, on a national scale, a disciplined work "collective" with the technical skills to promote DDR industrialization and "build socialism."[134]

So from now on, talk among SED educators was about the "new socialist school," not the "new democratic school." And in the SED's headlong rush to adopt Khrushchev's educational ideas, the continuity in the DDR between the era of Stalin and his successor was evident. When scattered protests surfaced about the new curricula, the editors of *Moskwa* made clear that recalcitrant educators had better guard their groins—and necks: "Revisionism must be exterminated. Either we kill it, or it will kill us." Ulbricht himself referred to "the weed of revisionism" among economists and legal theorists in the Academy of Sciences and elsewhere.[135]

So now the second Russian revolution in DDR education, led by Ulbricht—the quintessential polytechnical *Mensch* and organization man himself—went into high gear, resulting in changes even more far-reaching than in 1948/49. The "special road" for DDR education was another *Autobahn* to Moscow. In addition to the polytechnical school for all children, all teachers were compelled to present their lessons from an atheistic, materialist perspective. Centralized educational control increased, and the "socialist class struggle" was taken to the villages: the *Dorfschule*—the DDR version of the "little red schoolhouse"—which, in many outlying areas, had been virtually ignored and subjected to little ideological pressure from SED functionaries, was now fully integrated into the system.

Right down to elementary classroom lessons, centralized control and regimentation prevailed. Each teacher was expected to apply the disciplined rhythms of the factory: the polytechnical lesson plan would run like a cog in the new Seven-Year Plan, introduced in 1959. Everything was planned to the minute from East Berlin: Seven minutes to review homework, 30 minutes to explain the new assignment, 5 minutes to handle administrative details, and so on.[136]

As early as 1956, SED educators had begun to discuss the widespread implementation of polytechnical education. But the revisionist campaign had delayed this second educational revolution; now its time had come.

Throughout 1958, the SED employed top party functionaries, including Central Committee members, to promote polytechnical education as the solution to all the DDR's woes. In an SED teachers' conference in April, Ulbricht launched the slogans of his campaign, "Educate the Educators!" and "Education Toward Willing and Acting as Socialists," which were aimed at overcoming doubts among rank-and-file teachers and parents about the decision to downgrade academics and promote polytechnics. The SED teachers' conference explained to cadre leaders the fine points of the upcoming polytechnical education and of their new roles in atheistic education and the *Jugendweihe*, the agitation for which provoked, predictably, yet another mass exodus of experienced faculty. (In exchange for grants for special projects, however, the Party did win over the first sizable group of Christian teachers to public support for the *Jugendweihe* and the idea of a cooperative "church in socialism.")[137]

In September 1958, teacher training was centralized and streamlined. Humboldt University became the key institution for most teacher training; Marxism-Leninism became a formal, university degree program, rather than just a degree program in Party schools. In October, the polytechnical experiment went into effect. Teacher training now included internships in industry and agriculture, thereby assuming a definite polytechnical character. All elementary school graduates and *Abitur* holders who wanted to become teachers were required to do a "practical year" in industry or agriculture.

DDR students were brought to rein by alternating sticks with carrots. In 1957, student travel to the West was banned, except under special circumstances; open war was declared by the Secretary for Higher Education against the irresistible compulsion of certain student circles to travel to the "NATO-Atom Bomb Republic"—the BRD.[138] In 1958, local school boards were formed to assist university admissions committees. These boards assembled data on applicants' activities outside the school, often unknown to teachers, thereby improving the odds that only "reliable" students were accepted for university. That year, all students were also required to sign the following loyalty oath upon matriculation, which a western scholar referred to as "the perfectionizing of *Gleichschaltung*"[139]:

> My course of studies is an award from our Worker and Peasant State. Therefore I assume the duty to actively support the politics of the government at all times and to gain a basic knowledge of the foundations of Marxism-Leninism, which, after the end of my course of studies, I will put at the service of the further socialist construction of the Worker and Peasant State.
>
> During my course of studies, I will also participate energetically in the socialist construction of industry and agriculture. I am ready to contribute to strengthening the DDR's defense preparations.[140]

The carrots came in the form of official titles and public office. By the mid-1950s, the DDR began to look, from the outside, like a society ruled by youth. Although thousands of young people were emigrating, rapid advance was available to FDJ leaders; they could gain high state offices 10 to 20 years earlier than their peers in the West. More than 8,000 young people between 18 and 25 held public office, including 11 mayors and 78 government department heads. A 23-year-old Blueshirt was mayor of Potsdam, another Blueshirt was mayor of Leipzig, and dozens of Blueshirts occupied top positions in the *Land* parliaments. In 1950, the SED had also reduced the voting age from 21 to 18, further contributing to the illusion that DDR youth were running state policy.[141]

By the decade's close, 65 percent of DDR university students were drawn from the "worker and peasant class." ("Worker" had been redefined to include the children of Party functionaries.) A majority of these students were docile or loyal to the state, fully aware that they owed their privileged positions to the regime. Their intellectual horizons were more limited than those of the previous student generation; they were welded-to-order *Planmenschen*, products of the SED's relentless, and now partly successful, ideological offensive.

A trio of SED policies, systematically pursued to gain the upper hand with a prominent minority of East German youth, had produced these model young communists: ideological re-education in the schools, complete control of the youth organizations and extracurricular activities, and the apparent investment of early responsibility for state affairs in youth leaders.

Looking back in his memoirs on DDR student life in the early 1960s, Hans Mayer, the great German literary scholar at Leipzig University, who committed *Republikflucht* in 1963, bemoaned the intellectual decline of his last generation of DDR students:

In the fifties, everything new that could be found in our university library was read. Especially if there was a smell of bourgeois decadence about it. Because I was known to the major West German publishing houses, I received beautiful book packages as gifts. In the university library and the bookstore, [the novelist] Uwe Johnson and his friends systematically handled the orders. They were always up to date. That changed at the turn of the sixties, quite noticeably after the erection of the Berlin Wall. Now the state secretaries [of education] became petty autocrats, which for so long had been impossible and inopportune. The new students did not at all resemble the first generation of postwar children of the workers, which, as Brecht had put it in Leipzig, never let themselves be 'degraded into buddies.' Now the ambitious ones entered the classroom. They were FDJ students eager to get to the top. Suddenly my [teaching] assistants ascertained that all suspect books and authors, which until then were always borrowed and reserved long in advance, stood unnoticed on the book shelves.[142]

The "new socialist school" and the "new socialist intelligentsia" were now realities. A new line on education had been laid down, and it was given statutory form in the 1959 "Law on the Socialist Development of the School System," which superseded the 1946 Education Act and codified the central role of polytechnical education and "the socialist school" in DDR society. It promised that DDR planners would soon be producing their quotas of "students of the new type" like pig iron and potatoes:

> The transition from the anti-fascist democratic school to the socialist school became historically necessary for the realization of socialism. The successful building of socialist society requires high worker productivity in all branches of the people's economy.
> This is reached by applying, in ever stronger measure, the insights of modern science and the achievements of the highly developed technology of socialist production in industry and agriculture. . . . The common polytechnical high school educates the rising generation to love work and working people, and to contribute to the many-faceted development of their intellectual and bodily capacities. It teaches the younger generation the lessons of German history and educates them toward peace and friendship with all peoples, especially friendship with the Soviet Union.[143]

Similar to the rhetoric trumpeting *die neue schule* upon passage of the Education Act of 1946, the establishment of the "common polytechnical school" in 1958/59 was proclaimed by SED educators as the glorious culmination of a great radical tradition, this one stretching from Thomas More to Owen, Marx, Lenin and, above all, Krupskaya—who was also back in vogue in the "back to Lenin" climate of the late 1950s.

"Always prepared for the triumph of socialism!" proclaimed the JP slogan for 1958.[144] Indeed, optimism was in the air in 1958/59, as school reform and economic growth suggested the growing pains of DDR socialism might be nearing an end. Industrial production grew by a spectacular 11.3 percent in 1958—the year postwar food rationing finally ended—and by 12.6 percent in 1959, when the refugee total dropped to 143,917, the lowest number since 1949.[145] In 1959/60, land collectivization, often brutally executed, also rose to 85 percent; Ulbricht celebrated this surpassing of capitalist backwardness in agriculture as "the socialistic spring."[146] With church leaders and Christian teachers no longer a formidable opposition, participation in the *Jugendweihe* reached 70 percent; "Grow beyond your own limits by growing into the fabric of society!" urged the newest SED slogan promoting the *Jugendweihe*.[147] The SED also instituted a socialist naming ceremony that resembled Christian baptism, and a group of Protestant church leaders accepted a government grant to explore ways to form a state church separate from the main body of the German Evangelical [Lutheran] church.[148]

To the SED leadership, the vision of a socialist DDR seemed within reach in 1958/59. The November 1958 election—conducted under the slogan, "Plan, work, and govern with us"—broke all records: 99.8 percent support for the single list. Revisionism having been defeated, the Party took on the churches as never before, preparing to transform fully the private realm of DDR life according to Ulbricht's so-called Ten Commandments of Socialist Morality:

1. Thou shalt always defend the international solidarity of the working class as well as the permanent bonds that unite all socialist countries.
2. Thou shalt love thy Fatherland and always be ready to defend worker and peasant power with all thy strength and capacity.
3. Thou shalt help to eliminate the exploitation of humans by one another.
4. Thou shalt perform good deeds for socialism, since socialism produces a better life for all working people.
5. Thou shalt act in the spirit of mutual support and comradely cooperation during the construction of socialism, respect the collective, and take its criticisms to heart.
6. Thou shalt protect and increase the property of the people.
7. Thou shalt always pursue ways to improve thy performance, be thrifty, and strengthen socialist work discipline.
8. Thou shalt rear thy children in the spirit of peace and socialism to become citizens who are well-educated, strong in character, and physically healthy.
9. Thou shalt live a clean and decent life and respect thy family.
10. Thou shalt exhibit solidarity with all those people who are fighting for national liberation and defending their independence.[149]

With the foundations of socialism established on all fronts, the triumph of socialism seemed to Ulbricht and other Party loyalists no more than a question of improved efficiency, of "perfectionizing *Gleichschaltung*," as one West German scholar phrased it.[150]

But it was precisely Ulbricht's conviction—shared by Khrushchev, who since 1957 had ruled as the undisputed CPSU boss—about the superiority of communism to capitalism that would soon undermine the DDR's relative stability. Bolstered by their own intra-Party successes, Ulbricht and Khrushchev drew confidence from a variety of events—the launching of Sputnik in 1957, the improving Soviet and DDR economies in 1958/59, Castro's 1959 victory in Cuba, a wave of neo-Marxist national liberation movements in Africa and Asia around 1960, and the rocketing of Yuri Gagarin into space in 1961—all of which emboldened both men to push for an end both to Allied occupation of West Berlin and the right to western access to Berlin at all. A decade and a half after the war's close, the bickering Allies had still not signed a peace treaty with Germany. Khrushchev wanted a peace treaty that would turn West Berlin into a "free city" without troops—but, given its location in the heart of the DDR, the western Allies justifiably viewed the proposal as tantamount to surrendering their "island of freedom" to communist domination.

And so, just after the DDR celebrated its 10th anniversary in 1959 with an incipient feeling of permanence and identity, its worst crisis since 1953 erupted. Khrushchev railed that Berlin was "a bone stuck in our throat"—and he meant to cough it out by driving out the western Allies.[151] In the context of new U.S.-USSR crisis resulting from the Soviet shootdown of an American U-2 spy plane over the Urals in May 1960, Washington's abortive Bay of Pigs coup in Cuba in April 1961, and the defeat of pro-American forces in Laos in May 1961, Khrushchev's proposals about Berlin rekindled uncertainty about Berlin's future. Rumors flew that the USSR and DDR would soon sign a separate peace treaty, which would automatically seal the borders—leaving West Berlin to be swallowed up by the DDR. Overwhelmed by dread that the Iron Curtain's last door to the West would slam shut forever, East Germany suffered an epidemic of *Torschlusspanik* (fear of gate-closing), provoking a greater mass exodus of East Germans than ever before.

With the new stampede, DDR economic growth slowed to a halt. The ambitious Seven-Year Plan, drawn up only two years before and designed to double East German industrial output, was now shelved; due to labor shortages, only 8 to 10 percent of DDR factories were fulfilling their quotas. By the summer, a state of emergency was declared in many agricultural areas, and the SED called on industrial workers, students, and even schoolchildren to work the fields.

Throughout June and July, Ulbricht tried to halt the emigration flow by every conceivable means—short of ringing down the Iron Curtain. Many of the restrictions were attributed, absurdly, to a "flu epidemic" supposedly raging throughout West Germany. Police staffing increased sixfold at all crossing points into West Berlin, in order to check the special stamps on ID cards that noted the increased travel restrictions and rigorous curbs imposed on passage into Berlin from the surrounding countryside. New regulations required *Grenzgänger* to obtain permission to work in West Berlin. DDR television featured show trials of "confessed" western "recruiting agents" and staged interrogations of alleged western "kidnappers."

All to little avail: Record numbers of the best-educated DDR citizens, including the cream of East German youth, continued to flee. East Germans joked that the first three words eastern newborns were learning were "*Mutti*," *Vati*," and "Marienfelde"—the latter being the name of the main refugee center in West Berlin.[152] One provincial optician reportedly pinned a notice on his office door on the day he fled West: "The near-sighted should go to the eye clinic. The far-sighted should follow me." By August 1961, 207,000 refugees—half of them under 25—had taken his prescription; in the first 11 days of August, 16,500 sought haven, including a supreme court judge, Horst Hetzar, who left (along with his nine family members) because "the administration of law has descended to such a level that one is ashamed to be a lawyer there." On August 7, Khrushchev boasted about a USSR "superbomb" that could reduce Germany "to dust" and roared that the Red Army would mass on the DDR's borders if the West continued to claim a presence in Berlin; any attempt to enforce western Allied rights to Berlin would lead to an apocalyptic war against the West, in which "the culture and arts of Italy" would be destroyed and "the Acropolis would be in the line of fire."[153] Khrushchev also dispatched a new supreme commander of Soviet forces to East Berlin: stocky, taciturn Marshal Ivan Stepanovich Koniev, dubbed "the Tank" in the USSR, a man well known to East Germans as the general who had crushed the 1956 revolt in Hungary—and led the Ukrainian armies that invaded Berlin in 1945.

Ivan—"Big Ivan"—was definitely back, murmured frightened easterners.

Koniev's return, along with Khrushchev's belligerent rhetoric, pushed the eastern flood tide still higher. During the second week of August, DDR refugees were rushing out at the rate of almost 3,000 per day; on August 12, more than 4,000 crossed the border—the greatest number on a single day since June 17, 1953.

The DDR was bleeding to death. Ulbricht would have do something; East Germany was becoming, as an American journalist observed, "the disappearing satellite."[154]

East Germans' *Torschlusspanik* was well-justified. Not much longer would the far-sighted be able to follow the clear-sighted optician; Brecht's cynical refrain in *The Good Woman of Setzuan* took on a new meaning:

> What rapture, oh, it is to know
> A good thing when you see it
> And having seen a good thing, oh
> What rapture 'tis to flee it.

On a clear, warm mid-summer night, the rapture—or at least solace—of knowing, just *knowing*, that you could flee if need be, evaporated. The DDR didn't disappear; the escape hatch did.

Ulbricht finally took action to staunch the bleeding, and he took almost everyone by surprise. During the night of August 12/13, 1961, on another 10th anniversary, indeed to the very day of the 1951 World Festival of Youth and Students—as if History had decided to give richly symbolic testimony to the chasm between agitprop and actuality—the men in the House of Unity moved, stealthily but this time definitively, to seal the hemorrhage of Berlin from the eastern side. And thereby wall off the crippling flow—for decades to come.

Die Schandmauer (wall of outrage), the West German media would name it; in the official Ulbrichtian/Orwellian nomenclature of the DDR it would become *der antifaschistische Schutzwall* (the anti-fascist Wall of Protection).

And in the years to follow, the mandatory marksmanship courses in school would prove themselves useful in a new way, as hundreds of human beings heading for the Wall would be shot by their countrymen—East Germans killing East Germans trying to escape its unwelcome protection.

3

After the Wall

Pride before the Fall, 1961–89

We cannot outline the future of socialism.
What socialism will look like
when it takes its final form
we do not know and cannot say.

Lenin, 1921

Alas, we
Who wished to lay the foundations of kindness
Could not ourselves be kind.
But you, when at last it comes to pass
That it is possible to help one's fellow man,
Do not judge us
Too harshly.

Brecht,
"To Our Descendants," 1938

No one intends to build a wall.

Walter Ulbricht, June 15, 1961

The Fenced-In Playground

East Berlin. August 13, 1961. As the sun peeks over the horizon on this beautiful Sunday morning, most East Berliners sleep on, but some rise for work; a few thousand of them are *Grenzgänger*, who cross town—quite legally—to work in the "other" Berlin, mostly as hotel and restaurant employees and in other service jobs made lucrative by the uneven exchange rate. Each day they make the trip to West Berlin—by foot, by bicycle, by S-Bahn and U-Bahn, showing their DDR identity cards and special work permits to the bored *Grepos* (*Grenzpolizei*, border police) stationed at the gates.

But this morning the *Grepos* are not bored; today, as the would-be commuters discover as they reach streets and subway stations along the East Berlin border, no *Grenzgänger* will cross.

"*Die Grenze ist geschlossen!*" people scream to each other in the early-morning stillness. "The border is closed!" No subway cars are running westward; *Grepos*

111

guard the U-Bahn tunnels to prevent subway commuters from fleeing to the West on foot; *Vopos* turn back *Grenzgänger* at every checkpoint.

The SED has apparently found a way to secure its future and halt the flight of DDR and skilled labor—by walling them in.

WHO HAS THE YOUTH, HAS THE FUTURE!

As the *Grenzgänger* stumble home and the DDR capital—*"die Hauptstadt der DDR"*—awakens to the nightmare, it is as if a tremendous howl—the anguished wail of cornered, trapped, desperate animals—has gone up throughout East Berlin—as it soon will over the DDR. For almost a decade, East Germany's 600-mile border has been sealed by barbed wire and 12-foot electrified fencing; just inside the fence is a strip of land about 50 yards wide that is cleared of brush, dotted with mines, and covered by machine guns in high watchtowers. And so, most aspiring refugees make their way to East Berlin, where many of the streets and subway stations along the city border are guarded casually, if at all. Here the task is comparatively easy: as everyone knows, one can often just cut through a back yard, or hop the subway and ride it for a stop or two, till it reaches the West. And so, the *Grenzgänger*, like most East Germans, have always thought there would be time to pack their bags hurriedly, if it came to that; they have always assumed the day of decision was theirs to choose, if necessary.

They were wrong—and now it is too late. Overnight, their world has changed, utterly.

It was an operation conducted, as bitter western columnists put it, with Red Prussian efficiency.[1] Early Saturday evening, *Vopos* had been summoned, without explanation, to their barracks; Soviet troops, under the command of Marshal Koniev, had been placed on full military alert. By midnight, the operation—so secret that it bore no code name—had officially begun. The planning group, under Erich Honecker's direction and including SSD chief Erich Mielke and General Heinz Hoffmann of the Ministry of Defense, issued envelopes marked "Top Secret" to all company commanders. SSD agents immediately took up posts at all major intersections between the Soviet and western sectors. At one A.M. NVA troops—most of them FDJ members and staunch DDR loyalists under the age of 25—arrived at scores of border points to unload barbed wire, concrete posts, stone blocks, picks, and shovels.

West Berlin had long been surrounded by a forbidden zone similar to that separating East Germany from its neighbors. Now, informed that the Warsaw Pact nations had finally decided to stop the West German exploiters and militarists by sealing the border, politically reliable factory brigades and *Vopos* worked diligently through the night to close all passageways in the circumference of West Berlin's 103-mile border. At four A.M. West Berlin radio issued the first panicky news reports of the commotion in the streets.

The Iron Curtain had finally fallen. And 17 million people were now trapped behind it.

Among the *Grenzgänger* suddenly trapped were teachers and students from East Berlin who commuted daily to West Berlin schools and universities. (All West Germans and West Berliners who happened to be in the east were allowed to return to the west.) Forty of the 100 *Grenzgänger* teachers, and a few hundred of the 2,400 students, were visiting the west when the Wall went up; almost all of them decided to stay. The rest of the students were transferred to eastern schools, where new committees were appointed to eradicate western influences; the remaining 60 *Grenzgänger* teachers lost their jobs, in spite of the DDR teacher shortage. Politically suspect, they were required to take miserable jobs at bare subsistence level. But even worse off were the retired teachers who lived in the east but had taught in West Berlin—their West Berlin pension checks were not honored, and so they were completely dependent on the government.[2]

Yes, finally, believed the SED leadership, with their escape hatch finally sealed, DDR educators and students—and, likewise, the rest of the population—would cooperate with the government and accept that the DDR's future and theirs were the same. Young people would begin to regard East Germany as their *Heimat*—since they now had no other choice.

Yes, now the DDR would become, as Christoph Hein later called it, "the fenced-in playground that was my home." The West German media, however, would choose a more ominous term—"the Barbed-Wired State"—and dub August 13 *Stacheldrahtsonntag* (Barbed-Wire Sunday).

"August 13." Like "June 17," the date would go down in German history without any need to mention the year, let alone the allusion: Everyone knows the referent.

Ulbricht had long urged the Wall on his Warsaw Pact allies, who worried that such an expedient might trigger war and, in any case, would become a burdensome anti-socialist propaganda symbol. But Khrushchev's tour, incognito, in a Mercedes-Benz limousine through prosperous West Berlin in late July finally convinced him that Ulbricht was right: the lifeblood of his showcase socialist state was flowing into—and then out of—Berlin, this open wound in the center of communist Eastern Europe. Nothing short of a Wall could staunch the hemorrhage, and failure to check it would mean the death of the DDR. "I will remove this splinter from the heart of Europe," Khrushchev growled; at the Warsaw Pact meeting in Moscow on August 3–5, Khrushchev's word prevailed.[3]

And so, under the capable direction of Erich Honecker, now the Number 2 man in the SED in charge of national security, the "splinter" was removed smoothly—and a concrete and barbed-wire bandage was expertly applied around the circumference of West Berlin. As Ulbricht would later boast: "The operation went off with less damage than a rock'n'roll evening at the Sportpalast." Until just two hours before the midnight venture, no more than 20 top advisors had even known about the plan. Secrecy was vital: the word "wall" was never spoken (except by Ulbricht, whose June 15 slip at an international press conference went unremarked); indeed, not a single word about the operation had even been committed to paper until that Saturday evening.

August 13: *Stacheldrahtsonntag*. As morning wears into afternoon, wrecking crews are still tearing out rails and putting up concrete barriers and barbed wire. By four P.M., as temperatures soar into the low 90s, the incendiary materials for a potential conflagration are heating up along the barbed-wire boundary: Half a million Berliners, east and west, are massed along the sector line. The *Vopos* keep East Berliners well back from the ongoing construction; the West Berlin police restrain West Berliners, who are calling for action. A total estimated force of

533,000 East German troops and paramilitary police stands poised, waiting for trouble—from the east or west. But where are the 40,000 western troops stationed permanently in West Berlin for just such an emergency?

In their barracks. Pending orders from their national capitals, and to minimize the risk of unauthorized escalation, Allied military officials have confined soldiers to their quarters. From the western Allies' viewpoint, there is little else that the West can do. Is interference with the Wall—which, after all, stands on the eastern side—worth the risk of World War III? No. The West will act to prevent a Soviet takeover of Berlin or to maintain free western access routes to the city. But the West has long considered East Berlin to be, in practical terms, part of the DDR.

Within easy earshot of the *Vopos* and workmen fortifying the barbed-wire wall, dozens of West Berlin students holler: *"Hangt Ulbricht!"* ("Hang Ulbricht!"). *"Der Spitzbart muss weg!" "Ivan muss weg!"* Jeering at the DDR work crews, the students chant rhythmically: *"K-Z Wäch-ter! K-Z Wäch-ter!"* ("Concentration camp guards!"). And they mock Moscow's latest technological triumph—the first manned space mission, flown by cosmonaut Gherman Titov:

> *Keine Butter, keine Sahne,*
> *Aber auf dem Mond eine rote Fahne!*
> [No butter, no cream,
> But a red flag on the moon!]

One placard sums up the feelings of many older Berliners: *"Ulbricht = Hitler."* The drawing cleverly makes the appropriate adjustment to Ulbricht's goatee. One East Berlin escapee tells an RIAS reporter: "The DDR has become a worse Gestapo state than the Hitler regime."

All day long, East Berlin radio has been repeating the Party hymn ad nauseam:

> *Die Partei, die Partei*
> *die hat immer recht!*
> [The Party, the Party
> It's always right!]

To the rhythm of this background music, "troublemakers" have been dispersed by tear gas bombs and water hoses; the SSD has arrested thousands.

At the rapidly ascending Wall of Protection, itself protected from East German protesters by a wall of *Vopos*, all is socialist brotherhood. Courteous blue-shirted boys and girls from the FDJ and JP line Unter den Linden—on which new linden trees, planted a few years ago, are growing—gratefully bestowing flower bouquets and refreshments on the sweating comrades at "the front." And indeed, sections of East Berlin still evoke the war front of 1945—street rubble from the Battle of Berlin remains everywhere, miles of it still not cleared away, 16 years after the war's close. The once-ubiquitous 10-foot portraits of Stalin and Pieck are, however, gone at last; only those of Lenin, along with a few of Ulbricht, remain. But the red signs still proclaim: *"Der Sozialismus siegt!"* ("Socialism is winning!").

At "the front," the hard-working "victors" take a break. NVA soldiers leave their mounted machine guns and thank the children for the soft drinks and pastries. Whereupon the Blueshirts, honoring the heroic "fighters for peace," burst into the theme song for the day: *"Die Partei, die Partei! / Die hat immer recht!"*

As construction continues in the days to come, the East German government consolidates its victories—material and psychological, military and political. In his frequent radio broadcasts, Ulbricht explains that many lives are being saved by the construction of the "anti-fascist wall of protection." West Berlin had become a den of terrorists serving imperialist intelligence forces. DDR citizens were, in effect, being kidnapped by "slave traders," West German recruiting agents who "lured" them across from East Berlin (which Ulbricht refers to as "Free Berlin" and "the Democratic Sector") into the West, where they were forcibly inducted into the West German army or forced to work in western munitions factories. "IT'S GREAT HOW EVERYTHING WORKED OUT!" headlines *Neues Deutschland.* "Thank you, Comrades of the People's Army, thank you, Comrades of the Battle Units! . . . When peace is endangered, Walter Ulbricht does not hesitate." Proudly, Ulbricht quotes *Izvestia*, which raves that "millions" welcome the border closing as a blow to western spies and saboteurs. Ulbricht's words anticipate the official Party line that will soon be worked out to explain August 13. DDR schoolchildren will later learn about this day in their 10th-grade history books:

> When other developments endangering peace in Central Europe arose in 1961, especially along the open border between the DDR and West Berlin, the DDR was forced to seal off its borders. . . . The measures taken on 13 August 1961, in coordination with the USSR and the Warsaw Treaty countries, removed this threat to peace and put an end to direct attempts to disrupt the country's political and social life.[4]

But in the meantime, the JP and FDJ rally to defend Ulbricht's Wall. JP leaders offer soccer balls and track suits to children who inform on attempted escapees. FDJ schoolboys climb on rooftops, tearing down any antennae used to watch West German TV, so that East Germans "blinded by enemy propaganda" can come to their senses.[5] "Anyone listening to western radio or TV is a traitor," editorializes Leipzig's *Sächsische Zeitung.*"[6] Thousands of FDJ university students go into the fields to "enlighten" farmers about the political necessity for the Wall. FDJ leaders call for two million immediate army volunteers and recruit 48,000 new volunteers for the NVA before the close of August—no conscription exists in the DDR. By September, the NVA will expand by 70 percent to 170,000 men, and Ulbricht will reopen three Soviet occupation-era forced-labor camps for young men who refuse to "volunteer" for service.

Overnight, the torrent of East German refugees drops to a trickle—an elderly couple crawl on their hands and knees across a cemetery, as *Vopos* string barbed wire 20 yards away; a young family swim across the Teltow Canal, four-year-old son perched on his father's shoulders. The escape total on *Stacheldrahtsonntag* numbers no more than a few hundred, however, and no more than a few dozen on August 14. The minimum penalty for attempted escape is imprisonment: 3 to 10 years of hard labor, usually accompanied by retribution visited on one's family.

Yes, to the East German government it is *"der antifaschistische Schutzwall."* "The Anti-Fascist Wall of Protection." In the months to come, the Wall will ultimately snake for 28 miles through the heart of Berlin, slashing its way across main highways and back alleys, inflicting its schizophrenia on whatever it traverses. "Protecting" East Germans "for their own good," it amputates proud squares, desecrates graveyards and gardens, deforms entire street fronts into sickly concrete slabs, divides families and friends.

The West Germans call it *"die Schandmauer."* "The Wall of Outrage." Khrushchev and Ulbricht may have gotten away with building it, the West concedes. But, as the Warsaw Pact allies feared, the political cost is enormous: Almost every nation outside the communist sphere condemns the Wall, which now stands as a tremendous propaganda symbol to be exploited by the West, a graphic admission of the moral and economic bankruptcy of communism, of its utter failure to survive except by threat and terror.

So be it: The apparent admission of failure is a price Ulbricht willingly pays to save his dismal little satellite on the Elbe. Now the East German work force is captive; Party orders can be enforced with maximum repression—and without concern about stampeding millions into fleeing *drüben.* Now, at last, the DDR population level will stabilize. So DDR planners can, at long last, really plan: They can calculate accurately their economic outlays and manpower levels, free from worry that—tomorrow or next week—half of the skilled workers and the technical elite—and the youth—will hop the S-Bahn and head west.

The Wall has saved the DDR, which has lost more than 4 million citizens since 1945; but it has also upped the ante. For in walling in the population it has also walled out the endlessly cited alibi with which the government has rationalized away all failures: the emigration problem. Treating massive emigration as a cause rather than effect of their policies, SED officials have always fallen back on it as an "explanation" for their every blunder.

And so, "after the Wall," now what? The phrase, once so common as a marker of events in the 1960s and '70s, possesses a different, hopelessly overdetermined resonance in the wake of the events of 1989. But in 1961, "after the Wall" means depression for the DDR populace and gritty determination for SED leaders. "After the Wall," the Party has no excuses; it is up to SED planners to prove what they can do. Now that the Party has built the Wall, can it finally "build socialism"?

For the world battle between capitalism and communism is to be fought out—in microcosm—on German soil. "We will bury you!" Khrushchev once declaimed, with his typical bombast, promising that communism would soon outdo capitalism—not only in space technology but economically and every other way. Ulbricht has often said the same about the long-term superiority of DDR socialism to BRD capitalism. "After the Wall" he finally has a chance to prove it.

So: Can the German communists compete? And, production quotas and living standards aside, what can they do—cheaply, quickly, and yet effectively—that will alter their international image as a nationwide concentration camp?

August 26, 1972, just 11 Augusts later: Success—or, at least, the *Schein* of Success.

At the Twentieth Olympiad in Munich, on the soil of the class enemy, along with 1,200 athletes representing 124 nations of the world, DDR athletes triumphantly enter Olympic Stadium—which has just been built on the spot where Chamberlain landed in 1938 to meet Hitler. Before one hundred thousand spectators and more than one billion TV viewers, the cream of DDR youth—the nation's Olympic team—steps smartly to the sound of "On the Elbe." Just weeks previously, *The Times* of London predicted—in light of recent international performances— that the world was about to witness the birth of "the golden age of DDR sports." And the SED midwives in DDR athletics know it. Boasted one East German sports official to a West German newscaster before the Games: "Tell the maestro to practice our national anthem. He'll be playing it often." Crowed another, referring to the once-scorned DDR flag: "We'll show them what a hammer and compass are."

Only hours after the opening parade, the first DDR Olympians mount the victory stand, standing tall as their national anthem, "Arisen from Ruins," is played for the first time at an Olympiad by—oh, Sweet Victory!—a West German orchestra.

> German youth! The best hope
> of our People is embodied in you.
> You will become Germany's new life
> and the sun, more beautiful than ever,
> will shine over Germany,
> will shine over Germany.

For the first time in history, the DDR's own flag—the black-red-gold with hammer and compass—billows in the wind inside an Olympic stadium, waving acknowledgment to the desolate past and greetings to the ever brighter future.[7]

Conceding this historic first, taking place over the energetic protests of the BRD, some West German media commentators speak condescendingly of the First German Workers' and Peasants State—perhaps better termed, they suggest bitingly, the First German Sports State. The new spirit of détente notwithstanding, some sportscasters still embrace the Cold War *Querelle allemandes*, referring patronizingly to the "so-called" DDR; or to the "East Zone," or even the "Soviet Zone"; DDR visitors in Munich are indeed called *Ostzonler* (East Zoners). (The term *Ossi* will not emerge until 1989/90.) A few sportscasters speak provocatively of the *"Arbeiter- und Mauerstaat"* (Workers' and Wall State) and hail the first West German medal winner as "the champion of the nation"—long after several DDR medalists have mounted the victory stand.[8]

But whether the West Germans like it or not, the DDR will prove itself without a doubt first in German sports. In the next 15 days, "Arisen from Ruins" will salute DDR medal winners 66 times. The DDR will far outdistance the fourth-place BRD (40) as it finishes third, behind only the USSR (99) and the United States (94) in the medal sweepstakes—leaving the rest of Europe departing Munich "with less than even Neville Chamberlain got," as two American reporters joked.[9]

And indeed, the East German sports machine is awe-inspiring. From the first day of the Games, the military discipline and the athletic achievements of the little nation on the Elbe astound the world. In their Olympic quarters, House 44, the DDR Olympians rise each day at dawn, with military precision, to the sound of reveille—the only team in the Olympic Village to do so. Later each day, the hammer and compass are hoisted time and time again—more frequently, in fact, than even those of the United States and the USSR, each of which is almost 200 times larger and 15 times as populous.

The victories belong, overwhelmingly, to young athletes who are both under the age of 25 and faithful FDJ members, and thus the DDR's athletic success seems also to represent a triumph of SED youth and education policy.

Perhaps the most notable DDR victory in Munich is that of Wolfgang Nordwig, a former mechanic studying at the University of Jena, who sets a new Olympic mark in the pole vault with a leap of 5.5 meters, defeating 1968 Olympic victor and future "Breakfast of Champions" hero, the American Bob Seagren. The Breakfast of Champions proves no match for the Factory of Champions.

And the Factory produces in almost every sport. Most impressive is DDR rowing, which produces such consistent success that the West Germans refer to "the great assembly line of DDR boating."[10] East Germany is the only nation to have its crews reach the finals in all seven Olympic boating classes—and not only that, but also to win medals in all seven classes (three golds, a silver, and three bronzes). A post-Games West German review of the Munich Olympics will sum it up as a feat "without comparison in recent decades."[11]

But the DDR proves almost as strong in the Olympic showcase events: track and field and swimming. In the javelin, 22-year-old Ruth Fuchs, the reigning world record holder, breaks all Olympic marks with the second longest throw in history; her 18-year-old teammate Jacquelin Todten places second. Renate Stecher, 24, world record holder in the 200-meter dash, glides to victory, as does Roland Matthes, 25, who garners gold medals in both the 100- and 200-meter backstrokes. Probably the 400-meter freestyle in women's swimming, however, furnishes the most delicious frisson of satisfaction for DDR sports functionaries and the loyal fans back home: Monika Zehrt of Saxony captures the race in 51.08 seconds, almost shattering a world record; a close, indeed heartbreaking second is Rita Wilden of the BRD. The *Schadenfreude* owes to the fact that Wilden, also a native Saxon, is a "renegade" who committed *Republikflucht* along with her family when she was a little girl, leaving the DDR shortly before the Wall went up.

Yes, now the whole world knows what a hammer and a compass are. It is indeed a sweet moment for East Germany, both athletically and politically. As two decades of Cold War struggle on and off the playing field gives way to détente and a historic treaty of BRD-DDR cooperation to be signed this December, the DDR is now on the verge of gaining official diplomatic recognition from all the major powers of the globe—an acknowledgment of its legitimacy that West Germany had fought throughout the 1950s and '60s by every means: from the Hallstein Doctrine, which broke relations with states that recognized the DDR, to a BRD-inspired campaign by NATO countries to refuse visas to DDR teams and to cancel international awards ceremonies if DDR athletes triumphed.[12] Only recently has the BRD let up, as the Social Democratic Party under Willy Brandt and the SED under Erich Honecker have begun to pursue détente in the form of *Deutschlandpolitik*, exhibiting a flexibility and pragmatism absent in the Cold War battles fought by the older generation under Adenauer and Ulbricht. One key to the DDR's diplomatic breakthrough has been its triumph in their marathon of "Olympolitics"[13] and the international prestige gained by its sports program. Three times smaller than Poland, five times smaller than France, the DDR is nevertheless the ruling sports power of Europe.

"Diplomacy through Sports," the West German media sneeringly, if accurately, term the DDR's political uses of athletics. But the tactic has worked: The heroes on the playing fields have compensated for the corpses on the mine fields, as DDR Olympic medals have made the international community forget—or, at least, overlook—the barbed-wire fences, the automatic firing devices, the watchtowers, the guard dogs, the death strip separating east from west. In head-to-head competition, year-in and year-out, the DDR has become such a *Sportmacht* that western athletics can no longer plausibly ignore its existence. This time—in its athletic program, if seldom elsewhere—DDR planning has worked brilliantly.

With the same organizational genius and a monomaniacal single-mindedness that erected the Wall, the SED leadership began, decades earlier, to draft doctors and chemists and biologists and mathematicians to assist the campaign for elite athletic performance. Obsessed with medals, Olympic functionaries shrewdly concentrated their early efforts in areas where the competition was thin, such as women's events and newly instituted Olympic sports (bicycling, wrestling, rowing, skating). And as the medal counts mounted, the DDR gradually gained official recognition from international sporting associations. From there it set about getting its sports functionaries placed in executive positions in almost every important athletic association, posts that could then be used as a base for pursuing larger political goals.[14] After the sports breakthrough, international diplomatic recognition was just a matter of time.

"TO LEARN FROM THE SOVIET UNION / MEANS LEARNING TO TRIUMPH!"

But the more difficult planning lay far beyond diplomatic strategy. So what accounts for the DDR *Sportwunder* (sports miracle)?

The "essential recipe for success" is the role of the schools.[15] Nursery school teachers scout for talent over a three-year period; by school age, the coaches are ready to step in, with some schools sponsoring Spartakiads, or mini-Olympiads, for children as young as five. "In the spirit of Socialism, Peace, and Friendship and for the honor of the German Democratic Republic and the Glory of Sport" runs the Spartakiad oath that the children recite before competitions. Top-performing 2nd- and 3rd-graders eligible for the sports schools receive a 10-day battery of tests from doctors, psychiatrists, and coaches; computers measure abilities ranging from endurance to lung capacity, after which experts assign children to sports based on their physical aptitudes, regardless of the child's preferences. Parents must sign releases that grant the state complete charge of their children, whom they may visit twice a month; in exchange for this waiver, savvy parents often extricate special state favors such as bigger apartments.

In the sports schools, academic classes are organized around 35-hour-per-week training schedules, which feature a coach/pupil ratio of 1 to 3. (In the West, it is at least 1 to 20.)[16] Every pupil receives a monthly stipend in exchange for a promise to "fulfill the plan" developed for him or for her; steadily rising sports achievements satisfy the student's responsibility as a citizen to meet the "class contract" and "work norm." Students who fall short are said to "have no perspective any more"; they are dismissed, and return to a common 10-year polytechnic school. Sports school graduates who continue to "fulfill the plan" and have the "perspective" to win an Olympic medal skip military service; they receive special *K-Stellungen* (*Kader-Stellungen*, cadre positions) as university students or in big industrial firms like VEB 7. Oktober. The positions are only a facade to preserve their amateur status; athletes show up for a few days or weeks per year to hoist a few beers with the students or workers. DDR athletes live together and are not permitted to listen to western radio or watch western TV; the Party controls their access to all information.[17] For all these reasons, they are among the country's most loyal citizens.[18]

"*Bei uns*," remarks the editor of *Sportecho*, "*ist immer Olympia*": "Here it's always the Olympics."[19] Indeed, the Olympiad is more than just a Game in the DDR; it is what the whole country is oriented toward, what the populace waits for and identifies with—since for so many years nothing else has brought international respect or recognition. Although the regime's emphasis is clearly on creating a sports elite, it has also managed to promote popular identification with its athletes—who are the DDR's version of movie stars. So sports are an especially important dimension of DDR youth policy: Not only are almost all DDR Olympians in their teens and 20s, but they are also held up as role models for DDR youth.

All this testifies to both the overall failure and success of the SED: before the late '60s, the DDR seemed to most of its citizens to have so completely failed in everything except sports that many citizens could identify *only* with DDR sports; but communist ideology and planning have also played a role in the SED's success in fostering a national sports consciousness. Whereas western organizations such as the American Council for Physical Fitness issue unheeded pleas for a few more push-ups and sit-ups, SED leaders have aggressively promoted sports, not only in the schools but also in prestigious sports clubs, organized by profession, such as those sponsored for soldiers (*Vorwärts*), civil servants (*Einheit*), farmers (*Traktor*), miners (*Aktivist*), textile workers (*Fortschritt*), and academics (*Wissenschaft*). (The most successful club, with hundreds of medals won by its members in Olympic and other international competitions is *Dynamo*. Sponsored by the SSD and the *Vopos*, its president is Erich Mielke, chief of the secret police.) And so, the population has become not only a nation of spectators but also of participants.

Not just polytechnical but also physical education is an integral part of the SED program for "the new human being." Lenin was a fitness fanatic and a keen sportsman: a walker, a marksman, a skater, a mountaineer, a cyclist, and a fisherman. (Here too, *der Spitzbart* imitates the Master, doing a program of calisthenics and jogging every morning.) For as Ernst Thälmann, then head of the KPD, touted the political value of physical education in 1930: "Bodily training and bodily toughness enable proletarians to develop special capacities for resistance and defense that are invaluable in the class war."[20]

After the erection of the Berlin Wall, the Party promotes sports primarily for economic reasons. Just as elite sports has brought socialism its due international prestige, mass sports will strengthen the economy: "regular participation [in mass sports] raises production" by maintaining workers' health and energy levels, the FDGB (*Freie Deutsche Gewerkschaftsbund*, Free German Labor Union) reminds its members in Rule 1 of its "Ten Rules for an FDGB Functionary."[21] Calling on Lenin's inspirational example, Chairman Ulbricht issues a constant stream of slogans in the 1950s and early '60s promoting the collectivization of physical education:

> *Für Frieden und Sozialismus*
> *Für Gesundheit und Lebensfreude*
>
> *Jeder treibt Sport!*
> [For Peace and Socialism
> For Health and Joyful Living
> Everyone plays sports!]
>
> *Das ganze Dorf treibt Sport!*
> [The whole village plays sports!]
>
> *Mein Urlaub—kein Urlaub vom Sport!*
> [My vacation—no vacation from sports!]
>
> *Jeder Mann an jedem Ort*
> *Jede Woche einmal Sport!*
> [Everybody in every place
> Play sports once a week!][22]

By 1968, the SED has upped its expectations to "*Jede Woche mehrmals Sport!*" ("Play sports several times a week!"). The FDJ and other youth organizations have pushed both elite-level competitiveness and mass participation. By the 1970s, 97 percent of 10th-graders and 82 percent of 5th-graders can swim. Indeed, 3.3 million DDR schoolchildren—80 percent of the nation—are participating in the national Spartakiad, whose championship events are held biennially in Leipzig with all the trappings of the real Olympics (village, torch, doves, etc.), making the Spartakiad another invaluable venue for spotting athletic talent. Amazed by the commitment of DDR coaches, teachers, and students, one American sportswriter writes home: "As a talent search it's the New York Yankees scouting system in its heyday—but run by tough Teutons. . . ."[23]

In the Olympic swimming hall at the Munich Games, one group draws special attention to itself: the 2,000 DDR tourists. The only national group to carry flags, they wildly brandish the hammer and compass, rooting for their national heroes. These, the first DDR tourists ever to visit West Germany, have been meticulously selected by the SED—though not all of them are Party members. Carefully segregated from the other Olympic tourists, the *Ostzonler* travel together in groups and are quartered in two small villages 100 km from Munich (ironically, the very locale where the first All-German Ski Championships were scheduled for 1953—before their cancellation in the aftermath of June 17). Probably on Party orders, the *Ost-zonler* studiously avoid all contact with West Germans.[24] As one Bavarian native remarked, after a frustrating attempt to engage a DDR citizen in conversation: "It's as if, whenever we meet, we have the Wall standing right between us."[25]

And it was true: Even as the Cold War mentality faded, the intra-German rivalry on the playing field remained intense, above all on the DDR's side. The struggle against the class enemy had moved from the streets of Berlin to the stadia and swimming pools of East Germany. Or as one DDR athlete who defected in the early 1970s put it, in a statement much-quoted in the BRD press: "The ideological stance in [DDR athletics] is that, if we finish next to last, then West Germany must be last."

"You are diplomats in warm-up suits," SED officials told DDR Olympians. In indoctrination pep talks at Munich—"political drills" for the Games—athletes chant the prescribed slogan:

Schlagt die Imperialisten und den Klassenfeind auf eigenem Boden!
[Defeat the Imperialists and the Class Enemy on Their Own Home Turf!][26]

"The best answer to the reactionaries in Bonn who claim sole representation of Germany," Ulbricht had declared in 1960, "are DDR sportsmen on the victory stands of the European Games and of the world."[27] By 1971, Honecker, now SED chief, could tell Party members: "Our state is respected in the world . . . because of the excellent performances of our top athletes." A sports elite—cadres of athletes "running for socialism," "swimming for socialism," "rowing for socialism"— had brought world respect to socialist Germany.[28]

History had seemingly validated the already-quoted, oft-repeated, early postwar statement of the young FDJ chief, Erich Honecker: "Sports is not an end in itself for us, but a means to our end."

And the end had justified the means. The DDR emerged from the 1972 Games a clear winner in Olympolitics as well as athletics, having further burnished, and by now, substantially refurbished, its image—doing so, as it were, in record time.[29]

The DDR: from *Stacheldrahtsonntag* to *Sportwunder*. After the Wall went up in 1961, the DDR economy did indeed experience the sharp economic upturn that Ulbricht had predicted, which—along with the embrace of détente by Moscow, Washington, and Beijing—made the historic agreements in the early 1970s between Bonn and East Berlin possible. But DDR sports served as a key Leninist transmission belt toward DDR recognition; the DDR's international sports triumphs gradually made it inevitable that such a *Sportwunder* would be recognized by its capitalist inferiors. Within little more than a decade, this small nation transformed its reputation from that of a national concentration camp to a national sports stadium, from that of the Barbed Wire State to the Olympia on the Elbe.

The Wall and the Sports Factory of Champions: those were the two features of the DDR known for decades throughout the world. The SED leadership bet that the triumph of the latter could expunge the treachery of the former; but it was a losing gambit. "Something there is that doesn't love a wall / That wants it down," wrote Robert Frost. No matter how many medals the Factory produced, the DDR populace never ceased to want "it" down—the Wall and, ultimately, the Party and government that erected it.

"The fenced-in playground that was my home." Once again, Christoph Hein's characterization of the DDR shortly "after the Wall," i.e., after November 1989, comes to mind—though nobody, even ironically, viewed the DDR as a "playground" in the 1960s. And in the context of the DDR's sports gamble, the metaphor evokes a quite complex set of impressions. For the playground surrounded by barbed wire and concrete included not just guards and dogs within its walls, but also the world's leading "diplomats in warm-up suits," whose accomplishments became more and more impressive as the decades passed—the periodic reports of state-administered doping of athletes notwithstanding. Beyond their athletic, political, and diplomatic achievements was their decisive contribution to the DDR national identity. Partly because of the DDR sport successes beginning in the late 1960s and continuing into the 1980s, a feeling of distinctive national consciousness, if not patriotism or pride toward the "socialist Fatherland," emerged among East Germans, at least among non-dissidents.[30]

In hindsight, however, this period amounted to a long, prelapsarian moment of Pride before the Fall of the Wall. For the SED's calculated tradeoff—medals for the *Mauer*—would ultimately pay off only temporarily: a shady, bargain-basement international facelift had been conducted by the government at the price of suppressed popular outrage about the Wall around the playground. And so a frustration would slowly grow until the People finally razed it—Wall and playground altogether.[31]

For just as the sports elite, coddled from their earliest years in the special sports schools, contributed to the sense of national consciousness and socialist identity, so also did the privileged athletes provoke national anger and indignation,[32] especially as socialist sports morality gave way to state and individual profiteering from western trade and advertising contracts.[33] And just as the sports schools were only one example of the DDR turn toward special schools for the gifted, so too was the sports elite only one category of the educational and technical elite—whose privileges likewise invited both popular admiration and disgust.[34]

The rise—and the fall—of the DDR is mirrored in these shifting relations, in the ever intensifying dynamic between collectivism and elitism, ideological orthodoxy and economic aspirations, the pieties of the old Marxist religion and the imperatives of the new "technical-scientific revolution." By the 1970s, the Party was coming, more and more, to emphasize the latter halves of the dynamic, a policy choice that finally fueled contradictions whose explosive potential, by the late 1980s, no Leninist two-stepping or dialectical dancing could contain.

At the crossroads of these byzantine contradictions stood the biggest nationalized Factory, DDR education. With everything, finally, firmly in place—until 1989—the highlights of the picture can be sketched in quicker, broader strokes than heretofore. But each of them reflects a key moment in three decades of East German education "after the Wall," comprising a narrative that constitutes, once again, another history of the DDR in microcosm.

Rearing the Technical Elite

A revolutionary is a comrade with a heart of fire and a brain of ice.

Lenin

You say you want a revolution
Well you know. . . .
You better free your mind instead.

Lennon and McCartney

"I'm 20!" announced the DDR in 1969, celebrating its emergence from troubled adolescence with 100,000 posters of a gorgeous, glowing *Fräulein* proclaiming the same. To prepare for the birthday party, the German Military Publishing House in East Berlin printed a 380-page poetry anthology titled "You, Our Darling!" JP students cleared and cleaned the streets under the slogan, "More beautiful cities and communities—join us!" Jubilee week, which featured more than 700 political and cultural meetings, culminated on October 7 with the "Rally of Young Socialists," as tens of thousands of long-haired boys and mini-skirted girls—"the children of the Republic"—paraded through East Berlin streets. Under the beaming presence of Leonid Brezhnev and comrades from 84 nations, one SED functionary after another extolled the DDR as a paradise for its "young revolutionaries"—"The Land of Learning," "The Land of Youth," "The Land of Sports."[35]

For the '60s was the decade of youth in the DDR just as throughout the West. In fact, to establish that the State and DDR youth had the same interests, the Party had already, with the passage of the 1964 *Jugendgesetz*, introduced special slogans proclaiming its new trust in the young guard:

> *Vertrauen und Verantwortung der Jugend gegenüber!*
> [Trust and responsibility to the youth!]
>
> *Die Jugend hat das Wort!*
> [The youth have the word!]

Unfortunately for SED ideological purity, however, most DDR youth had begun to repay this official trust in western notes. To them, the word—or the Word—was: rock'n'roll.

Before the Wall, a vibrant club scene had grown up mostly on the western side of divided Berlin, featuring combos from the West that played jazz, blues, and the hottest new rock'n'roll. "Teens and Twens" from East Berlin would slip over to West Berlin on weekends to enjoy the night life, stepping and swaying and rockin' 'round the clock. After the Wall, even the few western-style clubs in East Berlin were closed; frustrated DDR youth resorted to private dance parties with rock'n'roll smuggled in by western relatives and friends, and to practicing in their bedrooms the new dances they saw on forbidden West German television.

In 1961/62 a new dance craze swept the world, not excepting East Germany: *Der Twist.* "You should see my little sis," sang Chubby Checker—an unlikely candidate for cultural subversion—"she really knows how to dance / She knows how to Twist." Hip DDR disc jockeys surreptitiously slipped Twist records into their officially approved late-night programs; DDR youth twisted the night away.

SED officials sprang to the barricades. At a 1961 conference for school officials, a Party dance spokesman argued that the wild gyrations of the Twist disclosed its paramilitary purposes, for it was being "used as an instrument of the imperialists in West Germany in order to prepare young people for war."[36] In June 1963, Horst Schumann, Honecker's successor as FDJ chief, fretted that the Twist had turned into "the king of dances" among East German youth; it was a measure of the distance of middle-aged apparatchiks from everyday teen life that Schumann merely *suspected* that DDR "boys and girls in reality believe something quite different" from the old communist slogans. Hostile to western imports and still reeling from the fight against the *Hotmusik* and jitterbug, bewildered SED commissars were still rhapsodizing about the supposedly socialist virtues of the "Leipzig *Lipsi*," which had proven a dud. The FDJ Central Committee officially declared the Twist an anti-communist weapon "disseminated by the American secret services to [infect] us through the ether." To the official music magazine *Melodie und Rhythmus*, the Twist was "NATO music" revealing "the rotting character of the Bonn state." It was degenerate imperialist hip-weaving, the "outgrowth of capitalist decadence, the erotic death throes in the decline of a condemned, decaying world." An alarmed Ulbricht declared at an FDJ conference that "Western bacteria" in the form of rock'n'roll had "invaded" the minds of DDR youth.[37]

But soon the SED leadership gave up trying to enforce its rock'n'roll quarantine; though *der Twist* remained officially taboo for a while, its music was widely admitted into the DDR under the false classification of "foxtrot." Instead, the Party tried a homeopathic remedy: If you can't beat the new beat, reasoned SED leaders, then dance to the music.

And so the Party set about producing its own Twist records, e.g., "Our Love," "The Yodel Twist," and "Seven Thousand Head of Cattle." Now even the FDJ chief himself was photographed doing the Twist. "The Twist is fundamentally abused for anti-humanist ends in the West," declared a Party rock'n'roll spokesman, "whereas here we have liberated this interesting new rhythm from such corruption," testifying once again to "the renovating power of socialist society." (No Party ideologue specified exactly how its socialist revisionist music—termed "rock around the Bloc" by one American historian—differed from its western counterparts, except to reiterate as a virtue the self-evident truth that it was not produced by a capitalist music industry.)[38]

Yet now an even more contagious epidemic hit DDR youth: Beatlemania. During 1960–62, the Beatles had made brief forays from their native Liverpool to play seedy Hamburg clubs, though they had not yet become known to the wider German public. Especially given the group's recent presence in West Germany, however, East German teenagers were happily susceptible to the paroxysms of ecstasy that convulsed all of Europe during the Beatles' first continental tour and the release of *Meet the Beatles* in autumn 1963. By mid-1964, even *Neues Deutschland* had embraced the Beatles as "four likeable boys," whose "healthy naïveté" was a suitable model for DDR rock'n'rollers. For SED policymakers were now promoting a homegrown variety of western-sounding German rock'n'roll, as one feature of a native German version of the private life attractions that DDR youth identified with the West. The new beat was welcome, as it had always been, the Party announced: "It would never occur to anyone to prescribe to youth how they should express their feelings and moods in dance or tango rhythms. Whatever way young people choose is up to them."[39] Of course, the future would inevitably belong to the DDR and its vision for youth. As one SED leader rosily predicted:

> In the future, people in the DDR will seldom sing western rock music. Rather, in both German states, they will sing rock music from the DDR, with texts that correspond to our lives and feelings.

But here again, it was not to be. The popularity of the Beatles only spread, further exposing the East German body politic to the new British (and American) invasion. Officially approved home-grown German rock'n'roll could not compete with the Beatles. And the Fab Four themselves were growing less "likeable" to DDR authorities (as they were to authorities all over the world). Irony and a dangerously anarchistic freethinking had crept into their sunny songs. The "healthy naïveté" of "Twist and Shout" had darkened into the brooding skepticism of "Nowhere Man." By 1965, the Party was deploring "rock vagabonds," who would hang out on street corners, holler unapproved slogans, and disturb the peace of decent DDR citizens. Especially frustrating for the SED were boys who adopted Beatle haircuts—or "Marx haircuts," as DDR youth sometimes referred to their locks, impishly (and disingenuously) citing as their model the hirsute hero of their civics textbooks. Long-haired boys were pulled out of dances by *Vopos* and escorted to nearby police stations, where barbers trimmed their hair to acceptable lengths. Erich Honecker himself, now SSD chief, warned DDR youth against taking western rock "for the musical expression of the era of the technical revolution." And *Neues Deutschland* now cautioned against the slippery slope that began with Beatle haircuts: "One of the main tactics of imperialism . . . is the supposition that DDR youth can be demoralized. . . . Moral subversion easily leads to political subversion. The transition is often completed very fast. . . . In Vietnam bombs are falling!"[40]

But there were guitar-toting guerrillas at home, too, and these the SED treated with much less respect. Explicitly subversive—and far more inflammatory and dangerous than the Beatles—were the provocative ballads of 29-year-old Wolf Biermann, a popular folk singer who had drawn 120,000 youths to an outdoor concert in 1964.[41] Honecker attacked Biermann's "so-called poems," which reveal "his petty-bourgeois, anarchistic outlook, his sense of superiority, his skepticism, and his cynicism. . . . Biermann betrays basic positions of socialism with his poems and songs."[42] Other top functionaries condemned Biermann's work as "American-style pornography" and "toilet-stall poetry."[43] Politburo candidate member Horst Sindermann, DDR press and radio chief, made the warning to Biermann and his followers more personally ominous: "Herr Biermann shouldn't be surprised, if instead of the milkman, some other people one day are standing in front of his door."[44]

By late 1965, FDJ chief Schumann was regretting the FDJ's former laxity, admitting that he had provided "totally erroneous ideological guidelines" toward western lifestyles and music. The FDJ worried about the "damaging" effects of western rock music on youth, which, along with "negative" western TV programming, spread an "ideology of skepticism and doubt." In a seven-hour Central Committee speech in December 1965, Erich Honecker linked the rise in DDR youth crime to the FDJ's wrongheaded promotion of rock'n'roll, which "overlooked that the enemy exploits this type of music to drive young people to excesses through the use of exaggerated beat rhythms." The General Secretary himself bemoaned "the eternal monotony of 'Yeah, yeah, yeah.' " Western jazz and rock'n'roll, Ulbricht now pronounced, represented "the culture of apes."[45]

The hard anti-West line returned. *"Zuverlässigkeit statt Kühnheit!"* ran a new Party slogan: "Reliability, not boldness!" In 1967, already announced LPs of Nat King Cole, Frank Sinatra, Ella Fitzgerald, Billie Holiday, and Dave Brubeck were canceled; American jazz could only be played on DDR radio in translation. Even once-approved anti-war American stars such as Bob Dylan and Joan Baez—indeed, even Pete Seeger, who had received the DDR Peace Prize and sung before ecstatic audiences during his March 1967 visit—disappeared from the airwaves. Although the American protest singers directed their songs against Washington and Wall Street, Minister of Culture Klaus Gysi feared that DDR youth might turn the rebellious lyrics against authorities at home, since they were incapable of distinguishing "the clear class border between socialism and capitalism."[46]

And so, although DDR teens continued to adopt western dance fads and listen to jazz and rock'n'roll at home, it was back to Soviet folk songs and Young Pioneer marches on DDR radio and TV. As one American historian summed up the doublespeak imposed on teens at this time:

> [M]ost young people lived in two worlds, the public and the private. In the public world they outwardly conformed, said the right things, and concentrated on promoting their own careers. In private, they regarded leading SED functionaries as peddlers of myths or half-truths, even cynics or hypocrites. Satisfaction in life came from cultivating the private life with its totally different value system.[47]

And the increasing feelings of hypocrisy and alienation on the part of East German youth were not misplaced: the 1960s were a decade of extreme tension between ideology and praxis, between rhetoric and action on the part of the SED leadership. "The basic principle" of socialist society, the Party reaffirmed in 1965, is: "Everything with the People, everything through the People, everything for the People."[48]

But the People's most urgent practical problem, of course, continued to be the DDR economy, whose collapse in early 1961 had both reflected and accelerated the mass exodus. The SED's proposed solution had been a technical-scientific revolution, and it wanted its "young revolutionaries" to step to socialist marches, not rock'n'roll tunes: it wanted a nation of youth who would join its technical-scientific revolution, not the West's decadent cultural revolution.

SED leaders envisioned an economic revolution in which advanced technology would "build socialism." Of course, first they would have to build an educational elite, from which what Milovan Djilas called the "new class" of scientists and technical experts would come. This new socialist intelligentsia would consist not of radical humanists or Marxist-Leninists, as in earlier eras, but rather of the best polytechnical *Menschen*, each making a specific technical contribution to the planned society.

But building an educational elite had posed ideological problems: the necessary introduction of special schools and schooling clashed with the idea of a uniform, common school system. As the "technical-scientific revolution" superseded the "workers' revolution," a gap widened between "the workers" and "the People," a political embarrassment that smacked of the feared "revisionism" of the 1950s.

And so the SED leadership dropped the curtain on DDR education, which disappeared from public view after 1961, *never* to reappear until the fall of the Wall.[49] SED leaders treated education as a national secret comparable to the military. As Freya Klier later wrote of this period:

> Education simply ceased to have a public dimension. This whole area was gradually put under water—systematically, when Honecker gained power. By the end of the 1970s, the DDR school found itself in a taboo zone; the degree of public openness about it roughly approximated that for the National People's Army. Forced course corrections occurred and had to be executed as inconspicuously as possible. The leadership didn't want to let either the "class enemy" or its own populace see much in this eminently important area. What was public now became only that which was explicitly directed to the public.[50]

Even after the breakthroughs in détente between the BRD and DDR in the early 1970s, East German education remained largely behind the Wall, off-limits to unofficial eyes.

Thus, in the decade after the Wall's erection—with the crippling refugee outflow halted, the SED's top leadership stable and pliant under Ulbricht, and a wall of secrecy covering their activities from their own people's view—SED educators could advance decisively toward their seemingly infinitely deferred goal of locking up their capture of "the citadel of learning." During this fifth phase of DDR educational history (1961–71)—which corresponds to Ulbricht's final decade in power, before Honecker's accession in 1971—East German education entered yet another new epoch. Just as the "anti-fascist democratic" era of the 1940s had given way to the "polytechnic" era of the late 1950s, the 1960s would witness the rise of the "systematic" era, as West German educators came to call it. First *die neue schule* of the early postwar era—the "democratic school"—had been replaced by the "socialist school"; now would come the socialist *system* in education, i.e., the uniform socialist educational system, a comprehensive transformation of schools, universities, and technical training institutes into a smoothly running unit closely coordinated with industry and agriculture. And thus the final triumph of socialism in the First German Workers' and Peasants' State. Education would thereby "build" the socialist society: schooling and production would cooperate at all levels. "Polytechnics" would not be restricted to education; it would become a way of life.

And a drab life it would be, though even that would come as a welcome relief to the many East Germans who, after more than a decade of ceaseless turmoil, longed simply for a measure of quiet and stability. No more the militant maroon and the officious crimson of what hostile western journalists had called "Red Fascism" during the Stalinist era and "Red Prussianism" thereafter. Now, by the mid-1960s, except for the occasional washes of western popcult brightening its monochromatic wall, "the DDR Way of Life" would weather and fade into its enduring color: the somber, washed-out gray of polytechnical socialism.

The impetus for the renewed commitment to polytechnics was a 1963 SED report that detailed the weaknesses in DDR polytechnical education and urged comprehensive reforms. The resulting debate within the Party led to the February 1965 "Law on the Unified Socialist Educational System," the third and final DDR education act of the postwar era, which extended and superseded the legislations of 1946 and 1959. The 1965 Education Act stressed the importance of polytechnics "in the new socialist age" for pre-schoolers, schoolchildren, work-study apprentices, and university students. It heralded the emergent era of the "technical-scientific revolution":

The most important goals in the comprehensive construction of socialism involve the mastery of the technical revolution, the development of the national People's Economy, and the raising of production and worker productivity through the highest quality of science and technology. . . .

The sciences are experiencing an extraordinary upturn. They embrace more and more new regions of knowledge and pervade them utterly. The intervals between scientific discoveries and their industrial usage are increasingly shortening. Complete mechanization and automation, linked to . . . the application of electronics and cybernetics . . . are the basic characteristics of the present technical revolution. They place high demands on the education of human beings in socialist society. The requirements of science and the technical revolution, the conscious application of the economic laws of socialism, and the shape of socialist community, democracy, and culture define the development of the new, essential . . . human education of our time. . . .

These objective laws of the social development in the German Democratic Republic require unifying the educational system and the comprehensive buildup of socialism. They demand appropriate education and culture corresponding to the modern state of science and technology. This will enable human beings, above all in work, in the community of the working people, to educate one another to become [socialist] personalities, who will be loyal to their socialist Fatherland, the German Democratic Republic, and be ready to strengthen and defend it. Thus the technical revolution and the striving after an educated nation will, under the comprehensive construction of socialism, become a unity. . . .

To achieve these goals it is necessary to create a unified, socialist educational system.[51]

Steps toward the systematic integration of DDR education had already begun by the late 1950s, especially after passage of the 1959 Education Act. Nevertheless, the actual execution of educational transformation mandated by the 1965 Act entailed some considerable readjustment.

Under the new unified socialist educational system, the unity started young: Socialist education began in kindergarten, where children made beds and set tables together, working collectively rather than individually. Beginning with 1st grade, all children learned arts and crafts with paper, leather, wood, metal, and other materials; eventually they did weaving and learned electronics. DDR polytechnics included the teaching of horticulture and agriculture, with each individual contributing to the collective: e.g., each student tended a tiny plot of the school grounds—planting vegetables, sowing, watering, and weeding the little gardens. In the upper grades of the 10-year POS, a seventh of the school week was devoted to instruction in socialist principles of production; here teachers formally introduced the ideals of communist sharing for the developing socialist consciousness. By 9th grade, students spent at least one day per week in co-op programs as apprentices in industry and agriculture; now they also received intensive lessons in "socialist patriotism" and Marxism-Leninism. Gifted students had already entered, sometime between 1st and 6th grades, "special schools" for specific subjects— math, sports, music, dance, or foreign languages—whereby youthful talents were cultivated so as to best serve the state.

In this way, the SED set out to effect educational transformation without precipitating drastic political changes, and to adapt Marxist-Leninist ideology to the new economic imperatives without appearing to adopt bourgeois, class-oriented, "Western" policies promoting the privileged. Any new policy favoring a technical-scientific class would need to be reconcilable with the Marxist allegiance to the working class. And so the SED introduced a strictly delimited set of educational innovations allowing for openness to economic developments outside the DDR and Soviet bloc, but which did not tolerate political openness. Focusing on economic reform, the SED acted to preempt any revisionist challenge to its authority by dismissing overt political reforms. Former allegiances would never be explicitly repudiated, merely downscaled in emphasis, and sometimes quietly abandoned. And yet, as the inevitable result of altering their labor focus from increased worker opportunities to productivity gains, SED educators shifted their political priorities dramatically, from ideology to science and technology.

Fortunately for the SED leadership, Khrushchev—flushed with the success of the USSR's technological advances symbolized by Sputnik and Yuri Gagarin—had already taken the lead; Ulbricht could, once again, lead by following. This shift in policy entailed an adjustment of DIAMAT philosophy. Classical Marxism-Leninism had posited a base/superstructure model of productive forces and relations: the institutions of the industrial economy formed the determining base, and all noneconomic institutions constituted the dependent superstructure. At the Twenty-Second Congress of the CPSU in October 1961, however, Soviet philosophers revalued science in Marxism-Leninist theory to a force of production, thus transferring it from the superstructure to the base. The use of atomic energy, the space flights, and the innovations in automation and cybertechnics signified the beginning of the new era, known throughout the Soviet bloc as the "revolution" in science and technology. This era, argued CPSU ideologists, corresponded to the postwar dawn of world communism, led by the USSR.

Following the CPSU, therefore, the SED reclassified science as a force of production in the mid-1960s. Only socialism, declared Khrushchev and Ulbricht, could fully exploit the technical-scientific revolution. SED hard-liners and ideologists, accurately sensing that the rise of cybernetics meant their own loss of authority and status, resisted the scientific turn; but with Ulbricht's enthusiastic endorsement, its advocates carried the day. The result was yet another formal change in economic policy: the SED introduced Soviet "Libermanism," the New Economic System for Planning and Leadership of the People's Economy, known as NOS, which made central planning more efficient by concentrating on individual and local needs and desires.

Conceived by Yevsei Liberman, a Soviet professor of economics, NOS constituted a sharp departure from classical Marxism-Leninism in its acceptance of economic incentives; in an earlier era it would surely have been branded as heretical "revisionism." Liberman argued that workers and factory managers should be evaluated by the amount of profit they returned to the People, changing the Marxist maxim, as it were, to "From each according to his ability; to each according to his *productivity.*" Liberman argued for economic decentralization, the application of international business principles, more material incentives for workers, and greater consumer satisfaction. He urged assessing individual workplace and factory productivity, rather than evaluating entire industrial and agricultural sectors, and awarding workers bonuses on the basis of their productivity. He also sought to redesign state planning to produce what citizens wanted to buy, rather than fulfilling quotas by producing unsalable goods.

Thus NOS was another move toward economic, if not political, liberalization—indeed it took its inspiration from Lenin's own liberal New Economic Policy (NEP) of the 1920s. Libermanism revived the spirit of the New Course begun by Malenkov after Stalin's death as well as in the DDR in June 1953—and abruptly canceled by Ulbricht after the events of June 17. Such policy reversals were by now familiar in the communist world: just as Stalin had junked Lenin's NEP, so too had Ulbricht scrapped the New Course in favor of a return to Stalin's heavy-handed Build Socialism campaign, and would now embrace NOS. And much as in the case of the Build Socialism campaign, Ulbricht instituted this newest economic panacea in a far more thoroughgoing, comprehensive fashion than did the Kremlin itself, which soon came to fear that Liberman's decentralizing proposals might weaken the CPSU's own authority.[52]

And so, East German education, under NOS, began the systematic development of a socialist intelligentsia of scientists and technical experts, which Ulbricht hoped would lead the DDR to an economic boom. The SED called for an expansion, by the end of 1960s, of the number of scientists by 250 percent and of engineers by 350 percent. Consequently, the prestige—as well as the total—of scientists, engineers, and economists rose sharply. More importantly, so did the economy: by September 1967, all DDR workers enjoyed a five-day week at higher living standards than ever before: after the Wall, weekly incomes rose almost 20 percent, with no inflation.[53] The greatest success of the economic "revolution" was in the increased production of consumer goods. By 1969, 66 percent of DDR homes had TV, up from 5.1 in 1958; during the same period, percentages skyrocketed of households that possessed refrigerators (2.1 to 48) and washing machines (1.6 to 48): the output of the DDR, with only 17 million citizens, now exceeded the 1936 output of 67 million Germans. And all of this had been achieved not only amid the ruins of 1945 and without Marshall Plan aid, but indeed after paying the USSR roughly $30 billion in reparations (West Germany paid nothing) while enduring, until August 1961, the flight of four million able-bodied workers.[54]

These successes notwithstanding, the stress on technical expertise widened the gulf between the intellectuals and the workers, and the SED became a "party of the new type" in a way not publicly admitted: an elite, rather than a mass, party. The membership of the intelligentsia in the SED doubled to 20 percent during the 1960s; all Party secretaries of district and local committees and 93.7 percent of SED secretaries in large industrial firms possessed higher education and Party college degrees by the late 1960s.[55] Indeed the majority of Party functionaries now came from intellectuals' families: Germany's First Workers' and Peasants' State had become the First Apparatchiks' State.

Moreover, despite the growing status of educators, widespread unrest still prevailed, especially among teachers. The teacher exodus continued as the 1960s progressed—no longer leading, of course, to the West but rather to other occupations. Most teachers simply did not want to be Party propagandists, however much they might initially have been willing during their student years to promote socialism and atheism. Now teachers were leaving the profession not for better jobs in the West but rather because they wanted to be *teachers*—and could not be, given the Party's priorities. Those faculty who remained often became "inner emigres," accommodating Party regulations with robotic lifelessness. As DDR psychologist Hans Joachim Maaz later defined the plight of East German teachers in *Der Gefühlsstau*: " 'Teacher': a diagnosis, not a profession." Klier estimates that between one half and two thirds of DDR teachers left the profession between 1961 and 1987, largely due to the lack of academic freedom:[56]

> The prescribed black-and-white program was "Seeing-Experiencing-Recognizing-Judging." Peace, democracy, security, and solidarity were identifiable on this side of the Wall, and hatred of humanity, poverty and humanity were on the other side of the Wall.
> To be a teacher, you had to be a cadre member. To get a high post, you didn't need special knowledge or teaching ability, but rather a class perspective. That was also the case for positions in higher education, for editors of specialized journals. . . . The Party needed peace and reliability in the school staff, so that the [ideological] invasion of the schools could be most effective.[57]

This ideological "invasion" caused particular problems in an important area related to the technical-scientific revolution: the physical sciences. In a series of 1962 lectures, Robert Havemann, a physical chemist at Humboldt University, argued that Soviet and SED philosophers (dubbed "DIAMATniks" by DDR students), were clinging to positions of "vulgar materialism" and "mechanistic materialism" that already decades ago had "resulted in the discrediting of DIAMAT among scientists of the world."

As had SED ideologists who theorized about the DDR technical-scientific revolution, Havemann took as his point of departure the Twenty-Second Party Congress of the CPSU in October 1961. But Havemann seized on an announcement in Moscow which Ulbricht had soft-pedaled, one that was much more dangerous to the SED: the second round of de-Stalinization launched by Khrushchev.[58] To prevent ossification into dogma, maintained Havemann, Marxism-Leninism had to take account of modern developments in the natural sciences. Orthodoxy could only hurt the basic sciences, whose research and development required freedom of inquiry. Marxism-Leninism had no subject matter of its own; the dialectic was a method, and progress in its application depended on the results of other sciences. Havemann warned against ideological orthodoxies of all sorts, ridiculing Party ideologists as the "Central Administration for Eternal Truths."

As dangerous as these criticisms were, Havemann was in a good position to deliver them: he had been a respected scientist as well as a Party member in good standing for three decades. Son of a conservative nationalist teacher, the 22-year-old Havemann had joined the KPD in 1932. During the war, he worked by day as a physical chemist at the Kaiser Wilhelm Institute in Berlin, then organized resistance groups by night. In 1943, he was arrested by the Gestapo and sentenced to death; he won a reprieve and was jailed in Brandenburg Prison, with a special laboratory set up for him—near Erich Honecker's own Brandenburg cell—after his friends persuaded Reich authorities that Havemann's scientific expertise was indispensable to the war effort. Liberated by the Russians in 1945, Havemann returned to the Kaiser Wilhelm Institute—now in American-occupied West Berlin—and was promoted to director by American authorities, only to be removed in 1948 when he made pro-Soviet statements to the press. Before and after the founding of the DDR, Havemann stood loyal to "the better Germany": Volkskammer representative (1949–63), Kulturbund member, and recipient of the second-class National Prize and the Fatherland Merit Medal in Silver. He urged West Berliners to boycott the Marshall Plan, persuaded qualified colleagues to fulfill their national duty by contributing to the DDR atomic program, and lionized Stalin in the *Tägliche Rundschau* as "the greatest scientist of our time."

Unlike most Party leaders, Havemann was highly respected by non-Party scientists and by the younger technical elite in industry. Moreover, he was a fearless, charismatic speaker. His Friday afternoon lectures were popular with students (and unannounced SSD auditors),[59] sparking lively discussion at Humboldt University and drawing auditors from as far away as Jena and Leipzig. "You can command human beings and prescribe to them a great deal," Havemann declared, "but you can't prescribe to them what they should think."[60]

The professor was speaking from personal experience. A defender of Ulbricht's harsh measures on June 17—indeed Havemann had been one of the government spokesmen who had addressed the workers in the streets on June 16 and had been shouted down by them—he had been an unwavering Party loyalist until 1956 when his eyes were opened by the events in Hungary. When *Forum*, the FDJ newspaper, tried to humiliate him and discredit his SED criticisms of the 1960s by publishing a long list of his previous professions of faith to the regime, Havemann sent a simple, one-sentence reply:

Yes, I was wrong—that's why I was a Stalinist and became an anti-Stalinist.[61]

Havemann was not blind to the Orwellian character of the DDR. A Party member's support for the Party line amounted, he declared, to "Unfreedom as Necessity," "the leitmotif of Stalinist pseudo-socialism."[62]

But Havemann remained a Marxist, albeit a "revisionist" like Leslek Kolakowski and Adam Schaff in Poland, Eduard Goldstücker in Czechoslovakia, Ernst Fischer in Austria, and Roger Garaudy in France, all of whom Havemann quoted and admired. Havemann continued to believe, as Sartre expressed it in his *Critique of Dialectical Reason* (1960), that Marxism was the "horizon" toward which the modern world and all other philosophies were heading.[63]

Despite his fierce criticisms of the Party—even including comparisons between it and the NSDAP[64]—Havemann remained true to his vision of the DDR as "the better Germany." He never sought asylum in the West, even though he was kept under virtual house arrest for the last decade of his life, until his death in 1982.[65] In the mid-1960s, he went on to explain his change of heart toward the SED, in words that recall those of Alfred Kantorowicz, words that testify to the onetime power of the Marxist dream to capture even the strongest minds—and of the internal battle of wills that must ensue to oust the Thought Police agents after "they get inside you." Coming from a man of such great integrity and fortitude, and illustrating a much further phase of the process of "working through" the "God That Failed" disillusionment than did Kantorowicz's testimony, Havemann's statement is a stirring declaration of hope:

If one changes his opinions on important questions, it isn't enough to set forth the new views and criticize the old ones. One must inquire as to why one thought differently before, why one today thinks differently. . . . One must lay the change in one's thinking before others in all openness. Whoever seeks to give the impression that he never erred is behaving dishonestly and deserves no credit.

Before what held force for me was the principle: Truth is "partisan." I held every thought that wasn't "Marxist" to be threatening and false. Naturally I wasn't so arrogant as to judge whether certain opinions merited the characterization "Marxist" according to my own thinking. That decision was a matter for the Party. I was reared to unconditional modesty toward the collective wisdom of the Party. I believed: *Die Partei hat immer recht.* . . .

Before I was of the opinion that one could recognize a good comrade by how fast he could understand new insights of the Party and publicly campaign for them. The bad, uncertain comrades, on the other hand, were recognizable by their immodest superiority, whereby they objected and asked completely pointless questions, which one had best not even answer. The worst cowards of all, however—who already stood with one foot in the camp of the class enemy—were the unfortunates who risked criticizing the leading comrades of the party, indeed criticizing even the leading comrade. . . .

Year after year I believed myself to be a good Marxist. Precisely because I believed that, I wasn't. Today I don't believe it any more. I am in doubt, restless. I am trying to think through everything. . . .

Before [1956], [criticism of] the Party leadership was taboo for me. The Party had the right to censure and to suppress all opinions that it didn't share. Today I know that all of us, outside and inside the Party, have the right and the duty to form an independent judgment, as I have explained in my lectures.[66]

Published in the West in 1964 as *Dialectik ohne Dogma (Dialectics without Dogma)*, and quickly soaring near the top of *Der Spiegel*'s best-seller list, Havemann's lectures criticizing dialectical materialist dogma represented still another doomed attempt—in the footsteps of Ackermann, Leonhard, Harich, Bloch, Lukács and numerous others—to mark out a "third way" between SED Stalinism and western capitalism. "A spectre is haunting Europe," announced Havemann, echoing the classic lines in *The Communist Manifesto*, "the spectre of *humanistic socialism*, the spectre of the Third Way."[67]

But the call raised only the full fury of the DIAMATniks and SED Thought Police against Havemann. "Why should we permit this Socrates—he is not as smart as Socrates!—to despoil our children?" demanded Hanna Wolf, director of the SED Party College in Berlin. Like his predecessors, Havemann was branded a heretic and a revisionist for defying the "Eternal Truth" of the Party leadership's infallibility. He had warned in his lectures against the Party's approach to dissents becoming a "papist Inquisition toward Galileo"—and now the Italian communist newspaper *Unita* admiringly compared Havemann himself to a freethinking, Marxist Galileo.[68] Havemann advocated "ideological coexistence" with the West, which he defined as "engagement with what others think" and "presuppos[ing] freedom." "Reactionary regimes," Havemann declaimed to his students, "have striven at all times in history to keep the People ignorant."[69]

"The Party," replied Horst Sindermann of the SED Central Committee, "can't leave rotten eggs lying in the nest."[70] Havemann was thrown out of the SED in October 1964 because of "continued damage and an outlook foreign to the Party." He had already lost his post as Director of the Berlin Institute for Physical Chemistry for insisting on academic freedom of information and expression. "Under the cover of criticizing 'inadequacies' [in Marxism-Leninism]," explained SED Ideologist Kurt Hager, "Havemann wants to disseminate, in organized fashion, skepticism."[71] When Havemann criticized the SED in a December 1965 *Spiegel* article, suggesting both that the DDR establish opposition parties and the BRD readmit a reformed KPD (which had been banished in West Germany since the mid-1950s) as moves toward possible reunification, he was summarily dismissed from the Academy of Sciences.[72] No general protest in the universities answered the expulsion of Havemann, who had become the conscience of the post-Wall era, the Harich *and* Bloch of his generation. The intellectuals and students, let alone the general population, raised barely a whimper.

Thus did the long period of brutal force and terror tactics slip into the age of wearied accommodation: this was the key change in the attitude of the DDR populace "after the Wall." The new generation of students had been carefully screened for ideological conformity; more vocationally and technically oriented than earlier generations, neither they nor the technical elite interfered in political or Party decisions that fell outside their narrow spheres of interest. Calibrated and synchronized by Party leaders, the technical-scientific "revolution" was, finally, starting to hum along smoothly.

Looking back from 1990 on her DDR university days in the mid-1960s, Freya Klier spoke of her generation's experience of dogmatic "scientific socialism" as the core curriculum,[73] confirming Havemann's critique and suggesting how—in the same way that he himself had once coped—they fitted themselves to their Procrustean-Stalinist beds:

> Everyone who began his studies after 1961, and stayed the course, left the university damaged. . . . "Scientific communism" lasted for all of us at least three years and was not a matter of a creative engagement, but of the SED's cramming its power-preserving, self-dignifying doctrines [into us]. All of us prettified and rationalized this, in order to keep our scholarships and because we didn't know anything else. The horizon of our thinking was systematically shrunken during these years.[74]

Given this mentality, it is hardly surprising that Havemann's official unpersonhood excited no university protests; even more revealing of this slide into public resignation and inner emigration was the indifferent response of DDR students to the revolutionary events of 1968 in neighboring Czechoslovakia: the "Prague Spring."

In January 1968, the liberal Aleksandr Dubček replaced pro-Soviet hard-liner Antonin Novotny as First Secretary of the Czechoslovakian CP. Now the long Prague winter of Stalinist discontent ended, and a long-deferred process of de-Stalinization began in earnest. Dubček's program of reforms, dubbed "socialism with a human face," included freedom of travel, freedom of speech and the press, the speedy rehabilitation of victims of Stalinism, and free-market incentives. Tito voiced immediate support for Dubček's humanistic socialism, but in March, Moscow and the other Warsaw Pact nations emerged from a Soviet bloc summit meeting held in Dresden to castigate the reforms.

"A thaw is a dangerous climate for politicians," Havemann remarked. "When the old ice melts, a new, thin ice then exists."[75] In the spring of 1968, Ulbricht knew the ice was thin, and he took proper precautions that the warmest southeast winds from Prague did not reach the DDR. Indeed the SED—fully aware that Czechoslovakian intellectuals around dissident magazine *Kulturny zivot* had inspired Havemann's own thinking five years earlier—became one of the fiercest critics of Dubček's Prague Spring. Playing it safe, Ulbricht forbade entry of the German-language Prague *Volkszeitung*, and eventually also banned university student meetings; he even went so far in March as to prohibit FDJ-sponsored marches against the Vietnam War, fearing that they might turn against the regime, as had happened in Czechoslovakia, Poland, and West Germany.[76] Fearing unrest in the

DDR after the Easter week assassination attempt by a right-wing youth on 28-year-old Rudi Dutschke, the radical student leader at the Free University in West Berlin, SED restrictions on student freedoms tightened further. While revolution-minded students from Paris to Tokyo to New York to West Berlin were barricading university buildings and skirmishing with police, not a peep was heard from DDR students. Asked about the prevailing climate of order and discipline in the DDR, a proud Ulbricht announced, "All students here see only progress and sing happy songs"—like the FDJ's "Tell me where you stand!"

For the DDR revolution was long over—a revolution from above. When non-FDJ students did issue scattered calls for youth activities outside the sponsorship of the FDJ, the Minister for Higher Education replied: "Only a united youth organization led by the Party of the working class can measure up to its historical responsibility of bringing about the worldwide victory of socialism." The socialist student, declared an FDJ leader, "is class conscious, trained in modern ways, well adjusted . . . , and above all full of revolutionary passion."[77] At long last, the DDR "young revolutionary" had met Lenin's exacting standard: a comrade with a heart of fire and a brain of ice.

RELIABILITY, NOT BOLDNESS!

TRUST AND RESPONSIBILITY TO THE YOUTH!

THE YOUTH HAVE THE WORD!

The season of hope in Czechoslovakia, however, was far advanced; only brute force could freeze its progress. "They want to be national heroes," said Ulbricht of the Prague reformers. "We'll soon make heroes of them."[78] In July 1968, the Warsaw Pact nations, excepting Yugoslavia, issued a condemnation of the Prague Spring, followed by the announcements of the Brezhnev Doctrine, which authorized the CPSU to set the "line" for international socialism. An SED Politburo resolution of July 25, 1968, Ulbricht cautioned Dubček's supporters that they underestimated the "anti-socialist forces at work in their country. . . ." Ulbricht visited Dubček on August 13, warning him personally that harsh measures awaited him if he proceeded on his course.

The wait was a short one. With the NVA at its side—evoking bitter memories for Czechoslovakians of the last time, exactly three decades earlier, that German troops had invaded Prague—the Red Army marched into Czechoslovakia on August 20/21, crushing all anti-Soviet opposition and jailing Dubček and his followers. On August 22, *Neues Deutschland* falsely "exposed" Dubček as a paid agent of the West and thanked the SED "Party leadership for their Leninist vigilance toward the machinations of the counter-revolution."[79] To avoid comparison with Hitler's Czechoslovakian invasion, no DDR publication mentioned that two NVA divisions had marched on Prague.

Thus far public reaction in the DDR largely resembled that of October/November 1956: hope, then dejection and disillusion. But similarities to the events of Poland and Hungary ended there: little protest followed.[80] Instead, both professors and teachers decried the Czechoslovakian "counterrevolution" and praised the interventionist "act of peace." Declared a professor of People's Law: "The sovereignty and independence of socialist Czechoslovakia now lie in safe hands."[81] Except for a few scattered outcries by the children of prominent dissidents—including Havemann's two teenage sons, who did nothing more than daub Dubček's name on a few signs—the "young revolutionaries" of the post-Wall generation barely responded. In Erfurt and Gotha a few hundred youngsters gathered in the streets and shouted anti-Ulbricht slogans until the police arrived. In East Berlin, youths surreptitiously distributed leaflets condemning the invasion; in Frankfurt an der Oder, someone scrawled, "Up with Dubček—Down with Ulbricht."

Just a few years earlier, such protests would have been considered child's play; but, in the climate of wintry neo-Stalinist reaction provoked by the Prague Spring, the Party's response was swift and harsh. In late October, a series of secret show trials of 100 students and young intellectuals began. The defendants, who had variously expressed their solidarity with Dubček's reform communism—distributing anti-SED leaflets, painting walls with pro-Prague doggerel, and shouting pro-Dubček slogans in the streets—included the children of high-ranking Party functionaries as well as non-Party intellectuals and vocal dissidents. Among them were the 23-year-old son of the Deputy Minister of Culture (whose own father reported him to the SSD); the 18-year-old daughter of the director of the Institute of Marxism-Leninism; the two sons of Havemann, whom the defense cited (unsuccessfully) as a "harmful influence" in its plea for leniency;[82] and a 20-year-old niece of Helene Weigel, widow of Bertolt Brecht and now director of the Berliner Ensemble. Charged with "instigation hostile to the state," "smearing inflammatory slogans on buildings," and aiming to "incite citizens of the German Democratic Republic against the socialist social order," the defendants received jail terms—sometimes suspended on condition of future proper behavior—ranging from 20 to 27 months.[83]

The Central Administration of Eternal Truths had, once again, handed down its unerring verdict.

THOU SHALT RESPECT THE COLLECTIVE AND TAKE ITS CRITICISMS TO HEART!

THOU SHALT PERFORM GOOD DEEDS FOR SOCIALISM, SINCE SOCIALISM PRODUCES A BETTER LIFE FOR ALL WORKING PEOPLE!

THOU SHALT PROTECT AND INCREASE THE PROPERTY OF THE PEOPLE!

Many western observers speculated that Ulbricht had played a key role in the decision to invade Czechoslovakia. Not only did he convene the Dresden summit meeting of the Warsaw Pact in March, but he also made two special trips to Moscow to protest Dubček's reforms; certainly the "Prussian corporal," as the Czechoslovakians mockingly called him, saw the Prague Spring as a threat to his power and even to that of the SED. After the Czechoslovakian "counterrevolution" was suppressed, Ulbricht, as in 1956, left nothing to chance. This "Friend and Champion of the Youth," as Party newspapers called him and FDJ jingles affirmed ("*Wer ist mit uns jung geblieben? / Walter Ulbricht, den wir lieben!*" ["Who has stayed young like us? / Walter Ulbricht, whom we love!"]), launched a vigorous campaign to bring the youth and intelligentsia fully back into "revolutionary" lockstep. Father Ulbricht argued that the protests had been precipitated by those, like Havemann, who urged the "third way" of "ideological co-existence" with the West.[84] Ulbricht sought now to create a new "reliable young guard of revolutionaries." Announcing his goal in an impassioned October 1968 speech delivered to 150,000 JP members, he recommended "sausage communism" to them: "A tasty sausage in a solid package is preferable to the People than the coffee grounds of anti-socialist intellectuals made in Prague!" Then the JP, wearing KPD uniforms from the 1918 revolution, marched from Marx-Engels Square down Unter den Linden in a torchlight parade. Having given the JP food for thought, Ulbricht now updated his 1958 list of socialist commandments, appending four new, centrally administered Eternal Truths showing how a Young Pioneer was *ipso facto* an upstanding "young revolutionary":

> A young revolutionary proves his loyalty to his socialist Fatherland, the German Democratic Republic, through deeds.
>
> A young revolutionary heeds the motto, "Knowledge is Power," and seeks a higher education.
>
> A young revolutionary steels his character and strives to become an industrious member of socialist society.
>
> A young revolutionary is a true friend of the Soviet Union and a glowing champion of socialist internationalism.[85]

Such Party calls to serve socialism as "a matter of honor, of glory, and of heroism" continued to be sounded into the 1970s. But the times had changed; hypocritical calls for revolutionary loyalty had lost their power to move East Germans. As Klier noted, such old Marxist shibboleths provoked "only a flood of jokes . . . Hardly a soul would now raise either cheek of his backside for the honor of the Party."[86]

Still, Ulbricht's relentless "revolution" from above continued. "National defense" needs in the wake of the Czechoslovakian "counterrevolution" prompted him to take decisive action to expand compulsory military training for the 200,000-man NVA. Under a newly authorized program, a four-year pre-army training course was made compulsory for all male youths. For the first time—now that conscription could no longer drive male youths westward and that the labor shortages were easing—an 18-month draft into the NVA became mandatory, after which paramilitary service in *Betriebskampfgruppen* (factory fighting groups) or call-ups for reserve duty were slated. Henceforth, millions of DDR males aged 14 to 60 would be subject to immediate call-up for active or reserve duty.[87]

By early 1969, all pathetically modest vestiges in the DDR of the "counterrevolutionary" Prague Spring had been swept away; at the 20th anniversary celebration of the DDR in October 1969, Ulbricht showed himself in firmer control than ever.

And, finally, in this anniversary year, the longest battle in DDR education had also met with victory. As the rector of Humboldt University put it: "On the table of offerings to the Republic this year we've placed a new university."[88] The "university of the new type" had arrived: the Marxist-Leninist, polytechnical, "praxis-oriented" university, featuring close ties to industry and agriculture.

In the Land of Learning, the citadel was in secure hands.

The next several years would be known as "the Good Years" in Ulbricht's Reich, especially among Party members: growing prosperity, peace at home, increasing acceptance abroad. The biggest new success was the economy, which in the early 1970s experienced a boom similar to the BRD's *Wirtschaftswunder* of the 1950s.

Modest prosperity reigned. With a GNP of $14 billion that was rising at a healthy six percent annually, the DDR had indeed "arisen from ruins" to rank fifth among economic powers in Europe, second only to the USSR within the Soviet bloc, and ninth in the world.

Much of the credit for these successes owed to the policies of Ulbricht, whom even his enemies reluctantly acknowledged was the Lenin *and* Stalin of the DDR: Spirit *and* Welder of the nation. Hegel had once said that Germany would need a *Zwingherr*—a heroic oppressor—to impose greatness and unity on the nation.[89] Earlier generations of German historians had awarded Bismarck and Hitler this dubious honor; but now Ulbricht, as his lavish 75th birthday celebration in 1968 and his ubiquity during the DDR's 1969 anniversary gala demonstrated—again evoking uneasy whispers within even the SED leadership of a Stalin-like cult of personality (and even talk of "Ulbricht's Reich")—was coming to seem to many even better qualified. Outside the Party and even in the West, hatred had turned into a grudging respect for Old *Spitzbart*, for with the passage of years his caution and unctuousness toward Moscow had come to appear to be patience and even cleverness and foresight—and had, finally, delivered undeniable results.[90]

And yet: Alas for Ulbricht, his days in power were numbered: he would not reap the full glory of the DDR's triumphs. The man who had always shown extreme circumspection and vigilance, especially toward the Kremlin, would be undone by his own hubris.

In the years after Khrushchev's fall from power in 1964, Old *Spitzbart* increasingly irritated Premier Leonid Brezhnev and President Aleksei Kosygin. Especially annoying to them were Ulbricht's frequent reminders that he had headed his country longer than any other Soviet bloc leader and that no other living communist leader had ever met the great Vladimir Ilych.[91] Moreover, the new CPSU leaders bristled at Ulbricht's growing personality cult; they upheld the Leninist principle of collective leadership far more than even Khrushchev. Nor did the new keepers of the Kremlin approve of Ulbricht's tendency to try to elevate the DDR above its traditional junior-partner status vis-à-vis the USSR. Indeed, Ulbricht's seniority among Soviet bloc leaders and the DDR's expanding economic strength induced him to imply occasionally that East Germany could serve as an alternative model for communist nations, an ironic example of Ulbricht himself touting a version of the allegedly counter-revolutionary "special German road" to socialism.

Such personal tensions exacerbated the substantive differences between Brezhnev and Ulbricht over *Deutschlandpolitik*, the main policy issue that divided them: Ulbricht wanted a settlement on West Berlin and relations with West Germany highly favorable to the DDR; the USSR wanted a deal with West Germany that chiefly promoted Moscow's own geopolitical and economic interests. Brezhnev prevailed, of course, and Ulbricht lost his Party position as First Secretary in May 1971, retaining only ceremonial state posts.

Indeed fate dealt the weakening 78-year-old Ulbricht a harsh blow: he did not remain in power long enough to gain lasting credit for the policies of his final decade, policies that would soon bring the DDR worldwide diplomatic and athletic recognition. Forced out by Brezhnev, he fell overnight from his towering height, becoming now an unperson himself—"a political corpse," remarked one observer—from virtually the day of his demotion. "De-Ulbrichtization" was swift and thoroughgoing; whereas the basic SED ideology manual of 1971 quoted him more than 100 times, the 1973 manual contained not a single reference to him.[92] "*Walter Ulbricht—das sind wir alle!*" the old Party slogan had run. "Walter who?" would soon be closer to the mark.

And with his death in August 1973, Ulbricht did not even live to witness his dearest, decades-long dream become reality: the DDR's entry into the United Nations in September and its formal exchange of diplomatic representatives with Bonn the following June. Like Moses, the SED patriarch had delivered the DDR its Ten Commandments (plus four) of socialist morality and had led it out of the desert of economic chaos and diplomatic nonrecognition; but he would not live to enter the Promised Land of universal international acceptance and respect.

Instead Erich Honecker would be the Joshua who would preside over the breakthroughs with the West—the triumphs at the Munich Olympics, the reception of dozens of western ambassadors in East Berlin, the 1987 state visit to Bonn. Ulbricht's favorite ever since 1958, when he had sided with Ulbricht against Ulbricht's moderate Politburo rivals, Honecker had been the official SED *Kronprinz* since the Seventh Party Congress in 1967, and had bided his time to succeed Old *Spitzbart*. Like Ulbricht, Honecker had been no fan of Willy Brandt's *Ostpolitik;* he had criticized the West German SPD leadership ferociously during 1969/70, fearing (correctly) Brandt's strategy of liberalizing the DDR by enmeshing it in diplomatic and economic agreements with Bonn. But Honecker still had the flexibility that the aging, prideful Ulbricht had lost by 1971: the younger man quickly grasped that Brezhnev was determined to have a comprehensive treaty with West Germany as part of his western détente initiative, and that only a pliable partner as SED head would be tolerable to him.

At the Eighth Party Congress in May 1971, Honecker secured his authority, replacing numerous Ulbricht footmen with his own old "FDJnik" cronies. Among his advisers was his wife Margot Honecker, head of the Ministry of Education since November 1963, candidate member of the Politburo, and the only woman in the Council of Ministers.

Working together throughout the 1970s and '80s, the Honeckers would always take special interest in education and youth issues. And together, they would superintend the era of "real existing socialism"—when fully developed socialism became, at last, a purported reality in the First German Workers' and Peasants' State—and marked the final long movement in the rise and fall of the DDR.

The Herr und Frau Honecker Era

Erst kommt das Fressen, dann kommt die Moral.
[First grub, then morality.]

Brecht,
The Three-Penny Opera (1928)

On August 3, 1973, a feeble, 80-year-old Walter Ulbricht died of heart failure in the Wandlitz hospital in East Berlin, a fact little remarked, indeed scarcely noticed, even by SED officials: Ulbricht had been politically dead for two years.[93] Less than a mile away, in the former Walter Ulbricht Stadium, recently renamed the Stadium of the World Youth, festivities at the 10th gathering of the quadrennial World Festival of Youth and Students continued without even a moment of silence; at the Youth Ball that evening the only official notice was a sign announcing that "Walter Ulbricht's last wish was that this festival be conducted successfully to its end."[94]

The World Festival of 1973 was the first youth festival that the DDR had hosted since 1951—and the largest international event of any kind of the entire Honecker era.[95] And it was Erich and Margot Honecker's particular triumph, the SED's jubilant unveiling of the newest "new Germany"—an internationally recognized DDR—before the world. "The host of this tremendous gathering is our German Democratic Republic," announced Honecker in his greeting to Festival delegates, "and this year we now have almost 90 countries that have established formal diplomatic relations with us." The nine-day Festival, wrote *Der Spiegel*, "illustrates the end of the Era of Ulbricht, and the openness, even opulence, with which the DDR this week presents itself to the world."[96]

Another new era was at hand.

On Saturday, July 28, 100,000 young people from 130 countries—led by the Vietnamese delegates, who ignited strings of firecrackers to symbolize American guns firing on their people—marched from Alexanderplatz through the Karl Marx Allee into the Stadium of the World Youth, their placards blazoning the Festival's theme: anti-imperialism. "Away with the U.S. Bases." "All Hail the Memory of the Martyrs of the Sudanese National Democratic Front." "We ALL Decide the World's Future." Evoking memories of the Soviet-sponsored Olympiads of years past, a runner carried a "Solidarity Torch" into the stadium, lighting a "Solidarity Flame," whereupon 100,000 Blueshirts clapped their hands and shouted in unison: *"Friede, Freundschaft, Solidarität!"*

Familiar Party lines prevailed in the Festival agitprop. The official slogans of the Festival sounded no new notes: "Anti-Imperialist Solidarity, Peace, and Friendship!" "*Volk*, Youth, and Students of the DDR Are Building Socialism!" An official "solidarity opera" celebrated a workers' strike; the anti-imperialist theme of the "Festival of Happiness," as the SED proclaimed it, was also trumpeted in the official anthem, specially written for the Festival by a loyal teacher:

> *Festival des Glückes*
> *Freundschaft uns vereint!*
> *Festival des Kampfes*
> *Schlagt den Klassenfeind!*
> [Festival of Happiness
> We are united in friendship!
> Festival of Battle
> Defeat the class enemy!]

The Young Pioneers of Socialism attended official functions, lots of them—the FDJ had organized 1,542 political and cultural events, many of them meetings to express "solidarity" with the youth of Vietnam, Laos, Cambodia, Mozambique, and numerous Third World nations. "United in friendship," delegates joined discussion groups devoted to Young Health Workers, Young Technicians and Engineers, and Young Metal Workers; university youth checked in regularly at the Students Accuse Imperialism Center. *Gemütlichkeit* reigned; no imminent East-West confrontation threatened to disturb it. But this did not prevent long-haired Blueshirts from arguing spiritedly in the streets with long-haired *Jusos* (Young Socialists, affiliated with the West German SPD) about the wisdom of gradualist versus revolutionary roads to the socialist utopia.[97]

In contrast to the 1951 Festival, which welcomed a lonely tribe of only three dozen American delegates—mostly from New York City—more than 300 Americans from 30 states attended the 1973 Festival, almost half of them black. Angela Davis, honorary chair, a striking presence in her Afro and flowing dashiki, stood proudly next to Herr Honecker as he hailed her as a representative of "the Other America." Fellow "Other Americans" included Jarvis Tyner and Stoney Cooks of the Young Workers Liberation League, affiliated with the American Communist Party; actors Ossie Davis and Ruby Dee; and the Rev. Ben Chavis of the Wilmington Ten. "The Festival is an eloquent expression of the changed relationships in the world," Angela Davis proclaimed, adding that "the magnificent victory of the Vietnamese people over the U.S. government" testified to "an erosion of the strength of imperialism." Later she told the press: "I have had three unforgettable experiences in my life: my experience as a member of the Communist Party, my release from prison by the power of international solidarity, and the Youth and Student Festival in Berlin."[98]

The "Festival of Happiness" was unforgettable for more than political reasons. The buoyant atmosphere in the Land of Youth resembled less a traditional communist rally than Woodstock on the Elbe, a brief DDR Summer of Love. At least 500,000 East and West Germans—plus 150,000 foreign visitors and 25,646 official foreign guests, among them such international celebrities as Yasir Arafat—cavorted and kissed in the Alexanderplatz fountains, roamed up and down Karl Marx Allee, and shouted "*Freundschaft!*" on Unter den Linden. Pegging their transistor radios to the DDR's western-oriented Youth Radio DT 64, the young Builders of Socialism relaxed to the deafening beat of western and East bloc rock bands. Or they sat in the grass, listening to The Puhdys perform their melodious socialist realist hit, "Ahead is the Future," or to the hard-driving Klaus-Renft-Combo condemn imperialism in "The Chains Grow Tighter."[99] (In the spring of 1973, the DDR had begun, once again, pushing its own German rock, officially supervised by the *Section Rockmusik* of the Ministry of Culture.)[100]

"This will be a party of joyfulness!" Erich Honecker had declaimed on opening day. Was this the Erich Honecker who had fought rock'n'roll in the 1960s? Who had masterminded the construction of the Wall, hounded the intellectuals, and figured prominently in the fall of Dubček and the death of the Prague Spring? The model apparatchik who had so perfected his invisibility under Ulbricht that DDR burghers didn't even have any jokes about him?

On the face of it, Honecker had hardly seemed the man to lead the DDR into the new era of détente. Lacking Ulbricht's standing both nationally and internationally, Honecker had never run a ministry or held formal office after leaving the FDJ in 1955. True, he had overseen the SSD and NVA throughout the 1960s, reporting to the Politburo on activities in three crucial areas: state security, the armed forces, and youth affairs. But his grasp of economic and technical questions was limited; he was a strategist and ideologist. He was known, like Ulbricht, to have feared the embrace of the West German SPD after Brandt became chancellor in 1969, interpreting Brandt's *Ostpolitik* as "wanting to get a foot in the other fellow's door. First they want to make themselves look open-minded and objective, then they want 'contacts' below what they call the threshold of international recognition to lull our potential vigilance."[101] And in February 1970, even as inter-German détente loomed on the horizon, he had launched an even more violent attack on the SPD leadership, fearing with Ulbricht that uncontrollable pressures for domestic liberalization would follow.

All this notwithstanding, Moscow had accepted Ulbricht's choice of successor without demurral. The Kremlin was pleased by the new leader's embrace of Lenin's principle of collective leadership and explicit disavowal of a cult of personality; in a deliberate, and, of course, politically necessary move, Honecker had assumed at first only one of Ulbricht's offices, his Party title. Ulbricht's state offices had gone to other politicians, such as Prime Minister Willi Stoph, Honecker's main rival. Stoph had led the way to *Deutschlandpolitik* and met personally with Willy Brandt in March 1970 in Erfurt; the tension between Stoph and Honecker was an open secret in East Berlin. DDR power politics in the 1960s thus resembled that of the USSR a decade earlier, when Brezhnev and Aleksei Kosygin had vied for supremacy. Just as Brezhnev, using the Party as his base, had outflanked Kosygin by the late 1960s, so Honecker, as Party leader, outmaneuvered Stoph within two years. It was a Honecker fully in control who greeted the 1973 Festival—a very different Honecker than the invisible apparatchik of the Ulbricht era.[102]

In 1971, when he was named First Secretary of the SED, Honecker had seemed the quintessential Number 2 man—indeed, in American terms, a career vice president: modest, diligent, unassuming, obedient. One of his few touches of personality was his old-fashioned Saarland straw hat. Little noticed previously, it began to draw frequent public comment across the border. Western commentators observed that it evoked a vague nostalgia among Germans, as though alluding to Honecker's youth in the West and the tragedy of divided *Deutschland;* indeed it softened his hard-liner reputation, helping project a solicitous, even warm image.[103] For nearly a decade, this new reputation would grow. Honecker himself was known to be nostalgic, and Party stories began to circulate about how young Erich had delivered newspapers for the KPD when he was eight, how he had shunned religion for Marxism and played as the little drummer boy in the KJVD brass band,[104] how *die Nummer Eins* of the Party, as he would now be called, relished traditional German pork knuckles and sauerkraut washed down with buttermilk, loved hunting, and enjoyed playing the card game *Skat.* Given his origins in the Saarland, now part of the Bundesrepublik, the West German press dubbed him "our German brother" and "*unser Erich*"; some DDR citizens, half-affectionately and half-mockingly, would privately refer to their leader—often with a wide grin and quick shake of the head—as "Honi."

No one had ever referred to Ulbricht—except with withering ridicule—as "Walter," let alone "Ulbie." The difference was refreshing to many DDR citizens. Formerly viewed as the contemptible architect of the Wall and the dutiful son of Ulbricht, Honecker now came to be seen as a *Hoffnungsträger* (carrier of hope) and a liberal. His "former" calculating ambitiousness and rigid conservatism were generally excused in the West as the cold warrior role required of Ulbricht's protégé. Western reports of the machinations that enabled him to rise so quickly after 1945, revealed in a 1971 Honecker biography by a former FDJ assistant who had defected, were largely overlooked; vague charges that Honecker was involved in the SSD kidnapping of onetime FDJ colleague and rival Robert Bialek were ignored.[105] By now, Honecker was firmly entrenched. He owed his rise to Ulbricht and his durability to his own patronage power; like Stalin, his onetime "beloved leader of the workers of the entire world," he had amassed a legion of loyalists in the Party apparatus due to his influence over appointments.[106]

And no one was more loyal to the Party than his wife and comrade, Margot Honecker, Minister of Education. But the "First Lady" of the DDR, as she was known in the western European press, was less popular than "Honi," her fierce conservatism and ideological tenacity, if anything, outdoing that of her mild-mannered husband. "It is our task to pass on those spiritual and moral values to youth that will produce a socialist society," she declared, defending her forced adoption policy, whereby children of politically suspect parents were given to loyal SED families.[107] To her, the purpose of education was nothing more or less than the formation of "socialist personalities."[108]

Like her husband, Margot Feist was born into a communist family. But she grew up in Halle on the Saale in Saxony-Anhalt, a region that would become the DDR. Her father was a shoemaker and, even during the Nazi era, a communist functionary in the illegal KPD (and served a seven-year prison term for high treason, including four years in Buchenwald).[109] Offered a training practicum to become a teacher in 1941, 14-year-old Margot turned it down, instead taking nonideological jobs as a telephone operator and typist. After the war's end, she joined the KPD and founded an anti-fascist youth committee in Halle; by 1946, she was a member of the FDJ regional leadership. She was just 22 years old when, in 1949, as head of the Young Pioneers and the youngest FDJ delegate in the *Volkskammer*, SED authorities chose her to congratulate Wilhelm Pieck in a public ceremony on his inauguration as the first president of the DDR. In 1950, she became secretary of the Central Committee of the FDJ, where she worked closely with her boss, Herr Honecker. Erich left his wife, Edith Baumann, a Social Democrat, for Margot, who bore his second daughter in 1951;[110] Honecker soon divorced his wife and married Margot in 1953. She advanced quickly thereafter: department head in the Ministry of Education at 27; candidate member of the Politburo at 29; Assistant Minister of Education at 31. In 1963, at the age of 36, she rose to Minister of Education and a full member of the Central Committee; she became the so-called First Lady of the DDR in 1971.[111] Known for her charm and elegant style, Frau Honecker's blue-rinse hair and expensive clothes distinguished her in the drab SED Central Committee; she defied the clichés of the joyless, repressed communist female functionary, even when she exhibited rabid constancy to the Party. Unlike her inconspicuous predecessor, Lotte Ulbricht, Ulbricht's second and long-time wife, Margot cultivated a high public profile and wielded considerable political influence, especially among hard-liners, even beyond education: for style and clout, she became something close to a DDR combination of Raisa Gorbachev and Hillary Rodham Clinton.

Erich and Margot: carrier of hope and purveyor of ideological orthodoxy. Together they embodied the contradictory DDR in the early 1970s and its attempted reconciliations: liberalism toward western culture and fidelity to Marxism-Leninism. The 1973 Festival demonstrated the new unwritten "don't ask, don't tell" commandment for "young revolutionaries" during the early Honecker era: Thou art granted a western "private" life, if thou leadest a communist life in public.

Two liberal domestic programs launched during 1971–73 bolstered Erich Honecker's image as a *Hoffnungsträger*. Downplaying the technical-scientific revolution and the buildup of industry in his opening speech at the Eighth Party Congress in May 1971, Honecker had instead stressed consumer satisfaction, inaugurating a new policy, dubbed "consumer communism" in the West.[112] "A Better Quality of Life for the Citizens" was Honecker's slogan for a program that emphasized the service sector and extensive business cooperation with the West. Ulbricht had promised, and partly delivered on, "sausage communism"; DDR citizens, impressed with the smorgasbord of western wares newly available in the early '70s, welcomed what they termed Honecker's "goulash socialism."

If "consumer communism" gained Honecker favor from the DDR populace, his declaration of openness to artistic experiment and the literary avant garde won him supporters in the intelligentsia. Soon after his elevation to First Secretary, in December 1971, he uttered two sentences that created an excited stir: "If the starting point is the firm position of socialism, there can, in my opinion, be no taboos in the field of art and literature. That concerns questions of content as well as of style—in short: the question of artistic excellence."[113] In later years, exegetes would pore over every phrase in these sentences: What did "in my opinion" mean? What defined a "starting point"? What constituted a "firm" socialist position?

Was this yet another side of the new Honecker in the making? In the 1950s and '60s, Honecker was known to have had little respect for intellectuals, artists, and professors, once provoking Johannes Becher to dismiss him as "an arrogant, egotistical numbskull."[114] The "correct class perspective," Honecker held, was "more important than book knowledge."[115] Still, despite the uncertainties over Honecker's sudden turn, the immediate effect of his new dispensation was to set in motion a cultural thaw that soon witnessed the publication of such works as Ulrich Plenzdorf's *Die neuen Leiden des jungen W.* (*The New Sufferings of Young W.*), a work updating Goethe about an East German Werther; Carl Heinz Danziger's *Die Partei hat immer recht*, a systematic assault on the SED literary Establishment; Stefan Heym's *Der König David Bericht* (*The King David Report*), a trenchant satire of Stalinism; and Völker Braun's *Unvollendete Geschichte* (*Unfinished Story*), a controversial novella sharply critical of both the Party and the socialist state.

Moreover, as we have already seen, the foreign policy breakthroughs associated with *Deutschlandpolitik*—policies that had, until 1971, been more resisted than supported by Honecker—worked to his advantage during the early 1970s. "Honi," rather than the forgotten *Spitzbart*, was generally credited with bringing the DDR "in from the cold"; until 1973, the year of Ulbricht's death, the DDR had remained in relative isolation. That year alone, in the aftermath of the Basic Treaty signed in December 1972 with the BRD, 54 nations recognized the DDR; in the previous 24 years, only 40 nations had done so, most of them communist. In 1973, Honecker began to speak of "real existing socialism," and many DDR citizens believed—now that Ulbricht was gone—that while it certainly did not yet exist, "real" socialism might at least now really begin to exist.

Hope sprang eternal even among liberal educators and students. Indeed the honeymoon with the intellectuals carried over partly into education and youth policy, which now entered a sixth period (1971–77) characterized by a more liberal stance toward western-imports in youth culture, alongside an insistence on ideological orthodoxy outside cultural matters. Now came a philosophical turn away from cybernetics toward Marxism-Leninism, as communist morality received greater attention than DDR polytechnics. Now came a growing stress on the duties of "young revolutionaries," as ideologists decided that high worker performance and political reliability were fully compatible. Now came a drive to create an elite Party *Apparat*, as the SED consolidated its hold on every major institution of society.

The shift in priorities reflected Honecker's own predilections. As the "systematic era" of integrated polytechnical education gave way to the "early Honecker era" of ideological adjustment, the downgrading of the scientific-technical revolution resulted in a more relaxed period for most DDR students and educators, especially non-Party members, one of increased private freedoms and greater public responsibilities.

In January 1974, the SED passed a new *Jugendgesetz* (youth law), the "Law on the Participation of Youth in the Shaping of the Developing Society," which superseded the 1964 *Jugendgesetz* and represented the most significant youth legislation of the Honecker era. Combining indulgence of western culture with Marxist-Leninist orthodoxy, it typified the balancing act that the SED was attempting in all policy areas. Article 30, for example, enjoined the FDJ to provide "good-quality discotheques" and to improve standards of popular entertainment. But the 1974 *Jugendgesetz* also codified Ulbricht's Ten Commandments and four precepts, giving legal expression to the increased duties of "young revolutionaries":

> The three revolutionary tasks facing the younger generation are to strengthen friendship with the USSR, to demonstrate anti-imperialist solidarity, and to shape advanced socialist society. Their fulfillment requires the readiness to serve, initiative, and a clear political perspective.[116]

Enshrining such responsibilities in the 1974 *Jugendgesetz* testified not only to the Party's new emphasis on Marxism-Leninism, but also to the growing confidence of the Party in DDR youth.

WE ARE UNITED IN FRIENDSHIP!

TRUST AND RESPONSIBILITY TO THE YOUTH!
THE YOUTH HAVE THE WORD!

Just a few months earlier, the World Youth Festival, at which a draft of the new *Jugendgesetz* had been circulated, had demonstrated how DDR youth were already serving as good comrades to the USSR and contributing to anti-imperialist solidarity; both goals were also reflected in the increased economic cooperation between the DDR and the Soviet bloc. Trade between the DDR and the USSR increased by 50 percent between 1971 and 1975; trade with COMECON (Council for Mutual Economic Assistance) countries increased by 90 percent between 1972 and 1975.[117] The 25th anniversary of the DDR's founding in October 1974—by which time the DDR was recognized by 104 nations, including the United States a scant two weeks earlier—announced a crucial change in the 1968 constitution, one that brought the DDR and USSR even closer—and separated the DDR and BRD even further. Article 1 of the 1968 constitution had stated: "The DDR is a socialist state of the German nation." The revision specified: "The DDR is a socialist state of workers and peasants." As part of *Abgrenzung* (delimitation), Honecker's policy to reap economic advantages from the West while restricting its political influence on the DDR, mention of German reunification and of the "German nation" was now deleted. The word "German" was also replaced by "DDR" in the names of numerous state institutions. For instance, the German Academy of Sciences became the Academy of Sciences of the DDR. The National Front of Democratic Germany became the DDR National Front. German Radio became Voice of the DDR.[118]

But the technological race conflicted with such political decisions and led to worrisome, undialectical contradictions: Even as the SED was disengaging from the West and integrating more fully into COMECON, the equally important goal of keeping economic pace with the West—whether in consumerism or in the technical-scientific revolution—clearly demanded doing the reverse.

As Freya Klier points out, the DDR's pseudo-egalitarian pedagogy had backed it into a corner. Two key slogans of yesteryear continued to have psychological force: "Reliability, not boldness!" and "We leave nobody behind!" Pedagogy based on those mottoes had created an elite of conformists, unfamiliar with creative thinking and uncomfortable with entrepreneurial decision-making.[119] Now, as Cold War pedagogy became clearly outdated, educators rushed to develop a new didactics that echoed the once-despised bourgeois "endowment" theories associated with aptitudes and gifts. The old SED bromide had been: To everyone and everything the same. Now the new faith proclaimed: Some children are different. The old SED dogma had been: There are no differences in gifts or in development. Now the new doctrine held: Children are variously gifted. The old SED shibboleth had been: The teacher represents the Party's will. Now the new wisdom maintained: Students and teachers are partners in learning, and the teacher too is an individual.

But "the new continent of individuality," as Klier notes, was explored only in the case of a few thousand gifted students or exceptionally valuable teachers. Now the system would happily "leave behind" the 2.6 million "average" achievers. But preferential treatment presumed a "firm class perspective"; even as the Party urged

intellectual innovation, its tight screening process and school indoctrination practices ensured political reliability. Exceptions would, however, be tolerated for the
elite athletes, students, teachers, and coaches who produced or guided coveted
Spitzenleistungen (top performances). As Klier puts it:

> The highly gifted child need not be an obedient Young Pioneer, and even
> disapproved characteristics like unwillingness to conform or reservations
> about the FDJ could be tolerated if he or she possessed scientific talent. . . .
> The elite students enjoy the privilege of being seen as individual personalities.
> Nobody gets excited if they use a western bag for carrying their lunch.[120]

And so, students who attended special schools received a reduced period of military service; top athletes or *Abitur* examinees skipped the army altogether. (But
average students who barely qualified for university and expressed "conflicts of
conscience" about military service often had to spend double the time—three
years—in a non-combat military assignment before gaining university entrance.)
This exceptionalism was even enshrined in the new DDR pedagogy. One manual
for special schools for the gifted advised teachers:

> Gifted, especially highly gifted children, possess a different personality struc-
> ture. We are responsible for recognizing this distinctive shape of conditions
> and developing distinctive pedagogical responses to them.[121]

By the 1970s, as education became ever more important for producing the politically reliable technical and Party elite, the majority of elementary and secondary
school teachers came from two sources: teachers' and *Stasi* families. An amazing
40 percent of all women students in higher education were daughters of DDR
women teachers. Class differences between the educated and workers in the Workers' and Peasants' State widened further, even though the SED now defined all
Party functionaries as "workers" and called anyone who had ever held a full-time
manual job (even 50 years previously) a "worker."[122]

Meanwhile, Herr and Frau Honecker's honeymoon with the DDR public appeared as if it might turn into a tolerably decent marriage. Although growth had
slowed after the 1973 Arab oil embargo, the economy was still strong. *Abgrenzung*
was integrating the DDR more completely into the socialist bloc without preventing beneficial economic cooperation with the West. Scattered "troublemakers" and
asozial (anti-social, delinquent) youth were still around; but workers, intellectuals,
and students were generally quiet. The single unsettling issue was a new problem
with emigration: in August 1975, both Honecker and Brezhnev had signed the
final agreement of the Helsinki Conference on European Security and Cooperation,
which guaranteed freedom of travel to citizens of signatory nations. Though few
in the West expected a DDR policy change from this, 100,000 DDR citizens had
taken the commitment seriously—much to Honecker's public embarrassment—
and applied to emigrate. After an initial period of relaxed regulations that generated hopes of greater liberalization among DDR youth, Honecker tightened emigration criteria, effectively disqualifying all applicants who did not already have

families in the West. So the illegal escape attempts continued. In 1976, at least 10,000 citizens—1,000 of them between 15–20 years old—sat in jails as political prisoners, guilty of illegal attempted escape to the West.

Nevertheless, after the DDR's spectacular second-place finish in gold medals (trailing only the USSR) at the Montreal Olympics in the summer of 1976, Honi's popularity and power crested to an all-time high. His authority among Party members was so great that he added to his portfolio that fall the leadership offices of the other two key DDR institutions: the National Defense Council and the Council of State. Within just five years, he had attained a level of power that took Ulbricht more than 15, and without Party purges—and without a single rival in sight. As if to top off his success, the single list received still another all-time high of "yes" votes in the 1976 election: 99.86 percent.

But the popularity of the General Secretary came to an outraged end on November 17, 1976, when he moved against protest-singer Wolf Biermann—still a prominent "troublemaker" after a decade of official censure—stripping him of his DDR citizenship while he was on a tour of West Germany.[123]

Biermann had not appeared in concert in the DDR since 1966,[124] and was still prohibited from recording or publishing in the DDR. But he was nonetheless managing to get his recordings and writings smuggled to the West, from which they soon reached the DDR via radio and underground publications. And he was still tweaking the SED with singles like his 1967 "Stasi Ballad" (addressed to "My truest fans . . . / Who ensure my immortality").[125] His albums, such as *No Use Waiting for Better Times* (1973) and *Chaussee Street 131* (1975)[126]—both recorded for CBS Records—were immediately condemned by the SED as "pornographic" and "anti-socialist." Still, on condition that he forego playing his more "objectionable" songs, Biermann had received permission to appear at a Cologne concert to be attended by 6,500 fans and broadcast live on West German radio and TV. Defiantly playing his preferred repertoire anyway, Biermann then learned that the SED had taken the opportunity to lock him out of the country. (Many observers later argued that the unexpected deal was a ploy to lure Biermann to leave the DDR: knowing that—agreement or no agreement—Biermann would be Biermann, the SED would have an excuse for refusing him re-entry for publicly "defaming the DDR.")[127]

But Honecker was totally unprepared for the national and international outcry against his move. Biermann was more than just a popular singer. Originally from Hamburg, 17-year-old Wolf had emigrated to the East in 1953, arriving on March 5, the day of Stalin's death.[128] Traveling against the flow of refugees that year, Biermann continued to believe—despite the evidence of June 17[129]—in the dream of *das bessere Deutschland*, of a communist Germany, his father's dream. "I was looking for a Fatherland," he later explained. "Or should I say, the land of my father." Imprisoned by the Nazis for being both Jewish and communist, Dagobert Biermann had been a shipyard worker, whose Party assignment was to sabotage ships carrying weapons for the Nazi bomber squadrons of the Legion Condor, which Hitler was sending to aid Franco in the Spanish civil war. Arrested and sent to a labor camp, Biermann Sr. was murdered in 1942 in Auschwitz, as were

20 of young Wolf's relatives. For years afterward, Frau Biermann would tell her son every day: "Wolfie, you must never forget your father's murder."[130]

Biermann never did. In his early 20s, he began composing songs condemning social evils and state tyrannies of all sorts. His mother's admonitions fed the rage in his protest songs, which often seemed like diatribes or tirades to outsiders. Bristling with curses and cacophony, they had little melody, swinging from ecstasy to melancholy. All this made the idealistic, sometimes disillusioned Biermann— a short, rumpled man known by his droopy Mexican moustache and Spanish guitar—seem like a miniature German Don Quixote. His spiritual mentor was Brecht, the radiant "sun"[131] that he never met and whose death in 1956 came a year before Biermann began a stint as an assistant to the new director of Brecht's Berliner Ensemble. Biermann developed his stage presence as an actor-director at the Berlin Workers' and Students' Theater during 1961/62, where he worked while studying economics, philosophy, and mathematics at Humboldt University (1955– 63). From the SED's standpoint, of course, Biermann should have studied diplomacy. An SED candidate member, Biermann was disqualified from Party membership in 1963; authorities banned him from performing, publishing, and foreign travel after the SED Central Committee attack on him in December 1965.

Nevertheless—or precisely for these reasons—Biermann enchanted a new generation. Already a folk hero to DDR youth by the late 1960s, Biermann the rogue troubadour might have become the dissidents' successor to Havemann, indeed the public conscience of the '60s generation—a lowbrow Harich or even a pop Brecht. Instead, he was forced to lay low. For the SED, Biermann too, like Harich, had crossed the line from dissident to renegade, a mistake that Havemann and Brecht never made; and unlike the elder pair, neither Biermann nor Harich were protected by a history of distinguished service to the Party, high international prestige, or close connections with SED higher-ups or the CPSU elite in Moscow.

Still, Biermann's forced expatriation unleashed a storm of protest, abroad as well as at home. The organs of the French, Spanish, Italian, and Swedish CPs criticized the SED's decision, as did leading left-wing personalities such as Sartre, de Beauvoir, Yves Montand, Ernst Mandel, Peter Weiss, Rudi Dutschke, and even Joan Baez, who had, in concert, publicly castigated the SED's silencing of Biermann when she played East Berlin in the early 1970s. Factory workers in West Berlin issued calls for solidarity with Biermann. In the DDR itself, a dozen intellectuals immediately released an open letter objecting to his expatriation; 150 more artists signed within days. The signatories included Christa Wolf, Stefan Heym, Stephan Hermlin, Sarah Kirsch, Günter Kunert, Heiner Muller, Rolf Schneider, Jürgen Fuchs, and Jurek Becker. Havemann, a friend of Biermann, also signed, and then published an article in *Der Spiegel* that criticized Biermann's expatriation.[132]

The organized protest was the most serious since 1956. But the Party leadership withstood the international criticism and responded to the domestic opposition harshly: Biermann's supporters variously endured imprisonment, house arrest, and expulsion from the DDR Writer's Union.

Honecker's "blue period" was over. Now it was back to leaden gray, as a new cultural winter set in. Havemann was put under 24-hour surveillance; dozens of artists and intellectuals now chose exile and followed Biermann westward during 1977/78: actress Eve Marie Hagen (one of Biermann's many lovers) and her singer-daughter Nina Hagen; actresses Dagmar Graf and Katharina Thalbach; Berliner Ensemble director Einar Schleff; comedian Eberhard Cohrs; composer Tilo Medek; rock star Klaus Renft, lead singer in the Klaus-Renft-Combo; film star and ballad singer Manfred Krug; writers Siegmar Faust, Bernd Jentzsch, Erich Loest, Klaus Schlesinger, and Jurek Becker; acclaimed poets Reiner Kunze and Sarah Kirsch; and author Thomas Brasch, the deputy culture minister's son who had been jailed in 1968 for his pro-Dubček gesture. Rudolph Bahro, a DDR economist and youth official, was jailed for two years, before being exiled for publishing in *Der Spiegel* passages from his manuscript, *Die Alternative*, a severe critique of the Party apparatus of the USSR and DDR.[133]

The intellectual exodus put an end to Honecker's program of cultural liberalization, and he would never recover the intellectuals' support; in the next decade at least 350 artists and cultural figures left the DDR.[134] Indeed, as had happened before in the DDR, Honecker's loosening of the reins had ultimately led to a heightening of tensions in his relations with the intelligentsia. As in the Ulbricht era, dissident intellectuals were hereafter treated as enemies of the state, though they were usually exiled rather than jailed (or, if possible, *freigekauft* [bought free] by the BRD, i.e., "sold" to Bonn, at prices ranging up to $20,000). A revision in the criminal code made passing information to western journalists punishable by 2 to 12 years' imprisonment. All this contributed to the continuing exodus of the DDR's leading intellectuals. "Our Erich" had reverted to type: dogmatic conservative.

Honi and Margot's Good Years with the DDR public were now over too. The discord spilled into violent public expression in 1977, during the October 7 celebration of the DDR's founding. Chanting "Wolf Biermann!" and "Russians go home!" 3,000 young people at an Alexanderplatz concert rioted, resulting in hundreds of arrests and 200 injuries; four *Vopos* and nine youths died in the melee. It was the first instance of mass unrest in DDR streets since 1953.[135]

The Alexanderplatz brawl revealed that, beneath the placid gray surface, little had really changed since 1961—or 1953. To mollify restless youth, the SED made some concessions in pop programming: formerly scorned, ideologically incorrect western music was now played, even at political rallies; soon even disco and new wave were in. Soon FDJ official Hartmut König could rewrite history and proudly declare: "German rock had its birthplace in the DDR." The Party temporarily drew the line at punk, however, with bands like Itch in Magdeburg and Sewage in Weimar limited to small venues.[136] But in the next decade, punk and every other western music craze would sweep the DDR. "Agit-socialist" rock groups like Karat and Silly would garner state recording contracts and promotional tours in the West if their music contained enough thumps at neutron bombs and Reaganism; in 1980, *Neues Deutschland* would eulogize John Lennon lavishly as a proletarian champion and Vietnam War opponent.[137] At the same time, aggressive *Szenesprache* ("scene" language)—featuring German youth slang like "*Scheissspiesserladen*" ("shitty philistine joint") and "*Null Bock*" ("no way" or "I don't wanna")—would fill the song lyrics of bands like Rosa Extra.[138] And the new-wave band Pankow would replace Klaus-Renft as the star bad-boy group of the 1980s, with hits like "*Komm aus'm Arsch*" ("Out of the Ass") and the album *Hans Makes Good*, the story of "Hans Nihilist," roaring the rage of a generation.[139]

With the reins loosened on DDR popcult programming, East German youth seemed mollified. No new instances of violence erupted, and most foreign observers dismissed the Alexanderplatz incident as little more than a Friday night of drunken revelry. Within the SED and the Soviet bloc, Honecker still appeared invulnerable, indeed perhaps stronger than ever. When he turned 65 in August 1977,[140] West German commentators judged him at the zenith of his power.[141] Not only did he now possess the leading offices of the Party and state, but he also enjoyed Brezhnev's unwavering support—a level of power and prestige that Ulbricht had not attained until near the end of his career.

Under the circumstances, it was therefore understandable that neither Herr nor Frau Honecker had worried overmuch the previous August about a tragic incident near Margot's hometown of Halle, which, however, aroused much distress among church leaders and church youth. As a protest against communist barriers preventing religious instruction in school and young Christians' admission to higher education, Oscar Brusewitz, a pastor and youth minister previously jailed for helping youths in trouble with the authorities, doused himself with gasoline and set himself afire in the town square of Zeitz. A sign at his side read: "The churches accuse communism of oppressing Christian young people."[142]

Neues Deutschland reported the death as a private matter—the suicide of a "mentally disturbed man"—but thousands of grief-stricken East German Christians found in Pastor Brusewitz's self-immolation an expression of the acute despair and anger they felt toward the SED and its Christian youth policy, as well as of their frustration toward their own church leaders' acquiescence in SED restrictions.[143] Still, no one took the dramatic death as the prelude to a requiem for the regime. Or as the catalyzing spark of a national conflagration.

But the pastor's cries were the first tongues of fire, a lighted candle to the tinderbox of DDR discontent, which would smolder quietly for a dozen years, ultimately to blaze forth and climax in a Wagnerian, self-consuming, empyrean end.

The Revolution of the Candles

Theory, my friend, is gray—but green is the everlasting tree of life.

Lenin,
Collected Works, vol. 20[144]

The Wall will be there in 50, and still in 100 years.

Erich Honecker,
January 15, 1989

In the spring of 1978, full-scale *Gleichschaltung*—the term that former FDJ Chief Erich Honecker had used, without concern for its Nazi overtones, in a speech thirty years earlier to describe the SED's ultimate political goal—appeared near complete. Every major DDR institution was now integrated into the socialist system—except one: the church.

With the erection of the Berlin Wall, and especially after *Abgrenzung* began in the early 1970s, SED policy had isolated the churches from western influences, forcing East German churches to abrogate ecclesiastical ties with West Germany's "NATO churches," with which they had previously shared bishops. Over the years, SED policy had successfully undermined much of the influence of the churches within the DDR; Lutheran church membership had declined from 80 percent of the DDR population (or 14 million) in 1945 to 30 percent (5 million) in 1978, and Catholics constituted a miniscule 7 percent (1.2 million) of the population. Atheistic, Marxist-Leninist rituals substituted for Christian sacraments—e.g., the *Jugendweihe*, the *Namensweihe* (socialist baptism), the *Eheweihe* (socialist matrimony), and even socialist funerals and wakes. For a majority of the population, these secular rites—conducted in festive rooms, featuring notable speakers and music from Bach or Handel, and completely paid for by the state—gradually replaced traditional religious ceremonies; indeed, by the mid-1970s, *Jugendweihe* participation stood at 95 percent, with church leaders no longer publicly voicing resistance to it. But religious opposition to the regime flickered here and ignited there (e.g., Brusewitz's self-immolation).

Now Honecker moved to neutralize this last potential center of dissidence. Despite his recent failure at liberalization with the intellectuals, Honecker envisioned no comparable difficulties with church-state détente, because he saw no evidence of loose-lipped Biermanns in the churches' ranks and believed that, in the main, the SED's long-term church policies had already succeeded.

And so, on March 6, 1978, Honecker held an historic meeting with Bishop Albrecht Schönherr, head of the Evangelical (Lutheran) Church. Schönherr identified with the Confessing Church and Reformed theological tradition and was a disciple of Dietrich Bonhoeffer, who had criticized the political passivity inherent in the Lutheran concept of the "two kingdoms," which taught respect for state authority as well as Almighty God and His church. Defying Hitler, Bonhoeffer had held that the church owed no allegiance except to God,[145] breaking with most Lutheran (and Catholic) congregations in Nazi Germany, which had prayed until the war's close for Hitler's armies. By the end of the war, Bonhoeffer himself was imprisoned in Buchenwald as a conspirator in the July 20 movement to assassinate Hitler; he was executed in Flossenberg in April 1945, just days before the camp's liberation by Allied armies.

Unlike the most radical church dissidents, Schönherr did not equate the SED with the Nazis. Declining either to support or oppose the government, he tried to chart his own third way between the pro-government stance of mainstream Lutheranism and the oppositional stance of the Confessing Church and the Reformed tradition. Schönherr embraced the role of the "*Kirche nicht gegen und nicht neben, sondern im Sozialismus*" ("a church neither against, nor alongside, but in socialism"). The nuance was ignored by SED leaders, however, for whom Schönherr's new concept of the church "in socialism" was good as support. To the Party, the new concept meant that the church had disavowed a political role, accepting the traditional Lutheran doctrine of "separate kingdoms" between church and state.

For consenting to abstain from interference in political or state affairs, Honecker granted church leaders important concessions: church kindergartens, radio and TV time for special church events, state aid for church buildings and cemeteries, church control of seminaries, and official acceptance of the internal autonomy of the churches and of the principle of religious freedom.[146]

Church-state détente signaled a change in SED agitprop tactics: "The premier question," declared Klaus Gysi, head of the State Secretariat for Church Questions, "is not how to spread atheism, but how to win Christians to a socialist way of life."[147] A major consequence of this change was increased financial support for the churches. In pre-war Germany, the government had supplied 40 percent of church funding. By the 1960s, however, East German churches received less than 10 percent of their funds from the state, leaving them to depend on their western counterparts for support. Now, to reward their new "independence," the SED agreed to increase state support for church reconstruction and such activities as care for the elderly and the disabled. Inadvertently, the SED was revivifying—with media access and even financial support—the "gendarmes in cassocks" that Lenin had railed against, the alternative institution that would ultimately bring down the SED.

With the churches and the intellectuals apparently in hand, the way now seemed paved for the DDR's ambitious program of forming "socialist personalities" through education and youth policy to progress apace into its seventh and, as it would turn out, final stage (1977–89). During this increasingly embattled period, as western youth culture expanded beyond private life and increasingly encroached on DDR public life, SED educators fought the advance by remilitarizing the schools and stepping up youth indoctrination: Education for Socialist Patriotism evolved into mandatory *Wehrerziehung* (defense education), and Marxism-Leninism was integrated even more widely and systematically into school curricula.

Wehrerziehung had already been introduced in the 1950s into extracurricular activities via the GST, the paramilitary sports organization for youth, which had for a quarter-century been pressuring students, with only mixed success, to take up military exercises. In 1972/73, SED educators had already adopted new, optional courses for girls in emergency first-aid and for boys in firing practice and field training (totaling four hours per week). Beginning in September 1978, however, these courses became compulsory for 9th- and 10th-grade students, making the DDR the only country in the world whose core curriculum including training its 15-year-old schoolboys to kill. The new hard-line policy was the brainchild of Frau Honecker, who was dissatisfied with the apathetic response of her "young revolutionaries" to the 1974 *Jugendgesetz* and who rejected her husband's advice to relax indoctrination.

The remilitarization campaign in the schools was a ticking time bomb. Indeed, just as ideological indoctrination in the schools had been the single major factor precipitating East Germans' flight to the West in the 1950s and early '60s, mandatory *Wehrerziehung* would prove the biggest catalyst to an unexpected grassroots movement in the 1980s: a peace movement growing out of the Lutheran churches.

That was all to come. The 30th anniversary celebration of the DDR in October 1979 went off like clockwork, another gala affair attended by Brezhnev, complete with torchlit procession, military parade, and the traditional 10-foot, socialist-realist portraits of the top Kremlin guest. Even as late as 1981, the determined attempt, on the 20th anniversary of the *Unding* (monstrosity), to glorify August 13 as a day of national celebration met with modest success.[148] The Wall was Honecker's own handiwork, and he would always remain proud of it. Before red banners draped from East Berlin shops and houses ("Everything for the Well-Being of the People!"), he honored the brave "border guard heroes" and praised his own midnight masterstroke as the key milestone on the way from the Cold War to détente. Scattered murmurs of protest against "DDR militarism" were heard during 1979–81 from a few church leaders. But church-state relations remained, in general, cordial.

The rise in Poland of the Solidarity trade union movement in August 1980, and the increasing outspokenness of the Polish Catholic Church thereafter, kindled the first sparks of East German activism. Unlike Poland, however, the DDR was overwhelmingly Protestant. Indeed it was the only Protestant nation in Eastern Europe outside the USSR,[149] and this meant that DDR protest remained less organized and more populist, i.e., more focused on questions of individual conscience and less dependent upon protest leaders or influential clergy than in Catholic nations.

Ironically, the decisive impetus for the formation of an East German protest movement came from the DDR's indomitable atheistic humanist, Robert Havemann; the peace "movement" can properly be dated from his last public act: Havemann's open letter to Brezhnev in November 1981, written two months before Havemann's death, in which he appealed for world disarmament and the withdrawal of both NATO and Soviet troops from Germany.[150] Havemann's plea fell on deaf ears abroad: Not only did neither side withdraw troops, each proceeded with plans to place nuclear missiles on German soil.

But a candle had been lit at home. The DDR peace movement remained small in 1982/83: where Bonn's streets rang with the shouts of 300,000 West Germans marching to protest the planned installation of U.S. Pershing missiles, 15 or 20 people would sit quietly in the Nicolai Church in Leipzig, discussing nuclear free zones. The Dresden Peace Forum, initiated in January 1982 by Rainer Eppelmann, was able to attract 2,000 signatures for a petition that called for stopping the production of children's war toys, replacing military instruction in school with "peace education," instituting a 24-month "peace service" alternative to the 18-month military draft, and ending military displays on public occasions. Eppelmann, a Lutheran youth pastor in East Berlin—whose uncanny physical resemblance to Lenin far exceeded that of the late *Spitzbart*—delivered the graveside oration at Havemann's funeral. The candle—soon the torch—had been passed.

To Bishop Schönherr's chagrin, Eppelmann quickly became the unofficial early leader of the peace movement. (Later in the year Schönherr would retire, to be succeeded by Werner Krusche, a more outspoken leader with a record of anti-Stalinist defiance.) Eppelmann upset Schönherr's careful placement of the church "in socialism," holding that Luther's two kingdoms could not be separated and that no tidy line existed between preaching the Gospel and living it. Indeed, Eppelmann's prominence in the peace movement signified that the center of DDR dissent was shifting from the intelligentsia to the clergy, from the seminar room to the church pew, from Marx to Bonhoeffer.

On February 14, 1982, 6,000 Dresdeners—mostly young people—chanted *"Frieden schaffen ohne Waffen!"* ("Make Peace Without Weapons!") and sang "We Shall Overcome" and John Lennon's "Give Peace a Chance," as they solemnly marched, candles in hand, to the ruins of a war-damaged church to commemorate the 37th anniversary of the Anglo-American bombing of Dresden. Unbeknownst even to the protesters themselves, *die Revolution der Kerzen*—the Revolution of the Candles—had quietly begun.[151]

The church had found its niche "in socialism." To counter the state's Education for Socialist Patriotism program, the churches organized discussions on the theme of Education for Peace. Now the church, benefiting from its access to radio and TV, began to attract dissident nonbelievers: it was the only institution in this closed society in which citizens could express themselves openly and safely. At the July 1982 *Kirchentag* (church congress) in Dresden—the first of its kind since 1954—20,000 persons attended peace and disarmament workshops; later in the year church dissidents issued the first calls for unilateral DDR and Soviet disarmament.

In the summer of 1982, the SED began to take the nascent peace movement seriously, organizing the first state counter-rallies of 100,000 or more youth. One historic moment occurred when Margot Honecker and 30,000 Thälmann Pioneers gathered in Dresden on April 16 for a rally commemorating Ernst Thälmann's birth, chanting the new FDJ line: *"Der Friede muss bewaffnet werden!"* ("Peace Must Be Armed!"). Meanwhile, a few dozen church members marched through nearby streets, wearing peace badges proclaiming *"Schwerter zu Pflugscharen!"* ("Swords into Ploughshares!")[152] and chanting "Make Peace Without Weapons!" Before the decade was out, these slogans would be on the arms and lips of millions.[153]

Now that they were finding their voice, church youth and youth ministers tackled a number of issues: First, the lack of a socialist peace service. Although conscientious objectors could serve in DDR military building units, rather than in the armed forces, many religious believers wanted to fulfill their state responsibilities through social work. Second, mandatory *Wehrerziehung* in the schools. The churches objected to both the compulsory pre-military education (which they derisively called *Kommandopädagogik* (commando pedagogy). They also criticized the official disapproval of pacifism, which they viewed as a symptom of the wider militarization of society, exemplified, as they pointed out, by the proliferation of war toys and games for children and by lavish DDR military parades. Third, nuclear stockpiling in Germany. Church youth advocated nuclear disarmament. Worrying that no progress might ever be made until one side took the first step, some young people even urged unilateral disarmament.

Finally, the churches linked ecology and theology, embracing the polluted environment as a damaged part of divine creation needing spiritual care. It was East German church members who published the first reports on DDR air and water quality; the first "environmental library," consisting of a few handouts, was set up in East Berlin's Zion Church. The peace movement thus widened into the "eco-peace movement." The churches were now defining their spiritual "sphere" ever more expansively; but so long as they avoided provoking the SED, the state had no justification to intervene.

Thus, despite close cooperation between the SED and church hierarchies—the last high point of church-state harmony occurred on the planning to commemorate the 500-year anniversary of Luther's birth in November 1983, which the SED linked to its centenary of Karl Marx's death,[154]—the peace movement continued to build. It surged after the DDR, along with the rest of the Warsaw Pact, accepted Soviet missiles in October 1983. Soon the SED claimed a monopoly on disarmament policy, holding that an unofficial "peace movement" endangered the national security. "Peace is our state policy!" announced SED leaders. "Make Peace Against NATO Weapons!"

Now SED authorities declared the Swords into Ploughshares badges provocative and pacifist ("The sword must be held just as firmly as the plough," insisted one SED functionary), and *Vopos* were authorized to rip them off the clothing of DDR marchers, as well as to arrest repeat violators. Teachers searched schoolchildren's book bags; university students caught with the emblems faced expulsion. Still, church leaders preached "*Keine Gewalt!*" ("No Violence") to the youth, and the candlelight vigils went off largely without incident during 1984–86. Indeed, even a respected commentator such as Theo Sommer, editor of *Die Zeit*, could mistake East Germans' sparks of interest in alternative politics for a brightening of the national mood, when he discerned during his summer 1986 visit "a more self-confident, relaxed atmosphere, gray giving way to friendly colors—the oppressive melancholy has gone."[155]

It hadn't, but athletic and diplomatic achievements on the international scene distracted outsiders' attention from domestic conditions, as did the contrasting upheaval elsewhere in the Soviet bloc, not excepting the USSR itself. The rapid turnover in the Kremlin in the mid-1980s—Brezhnev's death in 1982, the brief tenures of Yuri Andropov (1982–84) and Konstantin Chernenko (1984/85), and the rise of Mikhail Gorbachev to CPSU General Secretary in 1985—camouflaged the mass discontent simmering in the DDR: living standards were stagnating, the intelligentsia was a constant problem, and the great diplomatic breakthroughs of earlier years were old laurels.

With Gorbachev's rise to power in 1985, East German dissidents once again, as in 1956, received support from an unlikely source: the Kremlin. Gorbachev made it clear that reform was both desirable and possible. By 1987, his liberalization program, especially his policies of *glasnost* (openness) and *perestroika* (restructuring)—put the Kremlin and SED publicly at variance with each other for the first time in their histories. A generation gap separated Honecker and Gorbachev, who at 55 was the first Soviet leader who had not fought in World War II or held office under Stalin. Asked by West Germany's *Stern* in April 1987 about the SED's reluctance to follow Gorbachev's liberal leads, DDR Politburo member and ideology chief Kurt Hager remarked: "If your neighbor renewed the wallpaper in his flat, would you feel obliged to do the same?" Hager went on to cite, in earnest, the KPD's postwar statement of June 1945—its opening exercise in *Scheindemo-*

kratie—which argued that, given their distinctive historical developments, it would be misconceived to impose the Soviet system on Germany. Now the tables had turned; now it was the Soviets themselves falling into the trap of "revisionism," seeking the illusory "third way." And so now, ironically, it would be DDR Party leaders, rather than dissidents—who would resurrect the idea of a "separate German road" to socialism.[156]

Clearly the Honeckers felt no obligation to repaper their own Wall from good old SED leaden gray to the new Kremlin silver-gray. But in mid-1987 its edges began to peel. On June 6, 7, and 8—a week before Ronald Reagan's famous "Tear down this Wall!" speech at the Brandenburg Gate in West Berlin—a more hip set of western emissaries provoked an even stronger reaction among DDR youth. For three straight nights—as 60,000 West Berliners listened to open-air concerts by British rockers David Bowie, the Eurythmics, and Genesis—4,000 DDR teens struggling to hear the music clashed with *Vopos* on the eastern side of the Wall, just 350 yards away and in full view of western TV crews. Not "daring to trust" the youths that close to the Wall, *Vopos* bloodied dozens and arrested hundreds every night, many of whom sported Mohawk punk haircuts and mockingly sang *The Internationale* or shouted "*Bullen raus!*" ("pigs out!") and "*Die Mauer muss weg!*" ("The Wall must go!").

PEACE MUST BE ARMED!

PEACE IS OUR STATE POLICY!

TRUST AND RESPONSIBILITY TO THE YOUTH!

As they were dragged off, thousands of teens chanted—within easy hearing range of the Soviet embassy: "Gor-bi! Gor-bi! Gor-bi!"

Yes, it was a long way from the "Ivan go home" calls of just a few years earlier, let alone from June 1953, when thousands stood in front of the same Soviet embassy and derided the Russians. Indeed, for DDR youth, "Gorbi" was now far more popular than "Honi" had ever been.

Two weeks later, Frau Honecker made it clear that DDR education would reject the sovietized "third way" and take the separate German road. She warned that attempts to liberalize the DDR under the pretext of *glasnost* would be repulsed; she was well aware that it was Gorbachev himself, far more than Reagan or western music, who threatened the regime. "It is an incontrovertible historical truth that socialism has brought working people the highest degree of democracy in history," Frau Honecker declared. "Anyone who flirts and plays with this under the flag of freedom, the motto of more openness, and challenges the basis of democracy and freedom, will be shown his limits by the working classes." DDR children's hearts should be ablaze with complete dedication to socialism; their minds should be coolly alert to hypocritical western attempts to twist the ideas of freedom and democracy, she continued. The idea of a "third way" was still intolerable: "Time and time again we must explain that communism and capitalism cannot be mixed."[157]

And now Erich Honecker was positioning himself as the international standard bearer for communism. Indeed, by the mid-1980s, Honecker had been received in Paris, Tokyo, Helsinki, and even by the Pope in Vatican City. His crowning moment came with his September 1987 visit to Bonn, during which West Germany effectively gave the DDR official recognition: the DDR flag was raised before the chancellor's office and the West German army band played the East German national anthem. And for one final time, the Saarland straw hat imbued the scene with nostalgic warmth, as "our Erich" made a sentimental journey to his hometown of Neunkirchen, where the slight 75-year-old man with swept-back, thinning hair saw again the modest green wooden house of his boyhood, ate his favorite crumble cake at his sister's, spoke with his sister and old friends in the local dialect, sang ballads from his KJVD days, and openly wept.[158]

Upon Honecker's return from his nostalgic *Heimkehr*, however, he found a house increasingly divided, as secular intellectuals and FDJ youth openly joined the peace movement. On January 17, 1988, hundreds of protesters tried to enter the annual SED march commemorating the 1919 murders of Karl Liebknecht and Rosa Luxemburg. The uninvited marchers unfurled banners reminding DDR citizens that Luxemburg had supported free speech and the right to differ. Dozens of protesters were arrested and jailed; 54 of them were expatriated to the BRD within a week, in many cases *freigekauft* by Bonn. By mid-1988, Honecker found himself in the absurd position of banning the USSR youth magazine *Sputnik*, which was widely used in DDR Russian language classes; in the spirit of *glasnost, Sputnik* had begun publishing articles comparing Stalin with Hitler. In November, eight FDJ students at East Berlin's elite Carl von Ossietzky EOS, the Eton of the DDR, organized a petition opposing the annual military parade to celebrate the anniversary of East Germany's founding. FDJ officials pressured their local members (numbering virtually the entire school body) into voting the youths out of the FDJ; an FDJ official compared the group to neo-Nazi desecrators of graves. Then Frau Honecker stepped in and personally ordered "the ringleaders of dissent" expelled and the responsible administrators disciplined. Within days, four students were summarily expelled, two others were sent to other schools, and two were issued reprimands. Meanwhile, the school principal, who had also permitted the creation of a speakers' corner for students to discuss difficult questions of politics and history, was disciplined.[159] The order came down: The wallpaper stays ash-gray.

TRUST AND RESPONSIBILITY TO THE YOUTH!

THE YOUTH HAVE THE WORD!

EVERYTHING FOR THE WELL-BEING OF THE PEOPLE!

Yes, it was a long way from that honeymoon season in 1971 when Herr Honecker announced that there would henceforth be "no taboos."[160]

The handwriting on the Wallpaper became near-legible in early 1989. The year began with the arrest of 80 marchers in Leipzig. "The Wall will be there in 50, still in 100 years," declared Honecker in mid-January, angrily replying to a chorus of western calls—from U.S. Secretary of State George Schultz, British Foreign Secretary Geoffrey Howe, and West German Foreign Minister Hans-Dietrich Genscher—for its razing.[161] A few days later, another would-be escapee—the last, as it turned out—was killed as he tried to scale the Wall. In February, the churches balked: Church-state relations snapped when Bishop Werner Leich stormed out of a fruitless Politburo meeting. Hereafter the Lutheran Church was not just in, or even alongside, but rather *against* SED socialism. In April, the previously silent

Catholic Church joined Lutheran bishops in an ecumenical protest against SED policies on travel, press freedom, and human rights. Now the churches had a united front, and the DDR was fast catching up with its communist bloc neighbors. A new spectre was haunting Eastern Europe: "the spectre of dissent," as Vaclav Havel, the Czechoslovakian playwright and later president, said. With the first multi-party elections in Poland in June 1989, after which a Solidarity-led government was formed under the leadership of Lech Walesa and the free trade union movement, the reform movement spread like wildfire throughout Eastern Europe.

But SED educators stood fast. *"Rote Fahnen gegen weisse Kerzen!"* cried SED loyalists in reply to the churches. "Red flags against white candles!" With Herr Honecker still recovering from gallbladder surgery, Frau Honecker, now widely referred to as "The Witch" and "the lilac dragon" by DDR citizens,[162] led the would-be firefighters. On her orders, 2 million FDJ and 500,000 JP took an "oath of allegiance" to the "socialist Fatherland." Teachers and FDJ functionaries administered catechisms to students that made the Party line clear.[163] In a five-hour speech on June 13, delivered before 4,300 SED functionaries at the Nineteenth Pedagogical Congress in the Palace of the Republic in East Berlin, Margot rallied the educational elite. Fighting fire with fire, she delivered a scathing, grotesque denunciation of the churches and dissidents, whom she called "enemies," "traitors," and "counterrevolutionaries" who sought "not a strengthening of socialism, but a return to capitalism." "Why shouldn't we say clearly to our youth," Frau Honecker told the teachers, "that they create grave worries for us when they contribute to the counterrevolutionaries' plans under the slogan of 'diversity'? It is proper that our youth be able to draw fine distinctions between what is revolutionary and what is counterrevolutionary."[164]

All this came just a month after local elections garnering 98.85 percent for the SED (elections later shown to have been fraudulent), and just a week after Herr and Frau Honecker, almost alone among world leaders, publicly supported Deng Xiaoping's bloodbath in Tiananmen Square, where the communist government had crushed the Beijing student protests with tanks. Now, in bloodcurdling language seldom heard since the era of high Stalinism, Frau Honecker lashed out at reformers such as Poland's Solidarity and Czechoslovakia's Charter 77, insisting that nothing fundamental would ever change in the DDR, in education or anything else. DDR education would continue, she insisted, to produce youth "who campaign for socialism, with word and deed—if necessary, with gun in hand."[165]

PEACE MUST BE ARMED!

PEACE IS OUR STATE POLICY!

RED FLAGS AGAINST WHITE CANDLES!

Frau Honecker's verbal pyrotechnics drew a formal protest from Chancellor Kohl, and even the visible displeasure of Gorbachev, who was visiting in Bonn that day. But, for a brief moment, it had its intended effect at home: intimidation. Fearing to jeopardize their privileges and scholarships, few educators and even fewer university students—except for church youth—joined the active opposition. Nevertheless, given such public provocations, the ferment throughout Eastern Europe, and her husband's illnesses (which left the SED adrift at the top), events in the DDR now advanced like an avalanche, as developments elsewhere in the Soviet bloc began to work against the SED and as the DDR public joined the church youth in the streets.

The crisis began unexpectedly. On August 8, 1989, 500 East Germans vacationing on the Hungarian-Austrian border suddenly fled across it to Austria, from which they made their way to West Germany. On August 9, as more East Germans crossed into Austria and began flooding the West German embassy in Budapest, Hungary announced that it would grant asylum to any and all East Germans. By August 13, the 28th anniversary of the building of the Wall, more than 55,000 citizens had fled, most of them young people,[166] the largest number in 28 years. Indeed 1.5 million people—nine percent of the DDR population—had applied to emigrate. The wheel had come full circle, back to August 1961: the DDR was, once again, bleeding to death. Western journalists quipped that the DDR anthem should be changed to "*Auf wiedersehen*"; the proper gift for DDR relatives this year, they advised, was a new set of luggage.

On September 10, *Neues Forum* (New Forum), the dissident group headed by Jens Reich, a member of East Berlin's Academy of Sciences, announced itself publicly. Within the next few days, leading intellectuals, including Party members, issued calls for urgent reforms, especially in education. "Our children are brought up in school to lie," Christa Wolf declared in a widely quoted article. By September 26, the small Monday evening vigils in Leipzig had become a candlelight march of 7,000 citizens, the largest mass protest in the DDR since June 1953. The little sparks of faith that had begun in church basements were now ablaze in the streets: the candles' simple message of peace and justice was lighting the night.

Still, the regime's fall did not seem imminent: polls conducted in October 1989 showed that almost 70 percent of West Germans did not expect reunification by the year 2000; western estimates of East German expectations were similar.[167] Anyone in attendance at the 40th anniversary celebration of the DDR's founding on October 7—which featured, amid thousands of *40 Jahre DDR* banners, a torch-lit parade of 100,000 FDJ members—could have been forgiven for believing the SED still had a firm grip on power. True, church leaders had declined invitations and Gorbachev had snubbed Honecker, sparing time only for a brief conversation in which he warned Honecker that the USSR opposed the use of force against the protesters: "Honi" could expect no support from "Gorbi." But the combined force of the NVA and *Vopos* stood at more than a half million. "*Den Sozialismus in seinem Lauf hält weder Ochs noch Esel auf,*" Honecker declared, in one of his last public statements. "The course of socialism stops neither for oxen nor jackasses."[168] In plain German: "The future still belongs to socialism."

Perhaps; and yet Honecker himself already belonged to the past. The anniversary celebration was, in reality, the Last Hurrah for the infirm 77-year-old, whose very appearance would soon seem symbolic of his regime's frailty.

Still, the spectre of another Tiananmen Square was on everyone's minds. On October 8, in Plauen, after 30,000 people had peacefully protested the day before against the DDR's 40th anniversary, local newspapers warned darkly of swift government retaliation.[169] On October 9, after meeting with a visiting Chinese Politburo member, Honecker publicly—and ominously—compared the "counterrevolutionary rebellion in Beijing" to the "present campaign of defamation" against the DDR. That Monday evening, 150,000 Leipzigers bathed the streets in light, chanting *"Wir sind das Volk!"* ("We are the People!"). Over the next days, the peace marches grew, as the Revolution of the Candles swept through Dresden, Berlin, Halle, Jena, and other cities.

The "Chinese solution" was not applied, and now a remarkable change came over the DDR *Volk*: the polite peace marches turned into raucous *Demos* (demonstrations). Since 1953, the only slogans seen and chanted openly in DDR streets had been the hopelessly bland and boring shibboleths of the Party. But now, arisen from the ruins of the debased East German *Sklavensprache* came *Demosprüche*, sayings at the *Demos* that were of, by, and for the People (*das Demos*).

So now, in the streets, the public German language returned to life: colorful, rich, hilarious, witty, as evinced in an astonishing variety of political jokes, puns, and satire.

The Revolution of the Candles had become the Revolution of the *Demosprüche*. And "our Erich" became the first of the SED *Bonzen* to be publicly tarred as a figure of fun. Jokes about the SED General Secretary had grown plentiful since the early '70s, but—like the Ulbricht gags during the reign of his predecessor—they had always circulated privately. Now the Honecker humor—by turns light-hearted, bitter, and ironic—burst forth on thousands of marchers' placards and lips:

> *Erich, lass die Faxen sein*
> *Lass endlich perestroika rein!*
> [Erich, stop finally with the buffoonery
> Introduce *perestroika*!]

> *Die Demokratie in ihrem Lauf*
> *Hält weder Ochs noch Esel auf!*
> [Democracy stops neither for oxen nor jackasses!]

> Dear God, make me deaf, so that I can't hear RIAS.
> Dear God, make me blind, so that Hungary I can't find.
> Then deaf and blind,
> I'll be Erich's dearest child!

"On his last day in office," the joke went around, Erich drives his tractor throughout the DDR. The People ask him why he is on the road alone. Erich says, "I'm looking for followers!"[170]

Even within the Politburo, however, Honecker now found few followers. And so, in a surprise announcement on October 18, Honecker resigned, purportedly on grounds of "poor health," though actually under severe pressure from his Politburo colleagues.[171] The street barbs against him did not stop, however, but only changed to the past tense:

Q: What was the difference between a skilled worker and Honecker?
A: The worker never came, and Honecker never went.

Late in the summer, Erich wanted to emigrate to the BRD.
Why?
He wanted to be with his *Volk*.

And the jokes only multiplied:

> George Bush, Mikhail Gorbachev, and Erich Honecker once flew together in an airplane to a UN meeting in New York. Suddenly the plane ran into turbulence and seemed about to plummet. Bush prayed to God for help. God appeared personally and said: "You can all be saved, when you divest yourselves of whatever is dearest and most precious to you. Spontaneously, Bush reached for his checkbook, kissed it, and threw it out the window. Erich took out of his coat pocket his Party book, kissed it, and threw it out the window. And Gorbachev turned, kissed Erich, and. . . .

> What was a meeting of Honecker's aged Politburo like? The agenda contained the following items:
> 1. Carry in the members
> 2. Synchronize pacemakers
> 3. Sing together: "We are the Young Pioneers"
> 4. Practice: Eulogy for the Next State Funeral
> 5. Carry out the members

"Erich, hol die Margot heim!" taunted protesters throughout the week following his resignation: "Erich, take Margot home with you!" And so, Frau Honecker also resigned, along with the entire 41-member cabinet, on November 3. "Mandatory 10-Year School Punishment" read Leipzig posters waving her goodbye.

Egon Krenz, Honecker's longtime heir apparent, now took over. A former FDJ chief (1975–83) who handed over control of the organization only at the ripe age of 46, Krenz bore the mocking sobriquet *der Berufsjugendliche* (the professional youth). In classic apparatchik style, Krenz maneuvered to win all three of Honecker's offices: General Secretary of the SED, Prime Minister, and Chairman of the Council of State. While insisting that the SED would remain the only party in the DDR, Krenz also began tentative measures to introduce *glasnost*. But now Gorbachev's October 7 warning to Honecker proved all too true: "He who comes too late will be punished by History."

It was decidedly too late. Dismissed by reform leaders as a rubbery *Wendehals* (wryneck, i.e., turncoat or quick-change artist), the man who had flown to Beijing to congratulate Deng Xiaoping after the Tiananmen Square massacre lasted less than two months. Krenz lamely expanded travel abroad to 30 days; the dissidents hooted. He lifted the ban on *Sputnik* and other publications; the dissidents scoffed. He secured Central Committee approval for freedom of assembly and association; the dissidents jeered. Ever bolder, they referred to the ZK (*Zentralkommitee*, Central Committee) as *Zirkus Krenz* (Krenz's circus), and dubbed the new General Secretary himself "Krenz Xiaoping." Indeed the ridicule of Krenz's name, background, and even physical appearance (especially his toothy grin) was endless:

Reforms, yes, but *unbeKRENZt* [not limited]!

Zirkus Krenz: the performance is over!

Blumen statt Krenze!
[Flowers instead of garland wreaths (*Kranze*)!]

Away with the *Krenz*truppen [border or "Krenz" troops]!

Enough of the Ego(n)centric!

eGOn!

Egon—BEGONE!

Egon, remember Erich and Walter
Go before your *Greisenalter* [old age]!

Demokratie ohne Krenzen!
[Democracy without limits (*Grenzen*)!]

What little Krenz never learned, [big] Krenz will never learn.

China Lob und Wahlbetrug
Egon Krenz, es ist genug!
[Praising China and rigging the elections
Egon Krenz, we've had enough!]

From Egon's arithmetic book: $100 - 20 = 98.85$
   (on the falsified May 1989 elections)

Support our Egon in the next election: 105%!

EGON—what does that mean?
Er geht ooch noch! [He'll go too!]

Grandmother, why do you have such big teeth?

Egon, first do something! Then smile!

As long as Krenz rules, we'll demonstrate!

And they did. What the Russians had once deemed absurd was now reality: a revolution on German soil. Gorbachev had fomented what Lenin and Stalin pronounced impossible; East Germans were no longer shy about walking on the grass—indeed, they were trampling it. "Put trust in our policy of renewal," pleaded Krenz in a November 3 television address. "Your place is here. We need you."[172]

But a skeptical DDR *Volk* decided that control was better, and that their place was in the streets. On November 4, a million citizens marched in East Berlin, including tens of thousands of educators and students, whose objects of wrath included the schools and youth organizations.[173]

To learn from the *Volk* / Means Learning to Triumph!

I want to be—me!

I want to have a voice in how I'm educated!

Teach our children to stand up!

Zensoren auf die Traktoren!
[Censors—to the tractors!]

Wir wollen kein Foltsbildungsystem!
[We don't want an educational persecution system!]

Schluss mit der Volks(miss)bildung!
[End People's (Mis)education!]

Frei, deutsch, jung = ohne FDJ!
[Free, German, young = without the FDJ!]

FDJ—You need a facelift!

Wir sind nicht traurig ohne Aurich!
[We won't be sad without (FDJ head) Aurich!]

40 Years of kindergarten are enough!

Demilitarize the schools!

Peace education instead of *Wehrerziehung!*

Church youth, above all, felt a sense of triumph. *Marx ist tot und Jesus lebt!* they cried throughout the streets of Berlin and other cities: "Marx is dead and Jesus lives!" Party calls for "red flags" died away.

The end of SED rule now flared on the horizon: a revolution by candlelight, a tyranny in twilight. History had never witnessed a revolution like it: millions marching without incident, armed with nothing mightier than candles and catchwords. "*Vernunft der Strasse,*" the novelist Christoph Hein termed the peaceful protests. "The reason of the streets." Things had come a long way from the night in November 1950, when 18-year-old Hermann Flade stuffed a few handmade circulars critical of the SED in neighbors' mailboxes—and paid for his effrontery with a death sentence grudgingly commuted to 15 years in prison. The same Germans whom Bolshevik leaders had joked would never even tiptoe on a lawn were now a street-smart—indeed smart-alecky—*Volk.*

Now the Word(play) about to set them free raised its voice in every town and village in the country. Perhaps the biggest issue for DDR *Bürger* was travel. "What illness is worse than AIDS in the DDR?" they joked. "The Buda-pest!"

And indeed, the Hungarian fever was now epidemic. By the first week of November, tens of thousands of DDR citizens were heading for Hungary or Czechoslovakia in hopes of gaining passage to the West; others were chanting "*Wir bleiben hier!*" ("We're staying!") as they escalated their demands for freedom of travel. "*Visafrei bis Shanghai!*" chanted the marchers: "No visa until Shanghai!" "*Ohne Visa bis nach Pisa!*" ("Travel to Pisa without a visa!"). "*Mit dem Fahrrad durch Europa / Aber nicht als alter Opa!*" ("A European bike tour, but not when I'm an old Granddad!").

On Thursday, November 9, 1989, Politburo member Günther Schabowski ended an hour-long press conference with a stunning announcement: in the face of 2.7 million exit visa requests, the DDR would open the Wall.

That evening, thousands of honking little Trabis—the state-manufactured auto of the DDR—chugged happily into West Berlin. For the first time in 28 years, East Berliners could cross the death strip unimpeded, leaving behind the confused border guards and running a gauntlet of welcoming West Berliners, who met the spluttering Trabis with congratulatory bangs on their rooftops—as well as fistfuls of ripe yellow Dollar bananas. And as East met West in that wondrous scene, future and past also converged: If the big Dollar banana would soon represent the symbol of the eastern German future, the tiny Trabant would soon stand as the emblem of the DDR past.

The SED leadership seems to have believed—naïvely—that the decision to open the Wall might stabilize the regime and stop the DDR exodus, that the prospect of such an immense flood of emigrants might prompt Bonn to suspend DDR citizenship rights or act to limit the tide. But it was not to be: the world community and DDR citizens themselves saw the opening of borders as an admission of the desperate weakness of the SED. As West Berlin writer Peter Schneider later observed, the regime had, ironically, thus both erected and eradicated the Wall for the same reason: to stop East Germans from fleeing.[174]

And now, a second crucial transformation came over the DDR citizenry: the revolution to overthrow the DDR dictatorship gave way to an urge to reunite with the BRD and enjoy the fruits of capitalism. Armed with DM 100 in *Begrüssungsgeld* (welcome money) from the West German government, one million DDR citizens swept through West Berlin during the weekend following November 9, gawking at the store windows and buying everything from CDs to pretzels. Events had taken an unexpected turn: After 40 years in the communist wilderness, DDR citizens had entered the consumerist Promised Land. The Revolution of the Candles, and the Revolution of the *Demosprüche*, had become, within hours, the Banana Revolution.

Thus did the SED's decision on the Wall catalyze German popular thinking on reunification and soon prove the beginning of the real end—the end of the DDR, the last and greatest addition to the 1989 necrology. Marxism, not just Marx, seemed forever dead. The cries of *"Wir sind das Volk"* soon changed into *"Wir sind ein Volk."* Within days, membership in the SED dropped from 2.4 to 1.2 million. *"Demokratie statt Bonzokratie!"* ("Democracy instead of Bigwig Rule!") shouted the protesters, who began referring to the SED leaders' residential area in Wandlitz, an East Berlin suburb, variously as *"Bonzograd,"* "Honecker-City," and *Volvograd."* (The latter name alluded to the high number of Volvos driven by Party leaders.)[175] Some Politburo members, such as ideology chief Kurt Hager, came in for special treatment. "We need architects of reform, not carpet-makers!" *"Reformen á la Hager / Sind uns zu mager!"* went one chant ("Reforms á la Hager / Are too meager!"). With the late-November revelations of the luxurious lifestyles that the SED *Bonzen* in Wandlitz had enjoyed, the Party—not just Honecker, Krenz, and the Politburo, but the SED itself—became the target of protesters' wrath.

SED—das tut weh! [that hurts!]

SED—Geh! [Go!]

SED—Sicheres Ende DDR! [A certain end for the DDR!]

SED—Nee! [No!]

SED—Ade! [Bye-bye!]

SED, gib acht,
Das Volk ist die Macht!
[SED, pay heed,
The People are the power!]

S wie Sauwirtschaft, E wie Egoismus, D wie Diebstahl = SED!
[S as in a disgusting economy, E as in egoism, D as in theft = SED!]

40 Jahre Lug und Trug
SED—es ist genug!
[40 years of lying and deception
SED—that's enough!]

Kommt raus aus Wandlitz
Und zeigt euer Antlitz!
[Come out of Wandlitz
And show your faces!]

Dem Land ein neues Antlitz
Ohne Kalk aus Wandlitz!
[A new face for the nation
Without the slime in Wandlitz!]

Privileged Ones of all countries, remove yourselves!

Our *Volk* need the SED like a fish needs a bicycle!

Away with the *Wendehälse* [turncoats]!

SED allein—das darf nicht sein!
[The SED must not rule alone!]

Partei Monopol macht hohl!
[A party monopoly is a bankrupt policy!]

Demos müssen sein
Sonst schlafen die Reformen ein!
[There must be demonstrations
Otherwise the reforms will cease!]

Whoever votes SED will be punished by Life!

Desperate, Krenz called a full Party congress, at which the SED formally expelled Honecker and announced a name change, first to SED-PDS, then a few days later to PDS (*Partei Demokratischen Sozialismus*, Party of Democratic Socialism). Gregor Gysi, a lawyer and son of the former minister of culture, took over the Party leadership and spoke at the podium with broom in hand, reassuring listeners that he would clean house. Still, the onslaught from the streets did not stop; indeed by now it had gone far beyond criticism of the SED *Bonzen* to a blistering attack on the Party itself.

> *SED—stalinistisch, egoistisch, diskriminierend;*
> *PDS—perspektivlos, demokratiefeindlich, stasifreundlich*
> [SED—stalinist, egoistic, discriminatory;
> PDS—hopeless, hostile to democracy, friendly to the *Stasi*]
>
> *PDS—Pleite des Sozialismus, Partei der Stalinisten, Pack*
>   *deine Sachen!*
> [PDS—Bankruptcy of socialism, Party of Stalinists, Pack up!]
>
> *PDS—Parasiten, Diktatoren, Stalinisten!*
>
> Don't Gysi, Be Happy!
>
> Don't worry, take Gysi [away]!

Verify, not trust, was the aim of DDR citizens now, fed up with Marxist-Leninist "dares" to trust:

> Trust is good, changing officials is better, democratic elec-
>   tions are the best!
>
> *Gestern noch hauen—heute vertrauen?!*
> [Still beating us yesterday—and trust you today?!]
>
> Mistrust is good, control is better!
>
> Vomit out Stalin!
>
> *Von Arkona bis Plauen—der SED kein Vertrauen!*
> [From Arkona to Plauen—don't trust the SED!]
>
> *Q:* What is the difference between Lenin and Gorbachev?
> *A:* Very simple: Lenin wanted to make communists out of
>   workers. Gorbachev wants to make workers out of com-
>   munists!

The *Wende* (turn) had arrived. "Really a *Wende*! Not just bananas and travel permits!" cried the demonstrators. "The issue isn't bananas anymore. *Es geht um die Wurst!*" ("It's sausages"; i.e., do or die!). As revolutionary protest suddenly gave way to reunification calls, and then reunification proposals, and then reunification negotiations, plans, and timetables, it would soon become the *Wende* in the *Wende*, and the *Wende* in the *Wende* in the *Wende*. And on and on.

Now the wheel was turning fast; ironies piled upon one another as the revolution came full circle. Three of the richest moments at the close of annus mirabilis 1989:

November: With the fall of the Wall, the People's Chamber comes to life for the first time in its 40-year history. Delegates begin asking questions and even criticizing SED leaders. On November 13, under the glare of flashing TV lights, 82-

year-old Comrade Major General Erich Mielke, Minister for State Security since 1957 and Politburo member since 1971, is called to account for his state within a state, an empire including 2,000 properties, 130,000 full-time employees, and 1.2 million informants. In what turns out to be his valedictory speech, before he is hauled off to one of the prisons he used to administer, he describes his *Stasi* agents: "We are the sons and daughters of the working class. We did it for you." The People's Chamber delegates hoot and jeer. "Believe me, believe me," Mielke pleads. "Comrades. . . ." A heckler shouts that he's no comrade of Mielke, who sputters and then blurts out: "*Ich liebe Euch doch alle!*" ("But I love you all— really!").[176]

December: In yet another sign that the times really are a-changing, Wolf Biermann returns to the rapidly disintegrating DDR, giving his first public performances in 23 years. On December 1, 800 fans jam into Leipzig's Massenhalle 2 to glimpse the Biermann legend, as millions more tune in on TV. Just days before the Wall came down, ideology chief Kurt Hager and the Krenz government had declared Biermann an "anti-communist rowdy" and had refused him entry at Checkpoint Charlie; now Krenz sees liberalization as the only, if slim, chance to remain in power.[177]

Playing taps for tyrants is a Biermann specialty, and Wolf arrives, with a new number for the occasion: "The Ballad of the Rotten Old Men":

> Hey Krenz, you happy Cold Warrior
> I don't believe you, not one word
> You cheered the tanks in Beijing
> I saw your toothy smile at the mass murder. . . .
>
> Hey Hager, Professor Flying Carpet
> I don't believe you, you rotten old man
> Now our own words roll smoothly out of your mouth
> In new phrases you deliver your same old shit. . . .
>
> Hey Honi, you left for health reasons
> I don't believe any of this
> You always had the worst kind of disease
> The Stalinist syphilis.[178]

By turns bitter and nostalgic, Biermann ends the concert with an old song, "Or Maybe I'm Wrong," whose last stanza goes:

> Perhaps when I'm there
> At the end of the road
> And the race has been run
> I'll be back at square one.

January: The feeble object of Biermann's wrath, a poor KPD miner's son and now a homeless Stalinist pariah, may have had similar feelings. With thousands of East Germans still pouring into resettlement camps in the West, Erich and Margot Honecker are reduced to asylum seekers too. Expelled from palatial Wandlitz, having nowhere to go, and under constant attack from all sides, the Honeckers receive shelter in Lobetal, northeast of Berlin. In this little Bethlehem of the DDR, under the roof of a Protestant pastor whose son had been denied higher education by Margot's policies, the fallen atheist pair meekly accept Christian alms.

Asked about the rage felt by many villagers at the thought of helping the former First Couple, a Lobetal social worker tells the press: "We take in the homeless, the mentally handicapped, and alcoholics. So why not also our head of state?"[179]

Figure 1. On 7 April 1946, the KPD and SPD united in Mecklenburg. The portraits (*from left to right*) of Ernst Thälmann, Friedrich Engels, and Rudolf Breitscheid represent the respective communist and socialist allegiances of each party and their roots in a common collectivist tradition. Embracing the new party promoting socialist unity—which was to become, within three weeks, the SED—the KPD renounced (the otherwise common) pictures of Lenin and Stalin and omitted every reference to Marxism-Leninism. Beneath the portraits stand the banners: "The Unity of the Working Class Guarantees the Unity of Germany." The banner on the table reads: "Both currents of the German worker movement must unite." (Photo courtesy of Deutsches Historisches Museum, Berlin)

Figure 2. A page from a photo album honoring President Wilhelm Pieck and reporting on the activities of the FDJ in Saxony-Anhalt, 1950. The scene depicts the work of East German postwar reconstruction and is encircled by the new DDR national hymn, which had been formally sung for the first time on 7 November 1949, the 32nd anniversary of the Great Socialist November Revolution. President Pieck had asked the DDR's distinguished poet and future Minister of Culture Johannes Becher to write the hymn, which was set to melody by Hanns Eisler.

The hymn, which embodied the sense of promise felt by many DDR citizens in their new socialist land, was affectionately (and sometimes cynically) known as "The Waltz of the Ruins." The melody was near-identical with the tune "Goodbye, Jonny," which the singer Hans Albers made famous in the West German film "Water for Canitoga." (The similarity drew frequent charges of plagiarism.) The first stanza, which is portrayed here, reads as follows: "Arisen from ruins / and turned toward the future / let us serve the Good, / Germany, united Fatherland. Extreme need compels us to cope / and we cope in a spirit of unity. / For it will yet pass / that the sun, more beautiful than ever, / shines over Germany." (Photo courtesy of Deutsches Historisches Museum, Berlin)

Figure 3. The FDJ parades through East Berlin during the German Rally of May 1950. In the background stands the Ministry of Justice, which was undergoing reconstruction. The ten-foot poster portrays a heroic Stalin, who is gesturing with raised forefinger in the in the manner of Lenin. The banner on the left reads: "We thank Stalin, the friend and helper of all peace-loving peoples." (Photo courtesy of Deutsches Historisches Museum, Berlin)

Figure 4. This poster was commissioned to celebrate the fifth anniversary of the founding of the SED in April 1951. The Unity Day anniversary of the SPD and KPD, which had combined to form the SED, had occurred on 21–22 April 1946. The poster reads (*from top to bottom*): "Five Years of the SED." "Five Years Battling for Peace, Unity, Reconstruction." The four leading heroes of the Stalin-era SED are pictured on the DDR flag: Marx, Engels, Lenin, and Stalin. (Notice that the German leaders depicted in the SED of the 1940s [see Figure 1] have been replaced by Lenin and Stalin—a clear sign of its "Stalinization" and of the SPD's secondary status in the SED by mid-century.) (Photo courtesy of Deutsches Historisches Museum, Berlin)

Figure 5. This classroom scene features the JP (Young Pioneers) of the Pfaffenheimer school in Chemnitz, 20 March 1952. These JP members are writing to West German pupils as part of the DDR initiative "Your Letters across the Border." An agitprop statement announcing the initiative began: "Your letter is a sharp weapon of enlightenment in the battle for unity and peace." Some of the pupils are wearing their Young Pioneer blue scarves, as the teacher observes their letter-writing. On the wall, in the back of the room, runs the theme of German reunification that the letter-writing campaign promoted: "The Promotion of the Present: Germans at One Table."

The letter-writing initiative began after the "Stalin Note" of 10 March 1952, in which Stalin offered to sign a treaty that would promote a "unified, peace-loving and democratic Germany" and support German reconstruction. His main condition was that a reunited Germany would remain neutral. Chancellor Konrad Adenauer of West Germany, along with the U.S. government, rejected Stalin's overture. Nonetheless, the treaty offer benefited Stalin politically, making it easier for him to blame the division of Germany on the western powers and thereby to integrate the DDR into the east bloc. (Photo courtesy of Deutsches Historisches Museum, Berlin)

Figure 6. A 1952 poster reflects Stalin's cult of personality in the DDR at its zenith. Stalin is lionized as a great statesman, a decorated military hero, an international father figure loved by children. Wearing their blue neck scarves, these three Young Pioneers stand for his adoring East German public. The poster reads: "Stalin: He Is Peace." (Photo courtesy of Deutsches Historisches Museum, Berlin)

Figure 7. A 1953 poster depicts an FDJ ceremony honoring excellence in examinations demonstrating knowledge of Marxism-Leninism. The FDJ girl is being awarded an FDJ pin, on which appears the phrase (not visible here) "For Good Knowledge" imprinted on an open book, with the FDJ flag placed behind it. Running across the bottom of the poster is the statement: "Acquire the Award 'For Good Knowledge.'" On the left is a so-called Red Corner, a socialist altar to Stalin and Marxism-Leninism. Common in early postwar DDR schools, it typically featured portraits of the communist pantheon of heroic party leaders, bedecked with flowers and the classics of M-L.. Above the Stalin portrait run the words: "Fulfill the Legacy of the Great Stalin!"

FDJ pins were awarded in bronze, silver, and gold for mastery of socialist topics in oral examinations. The topics included the history of the FDJ and the Komsomol, fundamental questions of M-L philosophy and political economy, youth policies of the SED, and the biographies of Marx, Engels, Lenin, and Ernst Thälmann. (Photo courtesy of Deutsches Historisches Museum, Berlin)

Figure 8 (above). Scene from the Fourth Party Congress of the SED, held from 30 March to 6 April 1954. Bannered across the stage (from left to right) is the SED slogan adopted for the occasion: "The strength of the Party lies in its indissoluble alliance with the masses. The strength of the masses lies in their union with the Party." The scene shows numerous Soviet and East European leaders in attendance; SED leaders include First Secretary Walter Ulbricht *(ninth from left)* and Minister President Otto Grotewohl *(eleventh from left, standing before the second microphone).* The M-L pantheon enshrined above the stage depicts Marx, Engels, Lenin, and Stalin—the latter of whom had not yet been dethroned from his exalted status and still enjoyed a "cult of personality." The Fourth Party Congress approved the DDR government's so-called New Course, a short-lived turn toward moderation that followed in reaction to the 17 June 1953 worker rebellion against the state. (Photo courtesy of Deutsches Historisches Museum, Berlin)

Figure 9 (below). This mandolin youth group entertains citizens in Erfurt during the DDR People's Opinion Poll on 27–29 June 1954. The DDR government's campaign behind the vote, which sought to organize opposition to West German membership in the newly forming econom-ic Common Market, was called "For the Peace Treaty and Against the EVG." The poll specifically concerned the question of a peace treaty to reunify Germany and support the withdrawal of the occupying troops. Not surprisingly, the poll showed DDR citizens overwhelmingly in favor of the ongoing Soviet effort to unify their country (and thereby keep West Germany not just out of the EVG but also excluded from NATO, which Bonn was to join in 1955). Above the doorway reads: "Peace Yes, War No." The sign on the front door reads: "We are voting this June for peace." The sign behind the mandolin players runs: "Parents! Think when you submit your vote on the happi-ness and future of your children!" (Photo courtesy of Deutsches Historisches Museum, Berlin)

Figure 10 (above). This neighborhood voting group, the Stalinallee 191 in East Berlin, is lined up to vote on 17 October 1954. The vote is to reaffirm their support for the loss of Germany's far eastern territory to Poland by the redrawing of East German boundaries at the Oder-Neisse River. This government photo was originally affixed with the caption: "The community members of Stalinallee 191 are going decisively together to the election." Above the entrance to the voting center in District 24 of East Berlin is a sign: "In support of the Polish-German Oder-Neisse Peace Boundary and Against the Warmongers." (Photo courtesy of Deutsches Historisches Museum, Berlin)

Figure 11 (below). These *Jugendweihe* pupils are admiring their certificates of participation on 27 March 1955, the month during which the ceremony was launched as an official DDR youth ritual. These pupils attended schools no. 7 and no. 22 in the Kopenick section of Berlin, which was the first DDR city to host the ceremony. It took place in the Erich Weinert Club in Kopenick, with Paul Wandel, Secretary of the Central Committee of the SED and former DDR Minister of Education, as the featured speaker for the occasion.

Figure 12. The Fifth Party Congress of the SED met from 10–16 July 1958 in the Werner Seelenbinder Stadium in East Berlin. The SED slogan for the event (depicted in center) ran: "Socialism Is Winning." Male and female *Aktivisten*, idealized models of the DDR worker in socialist realist style, surround the Party banner. SED General Secretary Walter Ulbricht speaks at the podium *(below center)*.

The SED Fifth Party Congress was the first major Party gathering during which Ulbricht held unchallenged power and could rule without opposition. The Congress occurred in the wake of the show trials (of Wolfgang Harich, Walter Janka, and others) and Politbüro expulsion of Karl Schirdewan in 1957. The Congress ratified Ulbricht's decision to adjust DDR education precisely to the Soviet model and adopt mandatory, universal polytechnical education. (Photo courtesy of Deutsches Historisches Museum, Berlin)

Figure 13. The Reiterweg neighborhood community of Potsdam marches to the polls for a local election, 1961. The banner reads: "We are voting today for tomorrow." The boy on the far right is wearing the blue scarf of the Young Pioneers. (Photo courtesy of Deutsches Historisches Museum, Berlin)

Figure 14. These schoolgirls from the Carl von Ossietkzy School in Pankow are the model East German youth of Berlin's elite EOS (advanced secondary school), 1963. The placard above the entrance to the school features one of the DDR's leading youth slogans of the 1960s: "Trust and Responsibility to the Youth in the Comprehensive Development of Socialism." Ossietzky, an outspoken anti-fascist critic of Hitler, was exalted in the DDR for receiving the 1936 Nobel Peace Prize while in jail. (Photo courtesy of Deutsches Historisches Museum, Berlin)

Figure 15 (left). Annaliese Saupe of Plauen, c. 1996. Born in 1912, Frau Saupe was one of many little-known citizens who acted heroically during the "unbloody revolution" in the DDR during October-November 1989. Plauen was the first city to rise up in protest against the DDR regime on 5 October 1989.

Frau Saupe had participated in the anti-government protest demonstration. With the help of her 91-year-old husband and her son, who developed their photographs of the demonstration, Frau Saupe smuggled the photos plus her news report of the event in her underclothes and took the train across the border to Hof in West Germany, where it was all published. Thus did Frau Saupe, at the age of 77, contribute to the downfall of the DDR regime. And thus did the world first learn about the new level of protest afoot in the DDR. (Photo courtesy of Annaliese Saupe)

Figure 16 (right). Annaliese Saupe of Plauen, c. 1946, when she became a *Neulehrerin* in the first year of the DDR's early postwar campaign to hire progressive, working-class teachers. (She was one of only four Plauen schoolteachers in 1946 to hold an *Abitur*.) In 1958, she was fired for her criticisms of communism and her open practice of her Lutheran faith. (Photo courtesy of Annaliese Saupe)

Figure 17. The renovated Nietzsche Haus in Weimar, 1999. Here at Humboldtstrasse 36, in a house then known as the Villa Silberblick, the philosopher Friedrich Nietzsche spent the last years of his life. His sister Elisabeth turned the home into the site of the Nietzsche Archives even before her brother's death in 1900. In this picture of the library, which was originally designed by Belgian *Jugendstil* architect Henry van der Velde, a mammoth white marble bust of the philosopher rests atop a six-foot pedestal. To its left, built-in bookshelves cradle volumes of Nietzscheana. The Nietzsche Haus, which had been closed by the Russian Army on entering Weimar in 1945, was reopened to the public for the first time in May 1991. (Photo courtesy of Stephan Schwarzkopf, Weimar)

Figure 18. The Friedrich Schiller Gymnasium in Weimar, formerly known as the Schiller EOS, 1999. During the DDR era, the Schillerschule was the leading school in Weimar and its only EOS. Its auditorium features windows into which classical German writers and artists are carved; a Nietzsche window was added by the Nazis in 1936, removed by the Communists in 1958, and reinstalled on the anniversary of Nietzsche's 100th birthday in October 1994. (Photo courtesy of Stephan Schwarzkopf, Weimar)

PART II

(POST)SOCIALISM WITH A GERMAN FACE, 1989–95

The human soul is virtually indestructible, and its ability to rise from the ashes remains as long as the body draws breath.

Alice Miller, *Am Anfang war Erziehung* (1980)
(*In the Beginning was Education*)

4

After the Wall II

The Fall and Rise of an Educational System

What belongs together is now growing together.

Willy Brandt, November 10, 1989

It will take longer to tear down the wall in our heads than any wrecking company will need for the wall we can see.

Peter Schneider,
The Wall Jumper (1983)

Accursed Volk! Just when you gain freedom, you break yourself into two pieces!

Goethe, 1831

Trabulations, or Lurching Toward Unity

In the fall of 1990, a hit movie comedy opened to packed houses in eastern German theaters. *Go, Trabi, Go!*—the producers gave the film an English title—celebrated with rollicking *Weltschmerz* the misadventures of Georg, a hapless baby-blue Trabant 601—whose jinxed capers make him the undeniable screen successor to Herbie, the Disney VW Beetle of the 1960s. Georg stalls pitifully on the *Autobahn*, is shorn of his bumper in Munich traffic, is robbed of all four tires by pranksters during a camping stop, and even gets mistaken for scrap near an auto junkyard, an obvious metaphor for the DDR running out of gas—as it lurches toward unity.

Go, Trabi, Go! begins with DDR German teacher Udo Struutz deciding to fulfill a long-deferred dream: his first journey to the West will be to travel from his hellhole hometown of industrial Bitterfield, the dirtiest city in all of Eastern Europe, to balmy Naples, thereby tracing the footsteps of his beloved Goethe, whose *Italian Journey* recorded his own (less quixotic) southern pilgrimage from Weimar in the 1780s. Herr Struutz packs his wife and daughter into little Georg, a family member for 20 years whom Herr Struutz lovingly wipes down with his own washcloth. "See Naples and Die!" scrawls Herr Struutz on Georg's trunk, recalling Goethe's clarion call to self-actualization: *"Sterbe und werde!"* ("die and become!").

The adventure turns out to be a story of Innocent *Ossis* Abroad and their psychological collision with the West. Numerous scenes in *Go, Trabi, Go!* allude to the region's plight: putt-putting along on the *Autobahn*, little Georg strains to do his maximum speed of 60 mph as contemptuous Mercedes-Benzes, Porsches, and

BMWs fly by; broken-down in Bavaria, Georg costs the Struutz family a steep (an outrageously inflated) price for repair, which the intrepid socialist entrepreneurs earn by charging curious Bavarians DM 5 for a "Trabi Peep Show" and a five-minute joy ride in Georg. Reassuringly, the Struutz family eventually does reach its destination, albeit with the accident-prone but indomitable Georg—now minus his top—as a breezy convertible.

East Germans loved *Go, Trabi, Go!*[1] They had always had a love/hate relationship with the 26-horsepower, plastic-frame, little two-stroke-engined *Trabant* (satellite), an early achievement of the DDR's "scientific-technical revolution." Named in honor of Sputnik's maiden flight, the first *Trabant* had rolled off the Zwickau assembly line in 1957. Its design and construction—featuring the world's first mass-produced plastic body—remained virtually unchanged for the next 30 years. Long mocked in the West as an ugly, fume-spewing jalopy, the Trabi symbolized the backwardness of DDR technology and of DDR life in general. No product was so widely associated with the DDR—and so widely ridiculed—as the Trabi: "plastic bomber," "crutch on wheels," "asphalt bubble," and "Zwickau cardboard," DDR citizens called it. Trabi jokes, like Ulbricht and Honecker jokes, had made the rounds for years in the DDR.[2] But the ridicule was tinged with affection, for the Trabi was also loved like a weirdly funny neighbor or an endearingly daft old aunt or uncle, especially so because it was practically the only immediately recognizable symbol of DDR identity. And unlike DDR political humor, Trabi jokes could be openly shared and freely embroidered:

Why are there no terrorists or bank robbers in the DDR?
Because of the 10-year delivery wait for a getaway car.

The Trabi is supposed to be renamed the "Luther."
Why?
Because Luther said in the Reichstag in Worms, "Here I stand, I cannot do
    otherwise."

Why does the Trabi have a heatable back window?
So you can keep your hands warm while pushing.

An American orders a Trabi. Because he pays in dollars, he gets one delivered
    to him immediately. Astonished, he sends the Ministry of Foreign Trade in
    East Berlin a telegram: "Thank you very much for the miniature model of
    your automobile. I look forward to receiving the car."

A Trabi driver goes to a BRD radio store.
"I would like to have a radio for my Trabi."
"Well, that's a pretty bad trade for us."

A weasel asks the Trabant: "What are you, really?"
"I'm a car."
The weasel laughs: "Then I'm a thoroughbred racing horse!"

A manure pile asks the Trabant: "What are you, really?"
"I'm a car."
"Then I'm a pizza!"

The traffic light turns green, but the Trabi driver can't move.
The accident service comes and reports after a few minutes:
"OK, you can drive now. But in the future, take care that you don't have any
　gum under your tires."

Post-Wall Trabi bumper sticker: Zero to 60 in 15 minutes!

More seriously, DDR students joked about their diplomas in terms of the Trabi.
"My *Abi* is no better than our *Trabi*," a Leipzig pupil, Ulrike, told me in early
1990 with a weak smile. "Worthless."

Ulrike exaggerated. But the comparison was apt: as late as September 1989, a
Trabi was a coveted possession in the DDR. Many people waited up to 15 years
for the opportunity to purchase a Trabi, and were willing to pay $8,000 or more
for the privilege, the equivalent of some DDR citizens' wages for a year. And the
price was often double that on the black market. Ulrike's family had, unfortunately, bought one just weeks before the Wall came down, when a Trabi in the
driveway was still a mark of distinction.

By 1990, however, western cars were beginning to dot Leipzig streets, and the
DDR had severely scaled back production of the Trabi. Because most Trabis failed
to meet strict West German pollution statutes (they emitted 10 times the hydro-
carbons of western cars) and bore the stigma of the "backward" DDR, people were
selling them, if they could, for a few hundred dollars or less. Formerly a symbol
of DDR attainment, the Trabi was now a sign of DDR adversity.

As was the *Abitur*.

Nearly all DDR pupils, as we have seen, had attended the 10-year POS (*Polytechnische Oberschule*) and received a uniform, non-selective education through
the age of 16 (the exceptions being students gifted in athletics, dance, etc.). After
graduating from the 10-year POS, roughly 13 percent of pupils advanced to the
two-year EOS (*Erweiterte Oberschule*; 11th and 12th grades). It was from this latter,
elite group that candidates for university were chosen. Disastrously for the DDR
educational system, however—and for the educational fates of its graduates upon
the fall of the Wall—the academic elite was chosen more on the basis of ideological than intellectual criteria, and the two years of advanced education were more
political than philosophical in content.

The *Abitur* had been a mark of privilege in the DDR; only *Abitur* holders could
hope to be among the 10 percent of DDR students accepted to university on the
basis of projected economic needs and guaranteed jobs after graduation.

But now East German *Abitur* holders would compete with West Germans holding a degree of an entirely different nature.

In the early postwar era, most of the western *Länder* had returned to the tripar-
tite system of traditional German education, which emphasizes diversity and early
tracking. At the age of 10, West German students move from elementary school to

the *Hauptschule* (general education school), *Realschule* (technical school), or *Gymnasium* (academic school). By the 1980s, approximately one-third of West German schoolchildren attended *Gymnasium*, which provided extensive academic training and led to the *Abitur*.

It was with these students that Ulrike and her peers would compete in 1990, to attend one of West Germany's 61 universities. Or they could stay home and go to one of East Germany's own deteriorating universities—and then one day possess (according to the dire prognosis of many observers at the time) a near-worthless university degree.

Ulrike and other East German students were caught in another historic moment—or time warp: the abrupt fall and slow rise of yet another German educational system. For the second time in a half-century, German education east of the Elbe would again "arise from ruins" at the behest of a foreign power, this time not to "build socialism" but to capitulate to capitalism, this time at the hands of a power invited by eastern Germans themselves. In this first phase of the post-Wall history of eastern German education (1989–90), which coincided with the collapse of the DDR and its integration into a newly united Germany, a crisis in education developed within the tumultuous transition from dictatorship to democracy through which the region, several years later, would still be passing.

The opening of the Wall led to a brain drain of eastern students, skilled labor, and youth that even exceeded the situation before the Wall went up in 1961. Once again, young pioneers were going westward: People under 25 comprised the bulk of the immigration flow, abandoning East Germany and its educational system at the rate of 2,000 per day. Many emigres were young high school graduates who now believed an advanced education in the east would be a badge of inferiority; 16 percent were students at eastern universities. DDR degrees—prized because they had indicated Party approval and because their numbers had been severely limited by the socialist planned economy—plummeted in value as reunification neared.[3]

But for those who stayed, the schools and universities were a shambles of disorganization and confusion—and excitement. By December 1989, schoolchildren were no longer standing at attention and pronouncing *"Freundschaft!"* on a teacher's entrance; now a casual *Guten Tag* would suffice. They were skipping Pioneer meetings or dropping out altogether. FDJ activities in schools and universities fizzled out; at the Carl Ossietzky EOS (the elite school where in 1988 critical pupils had been disciplined on orders from Margot Honecker herself) FDJ membership dwindled from 170 to 10;[4] in the universities, no one paid attention any more to the FDJ or the pre-military GST.

At all levels, the curriculum was being turned upside down. Every teacher I interviewed during the fall of 1990 mulled in anger the same question: Are there no good features of the DDR system to save? Nothing worth keeping in education? Their answers were various: the generous program of paid kindergartens and after-school day care; the polytechnic principle, which established firm connections between classroom and world; the single, unified school system of the 10-year POS.

But virtually nothing would survive. Already by December 1989, pupils were boycotting Russian and demanding that English be taught as the first foreign language; *Staatsbürgerkunde* and *Wehrerziehung* were dropped from the curriculum in most schools by the end of the month. With events overtaking the SED interpretation of history, many EOS teachers went back to teaching ancient history, which they judged to be a safe "niche" in their subject. Lower-level POS history of the nineteenth and twentieth centuries was similarly replaced by a flight into a review of feudal or ancient history. The 11th- and 12th-grade EOS classes on the history of the SED and CPSU, respectively, were eliminated in favor of current events; the universities jettisoned M-L, and ineptly initiated new courses that no DDR university had ever offered: corporate finance, labor markets, non-Marxist philosophy. Professors were, at best, just a few pages ahead of the students. Students openly sneered at many teachers' and professors' attempts to look credible with the new subject matters, especially those *Staatsbürgerkunde* teachers who struggled with the new subject of *Gesellschaftskunde* (social studies), devoted to the study of personal choices rather than state duties.

To many students and staff, the shattering results of the educational transformation made East German academic life resemble Humpty Dumpty After the Wall—and the challenge of putting the educational system back together again would be greater than anyone realized. And for many older eastern Germans, especially the students and *Neulehrer* of the early postwar era, the experience of their children and grandchildren evoked memories of the Soviet occupation and the educational reconstruction of 1945/46: chaos, mass firings or layoffs, no suitable textbooks, ideological "re-education," and structural revamping largely determined from a foreign capital. Again they felt as if they were living in an occupied country.

The crisis in education and youth affairs signified the demise of the vaunted polytechnical education experiment of the DDR, but it was not an isolated phenomenon: it was occurring in the context of the DDR's national collapse. Already by late November 1989, talk of reunification filled the air. An extended look at the dying DDR and the new Germany lurching toward unification is instructive here, for the larger sweep of events—both the stories of the expiring DDR and the emergent, enlarged BRD—influenced mightily the upheaval experienced by educators and youth during 1989/90.

In November 1989, many East Germans recognized that their situation would get worse before it got better. Still, no one other than SED functionaries and *Stasi* agents expected to be much worse off than before. But due to worker apathy and emigration—as always, mostly of young people under 25—the economy suddenly spiraled downward into free fall. Industrial output in November dropped 2.5 percent from the same month in 1988. Meanwhile, unmet production goals doubled and the government announced a budget deficit of $70 billion. The sudden exodus of more than 300,000 citizens, a 2 percent reduction in the work force, generated severe consumer shortages of everything from lawnmowers to laxatives. The DDR health care system suffered an extreme loss of qualified people due to the mass exodus; at one hospital in East Berlin, 30 physicians, 60 nurses, and 30 members of the technical and housekeeping staffs left for the west; rates of departure from provincial hospitals were even higher.[5] And the labor crisis would stretch far into the future: by the end of the year, the flight of women of child-bearing age would precipitate an 8 percent decline in the DDR birth rate.[6]

Throughout the winter of 1989/90, reunification prospects exacerbated the crisis, as factories laid off workers to make DDR enterprises more attractive as joint ventures for western investors. Pensioners and unskilled laborers trembled for their once-sacred social benefits; obsolete factories feared for their survival. The tight discipline of the NVA disintegrated after the borders opened. Desertion was rife, especially among the youngest soldiers; a demoralized officer corps watched as NVA strength dwindled to less than 100,000 men by December 1989, a loss of 70,000 since the summer. In order to prop up the economy, officers assigned the remaining disgruntled soldiers to civilian jobs, replacing East Germans who had fled across the border.

Would the DDR stand? With the clarity of hindsight, it is easy to forget that the question of German reunification *was* a question. On November 9, Egon Krenz had dismissed the idea of reunification, as had a spokesman for the Kremlin. But in a mid-November 1989 poll, only 19 percent of DDR citizens had expressed trust in the Krenz regime, and the flood tide of emigration showed no sign of turning.

The East German government frantically attempted to ride the waves of public opinion. "*Hans Modrow auf Egons Platz / Alles andere ist nur fax!*" shouted the protesters. "Hans Modrow in Egon's seat / Everything else is just buffoonery!" "*Modrow bleibt, der Rest muss gehen!*" ("Modrow can stay, the rest of you must go!").

Modrow? Who was Hans Modrow?

A mechanic by trade who had also earned a doctorate in economics, and a Central Committee member since 1967, Modrow had never made it to the Politburo, even as a candidate member. As regional Party boss in Dresden (1973–89), he had clashed on many occasions over *perestroika* with Honecker, who had once derided him as the "Dresden Dubček." Modrow had advocated Gorbachev-style economic reforms since the mid-1980s. In October 1989, he had publicly supported the pro-democracy demonstrations. Practically the only higher-echelon communist who commanded wide popular respect, the quiet, gray-haired Modrow had won admiration from Party rank-and-file and non-Party members alike during his Dresden years for refusing the limousine and villa available to state Party bosses, instead choosing to live with his family in a modest three-room apartment—a difference that shone all the more radiantly after the scandalous revelations about the Politburo's perks in Wandlitz. Modrow, 61, had been finally admitted to the Politburo the day before the fall of the Wall. If the People wanted Modrow, Modrow they would have.

On November 17, the Volkskammer formally elected Modrow prime minister. On that very day, he announced his plan for alternative civilian service to the NVA for DDR youths. On November 19, 1989, Egon Krenz stepped down as SED General Secretary; the following week—with its membership dropping by tens of thousands every day—the FDJ severed its formal ties with the SED, kicked out its hard-line chief, and replaced him with a Modrow protégé. On December 6, Krenz surrendered his remaining posts of Chairman of the Council of State and head of the National Defense Council, clearing the way for Modrow to assume full responsibility for the country's reform.

Immediately dubbed "the East German Gorbachev" for his reformist views, Modrow became the great Red hope of the Party. But already by late November, unity had become the dominant demand of the weekly demonstrations in Leipzig. And the talk was more than revolution from below; West German Chancellor Kohl himself brought up the idea of confederation as a way to promote inter-German cooperation, thereby broaching a subject near-taboo in West German public discussion for almost two decades: reunification. Ultimately, though it was not yet obvious, this step would mark the beginning of the end—of Modrow's tenure, SED-PDS rule, and the DDR itself.[7] Although Modrow's term of office would last until April 1990, the DDR proved imaginable only as a socialist alternative to the BRD. Once faith in socialism died, the DDR did too.

Beginning in early January, Modrow's luster was partly tarnished by his plan merely to reorganize the *Stasi*, rather than abolish it outright. Modrow favored reform over dissolution, he said, because a revamped *Stasi* was necessary to combat the rise of neo-Nazism. Critics saw Modrow's move, however, as an attempt by SED holdovers to restore the hated old secret police. Reluctantly bowing to public pressure to get rid of the *Stasi* altogether, Modrow withdrew his plan. Still, that was not enough, especially after reports surfaced that 1,000 to 1,500 unemployed *Stasi* agents had been given jobs as East Berlin schoolteachers.[8] The idea of former communist state spies explaining the virtues of democracy to their children was just too much for many East German parents, who now proceeded to take matters into their own hands. "*Stasi an die Stanze!*" went the cries in the streets. "*Stasi* officials in the metal punchers!" On January 15, crowds of angry protesters invaded the 3,000-room *Stasi* headquarters in East Berlin, destroying files and furniture.[9] And unlike the case in October 1989, when most students—fearful of losing their stipends and subsidized rooms—obeyed university authorities and did not participate in the *Demos*, this time students were out in force in the street protests:

Stasi, Gestapo, KGB, [Rumanian] Securitate: all bloodsuckers!

Secure rights instead of State Security!

Gestern Stasi, heute Nasi, Maskenwechsel quasi!
[Yesterday a *Stasi*, today a Nazi, just a flip of the mask!]

Gestapo-Stasi-Nasi! Constitutional Protection. Always the same guys and methods. Will it never end!

An alert *Volk* is the best State Security!

Stasi + SED = mass emigration!

Stasi: produzieren statt spionieren!
[*Stasi*: produce instead of spying!]

Stasi: statt gucken und gaffen lieber hucken und schaffen!
[*Stasi*: instead of looking and gaping, try carrying a load and doing something!]

When do we get security from the Security?

Staatsicherheit durch Öffentlichkeit! [State Security through Openness!]

Stasi Leute, reiht euch ein
Ihr sollt nicht länger Büttel sein!
[You *Stasi*, fall in line
You're not going to be petty officials any longer!]

Student passions were roused especially by the buzzing rumors about how readily the schools and universities had cooperated with the *Stasi*. (And were still co-operating, as the East Berlin schools' friendly gesture to assist the newly unem-ployed agents evinced.) It was widely known that half of DDR teachers had been SED members (and more than 90 percent in subjects like *Staatsbürgerkunde*); at least 80 percent of senior university professors had carried Party cards. But now *Stasi* files documented that each East German school had one to three spies on its staff; even schoolchildren had been recruited. In the universities, professors had reported regularly to the *Stasi* on returning from any trip abroad; university stu-dents who had cooperated had mysteriously been blessed with good fortune in scholarship applications and competition for elite jobs.[10]

Another decisive *Wende* in the *Wende* occurred in late January. With the emi-gration figure at 2,000 per day—comparable to the level of August 1961—Modrow acknowledged the citizenry's lack of confidence in his leadership. In a televised address, he appealed to the opposition to join him in a coalition government. On January 26, the opposition parties and movements announced their willingness to share power under Prime Minister Modrow; among the new cabinet members was former dissident and Democratic Awakening leader Rainer Eppelmann, who be-came minister of defense. But now the masses on both sides of the border were speaking with one voice: An early February poll showed that 87 percent of East Germans and 81 percent of West Germans wanted reunification. The Germans had long referred to *Tag X*—that mythical day in the misty future when the two Ger-manies would reunite. Now *Tag X* seemed suddenly on the horizon.[11]

The breakthrough came with Kohl and Genscher's visit to Moscow on the week-end of February 10/11, when Gorbachev agreed in principle to a reunified Ger-many that would remain in NATO. Given the deteriorating economic and political situation in the DDR, East German elections originally scheduled for May were advanced to March 18, a move that smaller opposition groups belatedly realized favored the already well-organized major parties, the CDU and SPD (and even the PDS).

Meanwhile, the schools and universities teetered between ferment and chaos. Schools and even university departments lacked not just computers but copy ma-chines; even university students had grown accustomed to copying out, by hand, pages and pages of articles and books.[12] Most schools had few or no teaching materials. Many classes turned into defiant rap sessions about the evils of the DDR system and freewheeling discussions on the fate of the nation.

Perhaps the most ironic—and even comical—curricular feature of the educa-tional transition had to do with textbooks. In early 1990, West Germany sent 30 million used texts to the DDR—and the results were sometimes pure bathos: for instance, the history and politics textbooks from SPD-governed West German *Län-*

der were teaching DDR pupils not how bad—but how beautiful—"real-existing socialism" really was.

How did this happen? In the BRD, unlike in the DDR, educational policy was not centrally administered, but rather handled by individual West German *Länder*. Because of this, textbooks often differed substantially from *Land* to *Land*. All pre–1970-era West German textbooks had indeed roundly condemned DDR socialism, and most CDU-*Länder* textbooks continued to do so through the 1980s; beginning with the era of East-West *détente* and the Brandt-Honecker *Deutschlandpolitik*, however, several SPD-governed *Länder* specified that DDR chapters in textbooks were to be written from the "self-understanding" of the DDR government. The result was passages such as the following from a politics text: "Under socialism, people therefore live in prosperity and peace." Or take this classic example of the old theory of equivalence:

> How is a "free press" free? The American press is certainly freer than the communist press from government direction and the pressure of the ruling political party. The press of the communist countries is definitely freer than the American press from the influence of commercial advertising and from the power of private capital. The American press is to a greater measure free from censorship; the communist press is freer from pornography.[13]

Thus, rather than learning about the *Stasi*, SED privileges and corruptions, Moscow's iron-hand manipulations of its German puppet-state, and the real story of the 1953 workers' uprising and the erection of the Berlin Wall, thousands of DDR pupils still protesting in the streets against SED policies and overwhelmingly supporting reunification found themselves in an ironic, near-schizophrenic position: Now they were learning—via the textbooks of the former ideological enemy and even as their parents were deciding to vote the DDR out of existence and join the BRD—just how good they had really had it under the SED.[14]

Teachers too were learning—and relearning. Having been trained to treat pupils as collective beings and thereby create "socialist personalities," they were now being told to teach critical thinking and to treat pupils as individuals with their own unique talents. Russian and *Staatsbürgerkunde* teachers were also relearning in other ways. For instance, because Russian was scheduled to be reclassified as an elective in fall 1990, Russian teachers were retraining themselves to teach English or French. Since Russian had received more class hours per week than any subject except German and math before the *Wende*, the DDR's 15,000 Russian teachers, along with thousands of *Staatsbürgerkunde* and history teachers, now feared (with cause) that they would soon lose their jobs.[15] Some higher education faculty took steps to avoid that result; in the 60 institutes of the East German Academy of Sciences, secret ballots returned 50 percent of the old SED professors to their posts, which guaranteed that no wholesale purge of SED members would occur. But thousands of the DDR's 130,000 students were streaming westward; hundreds had enrolled in West Berlin alone. To stem the tide, Bonn offered $590 million to halt the flow.[16] And to help keep qualified young faculty in East German higher education, Bonn agreed to invest at least DM 2.3 billion over the next decade in faculty development.[17]

As the days wound down to the March elections, the national political scene altered radically. The Social Democrats were very popular initially as the party of Willy Brandt, who had done so much to improve inter-German relations in the 1970s. But as the central election issue became national reunification—a March poll showed that 91 percent of East Germans favored unity and only 5 percent were against—the party in power in Bonn, the CDU, gained support.[18] Many intellectuals, in both the west and east, supported Modrow's suggestion for a go-slow approach, perhaps a closer contractual relationship between the BRD and DDR, regarding such an arrangement as well-suited to the current state of relations between the two countries. But those relations were altering almost daily: East Germans were rapidly making it clear that confederation would not be well-suited to future relations.

The CDU campaigned on quick reunification and continuity of leadership, and it was widely believed in the east—by DDR youth too—that the CDU was best qualified to guide economic reconstruction. Politicians from the west made regular visits to the east. In a February campaign stop in Erfurt, Kohl was introduced as "Chancellor of our German Fatherland," as 130,000 ecstatic East Germans cheered. The growing support for the CDU leading up to the March 18 election thus soon translated not only into a condemnation of 40 years of DDR socialism but into a positive referendum on the capitalist system and Kohl's leadership qualifications, as the placards in DDR streets in February and March made clear.

Kommt die D-Mark / bleiben wir
Kommt sie nicht / gehen wir zu ihr!
[If the D-Mark comes, we'll stay
If it doesn't, we're coming to you!]

No second experiment. Reunification!

BRDDR!

Put an end to the empty 40-Year serialized Utopia!

The new federal state of Saxony greets its Chancellor!

Wir grüssen Helmut Kohl—nur Einheit tut uns wohl!
[We greet Helmut Kohl—only unity will work!]

Helmut und Hans, macht Deutschland ganz!
[Helmut and Hans, make Germany one!]

Better a Kohl plantation than another socialist Fatherland!

Better Kohl (cabbage) than mere vegetables!

Ein Volk, ein Reich, wie früher!
[One People, one Nation as before!]

Freiheit, Gleichheit, Käuflichkeit!
[Freedom, equality, economic competitiveness!]

DDR nicht verfassen—abschaffen!
[Don't reform the DDR—abolish it!]

Nevertheless, reunification opponents, though they numbered only a small minority, were also quite vocal. For many intellectuals and dissidents, reunification amounted to annexation, a betrayal of their hopes in October and November for a reformed socialist DDR. Their election slogans raised doubts both about an eastern future under capitalism and about the spectre of a right-wing Germany, doubts that would, little more than a year later, resonate in the populace deeply:

I'm going to keep my face, Herr Kohl! Another won't suit me!

Helmut, nimms nicht so schwer / Wir bleiben DDR!
[Helmut, don't take it so hard / We're staying the DDR!]

Do you want *den totalen Kohl* [the total Kohl]?[19]

Vom Stalin-Regen in die Gross-Deutsche Traufe?
[From the Stalinist (steel) frying pan into the Greater German fire?] [der Stahl-steel]

Better red than colorless!

We won't let ourselves be bought by Mickey Mouse, McDonald's, and Coca-Cola!

DDR—not for sale!

Wir lassen uns nicht BRDigen!
[We won't be broken in (*bändigen*)!]

Lieber rote Ruben als den Kohl von drüben!
[Better red beets than cabbage (money) from over there!]

Der Kanzler lenkt, aber wer denkt?
[The Chancellor is steering, but who's thinking?][20]

Better the Third Way than the Fourth Reich!

Right turn *verboten*!

Wir brauchen weder Krenz noch Kohl
Nur wenn wir selbst regieren wird uns wieder wohl!
[We need neither Krenz nor Kohl
Only when we ourselves rule will things go well!]

Wir wollen nicht verKOHLt werden!
[We won't have the wool pulled over our eyes!]

Gegen KOHLonie!
[Against becoming a KOHLony!]

Für unser Wohl ohne Kohl!
[For our welfare—no Kohl!]

On March 18, 1990, in the first free election in eastern Germany since 1932, 93.4 percent of East Germans voted, the highest turnout of any free election in German history. It was a stunning victory for the Alliance for Germany, led by the CDU, which received 47 percent of the vote; the SPD won only 21.8 percent and Alliance 90 only 2.9 percent. The PDS did surprisingly well, garnering 16.3 percent. The

CDU triumph was a resounding vote of confidence for Kohl, a clear statement by East Germans that they wanted a better life—i.e., the D-Mark—immediately. Kohl soon obliged, announcing that East Germans could exchange their wages, pensions, and personal savings for D-Marks at a one-to-one rate, up to DM 4,000 ($2,400), and at two-to-one for additional savings—an extraordinarily favorable deal given that the black-market exchange rate had been 5 to 1 or higher.

On April 5, CDU leader Lothar de Maizière took over the East German government from Modrow, thus becoming the first and last freely elected prime minister in DDR history. Maizière organized a coalition government that included the SPD and Alliance 90. One of the first acts of the new *Volkskammer* was to issue a statement acknowledging the DDR's joint responsibility for the Holocaust and apologizing to Jews, Poles, Slavs, and Gypsies. The new *Volkskammer* also reaffirmed the Oder-Neisse frontier with Poland and asked forgiveness for participating in the suppression of the Prague Spring.

Now events began to take on the appearance of the inevitable: it was just a question of exactly how and when reunification would occur. In the May 6 local elections, the CDU again led the field, paving the way for another significant step on the road to reunification: the currency union of July 1, when the D-Mark replaced the Ost-Mark.

Finally, however, at midnight on October 2, 1990, a giant (West) German flag was unfurled outside the old Reichstag building and the first words of the third verse of the West German national anthem, the *Deutschlandlied*, rang out—"*Einigkeit und Recht und Freiheit*," the crowd sang, "Unity and Justice and Freedom." Fireworks shot through the Berlin sky, as more than a million Germans converged again on the Brandenburg Gate to celebrate the long-sought arrival of *Tag X*, now officially named *Tag der Einheit* (Unity Day). East and West Germans sang old German folk songs and drank Berliner Weisse together in celebration. President Richard von Weizsäcker vowed that the nation would serve peace in the twenty-first century. To many observers, the celebration marked the end of the Cold War and European division. To a great extent because of the German October and November Revolutions, 1989 would go down as the most important year in modern history, rivaled only by 1789 and the French Revolution.

Now, at last, two Germanies were one; the Germans and the world, as an old Freiburg teacher of mine reminded me, could once again say "*Deutschland*."

But whereas euphoria, tinged with premonitions of anxiety, had been the predominant emotion of 1989, feelings in 1990 were already giving way to doubt. Even on October 3, at least outside Berlin, the underlying mood was reflective, even somber, rather than jubilant or even buoyant. The west was beginning to worry about the costs of unification; the east was plunging into a region-wide identity crisis.

Educators and students shared the new mood, which was pervaded by economic uncertainty. Between June and December of 1990, the East German economy shrank by more than a third, with a loss of 1.1 million jobs. Industrial output fell by 50 percent below 1989 levels and unemployment skyrocketed 15-fold (to 30 percent overall and 60 percent in some industrial areas). But in that same period, the West German economy boomed: growing by a spectacular 4.5 percent and creating 800,000 new jobs. Many East Germans began to feel less like free men and women than second-class citizens of the "KOHLony" against which the dissidents had warned. The road to October seemed to them, in hindsight, less a process of *Vereinigung* than *Anschluss.*[21]

Even as eastern educators still lacked textbooks for basic courses, the battle lines between west and east for the control of new nation's resources were forming. Plans were under way to gut the DDR sports machine, cutting at least 90 percent of the staff and coaching jobs.[22] Although Hans Joachim Meyer, the DDR's last Education Minister, had assured the 170,000 POS and EOS teachers that there would be no mass firings by the west-dominated screening commissions, teachers fretted for their jobs—especially after a prominent West German scientist, Heinz Bethge, the former president of the prestigious Leopoldine Academy at Halle University, remarked that most eastern professors owed their careers to collaboration with the SED or *Stasi,* and that 80 percent of DDR teachers and professors were SED members and at least 60 percent of them should be fired.[23]

The western attitude toward higher education seemed similarly severe. Surveying the landscape of DDR social science, Hans F. Zacher, newly elected president of the Max Planck Institute, unhesitatingly declared: "It is a desert." Even a few DDR professors joined in the criticism. Of the East German Academy of Sciences, Lutz Nover of the Institute for Plant Biochemstry in Halle concluded: "The Academy of Sciences is just a pile of old-fashioned Stalinists. . . . Sixty percent of them have no connection with science; they're there purely because they've been bought."[24]

Thus, while united Germany seemed poised to return to its prewar eminence in the sciences and become the second leading scientific and educational power in the world, political infighting over funding and jobs was growing fierce. In the west, educators feared that reinvigoration of the east would inevitably necessitate cuts in their own budgets. They also worried about massive overcrowding of their institutions and severe housing shortages in university towns from the wave of resettlers still flowing into western universities that were already crammed with 1.5 million students, double the number envisioned in the 1970s. In the east, the upcoming ideological *Überprüfung* (screening) of all educational staff by western evaluators generated fears of mass firings, evoking memories of the ruthless Soviet purges during the SBZ days. By October 1990, most M-L faculty had already been dismissed; other ideologically "tainted" departments—such as economics, history, and political science—were facing complete closure. Also enflaming East-West tensions was eastern resentment about the westerners' salaries: eastern teachers were receiving just a third ($655 median) of the salaries of western colleagues hired to teach in the east. (In most cases, however, this sum still exceeded East Germans' 1989 salaries.)[25]

Berlin—*Treffpunkt Berlin*—where east and west met, was the site of the most contentious disputes once the "purges" began.[26] At Humboldt University in East Berlin, professors and students spoke of a "witchhunt" conducted by the west. Because West Berlin already had two major universities and some legislators saw little reason to maintain a third one, there was even talk about abolishing Humboldt altogether. Throughout December 1990, Humboldt faculty and students marched against the dissolution of the law, philosophy, aesthetics, cultural studies, history, and teacher-training departments, which administrators planned to close, restructure on non-Marxist lines, and then reopen with new faculties. "The whole thing," editorialized *Neues Deutschland*, which remained a voice of the eastern Left, "stinks of a politically motivated settling of scores." At the head of a protest march from Berlin to Leipzig, students from Humboldt and Leipzig's Karl-Marx University carried a sign: "*Ossis* and *Wessis* have only interpreted the BRD differently: the point, however, is to change it."[27]

But East German voters were in no mood for any more big changes. Although eastern classrooms were already seeing T-shirts with the notorious caption: "I want my Wall back!" frustrated easterners were preparing to interpret the BRD in the same conservative terms as westerners. Sickened and exhausted by the prospect of yet another trip to the polls—this incessant voting!—easterners joined westerners in the nationwide elections on December 2, 1990, the first election in reunified Germany.

The election merely ratified the CDU's commanding position in the east as well as the west. Along with its sister party, the Bavarian CSU, the CDU won 43.8 percent of the vote; the SPD was a distant second with 33.5; the Greens garnered only 3.9 and the PDS 2.9. Still, despite the fact of another CDU electoral victory, a clear change in the eastern German temper was discernible in the eight months since the March election frenzy: from hope to apprehension.

Three decades of Trabis could not be overcome by a few months of fresh bananas. East and West were now united: but in name only, not in spirit. Honecker's blustery forecast of January 1989 that the Wall would be standing "in 50, still in 100 years" had proven laughably false, but a psychological wall remained—and threatened to do so for many years to come.

On Unity Day 1990, speaking on the Reichstag steps before millions of TV viewers, Prime Minster de Maizière had bid "farewell without tears" to the DDR. But perhaps the real end of the DDR came during a tearful though little-publicized moment the following April, when the last Trabi, No. 3,096,099, trundled off the Zwickau conveyer belt. In the face of stiff western competition, with most eastern Germans buying or trading up for western cars, VEB Sachsenring had spent the last year trying to modernize the Trabi, hoping that it might sell again with a metal body, a four-stroke, 50-horsepower Volkswagen engine, an upgraded transmission, and real springs. But despite Georg the Trabi's movie-stardom, and even at the bargain price of $4,000, there were few takers.

And so, nostalgia was in the air as 3,600 East Germans—including Saxony Prime Minister Kurt Biedenkopf and 50,000 newly jobless autoworkers—wept and jeered. It seemed that everybody had a story about his or her trials with the boxy four-wheel midget.

The offhand comment of one Zwickau bystander gave voice to the dread of obsolescence that many ex-DDR citizens felt about their own lives as they entered the brave new *Bundesrepublik*.

"It was a good car," he mused, "30 years ago."[28]

Ossification, or Purging through Merging

Der Schoss ist fruchtbar noch, aus dem das kroch.
[The womb from which that crawled is fertile still.]

Brecht, *The Resistable Rise of Arturo Ui* (1940)

Hopes ran high after the fall of Honecker and Krenz, and even after German reunification, that with the decline of the DDR, a genuine "sunrise in the east" might follow in eastern education. Former dissidents such as Jens Reich, head of New Forum and a researcher at the Central Institute for Molecular Biology in the East Berlin Academy of Sciences, had dreamed throughout the Revolution of 1989/ 90 of a "university of the new type" in non-SED terms—a university modeled on the SBZ's promise of university renewal of 1945/46 and in the *Reformschule* tradition that had flowered in Saxony and Thuringia in the 1920s. But it wasn't long before the would-be reformers grew disillusioned.[29] Most DDR students and professors—much like their Nazi-era forebears—had laid low in the early phases of the Revolution of the Candles; apparently it was too much to expect that they would now initiate thoroughgoing renewal in the universities.

Utopian hopes spring eternal, but no: a new beginning was not to be. In hindsight it is clear that a real transformation of eastern education would have required something like the authority of the Soviets in the SBZ after World War II—this time without the arbitrariness and injustices that followed. But post-unification education in the east resembled the early postwar situation in the western zones— not the SBZ—whereby, through local intransigence and bureaucratic entanglements, special interest groups frustrated full-scale reform. True, DDR school years no longer began with learning "We are the Young Pioneers / Marching on our way to socialism." Saturday classes had been dropped (the major source of DDR schoolchildren's "class hatred"); *Wehrerziehung* and the old textbooks had disappeared. But so too had free kindergartens and day care. Worse, there had not occurred a major overhaul of eastern personnel—with selected exceptions—let alone the once hoped-for rethinking in the west of the purpose of education.

Instead, the countdown to unity was followed by a meltdown to uniformity. In this second period of post-Wall education in the east (1991/92), "merging" the west and east—the Germany of the Mercedes and the Germany of the Trabi—came to mean *sub*merging east into west—and purging those eastern remnants that didn't easily integrate or dissolve. High aspirations now gave way to dashed expectations: the *Wende* of 1989/90 had been the euphoric year of good news; 1991/ 92 would be a time of *Wendekrankheit* (turnabout sickness), a period of resentment and despair in which easterners reacted angrily yet helplessly to the perceived economic discrimination and arrogance of westerners.

Now the old Honecker jokes, the SED and *Stasi* puns, and the Trabi gags gave way to a new genre of eastern wit. The new humor faced off east against west. Its staple: the *Besserwessi* joke.[30]

Q: What do you call a person from the old federal states who drones on in the new federal states about his extensive experience?
A: A BESSER-WESSI!

A *Besserwessi*—a pun on the term *besserwisser* (know-it-all, smart aleck)—is a *Wessi* who fancies that he or she knows everything better.

> So, dear course participant from the east, today I am going to teach you how one calculates with computers. Ossi, you begin: How many are 8 computers and 4 computers?

The esoteric Wessi:
> Ossi, don't you always have a feeling of magnetism when we're together?
> Yes, you repel me.

Wessi: I must ask you urgently not to mention to anyone how much money I'm paying you.
Ossi: No, I fear I'm just as ashamed of it as you are.

> The western recipe for success: Should the partners be of the same opinion, then the opinion of the Ossi applies. When the partners are of a different opinion, then the opinion of the Wessi applies.[31]

And with the new jokes came a new, western-style bureaucratese: the Orwellian vocabulary of BRD capitalism.

Abwicklung (winding down, wrapping up, liquidation), the epitome of government Newspeak, was the word of the hour.[32] Like DDR state firms, DDR schools and universities would now be *abgewickelt*, i.e., dismantled, dissolved, and reconstructed in the western image and likeness. (In this respect, the post-Wall DDR *did* resemble the postwar SBZ, as the 4 Ds (demilitarization, deindustrialization, denazification, democratization) were practiced by the Soviets. Pre-unification talk in Bonn of re-evaluating western institutions in light of the needs of a New Germany, perhaps with an eye toward adopting successful features of the DDR system, were heard no more; as more information emerged about the east's crumbling infrastructure and SED-corrupted institutions, the western system began to look surprisingly strong.[33]

To West German politicians, the DDR would simply have to be "wrapped up" according to the unification treaty. *Abwicklung*, however, is also sometimes translated as "liquidation"—as in a business liquidation—and the German word also bears a drop of the same murderous tinge as does our English usage. This connotation was not lost on thousands of enraged, depressed, unemployed, or underemployed easterners. In an astounding February 1991 poll, 90 percent of eastern Germans stated that they felt like second-class citizens; East Berlin playwright Heiner Müller spoke of the "submissive look of the colonized" in the faces of his eastern neighbors.[34] Unlike other former communist nations, whose states still existed and whose citizenry were conducting their own political renewal, many eastern Germans did indeed feel colonized by the west: the unheeded warnings about the east turning into a "KOHLony" through unification had proven true for them. *Abwicklung* seemed like a hostile takeover.

So the "five new federal states" would now be molded in the image of the eleven old ones. In the schools, the DDR uniform system of the POS and EOS would be abolished, and the West German system of differentiated, ability-oriented school-

ing would be adopted; in the universities, the curriculum and admissions processes would be totally revamped on western terms.

Amalgamating a communist and a capitalist educational system was soon to
prove an unprecedented and excruciatingly painful task. And insofar as merging
east into west entailed a psychological purging—the purging of the East German
past, the purging of East German identity—it was arguably the most painful aspect
of unification for eastern educators. For thousands of them, *Verostung* (becoming
eastern, "rusting out," i.e., "*Ossi*fication") was coming to mean accepting the par-
alyzing ossification of the eastern German spirit. *Verostung* was thus actually a
widely resisted process of what could also have been called *Verwestung* (becoming
western), for it signified an acquiescence to the supremacy of the *Besserwessi*,
whose agenda was to clone the western infrastructure in the east, i.e., to *wessify*
it.

The full costs and implications of reunifying the two educational systems were
only belatedly grasped by the CDU, Chancellor Kohl, and the western and eastern
populaces. Sharp differences on two separate yet overlapping and interacting issues—political background and training qualifications—confronted educators trying to evaluate DDR institutions and integrate the eastern and western school and
higher-education systems.

In the schools, battles raged between those who insisted on a thorough house-
cleaning and those who claimed that they too had been victims of the system.
Many teachers felt that the Cold War victors were dictating terms to the vanquished. Press accounts reported two angry, sharply opposed groups of eastern
teachers: those favoring amnesty, who charged that the west, planning a witch
hunt, had no conception of what it was like to work in a police state; and the new
hard-liners, who vowed that *this* time the guilty would publicly acknowledge their
roles in the totalitarian past, which had seldom happened under western (or even
SBZ) denazification.

Probably a majority of eastern Germans sided with the hard-liners; in an EMNID
survey in July 1991 in Saxony, 71 percent of citizens demanded the firing of "politically unfit teachers."[35]

But already, the appetite for justice—or revenge—was slackening; many of the
students who had been victimized by Party- and *Stasi*-loyal SED teachers were by
now starting over in the west. Others, who had stayed, just wanted to get on with
their lives and succeed in the new system; they and their parents feared that firing
politically suspect yet competent teachers would hurt even further their *Abitur*
performance and thus their chances to study in the west. Or their job prospects
at home: parents and students were well aware that, for the 120,000 graduates in
1991, there were only an estimated 40,000 eastern job openings.[36] And so
thousands of them wrote letters and even demonstrated on behalf of teachers
whom everyone knew had been strict Party-line mouthpieces. As one frustrated
reform-oriented teacher conceded: "The time of forgetting has begun."[37]

The result was that school personnel changed much less than feared—or
hoped—after the collapse of communism. The five *Länder* conducted their screening processes of teachers independently. For the most part, the only teachers
sacked were former *Stasi* agents and some former school inspectors and cadre

leaders. Since each school seldom had more than one or two *Stasi* teacher-spies, a school inspector, and a cadre leader, the purged group amounted to a small fraction of the 165,000 teachers in eastern schools.[38] The big exception was in CDU-dominated Saxony, where Education Minister Stefanie Rehm sent *blaue Briefe* ("blue letters," i.e., pink slips) to 7,000 (of 52,000) teachers in 1991—*all* of those who, "at any time, actively and unreservedly executed SED policies."[39] She required bodyguard protection after receiving numerous death threats.[40]

The paradoxes were uncanny and unnerving. In Berlin, for example, former SED-loyal teachers were allowed to keep their jobs, while numerous DDR teachers who had opposed the regime and fled the country before 1990 remained jobless. Until Unity Day 1990, DDR teaching qualifications had gone unrecognized in the BRD, so DDR refugees who wanted to teach in the BRD had to spend two years in retraining programs. But now, with the GEW—the eastern labor union—defending even former *Staatsbürgerkunde* teachers and demanding that the state retrain them for other school subjects, there were no jobs available for the newly requalified refugee teachers. "The victims are being punished," sighed one such jobless teacher, "and the culprits are being rewarded."[41] From his point of view, it was a thin coat of paint, indeed, slapped onto the little Red schoolhouse. A new generation of *Neulehrer* was not to be.[42]

In the universities, tensions ran, if anything, even higher—for students as well as professors. Suddenly, university students felt a dizzying freedom and a charge of *Zukunftsangst* (fear of the future), just like the rest of the eastern population: Whereas East German universities had fitted students into highly regimented programs of study, closely monitored by professors charged with keeping them on the four-year track, eastern students found that western German universities valued student initiative and self-sufficiency, and granted them a level of casual autonomy reserved in America for graduate students: in the humanities, students could take almost any courses they chose, in any order they chose. They had little contact with and received little guidance from their professors; they sat for "exit" exams largely when they themselves determined they were ready—and they often weren't ready for six or even eight years. And because they knew they would enter an uncertain, highly competitive job market, the classroom itself was a tough, competitive market that determined distinctions and jobs.

And for thousands of eastern faculty, *Zukunftsangst* became the anti-utopian present. By January 1991, six of the 55 eastern institutions of higher education had been closed, including East Berlin's noted Bruno Leuschner College of Economics, where 36 professors of Marxism-Leninism were forcibly retired. Of 200 lecturers, half were compelled to resign; most of them, however, were then permitted to take a two-year MBA course, and some were rehired if they passed the courses. (In their places, 44 western instructors lectured in subjects unknown or condemned in DDR days: strategies of marketing, entrepreneurial finance, and corporate management.)[43] Once again, Saxony proved the toughest *Land*, dismissing 14,000 higher education faculty by mid-1991; at Karl-Marx University in Leipzig—soon to be returned to its original, pre-1953 name, Leipzig University—a western dean initially sacked all DDR-era lecturers.[44] Journalism, M-L, and economics had already been eliminated, and their faculty dismissed or forcibly retired, receiving the same benefits as did schoolteachers in similar categories.[45]

The dictatorship of the professoriat did not exactly wither away, however. Its survival was guaranteed by actualizing the old word *Seilschaft* (roped-together mountain climbers), which became the newest Newspeak term for SED comrades who hung together and pulled for each other.

SED corruption in institutions of higher education had been—and continued to be—pervasive. The northeastern state of Mecklenburg-Vorpommern, the poorest land in the new BRD, for example, had a bloated staff of 15,000 professors and lecturers for a student body barely numbering 13,000. The new Minister of Culture Oswald Wutzke, a priest catapulted into the job by the paucity of untainted politicians, announced after reunification that four of the six institutions of higher education in Mecklenburg-Vorpommern were to be *abgewickelt*. The move was evidently justified, but when politics intervened, Wutzke capitulated before a pressure campaign organized by old SED comrades. In the end, he made only token firings, costing *Land* taxpayers more than $100 million; some Mecklenburgers outraged by his sunny reassurances that everything would still work out fine began speaking of a "Wutzke" as "the shortest distance between two cow piles."[46] SED teamwork was in further evidence at Rostock University, where the selection of faculty leaders was done by a vote of the general faculty—the vast majority of whom had been SED members. So 80 to 90 percent of the university council consisted, unsurprisingly, of former SED members. And unsurprisingly, aside from abolishing M-L, *Abwicklung* at Rostock was purely cosmetic.[47]

Still, by the end of 1991, 109 departments in 37 institutions of higher learning throughout the former DDR had been *abgewickelt*, to the evident approval of western educators.[48] Affirming the dismissals, Johannes Niermann, professor of pedagogy at the University of Cologne, caused a stir when he declared that former DDR professors were "incapable of acting and thinking beyond what they have been taught in the last 40 years." Harald Fritzsch, formerly a leading DDR physics professor who had fled to Munich in the 1970s, argued that the DDR's senior science faculty had been worse than those of any other East European nation: the DDR had been the only East bloc country that had introduced explicit political criteria and quotas for senior faculty promotions, whereby a certain percentage of full professors had to be SED members; DDR faculty at western conferences, the so-called *Reisekader* (traveling cadres), had been chosen strictly on the basis of Party loyalty and receptivity to *Stasi* collaboration. Fritzsch did not discuss the humanities faculty, but national Education Minister Jürgen Möllemann had already delivered the coup de grâce on them: some eastern scientists might be competitive, speculated Möllemann, but one could "forget about the contents of the liberal arts."[49]

These salvos provoked bitter rejoinders. Detlef Ganten, director of the new National Laboratory for Biomedical Research in East Berlin, observed that "if we evaluated the universities in the west as rigorously as we have evaluated" DDR education, "half of those universities would be empty overnight."[50] Ulrich Reinisch, head of Humboldt's School of Liberal Arts, suggested that the western criticism was part of a carefully orchestrated "barrage of attacks on the liberal arts" in eastern Germany.[51]

"*Keine kollektive Schuld!*" ("No collective guilt!") became the slogan of eastern faculty in both the shut-down and surviving departments. But could individual evaluations have worked? Like harried, wearied tenure committees, small groups of western scholars did appraise thousands of DDR professors individually during 1991/92. But for the most part these evaluations were superficial, extending the benefit of the doubt, whenever possible, to the professors. (Even so, some individual dismissals were subsequently overturned on appeal.)

And as it turned out, though DDR fields like (socialist realist) architecture and sports medicine were judged "a crime against humanity,"[52] western evaluators decided that the casual denigration of DDR scholarship proved only partly true. This was especially so in the sciences, as the 10-month study of eastern higher education by the German Science Council, completed in July 1991, concluded. According to the evaluators, some eastern research—especially mathematics, geology, and certain medical fields—was of excellent quality; due to the DDR's joint space program with Moscow, DDR astrophysics was judged to be superior to its West German counterpart.[53]

Still, the Science Council did not abandon the policy of *Abwicklung*. Its main focus was upon scientific research in the east, much of which had been carried out by East Berlin's Academy of Sciences. Formerly the Prussian Academy of Sciences, founded by Leibniz in 1700 and the prewar home of such figures as Max Planck and Albert Einstein, the Academy had been refashioned after the Soviet model in 1945 and vastly expanded. In 1968, following the Soviet bloc policy of promoting economies of scale in research, most research activity was removed from universities to the Academy, which by 1990 consisted of 120 research institutes, 17,500 scholars and researchers, and 30,000 staff.

The scale was hardly economical, however: the Academy's labs were overstaffed by a factor of three compared to the west.[54] Moreover, only SED members, after clearance through *Stasi* background checks, had been eligible for promotion to institute directors. The SED could and did impose its own candidates in a Party-controlled process even stricter than in USSR science (where the CPSU could only veto candidates). Molecular biologist and dissident Jens Reich, for instance, had failed to pass the *Stasi* vetting in the 1980s because he maintained unauthorized western contacts. (In an earlier age, of course, he might well have been fired or even jailed.) The Science Council's final recommendation called for cutting the number of research institutes in the Academy by more than half (including purging 7,500 of 8,500 junior researchers). Only a third—about 10,000 researchers—of the Academy's scientific personnel would be retained.[55]

The recommendations further called for bringing research back into the universities. And so some of the Academy's research programs were transferred to eastern and western universities, arousing the suspicions of some eastern researchers who thought they discerned the western evaluators' real purpose: to undercut eastern competitiveness by dismantling excellent research facilities that might have contended successfully with their western rivals for scarce funds.[56]

In the non- and social sciences, all remaining ideologically "tainted" university departments, i.e., M-L, law, economics, journalism, and pedagogy—would be immediately *abgewickelt*. An individual screening of faculty in other departments would follow. Evaluators would scrutinize questionnaires distributed to all eastern academics and researchers, who had to provide information on *Stasi* collaboration, SED service, and/or other kinds of political activity.

The main *Abwicklung* controversy in eastern higher education, however, continued to involve the former jewel in the crown of DDR academe, the onetime elite SED "university of the new type": Humboldt University.[57] After the CDU victory in December 1990, which led to the decision by the Berlin City Senate to abolish six departments, the university competed in early 1991 for funding with western Berlin's two established universities—the Free University and the Technical University.

The calls for Humboldt's complete abolition faded in 1991, but Berlin politics made a comprehensive *Abwicklung* of Humboldt impossible. Decisively seizing the initiative, supporters of the SED old guard at the university promptly turned western ideals of academic freedom to their advantage, declaring that the Berlin City Senate's decision to fire "tainted" professors constituted "a brutal assault" on the "autonomy of the universities"—a notion not much regarded in the Ulbricht-Honecker days, as western observers archly noted.[58] Protest activities increased. Humboldt students protested to save their professors' jobs by occupying offices and circulating petitions to recall Berlin politicians promoting *Abwicklung*. Another protest gesture was to boycott classes, especially those taught by distinguished, newly arrived western professors, further sharpening east/west tensions.[59]

The chief opponent of *Abwicklung* was Heinrich Fink, the first freely elected rector at Humboldt. A former theology professor who enjoyed a reputation as an inspiring teacher among his students, Fink had been the only non-SED member of Humboldt's Faculty Senate and among the few DDR professors to march in the streets in early October 1989. As the new rector, he at first sought a democratic self-renewal at Humboldt by imploring "politically unfit" professors to quit voluntarily. (At least 150 of the 780 senior Humboldt faculty had worked as informants or officers for the *Stasi*.[60]) Few heeded his request; but Fink opposed any interference in university affairs from the Berlin City Senate. The result was that politically suspect faculty continued to teach at Humboldt. The old-boy SED *Seilschaft* also went into action: by early 1991, 2,522 tenured staff had been fired, their departments officially *abgewickelt;* within months, roughly 700 of them—including 146 of 268 old M-L faculty—had won legal appeals and were secure again, back in their old jobs, or in newly created positions.[61]

The educators' battle of Berlin was joined. In early 1992, the Berlin City Senate enacted a special supplementary law to the unification treaty in order to cut Humboldt staff from 8,000 to 1,740; once again many faculty stymied execution of the measure or won back their positions on procedural legal issues. Protesting the "campaign of annihilation," Humboldt students went into the streets. Their success was partial: The majority of professors kept or regained their jobs. But the saga ended in December 1992 on a bitter note: Fink himself lost his own appeal against dismissal. *Stasi* documents had code-named him Heiner, an IM (*inoffizieller Mitarbeiter*, unofficial employee): an informer. As "IM Heiner," Fink had finked on students and colleagues for years.[62]

Financial woes lay at the heart of the educational disputes in Berlin and elsewhere in the east—and in the west, too. The incessant migration of eastern students was hurting the western economy too: straining health and welfare services, aggravating housing shortages, and overburdening schools and universities. The situation was so dire that, in April 1991, Hans Uwe Erichsen, president of the German Universities Conference of Rectors, declared that "a collapse of the German university system" was on the horizon, unless Bonn acted immediately to reduce overcrowding and restore budget cutbacks. Western universities' resources had been strained before the influx of easterners: between 1977 and 1991, the western German enrollments had climbed 70 percent; by contrast, faculty totals had risen only 6 percent and university funding only 18 percent.[63]

Meanwhile, outraged western educators noted, some eastern universities had hundreds of student *vacancies*—and had begun to place ads in mass-market magazines to attract students, playing up their low faculty/student ratios, inexpensive living costs, and uncrowded classrooms.[64] With short-staffed western universities bursting at the seams, eastern universities (which had always been over-staffed by West German—and American—standards) were guaranteed another $200 million per year through 1995 to revamp facilities and hire "politically unburdened" faculty.[65]

Eastern educators argued that these infusions were barely sufficient to cover library shortages, collapsing buildings, and basic retraining for staff, let alone to boost eastern universities to levels competitive with the west. Unification had raised government spending in education by 50 percent, from DM 4.2 billion in 1990 to DM 6.1 billion in 1991, with student grants raised from DM 1.8 billion to DM 2.8 billion. Still, this outlay amounted to less than 10 percent of Bonn's total earmarked for eastern German reconstruction. Educators in both west and east pleaded that it wasn't enough.[66]

But the government had more pressing concerns. Having decided to direct the bulk of its effort toward revitalizing the ailing industries and infrastructure of the east, Bonn was becoming increasingly agitated over what was developing into the biggest recession in western Germany in the postwar era. Although the economic downturn was both partly caused and partly exacerbated by the eastern educational crisis of 1991/92, the German economy was under the severe strain of numerous other obligations and burdens, both general and specific: the east's overall economic collapse, the European-wide recession, Germany's $10.6 billion contribution to the Gulf War, its payment of $38 billion for Soviet troop withdrawal and USSR economic aid, a $20 billion grant and loan package to Eastern Europe,[67] and the initial expenses of an estimated $55 billion transfer of the central government from Bonn to Berlin by 1999. In 1991 the western German inflation rate jumped to its highest level since 1981, averaging 3.5 percent (up from 2.7 percent in 1990 and 2.8 percent in 1991); the December 1991 rate was so alarming (by German standards)—4.2 percent—that the Bundesbank raised its two key interest rates to their highest levels since 1948.

Thus did the German economic juggernaut screech to a standstill. After its strongest economic performance in 15 years in 1990, united Germany posted a $21 billion deficit in 1991, the worst figure in a decade; the merchandising trade surplus also fell sharply, from $66.2 billion in 1990 to $12.8 billion in 1991. The eastern economy produced less than two-thirds of its 1989 output; the western economy declined in each of the last three quarters of 1991. "All the scholars published books on how to transform capitalism into socialism—not the other way around," lamely explained Jürgen Möllemann, who had left his post as Education Minister to become Economics Minister. "We're learning by doing."[68]

The learning curve was steep. Chancellor Kohl had expected a second *Wirtschaftswunder* in the east after the currency union of July 1990, comparable to that which followed the June 1948 currency union in the western occupied zones. But the predicted miracle turned mirage: D-Mark diplomacy had generated an eastern boom in consumer demand—but only for western products. Because monetary union had not been linked to a strategy for building up the east's own productive base and halting the flow of resettlers, it resulted in increased consumption without sustained growth. With westerners still earning from 33 to 50 percent more than their eastern colleagues for the same work in 1991, the mere presence of the D-Mark in the east was not enough to stop the flow of economic refugees to the west, a flow which had now exceeded one million people since 1989.

So long as the outflow of the best young easterners continued, a second German economic miracle could not occur. Moreover, Bonn estimated that as many as 150,000 eastern Germans in the west had not found regular employment.[69] Instead of a second German economic miracle, observers were beginning to talk of a second Mezzogiorno—"but without the pasta and the sunshine"—an industrially backward eastern Germany permanently dependent on financial infusions from the west, much like Italy's long-depressed south today, even a century after Italian unification.[70] Now fears emerged of a permanent *Wohlstandsmauer* (wall of prosperity) dividing east and west. At minimum, everyone agreed that Bonn had drastically underestimated the costs and time for eastern reconstruction. The new reckoning: $1.5 trillion over the next decade.

But talk of that scale of sacrifice provoked outrage in the west, especially when Kohl announced that Bonn would levy—on western *Länder* only—a 7.5 percent emergency, one-year income tax specifically for eastern reconstruction. But easterners looked at westerners' anger with contempt: *Wessis* still had their country; *Wessis* still had their culture; *Wessis* still had their jobs. Eastern unemployment, by contrast, climbed in late 1991 toward 50 percent in some regions, a rate almost twice that of the Great Depression; youth unemployment was even higher. Strikes and work stoppages idled tens of thousands of disgruntled workers. The suicide rate doubled.

And so, the demonstrations in Leipzig, Chemnitz, Schwerin, Cottbus, Plauen, and across the east began anew. This time, however, eastern Germans were not protesting against the SED and the *Stasi* but against Bonn and unemployment, the *Besserwessi* exploitation of the so-called *Beute-Ossi* (Booty-Ossi).[71] Beginning in March 1991, more than 70,000 people gathered in eastern German cities to protest the economic devastation of their region. Again, Leipzig demonstrators pledged to turn out every Monday to march.

But the marchers of 1991 were grim-faced, not joyous. The economic tragedy was rapidly turning the east into a political powder keg, provoking warnings from eastern politicians that the economic catastrophe might soon turn to violence, especially given the discontent of bored, unemployed eastern youth.

It soon did. Although reunification had stimulated no positive upsurge of German nationalism, it now triggered an explosion of *Ausländerfeindlichkeit*.

This problem was fundamentally a youth problem, and it was aggravated—some left-wing spokesmen said "caused"—by the collapse of the communist youth organizations. And it was also aggravated—some right-wing spokesmen said "caused"—by the sharp rise in foreign immigration since 1989. Germany was an attractive immigration target because of its central location, its prosperity, and its easy asylum law. The German constitution granted automatic entry to those claiming to flee persecution—since the fall of the Wall, more than 400,000 Poles from Eastern Europe and the Balkans and 1.5 million ethnic Germans from the USSR and Eastern Europe had arrived. (France, Italy, and Switzerland accepted only token numbers of Yugoslavian refugees; the U.S. agreed to harbor only 1,000 Bosnians and the British refused a request to take a mere 175 Bosnians stranded in Austria.[72]) By mid-1991, Germany was receiving 60 percent of all requests for asylum in the EC, three times the number of any other country, and applicants were legally permitted to stay at state expense for three to five years while their cases were considered.[73] Total cost: $2.5 billion.[74]

And yet something other than immigration pressure was fueling the hatred: *Ausländerfeindlichkeit* was most acute in eastern Germany, where foreigners numbered only 80,000, just one-half of 1 percent of the population, less than a third of the total number of foreigners in West Berlin alone. (In the west, foreigners made up 10 percent, or 6 million.)[75] In addition to the still worsening eastern economy,[76] a major contributing factor to the region's *Ausländerfeindlichkeit* was the sheer boredom felt by eastern youth. After the DDR youth organizations had been dissolved, no replacements had emerged. Eastern youth complained that there was nothing to do. Their favorite radio station, DT 64, which had introduced western music to the DDR, was phased out in April 1992 because it had served the SED. Church youth organizations remained small; interest in churchgoing and church activities rapidly dwindled after the fall of the Wall. To a great extent, then, the violence was a problem of youth who were angry and jaded and whose respect for authority had plummeted in the chaos of the post-reunification transition. They vented their frustration and rage on foreigners, especially asylum seekers.[77]

September 24, 1991: Hoyerswerda is the scene as dozens of rightist youth gangs, cheered on by hundreds of town residents, attack two apartment complexes housing 230 Vietnamese and Mozambican workers brought into the DDR under SED labor contracts. The police make 83 arrests; capitulating to the racists, however, town authorities bus the foreigners to an army base outside of town. Young neo-Nazis, many of whom have never spoken to any foreigners except for an occasional

Eastern European tourist, jubilantly proclaim Hoyerswerda *ausländerfrei* (foreigner free).

October 13, 1991: Greifswald witnesses 30 skinheads beat a Moroccan man; elsewhere in the east, right-wing youth gangs assault foreigners' hostels. Bonn announces that anti-foreigner violence has skyrocketed from 26 incidents in January to 900 in October. Violence against foreigners has reached a level not seen since the Nazi era.

November 9, 1991: In observance of the 53rd anniversary of *Kristallnacht*, more than 100,000 demonstrators in Berlin, Rostock, Schwerin, and Gera, as well as numerous western cities, march against violence and for peace. Neo-Nazis in Leipzig and Halle parade in counter-marches, engaging in vandalism and arson after confrontations with 1,500 police and left-wing militants.

As 1991 wound down, right-wing German politicians evoked the language of racial purity to decry the *Überfremdung* ("over-foreignization") of Germany. Calling for Germany to restrict immigration or halt it altogether, the Bavarian Minister of the Interior, Edmund Stoiber (CDU), dubbed Germany a *durchrasste Gesellschaft* (racially saturated society). Such terms possessed an eerie resonance, given Germany's twentieth-century history, the rise of racially motivated crimes, and the "ethnic cleansing" under way in nearby Bosnia. By the end of 1991, German anti-foreigner violence had risen 500 percent over 1990, totaling 1,527 criminal offenses, including 275 acts of arson, 135 injuries, and three deaths.[78] According to the German Ministry of the Interior, more than 97 percent of the perpetrators were under the age of 30: 21 percent were under 17, 48 percent were 18 to 20, and 28 percent were 21 to 30.[79]

Into the void of meaning and authority entered a neo-Nazi youth culture marked by rigid dress codes, violent computer games, and hate-filled skinhead fanzines. Bomber jackets, crewcuts, short haircuts or bald heads, white (i.e., "Aryan") shoelaces in black boots were de rigeur. High-tech rightist youths learned that genocide can be fun. Bearing the legends "Adolf Hitler Software" and "Made in Buchenwald," underground computer games such as "Aryan Test" and "Total Auschwitz" gave rightist youths instructions on how to gas Turks or be a concentration camp commandant.[80] "Skinzines" (underground rightist magazines) strengthened the skinhead subculture with news of "comrades" and activities worldwide. Titles included *Macht und Ehre* (Power and Honor), *Schlachtruf* (Battle Cry), *Totenkopf* (Deadhead), *Glorreiche Taten* (Glorious Exploits), *Aufstand* (Rebellion), and *Endsieg* (Final Victory).[81]

But the galvanizing force in the skinhead scene was music, a.k.a. "hate rock."[82] Also known as "Oi music"[83]—a cross between punk and heavy metal—neo-Nazi rock featured at least 50 nationally known *Fascho-Bands*. Groups such as Volkszorn (the People's Anger), Endstufe (Final Stage) Noie Werte (New Values), Kahlkopf (Bald Head), Sperrzone (Prohibited Zone), and Zyklon B (the poison gas used in Nazi gas chambers)—commanded their greatest popularity in the east. Some bands even had mainstream appeal: the album *"Heilige Lieder"* (*Holy Songs*), by Böhse Onkelz (Evil Uncles), made it into the Top Five in the German pop charts in late 1992. And the beliefs they espoused had mainstream appeal, too: according to an October 1992 study by the Cologne Institute of Empirical Psychology, a third of all German youth between 16 and 20 held racist views or were susceptible to anti-foreigner propaganda, double the number in 1990. (Indeed four of the seven aforementioned skinhead bands were from the west.) Between 25 and 40 percent of those interviewed expressed "understanding" for the right-wing youth.[84]

Störkraft (Destructive Force) pandered to the prejudices and became the top band in the German skinhead scene during 1991/92. Störkraft had several provocative hits, such as "Fighting Dog," in which an angry dog barks and growls behind the following shouted lyrics:

> Bad times for the scum in this country
> The fighting dog has them firmly in hand
> Quaking with fear they stand before the wall
> The fighting dog is lying in wait
> Without mercy and without morals
> Hellish torment awaits them
> Don't try to flee, you won't escape him
> Your descent is written on his face
>
> Fighting dog
> Savage beast of German blood
> Fighting dog
> Tremble and watch out![85]

Störkraft's emblem was an eagle perched on a cross over the words "white power," the power of the future, as "Kraft für Deutschland" (Power for Germany) expresses:

> We fight shaved, our fists are hard as steel,
> Our heart beats true for our Fatherland
> Whatever may happen, we will never leave you,
> We will stand true for our Germany,
> Because we are the strength of Germany
> *Deutschland erwache!* (Germany awake!)

Or take "Saviors of Germany," in which the band Radikahl—a pun on the German words both for "radical" and "bald"—projects a similar faith in the saving power of the blond beast and the Nazi equation of *Blut und Ehre* (blood and honor). The last stanza trumpets Hitler's campaign slogan of the early 1930s:

> O my poor Germany, you've come to this
> And there's no one, no one near or far to free you
> But things can't go on this way
> I can't stand this filthy breed any longer
>
> We are the saviors of Germany
> I'll fight for my *Heimat* like a wild beast
> With new blood and honor our greatest pride
> We are hard as German oak

I won't surrender my country to these lackeys
You'll have to kill me first
My children will be proud of their land
And won't be afraid of the pathetic swine. . . .

Deutschland, Deutschland, erwache! [Germany, awake!]
Or else we'll be sorry
Not until you make our pride your own
Will you really understand.
Not until you make our pride your own
Will you really understand.[86]

Not content with defending the *Heimat*, Radikahl also expressed a yearning for *Lebensraum*. In their song "Swastika," the band's plea for "understanding" included nominating the *Führer* for a Nobel Prize.

Give Adolf Hitler, give Adolf Hitler
Give Adolf Hitler the Nobel Prize
Raise the red flag. Raise the red flag
Raise the red flag with the swastika

Even as a boy, it was clear to me
That this symbol was my guide
And today I still feel just the same
There's only one and you're it

As on the German flags of old
It leads me down the right roads
For me, what matters hasn't changed:
Race and pride and swastika!

Everywhere I go you'll see it
Those who are different won't understand
There's no other sign that I like so much
Long may it soon wave over the entire world.

And consider Werwolf's "People, Wake up, Stand up."

Foreigners, German immigrants, and asylum seekers . . .
They are being favored in everything
Is this supposed to continue?
Free us from this miserable plague

In what passed in this milieu for a thoughtful consideration of German culture came Endstufe's "Winter in the BRD":

Times are tough for the German people
Foreign troops still occupy our land.
Forty years of calamity and corruption . . .
German culture—where is it these days?

> Will there ever be a Germany again
> That's worth living in?
>
> This state is ashamed of German history . . .
> No matter what we say
> The face of the government never changes
>
> We've got as many foreigners as grains of sand
> Pimps, junkies. Though it's all forbidden
> Believe me, Christians, praying won't do any good
>
> It's winter in the BRD.

This was extracurricular Education for Hate—and in the old homegrown Nazi style, updated for the '90s. Glorifying violence and hating everything un-German, this was music a long way from the "corrupting" foreign influence of *der Twist* and the Beatles, music that might leave one wishing for the innocent days of the DDR commissar censors. Although neo-Nazi rockers publicly claimed to be against violence, their lyrics suggested otherwise. And so, sometimes, did their direct effects. At many skinhead concerts, bands led fans in swastika flag-waving and chants of *Sieg Heil*! Five members of the band Tonstörung (Sound Disruption) received suspended sentences for inciting racial violence when fans attacked a Turkish wedding party after a 1992 Tonstörung concert.[87]

Understandably, with 80 percent of neo-Nazi rock concerts staged in the east, foreign students and academics there grew terrified.[88] Many African students simply did not leave their apartments after five P.M. for fear of being attacked by an *Ost-Skin*. One skinhead announced, á la America's David Duke: "We have no objection to Africans going out as long as they do so in Africa."[89] A survey of Saxony youth by the Central Youth Research Institute in Leipzig showed that one in eight schoolchildren thought that the National Socialist ideology "had its good side." Nearly half of youth apprentices and 23 percent of schoolchildren affirmed the slogan "Foreigners Out!"[90]

And as the tide of foreign immigrants continued to rise in 1992, so too did the pitch of such slogans and of German violence against foreigners.

August 25, 1992: Rostock neo-Nazis cap three straight nights of violence by firebombing a 10-storey hostel in the Lichtenhagen neighborhood occupied by Vietnamese guest workers. "*Ausländer raus!*" ("Foreigners out!") chant a thousand youths. "*Deutschland den Deutschen!*" ("Germany for the Germans!"). "*Sieg Heil!*" Conspicuous throughout the reign of terror are Böhse Onkelz T-shirts and music. A Social Democratic leader notes that 25,000 eastern Germans, half of them unemployed, live near the hostel. Rostock's unemployment hovers near 40 percent; Lichtenhagen's rate is 57 percent.

September 6, 1992: Eisenhüttenstadt—the onetime Stalinstadt—suffers a confrontation between police and 40 rightist youth heaving firebombs at a foreigners' hostel. A few miles away in Guben, 100 riot police drive back 60 youthful rioters outside another refugee hostel.

October 25, 1992: Greifswald rightists disrupt a peace march against violence organized by university students. A 16-year-old girl is severely injured, hit over the head with a baseball bat; police arrest 33. A new Orwellian slang for racial beatings emerges: skinheads joke that their victims were *aufgeklatscht* (slapped up). Meanwhile, skinhead terms such as *Holo*—a linguistic Final Solution to abbreviate the Holocaust—ring through the streets. "*Der Holo wird beendet!*" ("The Holocaust has been finished!"). A survey of Germany's 40,000 Jewish citizens is published: 33 percent feel threatened by the right-wing extremism; 75 percent say that the government is doing too little to stem it.[91]

November 23, 1992: And now Mölln, near Hamburg, shows that the west is gripped by the rise of the new Hitler Youth too, as the worst episode of anti-foreigner violence since reunification explodes. Rightist youth firebomb the home of three Turks—a woman and her two young daughters—all of whom are burned to death.

The Mölln neo-Nazi youth proclaimed that they have made their town *tur-ken-frei* (free of Turks). Having engorged themselves on rightist music, they have triumphantly fulfilled the edicts of bands such as Commando Pernod:[92]

> We are fighting for our German Fatherland
> And setting the asylum quarters in flames![93]
> If you see a Turk in a trolley
> and he looks at you challengingly
> Then simply stand up
> and give him a push
> and stick your knife in him
> seventeen times.[94]

Meanwhile, Endsieg's song, "*Kanaken*"—a derogatory term for foreigners—became a skinhead battle hymn against Turks:

> They eat only garlic
> and stink like pigs
> They come here to Germany
> and live on the dole
> They screw up everything
> all they touch turns to shit.
> They'll just have to be killed
> All else is pointless
>
> Throw them in a dungeon
> Or throw them in a concentration camp
> As far as I'm concerned, into the desert
> But get rid of them, finally, throw them in prison or
>   in concentration camps. . . .
> Kill their children, rape their women,
> Annihilate their race
> Only thus will they cringe with dread.

Germany was becoming what one American observer called "an Ellis Island of strife."

The 1992 refugee tally: 438,191 asylum seekers—a 70 percent increase over 1991—and 250,000 refugees from ex-Yugoslavia.[95]

In a *Spiegel* poll, 73 percent of Germans agreed that it was "especially important" to "get a grip on the foreigner problem."[96] Politicians pandered with Orwellian creativity, promising *aufenthaltsbeendende Massnahmen* (residence termination measures, i.e., deportation). The Bavarian premier warned that Germany had become a shelter for the "economic parasites" of the world.[97] Other politicians spoke of the Turks as not *integrationsfähig* (able to be integrated). The skinhead solution: purge them.

The 1992 violence tally: Nearly 1,800 racial crimes in Germany—this too a 70 percent increase over 1991.[98] (Add to this the 80 Jewish cemeteries desecrated in 1992—a figure, noted Ignatz Bubis, head of the Central Council of German Jews in Berlin, that exceeded the total in the years 1926–31.)[99]

But 1991/92 was not 1931/32, and the newly reunited BRD was not the shaky Weimar Republic: peace-loving German citizens let it be known that they would not be intimidated a second time into silence in the face of right-wing violence. Fed up with the deadlock between the CDU and SPD on how to respond to neo-Nazi violence and the immigration problem—the new coinages were *Politikverdrossenheit* (disgust with politics) and *Parteiverdrossenheit* (disgust with parties)—citizens again took to the streets.

In November and December 1992, millions of demonstrators marched peacefully through cities in the east and west: Berlin, Leipzig, Munich, Stuttgart, and more. They attended anti-racism concerts, such as Frankfurt's *Heute Die—Morgen Du* (Today Them, Tomorrow You), which featured the Skorpions and other leading German bands. Dresden youth launched a national campaign to fight xenophobia termed "Mission Courage"; Berlin students working as Santa Clauses posed for group photos with the sign, "Santa Is Against Nazis."[100]

On December 8, 1992, the German political leadership acted to curb the entry of asylum seekers and refugees, aiming thereby to defuse anxiety over immigration and curb rightist attacks on foreigners. The Social Democrats compromised in the face of public opinion. Officials at airports and border crossings would now turn away applicants from countries not deemed to engage in political persecution. In early December, the government outlawed a right-wing political party, and was making plans to ban other parties. Hoping to get a grip on other inflammatory causes of the violence, German legislators banned five prominent neo-Nazi bands—including Störkraft and Endstufe; sale and distribution of their "Oi music" were prohibited. Although the measures may violate American ideals of free speech, German legislators sought thereby to quell a key stimulus of the *Ausländerfeindlichkeit* among German youth.

At Christmas time, the Revolution of the Candles began again, now called *Lichterketten* (chains of light). In hope and even joy, and without songs or chants or banners or placards—in just the way that the Revolution of 1989 began—the candles now lit up western German streets too. Marchers braved freezing temperatures to carry candles and torches in the silent street vigils; stay-at-homes put candles in their windows to express solidarity against racism and xenophobia.

By the close of 1992, the call of 1989 was once again being heard in German streets. *"Keine Gewalt!"* ("No violence!"). But now it was sounding throughout the west as well as east.

Germany, lurching toward unity as 1990 ended, found itself slouching toward tolerance as 1992 drew to a close.

Memories of 1945/46 indeed. A half-century later, the wartime warning of Brecht in his anti-Nazi parable *The Resistable Rise of Arturo Ui* resonated deeply: "We overcame him but remember this / Before you hurry off to celebrate / Earth's womb still teems with prodigies." For all his cynicism and willingness to turn a deaf ear on June 17 and the crimes of Stalinism, Brecht was nonetheless right about the German Right:

> The womb from which that crawled is fertile still.

Or as "J," the 22-year-old anti-Nazi rapper from the east put it—in his feverish, hip-hop style—in "We are the Majority":

> Someone opened up the cage
> And out comes Germany again
> The beast that no one ever tamed.

The Unfinished Revolution

> You *Ossis* have been Germans now for nearly three years! When are you finally going to catch on?
> West Berliner Friedhelm Motzki, speaking to Edith, his Saxon sister-in-law

German humor is often said to be no laughing matter, but as 1993 opened, the top-rated and most controversial TV show on Tuesday evenings in Germany was an outrageous sitcom, *Motzki*, starring a bald, beer-bellied, retired driving instructor. A racist and reactionary, Friedhelm Motzki was the Archie Bunker of the German 1990s, complete with his own Edith ("that stupid cow from the east"), his late wife's sister, a college-educated woman and former schoolteacher who had come to western Berlin to keep house for Motzki after his wife's death. As did *All in the Family* in the 1970s, *Motzki*—the name derives from the slang word *motzen* (to grouse)—broke all taboos; Motzki blurted out in public prejudices that western Germans privately expressed to one another, thereby provoking laughter and embarrassment. Motzki had many pet peeves, ranging from asylum seekers and Turks to environmentalists and leftist youth. But the sloth of eastern Germans and the disaster of reunification topped his list. Of a dog who follows him home from eastern Berlin, he says: "He's from the east, and now he pretends I'm responsible for him." Poor Edith received the brunt of Motzki's outbursts. She was especially vulnerable, having taught at a school that catered to children of *Stasi* officials. "What do you want? Paradise?" Motzki harangues Edith, mocking the DDR's utopian pretensions. He continues: "Our money? But oh, as soon as you have to work for it, you're homesick for your socialism." In Motzki's living room hung a photo showing the Brandenburg Gate closed by the Wall—his picture of a return to paradise.

Motzki hit the German jugular. And not surprisingly, many indignant viewers felt that *Motzki* reinforced, not merely satirized, divisions between east and west. Numerous politicians, including Chancellor Kohl, President Rita Süssmuth, and PDS chairman Gregor Gysi criticized the show, with Süssmuth even calling for its cancellation; a citizen's suit lodged in a Hamburg court sought (unsuccessfully) to have *Motzki* taken off the air. A March 1993 poll showed that 60 percent of westerners and 67 percent of easterners thought the program should be stopped immediately; many eastern respondents called for candlelight protest marches against the show.[101]

Instead of canceling the show, easterners replied in the autumn of 1993 with *Trotzki*, about a Leipzig family headed by a taxi driver married to a scatterbrained shopaholic wife who thinks reunification means taking advantage of bargain sales. Broadcast by the Leipzig TV network MDR, *Trotzki* too received high ratings initially, though it was never so popular as its rival. *Trotzki*—derived from the verb *trotzen* (defy, be obstinate) and also evoking the name Leon Trotsky—preferred to mock easterners, in the good-natured spirit of *Go, Trabi, Go!* It did not adopt the biting satire of *Motzki*: e.g., the first call that Herbert Trotzki receives on the long-awaited family telephone is from a western family claiming to own his property; his own first phone connection is to a sex line. *Trotzki*'s opening episode featured all four family members feasting on bananas, then winning a quiz show prize for a trip to the west—and frustrating the quiz show host by their inability to decide where to go. China is out—the family has had enough of walls. Frau Troztki—an unemployed schoolteacher like Edith—is nostalgic for the family's DDR-era trips to Bulgaria. "What did I tell you?!" bemoans the game show host. "*Ossis!*"[102]

Many western Germans were saying something similar during 1993/94, and as the sitcoms reflected, the source of much of the frustration, exasperation, and anger between western and eastern Germans—between the *Besserwessis* and the (newly dubbed) *Jammerossis* (whining easterners) was economic. And as the unemployment plight of Edith and Frau Trotzki exemplified, the problems in German education and youth affairs must also be seen in an economic context.

In 1993, Germany entered a deep recession—its first since 1982 and its worst in decades. Unemployment perched at over 4 million in January 1993—the highest figure since the years of the Weimar Republic—fully 10 percent of the BRD's total population. By July, it was still rising, to 7.5 percent in the west—the highest level since the government began keeping records in 1949.[103] Western growth contracted 3.7 percent in the first quarter of 1993—the worst quarter since 1968. Because of the tremendous deficits that the government was running due to eastern reconstruction—Germany's federal deficit was 7.5 percent of GNP (compared with 4.5 percent in the U.S.)—one analyst dubbed the transfer payment program from Bonn "Reaganomics on the Rhine."[104] The cost for 1993 would be $112 billion, resulting in a GNP decline of 2 percent; more than 70 percent of the deficit spending would cover welfare and unemployment benefits for easterners.[105]

The situation was both worse and better in the east. The official unemployment rate stood at 15.3 percent, held low by the government practice of excluding people enrolled in government-sponsored retraining and make-work programs. As noted in the opening pages of Part I, the unofficial jobless rate was at least double that, hovering over 30 percent, indeed up to 45 percent if forced retirements and government work programs were included.[106] Industrial output was down 70 percent since 1991; productivity was a third of western levels. But the eastern GNP rose a healthy 6.2 percent in the first half of 1993. True, that represented a decline from the spectacular 10.1 percent in the latter half of 1992—and was still measured from near the region's economic nadir; industrial production remained 40 percent lower than before reunification.[107] Moreover, it was still mostly fueled by western transfer payments for welfare and public works projects. But it indicated a reversal of the downward economic spiral. Although a self-sustaining upturn was not yet under way, fears of the east becoming a German Mezzogiorno subsided. The long-term picture was hopeful: under the March 1993 "solidarity pact" worked out between Bonn and the western *Länder*, the east would be guaranteed massive infusions of capital for the rest of the decade.[108]

Still, angry easterners declared that they had been *verraten und verkauft* (betrayed and sold) by the west. Rolf Hochhuth's controversial play, *Wessis in Weimar: Scenes from an Occupied Land*, which opened in Weimar in July 1993 and portrayed western Germans as ruthless colonizers, gave vent to eastern rage. Hochhuth even constructed an imagined speech from the angry daughter of an eastern pastor to Detlef Rowhwedder, head of the *Treuhand*, implying that his April 1991 assassination was attributable to his own "liquidation" of easterners. The speech could have come from the mouth of *Motzki*'s Edith:

You leave the East Germans 10 percent but steal 90 percent, and for that you will be executed. You steal from the People. They are being robbed for the second time. Forty years ago, at the end of the war, by German Communists in the service of the Kremlin, and now [again]. . . . Something completely new in world history, a variant of colonialism that has never before been practiced against one's own people!

As if to upset easterners even more, a cynical new official euphemism, employing the language of economic reconstruction, gained currency to explain the tumultuous upheaval in easterners' lives: "*Sozialabbau*" (social dismantling).[109]

The situation of eastern education and youth continued to play an important role in the social and economic transformation.[110] By the end of the 1992/93 school year, 21 percent of eastern teachers had been fired or furloughed.[111] Moreover, although living standards were better than ever—the average worker in eastern Germany was earning as much as six Hungarians and 30 Russians—jobs were still hard to come by. This caused the migration of eastern youth to the west to continue. According to a survey by the Berlin Institute for Occupational Training, 10 percent of eastern youth, or 115,000 youth, most of them highly trained and well-educated, were still crossing the border in 1993; in Brandenburg alone, 75,000 had left since reunification. Even more dismaying, the survey found that 25 percent of the remaining 20-year-olds were thinking about going west. The young people gave their reasons: poor employment prospects, no possibilities for advancement, inadequate training. The survey estimated that the east was short at least 50,000 jobs for 16- to 18-year-olds. And thousands of easterners were forced to commute to the west daily or weekly for work.[112]

A related, much-discussed "youth problem" was the falling birth rate.[113] For instance, whereas 35,000 babies were born in Brandenburg in 1989, only a third of that number were born in 1993; eastern births were down by half since 1989 and marriages had fallen by 62 percent. The Brandenburg government was now paying parents DM 650 extra for every baby. Discussing the eastern *Sozialabbau*, one observer attributed the decline in births and marriages to "catatonic shock."[114] While acknowledging the uncertainty of eastern youth about their futures, other commentators ascribed it to the *Nachholbedarf*, i.e., the urge of eastern youth to spend their money on cars and vacations denied to them for decades.[115]

Thus, in this third phase of eastern educational history after the Wall (1993–95), the mid-term report card was mixed. The euphoria and anxiety of 1989/90, and the depression and despair of 1991/92 had given way to a complex mood compounded of resignation, grit, and hopefulness. On balance, the worst of the *Wendekrankeit* was over and progress was being made; but the after-effects were still being felt.

In the schools, integration proceeded apace. New syllabuses, introduced into most eastern *Länder* in 1993, resembled those in western *Länder*. For example, the German *Gymnasium* syllabus for Thuringia stressed a generic, rather than ideological, approach to literature. Nonetheless, numerous recommended authors and works on the syllabus probably would have been found in few western *Länder*. Teachers were encouraged to assign Hochhuth's *Wessis in Weimar*, Anna Seghers, Christoph Hein, Günter Kunert, Stefan Heym, Vladimir Mayakovsky, and even Wolf Biermann's ballads.

History classes also reflected both discontinuities and continuities with the DDR era. Gone were the "lessons of History"—or at least the old lessons. Thuringia pupils studying nineteenth-century history now heard relatively little about Marx, Engels, Liebknecht, Bebel, the Opportunists, or Eduard Bernstein. The past was no longer "another country" but rather the pupils' own Germany and Europe: the semester of nineteenth-century history in 11th grade was titled "From Status Society to Industrial Society." The emphasis was not on imperialism and pre-fascism; for instance, "the Bismarck era" afforded the pupil "insight into the relation between internal arguments and foreign policy possibilities in Europe." One unit was titled simply: "England as Industrial State." The words "proletariat" or even "class" did not appear. Nevertheless, 12th-graders studying twentieth-century history did learn new lessons of history, even if they were not explicitly formulated as such. The Thuringia history syllabus referred to the "totalitarian foundations of Leninism," contrasting it with the "basic democratic structure" of the U.S. and West German governments. Nazi Germany was also characterized as "a totalitarian state." "The Holocaust was an inhuman consequence of racial hatred and the misuse of power," said the syllabus, noting that the Holocaust was not to be historicized into a distant event but "should be made present." Departing from DDR practice, the syllabus emphasized the "diverse forms of resistance in the Third Reich," urging the teacher to "illustrate the Resistance in its entire breadth," i.e., not limit it to communist heroes. Finally, the 12th-grade units on the DDR reflected a western, or at least non-communist, approach to still controversial issues: June 17 was referred to as "the 1953 Crisis"—the phrase "workers' uprising" or "rebellion" was not used. Other topics included the DDR pre-Wall refugees' choice of "voting with their feet," the *Nischengesellschaft* (niche society) of the DDR, and "Gorbachev's reforms."[116]

The growing similarity of the syllabuses in east and west notwithstanding, however, cultural differences remained. Teachers involved in east-west teacher exchanges often noted them: western children don't learn so well because they have discipline problems, and have many extracurricular distractions and few incentives to study; eastern pupils are also becoming westernized, and now show up to school with Walkmans, Gameboy videos, and trendy clothes and shoes. Western teachers in the east reported that pupils had little initiative.

"They are used to having a teacher tell them what to learn," one Wittenberg teacher told me in 1994. "They are obedient, not defiant or even critical. They used to swallow everything, and they haven't yet unlearned that way of life."

Teachers themselves were also still trying to unlearn. A 1993 report showed that more than 42,000 teachers in Saxony alone were undergoing "re-education," which included taking seminars such as "The Third Reich in High School History Instruction" or "Economic and Political Structure of the BRD."[117] One report on the states of Mecklenburg-Vorpommern and Saxony-Anhalt showed that more than 2,000 teachers in the state of Mecklenburg-Vorpommern were attending continuing education language classes, not just in English and French but in Latin.

Because of their role in the DDR years as a cultural cadre, many teachers were perceived as cynical *Wendehälse* by pupils and parents. Commentators referred to the continuing need to break the old Party network—the SED *Seilschaft*—and for a rigorous *"Entstasifizierung"* of eastern schools.[118] As a spokeswoman for the Ministry of Culture in Saxony noted: "It's not credible for teachers who, just four years ago, were telling their students that these westerners were our deadly enemies now to be telling children that these are our good friends and we're part of the [NATO] alliance."[119]

Complicating the unlearning was the resentful feeling of many eastern teachers that they too, like other easterners, were second-class citizens. For instance, though teachers were extremely well off compared to the rest of the eastern population—the average teacher was earning DM 1,800 monthly, triple the average citizen's income of DM 500—the discrepancies between eastern and western teachers' workloads and salaries was still significant. Teachers in Baden-Wurttemburg and Bavaria were teaching 23 hours per week, whereas those in Saxony-Anhalt and Saxony were teaching 25 and 27 hours per week, respectively—and for 20 percent less pay. Moreover, no eastern teachers were tenured, and plans had not yet been formalized as to when they might receive tenure.[120] Western teachers already tenured who went eastward received their western salary plus a bonus (known derisively among easterners as *Buschgeld* [bush money]), making their total earnings almost double that of the average eastern teacher.

(Newly hired teachers from the west, along with western teachers not already tenured who went eastward, received the same pay as easterners.)

Another major task of unlearning for eastern pupils and teachers had to do with religion. The east was approximately 15 percent Lutheran and 5 percent Catholic. But the ignorance of and even hostility toward religion was even higher in many schools than these modest figures would suggest. For instance, at one Rostock school, only 5 percent of pupils had been baptized; 50 percent had no knowledge of the historical Jesus and 75 percent had never entered a church.[121] In an international survey in 1993, a majority of people in all western and eastern European countries—except eastern Germany—said they believed in God; only a quarter of easterners professed belief. "Eastern Germany appears to be an unreligious country," the report concluded. Only .2 percent, or roughly 3,300 pupils, out of a total of 1,164,000, were in religious schools in the east. The atheistic tradition (plus a lack of qualified teachers for the religious subjects) kept the numbers small. (More than 6 percent attended religious schools in western Germany.)[122]

My informal 1994 survey of a dozen classes in Thuringia, Saxony, and eastern Berlin found that 80 percent of eastern pupils were registering for Ethics—rather than Religion (Lutheran or Catholic)—exactly the inverse of the percentage in the west. The aforementioned survey of Mecklenburg-Vorpommern and Saxony-Anhalt reported similar results. In both states, most pupils were registering for Ethics, rather than for Catholic or Lutheran religion class; 300 new teachers in Saxony-Anhalt were being trained to teach them; 800 teachers were being trained in Thuringia. These teachers would also be teaching *Lebenskunde* (life studies) and an elective subject, "Philosophy for Children," which replaced *Wehrerziehung* and *Staatsbürgerkunde*.[123] One of the main tasks of both Ethics and Religion was to implement educational values that would counteract four decades of "*Feindbilder und Erziehung zum Hass*" in DDR schools, as one group of citizens in Magdeburg insisted.[124]

But those Pioneer afternoons and FDJ meetings had also had their positive sides, and many youth desperately missed the work groups and solidarity brigades. Into the identity vacuum swept a defiant wave of *Ostalgie*. Youth and even middle-aged adults sometimes dressed in their FDJ clothes. A few eastern Germans traveled proudly on their DDR passports, which were valid until the end of 1995. Easterners began buying up Trabis eagerly, as a second or third car for the household, and even forming "solidarity groups" of Trabi owners. "The Trabi is loved like never before," one Berlin mechanic told reporters.[125]

Ceremonies such as the *Jugendweihe* took on a new lease on life, becoming an expression of eastern identity, shorn of all socialist pieties. Nearly 80,000 eastern 14-year-olds were participating in the rite, which was now completely voluntary; including nearly 50 percent of 9th-graders in eastern Berlin. Instead of pledging to "work and struggle for the noble cause of socialism," these youth pledged to respect others. Instead of socialist book gifts, pupils received the non-Marxist *Vom Sinn des Lebens* (*On the Meaning of Life*), which includes chapters that soberly discuss the communist past (e.g., "World Change Since 1917," "DDR—State of the Youth?") Some *Jugendweihe* preparations included seminars with titles such as "Drugs Betray Everyone," "Facial Care and Makeup," and "How Tolerant Am I?"[126]

That question reflected both the anxiety and determination of school officials searching for ways to combat the ongoing problem of youth violence, racism, and neo-Nazi activity.[127] With racial tension at a postwar peak and the economy in a deep recession in 1993, dire comparisons were being made to the 1930s. Wilhelm Hankel, chief advisor of the office of Institutional Credit for Reconstruction, noted that eastern German unemployment figures and racial violence reminded him of 1931, when German unemployment reached 30 percent and the Nazis first won widespread popular support.[128]

Educators placed their hopes in curricular change. The most ambitious program launched by the schools involved a high-tech-cum-popcult package aimed at moving beyond textbook histories of the Third Reich.[129] Issued on an experimental basis to 900 schools by the Federal Center for Political Education, the package featured an interactive computer game—called "The Dictator," which showed the history of Nazi tyranny while challenging players to get involved in the underground resistance.

The most controversial part of the package was a 200-page glossy booklet titled *Hitler: The Comic Book*. In full-page colored pencil drawings, the comic book tells the story of the Nazi rise to power, the torture of Jews and Nazi political opponents in concentration camps, and World War II. It also features the actual words of Hitler, Goebbels, and other Nazi leaders. Designed as a supplementary text for 10th-grade history classes studying the Third Reich, the text was written by historian Friedemann Bedürftig.

Developed at a cost of $300,000, the Hitler book had received strong recommendations in the planning stages from observers outside and in the government, e.g., Nazi hunter Simon Wiesenthal, President Richard von Weizsäcker, and Chancellor Kohl. Unfortunately, although 35 teachers had tested the Hitler book and all had positive responses, distribution of the book was canceled in mid-1993; a second pilot program was canceled in mid-1994. Critics feared that its drawings, which included scenes of Hitler surrounded by adoring blond-haired youth and of Goebbels burning books, could be pulled out of the comic book and hung on bedroom walls of rightist youth or used as propaganda by neo-Nazis activists.[130]

The neo-Nazi violence continued, but the statistical declines aroused hopes that the problem would soon be in hand. Whereas 1992 had witnessed 2,285 acts of rightist violence—most of them attacks on foreigners—that killed 17 people (including seven foreigners), the figure for 1993 was 1,410, a drop of almost 50 percent.

Nonetheless, race and violence made headlines throughout 1993/94, as opponents sought to turn the tide against the neo-Nazi wave:

May 1993: Heavy clashes occur in Magdeburg between rightists and leftists commemorating the first anniversary of the death of a leftist murdered by skinheads; 43 people are arrested and three people are wounded. In Schwerin, gravestones are overturned before a memorial for German opponents of the Third Reich.[131] And in the biggest tragedy since Mölln last November, two women and three girls are killed in an arson attack on their home in Solingen. Peace marchers in Solingen chant: "Herr Kohl, shame on you!" "Where is the chancellor?" In Cologne, a sign reads: "Helmut, do something! We don't want another 1940!"[132]

October 1993: Duncan Kennedy, a two-time Olympic luger from New York, suffers a broken nose in a skinhead attack in a bar near Dresden. *"Heil Hitler!"* shout
the skinhead attackers. "We want blood! This time we're going to win!"[133] Since
the right-wing Republicans gained a frightening 8.3 percent of the vote in the
Hesse state elections in March, the threats carry weight. Journalists now speak of
a *Rechtsruck* (lurch to the right); one symptom of the newly confident right-wing
attitude is the mocking street chant *Holo!*—short for Holocaust, as in *Der Holo
wird beendet!*[134]

February 1994: Police seize more than 30,000 records, tapes, and CDs in a raid
on Rock O'Rama, a company based in the western city of Bruhl that features 28
right-wing bands on its label, including Störkraft. Several months earlier, Jorg P,
Störkraft's lead singer, was charged with inciting racist hatred and spreading Nazi
ideology in his lyrics.[135]

March 1994: A Lübeck synagogue is firebombed—the first synagogue attacked
since the Third Reich. Passover services were to be held here for the first time
since 1938. In the next days, 4,000 people march in Lübeck against the attack.[136]

May 1994: In Magdeburg, 4 persons are stabbed to death and 49 arrested in an
outbreak of violence against foreigners. One CDU official calls it "a new and horrifying high point" in German violence since the *Wende.* "Human beings are being
hunted down as they were in the time of the SA."[137] A few days later, 150 skinheads rampage through the streets, beating Africans and Turks.

The racial tension and violence were exacerbated by the continuing influx of
asylum seekers. With 6.3 million foreigners, Germany was now the western European country with the highest number of asylum seekers, who were still pouring
in at a rate of 30,000 per month. Fewer than 5 percent were ultimately found to
be truly persecuted in their homelands; in the interim, German taxpayers were
feeding, housing, and educating the refugees.

And the number of asylum seekers continued to rise: in the first quarter of 1993,
160,000 persons sought refuge in Germany, a rise of 36,000 over 1992. In response
to what politicians were calling the *Überfremdung* of Germany, pressure built for
a new asylum law to limit immigration—and after months of debate, it was passed
on May 27, just two days before the Solingen tragedy. Even before its passage,
however, the number of violent acts against foreigners was dropping: by 30 percent
(to 420) from the 1993 total. Nevertheless during 1994/95, youth violence remained a problem in German schools, especially eastern ones—part of the still
"unfinished revolution."

In the universities and technical colleges, educators had other problems to worry
about—though the general picture was better. At the April 1993 conference on
"Higher Education in the New Federal States: The Verdict After Three Years," held
at Humboldt University, participants drew five conclusions:

1. Eastern higher education is still carrying the "terrible burden" of the DDR
   years.
2. SED membership, which was in many universities as high as 80 percent,
   has unfortunately been "swept under the rug" by the western evaluators;

equally unfortunate is that evidence of *Stasi* activity constituted grounds for automatic dismissal.

3. Developments in the social sciences have been especially slow, partly because the scholarly evaluations took so long and many professors, once fired, exploited western German law to fight and get their jobs back. This has kept the "ideologically burdened" social sciences departments, above all, in a state of enduring uncertainty, even chaos.

4. Eastern students are more motivated and better supervised than ever; this is one of the brightest spots of university reconstruction.

5. Faculty-student relationships have improved too, now that SED politics is no longer a factor; this is partly attributable to the low faculty-student ratio, which means that eastern students receive much more personal attention than do their western counterparts.[138]

As the second and third conclusions evince, the conference took special account of the conduct of the higher education evaluation process, which was completed by 1993. To the surprise of most westerners, and even many eastern colleagues, the evaluators found that 60 percent of eastern university departments and research institutes had a high standard; this was especially the case in mathematics, physics, chemistry, astronomy, biology, and environmental science. By contrast, in the "ideologically burdened" disciplines, such as the social sciences and philosophy, as few as 11 percent of departments were judged to be good. The reorganization hit eastern R&D hardest: whereas 65,000 researchers were employed before the *Wende*, there were only 15,000 by 1993, a net loss of nearly 80 percent.[139] Regional rivalries also flared in the scramble for higher education and research funding: Berlin, Brandenburg, and Saxony won the lion's share; Mecklenburg, Saxony-Anhalt, and Thuringia came out the "losers."[140]

The rivalries were sharpest in Berlin, where the battle of east vs. west—Humboldt University vs. the Free University—continued in 1993/94. Some West Berliners voiced reservations about renewing Humboldt that echoed the sentiments of Friedhelm Motzki; typical of the western attitude was the remark of the FU rector when the Berlin Senate cut DM 50 million from the FU in 1993: "Building up the east means tearing down the west."

The FU worried about overcrowding; Humboldt administrators worried about being dominated by western faculty. Whereas FU classes were severely overcrowded, seminars with only 10 students and lecture halls with fewer than 100 auditors were common at Humboldt. Faculty layoffs at Humboldt had been extensive: in order to reduce the number of professors by 500, as mandated by the Berlin City Senate, two-thirds of the professors were fired.

By March 1993, only 37 percent of 1,230 faculty positions at the Humboldt were held by people who had worked there before the *Wende*.[141] Some faculty were rehired on a short-contract basis as "professors of old law"; their status remained uncertain. Others were replaced by "professors of new law," many of them westerners, who in 1993 numbered almost half the faculty positions. Several departments were mainly staffed by westerners. Surprisingly, these were sometimes the purportedly non-ideological subjects: for instance, whereas 13 of 28 faculty in

Germanistik were westerners, 20 of 22 positions in mathematics were held by westerners.[142]

But when the Berlin City Senate announced deep cuts in the higher education budget in late November 1993, both Humboldt and FU students responded: 2,000 students occupied city hall in protest.[143] The Senate's plans included reducing the length of study to nine semesters (the average was 14.7), persuading more students to attend technical colleges (*Fachhochschulen*) rather than university, and restricting admissions at Berlin's three major universities to 100,000 (a cut of 15,000).[144]

With the partial exception of such student protests in Berlin, however, it was as if events were in a time warp: Most western and eastern students still had little contact with each other.

Only 2 percent of western students, or 5,000—numbering one-sixth the total of 30,000 eastern students—were studying in eastern institutions. (By contrast, 15 percent of easterners had gone westward.)[145] And the western students were concentrated in just a few, special places: one-third of all western students were studying at Humboldt; westerners constituted 30 percent of the student body at the College of Film and TV in Potsdam-Babelsberg. Many Humboldt students were in the history department, which was mainly staffed by distinguished western historians, such as Heinrich August Winkler. With some FU students traveling across town to participate, some history seminars were populated almost totally by *Wessis*—or "*Wossis*," as some westerners following their fortunes in the east were now being tagged. Most western students in the east were pleased with the universities: Instead of anonymity, they received recognition from and regular contact with professors.[146]

Despite—indeed *because* of—the massive layoffs of eastern faculty, much of the work of the "unfinished revolution" in the universities, as the April 1993 Humboldt conference reflected, involved coping with the "terrible burden" of the past. "Ideologically burdened" faculty—a.k.a. former SED stalwarts—were believed to damage the democratic renewal, but mass firings were generally avoided because they provoked protests and undermined morale. Still, the investigations into *Stasi* informant backgrounds proceeded in some institutions. For instance, in mid-1994, University of Potsdam officials turned the names of a thousand suspected *Stasi* informants over to the government for investigation. At Leipzig University, 884 faculty were fired; in history alone, 50 of 100 academic staff were released, both for political and scholarly reasons; 22 of 30 staff members in the foreign studies bureau were fired for serving as *Stasi* informants. Estimates were that politically compromising evidence figured in half the resignations or firings of senior faculty.[147] Revelations about top-secret, formerly classified DDR dissertations earned front-page headlines; many of these doctorate holders were still faculty members.[148] But polls showed that, even as stories emerged of continued *Stasi* contacts—with well-known cultural figures and intellectuals such as Christa Wolf, Heiner Müller, Günter de Bruyn, Wolfgang Harich, and Peter Meyer, or politicians such as Wolfgang Templin, Ibrahim Böhme, Lothar de Maizière, Manfred Stolpe, and Gregor Gysi—easterners were fed up with such news; 57 percent said they would prefer that the *Stasi* files were permanently closed.[149]

For all that, the picture in eastern higher education had many bright spots. Instead of chaos, overcrowding, and boredom—largely the conditions in the west—there prevailed, amid the austerity, a sense of excitement and adventure: the feeling of "a new beginning." The reconstruction of eastern higher education constitutes "a feat without precedent," announced Hans Joachim Meyer, Science Minister of Saxony.[150] The 64 technical colleges and universities in the east received DM 3 billion annually; it was not unusual for a department to have a faculty/student ratio of 7:1. New buildings were going up everywhere: DM 81 million for a small new university in Frankfurt an der Oder; DM 260 million for new university buildings in Cottbus. Renewal was in the air: More than two-thirds of the 140,000 employees from the DDR era were fired or furloughed. "Never before has a similar transformation in German higher education history taken place," editorialized *Der Spiegel*, praising the "mostly familiar coziness" felt by the majority of students in eastern institutions by October 1994. Matthew Rossler, in charge of the reorganization of higher education in Saxony, proudly announced: "We are already on the level of many western German universities."[151]

At the same time that there seemed to be a mood of a new beginning for ambitious eastern Germans as individuals, a general apathy about the possibility and value of collective action also reigned. By 1994, the post-revolutionary "élan" was gone. The students who in 1990/91 had stormed the Erfurt parliament, organized a vigil at the Humboldt, and gone on hunger strike in Leipzig were gone or quiet: the *wessified* "Me" generation in eastern universities had arrived.

Campus interest in politics was now minimal. Only 12 percent of students voted in the 1994 Humboldt student elections and only 6 percent at Leipzig; indeed one survey showed that a third of eastern students at technical colleges didn't even know that their college had a self-governing student board. Journalists tagged the apathy *Politikabstinenz* (abstinence from politics); the ignorance and meager voting turnouts remind the American observer of the uninterest of most American students in campus government.[152]

But students did get exercised—in Berlin and throughout the country—about Bonn's plans to cut their stipends and impose limits on the length of their degree programs. Noting that, by fall 1994, overcrowding at the university meant that 1.8 million students were not able to pursue their preferred course of study, Chancellor Kohl went on record supporting the austerity measures, along with freezing funding for German higher education and providing better incentives for students to attend technical colleges rather than universities.[153]

In the weeks leading up to the October 16 national election, the SPD took the students' and universities' side: the SPD called on the government for a 4 percent rise in student grants and an additional DM 2 billion on research and education, with DM 400 million going to universities. "Hardly another country as economically competitive as Germany," said SPD deputy leader Wolfgang Thierse, "has so neglected its schools and universities as much as Germany in the last few years." Or as one student government leader put it, Bonn seemed to have three "mantras" for magically improving German higher education: "Do more research, sell technology, and make students leave sooner."[154]

The PDS also made education an important plank in its campaign platform, arguing that eastern schools and universities were insufficiently funded and dominated by westerners. With 130,000 loyal members—more than 90 percent of them former SED members, including many former *Stasi* agents and informers—the PDS was by far the largest party in eastern Germany. And with the eloquent and popular Gregor Gysi as chairman, the PDS continued to make inroads throughout 1994. Gysi capitalized on the resentment felt by eastern workers, who were earning an average of 65 percent of their western counterparts. In the June regional election, which was one of the most important referenda during a year that witnessed 19 elections—*Superwahljahr* (super election year) and, later, *Superqualjahr* (super ordeal year), the press dubbed 1994—the PDS won 15 percent in Thuringia, 16.5 percent in Saxony, 20 percent in Saxony-Anhalt, and 25 percent in Mecklenburg-Vorpommern. In some cities, the PDS vote was as high as one-third: Potsdam, Schwerin, Rostock, Frankfurt an der Oder. In eastern Berlin it was 40 percent. The PDS even captured the mayoralty campaign in Hoyerswerda.[155]

Despite strong student opposition nationwide, and an unemployment rate that stood at 8.8 percent in the west and 14.6 percent in the east, the CDU-FDP coalition prevailed in the October *Superwahl*, winning by a narrow margin of 10 seats (341–331) in the 672-member *Bundestag*. But with banners crying that eastern Germany had eaten "Kohl dust" too long, the PDS cast itself as the party of easterners and continued to grow stronger, this time gaining 20 percent of the vote in the east and capturing 30 seats, up from 17 seats in the 1990 election.[156] The star of the PDS was 81-year-old Stefan Heym, the eldest *Bundestag* delegate and a Jewish writer who fought with the Americans during the war and still held American citizenship. In his address to open the first session of the new *Bundestag*, Heym voiced the hope that he "could contribute to the development of a new, old nation."[157]

Hardly anyone seemed to remember another octogenarian who once dominated eastern politics and who had passed away just a few months earlier.[158] Indeed the death of Erich Honecker on May 30, 1994, after a long battle with liver cancer, went largely unmourned in the east or west.

Even before his fall from power in October 1989, Honecker had not been "our Erich" to Germans for quite awhile. After being stripped of his offices and residing in disgrace with a Protestant pastor near Berlin, he had lived in exile in Moscow in 1991. Extradited for trial to Germany by the Soviets, he was sent in July 1992 to Berlin's Moabit jail (where he was officially known as prisoner #244/92). Finally he was released on health grounds in January 1993, whereupon he flew to Chile to reside with Margot and his daughter Sonya in a $200,000 Santiago villa. At his Chilean funeral, the "Honecker Solidarity Committee" praised him for "stabilizing Central Europe" and supporting "liberation movements" in Vietnam, Cuba, Nicaragua, Mozambique, and Ethiopia. As Margot Honecker held back tears, hundreds of sympathizers threw red carnations, waved red banners, and intoned the *Internationale* and songs of the Young Pioneers. "*Para siempre, camarade Honecker!*" blazoned the farewell caption under the huge portrait of the deceased. "Forever, Comrade Honecker!"

But forever is a long time. Had the resolute atheist and brilliant planner masterminded his exit, hedging his bets on Eternity by keeping one eye on Christian salvation History?

For his gray wooden coffin was draped with the hammer and compass flag— and topped by a large crucifix.

5

Leipzig, 1990

Karl Marx-Universität, RIP:
Postmortems on the God that Failed

I

What was it like to be a junior faculty member and longtime SED supporter under the Honecker regime?

"I had a place secured, a paved road before me," came the answer, as if from a great distance. "You—you've spent your whole life competing. We haven't. My career track was clear—*Dozent*, then Professor, then *Ordinarius*. In time, if I were reasonably productive, it would have all been there. Now, no university in Germany will have me. Probably I'll have to emigrate. That's the only way to escape everyone forever asking me what I did in the Party and why I did it."

On a cold, drizzling, smoggy Leipzig afternoon in December 1990, Jürgen, a *wissenschaftlicher Assistent* (lecturer) in political science, sits in a dingy, second-floor cafe a few blocks from the Karl-Marx Universität, telling me in a low voice about his life as a Party activist and organizer at the University. Authorities have just announced that several departments—among them law, political science, journalism, and M-L, will soon be shut down; Jürgen expects to be released in six months. He has spent the last 10 years at the oldest university in eastern Germany, widely regarded as the second-leading DDR university after Humboldt University of East Berlin. Talk has been buzzing that Humboldt could soon be closed down altogether, since united Berlin doesn't need a rival to the Free University—and since old Cold Warriors at the FU have hardly forgotten being driven from Humboldt in the late '40s. Such a scenario would leave the Karl-Marx Universität the top university in the east.

But Jürgen's mind is elsewhere. Academic politics holds little interest for him now; it all seems curiously irrelevant.

Abwicklung is the order of the day in Leipzig, a city of 560,000, the second largest in eastern Germany. Those who served the Karl-Marx Universität in "ideologically burdened" departments, or who held Party offices, or who had contact with the *Stasi*, will probably not retain their positions. Jürgen admits that, even if he were to undergo an *Überprüfung*, he would "start with those three counts against me anyway." Fifty out of 100 academic staff members in history have already been sacked. Word has it that faculty screenings in Saxony will be particularly close, he says, given the CDU victory a few weeks ago. In protest against the *Abwicklung* of academic departments, leaders of the student body, which numbers 13,000, have blockaded the University and are organizing demonstrations. Last week students occupied the main buildings on campus; a dozen students went on hunger strike. Other students have boycotted classes in some "protected" departments. But Jürgen says that the measures will change nothing. The die has been cast.

As I watched Jürgen nervously flick the ashes of cigarette after cigarette, his palms wet and his wiry frame coiled over our little table, I felt as if I were present at a private reading of our generation's *The God That Failed*, that powerful collection of postwar memoirs of several leading ex-communist intellectuals of the 1930s and '40s. And more: as an English Ph.D., a scholar of George Orwell's work, and a teacher of courses in the history of utopianism, I felt also the frisson of uneasy recognition: Here was a man of precisely my own age (34), a student of his state's philosophy and literature, a onetime idealist who had spent his entire life desperately clinging to utopian illusions.

Who was he now? . . .

Even as we talked, the senior faculty at the University were drafting a motion dealing with their collective identity, themselves preoccupied by the same overwhelming question. They were voting, unanimously, that the University return to the hallowed name by which it had been known for more than half a millennium (before the communists renamed it in 1952): Leipzig University.

More than anything else, it was his understated, almost deliberately self-deflationary delivery that made Jürgen's words so powerful. Yet I now realize that it was I, more than he, who invested our three hours together with such dramatic significance: after all, he had been living in the aftermath of the spontaneous demonstrations against his Party by *das Volk*—the "Leipzig Miracle" of October 1989—for more than a year. But this was my first extended visit to an erstwhile communist country, my first real encounter with all that I had read. Though I was familiar with the painful history of the socialist movement, I had learned it largely through books. And so each living encounter brought on for me the visceral experience of déjà vu. *The God That Failed* and *1984* had both appeared in 1949. Had history stopped there? The repressed emotions, the incremental concessions, the everyday compromises: Was this the 1990s or the 1940s?

Through my mind ran Marx and Engels' famous sentence in *The Communist Manifesto* about the course of revolutions: "Venerable prejudices and opinions are swept away. All that is solid melts into air, all that is holy is profaned, and men at last are forced to face the real conditions of their lives and their relations to one another." And here was Jürgen, a good Marxist functionary, baring to me the story of his life.

But this wasn't what Marx meant, was it?

II

None of this is to say that Jürgen made any claims to having had an unusual connection with the Party. No, he was typical of his cohort of Party functionaries.

Yes, *that* was just it: he was typical.

Son of two Party members, Jürgen, like 98 percent of DDR children, attended a POS and entered the JP in first grade. Proudly donning his blue neckerchief on special Pioneer Days such as the national birthday of the Pioneers (December 13), he was the model communist boy scout. "*Immer bereit!*" ("Always prepared!"). Jürgen recalls that the Pioneer motto encompassed several kinds of commitment: "Always prepared" to study; "always prepared" for peace, friendship, and solidarity; "always prepared" for productive socialist labor; and so on. Little Jürgen could recite by heart the 12 Pioneer Laws ("1. Young Pioneers respect people. 2. Young Pioneers show respect for other nations. . . ."). After school, he participated in a variety of Pioneer activities; the JP sponsored "work groups" for chess, mathematics, singing, and various sports. The groups taught the child to think "collectively" and about the value of work outside the sphere of required schooling.

In 4th grade, Jürgen joined the Thälmann Pioneers, receiving his red neckerchief as he pledged to live up to the ideals and example of Ernst Thälmann. He was a "Timur Helper," running errands for retirees in his neighborhood and assisting them with household chores. And though he wasn't much of an athlete, Jürgen went to several summer camps, each one of them named after a famous German or East bloc socialist, in which he often sat around the campfire and sang folk and political songs. Every Wednesday afternoon, he attended Thälmann Pioneer meetings; at one memorable meeting, he was elected to the office of "Scribe"; his task was to keep records in the "group book." By the age of 11, Jürgen regularly helped organize the festivities for major national celebrations such as the 50th anniversary, in 1967, of the Great October Revolution.

After his *Jugendweihe* and entry into the FDJ in eighth grade in 1970, Jürgen held three different offices in his FDJ class: secretary, then deputy, then finally, culture functionary. His responsibilities included supervising the FDJ membership and organizing FDJ outings to museums. In school, he became the regular class representative to the Russian Olympiad; he excelled at Russian grammar, sang Russian folk and Soviet *Komsomol* songs with gusto, and could answer the FDJ equivalent of Trivial Pursuit questions such as "What is the main department store in Moscow?" Since 6th grade, he had written faithfully to a Russian pen pal; later he would sometimes go with his mother to DSF (*Deutsch-sowjetische Freundschaftsgesellschaft*) evenings, where he would talk to soldiers and their families in Russian.

"I enjoyed my years in the POS," Jürgen says with a smile. "I don't know whether I was a 'convinced socialist.' For the most part, I didn't associate the POS, or even Pioneer activities, with politics. Very little was directly political, actually. The group activities fostered togetherness and 'collective thinking.' You thought of the welfare of the group.

"Of course, the older you got, the more you realized what was politically acceptable to mention in public. Even my mother, who had little good to say about West Germany, always watched the ARD and ZDF channels on TV—and she would tell me never to say in school that we watched it. I would never say, 'Did you see that great movie on ZDF last night?' And neither did my other classmates.

You just didn't mention it. . . . Still, I never felt under any pressure to participate in the Pioneers or the Russian Olympiads—writing and language and music were always my pleasures."

Politics entered his life unmistakably, Jürgen says, with his entry into the FDJ and his matriculation to the Ernst Schneller EOS in Meissen, which was named after a KPD resistance fighter. The two summer camps that he attended during his EOS years were less like Boy Scout outings than army camps, featuring military exercises and use of small firearms. All but 1 of the 25 students in his EOS graduating class were FDJ members; 7 of them were "politically oriented"; 3 applied to the SED for candidate membership even before graduation. Whereas the POS teachers, especially in the early grades, had been little concerned with ideology, Jürgen says, many EOS teachers were *rote Socken* (Red socks, i.e., Party loyalists). Although his mother knew many of them through her SED circles, Jürgen never felt he could confide personal difficulties to them about family or politics; they were never *Vertrauensleute* (trusted persons).

"Almost all my EOS teachers were in the Party," Jürgen says. "Most of them were competent academically, but often they were limited by the curriculum. For instance, you could choose art or music in the EOS. I chose art because the teacher was intelligent and friendly. But she had to teach mostly Soviet art and socialist realism, and even when we briefly discussed ancient art, it was through an image of 'socialist antiquity.'

"Other teachers had less subtle minds and more overt agendas. My 11th-grade *Stabü* teacher specialized in *Feindbilder* [enemy images] of the West, and you received grades based on your political convictions. Sometimes he would have us watch a laughable TV show such as [Karl-Eduard von] Schnitzler's *Schwarzer Kanal* [*Black Channel*], which purported to analyze western events but was the most blatant, pathetic DDR propaganda—West Germans called him 'the Red Goebbels.' Nobody would ever sit through it if it weren't required—people joked that a 'Schni' was the unit of time it took to switch channels if you inadvertently saw his face on TV.

"Anyway, the *Stabü* teacher treated the weekly revelations of Schnitzler—or 'von' Schnitzler, I should say, and the aristocratic background of this 'worker's spokesman' elicited even more jeers—as if they were straight from Lenin's tomb. The *Stabü* teacher was an old army officer, the Reddest of the *rote Socken*, tolerating no deviations from the textbook's line whatsoever. NATO was bad, the Warsaw Pact was good. The Prague Spring was bad, the Wall was good. Bad Americans came through the Brandenburg Gate in August 1961, and courageous officers from our NVA—such as our *Stabü* teacher!—stood their ground, fended off the invasion, and in cooperation with loyal workers erected the Wall to prevent future assaults. For the most part, we believed what the history books said—without ever really listening to the *Stabü* teacher or acquiring a *Feindbild* of the U.S. or the West. It was all simply dead history to us, never talked about outside class or some official occasion.

"Curiously enough, though, I liked the old *Stabü* teacher—you knew where you stood with him. 'You are the socialists, the elite, the future leaders of society!

Behave like it!' he would thunder. Once he even asked me to apply to become an army officer! But I had no interest in that. All in all, I preferred him to the careerists, such as my 12th-grade *Stabü* and geography teacher—he was a real hypocrite! 'C'mon, tell me what you really think!' he'd say. 'We can all speak freely here!' And then—I say this in hindsight—he would report on any deviations to the Party officials at the school, which kept a *Gefährdetenkartei* [danger file] on political troublemakers and potential adult 'subversives.' It was clear to me even then that his every action was angled to become school principal or for some kind of promotion—and eventually he did become a POS principal somewhere."

Even before scoring a 1,2 on his *Abitur*—an A plus—it was clear to his family and teachers that Jürgen would go on to university. Both of his parents were college-level teachers; it was in the family. Undecided between *Germanistik* and philosophy, he chose philosophy when a friend of his mother, a professor of philosophy in Halle, persuaded her that his future was brightest in that subject. Jürgen joined his parents in the Party after gaining his *Abitur* at 19. Jürgen's mother, a radical and idealist with both feet planted firmly in the air, has been left hanging there. Among the first to be fired, she had been a senior M-L lecturer at a technical college in Karl-Marx Stadt, now also returned to its former name, Chemnitz. Jürgen's father, whom she divorced when Jürgen was 10, taught M-L in a Halle college that has also recently been *abgewickelt*.

"My mother is an economist who knows only Marxist economics—and it's been *aufgehoben* [transcended, canceled] by History," Jürgen jokes. He takes a deep drag of his cigarette and tosses his head back. "It's too late for her to do an *Umschulung* [retraining], or to begin over. Likewise with my father. Their lives are over.

"At 18, I still believed in socialism, I believed in its ideals," Jürgen says. "That's probably because my mother believed in it so passionately—my mother, a true believer, but also one of the few truly intelligent socialists I've ever known. But at least as big a part of me entered the Party for careerist reasons. Maybe 30 percent of us entered for the ideals—maybe 30. Seventy percent entered for the career advantages. After entering, maybe 10 percent stayed believers—maximum. My mother was one of the rare ones—the Idealistic Materialist! But most of us stayed for the advantages—it was simply much, much easier to make it up the ladder.

"By 19 I was already disillusioned—more by the timidity than by the lies," Jürgen goes on. "You knew what you couldn't say, you policed yourself. You never even thought outside those categories. Like *1984*. What, surprised? Yes, I've read Orwell. *Doppelzüngigkeit* [doublethinking]—that's exactly what it was, though we called it dialectics.

"It wasn't that the university was less open than the EOS. Just the reverse. We had a number of fairly free discussions in M-L about the future of socialism, even on controversial topics, such as whether the 'Law of History' meant that religion was dying out. No, it was that by now you had lost your innocence. Even the FDJ officials at the university would joke about FDJ activities—'OK, people,' they'd say, 'let's get this over with.' You'd have a half-hour meeting about some upcoming event, about which nobody cared, yet which let the FDJ official report to the Party that we met. Then we'd all go out for beers."

III

Jürgen's most difficult decision had come at the age of 30 when the Party offered him the three-year post of FDJ secretary at the University. He would be in charge of organizing youth meetings, evaluating students for Party membership, and keeping tabs on FDJ members.

"I never wanted to do it—I'm not really a political person. I refused, but they said, 'You'll do it, or no *Assistent*—let alone *Ordinariat*.' Finally, at my parents' urging, I gave in. I wanted the security, and I thought I could just go along and make things work.

"It proved to be nothing but a headache. Ridiculous. Old men telling young people what they 'really' wanted! For instance, in preparation for the DDR's 40th anniversary last October 7, [Egon] Krenz tells [FDJ chief Hartmut] Lange and the Berlin director of the FDJ to organize a youth festival. The Berlin director tells the *Bezirk* [district] leaders, and I get the word: 'Bring your best people.' But—of course—nobody wants to go. And I have to pressure and plead with them—all the while pretending that it's an 'honor' to be 'invited' to the 40th Anniversary Celebration. A bureaucratic nightmare—all *Doppelzüngigkeit*. Of course I knew I was living a lie—but by then it had been 15 years."

I ask Jürgen if, in his position, he had much contact with the *Stasi*. Folding his hands, Jürgen gazes out the window. "Not much," he answers. His eyes are fixed on the traffic below. "Once in a great while they would come around, just asking for information. We'd chat—I always considered it just a part of my duties—and of my duty as a socialist. Don't you feel that way about the CIA? . . . No? Well, I never knew anything very private or damaging about anyone. And I never again heard about whatever the agents were inquiring about—they never got back to you."

Tentatively, I inquire about Jürgen's specific contact with *Stasi* agents. He turns around, toward me. His voice is steady. He replies casually, "I'd rather not discuss that subject any further. What other questions do you have?"

Could you, in your position, ever criticize the Party?

"That was the one small advantage. Sometimes, if you couched it in the right terms and avoided making it a public criticism, yes. Then sometimes the higher-ups would listen—because now you too represented the Party. 'We must do this,' I might say—and I had a bit of leverage on the inside. But it was very little, really. It was a delusion to think we could ever reform the Party from within. And we knew the rule: Never criticize publicly, not even at a Party meeting. . . . Sure, the youth leaders were always questioning, always expressing reservations—but the older people would always be 'explaining' to us that X or Y had to be seen dialectically. And brilliant dialecticians they were!

"But I respected very few of them. They too were careerists, afraid to speak their minds. Yet—to stand up at a meeting and criticize Honecker directly?! Never. Your career would have been over with that very sentence. And anyway, what would it have accomplished? It would have been crazy. And far worse to leave the Party once you had joined than never to have joined at all. It was like the Mafia: once you were in, you were in for life. One or two senior profs did leave before 1988—when it first became possible to leave and survive—but you had to be outstanding to do that.

"People began to leave in 1988—no earlier. The young people welcomed Gorbachev, but the old people controlled the Party and wouldn't listen. They thought things would just go on forever as they always had. The Party defections came in droplets and then in waves. In 1988, two or three people at the University. In early '89, maybe 20. In the summer of '89, 200—by then, it was becoming too late to penalize faculty, because too many were leaving. And by November, leaving didn't mean anything anymore."

Jürgen admits that he stayed in the Party until January 1990. "Until 11:59," he says ruefully. He had still believed it might be possible to build a reformed Communist Party with a mass following.

"October 10, 1989—the day of the first big *Demo* here [when 50,000 Leipzigers marched peacefully through the streets]—we had a Party meeting scheduled. We canceled it just as the march was beginning—to save our lives! Funny, unlike many Party members, I was curious and rather supportive of the marchers. It even crossed my mind to join them—but everyone in the Party knew that observers were keeping tabs on the demonstrators, and that was enough to deter us. . . .

"To us, it still seemed possible then to reform socialism. Even after the citizens' committee occupied the local *Stasi* headquarters [in December] and began calling officially for the ouster of the Party. As late as January of this year, we were having Party meetings—as if we could abolish the SED and claim the People's support—just like that! As if a name change [to PDS, Party of Democratic Socialism] were enough!. . . . We were completely out of touch with reality. It was all a delusion—I was living in a *Schlaraffenland* [fool's paradise]."

But Jürgen says he was as surprised as anyone else about the revelations that began surfacing in late November 1989 about the corruption of the SED leadership. He'd had no idea of the full story—it had been kept within a tight little circle. However timid and hard-line he knew them to be, he'd had no idea that former Party and *Stasi* leaders had diverted hundreds of millions of marks to foreign bank accounts, had embezzled tens of millions for ski lodges and vacation villas. The stories during those winter months had filled him with anguish about the Party. Yet still he had stayed. . . .

Jürgen glances out the window again. The light is failing.

But Jürgen does not move. He does not rise from his seat.

Yes, still he had stayed. Some part of him, beneath all the careerism and *Doppelzüngigkeit*, still had believed in the collectivist god, still had trusted in the socialist *Schlaraffenland*.

IV

Stepping out into the rain, I remember Arthur Koestler's parting reflection in *The God that Failed*: The end does not justify the means; the means determine the end.

Walking back in the twilight to the University, I run into an acquaintance in the German Department there, Reinhard, a man slightly older than Jürgen. An *Assistent* who had withdrawn from the Party in July 1989 after the SED's public support for the Tiananmen Square massacres, Reinhard had been one of the very few Leipzig faculty who had been on the streets in early October '89 to protest.

We talk as I accompany Reinhard toward his office. I mention my impressions of my conversation with Jürgen, whom Reinhard knows slightly. Seating himself in his cramped office, whose centerpiece is a huge metal desk piled high with books and papers, Reinhard says that he too has read Orwell and Koestler. He mentions Koestler's *Sonnenfinsternis* (*Darkness at Noon*), the brilliant anti-Stalinist novel about the Soviet show trials and the totalitarian mentality, in which Rubashov, an Old Bolshevik defendant, abases himself, confesses to treasonous crimes he never committed, and accepts execution out of loyalty to his youthful communist ideals—his last act of devotion to the Party.

He himself has known Rubashovs, Reinhard says, nodding glumly. Koestler's psychological understanding of Rubashov and the logic of Party loyalty is acute, he says, though Stalin obtained his confessions by good old-fashioned torture, not via some mysterious process of self-incriminating confessions. We talk about Koestler's membership in the KPD of the 1930s, and the anguish and remorse that he felt when he realized that the Party was a fraud and a charade. In an existential sense, Rubashov *was* guilty, says Reinhard; his real crime was that he was willing to serve the Party until the end. Like Winston Smith in *1984*, Rubashov was as corrupt as the system that produced him.

We muse together on the Stalin cult, on the mass hallucination of those years, on the Party mentality. Then, suddenly, Reinhard swivels his chair and rolls over to a cluttered bookcase. Eyeing an old copy of *Neues Deutschland* stuffed between some books, he yanks it out. It is dated January 1989. With mock ceremony, Reinhard reaches into his inside coat pocket, pulls out a leather case, and with professorial fastidiousness, dons his glasses. He turns to me and smiles.

"As an exercise," he says impishly, "let's count the references to Honecker."

We go through the front page of the paper together. Total: 17.

"Definitely on the low side, I'd say," Reinhard pronounces. He shakes his head. Honecker was a long way from Stalin, he says. But how did he ever go along with such a system as that?

"Youthful ideals," I reply.

Reinhard does not respond. Instead he says: "If you had read [West German publisher Axel] Springer's *Bild-Zeitung* over the last four decades"—a mass cult rag amounting to a cross between our *National Enquirer* and *USA Today*—"you'd probably have gotten a more accurate picture of Germany than from *Neues Deutschland* or *Junge Welt.*"

The comparison stops me short, transporting me back again to the American literary scene: it is the early 1980s, and General Jaruzelski has just suppressed Poland's Solidarity movement. Susan Sontag comments in a Town Hall speech in New York that a *Reader's Digest* subscriber of the 1950s and '60s would have been better informed about the realities of communism than a *New Statesman* or *Nation* subscriber. A stunning claim! Sontag's observation—a mea culpa for her trip to Hanoi, her fear of criticism from radicals, her sentimental attachment to socialist pieties, her own moral blindness—triggered a firestorm of protest from the Anglo-American Left. Although her statement gave aid and comfort to the Right—as she had regretfully anticipated—its kernel of truth seemed to me undeniable. Why hadn't the democratic Left listened more closely to the waves of foreign emigres, the Cassandras from Koestler through Kundera and Kosinski, who had proclaimed the horrors of Stalinism? Why had leading liberal-Left magazines largely closed their ears—and their pages—to such voices?

Is there a Lesson—or Unlesson—in it all? Sontag drew one from from the crackdown on Solidarity: Communism is the most devious collectivism, a high-flown, "dialectical" fascism—"fascism with a human face," as she called it.

But is that it? Or is that just a new revisionism? Clearly, the emigres had been speaking an important truth, if not the whole truth. And the American Left had been living a lie—and with much less pressure to conform than SED members. Yet somehow this assessment seems to glide over the agonizing, visceral tug-of-war inside the souls of those like Koestler whose life stories appeared in *The God That Failed*, the years of love-hate through which most Party heretics—and believers—suffered.

How were you able to summon the strength to leave the Party? I ask Reinhard.

A long sigh. Reinhard tells me about his reaction to the Tiananmen Square propaganda in the DDR. Removing his glasses, he says he does not want to falsify his past.

"It was the vulgarity of it all," he says finally. "It was all so stupid—when you could see on West German TV what was really happening. . . . If they had presented it intelligently, the Party line might have been plausible. The stupidity of it all! As if Hitler and fascism were still the enemy! All presented so black and white! Like almost everything else, nothing they said corresponded to the complicated realities of the West—it was so dumb, so one-sided, so extreme. Your own TV set refuted it every night—as did your own relatives every visit. I just couldn't go on condoning the system, I had to do something. So I got out. I feared for my job, but I got out."

Reinhard pauses. He gazes absently out the window. It is dark outside.

Turning toward me, Reinhard looks at me intently, and then smiles.

"As my old grandfather used to say to us, there's just one thing wrong with socialism: *Es funkioniert nicht* [It doesn't work]."

We chuckle together. Still, I want something more than, or different from, such talk. But I don't know what to say.

Reinhard goes on talking, now addressing the recent national election in December that the CDU won decisively. He says he voted for the SPD in the election; he couldn't imagine supporting the PDS—and certainly can't imagine actually joining the new incarnation of "the Party."

I remark that numerous students at the University seem, however, to be showing renewed interest in socialism, in the PDS.

Could "the Party" one day rise again from the ruins? I ask. Did the god—or merely the Faithless—fail?

Reinhard looks out the window. Night has fallen. He turns back toward me. He nods, and then shakes his head.

"Yes, already one hears it everywhere—'That never happened under social-ism. . . . ' Socialism is a beautiful dream. Within 5 or 10 years, it will only become more powerful in the east again. As the dissatisfactions with capitalism mount, as the victims of competition become bitter, people will speak again of its vision of equality and social justice and brotherhood. . . . Ah, it is a beautiful dream—and one which can never work. But it will never die."

6

Plauen, 1990/1992/1994

From Schoolmarm to Revolutionary:
Annaliese Saupe, Old "New Teacher" and Local Heroine

I

"Oma der Revolution," a neighborhood child calls her. "Grandmother of the Revolution." And that she is: a revolutionary in love with the past, a revolutionary in love with a bygone Germany.

When I first met Annaliese Saupe in 1987, I had no idea that she had been such a hell-raiser: blacklisted by the Nazis, vocal critic of SED educational policies, fired for insubordination by SED school authorities. Nor could I have guessed what would lay ahead for her only two years in the future, when she would be lionized by neighbors for her derring-do against the SED during the Revolution of the Candles. With her hair coiled into a huge white bun on top of her head, her large brown eyes and quick smile, her slight limp and walking cane, her encyclopedic knowledge of grocery prices past and present, her antiquarian's passion for the history of her native region, her enduring love affair with Goethe and Schiller: Annaliese Saupe seems much like a *Hausfrau* and history schoolmarm—which is also just what she has been.

I met Frau Saupe in 1987 at a Goethe Institute talk near Freiburg, where she gave a presentation on Goethe's daily routine in Weimar. Struck by Frau Saupe's vibrance and energy, I struck up an acquaintance with her. Already 75 years old, she was a dynamo who could easily pass for a woman in her early 60s. She invited me to visit her in her hometown of Plauen, a small Saxony city of 85,000 in the old German region of Vogtland. But the paperwork for my tourist visa to East Germany dragged on beyond my six-week visit in West Germany, and I returned to the United States disappointed.

Nonetheless, we wrote each other, and in early December 1990, during the week of the first free elections in eastern Germany since 1933—in which Frau Saupe voted, now as then, for the Social Democrats—I finally had an opportunity to visit Plauen.

"Please don't leave Germany this time without coming to see me!" she had written me. "I have much to tell you!" Teaching was her family's vocation; she had been a teacher for 12 years; her first husband had been a loyal Nazi teacher, her second husband had been a (rather apolitical) teacher during the Third Reich era and DDR-era school principal for a total of 50 years.

And Frau Saupe had much to show me too, she said. She was busy assembling a private photo collection for a history exhibit in a local museum—snapshots that she and her son had taken, secretly, of the local demonstrations in 1989, and which she had smuggled, at great personal risk, to a West German newspaper. Against the denial of memory by a police state, against the obliterating forces of time and death murmured her eloquent plea to remember and to record.

II

If Annaliese Saupe looks rather grandmotherly, so be it: The streets of cheering grandmothers with their placards and unbowed schoolchildren with their lighted candles led to the Revolution of 1989. In the ranks of those thousands of local heroes was Frau Saupe. Fearlessly and unfailingly, she attended every one of the 22 weekly protest demonstrations against the SED held in Plauen between October 1989 and March 1990. After each Saturday *Demo* in October-November 1989 she stayed up all night, feverishly writing news accounts and developing photographs of the events. Then she stuffed everything in her underwear and smuggled it on Sunday morning across the border to Hof, Plauen's former West German "sister city," a town just fifteen miles away in Bavaria. As a retiree, Frau Saupe was permitted to travel to the West; border guards were usually lax in their searches of senior citizens. In Hof, Frau Saupe had found her way to the newspaper offices of the Hof *Frankenpost*, where she shared her work with its astonished editors, who in early October 1989 could hardly believe that a revolution was in the making and that a 78-year-old grandmother was risking her neck to document it and come to them with the story about it.

"If the border police had caught me," Frau Saupe says, "they would have jailed me immediately."

We are sitting in Frau Saupe's little living room, on the second storey of her modest home in the *Komponistenviertel* (composers' quarter) of Plauen. Her street is the Anton Bruckner Street, named after a distinguished nineteenth-century Austrian composer. The tumultuous events of a year ago seem a world away.

Eagerly, Frau Saupe shows me her smuggled stories in the *Frankenpost* and the Hamburg *Abendblatt*, printed merely under the byline "an eyewitness." Then she proudly unfolds the feature story about her heroics in the Plauen *Vogtlandpost* of May 1990, after *das Volk* had triumphed and the Revolution was already history: "Annaliese Saupe: The Woman Who Chronicled the Revolution."

But neither unsung nor sung heroines—nor even unflinching witnesses—are made in a day. For Annaliese Saupe, the process of gaining the courage to speak out began long ago. Born in 1912, shortly after the 40th anniversary of the Second German Reich and the famous Hamburg speech of Kaiser Wilhelm II insisting that Germany deserved "a place in the sun" among world powers, she has been for decades an "odd woman out," quietly refusing to go along with the crowd, questioning reigning orthodoxies, speaking truth to power.

A familiar, and yet an exceptional, story: A person goes her own way, and then one day the crisis—like the historic challenge of 1989—suddenly looms, and she is among those few who have committed the resolute daily acts of conscience and so possess the strength of character to speak. And the crisis unveils the person she has gradually become.

No politician or intellectual herself, as she readily acknowledges, Annaliese Saupe did not go in search of experience or consciously insert herself into the stream of German history. Nor has she had professional cause as a journalist or scholar to follow its course. No, as she put it, she was in 1989 "one of the little people who had simply had enough—and found the voice to say so."

How *did* she find that voice? I wonder. And the will to raise it? I see a hint in the folders—one for each of her research projects—containing dozens of neatly typed quotations and reports of her experiences in the DDR, before and after 1989. There are many exhortations from Goethe, the last western Olympian, and from Schiller, the poet of Liberty. Here a touchstone about the "ceaseless yearning for freedom" from Schiller's *The Robbers*, his stirring drama assailing corruption in high places. There a stanza from his "Song of the Bell":

> It is dangerous to wake the lion,
> The teeth of the tiger can prove fatal,
> But the most fearsome thing of all
> Is the human fanatic.

Frau Saupe presses her finger to a page containing maxims by Goethe, then nods her head: "None are more hopelessly enslaved than those who falsely believe themselves free." And from his *Faust*: "Old we grow indeed, but who grows wise?"

Here in front of me is a life, apparently obscure, that has endured and encompassed three-quarters of a century of History's march, a life variously touched by a vanished age of imperial grandeur, a Great War to end all wars, a failed communist revolution, a Great Depression that made its American counterpart pale by comparison, a fascist police state, a Second World War fought at the end on one's own soil, an occupation of one's homeland by enemy forces, decades of a communist dictatorship, the gradual collapse of that dictatorship in the face of mass protests, and finally the voluntary self-liquidation of the state and its incorporation by its long-estranged sibling and former ideological enemy.

What was it like?

As Annaliese Saupe told me the story of her life, I felt as if I had stumbled across a walking incarnation of modern German social history—complete with walking stick. For the framework of Frau Saupe's outwardly modest life inscribes the biography of a generation and a nation.

I hasten to point out that Frau Saupe did not present herself in these inflated terms: It was I, the bookish young American who visited her, who envisioned her on the horseback of History. But her range of experience and her diligent preservation of it prompted the apparition; and if it seemed to me that she had seen more, done more, felt more than a roomful of people, this was not because she had devoted her days to angling for her own "place in the sun"; no, she had lived her years in her own humble way as *Hausfrau*, schoolteacher, and good neighbor. However unassuming the tapestry of her life, it is nonetheless also extraordinarily rich, so much so that I immediately felt that hers exemplified not one life but several: the starving child of a defeated Wilhelmine Germany, the jobless young woman of the depression-era Weimar Republic, the alienated skeptic among Nazi true believers, the hopeful "New Teacher" contributing to the new socialist state, the ideological agnostic and DDR "enemy of the people," and finally the "Oma der Revolution."

That was the story she had "much to tell."

III

Annaliese Leonhardt was an only child, daughter of a Leipzig shoemaker and homemaker. Her parents were divorced when she was just two years old, and she was raised thereafter by her mother, who became a postal clerk. Frau Saupe's vignettes of her Wilhelmine childhood are vivid and poignant. Among her fullest memories are those about popular attitudes toward the German royalty. Like most Leipzig residents and Saxons, her family and neighbors had no great affection for Prussian princes—Saxons and Prussians had been enemies ever since the Saxons had fought on Napoleon's side in 1800—and most Saxons heartily disliked Prussian Kaiser Wilhelm II. But they had a deep fondness for their own Crown Prince Frederick August III of Saxony, especially after his wife the Duchess ran off with an Italian musician.

"He was so kind, so *gemütlich* [easygoing, genial]," says Frau Saupe. "Above all, he was so endearingly inept. Even as a child, I felt so sorry for him." She recalls his visit to Leipzig in the early 1920s, after Germany had declared itself a republic and had forced him to abdicate the crown. As the crowds cheered him ecstatically, he had said with a smirk: "My, you're a fine group of republicans now, aren't you?!"

Less pleasant for Frau Saupe are her memories of the atmosphere in Germany at the close of World War I, as arguments raged among her relatives about the wisdom of continuing a war of desperate expedients, about the German High Command and the competence of Ludendorff and Hindenburg, about the Bolshevik Revolution and the German victory at the Battle of Tannenberg, and about the "outrageously unjust" Treaty of Versailles. The 1917 Russian Revolution enflamed left-wing sentiments in Germany. Frau Saupe remembers her own frightening encounter with Germany's "November Revolution" in 1918, the unsuccessful coup engineered by the Spartacists (communists) just days after the Great War ended: how, as a seven-year-old, she had wandered one day into Augustus Square, where government troops in the streets faced off against Sparticist militia crouched on the roof of Leipzig's main post office. As she stood, dazed, her mother screamed "Anne!" and ran wildly to spirit her away from the potential crossfire.

But most of all, Frau Saupe recalls how she felt when the food shortages and food riots began during the potato famine of 1916–17, a consequence of the Allies' wartime "hunger blockade" of Germany, which had depended upon imports for a third of its food supply. Annaliese remembers her hunger.

"I was one of the starving children of the big city," Frau Saupe says of the famine that swept through Germany during the last years of the war. "The hunger was horrible! Nothing to eat except cabbage and turnips. We called it—rather unimaginatively!—'the cabbage-and-turnip-time.'" At the age of eight, sickly little Annaliese weighed less than 40 pounds. Dark bread, sausage slices without fat, a few potatoes, and lots of cabbages and turnips constituted her weekly diet; the government ration provided less than half the calories necessary for minimum subsistence. The food crisis destroyed the spirit of the home front: neighborhood children stole food from each other's homes; families with soldiers at the front turned into food scavengers. Annaliese's mother, also very sick at the time—the mortality rate for women jumped 50 percent during the war—worried whether her daughter would live. Death by starvation and death by malnutrition were common; by 1919, 3 percent of German schoolchildren were suffering some degree of open pulmonary tuberculosis. Fortunately, however, through a program organized by an office of the dismantled War Food Office, Annaliese's mother registered 10-year-old Annaliese in 1922 for a three-month visit to Holland, sponsored free-of-charge by sympathetic Dutch families to help German children victimized by the war.

"That trip saved me," Frau Saupe says. "I gained 17 pounds! It was the first time I had ever eaten—or even seen—an apple or a banana." Frau Saupe pauses and remarks on the need for the Germans of 1990 to help the asylum seekers pouring from poorer countries into Germany, and she shows me a picture of a Ukrainian family for whom she bakes and whose children she tutors in German. She has tried to pass on some of the kindnesses from strangers that she once received. "I've never forgotten how those Dutchmen—who, if anything, had certainly been hurt by our conduct of the war—treated me. I'll never forget the generosity of that family."

IV

When Frau Saupe dwells on the 1920s, she shudders. Intellectual mythology has it that the decade was "the golden age of Weimar," the age of Dietrich and decadence, of cabarets and culture, before the onslaught of the Great Depression, the Nazi takeover, and World War II. But outside Berlin and except for the avant-garde in theater and film, says Frau Saupe, there was little about which to be nostalgic—and certainly not for ordinary people. She pages through her mother's diary to the year 1923. Pasted in it are several clippings from the local Leipzig paper. The headlines startle: "Spartacists steal food; rioting near St. Thomas Church." "RM [Reichsmark] falls again; Is 'barter only' the rule?" And then, in her mother's handwriting: "21 August 1923: bread RM 480,000; potatoes [one pound] RM 50,000; margarine RM 900,000."

"After getting her wages, my mother would race to the grocer," recalls Frau Saupe of her home life in 1923, "because the next day everything would be doubled in price." As a 12-year-old, she herself often ran straight from school to the grocer with fistfuls of marks, only to be turned away. Largely as a result of war reparations payments and the savage penalties imposed on German trade by the Treaty of Versailles, the Reichsmark fell in 1922 from 16.2 to 7,000 to the dollar. (It had been 4.2 to the dollar before 1914. The DM exchange rate is roughly 1.5:1 today.) Faced with impossible budget deficits, Germany followed a practice already begun during the war: meeting expenses simply by printing more paper money. When the Weimar Republic defaulted on loan payments to France in the spring of 1923, French troops occupied the Ruhr and set up an economic blockade that cut off the Rhineland from the rest of Germany, sending the mark into the stratosphere: July 1923–RM 160,000 to the dollar; November 1923–RM 4.2 *trillion* to the dollar. "You've heard the stories of the men hauling wheelbarrows full of marks through the streets?" Frau Saupe asks me. "They were no exaggeration!"

Annaliese Leonhardt attended the Gaudig School—the best girls' school in Leipzig, and one of the outstanding girls' schools in Weimar Germany. Physical education and geography were her favorite subjects; she was a scholar-athlete. In 1929, at the age of 17, she captured the top prize in Leipzig track-and-field in the pentathlon.

Annaliese graduated in 1932, just after the National and the Darmstadter banks, two of Germany's largest, had failed, and unemployment had risen to 6 million. Inflation and the strictures of the Treaty of Versailles had plunged Germany into a depression more severe than that in any other country, and the extreme suffering generated popular support for extreme solutions. Before 1930, the fledgling National Socialist Workers Party had held only 4 seats in the Reichstag; in the 1930 elections, the Nazis gained a total of 107 seats. By late 1932, the Nazis were the largest, and the communists the third largest national party. Open warfare raged in Saxony streets between communists and Nazis throughout the Weimar era, but especially during the early 1930s. Plauen was a communist stronghold, and had even elected a communist mayor in 1927 (who would be interned in a concentration camp in the 1930s). Upon Hitler's ascension to power in January 1933, the crackdown was swift and merciless: outspoken Social Democrats and communists, including two of her own former schoolmates, were jailed or driven into exile.

V

The depression was the indispensable condition of Hitler's rise to power. It was so severe that, despite her *Abitur*, Annaliese could find no work. She was exceptionally well-educated, since only 2 percent of German girls before the war earned the *Abitur* (and only 10 percent of boys). She decided to teach herself stenography and typing, and in 1933 was hired as a secretary in a Leipzig business office.

That year she also met her first husband, Friedrich Flach. He was a student of Romance languages and physical education at the Universities of Hamburg and Leipzig, "a brilliant poet and remarkable athlete," Frau Saupe says. In April 1930 they married and soon moved to historic Plauen on the Elster. The capital of Vogtland in the thirteenth century, Plauen had become a hub of the European lace industry in the sixteenth century and the scene of the world's first lace-spinning machine in 1880. ("Plauener *Spitze*" [lace] is still known today throughout Central Europe). Also near the city is the Vogtland village where the first violin and the first German harmonica were made.

Soon the young couple took up residence in a house on the same Plauen street as Herr Flach's parents and aunts, the Anton Bruckner Street, located next to the Beethoven, Bach, and Klopstock streets. Here Frau Saupe has resided for the last

58 years. Herr Flach began teaching in the Plauen *Realschule*, and the marriage was, for a short time, an entirely happy one.

But politics soon intruded. Plauen had been a thriving textile center in the early decades of the century, but its economy tumbled after the 1920s, when European women lost their taste for lace. By 1935 the city suffered the highest unemployment rate (more than 50 percent) of any sizable German city. That same year, though Annaliese and her husband were not political people, school officials required him to join the Nazi Party or face losing his job. He did so, and to Annaliese's horror, became an ardent nationalist and enthusiastic supporter of Hitler.

"My husband believed that Hitler was our savior," Frau Saupe says ruefully. " '*Der Führer! Der Führer!*' A look of rapture would come into his face as he spoke the words. His beautiful pastoral lyrics and love poetry turned into hymns to the *Führerprinzip* [leader principle] and for *Lebensraum* ["living room"; i.e., expansion]. His parents and aunts parroted '*Heil Hitler!*' when Hitler and Goebbels delivered their speeches on the radio. I used to sit in my room and cry for hours. What has my family become?! What has Germany become?! . . . After a year or two I no longer talked with my husband or his family about it: There was no point to it. And they in turn treated me like a disloyal German, and as a child whose business was the kitchen."

Why was she so different? Only a perspective gained from her frequent trips outside Germany, concedes Frau Saupe, immunized her from the near-universal Nazi leader-worship.

"Because of my visits since childhood to my great uncle in Switzerland," Frau Saupe continues, "I knew what freedom of expression was. The fascination with Hitler stopped suddenly at the German border. . . . Almost everyone around me [in Plauen] had been happy about the annexation of the Sudetenland [in Czechoslovakia in 1936] and Austria [in 1938]. They said that the German people were seeking after World War I to become one people in a Greater Germany—Austria had voted to unite with Germany in 1919, but the Allies had invalidated the election. So now that we had the wherewithal to determine our affairs, why shouldn't we? What had prevented us? Only the punitive provisions of the Treaty of Versailles, everyone said. But no, my great uncle said. He was a strong anti-Nazi, he didn't want Switzerland to be part of the Reich, and he explained to me that Hitler was preparing for world conquest. He told me during every visit, which I continued until his death in 1940, how horrible the Nazis were. He always said that, if Hitler remained in power, none of us in Germany would inherit a *Pfennig* from him. From him I learned what humanism and democracy meant."

Meanwhile Herr Flach had become a reserve officer in the infantry, and with the outbreak of war in September 1939, the infantry called him up immediately to serve in Poland, where he received the Iron Cross for bravery in battle. He was a hero in everyone's eyes except her own, Frau Saupe says. Soon his commanders promoted him to the rank of major.

Frau Saupe opens the diary of her 29-year-old husband to the entries for 1939 and reads aloud his poem about the invasion of Poland, "We are marching":

> We are marching, we are serving
> The formation of a glorious Greater Germany!
> Your countryside, your spirit
> More than 1000 kilometers away.

She shakes her head, then turns away, holding back the tears. The poem moves her deeply—not because it is a moving poem, I suspect, but because of the memories of the man and the era that it evokes.

" *'Heimat! Heimat!'* " Frau Saupe exclaims. "That was his theme day and night. How impatient he was for war to break out! 'My smart little wife is anxious!' he would say. 'She's in the know, as always, isn't she?' . . . How could such a sensitive, highly educated man become so obsessed about German conquest? How could he imagine that Russians, Poles, and other Slavs were 'filth,' and that the Jewish people were subhuman?"

Frau Saupe falls silent.

I wait for her answer; but no answer comes. I broach the question that haunts her generation. Buchenwald is only 70 kilometers away, I whisper. Did your family know about the *Endlösung*?

But Frau Saupe does not hesitate; she has faced the question before.

"No. I knew about the camps, and I knew the Jews had been interned," Frau Saupe answers. "But I didn't know what was happening there. Believe me, many ordinary people didn't know. Not until the war was almost over. You were surrounded by a wall of propaganda, and I was a young mother at home with two babies [born in 1940 and 1943]. . . . Later I saw the films of the camps that the Americans showed in the theaters. Unimaginable horrors. . . . What my husband and his family knew I have no idea. I never found out. I'm sure he would have heard about it, though, and must have somehow screened it out or rationalized it away. He was home for only a few months between 1939 and 1945. And after the war began, neither he nor his family ever discussed anything with me except home and family."

Frau Saupe closes her husband's diary slowly, cradling it in her lap. Then she looks down, as if addressing it.

"How could a man lose his soul to these ideas?" she says, slowly pronouncing each word. She looks up. "What came over him?"

She searches in vain for the answer, as she has for 50 years.

Frau Saupe reopens the diary and finds another poem. "The Self-Evident Duty." She reads it aloud, then shrugs. "He was mesmerized, hypnotized. It was a cult." We both nod to each other. That unsatisfactory explanation will have to suffice.

On the second day of the Russian campaign in June 1941, a grenade exploded in Major Flach's face. Temporarily blinded and with one eardrum shattered, he lay for weeks in a hospital bed in Weimar, suffering excruciating earaches. But characteristically, when the Allied D-Day invasion pushed back the Germans in France in June 1944, and the Russians began to close in on Germany later that year, Major Flach volunteered from his hospital bed to serve on the eastern front. " 'To defend the *Heimat* against the Russian barbarians!' " barks Frau Saupe, imitating her first husband's delivery. Patriotic duty took priority over everything, she says, including his health and his wife and children.

"His pain was so terrible that he would suddenly put his head down and wail in anguish," Frau Saupe recalls of Major Flach's visits home after the disastrous campaign on the Russian front. "He was almost deaf—he couldn't even follow a dinner table conversation. You had to speak directly into his ear. He could never have taught in a classroom again."

Major Flach's final posting was near Dresden, shortly after the Allies had fire-bombed the city on February 13–14, 1945. Frau Saupe reads his last note home from the front: March 3, 1945. By now, the war was an insane lost cause, with half of Germany already occupied by the Allies, but the letter speaks of "trusting to Providence" and the "coming final victory."

"More Hitler than Hitler," Frau Saupe says in a low voice. Major Flach believed in the propaganda about the V2, Hitler's miracle weapon, she says, which the *Führer* was allegedly waiting to unleash until just the right moment and which would snatch victory from defeat. Frau Saupe folds the letter along the worn creases, and gently lays it down.

"It was a blessing for him that he didn't live to see the defeat of Germany," Frau Saupe says. "To him it was inconceivable that Germany could be conquered. Like Hitler, he would say, 'I do not know the meaning of the word "capitulation." ' Never could he have seen 1945 as a liberation."

In the final week of the war, Frau Saupe says, the entire company under her husband's command disobeyed his order, possibly communicated directly from Hitler's bunker, to attack a Russian regiment on the outskirts of Berlin. Her husband and a fellow officer executed the order alone, falling in combat on April 30, 1945: the very day on which Hitler committed suicide.

Back in Plauen, the Allies' own slaughterhouse of vengeance was proceeding apace. On April 10, 1945, long after air assaults could have had any strategic purpose, Anglo-American bombers, for hours, strafed Plauen, which, like Dresden, was in any case a city of no military importance. Three-quarters of Plauen lay in ruins. Ninety percent of the schools and 70 percent of the houses were pulverized. A fact little-known outside Plauen, Frau Saupe says, is that the city's wartime damage exceeded that of any other large German city—even Dresden. The air raid claimed more than 500 lives. By April 1945, Plauen, a city of 120,000 in 1939, was reduced through conscription, war deaths, and flight before the oncoming Soviet armies, to a population of 80,000.

"My children [two and four years old] in the bombed-out hospital, suffering cholera," Frau Saupe says, her voice shaking at the memory of those April days. The entire month is a blur. "I am so weak, I can barely stand up, I can't hold a cup in my hand. . . . No trains, no heat, no food of any kind. . . . I run to find my babies. . . . I carry them 15 miles to the hospital in Muhltroff. . . . We stagger through the woods together, we look for berries as the planes shoot at us. . . ."

She stops suddenly. It was the war, she says simply. Somehow she and her children survived. They were lucky. Others were not.

When the Russian soldiers arrived in July, Frau Saupe was summoned. She expected the worst: She had been the wife of a Nazi Party member and decorated officer. To her surprise, she was congratulated. The Russians had found her name on an anti-Nazi blacklist. Probably she was blacklisted, Frau Saupe thinks, due to her vocal criticisms of a prominent local Nazi and her refusal on two public occasions to give the *Heil Hitler!* greeting. And yet, ironically, it was probably only her husband's position as an officer that had saved her from jail or a concentration camp.

Because the Russians had fired all the judges and almost all of the schoolteachers in Plauen, they offered Frau Saupe a position as a magistrate or schoolteacher. She chose teaching. In early 1946, she began an eight-month teacher training course for *Neulehrer*, which consisted of four months of general education and four months of intensive Russian. Then she took up her post as a 7th- and 8th-grade teacher at the newly opened Julius Moser School, named in honor of a regional poet much admired by her late husband. And she looked forward to better times ahead.

VI

It all began promisingly enough—both for Plauen and for Frau Saupe. SBZ authorities decided to rebuild Plauen as a lace-making capital, make the city a regional center of a new electronics and precision industry, and print the Eastern European editions of *Pravda* there. Frau Saupe, a Social Democrat, welcomed the common call of the KPD and SPD in June 1945 to build an "anti-fascist democratic" educational system and to remodel the Nazi schools on the experimental progressive schools of the Weimar era.

But by the late 1940s, as we have seen, the KPD had undermined the SPD in the newly formed SED and, following Moscow, began insisting that DDR schools adopt exactly the centralized structure and rigidly orthodox ideology of the Soviet school system. Having been unwilling to swallow Nazi propaganda in silence, Frau Saupe was no more willing to fall in line with communist dogma. But in the early postwar years, a woman of her anti-fascist credentials commanded much official respect—and a *Neulehrerin* of her educational attainments was still a relative rarity. She was valued and needed. With many educated young men still in Russian camps and qualified teachers hard to come by (only 4 of Plauen's 350 *Neulehrer* in 1946 held the *Abitur*), school authorities tolerated Frau Saupe's criticisms of Stalinism and her open practice of her Lutheran faith.

By the mid-1950s, however, as Walter Ulbricht began trying to eliminate Christianity and especially the Lutheran youth groups—the *Junge Gemeinden*—from the DDR, the Ministry of Education introduced a stricter line for teachers: They were expected to patrol the anti-capitalist "cultural front." Unsurprisingly, Frau Saupe's iconoclasm provoked keen discomfort among her Party colleagues.

"Every year the pressure to conform increased," Frau Saupe says. "The spying, the cowardice, the 'groupthink.' " She sighs. "The children, of course, never knew anything different. Indoctrination, not education. It was a communist version of the HJ."

To illustrate her point, Frau Saupe recites from memory some slogans which schoolchildren learned in the Thälmann Pioneers and the FDJ: "*Täglich in Form, das Beste in Norm!*" ("Daily dedication to the job produces the best performance!"). *"Keiner ist zu klein, um Helfer der Partei zu sein!"* ("Nobody is too little to help the Party!"). Frau Saupe shakes her head, as if to say: "It is all so long ago and yet just yesterday." Then we look through an old Pioneer handbook just given to me by a current Plauen teacher. It contains the bylaws of the Thälmann Pioneers. We turn to "Bylaw #6":

> We Thälmann Pioneers are friends of the Soviet Union and maintain friendship with the children of all countries. We make friendship toward the Soviet Union—the vanguard of the forces of Peace and Socialism in the world—the fondest wish of all girls and boys! We value especially our close ties with the Lenin Pioneers [in the USSR]!

Unlike most other schoolteachers, Frau Saupe refused to join the SED or participate in any communist organization. Nor did she register her children for the Pioneers or the FDJ, an act of passive aggression since, by the late 1950s, two-thirds of all children—and practically every teacher's child—joined the Pioneers and FDJ.

Her school principal was not amused. In 1958, a trio of events converged to bring to crisis Frau Saupe's already tense relationship with her superiors. First, a schoolgirl denounced Frau Saupe for concluding a 3rd-grade astronomy class with the words: "So great is God's Creation." Second, a teachers' board publicly reprimanded Frau Saupe for sponsoring parents' evenings in her home for the *Junge Gemeinden*. Finally, most egregiously, although 90 percent of East German 14 year olds participated in the *Jugendweihe*, Frau Saupe—"a teacher no less!" fretted the principal—insisted that her son be confirmed in the Lutheran Church.

On the last school day in 1958, at the age of 47, Frau Saupe was fired from her job and informed that she would receive the minimum pension under law. Her second husband—in 1955 she married Herr Saupe, a schoolteacher in the nearby Kammler School—himself barely escaped being dismissed for his support of her decision. During the next two decades, the family supported itself on his salary and on her slim earnings from tutoring and secretarial work.

VII

A new life began for Frau Saupe in the late 1970s, after she turned 65. Her health was robust and, like other East German senior citizens, she was permitted to travel—and she could afford to travel, thanks to her resourcefulness. East Germans needed western currency to travel outside the East bloc—and geography was still a favorite subject of hers. And she was still a teacher at heart. So Frau Saupe prepared slide lectures for West German audiences on East German cities and cultural life, and above all on Goethe and Weimar. Her visits to West Germany, the United States, Italy, and other countries reminded her how precious were the "bourgeois" freedoms of travel, association, and expression—liberties sharply curtailed after the abortive workers' revolt in June 1953 and the erection of the Berlin Wall in August 1961.

Not until the 1972 treaty that relaxed relations with West Germany did the SED liberalize its policies on travel and emigration; even these measures, however, were accompanied by a new program of *Abgrenzung* (delimitation), an invisible wall of regulations designed to stem the heightened flow of "unwholesome" western goods and ideas. Liberalization and *Abgrenzung* functioned together like a series of steam valves, allowing for a modicum of freedom and for the venting of some popular frustrations without blowing the lid off the system. Small doses of openness periodically relieved sharp pressures without challenging the internal power structure. But after Gorbachev came to power in the Soviet Union in 1985, dissatisfaction with the Stalinism of the old guard in the SED (old-style "Stasinism") grew.

Like many citizens, Frau Saupe became upset with Party leaders for dragging their feet on reform. In the late spring of 1989, she, like others, watched in amazement and hope as the pace of events increased: In May, Hungary began to dismantle its border with Austria; in August, East German refugees flocked to Hungary, while others sought asylum in the West German embassies in Prague and Warsaw; in September, Hungary permitted 55,000 East Germans to escape (via Austria) to the West.

These events set the stage for the so-called October Revolution, and for the supporting roles that Plauen and Annaliese Saupe were to play. On October 1, the East German government arranged for 6,000 DDR refugees then in Czechoslovakia to travel in six special, closed trains from Prague to Hof in West Germany—but diverted through Dresden and Plauen, rather than direct from Czechoslovakia to West Germany. In this way, DDR officials apparently hoped to save face by pretending that the refugees were not "escaping" but were being officially "expelled." Plauen was the last city before the West German border, and Plauen citizens lining the tracks jumped on the trains. They had to be forcibly pulled away by local *Vopos*.

On October 3, as refugees continued to flood the Prague embassy, the DDR closed its border with Czechoslovakia, the last country with which it still had an open border. Two days later, a second closed caravan, this one with 11,000 refugees, traveled from Prague to West Germany via Dresden and Plauen. Fighting erupted in the Dresden and Plauen train stations; police beat one Plauen citizen brutally, and he died during the weekend in the hospital. Still, attention in East Berlin was focused elsewhere. Preparations were in full swing for Gorbachev's visit and the 40th anniversary celebration of the DDR. It looked as though the dissidents could once again be contained with a minimum of force: as in the spring and summer, security police repressed small counter-demonstrations in East Berlin and other major cities with little difficulty.

Little did the government realize, however, that just as the 40th anniversary parade was proceeding on October 7, 1989—as Gorbachev and Honecker kissed on the steps of the old Reichstag building in East Berlin—a mass demonstration was getting under way in Plauen whose consequences would lead to the fall of the Berlin Wall just four weeks later.

Frau Saupe's voice swells as she recalls those days of October.

"Saturday, October 7—it was a wet autumn day," Frau Saupe remembers. "When I went shopping, several different neighbors whispered to me: 'A gathering at three P.M. in the Theater Square.'"

She explains that a whispering campaign by neighbors and friends was virtually the only means of illicit communication in the former DDR. Just as few DDR citizens (apart from Party members and doctors) owned telephones, the public also had no access to photocopy machines—the churches possessed the only non-government copiers, and they were required to stamp every piece of paper "for church use only." As Frau Saupe spoke, I thought how difficult it is to run a modern economy under a dictatorship, and yet also how difficult it is to launch an organized revolution against a dictatorship: totalitarianism as mass paralysis.

"At two P.M. I took the streetcar into town," Frau Saupe continues, "and as we approached the theater, I saw thousands of people streaming toward the same spot, coming from all directions. Children, old people, mothers with baby carriages, fathers with little tykes on their shoulders! Everyone stood, waiting to see what would happen. The atmosphere was tense—just the day before the man whom the police had beaten [for attempting to board the closed refugee train bound for Hof] had died in the hospital. Everyone knew about it. . . .

"Suddenly several police cars drove toward us," Frau Saupe continues. "'Pigs! Swine!' shouted dozens of people. 'Freedom!' yelled someone, and thousands of voices echoed him. For the next hour we chanted 'Freedom!' together. . . . All the while a helicopter circled overhead, occasionally swooping down toward us. I knew somehow that it contained no bombs, only video cameras, but it terrified my granddaughter and many other people. . . .

"When we saw that the police were keeping back, we began marching down the Wilhelm Pieck Street toward city hall. Dozens of police with revolvers and guns, nightsticks, and German shepherds stood at the entrance. Two fire trucks, with their sirens at full blast, raced toward us, hosing down hundreds of people. As dozens of people advanced, several police beat them back with their nightsticks. At that moment, I think, the crowd was about to turn violent. . . . Abruptly, as if from nowhere, the minister of our Lutheran Church emerged from the crowd, begging, 'No bloodbath! No Beijing!'

"The police sensed the danger too. Tiananmen Square was in everyone's mind. The minister demanded a loudspeaker and ordered the police to back off, and to send away the helicopter and fire trucks. We waited several minutes, as the police deliberated. They finally withdrew everything, and the demonstration ended peacefully. . . ."

Frau Saupe lets out a long sigh, as if in triumph. A date that had come to represent a birthday of tyranny—October 7—is now baptized in her memory through that mass cry of "Freedom!" She muses on the aftermath of "October 7":

"The minister had arrived just in time!" Frau Saupe says. "His plea turned out to have consequences for the entire future of Germany! . . . On the way home I stopped to see a friend who had not been at the *Demo*. 'What I've seen this evening!' I cried. 'This has been the most beautiful day of my life!'"

But Frau Saupe's October 7 wasn't over yet. With the help of her 90-year-old husband, she typed out a story of the events. On Monday morning, she sewed it into her underwear, along with three rolls of film taken and developed by her son, and hopped the local train to Hof.

Frau Saupe winks, prepared to show me—in case I don't believe her!—exactly how she smuggled everything. She adds that she didn't have a *Pfennig* of West German money in her pockets; she walked the long road from the Hof railway station to the office of the Hof *Frankenpost*.

"No one at the *Frankenpost* had any idea what had happened in Plauen," she continues. "All eyes had been on the celebrations in East Berlin. There were no telephone lines between Plauen and Hof—and every phone call to West Germany would have been monitored by the *Stasi*, anyway. . . . The editors had no idea that this was the *Aufbruch* [revolutionary beginning]."

Fifteen thousand people attended that October 7 demonstration, almost a third of the adult population of Plauen. Immediately, the medieval-era Luther Church, standing next to city hall and towering above it, became a symbol of hope. Day and night people burned hundreds of candles and laid wreaths of flowers on its steps. Every Saturday at three P.M., the crowds met at the church. Quickly their numbers surged: October 14, 30,000; October 21, 50,000; October 28, 60,000. The newly formed Plauen citizens' council presented its list of demands to the mayor: freedom of travel and expression, a free press, abolition of the SED's monopoly on power, abolition of the *Stasi*, free elections, open borders, schools without communist ideology. By November 4, practically the entire city was on the streets, marching and chanting in unison, "The Wall must go!" "*We* are the people!" "Democracy Now!" "Egon, DO SOMETHING!" In the days after the fall of the Wall, the chants turned to "*Deutschland einig Vaterland!*" and "We are *one* people!" And before the month of November was out, East met West for the first time in Vogtland since 1951—Route 163, the old road connecting Plauen and Hof, was repaved and reopened. And construction was resumed on Route 183—known to locals as *Hitlers Unvollendete Strasse* (Hitler's Unfinished Road)—a planned *Autobahn* through Plauen on which construction halted on the eve of the war and was never completed.

Frau Saupe is proud of her townsfolk, proud above all that her adopted city, Plauen of Vogtland, was the first to launch a major demonstration against the Honecker regime—and that her native city of Leipzig carried the protests to their peaceful conclusion.

"Revolution was in the air," Frau Saupe says. "Saturday, Plauen; Monday, Leipzig; Tuesday, Dresden. Our proximity to the West German border, the refugee trains passing through to Hof, the fact that Hof is our *Partnerstadt* [partner city]—that's probably why we in Plauen were first."

There is pride indeed in Annaliese Saupe's voice. How differently she speaks of Germany from my West German friends—or even from my younger eastern acquaintances.

The cultural and economic ties between Plauen and Hof, a town of 15,000, stretch back to their days as medieval villages at the crossroads of Central Europe's main trading routes, Frau Saupe explains in a clipped schoolteacherly voice: The two communities were under joint rule in the thirteenth and fourteenth centuries. Beginning in 1986, in a mutual gesture of reconciliation in preparation for Honecker's 1987 visit to Bonn and to promote economic cooperation, East and West German towns began adopting each other as *Partnerstädte*. Originally wary of the idea, fearing that it might frustrate *Abgrenzung*, the SED's warming to it signified its feeling of invulnerability by the late 1980s. By 1989, 30 DDR and BRD cities or towns had "twinned," but the Plauen-Hof partnership was the only one between adjacent cities—and, even more so, between two towns with a rich shared history.

Frau Saupe pauses. Her smile thanks me for indulging her digression. She clears her throat: Now let's return to the Plauen of 1989, her businesslike air seems to say. Her voice lowers and softens.

"But what would have happened in the DDR, and in all of Eastern Europe, *if* the police had opened fire on us in Plauen that day? If the old Stalinist hard-liners had applied the methods of Berlin, Hungary, Prague, Poland? Would Gorbachev have sent in the troops against our men? Would he have risked intervening militarily in our affairs?

"If the SED, even at that late date, had come down hard, could it have contained the protest movement, limiting it to just a few days of mass unrest, as the Soviets did in June 1953? And as China had that very June? If the Party had done so that day in Plauen, then there might have been no Leipzig or Dresden. Yes, it would have been Tiananmen Square all over again. And then it might have been a civil war. . . ."

Frau Saupe pauses again, and it seems to me as if we stand together at an historical crossroads, as if on a single fateful day in 1989 her little city stood poised on the edge of time, at the nexus of the branching paths of two alternative futures for Germany and the world. Would it be civil war and perhaps lead to . . . ? Or, instead . . . ? Yes, the other path: By November 4, a million people marched peacefully and without disturbance from the Alexanderplatz down the Friedrichstrasse in East Berlin, and five days later the Wall was down.

But Frau Saupe puts it another way. Recalling a line of Goethe's—this one I did not see in her folders—after he witnessed the skirmish at Valmy in 1792, which later proved to be the decisive event which saved revolutionary Paris from capture by the Prussian armies, she declaims: "For today from this place there begins a new epoch in the history of the world."

No apology follows the rhetorical flight. Goethe, says Frau Saupe, would have understood the significance of October 7.

To this day neither professional historians nor ex-DDR politicians seem to know with certainty who in the SED power structure ordered the Plauen, Leipzig, and Dresden police to hold their fire in early October. All signs were that the government was prepared to commit something comparable to the Tiananmen Square massacres. Indeed the SED head in Gera in Saxony declared on October 3: "We'll deal with these miscreants after the 40th anniversary celebration, just as they did in China." On October 6, a news story in Leipzig quoted the police chief as "ready and willing to use our weapons against these counter-revolutionaries, if necessary." Two days later, Honecker himself announced, after a friendly meeting with high-ranking officials from Beijing, that "counterrevolutionaries" in the DDR would be dealt with just as severely as they had been in China. Weeks—and an era—later, several SED national leaders each claimed to have been the one to prohibit the use of force, among them Egon Krenz, who may have been warned by Gorbachev against it. But their stories are inconsistent; history may never know the full story.

Observers agree, however, as Frau Saupe puts it, that the decision "must have come from someone high up in Berlin, or even in Moscow," and also that, in retrospect, the decision not to crush the demonstrations spelled the end of the regime. That was the turning point. Why did the government back off? Was it fear? Was it restraint? Was it botched communication? Whatever the reason, from that week on, the marchers sensed that the government had feet of clay, and so they marched on and on until they swept the government away.

To prove how dangerous that momentous week was, Frau Saupe takes out her voluminous photo and clipping collection. She shows me the official report of the October 7 *Demo* in the regional Saxony *Freie Presse*, entitled "Unconscionable Provocation."

> . . . an illegal assembly of several hundred persons ended peacefully due to the decisive, thoughtful response of the People's Police. . . . The malcontents marched through the city, destroying store display windows, setting a People's Police car in flames, and vandalizing a fire truck. Thanks to the restraint of the security forces, who protected the city hall and the safety of the citizens, nothing serious developed.

Frau Saupe laughs derisively at the lies. "Typical!" she snorts. The "official estimate" of the number of protesters is 10,000, less than one-third the real total.

Frau Saupe shows me several photos from the local Plauen paper, the *Vogtland-post*, of the SED banners in the October 7 celebrations in East Berlin. How ironic they now sound! "Long live our Socialist Fatherland—the DDR!" "Forty years of the DDR—Work by the People, for the Welfare of the People!" Frau Saupe lingers with relish over a placard from the educational ministry: "Scholars! Students! High goals of teaching and research strengthen the DDR! We belong to the beautiful socialist community of Man!"

The clunky Marxist jargon contrasts badly with the salty language of the marchers in the streets, many of whose banners bore witty rhymed or punning slogans:

SED, das organisierte [V]erbrechen!
[SED, the organized crime (or vomit)!]

Niemand wird die SED vermissen, den sie hat uns 40 Jahre lang beschissen!
[Nobody is going to miss the SED, because you've screwed us for 40 years!]

Das Pulver ist verschossen, heran an die Wahrheit, Genossen!
[The game is up, so try telling the truth, Comrades!]

A gleaming smile lights up Annaliese Saupe's face as she recalls the autumn of 1989. "What an unforgettable, exhilarating spirit those days possessed!" she exclaims. She laughs suddenly. "The only time in 40 years that I ever experienced 'the beautiful socialist community of Man'!"

VIII

July 1992. My second visit to Frau Saupe. A warm reunion.

"I've been rehabilitated!" she announces, laughing, as we embrace. She presents me with her recent letter from the Plauen school board that apologizes for her dismissal from teaching—only 33 years late. "I'm no longer an 'enemy of the people'!" she says, grinning.

She reminisces fondly about teaching and her students. She is donating her time to German tutoring for a Russian girl newly come to Plauen; Frau Saupe stays in touch with dozens of former students from the 1940s and '50s. In fact, just 10 weeks ago, two dozen former pupils visited her—as they do every year on Holy Thursday. They are the 8th-grade graduates of the Class of '48. "My favorite class!" Frau Saupe confides. Up to 30 of her pupils have come virtually every year for the last four decades to see her—most of them Plaueners, but a few of them from as far away as Stuttgart, the Rhineland, and Switzerland, despite the difficulties that the DDR government imposed on western travelers to the DDR. My mouth falls open as she recounts this astonishing ritual, which she delivers in such a matter-of-fact style. "All of them are grandparents themselves now," Frau Saupe adds of her reunion guests. She smiles broadly, noting that graduates from other class years also visit her, but on a less formal, more irregular basis.

Then the smile disappears. Frau Saupe glances at the letter from the Plauen school board again and adds that, even though she has another letter from the 1950s stating that she was dismissed for her "Christian convictions," she has still received no official statement pronouncing her a "victim of the SED state." And she continues to receive the minimum pension under law: DM 484 per month. "Too much to die on, too little to live on."

Still, she considers herself a "*Glückspilz*" (lucky mushroom, favored one) of her generation.

"I was never jailed, and yet I was known to be—officially once and unofficially the second time—a victim of Nazism and communism," she says. "Many people suffered without it ever being acknowledged and without ever receiving satisfaction. They never knew how the *Stasi* or Nazi informants deprived them of jobs, promotions, educational and travel opportunities. . . ."

"Many elderly people here," Frau Saupe continues, "especially the men who fought six years in the war and suffered several more in the Russian camps, cry out: 'First Hitler, then the communists! Sixty years! They've stolen my entire life, these dictators!' But I can't say that. I've had good health and the chance to see a bit of the world. And I'm not burdened by shame or remorse about my activities with the communists or Nazis—I have a *weisse Weste* [a white vest, i.e., a clean past]. If you lost ten years of your youth to the war and its aftermath, or if you compromised yourself or simply swallowed the garbage that the ideologues tried to force down your throat, well then, yes, I can well understand the guilt and anguish. For some of those people, maybe it's true: the years are gone and wasted."

Do you feel that you've lived under a dictatorship all your life?

Yes and no, Frau Saupe answers. Yes, if one measures the DDR by the hopes attached to it in "Arisen from Ruins," that the socialist sun would one day "shine over Germany, shine over Germany." Yes, because after 1950, when the SED extinguished East German democracy by absorbing the other political parties, or after 1952, when it sealed its borders to the West [except through West Berlin], few thinking people could still hold that the DDR was *"das bessere Deutschland."*

"The dream of a socialist Germany, which I had once shared too," says Frau Saupe, "was gone."

But no, she continues, if one attempts by this question to equate German "democratic socialism" [the SED] with German "national socialism" [the Nazis]. No, because Honecker was not Hitler, the *Stasi* was not the SS, the corruptions of the SED were not the crimes of the Nazis. She adds that she has recently gotten word that she has no surviving *Stasi* or other government files: all state documents about her have been lost or destroyed.

"Bad as this state [the DDR] was," maintains Frau Saupe, "it never divided up people into racial and other groupings, and then pursued and executed them. There were no 'Final Solutions.' You could only equate the SED and the Nazis if you had no knowledge of the Holocaust or the Nazis' grand schemes for world conquest."

She pauses, her eyes drawn to the photo on the mantelpiece of the handsome young man in his major's uniform. She sighs.

"Three times my family lost everything and had to begin again—in the 1920s after the inflation, in '45 after the *Zusammenbruch* [collapse], and in '58 after I was thrown out of schoolteaching," Frau Saupe says. "And now, it's another new beginning. Some people call it another *Stunde Null*. For our family, it's mostly a spiritual beginning. But many families are starting all over again, both materially and spiritually—the unemployed, some former Party *Bonzen*, and *Stasi* agents.

"My life hasn't changed much since the *Wende*," she goes on. She could already travel abroad, she notes, and she doesn't hanker after western goods. But she notices the small changes in people's attitudes.

"I see the *Ich-Menschen* [I-people, self-seekers] everywhere now," Frau Saupe says. "We're losing our feeling of togetherness. Before, you rejoiced when a friend who had waited for 15 years finally got his telephone or Trabi. Now people look at their neighbors and they feel envy. They say: 'They have more than we do.' . . . People never used to lock their doors. Now they do. . . . Perhaps it all had to go, along with the worst of the old system. But now that we all have more money, what do we need neighbors for? You don't need to have friends now to help you fix your 20-year-old Trabi, or to give you a ride, or for a thousand other little things. Now you can buy everything. . . . Before, money didn't count for much. For heaven's sake, you couldn't buy anything with it, anyway! There was nothing in the stores!"

Plauen has yet to reverse its half-century economic decline. Most western companies, notes Frau Saupe, are waiting for eastern firms to go bankrupt before buying them up—and Plauen families can't wait forever for the economy to turn around. Thousands of Plaueners have moved to Hof, which is now booming, leaving Plauen with one of the highest proportions of old people in eastern Germany. "The mood here is depressed—just like the economy," Frau Saupe says. One exception to this trend is the West German wholesale textile manufacturer, Pfersee/

Kolbermoor of Augsburg, which purchased Plauen's famed lace and fabric factories in early 1991—and laid off the majority of its employees after the collapse of the Soviet Union, which had bought 40 percent of Plauen lace. Providing work for 14,000 Plaueners before the *Wende*, the factories now employ barely 2,000 workers. The only sizable new building in town is a McDonalds—Vogtland's first. Hamburgers are the big sellers, closely followed by its distinctive serving of *Klosse*, a Vogtland potato dumpling specialty.

"But is life really any better in the West?" Frau Saupe asks. A sharp note of skepticism is evident in her voice. She wrings her hands, thinking of her daughter in faraway Hanover. Like so many other eastern Germans since the *Wende*, her daughter's family has just relocated for employment reasons, seeking a better life in the West. But she is unhappy there, Frau Saupe says. "The people have no time, money is all that counts." A familiar charge from old easterners. But that would eventually be her daughter's fate even if she stayed in Plauen, Frau Saupe acknowledges. Creeping capitalism is slouching eastward, and East Germans too are starting to cultivate to the utmost the lesser things of life—shopping, travel, home furnishings—and mistake them for the higher things. She quotes a neighbor who, appalled by the affluent society, gives her a version of the philosophy of West Germany: "I consume, therefore I am."

We chat for a few more hours. Do I know that coffee costs just DM 6 now, when it was 40 or 50 even after the *Wende*? But bread is up from 78 pfennigs to almost 3 DM, and cream cheese from 55 pfennigs to DM 1.10. "At least we have fruit now," she sighs. She draws nearer and looks at me hard. "You know, a vegetarian like you would have starved in the DDR! If you don't consume enough, you'll be nothing!" I tell her that she is not the first *Hausfrau* to alert me to that fact. We laugh.

"Do you want to hear 'Annaliese's Advice for a Long, Healthy Life?' " she asks me.

I am all ears.

Frau Saupe runs down her list:

"1. Eat modestly. 2. Live a well-ordered life. 3. Challenge yourself mentally. 4. Laugh a lot. 5. Exercise!—I swim and walk as much as possible. 6. Memorize poems—I prefer Goethe and Fontane. But new poets too! 7. Develop hobbies that you love. My hobbies are to research the lives of famous people from Vogtland."

I tell Frau Saupe that some Americans would dub her list "The Seven Habits of Highly Fulfilled People." She laughs again, unaware of my allusion to a best-selling American self-help book with a similar title.

As I prepare to leave for the west, Frau Saupe launches into a detailed explanation of the name changes of the Plauen schools and streets. A school in which her first husband did a short stint of student teaching during the Third Reich—then called the Martin Bormann School, and during the DDR era renamed the Ernst Thälmann School—is now the Lessing Gymnasium. The Wilhelm Pieck Street, named after the first general secretary of the SED, is once again the Neundorfer Street. Swept away, in fact, are almost all the famous German and Russian communist names that once adorned practically every public place here. Otto

Grotewohl Square, Ernst Thälmann Street, Walter Ulbricht Square, the Yuri Gagarin High School: all gone. Gone too the *Platz der Roten Armee* (Red Army
Square), which Plauen wags called the *Platz der Armen Roten* (Poor Reds' Square).

"Some old people can't even find their way through the center of Plauen now!"
Frau Saupe says ruefully. She shakes her head. Symbolizing the difficult and sometimes comical shift from fascism to communism to democracy, the litany of old
and new names suggests the burdensome history behind and ahead: The problem
of spiritual as well as physical navigation in the age of Germany After the Wall.

IX

October 1994. I can't leave Germany without at least a whistlestop afternoon visit
to Frau Saupe.

"You've come just at the right moment!" Frau Saupe exclaims as I show up,
unannounced, on her doorstep. Before the front wall of her house now stands one
of the old, discarded border posts of the DDR, once used to mark the line between
west and east. A reminder, she says, of the narrow horizons that eastern Germans
once suffered.

Frau Saupe is a local celebrity this month. Plauen is commemorating the fifth
anniversary of the Revolution of the Candles. A regional TV crew interviewed her
last week. We watch a tape of the broadcast together; it features Frau Saupe as a
central actor in Plauen's story of October 1989.

"Like many people, she risked a great deal in the fall of 1989," begins the TV
announcer. "But Annaliese Saupe went a step further. She wanted the world to
know about the mass demonstrations under way in Plauen of Vogtland."

"Frau Saupe's first article hit with the force of a bomb," the editor of the Hof
Frankenpost tells the TV cameras. "News agencies from everywhere phoned us,
because nobody knew what was happening in Plauen. And then she came every
week thereafter.

"A courageous woman," the editor concludes. "If only more people like Annaliese Saupe existed!"

As we ride the bus into the city center, townspeople who have known her for
decades greet us, obviously sharing the editor's view. Everyone has seen the TV
special; they all trade stories of October 1989. Frau Saupe stops in at the bakery.
"Another one of my nicest pupils," she says, laughing, of the baker, a bald man
in his mid-60s.

Now Frau Saupe and I slowly follow the same steps through the streets as did
the marchers in October 1989: a pilgrimage to the *Rathaus* (city hall). Step by step,
she narrates the story that I heard in her living room four years ago. "More than
35,000 people were crowding this little street!" exclaims Frau Saupe. We are heading for the special historical exhibit on the *Wende* in the main foyer of the *Rathaus*.
The exhibit transports us backward in time: the barbed-wire fences, the 98.12
percent vote for the SED in the falsified election of May 1989, a letter from a citizen
group formed later that month to protest the election results, a respectful September 29 letter of protest to the mayor from the Lutheran pastor, a threatening

public letter of October 11 from the mayor, the plastic dummy of a *Vopo* raising a weapon, and dozens of photographs that Frau Saupe and her son took of the Plauen *Demos.*

In the middle of the foyer is a guest book, in which visitors have written their reflections. Frau Saupe and I page slowly through it.

"Be proud of what you risked that month, Plauen citizens, and never forget it!" writes one man.

"This exhibit moves me deeply," writes a woman. "Despite the hard times since 1989, it reminds me of what we fought for—and that things are indeed better. I thank the people who summoned the courage to speak out for freedom."

Frau Saupe leans down to write something in the guest book herself.

"Let this exhibit remind all of us of the 22 demonstrations in Plauen. Let us never forget what we used to suffer."

Returning home, Frau Saupe and I discuss the news—small and big—since our last meeting. Herr Saupe passed away shortly after my last visit—two years ago, at the age of 92. But otherwise, things are good—and getting ever better in Vogtland. Frau Saupe speaks with satisfaction. Even my vegetarianism is invoked to illustrate the point. It is still "worrisome" to her, but she's glad she's now able to accommodate me—"something I never could have done in the DDR."

Chancellor Kohl's victory in last week's election was encouraging, says Frau Saupe. She switched allegiances and voted for him this time, and she would have liked a bigger margin of victory for the CDU. She finds the criticism of Chancellor Kohl largely unjustified.

"When the Chancellor promised in 1990 that nobody in the east would be 'worse off,' he had no idea how badly off many people here really were," Frau Saupe says. "Certainly, he painted a rosy vision—such as when he said that the country-side would soon be blooming. But look! Things now *are* starting to bloom. Only his timing was off."

Her biggest fear is the PDS.

"Sometimes I wonder if we've really learned anything at all. I see many old SED *Bonzen* back in leading positions in the PDS. I know that people support them as a sign of protest, but it's a misconceived protest! It's a giant step backward, not forward."

More conversation about Goethe and Schiller, more photographs of the grand-children, more clippings from the newspaper about Plauen and Vogtland. I muse at length on one of Frau Saupe's quotations from Schiller's *Wallenstein's Camp*: "He who does the best for his own time has lived for all time."

Whether or not she is a heroine, I conclude, she is a witness. Yes, a witness and a chronicler of her age.

"If only more people like Annaliese Saupe existed!"

As she sees me to the door, Frau Saupe repeats another touchstone by her in-disputable hero, Goethe. It is my farewell gift from her: "What you have inherited from your fathers, earn over again for yourselves, or it will not be yours."

And from your mothers, I want to add, and from your grandmothers too.

7

Leipzig, 1991

Of Laughter and Forgetting:
A Faculty-Student Conflict of Generations

I

On a warm October afternoon in Leipzig, a hunched-over figure sits in the shadow of the monumental plastic sculpture *"Aufbruch"* ("Beginning"), a legacy of socialist realism that depicts a group of people struggling to move forward, as if awakening to political consciousness. Heike is tense; she gazes fixedly down at the ground, her hands clasped tightly in front of her. She is brooding on her quarter-century in the SED as a student and then professor here at Karl-Marx Universität—now, in 1991, again called Leipzig University.

"Nie wieder," repeats Heike. "Never again."

Never would she join the reconstituted SED, now called the PDS. Never again would she join *any* party or movement, of whatever political stripe. She is not quoting the campaign slogan used by the CDU in March 1990—already a bygone era—but is simply expressing a personal statement. Politics holds no interest for her. Her experience in the SED has disillusioned her toward—or, as she says, "inoculated" her against—party and ideological appeals. Permanently.

"I have learned my lesson," Heike says.

Looking up, she follows my gaze to the grotesque socialist realist sculpture, remarking that, since the *Wende* in 1989, she has been looking at it with a new eye. Across the courtyard stands a much older sculpture: a towering statue of Leibniz. Heike turns to it, deliberately, as if appealing to the wise old Leipzig professor—indeed to the classical spirit of the Enlightenment itself—for guidance and support. I'm still thinking about the marches that brought down the SED regime and East Germany itself, only two Octobers ago. Just a few yards beyond Leibniz is the sacred spot where the already historic marches arose and the *"We are The People"* chants against the Honecker regime began.

Heike, 46, a *wissenschaftliche Assistentin* (lecturer) in Slavic literature at the University, speaks in soft German—entirely free of Americanisms, unlike the speech of most West Germans—about her decades in the Party. Pale yet animated, her face is vital with expression, if lined with years; like many eastern German women, she wears no makeup.

"You had to have courage, and I didn't," she says simply. "You had to be a hero, and I wasn't."

As Heike spoke of the silent, daily, near-invisible compromises that she had made for reasons of career and family, I could not help but wonder whether I would have acted any differently in her place. I look again at the *Aufbruch* sculpture, then at the hundreds of students scurrying between buildings to catch their next classes. The scene resembles any urban American campus. How different were Heike's small, incremental concessions from my own? Her careerism? Her rationalizations? For me, an American literary historian and critic of European socialism, meeting Heike has meant an uncomfortable, provocative brush with *erlebte Geschichte* (lived history). And something more. Heike's soul-searching reminds me of Irving Howe's old joke: Marxism has died, only to be reborn in U.S. English departments. Do our literary Marxists know people like Heike? I'm none too sure. I suspect that Heike knows something that they—that I myself— ought not to forget. Hers is another story of the communist academic functionary in postwar Eastern Europe.

During the 1930s and '40s, Nazi Germany jailed in concentration camps, drove into exile, or murdered thousands of communists. Heike's paternal grandfather, a Viennese Social Democrat, spent four years in a Nazi concentration camp, and died there in 1943; his son became an impassioned communist, determined to live out his father's unlived political vocation. Leftists of her father's and grandfather's generations, Heike says, were fervently anti-fascist, and warned repeatedly and vainly about the slippery slope down which even tacit support for the Nazis would lead: Support for Hitler meant support for a European war, and support for a European war meant the ultimate destruction of Germany. Heike's row of dominoes reminds me of the 1932 KPD election poster, reproduced in all DDR history textbooks: "Who votes for Hindenburg—votes for Hitler! Who votes for Hitler— votes for war!" Oversimplified as the logic was, it must have seemed in hindsight prescient—and persuasive. As if History had spoken—and foolishly been shown the door.

"My father believed in communism, he believed in its ideals," Heike continues. To her father, she says, communism meant hope, communism meant enlightenment and progress, communism meant justice and equality for all. Even after World War II, her father regarded Eastern Europe as a fragile socialist seedling at the edge of a vast fascist desert. To him "capitalist" West Germany was virtually a fascist country—and indeed, because *Entnazifizierung* was never carried out there thoroughly, many former Nazis were leading comfortable lives in the West.

"My father believed that people like Ulbricht and Pieck had been right all along," Heike says. She does not mention one acute historical embarrassment to most orthodox leftists: the 1939 Nazi-Soviet Non-Aggression Pact, which suddenly put German communists in the awkward position of being in alliance with the Nazis, until Germany broke the treaty with its invasion of the Soviet Union in June 1941.

But I let it pass. Heike concludes: "My father even believed in the Wall—'an den antifaschistischen Schutzwall.' "

After the war, Heike's father had finished his studies in Vienna and become a professor of economics at the University of Graz, where he was one of just a few radical economists who took Marxism-Leninism seriously. He was an outspoken opponent of Austrian-born Joseph Schumpeter, the celebrated American defender of western free enterprise as a superior economic (if not moral) system (whose

Capitalism, Socialism, and Democracy exerted strong influence on Marshall Plan policymakers), and in later years, he was also a critic of the conservative, free-market school of Austrian economics championed by Ludwig von Mises and Friedrich Hayek.

Heike speaks with pride of her idealistic father. "When he spoke of 'building socialism' his face would light up," Heike says. She shakes her head and sighs. "It was a different age," she says of the early postwar period. "Then, it was still possible to believe." In late 1953, when the infant DDR called him to help "build socialism"—in the form of an offer to teach at the newly-refounded University of Rostock—Heike's father did not hesitate. Indeed an emigrant cousin of his, a brick-layer, was already touted by Party comrades as a local Adolf Hennecke, having received one of the highest honors accorded to model DDR workers, the Hero of Labor Star. It was a family obligation to join the socialist community, said Heike's father. Even as thousands of DDR citizens were rushing westward in the wake of June 17, he packed up the family and left Austria for Rostock.

At the time, Heike and her two older sisters were in their early years of grammar school. "We weren't going 'behind the Iron Curtain,' " she recalls of her father's explanation. "We were going to live in the great socialist experiment. . . . The DDR was a place where people were still trying to achieve a dream of decency and fairness for everyone."

Heike's early childhood in postwar capitalist Austria made her inevitably more critical of "the experiment" than most East Germans, she says, because she had a standard for comparison. She knew first-hand what life was like in the West; she understood its advantages in comparison with the DDR. Still, she also valued the egalitarianism, the sometimes daringly *avant-garde* intellectual atmosphere, and the skeptical spirit of anti-capitalist *Alternative* thinking in DDR life in the early '60s. Until the late 1960s, she says, she thought that the weaknesses of socialism could be overcome.

"Prague, August 1968—when the Russian tanks rolled in. That was the water-shed moment for me," Heike says. When the Czech Politburo under Aleksandr Dubček openly defied Moscow during the heady spring of 1968, Heike was en-tranced. She admired Dubček's Action Program, which renounced the Communist Party's legal monopoly on power, acknowledged other political parties, permitted freedom of the press, created market incentives, introduced small-scale private enterprise, and decentralized government control of industry—precisely those re-forms that a collapsing Soviet economy would compel Mikhail Gorbachev to pro-pose two decades later for the USSR itself as part of *glasnost* and *perestroika*. (A bittersweet joke made the rounds in Eastern Europe during the late 1980s: Q: What's the difference between Gorbachev and Dubček? A: 20 years.) Dubček's reformist socialism resonated with the liberal proposals that some of Heike's col-leagues discussed in local Party meetings, she says. In revulsion against a Soviet dictatorship that had dominated and exploited Czechoslovakia since the com-munist coup of 1948, progressive Czech leaders sought a "third way" between capitalism and communism: a nation both socialist and profoundly democratic. But the Soviet invasion in August meant that the Czech reforms never came to fruition.

Because Czechoslovakia was for many years the only country to which East Germans could travel without a visa—and because of its proximity on the southern border of the DDR, less than two hours from Leipzig—the events of August 1968 left an open wound on her generation, Heike says. The deepest anguish derived from the guilt of knowing that NVA troops had helped put an end to the Prague Spring.

"Right then, I concluded that '*das bessere Deutschland*' was a farce, an impossible dream," Heike continues. Her own idealism was dashed when the Prague Spring wilted. "Right then, I began to think about emigrating back to the West. And the thought never left me after that. . . ."

Heike pauses and looks away. Her grandfather had died in Auschwitz, she says, and her family had reacted by closing their eyes to the Gulag. Immediately she frowns, annoyed. No, that's too simple, her expression seems to say. But neither of us breaks the silence. Then she abruptly continues, picking up the narrative a generation later.

"Like my father, I couldn't look that nightmare [a failed socialism] in the face. 'Socialism *can't* be reformed from within'—again and again, that was the lesson, the lesson of all the uprisings in Eastern Europe before '68 and after. The system was Stalinism, not socialism. *Barbarism* with a human face."

Her allusion to *La barbarie de la visage humaine* takes me by surprise. I wasn't aware that the title of the controversial book by Maoist-turned-neoconservative Bernard-Henri Lévy had become a catch phrase in the east. Lévy is one of the Parisian *nouveaux philosophes* who was shell-shocked by the tumultuous events of 1968, a repentant leftist who proclaimed that the inevitable end of collectivism was totalitarianism.

"Or call it German-style '*Stasi*nism,' " Heike quickly adds. "We had already lost almost 3 million people before the Wall went up. If you're the government in a country of only 17 million, you don't then go and murder or drive out millions more. Yes, *Stasi*nism—Stalinism minus the camps and the physical terror. But barbarism just the same.

"But I couldn't bear to know that," Heike continues. "I was 22, I had just had my first baby. I pleaded with my husband [a Marxist-Leninist professor of philosophy] to consider emigrating to Austria. 'What about me?' he kept saying. 'What will I do there?' So we stayed."

II

For Heike, disillusion came with Prague 1968. But the rendezvous with disenchantment came, sooner or later, for nearly everyone, she says. And yet, there was no single shared moment, no common nationwide point of no return for renouncing the dream of *das bessere Deutschland*. And that was the hardest part, she says. Was the early postwar era of her father's generation really so different? I want to ask. But Heike effectively answers me: Each generation had its own unlessons, she says. Each generation had to unlearn and relearn for itself. Like those earlier communist pilgrims of the 1930s, who nurtured the flickering candle of Hope in exile or in concentration camps before the socialist sun rose over the eastern

German ruins in 1945—through the pyres of the purges, the show trials, the mass executions, the Nazi-Soviet pact, and all the rest—successive generations of DDR citizens had to pass their own trials by fire in order to confirm their blind, unconditional faith. The tests were hardest if you actually lived in a communist country and saw your friends and family disappear or fall "out of favor" with the Party. Political romantics abroad could wax theoretical about "real existing socialism," but eastern Europeans had to live under it. And yet, even when everything else had been taken from you, Hope remained. For, as Dubček later titled his autobiography, published posthumously: *"Hope Dies Last."*

But die it eventually did. For nearly everyone in the DDR, the moment of recognition eventually came, Heike repeats. As though it were a long-resisted and deathly unpleasant initiation ceremony for the recalcitrant idealist. Or a belated coming-of-age, a second and curative *Jugendweihe.* For Heike's paternal grandmother the date was 1953, when Russian troops ruthlessly suppressed the *Arbeiteraufstand* in East Berlin. For Heike's mother it was 1956, when the world turned upside down in the wake of Khrushchev's "Secret Speech," when the "Father of All Nations" suddenly stood revealed not just as a bad, "subjectivist" Party man but a murderer. For Heike's old Russian teacher it was 1957, when Ulbricht silenced Ernst Bloch and convicted Wolfgang Harich and his intellectual circle around the Aufbau Verlag, all of it eerily reminiscent of the postwar show trials elsewhere in Eastern Europe—indeed of the Soviet show trials of 1936–38. For Heike's older sisters it was 1961, when a desperate Ulbricht dammed up the westward flow of DDR migrants and erected *"den antifaschistischen Schutzwall."* For a younger cousin, then a law student at Humboldt University, it was 1976, when the expulsion of Wolf Biermann ended the intellectuals' honeymoon with Erich Honecker. Even for Heike's resilient father, always the idealistic hard-liner, the date with the reality of "real existing socialism" finally came: in the mid-1970s, as the DDR began to "sell out to the fascists," when the policy of *Abgrenzung* pursued by Honecker and Willi Stoph convinced him that the DDR would never offer a truly socialist alternative to the *Bundesrepublik.*

And for each of them, the depth of the disillusion reflected the majesty of the myth and the duration of the dream. For the vision of paradise over the horizon had proven nothing more than a tantalizing mirage.

So Heike stayed. She did her work at the University. She taught her classes. She fulfilled her committee obligations, one of which included helping to plan the academic ceremony for the University's 575th anniversary in 1984. She published some articles on East European literature, invariably according to "the dialectical and materialist interpretation of History. . . . I would never have thought to have done otherwise," she says. Enveloped in a chronic fatigue like the ubiquitous Leipzig smog, corroding from within like the brownstones on every city street, Heike fell distractedly into a mind-numbing routine. The years tumbled by. Bored and adrift throughout the late 1970s and '80s, she and her husband would attend their weekly Party meetings, coming home demoralized.

"There was nothing to do afterwards but drink," Heike recalls.

In the mid-1980s, as the SED *Bonzen* castigated as "bourgeois" the civil rights movements sweeping Eastern Europe and the USSR, the "Stasinism" of the DDR seemed hardly distinguishable to Heike from the Cold War decades under Ulbricht. She could only nod in agreement when she read Christoph Hein's description of their land: "a fenced-in playground"—supervised by the *Stasi* no less. Fearing mass emigration to West Germany and the possible collapse of the DDR if the Party eased its vigilant watchfulness, the nearly paralyzed SED leadership reacted by turning the DDR into a more secure—i.e., repressive—state than any other in eastern Europe, the USSR included. No *glasnost*, no *perestroika*. And more so than other East Europeans—even if less acutely than Heike herself—"we East Germans knew what we were missing," Heike says. Unlike the Bulgarians, Poles, Czechs, Rumanians, Hungarians, Albanians, and Russians, East Germans had a western measuring rod: the *Bundesrepublik*. It didn't matter that the DDR was the most prosperous state in the East bloc; daily life was a constant reminder of the gap between east and west: East Germans came into contact with West Germany at every turn. They watched West German TV, listened to West German radio, and received their (by comparison) rich relatives and visitors from *drüben*.

Like other young and middle-aged SED members, Heike and her husband also felt the DDR was, by the late 1980s, being left behind in the reformist wave in the East bloc. They seconded the few outspoken liberal voices in the SED, she claims, such as Dresden Party boss Hans Modrow. They were indignant when, in November 1988, the SED banned the German edition of *Sputnik*, the Soviet magazine that had turned reformist and had condemned the Hitler-Soviet pact of 1939. Still, they said nothing publicly. Meanwhile the SED elders ("the senile old men") continued to hide their eyes from the approaching deluge of History, Heike says.

Why did DDR leaders remain so willfully blind?

They didn't, really, Heike explains. Their near-paralysis derived from their vague awareness that there was no way out. To call the basic principles of communism and, more explicitly, the legacy of Stalinism into question threatened the legitimacy of the DDR and its self-definition as an "anti-fascist bulwark" far more radically than it threatened the USSR. The Soviet Union could always reject Stalin as Lenin's heir and appeal to a pre-Stalinist history.

Not so the DDR, which Stalin had single-handedly created out of the Russian occupation zone during 1945–49 and staffed with the cadre around Ulbricht. Moreover, the five East German *Länder* in the postwar Soviet zone had never any special relation before 1945; their existence was entirely the consequence of decisions made by foreign powers and contrary to the will of the majority of Germans: division and occupation. Unlike other Eastern European countries, then, the DDR had no separate national or linguistic or cultural identity to fall back on, through which it could legitimately claim sovereignty; the only real difference between the two Germanies was their political structure, and without the dream of a "socialist Fatherland" in the east, no compelling reason for two separate Germanies existed. Furthermore, West Germany's 1949 constitution explicitly called for a reunited Germany, and an illegitimate DDR would have no basis to resist the popular urge for western freedoms and economic prosperity. *Abgrenzung* had sought to wipe out a "German" national consciousness and inculcate a "socialist," "sovietized" national consciousness founded on the "good," *völkisch* German past—which ultimately came even to include partial rehabilitation of onetime enemies of progressive History such as Luther, Frederick the Great, and Bismarck. In the end, however, the search for a separate DDR identity failed, as the cries through the streets—"*Wir sind EIN Volk*"—made clear.

By 1989, SED leaders could vaguely decipher the Chinese handwriting on the Wall: Given DDR history, a diplomatic solution could have no foundation. Given the mass unrest, a political solution was no longer workable: "Stasinism" no longer sufficed; only the Tiananmen Square option—collectivism's "final" solution—remained. But, because Gorbachev opposed violence and SED higher-ups such as Egon Krenz evidently believed that the Party could retain control even while loosening its grip, the Party recoiled from Beijing-style butchery.

Yes, through it all she stayed, Heike says. With three children and a husband who couldn't fathom the idea of leaving, emigration or *Republikflucht* was never a real option. Her two older sisters, however, did not stay. They emigrated back to Austria in the mid-1980s, having waited three years for permission to leave. Even though they pursued their goal legally, they were regarded "as traitors, as 'enemies of the state,' " Heike says. From the week they applied to leave, they were prohibited from working in their professions (law and medicine)—even though moving to Austria, which was not a member of NATO or the Common Market, was not condemned nearly so severely by SED authorities as emigration to West Germany.

"I decided I just couldn't put my family through such an ordeal as all that," Heike says.

The words fall tonelessly. And then, her voice rising, Heike describes with awe the overwhelming autumn of 1989. Never in her own lifetime had Heike expected the Wall to come down. She had just, in the summer of 1989, taken her first trip to the West since adolescence, having been permitted to deliver a paper at a conference in Italy. A titanic battle seemed joined. Ronald Reagan's controversial 1987 speech ("Mr. Gorbachev, tear down this Wall!") was still ringing in European ears. And in mid-January 1989—just a few months before Heike's Italy trip—Honecker had made his much-quoted statement that the Berlin Wall would still be standing in the twenty-second century, "defending" the DDR against western imperialists.

"Do you think the Wall *could* fall?" several people at the conference in Rome asked her, Heike recalls.

"No, never, but maybe things are loosening up," she remembers answering. "The best proof of that is that I'm here, talking to you."

"No," she answers my question, with some irritation, it didn't occur to her not to come back.

But events were already beginning to overtake the SED leadership. By late summer, voting with their feet, East Germans vacationing in Hungary began to force their way into the West German embassy in Budapest, willing to abandon everything, begging for asylum.

Heike herself was long past hoping for "socialism with a human face," she says. Confused and ashamed, yet at the same time transfixed with fascination, she gorged on West German TV beginning in August 1989. She watched an ever-increasing number of East German refugees flee their homes and seek asylum in the West German embassies in Prague and Warsaw. She watched Hungary open its border with Austria, resulting in 55,000 East Germans escaping to the West. And she watched the weeks of peaceful demonstrations on her doorstep—the *Revolution der Kerzen* in Leipzig, the so-called City of Heroes, where the "October Revolution" began. Heike was too confused—and not hypocritical enough—to participate in the protests against the SED. She had been a *Nutzniesser* (beneficiary of the system).

But she watched. She watched throughout November, even after the Wall had fallen, as 300,000 Leipzig citizens marched peacefully through the streets, going from church to church carrying lighted candles. And almost as excitedly she watched the Velvet Revolution unfold in Czechoslovakia that same month, and culminate in the comeback of the deposed Dubček, who had spent most of the previous two decades repairing tools in a Slovak machine shop. She watched Dubček's triumphant return to Prague, as he stood on the balcony above Wenceslas Square, hand in hand with Vaclav Havel. The decent idealist was vindicated at last, as thousands jubilantly, indeed tearfully roared their approval. Hope died last—but was reborn in joy.

Heike's own joy was mixed with shame. And even fear: In 1990, she thought she might lose her job. (She did, however, keep it; her teaching contract, due to expire in mid-1992, was extended. She survived the political and scholarly *Überprüfung* required of all East German faculty.) Her husband, 57, has already been fired. His department was "wrapped up" summarily: *abgewickelt.*

" 'Early retirement,' he jokes, 'it's not so bad,' " Heike says, with a forced laugh. She pauses. "No, really he just sits at home and broods. The shame of it, and the guilt—never having taken a risk, never having stepped out of line, never having spoken up first. We'll take it to our graves."

She pauses again. Her voice is subdued and distant. "Nobody among us was a hero."

And then suddenly: " 'Police files are our only claim to immortality.' "

I flinch.

Heike says it is a line from Kundera, from *The Book of Laughter and Forgetting*, which she read in the early '80s and is now teaching in a class. Before 1990, the novel—available in the DDR in Czech only—remained under lock and key in the library, strictly off-limits to all except DDR Slavic scholars. The novel consists of a series of scenes in which time is measured back and forth from that legendary Prague Spring of 1968.

We talk about Kundera's novel and about Kundera himself—who eagerly joined the Czechoslovakian CP as a teenager, cheered the communist takeover in 1948, became an unperson after Prague 1968, and himself emigrated in the mid-'70s. And about the airless, claustrophobic character of DDR life under communism. And about the mortality of memory. Should one preserve, forget, or laugh away the painful past?

August 21, 1968. When the Soviet T-64s came rumbling in.

Heike glances away, then raises her head slightly. " 'The past is full of life, eager to irritate us, provoke or insult us, tempt us to destroy or repaint [*übermalen*] it.' " She is quoting Kundera again. She turns toward me and pats my notepad. She repeats the word "*übermalen.*" She smiles.

Heike mentions how Kundera's characters suffer from *litost*, an untranslatable Czech word signifying an abject state caused by sudden insight into one's own soul-sickness. She reaches into her book-bag for the Kundera novel and turns to a passage in which he writes of the Czech dissident Mirek: "He fought back his uncontrollable urge to reach far back into the past and smash it with his fist, an urge to slash the canvas of his youth to shreds." She pauses. Her own hands are clenched. Her voice drops; she recites from memory Mirek's thought before his arrest: "The struggle of man against power is the struggle of memory against forgetting."

Hesitantly, I mention the novel's protagonist, the unforgettable beauty, Tamina—exiled in Germany and working as a waitress—whose devouring passion is to retrieve the diaries that she abandoned in Czechoslovakia when she fled in 1968 after the Soviet tanks arrived. Heike nods gravely. Almost instantly, she finds the passage: "She has no desire to turn the past into poetry, she wants to give the past back its lost body . . . because if the shaky structure of her memories collapses like a badly pitched tent, all she will have left is the present, that invisible point, that mere nothing moving slowly toward death."

Heike closes the book, resting it atop my notepad. Her eyes bright with tears, she vouchsafes me the novel's closing line: "It takes so little, so infinitely little, for a person to cross the border beyond which everything loses meaning: love, convictions, faith, history."

Heike's voice is barely audible, but it floats onward, disembodied, dissociated. As if from a great distance, it speaks of the suffocating playground that was the DDR. About the exile from her homeland. No, about her twin exile: forced emigration from her ancestral *Heimat* of Austria and inner emigration from her adopted *Heimat* of eastern Germany. A daughter without a Fatherland. Within the border or beyond the border? It does not matter anymore.

Is this *litost*?

"The past—I can't laugh it away and I can't embrace it," Heike whispers.

The class bell slices the air, cauterizing the moment. Rising to leave, Heike glances at the *Aufbruch* sculpture, her face expressionless.

Mourning, remembrance, guilt, emptiness, homelessness, the vertiginous urge to throw off the past completely. *Nie wieder*: the unbearable lightness of being.

III

Minutes later, Gerhard, 25, a Ph.D candidate in the Slavic Department, greets me. We leave behind the *Aufbruch* sculpture, walking inside and up the stairs to his office cubicle. Gerhard speaks forcefully. He is a former student of Heike and says proudly that he is a PDS member—one of the few in a discredited, rump party that suffers the taint of the SED's failure, has shrunken overnight from 2.3 million members to 200,000, and boasts only 17 representatives in reunified Germany's *Bundestag*. Having joined the SED in 1985, Gerhard had only been a member for four years before it fell apart. His view is a minority one, he says, but the task for him remains: to keep the flickering socialist torch aflame. When I respond that Heike and other Leipzig faculty seem to want to have nothing to do with the PDS, nor with politics or a reformed socialism, Gerhard waves his hand dismissively. "They're from another generation," he says.

Gesturing for me to seat myself, Gerhard shows me a newspaper headline about the University's new rector, who has spent his entire career as a lowly lecturer in the chemistry department and was recently chosen to lead the University because of both his lifelong, public opposition to SED excesses and his reputation for integrity. "A good man," Gerhard allows. But Gerhard considers the rector overzealous in his commitment to "moral renewal" in the University via ouster of former communists.

He himself is one of the *rote Socken* (Red socks), Gerhard says with a grin. The phrase makes me think of doubleheaders at Boston's Fenway Park, but to Gerhard it's the old term among non-SED members for dyed-in-the-wool Party members, a term that post-unification anti-communists throughout Germany now apply derisively to PDS members. Gerhard is defiantly taking back the phrase from the conservatives. Yes, he favors pluralist democracy; no, he does not support the hardcore Communist Platform, a small group of Marxist-Leninists within the PDS—sometimes known by the conservatives' abusive term, *rote Arschlöcher* (Red assholes)—who still favor central planning, nationalization, and state ownership of the "means of production." But Gerhard is a local leader in the Young Comrades, the successor organization to the FDJ.

"Talk of 'renewal'!" Gerhard says. He considers PDS party chief Gregor Gysi a "genius." Gerhard rhapsodizes about Gysi's wit, his articulateness, his political intelligence. Gysi is no stuffy apparatchik, no Stalinist dinosaur. And indeed, with his sponsorship of rock'n'roll rallies and mascots such as Lulu the PDS clown, the 42-year-old Gysi—a Berlin lawyer who sometimes defended dissidents during the SED days, fought to legalize New Forum, and is now the youngest Communist Party chair in Europe—has repackaged the PDS as Germany's party of youth, fresh ideas, and fun. The Party—it is still known as "the Party" to many members—has reformed itself and fulfilled its 1990 campaign slogans: "Better Red than Colorless." "Left Is Lively." "Left Feels Good." And, considering its SED past, the PDS did well in last year's three elections: nearly 30 percent in East Berlin, nearly 16 percent throughout eastern Germany. In just two short years, Gerhard says, Gysi has completely refurbished the PDS image and renewed the "democratic socialist" idea. Gerhard takes the possibility of a "third way" and the name of the PDS, which emphasizes *democratic* socialism, seriously. Just because Soviet socialism has crumbled doesn't mean that socialism itself must be abandoned.

And the fact that the PDS has welcomed *Stasi* collaborators and former top SED members into its ranks—and, occasionally, even as candidates for public office—does not disturb Gerhard. "They bring valuable experience and deserve their own opportunity for self-renewal," he says evenly. Nor is Gerhard unduly concerned about the arrest of the PDS's two top campaign managers last year for diverting $72 million in SED funds abroad. Instead he notes sharply: "The West is wiping out everything we've had here, from our kindergartens and schools to our factories—the only thing 'East German' in the entire country now is the PDS!"

I mention my conversation with Heike about Prague 1968 and Kundera.

Gerhard's smile vanishes. "They're from another generation," he says again, a note of weariness, or perhaps annoyance, slipping into his voice. As an example, he cites the transformation of Günter Bernard, a Leipzig sociology lecturer and former SED member, who has completed his own 180-degree *Wende* from far left to far right and now is party chief of the Republicans in Saxony.

Suddenly Gerhard leans forward and grins. He says that when he thinks of Prague 1968 and middle-aged former SED members disillusioned with socialism since that date, another passage from Kundera, a scene from one of his stories, comes to mind and expresses his disgust with their quietism. Walking through downtown Prague, a man sees another man throwing up on the sidewalk. He comes up to him, shakes his head, and says: "I know just what you mean!"

Talk of the East German generation of '68 reminds Gerhard of Christoph Hein's *Der Tangospieler* (*The Tango Player*), which he read last year. A film version has just opened in Leipzig movie theaters.

Gerhard jumps up, goes into a cubicle across the hallway, and returns with a copy of the novel. I haven't read it; Gerhard explains that it is set chiefly during the spring and summer of 1968, and depicts the life of a 36-year-old Leipziger named Hans Peter Dallow, a Slavic history professor whose specialty is the study of the working class in postwar Czechoslovakia. Two years earlier, Dallow had filled in as a piano player for a student revue. Without knowing what he was getting himself into, Dallow had found himself accompanying—in public—a ditty with improvised lyrics satirizing an aged head of state—obviously Ulbricht. In a Kafkaesque irony characteristic of totalitarian injustice, Dallow then lost his university job and was sentenced to 21 months in prison. Now free in mid-1968, he is utterly mired in the past—and in self-pity. Indifferent to the world-shaking events in Prague, the history behind which he had spent years professing, he is furious with everyone he meets. Nothing is important compared to the personal suffering he has endured. An inner emigré, Dallow can merely mouth, over and over: "I was only the tango player." His only concern is to have his name cleared and his former privileges restored.

The wheel does indeed eventually turn again. News arrives that Dallow can replace an old department colleague who, upon being informed by his students about the Warsaw Pact invasion of Prague, had injudiciously expressed public doubt that the NVA would ever march against a socialist brotherland. The opportunistic Dallow does not hesitate to resume his career. Our final glimpse finds him happily ensconced in his old apartment, playing Chopin on the piano in sweet triumph, as he watches East German TV clips of Czech women and children welcoming Warsaw Pact troops with flower bouquets.

Gerhard waves the paperback at me. *Der Tangospieler* offers insight into the mindset of the disillusioned SED generation of '68 today, he says. They play at remorse; they gaze at their navels. Whether guilty or not guilty, they are Guilty in the end. Gerhard flips to Hein's description of Dallow's image of the word "future" and reads aloud: "an enormous sheet of paper, white and terrifying."

Tossing the novel on the desk, Gerhard leans back in his chair. "Their failures aren't ours," he says of Heike and his other teachers. "We are not afraid of the future." He reminds me not to forget Marx's warning about the need to break the grip of "the dead hand of the past." Gerhard believes in moving on, in building a better future. He is indeed "from a different generation." But what separates him from his elders is not just a few decades, but a chasm of experience. *Their* guilt—the legacy of years of disillusion and bad faith—is not his own, Gerhard says.

Gesturing expansively, his voice swelling, Gerhard declares: "Of course, they'll never make a mistake again; they'll never *do* anything again. It's perfect," Gerhard says, barely suppressing a derisive laugh. "If you do nothing, if you never get your hands dirty, you'll never make a mistake, you'll never be guilty! '*Nie wieder!*' they say. Of course! How easy! Bury yourself in guilt, run from it!"

That attitude, Gerhard claims, facilitated the wave of assaults, just three weeks ago in late September, against immigrants and refugees in the depressed eastern town of Hoyerswerda, near the Polish border. After the attacks, German police bussed the foreigners out of town, unable to guarantee their protection. Hundreds of locals had watched, and even cheered, as the asylum seekers' hostel had gone up in flames; despite outrage expressed by scattered voices, united opposition from Germans did not occur. The radical Right had thus achieved its aim: Hoyerswerda was now "foreigner-free."

Gerhard spits out the word: "*ausländerfrei.*" He looks hard into my face. "I'm still a socialist, still a utopian," he says. "Justice and decency for *all*! The ideals of socialism are still worth struggling for. We failed in the execution: the vision remains."

Another line from Kundera that Heike had quoted leaps out at me: "Totalitarianism is not only hell, but also the dream of paradise."

But I do not quote it. I listen and say nothing. For I am "only an American," I am from that Janus-faced thirtysomething generation between Heike's and his own. I breathe the unbearably lighter air of America—indeed, of the American academy—where all is permitted but too little has mattered, precisely the opposite of the heavy atmosphere that has formed both of them. But clearly, my intellectual world suffers from its own sorts of ideological conformity, doesn't it? Careerism? Status obsession? Gerhard races on:

". . . And when I think of the relationship between the West and the Third World, of the resurgent *Ausländerfeindlichkeit*, of the neo-Nazis on the march everywhere, I know we must *do* something, not merely run from the past.

"This country has been a microcosm of the whole world, a giant East-West laboratory to run one test over and over: Capitalism or socialism? Which will it be? And that's *still* the question. Capitalism doesn't represent the absolute truth! Capitalism hasn't succeeded! And socialism hasn't failed—it still hasn't even been tried.

"We're still a microcosm. By the way we treat the *Asylanten*, we reinforce or transform the relations between the industrialized and developing world. And those relations *must* be changed.

"Do I expect socialists to come to power in the next 20 or 30 years? No! Maybe never! But this much I do know: this capitalist system isn't capable of solving mankind's problems. When I think of this planet's future, of the children and of the Third World, I know this world mustn't—*can't*—go on as it always has."

I look across the table at that youthful face, in the springtime of Hope. None of its features betray any twisted or fanatical idealism. No marks whatsoever disclose any receding line from moral righteousness to the *Realpolitik* of reflexive expediency and revolutionary justice.

The human face of socialism, its sincere and earnest voice echoing in my ears.

8

Berlin, 1991

Dialectical Dilemmas in the Universities:
West Side Story, East Side Story

I

Western Berlin, October 3, 1991. *Tag der Einheit*: "Unity Day." The first anniversary celebrating German reunification.

Or perhaps "marking" reunification is a more accurate term. No jubilant talk of a New Germany, no flag-waving nearby. My forehead pressed against the cool glass of the third-storey living-room window, I watch a half-dozen skinheads swagger in the street below. "*Asylanten Raus!*" ("Asylum Seekers Out!") they chant. "*Deutschland den Deutschen!*" ("Germany for the Germans!"). Black jeans, jackboots, bomber jackets stabbed with Waffen SS insignias. Dirty blond hair clipped close on the sides, Hitler-style, with a single long forelock. Punk turned political with a vengeance. Waving swastikas, shouting the inevitable yet overwhelming "*Sieg Heil!*" they're heading toward the Breitscheidplatz, West Berlin's central square.

Behind me, the Thursday evening news. The sparkle of holiday fireworks gives way to the explosion of terror sweeping across the country. Shelters for asylum seekers torched in Karlsruhe in the southwest and Dusseldorf in the northwest. On the island of Rügen, in the Baltic, a dormitory for refugees razed and incinerated; two Lebanese children severely burned. A hostel for foreigners firebombed in Bremen. ". . . at least 16 racist assaults within 48 hours, bringing the number of attacks to 1,387 since the beginning of the year: the worst outbreak of violence since Hitler's Germany." The right-wing German People's Party, which has just captured an alarming six seats in Bremen's local elections, does not denounce the violence; its spokesman instead urges immediate restrictions on immigration. A conservative minister pitches Prime Minister Kohl's proposal to push through a constitutional amendment curbing Germany's liberal provisions for asylum, which have already opened the doors to more than 1.3 million foreigners since 1989. An interview with historian Golo Mann: "It's 1933 again."

But dinner is ready. Wolfgang, 44, a *wissenschaftlicher Assistent* (lecturer) in sociology at the Free University of Berlin, joins me at the window. He takes a long drag of his cigarette.

"The Hitler Youth of the '90s," Wolfgang says. "German Unity!?! Who knows what this 'new Germany' will lead to?" He turns his back on the receding parade of young *faschos*. "We Berliners are becoming Germans too," he says quietly. "Berlin is changing."

Wolfgang was 20 in 1968 when he came from Freiburg to Berlin to study at the FU. Isolated and vulnerable, West Berlin was situated in the heart of the German Democratic Republic, an "island within socialism." To make that island livable, Bonn poured billions of marks into it; by 1989, Bonn's financial support amounted to half the city's DM 35 billion budget. As an incentive to come to West Berlin, West German citizens who stayed for 12 years were excused from military service. A conscientious objector, Wolfgang immediately felt at home here: West Berlin, the cradle of West German pacificism and refuge for anti-war activists, dropouts, bohemians, gays, and eternal students. In the quarter-century he has lived here in Berlin, Wolfgang has seldom been back to West Germany except for short visits to see his father, a prosperous retired lawyer, and his mother, a homemaker. Secure in his job, Wolfgang worries about the changes coming over his adopted city.

" 'Berliners' and 'Europeans'—that's how we think of ourselves here," Wolfgang says. "We've never identified with the West Germans, with their narrow-mindedness and smug provincialism. Nor—heaven forbid!—with the earnest, dour, hopelessly conventional DDR—land of the people who never broke a smile. Given its isolation, you couldn't very easily come to or go from Berlin—it wasn't like going to Munich or Cologne. When you came here, you had made a decision. . . . We're Berliners and Europeans! Berlin has always been the cosmopolitan city, the center for refugees, asylum seekers, and *Andersdenkenden* (nonconformists).

"But now—it's all changing," Wolfgang repeats ruefully. He pauses. "If you're a black or a foreigner, you can't even ride the subway safely. It was never that way before." He glances out the window again, a few attenuated voices still wafting up to us. "Yes, Berlin is a fitting capital for the 'new Germany.' Germany is coming to Berlin."

I ask Wolfgang if he had supported the Bundestag's decision in June to move the capital from cozy Bonn (population: 270,000) to bustling, "imperial" Berlin—a metropolis of 4 million citizens, from which two world wars were launched.

"Bonn has been just a *Bundesdorf* [federal village]," Wolfgang says. "It's a genteel backwater nestled among ancient castles on the Rhine and secluded from the world. My father had a couple of offers to work in Bonn for the Christian Democrats, and he always said, 'In Bonn? Never. I'd die of boredom.' It's easy to see why—aside from the government, there's nothing much in Bonn except a candy factory.

"And then there's Berlin," Wolfgang continues. "In a new Europe looking eastward, it's crucial to have the capital here, in the center of Europe. Who knows better than Berliners what division really means? Berliners know. We know the east as well as the west, without feeling very much part of either.

"But more and more, we're losing our sense of specialness and realizing that we're part of East Germany. Geographically but also socially and psychologically. The *Fremdenhass* [xenophobia], the street violence, the unemployment, the special connection to East Europe—we're not any longer going to be a 'kept' city, fed by rich West Germans unconcerned with life in the east. Our problems are eastern problems: we resemble Leipzig and Dresden, not Munich. That's why it's so important that Berlin be the capital. We can't let the Bonn politicians just shrug things off. They must see up close what's really happening in the country, especially in the ravaged east. Germany must face the past, rather than pretend it never happened, as it looks to the future. *Ostpolitik* means something entirely different now. It doesn't mean for us anymore a role within a little *Bundesrepublik*—as a front man for the U.S. in the Cold War and as a showcase for capitalism. It means being the leading city in the economically most powerful country within a transformed Europe. We've been cast in a similar role before. This is the question: Can we play it properly this time?"

However much he may feel a Berliner or European when he's in Germany, Wolfgang concedes that he feels very much a German when he's abroad. I remark that it seems a tragedy that Germans can't recover some sense of fellow feeling, or even patriotism, without provoking either an orgy of nationalist fervor or national shame.

Gingerly, we approach the lurking question that shadows every German's conversation with foreigners: the issue of German identity. Wolfgang anticipates it. He feels no guilt for what his father and grandfather did 50 years ago, he says.

"But shame, yes, shame."

Immediately I spill out the sad spectacle that I witnessed in Holland a few weeks earlier: three German boy scouts, 12 or 13 years old, being taunted on the street by Dutch children shouting "Nazi!" I tell Wolfgang that it's awful that the world points a finger at the entire nation of Germany and at yet another generation of young Germans. And 46 years after the war has ended! Surely, if one hammers into a child for years on end, "You're despicable, you're a criminal," surely that child will eventually either embrace that role or lash out in defiance of it. Any society held in check by 12 years of Nazism and 45 years of communism would be vulnerable to extremism. I don't mean to justify the skinheads, I say. Just this: it's horrible that those boys, or you yourself, Wolfgang, should carry the sins of your fathers.

My outburst ends. Wolfgang shakes his head, then glances impatiently toward the window. We're not really of the same generation, you and I, I know he's thinking. History isn't so easy to escape! Would that it were! And our history, friend, is a long one. Those teenage skinheads are also part of it. A new start isn't easy.

But instead of responding as I expect, Wolfgang's answer jolts me, not in the least by his matter-of-fact delivery.

"We're the Jews of the world."

"What?!"

"Hitler turned us into the figure which the Jews had always been—the hated ones, the scapegoats," Wolfgang answers. "The Germans have become the Jews of the world. And it took nothing less than the Holocaust to do it. Nothing less than our mass-murder of them would have shifted the world's fingerpointing from them—as Christ's so-called 'murderers'—toward us. That was the sentence of Hitler on us for having failed him as 'Germans' and lost the war: To survive as 'Jews.' "

I ask Wolfgang if he expects the New Germany to end in another yet catastrophe.

" 'That things continue on this way *is* the catastrophe.' " A line from an essay by Walter Benjamin, says Wolfgang.

I don't know what to say. But Wolfgang won't let it rest there; he picks up the thread of his provocative claim and asserts calmly that it's understandable that "the Dutch and French too have a certain contempt for us."

"Imagine this," he continues. "Imagine that your grandfather committed a series of murders in the name of the family. Not just that *he* was a murderer—in that case it would just be a skeleton in the closet—but that he proclaimed those murders as a *family act*. How would the children in the victimized neighboring families feel about your family? . . . The *Endlösung* was done in the name of 'Deutschland,' committed precisely because the Jews and other peoples were *not* Aryans. It was a crime enacted as a German—and the consequences endure for us as Germans today. Yes, I can well understand that those other families too—the Dutch, the French—can't even bear to hear my name of 'German.'

"And yet,"—Wolfgang's voice rises, quivering—"that doesn't mean that I can't speak out against injustice today, that I can't criticize you or them! I won't let you say: 'Don't *you* criticize me! You people murdered the Jews!!' No, I won't stand for that. . . . You Americans sponsored a war this year in the Gulf which killed 300,000 civilians. To test your new weapons?! To keep the oil flowing?! You had no justification for your conduct of that war: it too was a crime against humanity. No, I won't let you—Americans, Israelis, Russians or whomever—I won't let you exploit the *Endlösung* to excuse your own crimes and to silence me! No, I'll speak out against inhumanity when I see it. And that doesn't mean that I've forgotten, not for an instant, what happened here in Berlin five decades ago."

The street is quiet. Now it's Wolfgang's voice that hangs in the air.

Hours pass, alternately in silence and in conversation. Finally I turn back to Wolfgang's claim. Wolfgang, I venture, doesn't the notion of the Germans as the "Jews of the world" imply an equivalence between the degree of victimage experienced by the Jews during the Holocaust and by the postwar Germans? And doesn't it suggest a "negative nationalism" on your part, Wolfgang, whereby you Germans, with a mixture of guilt and perverse pride, juxtapose the uniqueness of the Holocaust with a dark claim to your own special status as an "Evil Empire"? And doesn't that claim revive the old idea of the German *Sonderweg* (special path) in History, recasting it in post-Holocaust terms as a road of Evil?

Wolfgang looks surprised; he admits his analogy limps. He means it to startle, he says. But he adds that he wishes that, rather than reuniting politically, Germany could have become again just a *Kulturnation* (cultural nation), as it was before 1871, when Prussia under Bismarck reunified the numerous sovereign German principalities and formed the Second German Reich.

"Why a political union of Germany?" asks Wolfgang somberly. After all, a sense of "Germanness" goes back much further than Bismarck; its roots are in Luther and the Enlightenment. "Why couldn't we have had a cultural federation, something like the sense of relatedness among the English-speaking peoples? Or something like the British Commonwealth? Why isn't cultural unity enough?"

Neither of us has an answer; again the room falls silent.

By now it is long after midnight; too exhausted to sleep, we wander outside through the cool night breeze. Ah, *Berliner Luft*! Following the path of the skinheads hours earlier, we stroll toward the Kurfurstendamm (or "Ku-damm"), Berlin's most fashionable shopping and entertainment street, the center of the city's day and night life, like Fifth Avenue and Broadway rolled into one. We arrive at the Breitscheidplatz, that famous square containing the Kaiser Wilhelm Memorial Church, its bombed-out old nineteenth-century shell shoulder to shoulder with its modern, glass-and-concrete addition. Next to the church is the sprawling Europa Center, a flashing, psychedelic mini-Common Market of dozens of bistros and boutiques and sex shops, complete with indoor ice rink, Finnish sauna, art gallery, and the national cuisines of the 30 House of Nations restaurants. Do I know, remarks Wolfgang, that Rudolf Breitscheid was a Social Democratic Party leader and minister in the Weimar Republic who lost his life in Buchenwald concentration camp? No? Of course, I must know Kaiser Wilhelm I, with his muttonchop whiskers, the dignified old gentleman crowned Kaiser of the Second German Reich in 1871 at Versailles. And we should go to the Europa Center, which houses the Romanisches Cafe, named in honor of the legendary cafe—also located on this very spot!—where Berlin's leading poets and painters in the 1920s used to gather. . . .

Wolfgang rambles on. But I'm frozen: the scene transfixes me. Germanies and more Germanies swirl around us, as though the pictures from the evening TV are trailing us in the street. A density of superimposed images: the new economic superpower of "borderless" Europe, the stolid and prosperous former Federal Republic, the still-smoldering ashes of Nazi Deutschland, the promise and the tragedy of the Weimar Republic, the grandeur of fossilized Wilhelmine Prussia.

The story of modern Germany compressed into this single square, a postage-stamp palimpsest of German history.

II

Eastern Berlin—four days later—October 7, 1991. A would-have-been anniversary—along with old standbys like the "Day of the Co-Workers of Commerce" (third Sunday in February), the "Day of the National People's Army" (March 1), the "Day of the People's Police" (July 1), and the "Day of Public Health" (December 11). But October 7 was always the big event—great parades, long-winded speeches at the Marx-Engels Platz, colorful mass demonstrations for "real existing" socialism. Indeed East Berlin's biggest tool-making firm was named after the DDR's birthday—"*der Siebte Oktober.*" Yes, today would have been the 42nd anniversary of the DDR. Two years ago, Honecker and Gorbachev kissed and hugged in front of the TV cameras and declaimed the historic achievements of the DDR. Five weeks later, the Wall was down, and with it the DDR.

A humid *Altweibersommer* ("old wives' summer"; i.e., Indian summer) afternoon. Twenty blocks from the end of the Ku-damm and 40-odd years into the past, I walk through the center of old Berlin, half-seeing the postwar devastation of treeless Unter den Linden, once Berlin's main thoroughfare. My destination: the former Friedrich Wilhelm University (named for Frederick the Great), since 1949 known as Humboldt University after the famous Humboldt brothers, Wilhelm and Alexander.

Holger waves to me; he's standing in the front garden of Humboldt University, shading himself under the large gingko tree—planted by Alexander von Humboldt himself, Holger says. Red-haired with flecks of grey on the side and wearing steel-rimmed glasses, Holger, 36, is pleased to see me. He is a lecturer here in modern German history, and has much to show me at Humboldt. Slowly we traverse the grounds of the University, which occupies a restored palace originally built in the 1740s for Prince Henry, brother of Frederick the Great. Marble statues of honored Humboldtians inhabit the gardens: the physicist Helmholtz; the philologist Mommsen; and of course the brothers Humboldt, naturalist-statesman Alexander and educator-diplomat Wilhelm, the University's founder. Nearby is Hegel Square, known until the 1950s as the Courtyard, featuring the former home of the University's most distinguished philosopher, along with those of the physicist Max Planck, the novelist Gottfried Keller, and the theatrical producer Max Reinhardt. With a knowing smirk, Holger directs me to the palace's entrance hall, which still showcases a marble bust of the University's most famous alumnus, "K. Marx," Class of '41, inscribed with a bright word of welcome: "The philosophers have merely interpreted the world; the point, however, is to change it."

Die Herren Professoren in eastern Germany's most distinguished university have come down in the world, Holger remarks pointedly, and city-hall officials in Berlin are getting "the point" about putting theory into practice. That means that many Humboldt philosophers aren't doing much interpreting nowadays, since their own little world has changed radically: officials have already shut down several departments, including M-L and philosophy.

But Holger himself can't manage much more than a bemused, cynical laugh about the politics of the changes; it's too close to home. Last December's victory of the CDU emboldened conservative legislators in West Berlin to draw up legislation granting them authority to dismiss a whole array of other Humboldt departments too, among them law, economics, pedagogy—and Holger's department, history. Eventually, after a series of student rallies and sit-ins earlier this year, the legislation was narrowed to cover only those departments that the school did not plan to reinstitute: authorities ruled that individual faculty must receive due process if they worked in fields that would continue to be staffed at the University. But, even so, everyone is certain that draconian cuts in the targeted departments are in the offing. At least it no longer seems that the government will close Humboldt altogether, as some had feared because of its proximity to the Free University.

As we saunter toward the newly rechristened Opera Square—until last year still called Bebel Square (after nineteenth-century socialist leader August Bebel)—Holger launches breathlessly into the newest developments in the politics of *Abwicklung* at Humboldt.

But I'm gone again. Bombarded by names, by name changes, by changes of name changes, I'm years behind. I shiver, convulsively, trying to shake off the weight of History. With each step we're treading decades—for me, the spectacle is just as finely tesselated with historical association, minus the kitsch, as the Thursday night scene at the Breitscheidplatz. Hegel, the philosopher of history, would understand, wouldn't he? I'm overcome with sensory impressions, as if we're surrounded by an old *Wochenschau* newsreel spinning backwards, with the great figures of Berlin doffing their hats and prancing past us. Yes, I'm here with the gingko tree and the Humboldt alums along Holger's casual tour. But here are the Brownshirts: now, as Golo Mann said—what, four nights ago?—it's 1933 again, all right. Though Holger doesn't think to mention it, I know that Opera Square was the scene of the Burning of the Books—and I can't get the images of the chanting skinheads outside Wolfgang's apartment out of my mind. Here in the Opera Square—no, not yet Bebel Square—in March 1933, hundreds of screaming brown-shirted Humboldt students lit a bonfire and dumped tons of "un-German," black-listed books—the complete works of Stefan Zweig, Thomas and Heinrich Mann, Bertolt Brecht, Alfred Döblin, and dozens of others—into the blaze. All staged under the approving eye (and film cameras) of Dr. Goebbels, who heralded the atrocity as a sign of a glorious new Germany ascending from the hell-fire. The event is recalled by a small memorial that graces Opera Square and contains copies of a few of the books burned by the Nazis.

I stumble after Holger, who is waiting politely for me, and now we grab an empty table on the terrace of the Opera House Cafe, adjacent to the State Opera House. (It was the Prussian Opera House during the Second Reich, I know, and before that the Royal Opera House.) I look around at the casual scene. Plastic chairs, large umbrellas at every table. A warm evening. Weary shoppers lounging, sipping a *Berliner Weisse* or having coffee and cake. I anchor myself in 1991, and Holger and I queue for drinks and snacks. Inside are the well-heeled West German tourists, Holger remarks. He looks at me quizzically. As if restraining himself. He does not add "and Americans." We peer inside at the elegant dinner clientele, craning our necks to catch a glimpse of the pale pink walls, brass chandeliers, and plush upholstered chairs of the cafe's newly remodeled interior. Each room is dedicated to a Berlin composer—Lortzing, Mendelssohn, Nicolai. No socialist worker chic in this cafe; the renovated Opera House Cafe is recovering the Royal Opera House tradition. Make no mistake about it: this is the new East Berlin—open for business.

Holger is still preoccupied with the situation at Humboldt, where things are anything but thriving. He rolls a cigarette, lights it, stubs it out quickly, then rolls another. The University's staff will be slashed from 8,000 to 2,000 within three years, he says. To assure that entrenched Stalinist faculty are rooted out, Berlin's new "fire and rehire" education law authorizes city officials to dismiss *all* faculty hired under East German law. Any and all fired faculty are free to apply for any new jobs; any and all may be rehired if best qualified for the job. This happy ending seems unlikely, however, given the hordes of West Germans applying. Indeed, Heinrich August Winkler, a distinguished Freiburger historian, has just been hired, along with several of his hand-picked *Assistenten*, to direct the new Institute of Contemporary History at Humboldt. The resentment among Humboldt historians is keen, Holger says. It is all a bitter, if somehow not entirely surprising, turn of events. In 1949, West Berlin's Free University was founded by anti-communist faculty, forced out of the Friedrich Wilhelm University on ideological grounds. SBZ/DDR officials immediately retaliated by repudiating the imperial, Prussian (and allegedly "capitalistic") tradition of the University and changing its name to Humboldt.

"Yes, now the tables are turned," Holger says in his *Berlinerisch* patois. His easy smile has turned into a scowl. He tamps his cigarette on the table. "The *Wessis*—should I say '*Besserwessis*'?—are calling the shots." Holger fears that he and his colleagues are about to join the ranks of unemployed East Berliners, unofficially now totaling more than 40 percent.

"They've already refused to recognize degrees from the *Fachschulen* [technical colleges]," Holger says. His voice assumes a hard, sarcastic edge. He stubs out still another cigarette, grounding it down hard, as if enacting East Berlin's fate at the hands of the West. "Supposedly because they don't have anything equivalent in the west. You want to know the real reason? Competition. That's right: *fear* of competition. They talk about 'free' competition! That's a laugh!" His younger brother graduated from a *Fachschule* in eastern Berlin, Holger says. "He's just as capable and well-trained as any West German. But if there's an easy way to undercut competition, they'll do it. Any way they can."

An East Berliner all his life, Holger grew up in Kopenick, a red-brick district in southeast Berlin, a shabby but comfortable quarter never blighted, miraculously, either by Allied bombs or East German architects. His father and mother were both schoolteachers; as a 16-year-old Hitler Youth in April 1945, his father had fought in the Battle of Berlin. Like most East German children of his background, Holger joined the Party youth organizations, the Pioneers and the FDJ. At 18, he entered the Party. Conscientious and reliable, he studied diligently. He was admitted to Humboldt and eventually wrote a dissertation on the German workers' movement between the wars. At Party meetings, Holger says, he rarely spoke up. But privately, he says, he deplored the stodginess of the Honecker regime, supported Gorbachev, and favored liberalizing the Party. He didn't believe most of what the Party said. After all, he had been watching West German TV for years. But he had a job and the system functioned: that was enough. Yes, the system had been good to his family. And things might have remained so if the uprising in 1989 had led to an independent, socialist East Germany.

"But what's the point of thinking like that?" Holger says, stopping himself in mid-reverie. He's annoyed with himself for his dreamy flight from the unpleasant facts of real-existing capitalism. "That's just a *Gedankenexperiment* [thought experiment]. It would have taken years to straighten out our own mess and make it work, if it even *could* have ever worked."

The heated debate throughout the spring over moving Germany's capital, Holger adds, was really a post-factum debate about reunification. No one wanted to bring up the country's serious problems in the heady days of November '89 for fear of shattering the national mood of joy. Though the debate was inevitable, it had to be disguised when it came, lest it trigger a national identity crisis and disclose the deep ambivalence felt by westerners and easterners about coming together again. And so, the question: Bonn or Berlin? Since practically every eastern representative in the Bundestag voted in mid-June for Berlin, Holger said, the narrowness of the majority (338–321) showed how reluctantly the west embraced the east.

"No, a united Germany is probably for the best," Holger reluctantly concludes. "But we're contentious in-laws. You find your long-lost relatives, you have a big party—and then what do you do with them? You're not one big happy family overnight. . . . I, for one, feel more of an East German than ever. I don't think I'll ever be a *Bundesbürger*."

I'm still distracted by the skinheads swaggering through my head; I change the subject slightly and ask Holger about the nationalistic, right-wing German People's Party. How strong is it in Berlin? Last weekend in Bonn (October 5–6), neo-Nazis defaced Adenauer's grave with painted swastikas. Perhaps a symbolic attack on German democracy?

With a wince, Holger brushes the question aside; he says he's having trouble enough handling his own problems, let alone worrying about what's going on in Bonn. A quick spasm of pain seems to cross his face. So long as he is addressing marble monuments and textbook history, I realize, he remains the well-read historian and hospitable tour guide, armed with congenial if automatic responses; but turn the conversation to 1991, and it's clear that his own fate preoccupies him, leaving little room for other current issues. His job is all he really wants to talk about—as if by talking about it, he can find a way to hold onto it. His preoccupation reminds me of how difficult it is to think of anyone beyond oneself, when one's own security is threatened. And how difficult to see beyond the threat if— as is the case for millions of unemployed or soon-to-be unemployed eastern Germans—one has never known anything *but* job security. Wolfgang could speculate on the future of Germany in a new Europe; Holger just wants to know what his own future will bring.

"I wish it would just be *over*—I wish they'd just make a decision," Holger says. "Then at least I could begin a new life. Almost two years of waiting—and no word. In July, I filled out a long questionnaire, asking me to document practically every waking move I've made since I entered the Party. No word since. Just rumors, rumors everywhere. It's so corrupt. Like how the *Bonzen* at the *Treuhand* slip their friends the best deals. There's a disgusting lack of *Transparenz* [integrity] to this whole eerie process of transition. At Humboldt, at least half of us won't be rehired—but who knows according to what criteria? Nobody's saying. And everyone assumes that, if you just leave, you were probably hooked up with the *Stasi*."

Because history was one of the subjects most rigidly controlled by Party ideology, Holger knows that the chances of an eastern lecturer in history getting a job after the coming shakedown are slim. Still, he waits. And waits. And hopes. There aren't many other options. For him too, if in a less obvious sense, it's 1933 again— or worse.

"Under Hitler you could have left, and many people did go—to Paris, London, the States," Holger says. "But today? Where can we go? I'm so sick of it all—I'd leave the damn country tomorrow if I *could* get a job anywhere. But as soon as you apply, there comes that look on their face, as if to say, 'Oh, errr, ahem . . . you're from *East* Germany?' That's it, you're done for. They assume you're either incompetent or Erich Mielke [former'head of the *Stasi*]"—which on further reflection, Holger concedes, has come to seem tautological.

"Yes, it's even worse at Humboldt now than it was under our old idiots. . . . A few hours of joy in November '89, a few days of solidarity thereafter, then just a new set of problems. Just a new game, a new kind of corruption. All that mattered before was the Party. Now it's the Deutschmark.

"What do I believe in?" Holger echoes my next question. He glances away, distractedly, almost as if he is talking to himself. His voice is unsteady. He removes his glasses, places them on the table, turns them, repositions them again. Now it is Holger who seems to be caught in a time warp.

"*Nothing*," he answers. Like so many others with whom I've spoken, he says that institutions—Party, state, nation, church, academy—are empty husks to him. Holger pauses, scowling. He puts his glasses on again and eyes with distaste several well-dressed couples, in dark suits and flowing dresses, who are passing our table as they exit the Opera House Cafe. He adds in a low voice: "And they're empty for most of the skinheads too. That's the one thing we share.

"Who are their heroes?" Holger goes on, his voice rising. "There are no sources of authority here any more. Nor in the west. You asked about Adenauer. Nobody looks up to any public figure like most West Germans did Adenauer in the early postwar days. Love him or hate him, he was *der Alte* ["the old man"], the voice of Authority. For Christ's sake, they put the capital [Bonn] in his backyard because he demanded it! . . . These kids [the skinheads] aren't Nazis. They're a lost generation. They don't know who they are."

Holger recounts an old saw about the national character of Europeans. In England, everything that is not forbidden is permitted. In Germany, everything that is not permitted is forbidden. In Russia, even that which is permitted is forbidden. And in France, even that which is forbidden is permitted.

But since the Wall came down, Holger says, eastern Germans are outdoing the French: "Now we say: 'Everything that was once forbidden is *obligatory*!' "

The quip, Holger says, explains something about the right-wing breast-beating popular among East German youth. Under DDR communism, any expression of fascist sentiment was illegal; now Nazi salutes and Hitler haircuts are not only permissible but even de rigeur in some youth circles. Holger doesn't see it as a major threat yet. Not that the skinheads don't sometimes make his own skin crawl.

"They don't know who they are, but they know this much," Holger says. "They're sick of feeling shame. 'I don't want to feel ashamed to be white and German,' they're saying. Their parents, their teachers, their political leaders—the kids know that the older generation were all *Mitmacher* [joiners, conformists]. Until two years ago, the kids didn't yet know that. And the rage is just now coming out. That's why the authoritarian appeals are proving so successful today. 'Give me someone, *anyone* to believe in!' the kids are pleading. And I fear that, if no decent mainstream figures come, someone on the far right soon will."

The topic stimulates Holger's historical sense; he warms to the larger issues. The spectre of another outbreak of German fascism, he says, cannot be divorced from the absence of German pride in any periods or personalities of German history. The situation is worst in the east, Holger says. What Party leaders or political dissidents worthy of any respect did the DDR bequeath? None, he answers.

"Who are our 'decent figures' of the east? Who do we have to compare, in any way at all, with a Dubček or Havel, an Imre Nagy or a Lukács? With a Lech Walesa, or a Sakharov or Solzhenitsyn or even Gorbachev? We have no one. For all their faults and for all their critics at home, those are *figures* of whom postwar socialists elsewhere in the East bloc need not be ashamed."

No charismatic leaders emerged in the DDR in the fall of 1989, Holger notes. Instead the dissident movement spoke of pre-Weimar-era figures such as Luxemburg and Liebknecht—names that meant little to anyone under 60, the scope of their persisting influence a pathetic testimony of the desert of German socialist leadership since then.

And what about the cultural scene? Holger continues. Who are the "decent figures" there? Were there any "positive heroes" in the DDR? Holger's voice is sharp with irony: SED cultural gatekeepers used that term to enforce socialist-realist orthodoxy in the depiction of literary character. Holger jokes that *Held* (hero) was a word so abused by the SED that perhaps it should—not unlike the case of the Nazi abuse of *Führer*—be retired from usage in the east for the foreseeable future. Still, whatever the word, the question concerns him:

"Who were our 'culture heroes'? Who were the men and women admired by critically minded DDR citizens?" Holger asks, his voice rising. "*Were* there any at all?"

One by one we mull the possibilities. Holger repeatedly says that the West "misunderstood" or "exaggerated" the reputations of DDR intellectuals at home. Finally, leaving aside the charges of misunderstandings and exaggerations, he and I settle on a few names that may come to signify the DDR intellectual to the next generation. The short list is short indeed: Bloch, Havemann, Biermann. Holger pauses. Almost as an afterthought, he adds the name of Christa Wolf.

And Holger's verdict is harsh. He dismisses the candidates with a bill of particulars delivered with staccato-fire precision. Bloch was an "unreadable mystic," a Stalin apologist right up to Stalin's death, "timid" in his politics, not at all like Lukács but rather a vain academic's academic who fled to the West when the Wall went up; Havemann evolved from the Stalinist mouthpiece of June 1953 to a courageous activist, yet "lost himself in 'third way' dreams," even though he stands in hindsight as "the best DDR socialist of them all"; Biermann was—"and still is"—"perversely rebellious," an "aesthete," who, due to self-indulgence and lack of political seriousness, never fulfilled his potential to lead a younger DDR generation out of the SED morass; Christa Wolf was a Joan of Arc of dissidents in western eyes because she played with a few socialist-realist conventions and expressed certain feminist themes, but she was actually an SED-approved writer who helped legitimize the regime. Holger adds that he agrees with western critics who have interpreted Wolf's recently published autobiographical novel, *Was bleibt?* (*What's Left?*)—her story of her surveillance by the *Stasi* in the late 1970s—as the miscalculation of a self-absorbed "would-be martyr" who "had no respect for those who had truly suffered."

But there is also a fifth candidate, the consideration of whose merits Holger leaves for last.

"There was one name on every intellectual's lips as late as the mid-1960s, and even on a few lips right up to the end," Holger pronounces judiciously. Of course, he means to exclude discussion of the Party faithful's participation in the cults of

Pieck and Ulbricht, along with state campaigns to canonize "workers' heroes" such as Adolf Hennecke.

"The name was: Brecht. The question of the general effectiveness of the Party's propaganda about 'socialist heroes' aside—few thinking people believed it anyway—the failure of character of generations of intellectually minded DDR citizens is reflected in our blind hero-worship of Brecht. As an artist, of course, his work is powerful. He was the model of the engaged playwright, and even today, his insistence that the theater can effect political change and respond to social ills is worthy," Holger says. "But that was Brecht the artist. The man was charismatic, without a doubt, but look at his life! Talk about the disjunction between socialist theory and praxis! 'Nothing is more important than learning to think crudely,' he said. 'Crude thinking is the thinking of great men.' By that standard, Brecht himself was great—just as Stalin was great. And that, of course, was the standard by which he praised Stalin."

But as a democratic socialist, continues Holger, Brecht was deplorable: an opportunist, a hypocrite, and a cynic—indeed a spectacular example of all three, with his anti-capitalist plays staged here (in East Berlin), but his West German publisher, his Austrian citizenship, and his Stalin Prize money stashed in Zurich—just in case. Where did he spend the war years? Holger asks. In Moscow? No, in Hollywood!

"Of course, he called it *Realpolitik*—and so great was his power of mass manipulation that we accepted that. Leather jacket, tin-rimmed glasses, stubbly chin: publicly, he dressed and acted the proletarian." Privately, Holger says, Brecht lived comfortably and did Ulbricht's bidding—even lending the prestige of his name to the Soviet crackdown of June 17. And he was duly rewarded for it. The Berliner Ensemble proved to be a cult of personality in the artistic sphere hardly less sycophantic than the SED treatment of Party *Bonzen*. Brecht's influence proved fatal to a whole generation of admiring DDR citizens, says Holger—people like Biermann, who became caricatures of him.

But all that pertains to eastern Germans bereft of a usable socialist past based on DDR history, Holger stresses. The threat of a new round of German fascism in the New Germany of 1991 exists in the west as well as the east; and the absence of German pride in *any* eras or figures of German history includes West Germany and the pre-1945 German past too. For German history is a history of rents and ruptures, Holger says, warming to his theme. Turning professorial again, he cites a couple of western historians, acknowledging his agreement with them and commending their scholarship.

Holger explains that the jagged discontinuities of German history give rise, in turn, to the deep national longing for a "strong man" to suture them together or simply to reconstruct by fiat a plausible national tradition. Today a lack of consensus about almost every major event or figure in modern German history prevails. And that fact—not primarily the loss of two world wars—has thwarted the growth of a patriotic tradition and a stable identity. There's no pre-history, before 1945 or 1918, to retrieve, Holger says, which might serve as the basis for a positive, shared, healthy national identity.

"Germany is a nation without agreement not just on our heroes, but also even on our villains," Holger says. "Take Old Fritz [Frederick the Great]. Hero or villain? Some people see him as a tyrant, others as father of the nation. It's similar with old Kaiser Wilhelm I, Bismarck, Hindenburg. Even Hitler has his enthusiasts—as the kids on the streets are proving. And we've just discussed the dearth of DDR-era heroes.

"In the U.S., you all agree, more or less, who the good guys and bad guys are. Imagine if you had so much disagreement about George Washington or Thomas Jefferson! No, you see yourselves as having developed in a certain direction. You've worked toward each major stage in your history; you have a progressive trajectory. We don't—remember there was no 'Germany' before 1871; division is what we know best.

"So Germany never goes clearly forward or backward," Holger continues. "Our history goes in zigs and zags. Was the unification [1871] and the formation of the Second Reich a good thing? How about the defeat in 1918 and the abdication of the Kaiser [Wilhelm II]? Or the founding of the Weimar Republic? Or the destruction of the Third Reich? Or the formation of the DDR? Some people say yes, others no. As soon as people take into account the consequences, they often reverse their position. The consequences undermine the original event. So we zig and we zag. Ask East and West Germans today about the *Wende* and the wisdom of reunification. What will they say? Not the same thing as in November 1989. And you'll get no consensus."

But at least everybody agrees about the toppling of the Wall, I say. Holger is stopped short; he shrugs and does not reply.

Don't they? I wonder. But I keep the question to myself.

The Wall, or what's left of it, is just a few blocks away. No longer a Cold War metaphor or even tourist attraction. Just a curio.

The Wall. . . . The fragility of memory; the pale and fading past.

In the days of the Wall, a westerner's day visa to East Berlin expired at 2 A.M. Tonight, no worries. And no fretting either about passport officials, border police, or 15-foot-high barricades.

Holger and I get into his little two-stroke Trabi. We putt-putt our way up and down Unter den Linden to the Brandenburg Gate and back again to Humboldt. Crossing into West Berlin, we cruise along the Friedrichstrasse, not even slowing down for Checkpoint Charlie.

"Too bad you can't stay longer," Holger says, shaking my hand. The easy smile is back. Yes, too bad. Tomorrow Holger will attend a lecture on the *Wende*, delivered by the new Humboldt senior history professor from western Germany.

Tomorrow: October 9, 1991. Another roll of the German history newsreel, another turn of the German history kaleidoscope. Another date, another parade of names and faces.

And another round of marching and chanting too: a distant, fleeting, more hopeful historical moment. For the East German demonstrations against "real existing socialism"—and the last round of cheers through German streets: "*We* are The People!"—began tomorrow, two long years ago.

9

Leipzig, 1993

Of Sport, State, and *Stasi*:
Socialism with an Un-Beautiful Face

I

Back again in the so-called *Heldenstadt* (city of heroes), as the faded bumper stickers on a few cars remind me. Is the word now tinged with irony? Though the city is in the middle of a construction boom, Leipzigers are the first to tell you that the city's heroic image has been badly tarnished in the last few years.

A warm mid-September afternoon in the smoggy city center. I take a seat in one of the cafes that dot the streets near the University. Students sit inside with books in their laps, talking animatedly to one another. Across the street is the Leipzig railway station—before the war, it was the biggest in Europe—and the Gewandhaus, where the Leipzig orchestra plays. Kurt Masur, who helped negotiate with police to hold their fire against Leipzig protesters before the city's first mass demonstration—four years ago come October 9—is still conducting at the Gewandhaus. Otherwise, everything seems to have changed—the Leipzig smog excepted.

Ute, a 23-year-old, first-year *Germanistik* student at the University, enters and greets me. Once an accomplished teenage ice skater in a top *Sportschule*—indeed, at 16, a young *Privilegierte* (privileged one) on her way to joining the elite traveling *Sportkader*—Ute is still slim and athletic. She has come to tell me about her expulsion almost a decade ago from the elect Red circle, the causes of which, she told me on the phone, "I have lately been brooding about incessantly." She did not elaborate. I know only that the saga of her youthful rebellion against the State and her struggle to leave the DDR in 1988/89 had begun soon thereafter.

Reared in Weissenfels, a town near Leipzig, Ute was born into a family of athletes. In the 1950s, her father competed on the DDR national ice hockey team and her mother was a top handball player and member of the DDR national championship squad; Ute's older brother, Dieter, reached the Thuringia championship soccer team. Sports was the family's joy and preoccupation; in hindsight, Ute allows that her parents, who were unpolitical and little interested in affairs outside their immediate circle, turned to sports as a respite or even escape from Cold War agitprop and the ideological trench warfare between the early postwar DDR and *Bundesrepublik*.

"My parents simply wanted to live in peace," Ute says in a tired voice. She takes out a cigarette and lights up. "They never spoke for or against the state. They were never much interested in Party pronouncements." Ute's father joined the LDPD, the voice of liberal democrats in the DDR bloc party system. Like the other parties outside the SED, however, its effective purpose was merely to serve *Schein-demokratie;* it had no real power whatsoever. Ute remembers that her father had very little to do with the LDPD. "Perhaps that's why he was willing to enter it," she says.

Ute's father, who died in 1987, had led an unusual life of relative independence. Upon gaining his *Abitur* in the early 1950s, he could have gone on to higher education, but his own father had owned a small grocery store, and the state, after nationalizing the property, permitted the son and his wife to administer it under the auspices of the HO (*Handelsorganisation*, state business organization).

Ute attended the POS in Weimar and participated in after-school activities, especially sports, on the grounds of the local Pioneer House, where the Young Pioneers and older Thälmann Pioneers played after school. Strongly influenced by her father, and with his coaching, Ute's entry into competitive skating began at the tender age of seven, first in roller skating and then in ice skating. Despite the fact that her legs were of unequal length—which necessitated inserting a special right heel to even her leg length, creating an enormous strain on her young body— Ute dominated her rivals. Along with the other skater "prospects" in her school, Ute trained every day, often traveling to special ice rinks in other cities to compete. Skating was a passion that consumed all her free time and won her wide recognition; she became her class's "Sport Representative" in the Thälmann Pioneers and later in the FDJ.

Over the years, Ute watched, enviously, as friends left the POS for *Sportschulen*—potential athletic stars started professional training at different ages, depending upon the state's determination as to when intensive practice and expert coaching was advisable. Gymnasts started in 4th grade, swimmers in 5th grade; ice skaters, whose talents usually matured somewhat later, typically did not enter *Sportschule* until 7th or 8th grade.

Her own career began at the age of 12. At the Thuringia qualifying competition for ice skating, Ute expertly turned a triple Salchow, earning one of the top scores. She and her parents were thrilled when she was invited to attend the major district *Sportschule* in Erfurt, even if it was 60 miles from home. The invitation's language evinced the DDR's determination to endow this honor with the prestige of tradition; in 1981, like a distinguished scholar "called" to a chaired professorship at a leading German university, Ute, along with a dozen other female ice skaters from her region, was "called" or "nominated" to the Max Norgler KJS (*Kinder- und Jugendschule*), a *Sportschule* named after a KPD member and athlete who had died in a Nazi concentration camp.

The Erfurt *Sportschule*, which trained 900 students in 8th to 10th grades for all the major Olympic sports, was essentially an elite boarding school for athletes. Faculty and staff lived "on campus." Regular POS subjects were also taught, but these were secondary; the coaches usually doubled as teachers and considered the former role primary. Each athlete kept a health journal and received a full check-up every month at the health center on the premises—the medical care was the best that the state had to offer. Athletes trained year-round; in the off-season, Ute's group of six skaters ran 15 km per day. Parental visits were limited to an occasional weekend; students could return home for just two weeks in the summer, during which they were also assigned workouts.

The daily regimen was strict:

Six A.M.: Reveille. (Ute still remembers with distaste the shrill female voice "brightly urging us to 'Rise to a new day'!"—which uncannily evokes for me the morning warm-up drill instructress from Orwell's *1984*.)

Six-thirty to nine A.M.: Ice training.

Nine A.M. to one P.M.: School.

Two to six P.M.: Ice training.

Seven to ten P.M.: Study hall.

Ten P.M.: Lights out.

"I soon noticed that academics meant very little," Ute recalls. Every athlete had to belong to the FDJ; "study hall" was often given over to FDJ meetings. Teachers, all of them Party members, would lead discussions devoted to news analysis. Topics included freedom fighting in *Brüderländer* such as Nicaragua, western imperialism in El Salvador, and the American invasion of Grenada.

"Sometimes I felt like disagreeing just because of the arrogant attitudes of some of the discussion leaders," Ute says. "But I never said anything in public—it was pointless to say anything. It would just turn into a headache." Ute judged that it was better just to keep quiet and say little—silence was usually interpreted as agreement, and that would end a meeting sooner. "Besides, nobody really cared all that much about our ideological attitudes. The school cared about sports performances; only the older athletes had to support the state publicly." At 16, Ute couldn't say anything *against* the state, she says. "But I could be more or less indifferent and not get into any trouble at all. That was my father's approach—and my own."

Ute says that western TV was forbidden in the *Sportschule;* social activities were almost nil, limited to a film or a dance every other week in the cafeteria.

"Nobody, as far I recall, ever said, 'I want to watch western TV like other kids,' " Ute says. "I don't remember anybody ever having a western bent at all. Not that anybody ever said that Der Rote Oktober [Red October, a group that specialized in ideological rock] was their favorite group either! Their music was too political. But the Puhdys, Silly, and Pankow—I liked them, and so did many others.

"Nobody ever complained. We all knew why we were there. To become *Hochleistungssportkader* [top performance athletes]. People like Katharina Witt—the 'ice princess'—were national celebrities. We watched them on TV. The coaches knew her; they held up athletes like her as a model. 'Socialism with a beautiful face,' my brother Dieter and his friends called her. We knew what the rewards were. And the coaches and teachers reminded us every week that we were the *Privilegierten*. Even if we didn't always feel like it, we believed that we were the elite."

The peak moment in Ute's athletic career came when she made the semi-finals in her age group in the 1984 German Track and Sport Tournament, the DDR youth Spartakaiad, held every other year in Leipzig. Then came the kind of injury endemic to high-performance athletes. Attending a two-week training camp in Nordhausen with other top athletes, she trained harder than ever and injured her comparatively weak right leg. But her "perspective"—the word used in DDR sports jargon for one's *Sportkader* prospects—was still "good"; her coaches told her to rest. After several weeks, when her condition had still not improved, surgeons operated on her leg. The operation was successful; her hospital physician informed her that she could resume training within two months.

When she returned to the *Sportschule*, she began light training, hobbling around on her cast. But soon Ute's idyll was shattered. One day the head of the ice skating department called her in to see him. Her injury, he said, and her less-than-stellar—though still strong—performances forced him, reluctantly, to an unpleasant decision: she had "no perspective any more"; she would be dropped from her skater group immediately and put in the 10th-grade exit class for six months, after which she would be released. And so, not long after the February 1984 Winter Olympics in Sarajevo, in which the lissome 18-year-old Katharina Witt won her first Olympic gold meal in figure skating, Ute was out.

II

Ute was shattered. At 16, she felt she had "no perspective" anymore in life itself; all that she had worked toward, for almost a decade, had suddenly dissolved.

Why? Ute asked herself again and again. Why?! Just a few months ago, her "perspective" had appeared rosy. Why now?!

She couldn't come up with a good answer.

But her father arrived a few days later with the probable one: Dieter, 20, already in trouble for expressing public criticism of DDR life, had officially joined the Lutheran Church, had been confirmed in the faith, and (as an act of solidarity with several friends jailed on political grounds) had applied last month to emigrate. (Both Lutheran and Catholic dioceses could sponsor a limited number of emigrants from the DDR on religious grounds.)

DDR athletes had to come from families unswervingly loyal to the state and had to be without relatives in the "KA." Ute was being punished for her brother's defiance.

Ute was *orientierungslos* (adrift). Having finished her ten years of required schooling, she thought vaguely of getting a job near her parents in Weissenfels. She also applied, however, to the Friedrich Schiller EOS in Weimar, one of the best—and "Reddest"—schools in the DDR. Under ordinary circumstances, she should have been denied admission to the Schiller EOS because of her brother; but she guesses, in hindsight, that the EOS simply failed to contact the *Sportschule* for her updated records after her brother applied for emigration. So, upon receiving her letter of acceptance for 11th grade, Ute decided to pursue her studies for two more years and gain her *Abitur*, which would improve her job prospects.

It was one of those inexplicable screw-ups so characteristic of bureaucracy—and of totalitarianism generally, where so much was being watched and recorded that accumulation far exceeded the capacity for assimilation and action: the inefficiency of paranoiac hyper-surveillance.

Even now, Ute recalls her first weeks in the EOS with anguish. Not only was she far behind her age group academically and socially, but she was having heart and circulatory problems, the result of the abrupt halt of her training regimen and a too-short tapering-off period in the exit class. Moreover, when she thought of her old athletic acquaintances, most of whose "perspectives" were still bright, Ute felt pangs of envy for what might have been. Her Erfurt group of skaters would, in the next four years, produce a Winter Olympic champion, a World Championship gold medalist, and a runner-up in the European Championships. And Ute had been at their level.

Still, she discovered—in surprise, she says—that her first, main, and enduring feeling was simply one of relief: the pressure to perform was now off; at last she had the freedom of other girls. "And the freedom to smoke a cigarette!" she adds with a satisfied smirk, exhaling a long stream of smoke. Her feeling of *Glück im Unglück* (lucky misfortune) began after the DDR followed the USSR's dictates and refused to travel to Los Angeles for the 1984 Olympics. She recalls how older sports acquaintances, a few of whom were already assured a place on the DDR Olympic team, were devastated by the Soviet-led boycott.

"All that sacrifice, all that training—for what?!" Ute says. "I didn't want that kind of restricted life any more. But it's only in hindsight that I've realized what I missed by going to the *Sportschule*. I didn't have a normal youth at all. I didn't know how to relate to people outside sports, I didn't know how to relate except as a competitor! I never had a boyfriend—I never even had a date!—until I was 17. When I was small, everyone was always saying, 'Your school years will be the most wonderful time of your life.' But, no, that wasn't so for me. I had to catch up in practically everything."

And she grew appalled as she understood better the scope and nature of the DDR drug program for athletes. She says that she herself never took them; DDR ice skaters did not receive hormones until after 10th grade. But she had noticed— without yet fully understanding—the effects of drugs on other athletes at Erfurt.

"Although we ice skaters got only vitamins, I noticed right away that something was terribly wrong with the girl swimmers," Ute recalls. "At 14, they had shoulders as broad and muscular as adult men—and voices just as deep, which was doubtless why the coaches wouldn't allow most of them to give interviews. Before I left Erfurt, one older girl visiting an old teacher told me about how she was taking drugs to delay or advance her periods according to scheduled competitions. Later, I heard that most of the same things were occurring with the ice skaters. One girl even told me that the discus throwers and shot putters were instructed to get pregnant several weeks before an international track meet to increase their weight and strength—and thereby their throwing capacity. And then, of course, as soon as the track meet was over, they got abortions."

Ute falls silent. She stubs out her cigarette. She shakes her head.

"Unimaginable, isn't it? And I never heard—either at Erfurt or afterwards—of any athlete refusing the drugs or other coaching orders," she says. "I'm glad I didn't have to face that. At 16, I wanted to win just as badly as anyone else. According to the swimmers, the coaches told you it was necessary for top performance. Whether it was vitamins or hormones, you took them. You didn't question anything at that age—or even later. The coaches and doctors were prescribing it, the Olympic stars were doing it. They were our mentors and our models."

Complicating Ute's adjustment to a normal life, however, was her concern for Dieter, who had emigrated to West Berlin in late spring 1984, just before Ute left the *Sportschule*. Even though she was no longer in training, the school would not allow her to see him off at the Weimar railway station.

"Suddenly he was gone," Ute says. "I cried for weeks—I had hardly seen him since I was 13—and now, just as I was coming home and starting a new life, I thought I might never see him again."

She and her family did, but only in the face of strong opposition from the state—and even their own relatives. One of her father's cousins was a Leipzig city councilman and a leading regional Party man; he warned them to cut off all contact with "that black sheep" in West Berlin. Another cousin, who taught history in a Dresden college, said the same. Both families broke off all contact with Ute's family.

And only via elaborate subterfuges did she and her parents manage to visit Dieter, stratagems which, as their *Stasi* file would later show, did not go unnoticed by the authorities. As it turned out, they were right to suspect that their incoming mail from the West was periodically read by *Stasi* agents. And even if their business phone was not closely monitored, they, like all DDR callers, had to register to phone West Berlin, and the wait often took a full day.

The conditions were difficult. Dieter could not return to the DDR—nor, of course, could his family visit him in West Berlin. But working through Czech acquaintances, Ute's parents arranged family get-togethers in Karlovy Vary—still known to Germans as Karlsbad of the Sudetenland—a famous Bohemian health spa town of 25,000 in the corner of Czechoslovakia closest to the DDR, about two hours by car from Weissenfels. On the pretense that they were "taking a cure" or visiting friends taking one, many DDR emigrants would rendezvous with their families in this region; the local Czechs specialized in discreet German-German contacts—and turned a tidy profit at it.

"Every spring and fall—and on a few other occasions—we would drive to Karlsbad, or nearby, to meet with Dieter," Ute says. "Our border police were mean—they knew what was going on over there, even if they couldn't get the Czechs to do much about it and didn't know in each case when DDR families were meeting secretly. Police supervision at the border was draconian—I would always sit up front and flirt with them. Sometimes it worked. But sometimes it didn't—and, on those occasions, they would turn the car inside out, often for an hour or two, searching every nook and cranny, even our clothing. And searching for what? Nothing! And remember—we weren't even traveling to the West those times. Our destination was another 'socialist Brotherland.' They knew that they couldn't prevent us from traveling to Czechoslovakia. But they could make it so unpleasant that we'd think twice about going again.

"Then, once we got there, the Czechs milked us good—DM 20 per day just for the rooms. You had to pay DM. My brother always brought the money and paid for all of us. We only stayed two or three days, Friday to Sunday—we didn't want to attract undue attention. My father had to be back to open the store and I had school or work. A few times, though, given his schedule, we could only see my brother on a weekend that conflicted with my round of duty in the FDJ harvest campaign, when my group had to gather potatoes or beets or something. But I skipped it and saw him—though if the FDJ had known why I was absent, there would have been consequences."

A whole new world opened for Ute through her infrequent contacts with her brother. He enlightened her about western music. He spoke authoritatively about western books and dismissed most DDR literature as "Party trash." Although he had once been an excellent athlete himself, he now condemned DDR sports as blatant military education—though he did not defend NATO missiles or western capitalism. Ute had never met anyone who was "against the state" before. For her, Dieter became a rebel hero.

After gaining her *Abitur* from the EOS in 1986, Ute moved with a girlfriend to Leipzig and applied to study to become an ice-skating coach at the renowned German College of Physical Culture, the leading center for sports research in Eastern Europe and the only state university in the world exclusively devoted to physical education and sports medicine. Although she performed excellently on the entrance exams, she was refused admission—even though a fellow EOS applicant with lower scores and no *Sportschule* background was admitted.

"That was it. That time I had no doubt that the reason was my brother," Ute says. "Before that, I was still willing to compromise with the state. That experience was my breakthrough—and the beginning of my break."

III

The combination of the meetings with Dieter and this latest rejection quickly radicalized Ute. At first her rebellion chiefly took aesthetic form. By day, she worked in a "dead-end job" as a waitress near the University; on the weekends and at night she drew stares on the street, and sometimes hostile treatment from Leipzig *Vopos*, for dressing in black with a fiery orange punk haircut: In the DDR of the mid-1980s, such a gesture was understood by everyone as not just a cultural statement, but a protest against the state. That was especially the case in Ute's circle, which included members of a subversive youth group that dubbed itself the *Geschwister Scholl* (Scholl Siblings), named after the dissenting Munich University students, led by a brother and sister later executed by the Nazis.

By 1988, at 20, Ute had decided: She too would emigrate, even though success would mean—as in the case of her brother—never seeing her friends and parents again—except on brief, furtive visits to Czechoslovakia. She planned to expedite her emigration application via the same route that Dieter had taken: she too would cultivate church "sponsorship" to emigrate. But she—like her brother—had no interest in Christianity as a religion; she had never had any contact with it: the *Sportschule* generally prohibited Christians, and few Christians were accepted to the EOS. Although the ideology of M-L hadn't sunk in deeply, atheism had.

As had a pragmatic political sense: Ute saw that the churches had some "free space"—and she realized that they were the way out. So she began attending discussion meetings at the St. Nicholas Church in Leipzig, and also the "Monday Circle" meetings during her visits to Weimar, both of which were devoted to non-religious topics such as disarmament, ecology, and conscientious objection to military service; both of which were attended by many nonbelievers. She expressed an interest in being confirmed in Weimar, as her brother had been.

To Ute's surprise, Dieter discouraged her, convinced that the maneuver wouldn't work a second time. Doubtless the *Stasi* kept some kind of tabs on him; the state, if not the church, would balk this second time around. So Ute decided in late 1988 to pursue a different route to freedom, the only other way out short of going to jail and hoping that you would be *freigekauft* by the West Germans. An old EOS classmate of hers had met and fallen in love with a West German visitor and had been allowed to emigrate; Ute now determined to do the same.

Waitressing at the restaurant, Ute relates with a grin, she would chat up West German visitors who were male and unmarried—she was careful to ascertain their status—and explore whether her "rescuer" was truly "emigration material." The state generally assumed that sudden, grand East German–West German romances were bogus; Ute would have to meet a man willing to court her, write and telephone her often, visit Leipzig regularly, and marry her. The longer and better documented the courtship, the better the odds of state approval for emigration. To leave the DDR by this route, Ute would have to fill out a lengthy questionnaire about the origin and course of their relationship, complete with detailed written proof of its authenticity (love letters, logs of phone calls, etc.). It was an invasive procedure that invited the state into one's innermost private affairs, a bureaucratic nightmare designed to intimidate and to discourage the very thought of emigration. Ute would have to expose everything to the state—which she knew she could do only if the relationship were a theatrical fabrication. Ute was resolved. Belatedly, Dieter offered to find a partner among his West Berlin circle, but Ute declined the favor: She would conduct her "man hunt" herself.

And almost right away, she did meet her "rescuer": Heinz. Indeed the circumstances of the courtship surprised her—and tempered her growing cynicism about life.

Heinz was a *Germanistik* student in Göttingen. He lived just across the border in West Germany and was able to visit every month. She found herself, at the end of their first lengthy conversation, telling him the truth. She didn't want to share her life with him, she just wanted to emigrate.

"He was just so *good*," she recalls. "He said, 'I understand your situation. I just want to help you.' I loved him—and still love him—for that. He said he had met ex-DDR students in Göttingen. He was willing to phone and visit me every month—for years, if it meant that. We never slept together—he did it simply out of human feeling."

At first, Ute says, she held back a great deal from Heinz—even worrying that he might be a spy. But she soon came to think of him as a "second brother." His charity and power of empathy, Ute acknowledges, was one of those "*kleine Heldentaten*" (small heroic acts) that eventually brought down the DDR regime.

As it turned out, the regime fell before the scheme of Ute and Heinz was put to the test. The couple had agreed to "date" at least a year before Ute submitted the emigration application. But before the year elapsed, indeed just as Ute was starting to collect all the materials for the application, candles began to light up the Leipzig night, as thousands of marchers took control of the Leipzig streets. And on October 9, 1989, Ute, along with some acquaintances from St. Nicholas Church with whom she had stayed in touch even after dropping her plans for confirmation, fell in among their ranks.

And then—still an unexpected development just days earlier—the Wall fell.

Ute was free at last. But now that she could visit her brother, and even live in the west, she decided—perhaps paradoxically—to stay put after all. Now that she was free to travel, she didn't need to emigrate. Thousands of East Germans, including many of her friends and coworkers, were now migrating westward and enrolling in overcrowded western German universities. Along with two close friends, however, Ute applied to study *Germanistik* in Leipzig, rented a student apartment, and matriculated in September to the Karl-Marx Universität.

"Maybe it's all been for the best," Ute says. "Now I can read and study any writer I want. If I had gone to university in the DDR days, it would have been so limiting. As a *Germanistik* student, I could have studied German classicism and remained somewhat outside politics, or I could have pursued socialist realism: there was nothing outside or between them."

A long pause. We smile together. The end of Ute's cigarette glows in the twilight. As she starts to speak, a waitress places a small candle stand on our table.

"But it's not entirely a 'Happy End,' " Ute says abruptly, sharply accenting the English phrase. Her lips turn downward. She takes out a single piece of paper and turns it face down. Just this month, her brother—who now lives in eastern Berlin—received his *Stasi* file, which ran to more than 200 pages. She has brought a page of it to show me. Even though her family had always assumed that the *Stasi* kept tabs on Dieter, they'd had no idea of the extent of the surveillance. But now they know. Friends and classmates had spied on Dieter; even the family next door in Weissenfels had reported on her family to the *Stasi*. Ute, of course, is also mentioned frequently in Dieter's file.

"They knew everything about Dieter's life in West Berlin!" Ute says angrily. "Everything! Our 'friends' told them about his whereabouts at every turn! They regarded him as a *Verbindungsmann* (go-between), a poisonous influence infecting the family back home with 'western' values and attitudes."

Ute hands me the page. Peppered with grammatical and spelling errors, it is written in what Ute calls "proper socialist *Deutsch*." The file refers repeatedly to Dieter as "der E." I bend over the page and read silently:

Der E. was in Amsterdam last week with two of his mates. They met up with a couple of other expellees from the *Republik*. . . . Der E. is still working part-time in the [old age] home and at the theater. According to Stück [a cover name], der E. has broken off with Anke and now often spends nights with an actress named Gisela. She is 25, a student at the FU. According to Stück, . . .

Ute takes a deep breath and exhales. "We know who 'Stück' [drama, play] is," she says in an even voice. "A buddy of my brother from school in Weimar, a *ganz labiler Mensch* [quite unstable fellow] who had psychological problems after his release from prison. We've known him for ten years. And he was just one of their informants."

At least 50, possibly up to 100, friends and acquaintances—including members of the church groups in which she and Dieter discussed sensitive political issues—informed on Ute's family over a seven-year period, she says. Some of them are easy to identify: they are listed by name in Dieter's *Stasi* file. Those listed by name were not, technically speaking, *Stasi* informants. They did not sign contracts; they merely reported occasionally to *Stasi* agents and received token payments or favors. Professional informants, i.e., the actual IM—such as 'Stück'—received cover names, signed contracts specifying their services and responsibilities, and were well-compensated. The *Stasi* employed more than 200,000 collaborators, who carried various titles, known (according to status and function) by acronyms such as FIM (the IM supervisors)—and compensated accordingly.

Ute has applied for her own file, which may take months to receive. She has no doubt that it includes reports from her *Sportschule* and EOS classmates and teachers. She talks about the terrible feelings of anger and rage that grip her and her brother, who confided in friends, only to be deceived and betrayed by them.

Can you possibly forgive them? I ask.

"I don't know, I really don't know," Ute says in a low voice. She falls silent. The candle flame dances brightly as a soft breeze sweeps by.

She is lucky compared to some people, Ute says. We talk of *Stasi* victims such as dissident Heinz Eggert, a Lutheran minister spied on by his friends, falsely accused of child molestation, committed to mental asylums, and then pumped with drugs by a trusted doctor to disable his will. Perhaps even more unfortunate was peace activist Vera Wollenberger, imprisoned and then exiled from the DDR, and now a member of the Green Party in the Bundestag, who found out that her own husband had reported on her to the *Stasi* for more than a decade.

"I think I'd kill myself if I discovered something like that," Ute whispers.

And we talk of the newly discovered collaborators, among them leading political and literary figures such as former DDR premier Lothar de Mazière, now retired; Brandenburg Prime Minister Manfred Stolpe, still in office; avant-garde poet Sascha Anderson, now in disgrace; embattled playwright Heiner Müller; and writer Christa Wolf.

The news about Wolf has hit Ute hardest. Wolf, a graduate of Karl-Marx Universität in the 1950s, had been one of Ute's heroines—until January of this year, when Wolf admitted her work as IM "Margarete" during 1959–63 and then exiled herself to sunny Santa Monica as a guest of that wonderful socialist institution, the Getty Foundation.

Ute had defended Wolf against critics until recently, she said. Now Ute feels confused. Her contempt is mingled with pity: the *Stasi* had also spied throughout the 1970s on Wolf and her husband, referring to the couple as "Forked Tongue." Does that even the scale? Ute feels embarrassed for having spoken so passionately about Wolf's integrity, and has trouble even reading her anymore. Having always valued Wolf's "authenticity" (Wolf's signature term) and approached her as a moralist and critic of Party orthodoxy, Ute now finds that knowledge of Wolf's early IM years acts like "a dirty filter that discolors everything I've read by her."

I mention the problem of how to conduct "de-Stasification." Ute sighs. She has no solutions—or even suggestions, she says.

"What good does revenge do?" She can only speak personally, she says. "It's hard to trust, it's hard to believe anymore. Even now, I don't know how many—if any—of the friends with whom I'm still in touch betrayed me."

Ute pauses. She picks up the piece of paper and folds it gently.

" 'The past is not dead; it is not even past.' " Ute is quoting—the sentence, she says, is the first line of *Patterns of Childhood*, Christa Wolf's 1976 novel about her upbringing in Nazi Germany and her agonized struggle to work through it.

"Often I find myself speculating, spinning conspiracy theories out of innocent remarks," Ute says. "Or are they innocent? . . . I try to understand, but. . . ."

Ute's voice trails off. "Take the example of my family's next-door neighbors in Weissenfels. I haven't seen them since we got the *Stasi* file. But my mother, who had been trying to hold it all inside, had an argument with the wife one day last month. She got so mad that she finally told the woman off and called her a 'slimy *Stasi* weasel.' The woman denied it indignantly. My mother went straight upstairs and came back down and showed the woman several pages of Dieter's file that cited her by name. The woman turned white. She and my mother haven't spoken since then. They catch each other's eye on the street occasionally and quickly look away.

"I don't know how I'll react when I see this woman. Her husband drinks, she has no children, she is utterly alone. I think she used to gossip with my mother for hours partly out of loneliness, not just to report to the *Stasi*. I think she wanted attention and recognition. That may be why she was open to the *Stasi*'s overtures. She wasn't a Party member—she wasn't political at all. It was exciting and flattering for her to meet young *Stasi* men, have them taking down her words, and giving her little favors in return."

Ute looks away. The candle on our table flickers faintly in the dark.

"At my best," she says, "that's how I try to imagine it."

Weimar, 1991; Weimar/Röcken, 1994

Zarathustra as Educator?
To the Nietzsche Archives

God is dead.
Nietzsche

Nietzsche is dead.
God [Gott]

Better dead than read.
MarGott [Margot Honecker, DDR Education Minister]
[Graffiti on the western side of the Berlin Wall, 1988]

Signs and wonders. Greetings from the Phoenix.
[Letter from Nietzsche to Peter Gast, 1888]

I

"*Silberblick.*" Bright moment, lucky chance.

A sunny day in Weimar, November 1991. Hedwig, 38, waits solemnly for me in the town square still known as Karl Marx Platz (formerly Adolf Hitler Platz). A spirited, voluble woman, Hedwig has been eager to show me the cultural splendors of her hometown—the Goethehaus, the Schillerhaus, the Liszthaus, all lining the Frauenplan in the center of old Weimar. But today she is reluctant; today, warm morning rays beaming down upon us, Hedwig seems reserved as we stride along the Schillerstrasse toward the outskirts of town. Today our destination is Humboldtstrasse 36, the Villa Silberblick, home of the Nietzsche Archive, which opened in May to the public for the first time since 1945.

Hedwig hands me a May issue of *Die Zeit*. "The Banished One Is Back!" blazons the headline: The reopening of the Archives has been the cultural event of the year in Weimar. As we walk, I muse on the significance of the return to eastern German life of Friedrich Wilhelm Nietzsche (1844–1900): the author of notorious neologisms and catch phrases such as the Will to Power, the *Übermensch* (Superman), the Antichrist, master and slave morality, the blond beast, the free spirit, the last man, eternal recurrence, "God is dead," "Live dangerously!" "Become hard!" "philosophize with a hammer," and "beyond good and evil"; the writer who inspired thinkers such as Heidegger, artists such as Thomas Mann, and men of action such as Mussolini; the philosopher exalted by the Nazis and reviled by the communists.

No discussion of eastern German education "after the Wall"—and the ongoing political re-education of eastern Germans—would be complete without reference to the return of the writer regarded as the most important educator in Germany during the first half of this century. Indeed, *Nietzsche als Erzieher* (*Nietzsche as Educator*) was the title of a popular book in Wilhelmine Germany written by Walter Hammer, a leader of the Wandervögel (birds of passage) youth movement. And as Nietzsche returns to a powerful, reunited Germany, so too do the questions return about the controversial teachings of the author of *Thus Spake Zarathustra*, about his spectacular and worrisome influence on impressionable youth, about his ghastly fate in Wilhelmine and Nazi Germany, and about the lessons to draw from his repression in the DDR.

I am going to the Nietzsche Archive to explore these questions, concerned not only to learn who Nietzsche once represented for Germans but also to discover what he *is* for them once again, especially for eastern Germans. What does Nietzsche as Educator mean to them in the last decade of the twentieth century? And perhaps even more pertinently: Nietzsche as Re-Educator? What might they learn from the example of his history of reception?

Here again, I am approaching education under the broad German rubric of *Bildung*, whereby I seek to address "education" in the schools and universities, but also the process of "re-educating" a people. Just as any serious attempt to understand the "New Germany" struggling into being in post-1989 Europe can scarcely avoid examining the history and legacy of DDR education, so too can any full-scale inquiry into DDR *Bildung* hardly sidestep the issue of Nietzsche's exile and return to eastern Germany. *Ecce Homo* (*Behold the Man*), Nietzsche titled his autobiography—yet that has been impossible in his home state of Saxony since 1945.

II

> We have no way of preventing people from *darkening* us: the time in which we live throws into us what is most time-bound. . . . But we shall do what we have always done: whatever one casts into us, we take down into our depth—for we are deep, we do not forget—*and become bright again*!
>
> Nietzsche,
> *The Joyful Wisdom*

The Villa Silberblick: a stately three-story chateau overlooking Weimar. Here Nietzsche resided, shielded from the public on the second floor, during the last three years of his decade of mental illness. Silberblick literally means "silver view," from which derives the figurative meaning of an auspicious chance. Hedwig points out, however, that "Silberblick" possesses other meanings too. The word pertains to the gleaming residue of silver in the refining process, and in colloquial German, refers to a squint or cross-eye.

Vision, destiny, cosmology, purgation, pathology: Did Nietzsche—the philosopher of "radical perspectivism," the "mad genius" of modern German thought, the peerless aphorist and supreme prose stylist of German letters, the half-blind intellectual seer, the ill-fated posthumous victim of Nazi appropriation—appreciate the resonant irony of this overdetermined name? A previous owner christened the villa; we, if not Nietzsche himself, can appreciate the fitness of the residence's name. For *Amor fati!* (love of fate!) was Nietzsche's clarion call. And Providence has indeed proven no kinder to him in his afterlife than during his life.

Might the reopening of the Nietzsche Archive, however, suggest a turn of fortune? Nietzsche is indeed becoming bright again. Yet, at the same time, the *Heil Hitler!* salutes of young neo-Nazis are also on the ascent. Young *faschos* aren't quoting Nietzsche—yet. No right-wing intellectuals have cited Nietzsche to exculpate skinhead street terror—yet. Still, the militant gospel rhythms of Zarathustra's phrases march through my head: "A good war hallows every cause." "This world is the Will to Power and nothing besides." "What is evil?—Whatever springs from weakness." "Be hard and show no mercy, for evil is man's best force." "There are no facts, only interpretations." "Man is a rope over an abyss." "The oldest and healthiest of instincts: One must want to *have* more in order to *become* more!" "Nothing is true, so everything is permitted!"

It is bracing and incendiary language. In the present climate of political unrest in Germany, and given the availability of a potent arsenal of slogans already battle-certified through a century of ideological warfare, can the remilitarization and neo-Nazification of Nietzsche be far off?

The questions unsettle Hedwig. Yes, for just as The Banished One is now back, so too are the old fanaticisms and the newer warnings; so too is the dithyrambic furor that accompanied Nietzsche's reign as national philosopher in Wilhelmine and Nazi Germany—and the unavoidable fact of his burdensome legacy for Germans. Only recently have citizens of the former DDR begun to grapple with his ambiguous bequest, only since abandoning the pretense that East Germans had resisted Hitler all along, that the task of *Vergangenheitsbewältigung* (overcoming the past) was not their task at all because East Germans had no guilty past to overcome.

For these reasons, the return of Nietzsche means also the return of countless memories that eastern Germans have repressed since 1945. Now that the Nietzsche Archive is open, the question is finally also open as to whether and how eastern Germans will confront their Nazification of Nietzsche. For readmitting Nietzsche to cultural life in eastern Germany means admitting what had always lain behind East Germans' efforts to exorcise him: their reluctance to acknowledge that communist East Germany had also once been Nazi Germany. It means delving into their own secret archives: The newly opened Villa Silberblick is the DDR's intellectual counterpart of the newly opened *Stasi* files.

Might eastern Germans begin to face the past by facing Nietzsche? It will be hard indeed to confront the last century of German intellectual history without addressing him. And it will be impossible to face him by effacing the past: without confronting the gap between what *he* said and what was said *of* him, both before and after 1945, i.e., without seeing him whole, not just gobbling snippets out of context and swallowing the Nazi or SED lines on him.

As neo-Nazi youth once again rule the night in some cities in eastern Germany, the task of *Vergangenheitsbewältigung* has hardly begun. It must begin somewhere, and perhaps the most appropriate, if most painful, place to begin is with Nietzsche and the Villa Silberblick. Here in February 1932, Elisabeth Forster-Nietzsche, the dead philosopher's socially ambitious 86-year-old sister, received a rose bouquet from Hitler during the German premiere of *100 Days*, Mussolini's melodrama of Napoleon's final campaign. Here in July 1934, Hitler and reigning Nazi ideologue Alfred Rosenberg visited Elisabeth and presented her with a wreath for her brother's grave bearing the words "To a Great Fighter." Here in October 1934, on the occasion of the philosopher's 90th birthday—as Hitler posed for a now-famous photograph next to a white marble bust of Nietzsche—the Führer locked eyes with the creator of the Antichrist and received from Elisabeth her beloved Fritz's walking stick (along with a copy of the anti-Semitic petition that her late husband had presented to Bismarck). Here in November 1935, the Führer solemnly placed a wreath on Elisabeth's own grave, as the *Völkischer Beobachter*, the official Nazi organ, eulogized Weimar's grand dowager as "the First Lady of Europe." Here— next door—in April 1936, Albert Speer, Hitler's architect, began work on the Nietzsche Memorial (now a radio station), whose 90-meter high central hall would boast portraits of Hitler and Mussolini and bear the inscription: "From Adolf Hitler, 1938, in the sixth year of the Third Reich."

And near here in 1937/38—a 10-minute ride from the august Villa Silberblick— workmen completed construction of what would become the other "memorial" in the Weimar environs, on Etters Hill at Buchenwald: one of the first concentration camps in Germany.

Yes, all in Weimar. Weimar, the cradle of German culture, birthplace of the Weimar Republic, crematorium of German humanism—by 1930, it was already residence of the first Nazi minister and city council in Germany. "Believe me," wrote Elisabeth to a friend in 1935, "Fritz would be *enchanted* by Hitler."

The reverberations overwhelm. Yes, a trip to the Nietzsche Archive is a journey through modern German history, and it is but a short ride from the Humboldt-strasse to the camp on Etters Hill. Hence the whispered questions on the lips of visitors to the Villa Silberblick:

With Zarathustra Unbound, what repressed energies from the East German past will finally also be released? With the resurrection of the Antichrist, are the droves of disciples soon to follow? Will the philosopher of the Will to Power, the creator of the *Übermensch*, the trailblazer of modernism and postmodernism, soon return to German classrooms? Already Nietzsche is back in eastern German bookstores, but will he become a major presence in the region's intellectual life? Can Nietzsche possibly be discussed and taught without fixating on his history of reception in Wilhelmine and Nazi Germany? And might it not indeed be irresponsible and hazardous to teach his work *apart* from this context? (Even in western Germany, universities—let alone *Gymnasien*—have only recently and sporadically reintroduced Nietzsche into the curriculum.)[1] In short, now that East Germans can finally "behold the man," can they look him—and themselves—in the face?

And what of Nietzsche's critique of education? "I have no higher goal," declared the 29-year-old professor in an 1874 letter, "as somehow to become, in a great sense, an 'educator.' " Eight decades later, young Walter Kaufmann, a refugee from the Nazis soon to become the leading English-language postwar scholar of Nietzsche, could conclude in his landmark *Nietzsche: Philosopher, Psychologist, Antichrist*: "It is above all as an 'educator' that Nietzsche seems to us to confront posterity."[2]

Can one teach Nietzsche without taking seriously his views on education and self-development? "To educate educators!" proclaimed Nietzsche in his *Untimely Meditations*. "But the first ones must educate themselves. And for these I write!" He railed that German education was merely "imported knowledge" and had "nothing to do with Life!"

The last time German intellectuals took Nietzsche seriously, his teachings quickly contributed to the generation of both educational reform and youth movements. By the turn of the century, intellectually minded teachers and *Gymnasium* students were reading and taking positions on Nietzsche's writings, sometimes even as part of class assignments. Nietzsche's hatred of the deadening scholarship of his philological colleagues (*On the Future of Our Educational Institutions*, 1872) and his call to reinvigorate the classical humanistic tradition (*On the Advantage and Disadvantage of History for Life*, 1873) had a major influence on proponents and opponents of the so-called Pedagogical Movement of the Wilhelmine era. Advocates of pedagogical reform sought to separate church and school, promote free thinking, adapt the humanistic *Gymnasium* to the needs of the modern industrial world, and increase German competitiveness in international trade. Pedagogical reformers such as Ellen Key and Ludwig Gurlitt (who was known among educators as "Nietzsche's executor") urged liberal, *völkisch* school reforms designed to transform learning into a creative, democratic activity: the free unfolding of the personality, the attainment of *fröhliche Wissenschaft* (joyful wisdom). Their policy proposals included combining the humanistic *Gymnasium* with the more technically oriented *Realschule*, thereby to confront "history" with "Life" and elevate Germany into the front rank of European powers. Following Nietzsche—who, in addition to his lectures at the University of Basel, had taught six hours in a local Swiss *Gymnasium*[3]—they railed against the intellectual poverty of a Wilhelminian *Gymnasium* that was filled with churchmen and scholars who utterly divorced education from Life; German schooling of the future should abolish arid rationalism and academicism, and thereby prepare Germany for its leading place in the twentieth century. But critics of pedagogical reform such as Gustav Wyneken and the young Walter Benjamin rejected superficial institutional reforms and collectivist schemes, denouncing such proposals claiming "advantages" for "Life" in Nietzsche's name. "Youth for Itself Alone!" was Wyneken's slogan. Nietzsche addressed himself to the single individual and sought to create an international aristocracy of intellect, reform critics insisted, not to turn the humanistic *Gymnasium* into a highbrow finishing school, using a classical curriculum to dress up German provincialism with a little Latin and less Greek.[4]

In the early decades of the century, Nietzsche also influenced the so-called Youth Movement in Germany. "The Prophet of the German Youth Movement," one observer of the 1920s called him.[5] Nietzsche was taken up by the two chief youth associations of Wilhelmine Germany, the Wandervögel and the Freideutsche Jugend (Free German Youth), concrete expressions of the two positions on pedagogical reform: Gurlitt was the first chair of the Wandervögel's advisory council and Wyneken was the leading voice of the Freideutsche Jugend. The Wandervögel promoted *Lebensreform* (life reform), a back-to-nature movement opposed to everything artificial and corrupt in society. In *Nietzsche als Erzieher*, Walter Hammer wrote of Wandervögel boys thrilling to Nietzsche's "summons to the arena of struggle," and how they "stormed forward in the direction that Nietzsche pointed." The Wandervögel movement had "achieved Nietzsche's educational ideals"—which, in Hammer's view, were nationalistic, collectivist, and of pure German origin, and included practicing vegetarianism and abstaining from tobacco and alcohol. By contrast, the Freideutsche Jugend, a more intellectual and cosmopolitan organization, hearkened to Nietzsche's cultural sophistication, his internationalism, and his embodiment of the adventuresome "free spirit."[6] The latter organization considered the romanticism of the Wandervögel escapist and immature; given its intellectual orientation, it ultimately accorded Nietzsche a far more important place than did the Wandervögel. Without question, however, the enthusiasm of Wilhelmine educationists and youth leaders for Nietzsche—especially the reformers' and Freideutsche Jugend image of a nationalist, *völkisch* Nietzsche—helped set the stage for his state institutionalization by the Nazis in the 1930s, through the schools and the Hitler Youth.

All this may seem far in the past—and far removed from the immediate issues confronting young people in the new federal states—but for intellectually minded eastern German youth of today, it is utterly contemporary. For Nietzsche represents not only *the* past but *their* past—in all of its excruciating anguish—and not just since May 1945 but rather since January 1933. "What fails to kill me only makes me stronger": the Ordensburg Vogelsang, training center for Hitler Youth leaders, chose that line from *Thus Spake Zarathustra* as its motto. *Wille und Macht*—an obvious allusion to Nietzsche's *Wille zur Macht* (will to power)—was the title of the main HJ journal. But the Nazis ignored many other aphorisms of Nietzsche, e.g., "The surest way to corrupt a youth is to instruct him to hold in higher esteem those who think alike than those who think differently."

The challenge of coming to terms with Nietzsche isn't eased for Germans by his frequent expressions of contempt for his countrymen. From his self-imposed exile in Switzerland and Italy in the 1880s, Nietzsche showered reprobation on Germany and the Germans. Indeed, Nietzsche claimed (with no strong evidence) descent from Polish nobility—a little point about him that irks Hedwig, since her parents, caught in the wave of vengeance against the Germans that swept Eastern Europe at the war's close, were forcibly expelled by the Poles in 1945 from Silesia, now part of Poland. Declared Nietzsche: "The Teutonic *Deutschland über alles* is the stupidest slogan ever devised in the world." "Every great crime against culture during the last four centuries lies on the conscience of the Germans." "[T]his irresponsible race . . . has on its own conscience all the great disasters of civilization in all decisive moments in history." One shudders to imagine what thundering denunciations he would have rained down on German heads had he lived to witness the cataclysms of 1918 and 1945.

So Nietzsche is part of the long-overdue challenge in eastern Germany of *Vergangenheitsbewältigung*. His very name evokes the overpowering, numbing *shame* of being a German—an emotion long familiar to West Germans, but new to eastern Germans, since (in this rare instance) DDR citizens had welcomed the message their leaders had told them to believe: "We are guiltless of Nazism and the Holocaust." Because travel abroad was severely restricted and resident aliens scarce and near-invisible—the DDR was less than 1 percent non-German—East Germans led a sequestered, provincial life, rarely coming into contact with foreigners who would have punctured the fragile myth.[7] With Nietzsche back, everything that had been buried in the private records of the communist soul has been dusted off, ready for display.

Thus, Nietzsche's reappearance attracts all kinds of interpreters inclined to force timely concerns on him. He reminds eastern Germans of the intellectual and psychological wall between them and westerners, of the superiority and "sophistication" of "western" ideas, of the intellectual backwardness of the DDR's socialist realist fantasies and the naïveté of its Marxist illusions: Nietzsche is part of the eastern German *Nachholbedarf*. Indeed, no person, with the single exception of Marx, has had such a powerful impact on the minds of western *and* eastern Germany as Nietzsche. And no other individual, including Marx, is so controversial and so variously understood—and misunderstood. While events in Europe since 1989 have rendered Marx hopelessly out of date for most Germans, Nietzsche remains contemporary—or even "post-contemporary," as the current phrase has it.

Today, eastern Germans suddenly find themselves divorced from six decades of ideological banalities traded between the Right and Left, and cast into the brave new post-ideological world that Nietzsche envisioned. Nietzsche's main epistemological claims—that there is no coherent self, no stable identity between word and thing, and no fundamental continuity between temporal events—are central to both modernism and postmodernism, and have launched intellectual movements that have dominated the postwar West, among them phenomenology and existentialism (Martin Heidegger), French psychoanalysis (Jacques Lacan), linguistic philosophy and criticism (Jacques Derrida, Paul de Man), and poststructuralist historiography and cultural criticism (Michel Foucault, Jean Lyotard, Gilles Deleuze, Felix Guattari). Partly because of their repression of Nietzsche, easterners are playing catch-up in the task of understanding the history of ideas in the twentieth century. For unlike Marx, Nietzsche remains a thinker intimately relevant to the present. Indeed, our cultural condition is no more imaginable without him than was that of the nineteenth century. It is not, therefore, simply a case of D-marks über Marx, but of Nietzsche über Marx.

"*Ja, Marx ist* out, *und Nietzsche ist wieder* in!" Hedwig fumes.

In January 1889, the 44-year-old Nietzsche suffered a mental breakdown in Turin, Italy, from which he never recovered, though he lived on 11 years, in a vegetative state during the last 8. Throughout the spring of 1989, West German newspapers were announcing the 100th anniversary of Nietzsche's "intellectual death." Then—suddenly and unforeseen—impulsive Fate intervened, ushering a chaotic rush of events intertwining Germany and Nietzsche yet again: the fall of the Berlin

Wall, the collapse of the DDR, the return of Nietzsche to eastern German headlines, the reopening of the Nietzsche Archive.

1989: *Is* it merely an uncanny coincidence that the year of Nietzsche's outbreak of insanity coincided with Adolf Hitler's birth? And that their converging centennial anniversaries became the moment of the self-immolation of the DDR and of Nietzsche's phoenix-like rise from the ashes of Hitler's bunker? Is it just a quirk of history that the Villa Silberblick, last home of the Good European, reopened as Europe moved closer toward monetary unification? ("What I anticipate—and I see it gathering slowly and hesitatingly—is a United Europe," wrote Nietzsche in *The Genealogy of Morals*.) Finally, more darkly, is it also just an accident that Nietzsche is "in" again, just as the first serious outbreaks of neo-Nazi violence convulse eastern Germany?

"I am and ever will be a misunderstanding among the Germans," wrote Nietzsche in *Ecce Homo*. And in a June 1884 letter to Elisabeth: "I tremble when I think of all those who without justification, without being ready for my ideas, will yet invoke my authority."

"No philosopher is a prophet in his own country," I say to myself, as we turn into the Humboldtstrasse.

Pause.

Then, a whisper: "At least not *twice*."

And now: the "new" Nietzsche: More timely—or untimely?—than ever.

His star brightening once again? His long-awaited, second "lucky chance"?

Perhaps.

III

The injustice that has been done to him can never be repaired.

Camus,
"Nietzsche," *The Rebel*

"Prussian acid!" a friend of mine once called Nietzsche—only half-jokingly. Hedwig chuckles grimly as I explain the pun, with its touch of black comedy. Nietzsche grew up in the Prussian province of Saxony. His father, a Lutheran minister, christened him Friedrich Wilhelm after King Friedrich Wilhelm IV of Prussia, on whose birthday Nietzsche was born. The king went insane a few years later; Nietzsche's father suffered from a brain tumor and died. Nietzsche later dropped his middle name, along with his family's Prussian patriotism and strong Lutheran faith, but he did not escape the forenamed fate.

Amor fati! As we stand outside the Villa Silberblick, Hedwig jests darkly that my long-term scholarly contact with Nietzsche could lead to an end similar to Nietzsche's own. Nietzsche as spiritual cyanide? Is this visit my own "Prussian acid test"? Hedwig chides me for my keen interest in the philosopher. A German teacher in an eastern Berlin *Gymnasium* and an intense admirer of German classicism, she is less than enthusiastic about the reopening of the Nietzsche Archive. No, as happy as she is to introduce me to Weimar, the Villa Silberblick is not high on her sightseeing list. Why don't I go back for another visit to the Goethehaus?

Or visit the Schillerhaus or Liszthaus again, *um Gottes Willen*! Unlike her older brother, who has joined a Nietzsche reading group, Hedwig has no intention of joining the Nietzsche parade. No, she would prefer to spend her Weimar visit around the Frauenplan, where the Goethehaus and Schillerhaus lie within sight of each other.

"What *do* you see in him?!" she asks in exasperation.

I want to answer by unshrouding the Nietzsche whose prose soars and singes and sings, the Nietzsche who summons the seeker to "become who you are," the Nietzsche who transports his reader to exhilarating intellectual adventures through the superhuman energy of his formulations and the limpid clarity of his voice—the very same Nietzsche whose vitalistic *Lebensphilosophie* (life philosophy) inspired generations before 1933. Mine is the existential Nietzsche of "joyful wisdom"—and doubtless also the foreigner's Nietzsche: a figure little-stained by association with his more questionable German admirers.

But no, it does no good to tell Hedwig what she has already heard from countless other Nietzsche "apologists": that the Nazis blatantly distorted him for their own ends; that he is regarded in the West as the most significant philosopher of the last century, equal in importance to Kant and Hegel; that his chief influence was anti-authoritarian until the 1930s, exerted not only on liberal educators but also on progressive movements including feminists, anarchists, and SPD dissidents; that most German nationalists and militarists, especially the jingoistic Pan-German League, were wary of Nietzsche before World War I and dismissed him as a nihilist, immoralist, and friend of the Jews. . . . No, before I can formulate an answer, Hedwig adds—with some nostalgia—that, until 1990, scholars needed a *Giftschein* (poison certificate) to gain admittance to the Archive. One man's pleasure is, quite evidently, another woman's poison.

"And now it's becoming fashionable to read him again!" Hedwig sniffs disapprovingly. Nietzsche is "the newest intellectual fad!" Despite her rejection of so much DDR propaganda, Hedwig obviously lays the sins of the sons and daughters at Nietzsche's feet, granting the validity of the Nazi and SED claims that Nietzsche was Hitler's spiritual father. Admitting that she has never read Nietzsche, she says she feels no temptation to take up any bad habits.

Why does Hedwig insist on keeping Nietzsche a closed book? Her parents were both NSDAP members, she says; her older brother joined the SED. She herself wanted nothing to do with political parties or ideologies. Of course, this was a dangerous attitude in the DDR, where it was somewhat uncommon, at least in East Berlin, to teach German in a respected POS without SED membership. And even more uncommon to gain admission to a DDR Ph.D. program in *Germanistik*. Hedwig's Ph.D. thesis dealt with the influence of the 1848 revolution on the work of pianist and composer Franz Liszt (1811–66) in Weimar; her special expertise in music and German literature won her a position in a Berlin school.

I mention that Nietzsche is now being widely taught in eastern German classes in Ethics, especially for his "God is dead" theology. But to Hedwig, "Nietzsche" is an expletive to be deleted. She calls him a "degenerate"; since reunification, she says, many Weimar residents equate his name with the outbreaks of neo-Nazism, hatred of foreigners, German jingoism, and juvenile delinquency.

Hedwig's intransigence sets me back. It is hard for me to accept her formidable block against Nietzsche. In America today, Nietzsche is associated with popular culture, with alternative lifestyles, and with campus debates on political correctness and multiculturalism. Can this be the same Nietzsche whom Arnold Schwarzenegger—our cyborg *Übermensch*, our incarnation of the Will to Power—quotes ("What doesn't kill me only makes me stronger!") in the opening frames of *Conan the Barbarian*? The same Nietzsche whom Allan Bloom blames in *Closing of the American Mind* for student leftist dandyism and the trendy "lifestyle" revolution on campus—for casual sex, rock music, and the blurring of sex roles? The same Nietzsche whom my Texas undergraduates, exhilarated by his philosophy of "perspectivism," cite to defend their preference to "do your own thing"? The same Nietzsche whose face a colleague of mine spotted at a recent academic conference, printed on a T-shirt worn by a woman with purple hair in a punk haircut, under which ran the immortal line: "Nietzsche Is Peachy"?

No, that is not the Nietzsche whom Hedwig knows. She takes Nietzsche seriously. To Hedwig, "Nietzsche" means Brownshirts, not T-shirts.

Can Nietzsche be fully "denazified" in eastern Germany, to become again a philosopher free from the taint of association with fascism?[8] Or is there, for eastern Germans, too much in Nietzsche "that repels, too much 'Hitler,' "[9] too much latent Nazism and manifest war rhetoric for any full rehabilitation to be possible, for any reference untrammeled by a slight twinge, any admiration to go untinged by a touch of shame?

History sometimes entwines figures in a strange and unpredictable tradition. Whereas Germans once could hardly avoid hearing the Nietzsche in Hitler, eastern Germans today can hardly avoid hearing the Hitler in Nietzsche. Indeed, after 12 years of pro-Nietzsche Nazi propaganda and 45 years of anti-Nietzsche communist propaganda, Nietzsche's Nazi connection is firm in many eastern German minds: The associations with Hitlerism have raised to an almost insurmountable degree eastern Germans' perception of the "degenerate" in Nietzsche's work—and adulterated the pure, majestic voice that continues to move most non-Germans who encounter it.

Hedwig's indignation reminds me of my correspondence years earlier with West German scholars. Few letters surprised me more during my student days than to receive word that, even in the late 1970s, Nietzsche's work was still too controversial to be taught in *West* Germany's curricula. I knew that Nietzsche was persona non grata under the communists, but I had no idea that he was still unofficially taboo in the *Bundesrepublik*. This occurred at a time when he was all the rage in Paris and in the American academy, when he was being taken up by literary critics, psychoanalysts, linguists, anthropologists, and postmodern philosophers.

"If you want to study Nietzsche," a prominent West German scholar in *Germanistik* at the University of Konstanz wrote me, "by all means stay right where you are. Don't leave the U.S. That's where the Nietzsche scholars are." There seemed to be a note of admonition—and perhaps even pride—in his tone; as if to imply that he indeed hoped that I and my Nietzsche scholars *remained* on this side of the Atlantic.[10]

As Hedwig and I overtake two well-dressed, elderly ladies to enter the Archive, Hedwig lowers her voice and turns fully toward me. She repeats her verdict on Nietzsche: "*Ja, Marx ist* out, *Nietzsche ist wieder* in!"

As if to say: "*Now then*—are you satisfied?"

IV

The Villa Silberblick is an impressive building. Built in the mid-1800s, it was acquired in 1896 by a Swiss aristocrat as a refuge for Nietzsche and a repository for his papers. It was refurbished according to Elisabeth Forster-Nietzsche's specifications by Belgian architect Henry van der Velde, one of the leaders of the turn-of-the-century *Jugendstil* architecture movement. *Jugendstil* exhibited a high degree of craftsmanship, the use of organic forms, and a decidedly bourgeois sensibility, all of which van der Velde stressed in his redesign of the Nietzsche Archive.

The finished look, however, is one of classical, indeed Attic, elegance. Etched in brownstone is the family name, which rests above intricately carved, solid oak doors and contrasts with the red-brick and white-stone exterior; bronze doorknobs bear the letter "N." A similar restraint prevails inside, where stained glass windows bathe the public rooms in resplendent light. Particularly beautiful is the library, which exudes refinement and grace. A large golden "N" inscribed on the wall overlooks a green-tiled fireplace, sinuous couches in strawberry upholstery, built-in bookshelves, a grand piano, and glass cases full of Nietzscheana. Within this setting, the mammoth white marble bust of the Master is all-the-more commanding. Commissioned from the sculptor Hans Klinger, it rests atop a six-foot pedestal between the rear windows, contemplating the scene with Olympian disinterestedness.

What a spectacle! And all of it, ironically, conceived as a tribute to the simple life of the ascetic philosopher. Completed in 1904, the price tag was RM 50,000—at least a million dollars today—all of which Elisabeth had to beg and borrow. But she held that her brother (who would not live to see the renovations) had suffered a miserable nomadic existence before his breakdown and so deserved, despite his obliviousness to his surroundings, all the comfort that money could buy. A perhaps more telling reason for all the finery, however, was that Elisabeth's own tastes ran toward the luxurious. "Forster" means forest ranger; in later years Elisabeth's pretensions—which extended to riding through the streets with liveried coachmen—earned her the mocking sobriquet among Weimar residents of "Frau *Oberforster*" (head or senior forest ranger).

Even though eastern German intellectuals are finally taking notice of Nietzsche—and many visitors mill about the Villa Silberblick on this Sunday afternoon—no curator or even guide yet works in the Nietzsche Archive. Due to tight funds and a lack of trained personnel, the Archive has still to be assigned an official guide.

An old gentleman who lives in the Humboldtstrasse, a few doors down from the Archive, collects the admission price. Now in his 80s, Heinz Koch sits with a little cardboard box filled with change. A few strands of thin white hair, distributed equidistantly in matted rows, stripe his bald head. Herr Koch beams as he accepts my DM 5, his eyes dancing brightly beneath thick bushy white eyebrows, unconcerned that two of his front teeth are missing.

Hedwig drifts away, leaving Herr Koch and me to chat, and I ask him about the Nietzsche "renaissance." No more than a few thousand people have visited the Archive since May—far less than the Goethehaus admits in a single month, he says. I remark that it seems difficult to find Weimar residents who know very much about Nietzsche at all, that the Weimar *Gymnasium* schoolchildren shrugged their shoulders when I mentioned his name. Herr Koch nods. Hedwig, listening nearby, nods too—with seeming approval. "But my generation knows all about him and his family," Herr Koch adds.

Has he read Nietzsche? I ask. Yes, a wartime edition of *Thus Spake Zarathustra* as a soldier, and a popular anthology of Nietzsche's work before the war. No, not since then; do I not know? "To have mentioned his name, let alone praised him, would have raised suspicions of Nazi sympathies."

The stigma endures. Herr Koch leads me to a museum table to show me the last SED-supervised edition of the official Weimar picture guide (1990).[11] The expensively produced book features full-page color photographs and detailed descriptions of the galaxy of intellectual luminaries who once lived and worked in this almost-classical city-state of 63,000 residents.

Weimar. "The city of immortal fame," in Thomas Mann's phrase. In the late eighteenth century, under the benevolent patronage of Prince Karl August, Weimar became the residence of Germany's greatest literary figures: Goethe, Schiller, Herder, and Wieland. Featured in the picture book are numerous pictures of Johann Wolfgang von Goethe (1749–1832) and Friedrich von Schiller (1759–1805), their statues shoulder to shoulder in front of the German National Theater; the philosopher and poet Johann Gottfried von Herder (1744–1803); and the poet and novelist Christoph Martin Wieland (1713–1813). Also depicted are the painter and graphic artist Lucas Cranach the Elder (1472–1553), whose house is on the market square; the young Johann Sebastian Bach (1685–1750), Weimar chapel organist and court composer for nine years; Franz Liszt, the luminary of mid-nineteenth-century Weimar; Henry van der Velde (1856–1924); and Walter Gropius (1896–1957), leader of the *Bauhaus* school, a movement of functionalist architects in the 1920s.

Not a single mention or glimpse of Nietzsche.

Herr Koch points to a quotation from the East German novelist Anna Seghers, which opens the picture book: "The best and worst places of German history are here." Seghers didn't need to elaborate: Yes, it is a short ride from the kingdom of Art to the kingdom of Death. To the tune of Beethoven's "Ode to Joy," Aryan guards at Buchenwald marched their prisoners through the camp gatehouse, with its mind-numbing motto in cast iron letters: "To Each His Own." Bathed in Goethe's hymns to the Etters landscape, the camp commandant calculated the human, all too human, body count: 56,545.

Each year the SED had sponsored elaborate ceremonies on the anniversary of the liberation of Buchenwald: April 11, 1945. The ceremonies were designed to underline the regime's legitimacy by propagating an officially ordained "anti-fascism" that made "monopoly capitalism" in general and West Germany in particular responsible for Nazism and its crimes, thus exonerating East Germans of historic responsibility for what happened. The official rhetoric almost made it appear that wartime eastern Germany had been an occupied country with an heroic communist underground resistance movement—centered partly in Buchenwald itself, where Ernst Thälmann was executed.

But in 1990 mass graves were unearthed that contained the remains of the inmates of a Soviet concentration camp operating on Etters Hill during 1945–50. The inmates included not only suspected Nazi militants but also Social Democrats and other liberal opponents of the SED. Whispered rumors about these camps had seeped out for decades; publicized by the western Allies, the allegations were dismissed by the SED as anti-socialist propaganda. Rediscovery of the camps in the dying days of the DDR triggered a gruesome debate among East Germans about the comparative evils of the Holocaust and the Gulag: Which was worse, Buchenwald under the Nazis or under the Stalinists?

Herr Koch blurts out the question, then immediately retracts it with a shake of his head and a nervous laugh. The question overleaps the realm of the imaginable. He closes the picture book; he looks away.

"That question didn't exist last year," says Herr Koch, turning to look at me squarely. "No more than did the Gulag. In the DDR, Stalin's crimes never happened. They hardly existed, except as half-believed, half-denied rumor and folklore. Nobody knew about them—at least not officially—and that which people knew unofficially was seldom mentioned. *Nein*, nobody knew about them—nor about Nietzsche either."

"Why was Nietzsche the only one banned by the SED?" I ask. I hear myself racing on: Hadn't Schiller and Wagner also been glorified and rewritten by the Nazis? Schiller was proclaimed the Führer's "companion in arms." Wagner's *Die Meistersänger* was Hitler's favorite opera; the posthumous Wagner was court composer to the Third Reich. So why were Schiller and Wagner subsequently accepted, even honored, in the workers' paradise? Goethe and Beethoven had been similarly transformed by the Nazis into Teutonic geniuses, but the SED embraced them as socialist forerunners, or at least as democrats—Goethe's face graced the DDR's near-worthless bank notes; Beethoven's symphonies resounded throughout DDR concert halls. And what about all the others? The poet and monarchist Heinrich Heine had lashed out at communism—he was forgiven; his cordial personal acquaintance with the young Marx was recast as sympathy for revolutionary socialism. Even Hofmannstahl and Rilke, even Freud—even accommodators to or admirers of fascism like Gerhart Hauptmann, Stefan George, and Gottfried Benn!— were eventually admitted, however warily, into socialist intellectual society. Their explicit anti-socialism, their aestheticism and elitism, their outright contempt for the worker, were all explained away as symptoms of bourgeois protest or alienation within the capitalist order.

Was the stretch too great in Nietzsche's case? Was the posthumous Nietzsche so utterly enmeshed with Hitlerism that he could not be disentangled and repoliticized? Couldn't he too have proven ideologically malleable? Or is his language so provocative and his outlook so advanced that SED ideologues sensed that they had no choice but to ban him, that efforts to chastise his philosophy as the product of a decaying 19th-century imperialism, let alone attempts to convert him for the Left, could only fail?

Herr Koch nods again and points a gnarled finger toward a folder of clippings that the Archive has collected. He stops at a 1985 article from the respected *Frankfurter Rundschau* by Gerhard Zwerenz, a student and colleague of Ernst Bloch who had supported Wolfgang Harich's SED reform proposals in 1956—and fled Ulbricht's Reich in 1957:

> If Nietzsche had lived [in the 1930s], he would have been a Nazi party member, something like an intellectual version of [Alfred] Rosenberg. Perhaps he would have been shot with Ernst Röhm in 1934. . . . To take Nietzsche seriously is to resemble Hitler, who took Nietzsche seriously, albeit in the most naïve fashion: he styled himself an *Übermensch*. Many Germans followed him and did the same. Taking a thinker seriously is serious business: Lenin took Marx seriously, just as Hitler took Nietzsche seriously. Thousands of know-it-alls can rise up and criticize the logical errors involved in this kind of "seriousness": but the Lenins and Hitlers have history and reality on their side. Marx discovered the class struggle, out of which Stalin built the Gulag. Nietzsche preached the revaluation of all values, which led to Hitler and ultimately to the Holocaust. . . . Just as Marx led to Lenin and Stalin, Nietzsche led to Hitler.[12]

"*Marx ist* out, *Nietzsche ist wieder* in." Hedwig's words ring in my ears. I quote them to Herr Koch. Wordlessly, he flips to another article, this one from the local newspaper in Nietzsche's hometown of Röcken. Until 1990 the welcome sign on the village's outskirts had read: "Workers and farmers in socialist agriculture! Go forward to great achievements in the stalls and in the fields!" Today the sign reads: "Welcome to Röcken, home of the birthplace of Friedrich Nietzsche!"

Herr Koch cackles. His laugh is infectious; we grin at each other: the new welcome sign typifies the repainting of East German history since 1989. Such revisions are especially easy in Nietzsche's case, says Herr Koch, because even most Saxons don't know much about the man. Since 1945, even in his home state, Nietzsche had been an unperson without a country.

V

I know of no purpose better than being destroyed by what is great and impossible.

Nietzsche, *On the Advantage and
Disadvantage of History for Life*

"I am not a man," Nietzsche had written in *Ecce Homo*, "I am dynamite." As Germany lay in rubble in 1945, that prophecy too seemed fulfilled. At Nuremberg, the sins of the sister were lain at his feet; Nietzsche was, as it were, tried along with the leading Nazis—and found guilty. "The morality of immorality," one judge pronounced, "the result of Nietzsche's purest teaching. . . ."[13]

Soviet authorities in Weimar decided to encase and stash the dynamite, placing the Nietzsche Archive high on their blacklist as a center of Nazi propaganda. Major Oehler, its custodian, was arrested. He fell sick, was confined by the Soviet occupying army to a basement in a house near the Nietzsche Archive, and starved to death in the winter of 1945. For years Elisabeth's personal papers, correspondence, and diaries remained locked up in the newly organized complex of the National Research Center for Classical German Literature in Weimar, founded in 1953.[14] The Archive itself was turned into a guest house for visiting dignitaries and scholars. The Nazis had wanted to emphasize the similarities between Nietzsche and Hitler—and so too did the SED. It served both sides' purposes to do so.

Although Max Horkheimer of the Frankfurt School had attempted in the 1930s to bring Nietzsche into the fold of Critical Theory as a maverick leftist, his arguments never found favor on the Left. In the early 1950s, leading East European Marxist intellectuals united in their contempt for Nietzsche. Ernst Bloch pronounced Nietzsche "usable only for fascism." Georg Lukács said that Nietzsche was "the sworn enemy of the working class," the chief destroyer of reason, and the trailblazer for National Socialism. He would have "regarded Hitler and Himmler, Goebbels and Goering as moral and spiritual allies." Hitler was merely "the executor of Nietzsche's testament."[15] In 1956, Nietzsche's papers were finally made available to DDR and western scholars; but Lukács' verdict was in effect the nail in the coffin. In the official DDR publication, *German Literary History* (1974), Nietzsche is merely mentioned and dismissed as a "militant reactionary." In the SED's official 909-page history of Weimar (1976), Nietzsche earns a single paragraph, which condemns his "anti-humanistic, utterly individualistic, and irrationalist" teachings.[16] Like the Nazis, the communists took Zarathustra seriously: "Whatever falls—it should be kicked too!"

Nietzsche's works were not to be found in bookstores or in antiquaries. Instead they were relegated to the *Giftschränke* of libraries, where researchers were required to obtain an IG pass (*Internen Gebrauch*, for internal [scholarly] use only) to read him. Nietzsche entries in library card catalogues bore special stamps, either "Proof of purpose required" or "Limited borrowing." The books themselves—as in the case of George Orwell, Arthur Koestler, and other authors on the DDR "Index"—came affixed with a red circle: the mark of the censor's eye. Even his name vanished from East German periodicals; at most, liberal scholars might slip it past the censors in an essay on Schopenhauer or Thomas Mann. "Whoever thinks, above all whoever thinks a great deal, will never be a Party man," wrote Nietzsche in his *Untimely Meditations*. "He will think past and through the Party." Yet the strict SED party line on Nietzsche stayed firm for decades; no prominent SED intellectual thought past it.

In the early 1980s, however, DDR intellectuals began to broach tentative reconsiderations of Nietzsche. The unexpected breakthrough came in 1986 in the intellectual journal *Sinn und Form*, the flagship journal of the Academy of the Fine Arts, when Heinz Pepperle, a liberal professor of Historical Materialism at Humboldt University, drew a sympathetic portrait of Nietzsche that triggered the last major cultural debate in the DDR before the fall of the Berlin Wall. The argument resembled the public debate that would grip West Germany in 1987 about Martin

Heidegger, set off by the appearance of a biography by a former student, Victor Farias.

But the DDR Nietzsche debate never reached the wider public.[17] Fought in scholarly journals and conferences, it never made the review pages and letter columns of newspapers. That was not, however, due to public apathy. On the contrary: The SED judged that the Nietzsche dynamite was so explosive that the debate about him would have to be controlled and contained.

Pepperle's essay had urged no wholesale rehabilitation of Nietzsche. Indeed his proposals were mild—which suggests how controversial Nietzsche remained in the DDR, to the very end. Rather, Pepperle called Nietzsche "a philosopher of significance" and "an unquestionably honest character," who wrote "in an expressive, compelling language" and offered "a sharp critique of dying bourgeois culture." But Nietzsche was finally "an ideologue of his class" whose alienation under capitalism had provoked his outbreak of "irrationalism," said Pepperle. Nietzsche represented a symptom of the torturous transition from capitalism to imperialism in late 19th-century Europe. A familiar line.[18]

But even this stock approach to non-socialist thinkers was too much for SED ideologues such as Wolfgang Harich. Harich had emerged from prison in 1964 both a hard-line Stalinist and a vociferous critic of all modernist (and, soon, postmodernist) experimentation—an ideological and aesthetic orientation that turned Nietzsche into the quintessence of all he opposed. Harich pulled no punches: Nietzsche was a "Nazi worshiper," insisted Harich. His work "smells of Zyklon B," the poisonous gas used in the Nazi concentration camps. "He was a passionate war hawk and potential defender of Himmler. . . . A society can hardly sink lower than when it adopts Nietzsche as part of its general education. It should be one of the basic principles of intellectual hygiene that we ban all quoting of Nietzsche." Nietzsche was an "arch-reactionary," "inhuman through and through." The list of his crimes was long: master-race theorist, pre-fascist, misogynist, racist, anti-Semite, warmonger. Pepperle's interest in Nietzsche, said Harich, stemmed from a weakness for "western fashions." Harich wouldn't even let Nietzsche get away with a collapse into madness. Nietzsche "only pretended" to go mad, when it became evident to him that he was incapable of writing a systematic work of philosophy, said Harich. He escaped his failure by feigning mental illness: that was his only way out. He couldn't write a great work—just collections of aphorisms—and so he finally gave up. Nietzsche's legacy, Harich concluded, was "a giant trash bin." The prosecution closed by calling for the same sentence upon Nietzsche that Brecht delivered against the epicurean Roman general Lucullus in *The Trial of Lucullus*: "Into the abyss with him!"[19]

Not everyone agreed with Harich's formulation, but Party intellectuals toed the line. The word came down: "Better dead than read."

That line of graffiti—in English—on the western side of the Berlin Wall in 1988 sums up not only the finale of the DDR Nietzsche debate, but also Nietzsche's entire history of reception in the DDR. At the Tenth Writers' Congress of the SED in 1987, the verdict on Nietzsche became official, as representatives of the SED writers' organizations and of every relevant academic field entered the fray. Several young intellectuals demurred, and Stephan Hermlin, then president of the

DDR Writers' Congress, praised Nietzsche as "one of the most stimulating writers of the last hundred years" and worried about Harich's "reactionary retrogression." But most of the old guard held firm. Manfred Buhr, then Director of the Central Institute of Philosophy in East Berlin and known in the DDR as "the philosophy pope," concerned himself not with Nietzsche but with "the phenomenon of Nietzsche." Buhr argued that pro-fascist writers could never belong to the cultural inheritance of the anti-fascist DDR. "Serious" scholars could read "questionable" authors like Nietzsche in restricted sections of the library. But there would never be a DDR Nietzsche edition, let alone a DDR revaluation of Nietzsche.[20]

As late as 1987 that papal bull ex cathedra would have been the final word. But a series of factors converged in 1988 to thwart the SED inquisition and keep Nietzsche's name in the pages of DDR journals: the infiltration of postmodernism, the popularity of Nietzsche with Italian communists (Giorgi Colli and Mazzino Montinari had undertaken their Nietzsche edition with the Italian CP's enthusiastic support),[21] and the bicentennial of Schopenhauer's birth (another conservative, latterly rehabilitated German philosopher, who had exerted profound influence on Nietzsche). The old socialist realist arguments against Nietzsche sounded ever more lame. It was pointless, said some scholars, to ban Nietzsche as a "destroyer of reason" when postmodernism had thoroughly undermined the Enlightenment anyway.

But "Nietzsche can't be separated from his reception history," insisted Harich. "Whoever addresses Nietzsche addresses the politics of fascism." Harich suggested that "even to edit Nietzsche," as Colli and Montinari had done, branded one an "intellectual criminal."[22]

Seeking to prevent an erosion of Marxist dogma, Harich and Buhr concentrated their attacks upon Nietzsche's fatal influence on fascism. For them, the real issue was whether fascism was philosophically supportable. And because Nietzsche had been effectively used once before to make that claim, and because his work might conceivably lead again to the answer "yes," he was *verboten*. The fear in the DDR was that an edition of Nietzsche might have stimulated a revival of fascism. Instead, the Nietzsche taboo helped lead to the demise of the SED itself and to a revival of western capitalism.[23]

In hindsight, this vain, last-ditch attempt to save Nietzsche by liberals like Pepperle mirrored the scattered SED attempts before 1989 to save the DDR itself from self-detonating. The alternating mood between hesitant expectancy and harsh dismissal toward a Nietzsche rehabilitation disclosed the hopelessly closed-minded character of DDR cultural life. Although no one, of course, could have predicted it at the time, the closing round in the Nietzsche debate was the highbrow tremor of 1988 before the national earthquake of 1989.

"Who's Afraid of Friedrich Nietzsche?" headlined a West German review of a Darmstadt conference on Nietzsche in 1988 sponsored by the West German Communist Party. The headline referred to the suppression of Nietzsche's work by West German and DDR communists. The SED's Nietzsche debate, said critical West German intellectuals, was a debate about censorship, recalling the censorship debates over Heiner Müller's plays, Thomas Mann's essays (including his 1947 essay, "Nietzsche in Our Time"), Heinrich Mann's fiction, and the work of numerous other German and non-German writers, past and present. "The point isn't whether Nietzsche is an important writer or a 'phenomenon,' " declared one reviewer of the conference, "but when, finally, the SED will stop setting up ideological boundaries and walls, when it will stop policing freedom of expression and criminalizing certain books as 'forbidden literature.' "

The events of autumn 1989 provided the answer. Until the fall of the Berlin Wall, Nietzsche remained in the abyss, an unperson. Harich had even suggested that the Goethe-Schiller Archive sell Nietzsche's papers to the West and raze his grave in his village birthplace, Röcken in Saxony-Anhalt.

VI

"Blessed are the forgetful," wrote Nietzsche in *Beyond Good and Evil*, "for they get the better even of their blunders."

In the newest New Germany of the early 1990s, as the crimes of violence against foreigners and Jews uneasily evoked the political climate of the 1930s, that statement of the once and perhaps future philosopher-king of Germany also provoked worry, especially in the east. For the former East Germany sits at the crossroads of the two great failed experiments of the century, forever captured in the image of Buchenwald: Nazism and Stalinism—experiments allegedly fathered by the two great German minds of the nineteenth century, Nietzsche and Marx. Among Germany's fearful neighbors, the consensus has long been that Wagner, Nietzsche, and Hitler stand in the same relationship to one another as Marx, Engels, and Lenin. East German intellectuals shoulder the almost unimaginable twin burdens of both Nazism and Marxism-Leninism (or Stalinism). Indeed, that Nietzsche and Marx— the men whose work inspired 57 years of totalitarian rule in eastern Germany— conducted their advanced Ph.D. studies at eastern universities (Leipzig and Jena respectively), was an historical fact very tempting for ideologically orthodox eastern Germans to forget.

"If only Marx had come from East Germany and Nietzsche from West Germany," Weimar wags will tell you, "the DDR propaganda program would have been so much easier!" That Marx was born in Trier and not, say, in Karl-Marx Stadt (now, once again, called Chemnitz), that Nietzsche was born in Röcken and not, say, in Bonn—complicated the SED's exclusive claim to Marx and impassioned disclaimer of Nietzsche.

Is it Marx or Nietzsche? Leading German socialist intellectuals—Mehring, Lukács, Hans Günther, Johannes Becher, even DDR President Grotewohl—voiced that position. All of them took harsh, public stands against Nietzsche. For socialists, they said, the choice was clear: Marx or Nietzsche. You could not have both. Even though Nietzsche the Good European, the "gentle" Nietzsche, resembled the young, "humanistic" Marx of the 1844 *Economic and Philosophical Manuscripts* in his call for an end to nationalism and the birth of world citizenship, SED leaders portrayed the two as rival prophets of the Right and Left. Nietzsche and Marx never met, nor did they ever say anything specifically about each other. That gave the SED a free interpretive hand. According to the SED, Marx and Nietzsche created the ideological alternatives of our century via their contrary utopian visions of a workers' paradise and an aristocracy of Supermen.[24] So, East Germany was East Germany, and West Germany was West Germany—and never the twain would meet. You must choose, and you must never forget the implications of your choice.

The DDR could never admit that, before the Stalinist era, German and even Russian leftists (Max Gorky, Lenin's Minister of Culture Anatoly Lunacharsky) had admired Nietzsche as a thinker of the Left. Or that, at least since the 1960s, Nietzsche had been known throughout the West as a pioneer of Green politics, the counterculture, and alternative thinking.[25] Nietzsche—or a Nietzschean neo-Marxism—had replaced Marxism-Leninism in the left-wing pantheon. Western leftists had realized that Nietzsche's revolt against liberal democracy was far more radical than Marx's, who remained within the rationalist, metaphysical tradition. Thus skeptical Marxists, contemptuous of all large-scale conventional politics, wound up derationalizing Marx into an anarchistic neo-Marxist or aestheticized post-Marxist, and converting Nietzsche into a leftist. By the late 1980s, the SED was fighting internal skirmishes while the real war had long ago moved on to a different intellectual front.

Today, Marx *or* Nietzsche no longer appear mutually exclusive alternatives in eastern Germany. And yet, one must admit that it does seem, uncannily, as if their fortunes in Germany rise and fall in opposite directions: Whenever one swoops, the other soars. And now, since 1989, it is again Nietzsche's turn to take wing.

Indeed, Nietzsche *is* a phenomenon—though not quite in the way that SED intellectuals like Manfred Buhr once imagined. He represents the "phenomenon" of Germans'—especially eastern Germans'—ambivalent relation to their fate and their heritage. Nietzsche forces the question: What does it mean to be German— or to have been "East German"? In the former DDR, Nietzsche was a man without a country—but the DDR was a land without a history.

Nietzsche devoted much of his work to the problem of memory and forgetting. What ought we remember? What should we forget? The burden of the past, the danger of the future. How does a nation cope?

Accept the past and try to build on it? Simply wave it away, conclude that it doesn't matter?[26] According to Nietzsche, in the modern world the first alternative is no longer possible: "God is dead." The present is thrown into the vertiginous agony and euphoria of an unbridgeable break with the past; history has come to an end. All history has become "antiquarian"—you can't build on it, only observe it like a museum of memorabilia.

Has German history, in Nietzsche's sense, come to an end? Is the Holocaust its unbridgeable break with the past, after which nothing can be rebuilt? If so, that leaves only the second, postmodern alternative: not to let the past matter at all.

It would seem that the "Germany" of today is a story still being told. But is it? Psychologically, "Germany" does not seem to advance beyond the so-called *Stunde Null* (zero hour) of 1945: Germans and their neighbors are forever returning, given the slightest provocation, to the Nazi years and the Holocaust. If "Germany," as it were, "stopped" at zero, if it is "dead," if it can't be revived, if it can't get out from under its own ever-lengthening shadow, if there is no heritage on which to draw—what then? Then the possibility of a truly *new* Germany doesn't exist—and Germans can only rummage through the historical pawn shop, picking and choosing among the relics and discards of their past. As such, Germany is *the* quintessentially postmodern country, a scavenger among personalities and events of the past, none of which serves to build a history, let alone a heritage.

Yes, Nietzsche is a phenomenally problematic figure for Germans, but his name signifies less a *Schreckbild* (vision of horror) than simply that pressure point at which the accumulated anxieties of a people vilified for decades by the entire world have finally converged and concentrated. Nietzsche is merely the most quotable of a long line of extraordinarily ambivalent figures in German history, ranging from Luther and Frederick the Great to Bismarck and Wagner—and even beyond, to Spengler and Heidegger. Like them, Nietzsche signifies the phenomenon of *heritage*—and how one relates to it. And here enter the worries loosed by his example.

For the spiritual health of a nation can only be gained through a judicious modus vivendi with its past. In the 1950s, the DDR developed a new attitude toward German history. Trying to build a socialist society, DDR intellectuals had to *create* a pre-socialist past; they needed ancestors to fit a genealogy leading upward to the DDR itself. That German socialists now had a state of their own compelled a rethinking of the relationship between German socialism and German history. No longer could SED intellectuals find their entire identity in oppositional criticism; they had to create a story of the *German* past, not just the past of German socialism. They had to govern—and educate.

"We push our citizens to read," wrote Anna Seghers in 1961. "We speak of the national heritage [*Erbe*]. But do we guide our people sufficiently? What heritage is available for them to inherit? . . . We still haven't even started to address adequately the issue of *what* past our citizens should read—and how they can relate that past to themselves."[27]

In the 1970s, the SED made a start on that heritage. It constructed a "humanistic" pre-history of socialism. Above all, SED intellectuals distinguished "good" from "bad" bourgeois literature; even though their work suffered from ideological myopia, some pre-socialist or non-socialist—or even anti-socialist—writers were, if only implicitly, now praised as "critics of capitalism." True, capitalism had alienated them and warped their visions; but their very negativism was precisely a reaction against capitalism. They were humanists who could be integrated into the DDR "heritage."

East German scholars promoted the new view via a theoretical distinction in SED historiography between *Geschichte* or *Tradition* (history, tradition), which might be thought of as the whole of the past as it affects, consciously or unconsciously, the present; and *Erbe* (heritage), which is limited to those works and historical developments that helped create and sustain the DDR and socialism. The difference turns on the concept of *Aneignung* (appropriation), which mediates between the two regions of the past and constitutes the act of transforming a passively held tradition into an actively used heritage.

Luther, Frederick the Great, Bismarck, Wagner—and Nietzsche—had always been recognized in the DDR as part of German *history*. The decision in the 1960s and '70s to move the first four into the realm of "heritage"—and still to exclude Nietzsche—was not lightly taken. The DDR conception of heritage was political;

Erbe was a weapon in the continuing struggle with West Germany and the so-called forces of imperialism. The issue came down to which side—West Germany or East Germany?—represented the "real," the "good" Germany. "The DDR is to-day the embodiment of the best traditions in the German heritage," declared Erich Honecker in 1973. "The Farmers' Rebellion of the Middle Ages, the 1848 Revolution, the workers' movement founded by Marx and Engels and Bebel and Lieb-knecht, the heroes of the anti-Nazi resistance."[28] By reclaiming Luther, the SED was choosing to overlook Luther the theologian and defender of princely authority, and to lay claim to Luther the champion of freethinking and the peasant. By admitting Frederick the Great and Bismarck, the DDR was opting to downplay their imperialism, or rather approach it as a necessary and productive stage on the way toward socialism. By embracing Wagner, the DDR was willing to look past Wagner the mature anti-Semite and champion of Bismarckian imperialism, back toward Wagner the youthful supporter of the 1848 revolution.

But the SED could see no advantage in rehabilitating Nietzsche; he remained beyond the pale. "Nietzsche isn't our heritage, the heritage of the working class, the heritage of the anti-fascists," announced one SED intellectual after another. Nietzsche belonged to the *history* of Germany, they insisted, but not to the *heritage* of East Germany.

It needs emphasizing once again, however, that the "problem" of Nietzsche—and the question of cultural heritage—confronts not just easterners but all Germans today. Indeed, for more than five decades now, Germany has been a land where the burden of history tends to turn any symbolic gesture into a furious national—and even international—debate. Much of it is linked to the problem of Prussia—with which Frederick, Bismarck, and Nietzsche are especially associated. It served the purposes of both Bonn and East Berlin to vilify Prussia. Given the SED's urge to present the Third Reich as a logical heir to capitalism, Prussia had to be condemned—and with Bonn's desire to present the DDR as the totalitarian successor to Nazi Germany, Prussia—located in the heart of East Germany—also served as an attractive target.

Germany: A land of multiple personalities, divided for centuries and schizoid in recent decades—a land of dozens of principalities in the nineteenth century, a quadripartite occupied territory in 1945, a bisected nation in 1949, a reunified nation in 1990—modern Germany is a land with *too much* history. The DDR, a Stalinist creation sculpted from the rubble of the Third Reich, was condemned from the moment of its inception as being a land with a surfeit of history and a scantness of heritage, an endless firestorm of shattering events in its past and no capacity to fit the vestiges of a different, deceased order into its postwar consciousness.

And here again, evoked by the mere signifier "Nietzsche"—which generates the image of *Nietzsche in Trümmern* (Nietzsche in—and rising up from—the Rubble)—intrudes the dreaded apprehension that the entire German heritage is tainted and encumbered beyond renewal or redemption, that it cannot be salvaged. And not only the former DDR but also the current *Bundesrepublik* have long felt the impulse to *build* something out of the ruins, to engage in a massive psychological reconstruction. Though the DDR celebrated lavishly the 500th anniversary of Luther's birth in 1983, it yet remained uneasy about converting the princes' paladin into Comrade Martin Luther. Shortly before reunification, in July 1990, West Germans transported Frederick's body from Stuttgart to be reburied in his palatial retreat of Sansouci near Postdam in East Germany, fulfilling the last wish of Old Fritz in 1786—and officially affirming the legacy of Germany's greatest military monarch and Hitler's idol. In October 1990, a reunited Germany fêted Bismarck—the chancellor of "blood and iron," the tactical genius who united Germany in 1871 after maneuvering Europe into three major wars during 1864–70, the figure associated with German imperialism—with a gala exhibit in the Museum of History in Berlin, within a hundred yards of both Hitler's old chancellery and the rubble remains of the Berlin Wall.

And so, from Luther and Frederick the Great to Nietzsche—from Old Fritz to New Fritz—the tense associations persist. Nietzsche is simply a spectacular example of the difficulty of facing that past and facing it down.

Yes, how does a nation cope? Luther, Frederick the Great, Bismarck, Wagner, and Nietzsche *are* problematic figures. But so too is Thomas Jefferson, to name only one controversial American hero, the slave owner and founder of my alma mater, the University of Virginia, who has been the target of protesters and hunger strikers. American Caucasians have traditionally sought to spotlight the strengths and to downplay the weaknesses of awkward historical figures like Jefferson. In the age of multiculturalism, and now that African-Americans are powerful enough no longer to tolerate such selective history, the era of the Thomas Jeffersons remaining national heroes may be over. America's historical whitewashing always ran—and still runs—the risk of complacency, insensitivity, blindness, and self-congratulation; German history demonstrates, however, that the risk in the opposite direction—when a people (or the ethnic majority) can take no pride at all in their history—may also have a poisonous effect on the national spirit.

Germany and the United States have both long held themselves to be "special" nations, each with its own special path (*Sonderweg*) and destiny. Amid the ashes of the Third Reich, the United States decisively and permanently dislodged Germany from formal competition for that role, at least in its positive connotation. That both nations have conceived themselves "special" has much to do with their physical and spiritual isolationism, respectively. Geography has undergirded American exceptionalism, which has survived because the Atlantic and Pacific oceans have made us the unrivaled Great Power on our continent; Germany's distinctive intellectual evolution (traceable from Luther and Pietism, rather than Catholicism or the Enlightenment) and delayed political development (unification in 1871) likewise set it on its own different course.

For Germany had never followed the model of France and England toward humanism and political integration. And so, it was shockingly easy for the Nazis to invest the notion of the German *Sonderweg* with a new and sinister meaning, portraying their authoritarian government (*Obrigkeitsstaat*) as the fitting conclusion of Luther's insistence on obedience to the medieval prince. During World War II and after, the world adopted the same reasoning; the title of one American scholar's influential political history of Germany bore the much-quoted indictment: *From Luther to Hitler*. Finally, everyone simply accepted the line that

German chauvinists had promoted since Bismarck: the Germans' self-interpretation that they were special. So the years 1933–45 became not an aberration or interregnum, not a product of contemporary circumstances, but part of a deep Teutonic past, stretching back a millennium. The seemingly short-lived Third Reich really had, after all, survived for a thousand years.

VII

Hedwig and I return down the long and winding path of the Humboldtstrasse, back to the Frauenplan, into the center of Weimar. As we peek in at the Goethe-haus, I remark on how much more excited the visitors in the Nietzsche Archive seemed, especially the younger patrons.

"They want to 'live dangerously,' " Hedwig replies. Her voice lowers: "Germany has already seen twice where that leads."

Hedwig admits that Goethe exerts no shuddering fascination like Nietzsche; she is glad of it. What begins again with Nietzsche could end again with something much worse.

In the 1950s, Karl Löwith wrote that Nietzsche "is not as current as he was 20, let alone 50, years ago," and that "his teachings are not so tempting and powerful today." In 1968, shortly before the student protests, Jürgen Habermas commented that, while Nietzsche had once exerted "a peculiar fascination" upon leading "revolutionaries of the Right," "[a]ll that lies behind us now and has become almost incomprehensible. There is nothing contagious [about Nietzsche's influence] anymore."[29]

Those assessments have proven premature. In the 1980s, Nietzsche's most recent West German biographer could see past the amalgam of national guilt and wish-fulfillment that had inspired Löwith's and Habermas' vain hopes, observing that it was "uncanny" that Nietzsche is "more current today than ever."[30]

The latter judgment pertained even more strongly in the New Germany of the early 1990s. In the wake of the *Wende* of 1989, eastern Germany was the scene of the most recent round of Nietzsche's eternal German return. And those observers aware of his fateful roles in the past voiced hope that perhaps this time Germans—easterners and westerners alike—will heed the call of Nietzsche—the Educator, the Good European, the "gentle" Nietzsche of Zarathustra's Great Commandment:

My doctrine is: Love that thou mayest desire to live again—for in any case thou *will* live again!

VIII

October 1994. The resurrection of the Antichrist is on the horizon.

I don't want to miss Nietzsche's full rehabilitation during this second week of October, which is called "Nietzsche Week" throughout eastern Germany. And so, like hundreds of other curiosity seekers, I race from one Nietzsche event to another, all of them commemorating the sesquicentennial of Nietzsche's birth on

October 15. In Naumburg, an international conference of linguists meets in his honor. In Jena and Erfurt, writers hold public readings from Nietzsche's work. In Berlin, an orchestra ensemble devotes an evening to performing Nietzsche's musical compositions.

But the major events are hosted in Weimar and Röcken.

Or non-events: in Weimar, the week gets off to a bad start. The symposium that was to be a major cultural attraction of Nietzsche Week—an international conference on Nietzsche and his Jewish critics and admirers—is suddenly canceled, just three days before it is scheduled to begin. The topic "Nietzsche and Nazism" is again headline news in Germany—and Israel. Last week, Ernst Nolte, Germany's leading right-wing historian, made equivocal remarks about the Holocaust revisionists in *Spiegel* that provoked a storm of outrage in the Israeli media. Several Israeli participants who had, at first, welcomed Nolte's participation, responded by saying that they would not attend the conference unless Nolte's invitation was withdrawn. Andreas Schirmer, who organized the conference, tells me that the Weimar Endowment for Classical Culture was torn between disapproving Nolte's views and defending his free speech rights.

And so rather than rescind Professor Nolte's invitation, Schirmer and his colleagues finally decided to cancel the conference altogether. When we meet at the Weimar Endowment, across town from the Nietzsche Archive, Schirmer tells me that, given both the rise of German neo-Nazism and the ongoing debates about the fairness or unfairness of the Nazi appropriation of Nietzsche, a topic such as "Nietzsche and the Jews" was bound to be controversial. But he laments that Nietzsche's controversial reception history has again become an occasion for sowing distrust between the Right and Left, and also between Germans and Jews.

"The acrimony [among the invited scholars] runs so deep," Schirmer says ruefully, expressing dismay that the would-be participants even refused to submit papers intended to appear together in a published volume on Nietzsche.

Just a few blocks away in Weimar, however, another Nietzsche event goes off better—even though its speaker cautions his audience against re-elevating Nietzsche to the status of state philosopher. The occasion is the October 12 restoration by the Friedrich Schiller Gymnasium of its famous stained-glass "Nietzsche window." The window is a ten-foot glass portrait of the philosopher located in a wall of the school auditorium that faces out onto a main street in Weimar; it had been installed during the Nazi era. In 1959—by which time the Schiller school had become one of the elite "Red schools" during the DDR years—the communist principal ordered the Nietzsche window removed.

Professor Erhard Naake, the guest speaker for the evening—a former Schiller school student, a Schiller schoolteacher for three decades, and later a professor at the Weimar College of Music—told me later that he suspects that he never obtained a full professorship during the DDR era on account of his sympathetic stance toward Nietzsche. Asked by an audience member whether the New Germany should heed Nietzsche's words or not, Professor Naake smiles. He allows that the best answer would be to quote the philosopher himself. Professor Naake then selects a line from *Thus Spake Zarathustra*:

Thousands shout my name! I tell you: Go away from me and protect yourself from me—you honor me badly when you follow me!

Nonetheless, at the little shrine of Nietzsche's birthplace, Röcken, we followers, gathered two days later to honor Nietzsche's birthday, pay little heed to this counsel of Zarathustra.

On a warm Saturday morning, more than a thousand people crowd into the little Lutheran church in this tiny eastern German hamlet of 130 residents near Weissenfels, about 15 miles outside Leipzig. Many of the attendees are local residents gathered to honor a native son. The gala event is unquestionably the highlight of Nietzsche Week for the German public.

"I've never seen so many cars in all my life!" a boy exclaims as the ceremony commences. Luminaries throughout eastern Germany are scheduled to speak. But our host, the black-bearded village pastor—who lives in the very rectory where Nietzsche was born—notes that the organizers are "commemorating" rather than "extolling" Nietzsche.

Indeed the program refers to a "memorial event" rather than a "celebration." And the program title—derived from Nietzsche's clarion call in *The Joyful Wisdom*, "Become who you are!"—also seems chosen with deliberately subtle ambiguity: "How one becomes what one is."

No consensus on the vexing question of what Nietzsche "is"—or might "become"—emerges at the "commemoration." But virtually every speaker notes the importance of national memory and moral vigilance. The "past," the memorialists caution vaguely, must not be forgotten.

Reinhard Höppner, Minister-President of the state of Saxony-Anhalt, which sponsored the memorial event, greets the audience: "Nietzsche's influence has prompted new questions to be asked. Our questioning is more radical and our thinking is consequently different. Can one say anything more positive about a thinker, even if one voices many questions about his thinking? . . . Nietzsche urged us to remember. Before our reunified Germany falls into another round of smugness and self-forgetting, let us heed his words. Nietzsche can help us to overcome our tendency to self-inflation; he can help us to know ourselves better."

During a break, the crowd mills about in the rectory courtyard, waiting for the three P.M. inauguration of the new Nietzsche Museum, which has been built next to the rectory. "Are you a Nietzsche fan?" a woman from Austria asks me. She has come with three Cubans and two Frenchmen to the sesquicentennial event. "It's like a prayer meeting," says an elderly gentleman, noting that hundreds of people are carrying various works of Nietzsche and quoting aloud from them to one another. I ask a teenage boy why—like me—he is taking such extensive notes. He says that he is an 8th-grader from the local Röcken school and has volunteered to give the first school report on Nietzsche since 1945.

The boy and I notice that a man is hawking reprints of a 1912 postcard of Nietzsche's second childhood home in Naumburg (with Nietzsche's name misspelled "Nitzsche"—just as in the original, and thus a real collector's item, the man says). He is also pushing his self-designed telephone cards featuring Nietzsche's image, actually worth DM 6 in phone calls (which he sells for DM 30). Business is slow, however; there are few takers. Suddenly, the crowd's attention is drawn to another man, who sports a top hat and bushy moustache. He is buttonholing bystanders and introducing himself as—Friedrich Wilhelm Nietzsche.

What's going on? I ask. A nearby woman says that the Saxony-Anhalt state TV agency is covering the commemoration and that an actor has come dressed for the evening show, "Who am I?" The woman grimaces. "It's a sacrilege," she says. She takes in both the postcard/phone card salesman and the pseudo-Nietzsche with a dismissive wave of her hand. "They're turning the commemoration into a circus."

More than that—unfortunately. The wife of the village pastor shows me a small sticker, several of which have been found throughout Röcken today. "Go Right Before Left," proclaim the stickers. Members of the far-right Republican Party have left their message, she says. They want to claim Nietzsche too. The national election is tomorrow, October 16, she reminds me. She hasn't seen any neo-Nazis in Röcken, but she worries that Nietzsche's mantle might once again be captured by the German Right. I mention the canceled Weimar conference on "Nietzsche and the Jews"; she nods her head and says simply, "It worries me."

Seeing her husband, the village pastor, near the rectory, I request to speak to him about his experience of Nietzsche during the DDR years. Ironically, Hans-Jürgen Kant, 35, was one of the few DDR citizens who did read Nietzsche. Pastor Kant says that the DDR's few theology students were encouraged by the state to read Nietzsche's "God is dead" critique in *The Joyful Wisdom* and other works in order to gain sympathy for atheism; Nietzsche also entered discussions about the work of German theologians such as Rudolf Bultmann and Dorothee Solle on demythologization and secularization. The DDR imposed no "fascist interpretation" on Nietzsche in theology courses; Nietzsche was granted a limited place in the curriculum as a fierce critic of Christianity.

"But the church under the DDR never really exploited the limited freedom we had to pursue a radical reinterpretation of Nietzsche," Pastor Kant admits. "We had other, more serious worries under the communists!" Pastor Kant does note, however, that some of the activities of a secret "Nietzsche Circle" had been organized under the cover of the Lutheran Church, which had copies of Nietzsche's works. But he declines to discuss the topic further.

Does the pastor feel at home in the residence of Germany's famous Antichrist?

"Yes, I do," he says. He pauses and then laughs. "But I must say: Some of my house guests claim at times to hear Nietzsche's voice in the night! It makes them very uneasy."

Outside, in the rectory courtyard, the speeches to inaugurate the Nietzsche Museum are in full swing. A professor of German and representative of the Nietzsche Research Association, founded in 1990, declares: "We wanted to honor him with something more than a refurbished rectory. We wanted a museum, which symbolizes the task ahead: to recover what has been left in the past and forgotten. And this is the only proper course to take. For Nietzsche is the most important thinker in the entire world. And finally, Germany is honoring him as he deserves to be honored."

Yes, Nietzsche's re-embrace by German officialdom is under way. Another round of politicians and professors honoring Nietzsche—a few of them, I am told, the same figures who had blocked his rehabilitation during the DDR era.

Would Zarathustra have snickered or screamed?

Suddenly, however, the crowd's own smugness is rudely upset. The speaker, a tall, bearded man named Kai Schmidt, is a local politician and a former critic of the SED regime:

"We had a personal relationship to this rectory during the communist dictatorship."

The last two words trigger murmured remarks; Schmidt is breaking the unwritten taboo against plain-spoken criticism of the communist era at the "commemoration." Schmidt's "we" is an exclusive one: He is referring to those few members of the clandestine "Nietzsche Circle," an underground reading group that passed around copies of Nietzsche's works and was regularly spied upon by the DDR secret police. Professor Naake had told me about its activities. But Schmidt's speech marks its first mention in a public forum.

"We prayed here together, and we honored Friedrich Nietzsche's example as a freethinker," Schmidt continues. "Our first Nietzsche evening occurred in 1980. But we could only read him and speak about him in secret. Because of his misuse by the Nazis, the greatest philosopher of Germany was cast aside by the communists. We laid a wreath on his grave, here in Röcken, year after year; now we open this museum in his memory."

Then the mayor throws open the museum front door; the re-christening of the Antichrist is now official. Inside, the museum exhibits resemble those in Weimar; they too tell the story of Nietzsche's life, though they concentrate on his boyhood in Röcken. One exhibit, titled simply "F. W. Nietzsche," features the current work of 8th-grade students from Röcken's junior high school, who have written poems and reports for the sesquicentennial celebration that offer tribute to Nietzsche.

The area around the little church is now deserted. As I enter the church, lines of Nietzsche dance in my head. "I *want* no 'believers.' I have a terrible fear that one day I will be pronounced *holy*."

I muse once again on Nietzsche's extraordinarily complicated return to German politics and letters. Here in this church is where it all began. Here in these pews, Fritz spent countless hours as a small boy, listening to his father playing hymns on the organ and preaching the word of God. I look up at the biblical passage etched in stone on the church's left-side wall:

I live and you should also live (John 14.19).

And whether the echoes be ironic or fated, I am once again reminded of Zarathustra's own gospel of love:

My doctrine is: Love that thou mayest desire to live again—for in any case thou *will* live again!

11

Berlin, 1994

Bridge over Broken Glass?
A Journey to Germany's Sole Jewish High School

I

In the beginning was the memory.

"I'm still hesitant even to mention it," the young woman says in a low voice. We huddle closer together.

"East Berlin was, after all, the capital of our 'anti-fascist' state."

She pauses.

"And I'm even more anxious talking about it here—in this *Oberschule*."

She pauses again, then sets her shoulders and shakes her head impatiently.

"But, on the other hand, it *is* my family history—I can't do anything about that," she continues. "I don't believe in hiding it or repressing it—there's been too much of that down through the years. And so I do tell people about it. Because it's precisely my determination to confront my history that has brought me here."

Here: where—in a visceral, sometimes gut-wrenching way—past meets present, native meets foreigner, East meets West, Jew meets Gentile. And, above all, here: where—with as much good will and naturalness (and even a semblance of normalcy) as such an encounter can occur—Jew meets German.

For we are sitting in the first—and still only—Jewish *Oberschule* in Germany in more than 50 years.

We are talking in a corner in Room 212, the cramped teacher's conference room through which her colleagues pass as they leave to teach their classes. Frau Ulla Berhau, 33, has the morning free and is willing to talk to me.

A slight woman with short black hair cut in a close crop, Frau Berhau speaks in even tones and in a sharp Saxon accent about her past. Like many eastern German women, she wears no makeup, but her face lights up with animated expression as she tells her story, whose newest chapter has much to do with the historical challenges facing the Jewish *Oberschule* at Great Hamburg Street 27 in eastern Berlin.

"To build a school is hard," says Frau Berhau, "especially here in this street, especially for . . . us." She gestures toward the center of Room 212 and her colleagues as she pauses, then shakes her head again.

I wonder at the uncertain stress on *uns* (us). What does she mean? "Us Germans"? Or "us Germans and Jews"? Or something else?

313

I do not interrupt. Instead I listen as Frau Berhau relates in evocative detail (occasionally assisted by a couple of colleagues whose reading she interrupts to pose questions about the *Oberschule*) how the history of this school and her own family and personal history collided—and eventually made common cause.

For she has finally said "it" straight out:

"My father was an SS officer."

II

And the memory was made—indelible.

Eight A.M. A typical school morning on a beautiful, sunny October day at the Jewish *Oberschule* of Berlin. Commotion in the hallways as the school bell rings. Students dash to their seats; shouts and cries die to whispers.

Yes, for a moment, it seems as if life here is the same as in any other German school.

But the sights, if not the sounds, immediately belie the impression.

For as I absorb Frau Berhau's staggering confession, my eyes are drawn past her into the street outside the school, where Berlin police with bullet-proof vests and submachine guns stand at every school entrance.

History repeating itself?

Until the Nazi rise to power in 1933, the Great Hamburg Street, just a 10-minute walk from the Alexanderplatz, was a bustling scene of Jewish activity, the heart of Berlin life, where hundreds of boys received a classical German education that included instruction in all major secular subjects as well as in Hebrew and Jewish history. Indeed the present coed school, which reopened in August 1993, is located in the very same building that once housed the famed *Freischule*—the Berlin Jewish Free School—founded by the Jewish theologian and philosopher Moses Mendelssohn in 1778. The largest Jewish boys' school in Germany, the *Freischule* charged no tuition and admitted Gentiles; it reflected Mendelssohn's Enlightenment conviction that education teaches tolerance. The *Freischule* immediately became a model for similar schools in Germany in the last quarter of the eighteenth century, just as it has served as a model for the revived Jewish *Oberschule* today. Mendelssohn himself was an active pedagogue; he also supplied material for the *Lesebuch für Jüdische Kinder* (1779), one of the first readers for Jewish children; indeed many important religious and philosophical works by Berlin authors were published under the name of the Jewish Free School Press in the late eighteenth century.[1]

But after the decision of the Wannsee Conference in Berlin in January 1942, when top Nazis met and masterminded the "Final Solution" to the "Jewish question," Nazi education ministry officials closed down all Jewish educational facilities. After shipping the *Freischule*'s thousand pupils to concentration camps, the SS turned the school building into a main assembly point for Berlin Jews destined for Auschwitz or Theresienstadt. After the war, DDR authorities converted the building into a non-Jewish vocational training center.

And so a great Jewish educational tradition came to an end. And with it—almost—the Jews in Germany themselves. "German" and "Jew" were mutually exclusive terms during the Third Reich; Hitler had defined "German Jew" out of existence—and almost succeeded in making his definition become reality: a Germany *judenfrei* (free of Jews).

When the Wall came down in 1989, only 400 Jews—out of a population of 16 million people—lived in all of East Germany. Most of them were aged camp survivors, over 65; a Jewish wedding in the DDR was a great rarity.[2] A 1992 *Spiegel* report listed the number of Jews in urban areas in eastern Germany:

East Berlin: 208
Dresden: 59
Leipzig: 32
Magdeburg: 32
Erfurt: 24
Halle: 6
Schwerin: 4

Though the totals reflected the number of registered Jews in the Jewish *Gemeinde* (community) of the eastern states, and therefore probably underestimated the actual Jewish population of eastern Germany, they nevertheless prove sobering. The figures—not just in their smallness but in their very exactitude—reveal much about the story of postwar Jewish life: Jews were virtually museum specimens, and the practice of the Jewish faith was almost a subject of exotic interest.

The population figures of German Jewry from six decades ago tell a different story: In 1933, 660,000 Jews resided in Germany, one quarter of them in Berlin. Most Berlin Jews lived in the *Scheunenviertel* (barn quarter) of eastern Berlin, traditionally its Jewish sector. In the seventeenth century, the quarter lay outside the city gates; the area consisted of barns and cattle sheds. Still within the memory of many old Berliners, Hebrew and Yiddish songs once rang through the streets of the *Scheunenviertel*. A thriving German-Jewish culture—represented by more than a dozen German Jewish winners of the Nobel Prize, and by writers and actors such as Kurt Tucholsky, Franz Werfel, Jakob Wassermann, Stefan and Arnold Zweig, Max Reinhardt, Leopold Jessner, Richard Tauber, Kurt Weill, Elisabeth Bergner, and Fritz Kortner—helped establish Weimar-era Berlin as Europe's capital of cosmopolitan culture.

Across the postwar decades, the old Berliners kept the flame of memory alive. And by 1993, Berlin's Jewish culture was showing signs of a revival; most heartening to elder Berliners was that there were finally enough young Jews in Berlin to make special cultural programs for youth, and even a high school, feasible. An elementary school had already opened in the Great Hamburg Street after the Wall had come down. It was the first postwar Jewish elementary school in eastern Germany—and only the second Jewish school in all of Berlin, joining three existing elementary schools elsewhere in western Germany (in Frankfurt, Munich, and Düsseldorf). Now the time had arrived for the Great Hamburg Street to swing open its doors to high school students once again.

III

And the beginning was modest—and anxious.

When the *Oberschule* opened in August 1993, the entire high school consisted of a single 7th-grade class of 27 students, a third of whom were Gentile. In 1994/95, a total of 95 pupils in 7th and 8th grade attend the *Oberschule*, of whom 50 are Jewish. The adjacent elementary school contains approximately 100 students and is 80 percent Jewish. The *Oberschule* is adding a 9th-grade class in the near future; the administration will open a new grade level each year, as its students advance toward graduation. While some teachers would like to see the school accept more non-Jewish students, school policy specifies that all qualified Jewish children receive priority.

The school's location in the Great Hamburg Street places it in the heart of the *Scheunenviertel*. It lies just a few blocks from the famous New Synagogue, a Moorish-Byzantine-style, red-brick building with a cavernous ceiling topped by a golden dome and gilded star of David. The synagogue is in the Oranienburger Street, which lies just east of the old Berlin Wall, right behind the *Scheunenviertel*.

The fates of the Great Hamburg Street school and the New Synagogue seem linked by history. School and synagogue rose with the Enlightenment's aspirations and collapsed with the Nazis' truncheons. Dedicated by Bismarck in September 1866, the grand New Synagogue reflected the hope of a Jewish coming-of-age in Europe: now the star of David could be prominently displayed and German Jews could have great houses of worship in public places. By 1920, with Jewish life in Germany flourishing and pogroms bringing Russian and East European Jews westward, Berlin's Jewish population had risen from 20,000 to 171,000, making it the largest Jewish community in Europe and the fifth largest in the world.

Then, in a series of goose steps, a twisted cross destroyed that hope: The swastika's shattering blow fell on *Kristallnacht*—the night of November 9, 1938—when Nazi thugs desecrated and plundered the New Synagogue, razing 7,000 Jewish-run shops and set ablaze 1,200 other synagogues throughout Germany. Ninety-one Jews were killed. Following the rampage, 35,000 Jewish "provocateurs" were rounded up and sent to concentration camps; by the beginning of 1939, Berlin's Jewish population had fallen to less than 60,000.[3]

The horror of *Kristallnacht* marked the terrifying beginning of what would become the Holocaust, when Nazi policy descended from discrimination to annihilation. That night commenced the nightmare of the heretofore unimaginable, a nightmare that shattered German-Jewish relations utterly, a nightmare from which, almost six decades later, German and Jewish great-grandchildren are still attempting to awaken.

After *Kristallnacht*, the Nazis used the New Synagogue as a Wehrmacht army depot. Bombed out by the Allies in 1943, the synagogue lay in ruins for decades.

The DDR government never said much about the Jews, except that they were honorable "victims of fascism." In DDR historiography of the Third Reich, there were two classes of Nazi opponents: resistance fighters and victims. The Jews were always treated as victims—as anti-fascists of the second class.

In its 1988 commemoration of the 50th anniversary of *Kristallnacht*, with Erich Honecker and other Party bosses in attendance, the East German government re-inaugurated the renovated the New Synagogue as a center for the preservation of German Jewish culture, the Centrum Judaicum. To honor the event, synagogues throughout the world left their lights burning throughout the night. To many observers at the time, however, Honecker's rededication ceremony seemed more like a wake, given the paucity of East German Jews. Still, today the Centrum Judaicum, with its 60,000 volume library, houses a community college that offers courses in Jewish subjects to more than 15,000 Berliners—both Jews and non-Jews.

IV

And they saw that it was—might be?—possible.

A journey to Germany's sole Jewish *Oberschule* is a passage through a graveyard of memorials next to streets of sacrileges. In the footsteps of such a History, an atmosphere of faith and fear, hope and hesitation, desire and doubt pervades these school hallways. Sooner or later, someone voices The Question:

Can this experiment succeed?

The question caroms off the school hallways, into the courtyard, resounding throughout the *Scheunenviertel.*

The new school in the Great Hamburg Street, the golden dome raised high against the Berlin sky: symbols indeed of a courageous new beginning in the New Germany. Other signs: In 1990, the Jewish World Congress convened in Berlin for the first time in 60 years. In 1991, the Jewish communities of eastern and western Berlin, separated throughout the postwar era, were reunited. In 1992, on the 50th anniversary of the Wannsee Conference, a memorial to Holocaust victims was erected in the building in which the Wannsee planners had met.

And yet, if the Jews' new beginning in Berlin shines with faint hope, it is, admittedly, tinged and colored by anxiety. For History casts its dark and lengthy shadow in these streets. Like it or not, the past lives on in the present.

By the end of the war, only 20,000 Jews remained in Germany; today it is 60,000—still pathetically small, but nonetheless double the number of just five years ago. When the Wall fell, reunited Berlin had a Jewish population of 4,000, most of whom lived in the former West Berlin; by 1994, however, that number had more than doubled, to 9,200. The surge is almost entirely the result of a dramatic Jewish influx since the collapse of the Soviet Union in 1991: the number of Soviet Jews in Berlin alone now equals about one-third of the entire German total; roughly 20,000, most of them from Russia and the Ukraine, have entered Germany since 1989. (Despite sharp curbs on immigration imposed by Bonn in 1993, the German government has issued residence permits of unlimited duration to all immigrant Jews.) Equally dramatic is the change in the Jewish school population. Whereas 30,000 Jewish students attended community-run schools in the 1920s, and 200 did in 1989, approximately 700 Jewish children do so today.[4]

Unfortunately, the re-emergence of Jews in German society has been accompanied by a sharp increase in the incidence of anti-Semitic gestures—even though most young Germans have never met a Jew. For instance, in April 1994, skinheads defaced Jewish graves in the Oranienburger Street; since then, police tanks and large police wagons have been stationed in front of the New Synagogue and Jewish Community Center. The city's Jews do feel better protected and acknowledge that the measures are necessary, but the police presence has also generated a siege mentality for some Berlin Jews—as though the city itself had become a giant concentration camp in which Jews were now imprisoned.

The tension is palpable. In September 1994, police uncovered and stymied plans by the Palestinian terrorist Abu Nidal ("Father of the Struggle") to dynamite the New Synagogue and assassinate Ignatz Bubis, president of the Central Council of Jews in Germany. The incident electrified Jews throughout Germany, since Abu Nidal was reportedly responsible for killing or wounding 900 people in 20 countries.

Some prominent Jews urged that the Jewish community take aggressive measures to protect itself. The Jewish writer Ralph Giordano, author of *The Second Guilt*, called on Chancellor Kohl to arm Jews in Germany. Giordano, who had hidden in Hamburg throughout the war, said that he did not plan to hide again. Other observers believed that Giordano had contributed to a wave of hysteria among Jews, and that he had also soured some moderate Germans.

V

In the beginning was the Wall.

Born in 1961—the very year in which the Berlin Wall was erected—Frau Berhau was a child of the DDR and its "anti-fascist Wall of Protection." From the start, she says, little Ulla had the contradictory feelings both of being isolated and of being smothered in the DDR. Growing up in a small town in the *Erzgebirge* (ore mountains) near the Czech border, she felt far away from events. But once she began to confront and cope with her family's Nazi past, she felt nearly suffocated by the burden of History.

"My past has led me to this school," Frau Berhau says.

Frau Berhau pauses. Remembrance of Things Not Yet—and Never to Be?—Past? She lowers her gaze, as if surveying the morass beneath her, and then plunges in.

"My father was an SS officer and my mother was very proud of the fact. Not for ideological reasons—not because she was a convinced Nazi. Not for racial reasons—not because she was explicitly or outspokenly anti-Semitic. But because she wanted a strong, decisive masculine presence in her life.

"It's hard for me to talk about my father—not only because of what he believed, but because he died [in 1964] when I was only three years old. I have no memory of him." Frau Berhau says she has come to know him through the selective filter of her mother's memory.

Her father was "fed up" with the Weimar Republic of the 1920s, Frau Berhau says, which he saw as weak. How could he respect a government that would accept the humiliating provisions of the Versailles Treaty after World War I—terms that kept Germany in a subservient position: war reparations, war guilt, even occupation by foreign troops? Having been born in the Sudetenland (in Czechoslovakia), her father—as did most Germans—treated its 1938 annexation by Hitler as a great homecoming into the Greater German Reich. He entered the SS as soon as he was old enough, which was just after the victory over France in June 1940, when Hitler's prestige was at its height.

"He was 17 and, apparently, completely smitten with the Nazis and the glorious honor of being an SS soldier," Frau Berhau says. "He saw it as a great distinction to be accepted into the SS, because the SS was the elite corps; the SS soldiers were not only serious about returning Germany to her status as the first European power; they were the ones who were going to be doing it themselves. The army had to take you if you were able-bodied, but the SS had exacting physical—and racial—standards."

The war's end and aftermath, however, were quite inglorious for her father, says Frau Berhau. First he was dragged off to a Russian concentration camp, then he was taken to a Czech camp, from which he was released in 1949. But not before camp guards—taking a page from Nazi camp practices—pulled out many of his teeth for the gold and silver fillings. Adding insult to injury, he spent the last 15 years of his life disadvantaged in the "anti-fascist state" on account of his SS past.

Despite the role of ideology and politics in the family's fortunes, says Frau Berhau, her mother was an almost entirely unpolitical person.

"For instance, she never saw the SS in political terms. She wasn't interested in politics, she was interested in social honors. And it was a social coup, very prestigious, if your husband was an SS man. Her generation of women valued that especially highly. An SS officer had to project the image of being strong, healthy, and confident. And my father did so: He was a 'model Aryan specimen,' the ideal Nazi image. My mother's family prized his 'good Aryan stock,' since her own family traced its Aryan heritage back to 1600: they were 'pure.' So the Nazis' racial theories flattered them. Even today, my mother still uses the word 'Aryan' as a descriptive term, even a term of approbation for 'good breeding' and 'well-reared.' A 'good Aryan family.'

"Oh, the arguments we've had about it over the years! My mother was in the BDM. I cried about it when she spoke of it proudly, and then I fiercely criticized her. We argued through my teenage years. Always the same argument.

" 'You don't understand—we had to join it!' she would scream at me in defense. 'I would have been murdered if I hadn't!' 'That's absurd,' I'd say. Which it is. I'd say, 'C'mon, that's just an excuse. Plenty of girls didn't join and nothing happened to them.' At least 10 or 15 percent in every school didn't join. 'Oh, you just don't understand the 1930s at all,' she would reply. 'You don't know anything about it. It's all easy for you—you didn't have to live through it.' And so our conversations would often go."

Her mother's enthusiasm for Aryan racial theory, says Frau Berhau, coexisted peacefully alongside her absorption in the early history of the Jews.

"My mother was always interested in history, especially antiquity." Her mother's interest, quite literally, is antiquarian, Frau Berhau stresses. Her mother loves collecting historical facts and details. "If you accept the distinction, she was not a racist or even a Nazi, just a typical German woman of her time—largely nonpolitical, conformist toward Authority, and hypersensitive to Society's opinions.

And she remained partly frozen—even after the war—in the mind-set of bourgeois respectability from the 1930s."

Frau Berhau shared her mother's interest in Jewish life, an interest that deepened with private study. Frau Berhau avidly read the novelist and playwright Lion Feuchtwanger (1884–1958), a left-wing, pro-Soviet German author who dealt sympathetically with Jewish themes. Feuchtwanger's work was officially approved and widely available in the DDR. *Jud Süss* (1925), Feuchtwanger's celebrated play sympathetic to a Jew who refuses to convert to Christianity, and his Josephus trilogy of novels sharpened Frau Berhau's knowledge of Jewish history and the Jewish people.

"I wanted to understand where Christianity had come from," Frau Berhau continues. "I was always interested in the specific question, 'How do the Jews cope with their history, including their history in this century?' Because in the aftermath of the Holocaust, I knew that it was inextricably connected to the question, 'How do the Germans cope with their history?' And, of course, the two converged and became the basis of an identity question for me: 'How do I cope with my own history as a German daughter of an SS officer?' "

Two recent experiences assisted Frau Berhau's exploration of those questions and led directly to her application in the spring of 1994 to teach at the Jewish *Oberschule*. In May 1993, she attended a faculty development course sponsored by the Berlin Senate, "Jewish Life in Berlin from the Middle Ages to Today." In May 1994, she attended another course, "The History of the Jews in Brandenburg." She heard about the plan to reopen the Jewish *Oberschule* in Great Hamburg Street. The school might need teachers fluent in Russian, since so many of their students were from newly immigrant families from Russia and the Ukraine.

"For a person interested in Judaism, the news was a godsend," Frau Berhau says. She had taught German and Russian in DDR schools for a decade. Suddenly she realized that, even though the supply of former Russian teachers in eastern German far exceeded the demand—because the DDR had required the subject and it was a (little desired) elective in newly reunited Germany—her particular combination of interests and talents made her special. It gave her a sense of mission. As a former DDR Russian teacher who had lived in the USSR and was also informed about Jewish life, she had special qualifications to teach in the Jewish *Oberschule*. She resigned her tenured position in an eastern Berlin elementary school and immediately accepted her new job as a German and history teacher in the Great Hamburg Street school.

From the beginning, she served as a linguistic and intercultural bridge between Russian Jewish families and the non-Russian *Oberschule* staff. The need for such a liaison person was urgent: 20 of the 25 students in her German class are Russian and Ukrainian.

"Open religious practice was not permitted in the USSR, so they don't know much about it," Frau Berhau says. "I know much more about Judaism than some of the Jewish immigrants in the Berlin community." In the USSR, religious services occurred only occasionally and underground. The persecution ensured a sense of solidarity through negative identification with one another, but as a positive force for religious and historical consciousness, Judaism was rendered effectively inert.

Her mother supported her switch to the Jewish *Oberschule*, Frau Berhau says.

"She was even excited about it. And now she urges me to go to synagogue! For her, it reads like an intercultural adventure. And indeed it is, in a way.

"But my mother sees it all from the outside, as if it were only a gripping story, a fascinating historical saga. She feels no more personal relation to Jewish life under Hitler than she does to Jewish antiquity. She sees the problem of 'culprits' and 'victims' in simple terms and from the outside: it's all just 'interesting' to her, as if she's not at all personally involved in it. It's as if she keeps a wall around herself about it."

VI

And the Wall was—tall.

Frau Berhau has a special interest in Judaism that is connected with her personal struggle for religious freedom and represents another dimension of the ambiguous legacy of the SED and DDR.

"I'm a teacher because the Party wouldn't let me become what I wanted to be," Frau Berhau says. She pauses and looks out the window.

What was that?

"A minister!" She laughs, as I acknowledge my surprise.

"I really wanted to be a [Lutheran] minister," she says. "Our local minister encouraged me. I announced in 11th grade that I was going to be a minister and my teachers were at the end of their ropes! But we had to list two choices, and for my second choice I put down 'teacher.' So they pushed that on me. But at first, even that didn't fly with them. They said, 'You could be, at best, a butcher or a baker, but not a teacher!' Eventually they relented.

"I'm interested in the relation between Judaism and Christianity: how they mutually relate and how they cope. I'm still a Christian, even though I attend church only every month or two."

I ask about her relation to the Party, since German and Russian teachers were often regarded as the "cultural cadre."

Frau Berhau says she never joined the Party. Most of her friends did, but her Christian background gave her a reasonable excuse.

"And the Party didn't pressure me," she says. "Because the Party didn't want idealists. They were just problems, because they *believed* in communism. As soon as they saw what was happening from the inside, they knew full well that the DDR wasn't on track toward 'really existing socialism.' Idealists were far more dangerous than apathetic Party or even hostile non-Party members. Because the idealists believed in communism, but they didn't believe that it was being executed right in the DDR. And because they really wanted to transform the Party."

Young Ulla was too idealistic for the Party, and her chief allegiance was to the church, anyway. But she had belonged to the JP and the TP and the FDJ and all their ancillary youth organizations. And her participation had influenced her against the West.

"Yes, I did possess a certain *Feindbild* of the West, especially West Germany and the U.S. And so did my classmates. But by the mid-1980s, it simply wasn't credible to vilify the West in such terms any more: We all watched western TV programs and bought western products; we knew too much to be deceived by the blatant old propaganda."

The last time she gave full credence to the DDR version of events was in 1977, in her penultimate year at the Brecht EOS, when the school lavishly celebrated its 20th anniversary.

"Given the school's name, we had a relationship with the Berlin Ensemble, Brecht's acting company," Frau Berhau recalls. "And on May 1, the leading actors came to visit and we all honored Brecht. We sang the *Solidaritätslied* [hymn of solidarity, composed by Brecht]. We spoke of how the world was divided into 'oppressor' and 'oppressed' states. We praised DDR agitation for the liberation of oppressed Third World states such as Ethiopia and Cuba, all under the guidance of the 'glorious' USSR. You see, there was no '1968' in East Germany. Only a decade later did any kind of freethinking begin in the east."

No breezes of radical protest, no counterculture, no student movement blew over the Wall into the DDR until the end of the 1970s and the beginning of the 1980s, Frau Berhau says.

And so, Ulla's intellectual awakening began in college, during her studies at the Pedagogical College in Magdeburg from 1983 to 1988.

"Since I couldn't travel, I learned about the world outside the Wall from the foreign students," Frau Berhau says. "Many foreigners explained their lives in their native countries to me. They were the only contact we had with the outside world, and they were the living—even 'state-approved'—truth that our media were lying to us."

Eventually Frau Berhau secured a job in an East Berlin polytechnical *Oberschule*. She taught Russian and German to 7th and 8th graders. Many *Stasi* agents had children who attended the school.

"I didn't have too much room to maneuver. The best way to express disapproval of the standard line was simply to skip the author or work altogether. You could always say that you hadn't had enough time to get to the work. Better not to do anything than to deviate from the directive on how the work should be taught. Just not handle the work: That was the easiest and most convenient method of dissent."

But it wasn't always possible to operate this way, Frau Berhau admits. For instance, her teacher certification examiner was very strict: The examiner insisted that her student teachers adhere strictly to the Education Ministry's directives on content and approach.

"She was a true believer in the system," says Frau Berhau. She shakes her head in disbelief. "Right up to November 1989!"

VII

And the Wall crumbled—and yet remains.

Frau Berhau sees the differences between East and West in the presence of the Russian and Ukrainian pupils: Most German students take the *Gymnasium* track; almost all foreign students take the *Realschule* track. But even among the Germans, differences are evident: the eastern German students are much more traditional and respectful of authority than are those from the West. Geography also deepens differences. One third of the students are from eastern Berlin and know the neighborhood; two thirds are from western Berlin, where most Berlin Jews live—and hang around after school.

"Everything in the BRD is so different," says Frau Berhau. "I'm still adjusting." For instance, she says, when she taught Brecht's *Solidaritätslied* in DDR days, she treated it as a clarion call to DDR socialism; now she sees it simply as anti-fascist—rather than explicitly pro-communist.

"When I teach history, all the concepts are different. We talked in the DDR about the 'original classless society' and the 'slave societies' that followed; the West talks about the Stone Age and classical Greece and Rome.

"Everything was controlled in school through the group, the 'collective.' Old DDR colleagues say that the West is cold and individualistic. But that's not quite right. The fact is that you must be better organized here and more self-reliant. Because the *Zusammengehörigkeitsgefühl* [feeling of belonging, community togetherness] that we had in the DDR isn't here.

"It's hard for me to appreciate a variety of opinions. We had only one opinion—which was handed down to us, not thought through by us ourselves—and it was invariably right. So I'm not used to accepting lots of opinions.

"My pedagogical method was oriented toward a single question: How can I teach them so that they will be useful to society? As soon as any teaching called into question social norms or hurt Society, I stopped it. *Erziehung zur Gemeinschaft.* Education toward community-thinking. If you wanted to help the individual, you really couldn't. You had to suppress the uniqueness of the individual for the presumed good of Society. I was concerned with the *class's* best development.

"Today I see the individual student better. My teaching is much more varied and student-centered. I'm concerned with the personal development of each child. Now I try to give each child something he or she can take home. My new pedagogy promotes the free exchange of opinions in class. I think that different opinions aren't threatening; they enrich the class.

"My style used to be: X is right, Y is false. I had a *Feindbild* always available and operating, even if only subconsciously. The authoritarian mind-set is still strong in me. Many of us former DDR teachers are walking contradictions in the classroom. We say that the DDR was an oppressive, regimented nightmare, but we ourselves are still authoritarian and tied to the old ideology.

"But still I want to know: how does one *care*—and still tolerate so much—?" She stops in mid-sentence. Again the difficulty of distinguishing permissiveness and tolerance. What seems to be slack and permissive to Frau Berhau is tolerant and flexible to her western colleagues.

"—so much—well, all right, I'll say it—*deviation!* It seems often to me in this country [reunited Germany] that tolerance derives from a lack of caring—of genuine, deep concern. If you really care, you want to influence and even prevail. Nobody in the West seems to care about anything very much, nobody is passionate about anything—except their own small selves.

"It's a question of feeling adrift, without allegiances. It's difficult to support this state, the BRD. On the other hand, you don't have to support it. In the DDR, you did. The teacher was a political propagandist. You had to support it, conform, or make some compromising arrangement.

"But it's getting easier for me. I used to try to persuade the students to think in a socialist direction. Not any more."

VIII

And the broken glass—remains.

"My husband said to me, 'Can you imagine what your father would say if he knew you were teaching at this school?' I don't think he had changed many of his views developed in the 1930s." Frau Berhau pauses. She doesn't think he would view her decision with the same enthusiasm as her mother.

"For years I had been engaging in a dialogue within myself because of my family history, and now here I am at this school, where I'm confronted with that history every day. This school is a daily invitation to self-examination for me.

"Some parents can't talk to me; they know about my past, since I haven't hidden it, and that past is just too overwhelming for them. Small talk with me would seem to them an evasion of the wall between us; so they avoid me. At least for now. I understand the ambivalence.

"But most of the students do talk to me. And most of the Russian parents. They don't identify themselves with the Holocaust, and after all, I am one of the few Russian-speaking staff with whom they can have a substantive conversation. Moreover, I'm very interested in Russian Judaism and the Russian Jewish experience."

Her college experience had given her a keen interest in life outside the DDR and she had mixed frequently with foreigners. So frequently that she eventually married one: an Ethiopian student engineer. As a result of his experience, she became more sensitive to the problems of the Jews, and to Jewish perceptions of discrimination.

"My mother, of course, had problems with my choice of an Ethiopian husband. Not only because of her Nazi-influenced racial thinking. Most DDR citizens would also have had reservations, if only due to ignorance, because one seldom met foreigners in the DDR. There simply were very few, no more than 200,000, and they didn't interact with most citizens.

"All that is true. But, on that score, my mother was the exception: she had plenty of contact with foreigners. We had three [North] Vietnamese tenants living with us for several years. My mother was very friendly to them; she even treated them like her boys. But sons don't marry daughters: it was all fine, just as long as they had nothing whatsoever to do with her girls—or any German girls, for that matter.

"Fortunately, I was already pregnant before I told my mother about my Ethiopian boyfriend. It was too late to abort. So now she had a socially difficult choice: Accept an unwed mother or accept a daughter married to a colored man. I knew that, for her, it was just a question of which was worse, which was more embarrassing socially. To be the parent of a single mother? Or mother-in-law of a foreigner? What a dilemma for her!" Frau Berhau's laugh is heavy with sarcasm.

"Fortunately, she came to support what I had planned to do anyway—get married."

"But it's not entirely a happy ending," she adds quickly. Her husband is scared to go out in Berlin during the evening hours.

"Before the Wall fell, he had no fear at all," Frau Berhau explains. "He feels that people are prejudiced against him. He never felt this way before."

As another class bell chimes, Frau Berhau rises to leave for her noon class. She points out the window at the police guards.

"And he associates it all with the New Germany: the Wall is down, the 'anti-fascist state' has given way to right-wing terror in the streets. And he sees all this as a specifically eastern problem. He thinks West Berliners are much more tolerant, and he wants us to move there. Perhaps we will. But I've always lived in the east; I feel myself an easterner. I don't want to live in western Germany or western Berlin."

IX

And the memory was shared.

Back at the main administrative office, I speak briefly with Herr Uwe Mull, the principal, and at length with Frau Raissa Kruk, the assistant principal. Herr Mull is Christian; Frau Kruk is a Bessarabian Jew: Christian-Jewish dialogue in the principal's office too.

Frau Kruk takes me to her own office. She too understands the differences between east and west: she taught math and physics for 15 years in a West German *Gymnasium* in the Tempelhof district, before coming to the Jewish *Oberschule* two years ago.

We discuss the "experiment" of reviving the Great Hamburg Street school.

"To found a Jewish school in Germany is hard, especially for us, here in this street," Frau Kruk says.

Her statement echoes that of Frau Berhau, almost to the word.

But Frau Kruk's "us," I think, refers primarily to Berlin's Jewish community. Christians and Germans furnish welcome and much-needed support to the school in all capacities, she says, but the main challenge belongs to the Jewish community. Herr Direktor Mull recognizes that fact too, she says. And the biggest immediate challenge faces the Russian children and families, for whom everything is so new, so alien.

"I understand all that myself: I remember how it was for me when I arrived," she says.

But who are "us"? I ask her.

The problem is especially difficult for German-born Jews, she acknowledges, but all Jews living in Germany struggle mightily with the question. Many consider themselves to be resident Jews, who are living in Germany—Jews with German passports, something like a *yekke* abroad. The term refers to a Jew of German heritage living in Israel—such as Schalom Ben-Chorin, the only major Israeli author who writes in German—and sometimes has derogatory connotations. Some others see themselves as German citizens of the Jewish faith. Only a tiny number see themselves as most of their grandparents regarded themselves: German Jews, with a near-equal accent on both words. The chasm of History is not so easily bridged.

Frau Kruk sums up the challenges facing the school, one by one, as if they lay in the "In" box on her desk.

"To cultivate our roots. To remain open to Germans. Never to sequester or isolate ourselves from the society around us here. To turn Jewish life in Berlin into a living faith community. Not to let Jewishness slip into a museum piece forever located in the past. To integrate the foreign Jews into German life. And, finally, to acknowledge the ethnic diversity of our rapidly changing Jewish population."

Frau Kruk thinks her school's students are likely to be "more open to the world."

"It is a small school and yet there are students from Russia, the Ukraine, Azerbaijan, Israel, America, and elsewhere here. And the students interact and get to know one another's cultures and outlooks. And this promotes tolerance more effectively than anything we say in class. It helps us when we address topics such as violence against foreigners, anti-Semitism, and racism. The students can think concretely, in terms of their friends in the school, whom they wouldn't want to hurt or see hurt."

One of the most encouraging things, she says, is that elderly former pupils, now living on every continent, are coming back to visit the school. All of them are very moved by the experiment to revive the *Oberschule* in the Great Hamburg Street; some of them weep openly as they recall their classmates, many of whom died as children in the concentration camps. A welter of associations often overwhelms them as they pass through the halls of their youth. For instance, just last month, says Frau Kruk, a man in his mid-70s, who attended the Jewish school during 1933–39, before his family fled to London in the wake of *Kristallnacht*, made the pilgrimage.

Frau Kruk smiles broadly. Before leaving, she says, the alumnus announced that he intends to write a history of the school.

In the beginning is the memory.

12

Weimar, 1994

Difficulties with the Truth:
Coping with the DDR's Past in the New Eastern Classroom

> Whoever wishes to fight against lies and ignorance and write the truth today has at least five difficulties to overcome. He must have the *courage* to write the truth, even though it is everywhere suppressed; the *intelligence* to recognize it, even though it is everywhere concealed; the *art* to wield it as a weapon; the *judgment* to choose in whose hands it will be effective; and the *cunning* to spread it among them.
>
> Brecht, "Five Difficulties with
> Writing the Truth" (1934)

I

Eight thirty A.M. Another school day, another school—this time the Schiller Gymnasium in the Thomas Mann Street. It's a fine morning in late October. I greet Frau Losart, a German teacher, and Herr Gerrelov, a Russian teacher. They're happy to talk to me about changes at the school since my visit during the dying days of the DDR in the fall of 1990, when it was still the Schiller EOS, the only EOS in Weimar.[1]

Weimar has witnessed many changes since then, especially in education, including the transformation of three POS into *Gymnasien*: the Goethe Gymnasium, the Hoffman von Fallersleben Gymnasium, and the Sophiengymnasium. The classical names reflect the importance of German culture in Weimar. Indeed, "Weimar—the Heart of German Culture," runs the slogan in the official tourist brochure, which features, incongruously, both a picture of a young couple drinking Coca-Cola (the caption [in English]: "You can't beat the feeling!") and a pitch for a private bus tour line: "For more than a century," says the ad, in stately German script, Weimar "has been a magnet for all those who revere German classicism. . . ."

Or: those who mummify it. "*Stadt der toten Dichter*" (Dead Poets' City), journalistic wags from the west have dubbed Weimar instead. But the eastern and western slogans do, ironically, somehow fit together. For certainly the city's two biggest cultural drawing cards are its two greatest dead poets: Goethe and Schiller.

Not the least of the city's honors to the latter dead poet is the Schiller Gymnasium itself. Built in 1927, it was originally a *Berufsschule* (trade/vocational school) for girls; two years later, it became a coeducational *Realschule*. In 1936, the auditorium with its Nietzsche window was added, in honor of the city's third great dead poet.[2] In 1945, the school was used as an emergency hospital for soldiers wounded at the front. After the war, the Schiller *Oberschule* was the only school in Weimar to confer the *Abitur;* it became one of the first EOS in 1960 and a Gymnasium in 1991.

Since 1991, signs of progress in the school, as in Weimar and the surrounding state of Thuringia, are everywhere. Laughing as he relieved himself in the boys' rest room, Dietrich summed up for me earlier this morning the biggest advance in the last three years: "Automatic flush!" As he zipped up, he added: "Every room should have one! Especially those in which politicians speechify"—a reference to the national election held last week—since post-reunification politicians are "even worse than the old [SED] *Bonzen*." And people say that Bonn isn't doing anything for the eastern states?! Dietrich scoffs with mock-irony. Then the grin vanishes. The new bathroom tells the story of the west's ass-backwards priorities: *Wessis* know "everything about up-to-date technology and nothing about how to treat human beings." Pointing out the half-open window at the rusty fence surrounding the front of the school, he said as he left: "That's next to be overhauled. But I wish we'd keep it."

Indeed the state of Thuringia, the smallest and most "westernized" of the new federal states, is booming. It is the fastest growing region in all of Europe: the growth rate for 1993 was 11.8 percent. The official unemployment rate is still high—15.9 percent—but Thuringia has more immigrants than emigrants.[3]

In the faculty lounge, the two Schiller schoolteachers and I careen from topic to topic as other teachers come and go. The firings of DDR-era teachers: "I oppose this witch hunt against people with a Red background!" says Frau Losart, a petite woman in her mid-20s with a ready smile. Asked about the effects of *Abwicklung* on her own school, she admits that only the principal and another teacher were purged. Frau Losart graduated from the Schiller EOS in 1987, then studied German, history, and Latin at the University of Jena. Although the east still suffers from a surplus of German and history teachers, the Latin minor made her marketable. She is one of the lucky few university graduates who found a teaching position immediately upon graduation.

"Now you don't have much of a chance to teach in your area of study," Frau Losart says. "You always did before [in the DDR era]. That's why there's less interest in the schools and universities in learning. You can't make use of your degree, so now you study just for study's sake—just as in the west. And only a minority of dedicated students are really capable of that."

Herr Gerrelov, a Russian emigre from the pre-Wall era, laments that Russian is now, at best, the second or third foreign language—after English and, sometimes, French (and even, occasionally, Latin). Because French is "easier," many pupils prefer it, Herr Gerrelov says.

"Twenty percent of the kids still study Russian as a second language," says Herr Gerrelov, a short, black-bearded man in his 40s. "In 7th grade, you get 15 out of 90 pupils electing to take Russian. That's not many compared to the past. But there's one advantage: it makes the faculty-student ratio very favorable, given that we still have several Russian teachers." On average, he says, there are 30 pupils per class in English, 27 in French, and only 15 in Russian and Latin.

But Herr Gerrelov sees more cons than pros in "western-style" freedom in eastern schools.

"Before the *Wende*, there was much more discipline and order in the classroom, and many fewer distractions—no cable TV, no *Techno* [an aggressive teen TV series], no *Bravo* [a racy western teen magazine and TV show]. Pupils have no quiet at home now. It's overstimulating. Before, parents were calm and relaxed; now they are frustrated and nervous, especially the unemployed ones. In the DDR days, the pace was slower and people had a feeling of stability and the free time to nurture a family life. Pupils learned more in the EOS."

"But *what* did they learn?!" Frau Losart interjects. "Nowadays they can learn what's worth knowing. And for us teachers, there's freedom to teach outside a narrow, prescribed plan. Don't forget that! But it's true: the pupils haven't learned how to use their freedom at all. That's the main problem."

Attracted by the exchange, Frau Gammlich, another Russian teacher, joins our circle. She, too, is a Schiller EOS graduate. When I ask her about the Schiller EOS's reputation as an elite "Red" school, she confirms that only one classmate (of 80) in her graduating class did not belong to the FDJ. Frau Losart says the figure in her own class was similar.

Frau Gammlich, a soft-spoken brunette in her mid-20s, mentions that she has recently graduated from Leipzig University, which leads to conversation about her memories of the 1989 Revolution of the Candles, a time when the university was still called the Karl-Marx Universität.

"I couldn't participate in the Monday demonstrations in Leipzig," Frau Gammlich explains. "Every Monday evening I had a class. But I lived in the Karl-Marx Platz, down which many demonstrators would march, and I would hear the shouting on many evenings."

Would you have participated if you hadn't had class?

"I honestly don't know. Only a few students participated. All the students had anxieties about the police coming to pick us up—or beat us up. At minimum, we worried about losing our grants. Police officers stood before the main building of the University every day. I do remember a few class discussions about the *Demos*. We argued about them quite heatedly in a psychology class taught by a young *Dozent* whose father had participated in the June 17 uprising in 1953—and had disappeared. The *Dozent* never heard from his father again. That made the *Dozent* both angry and cautious toward the regime."

Frau Gammlich rhapsodizes about the exciting new curriculum that she experienced during her last years at Leipzig University: Solzhenitsyn, Pasternak, Alexandr Blok. Then the three teachers enumerate works by DDR and Soviet authors that were once curricular staples at the Schiller EOS but are no longer assigned today: Hermann Kant's *The Auditorium*, Anna Seghers' *The Seventh Cross* and *The Duel*, Becher's poetry, Louis Fürnberg's songs and poems, Erwin Strittmatter's fiction, Mayakovsky's verse, Sholokhov's *Fate of a Man*. Some DDR authors are still discussed, if seldom taught: Christa Wolf, Stefan Heym, Christoph Hein. During 1991/92, says Frau Losart, even works of undisputed artistic value by DDR-era writers were rarely taught at the school, though they were not officially discouraged, let alone proscribed, by *Land* education officials.

"People were still sick of DDR propaganda," Frau Losart explains. "But now the wave of *Ostalgie* sweeping here has resulted in a demand for us to teach 'our' authors too—and not just 'western' literature."

"But Brecht has always remained."

The low, richly toned voice is that of Frau Hintze, another German teacher, who chuckles as she comes up behind us. She and I shake hands. Four years ago, in the waning weeks of the DDR, we met in this lounge and addressed similar questions. She has arrived to take me to her 12th-grade double-period class on Brecht's *Life of Galileo.*

Another slight woman, Frau Hintze, 53, has taught at the Schiller school since 1978; both Frau Losart and Frau Gammlich are her former pupils. Frau Hintze recalls the old standbys in German: 12th grade: *Faust I* and *Faust II;* 11th grade: Seghers' *The Seventh Cross*, Kant's *The Auditorium*, Christoph Hein's *The Distant Lover* (titled *Dragon's Blood* in West Germany).

"Some books we couldn't even read, let alone study in class, because they weren't published in the DDR," Frau Hintze notes. She mentions Stephan Heym's *Five Days in June* (which deals with the 1953 uprising), Biermann's songs, and the work of Peter Hüchel, Günter Kunert, and Reiner Kunze (poet and author of the ironically titled *The Wonderful Years*, a chilling memoir of growing up in the DDR), the last four of whom "ceased to exist for us" after they left the DDR in the 1970s.

"Kafka was only introduced in the late 1970s," Frau Hintze recalls. "We teachers had to wait for the literary scholars to blaze the trail. Only long afterwards would such 'problematic' authors gain admission to the school curricula. That was also because the centralized curriculum required suitable secondary materials, and that took time to develop."

How about your pedagogical approach? Did you teach the DDR or socialist authors much differently then, as opposed to now?

"Not really," Frau Hintze answers. She looks at me quizzically. "What do you mean?"

Before I can reply, Frau Hintze hurries on. She handles Brecht as she did before the *Wende*, she says.

"I still emphasize his anti-fascism. We don't usually read his more aggressively pro-socialist works anymore, such as the "Soldarity Song" or *The Rifles of Senora Carrar*. But we still read *Galileo*. Come, let's go."

II

Ten A.M. Frau Hintze brings her 12th-grade class to order for the double-period class on Brecht. Posters of Herder and Schiller line the walls of the classroom, along with a portrait of a writer who would not have been seen here five years ago: Reiner Kunze.

On to *The Life of Galileo*. Treating the last three decades in the scientist's stormy life (1564–1642), the play opens in 1610, after Galileo has observed the phases of Venus and become a firm defender in the Copernican heliocentric theory of the solar system, despite the Church's position that the Bible supports the opposing Ptolemaic/Aristotelian position of a stationery Earth. Brecht then follows, with rough verisimilitude, the story of Galileo's tempestuous collision course with Rome. Warned by the Church in 1616 that he may investigate yet not publicize his heliocentric speculations—the Holy Inquisition's version of a "don't ask, don't tell" rule—Galileo obeys, remaining silent for several years. When the friendly Cardinal Barberini becomes Pope Urban VIII in 1623 and permits Galileo to write a book that will impartially present both the Ptolemaic and Copernican views, Galileo pens his famous *Dialogues* (1632), which ridicules the former and defends the latter. Summoned to Rome in 1633 to account for his defiance, Galileo recants his Copernicanism under threat of torture. But his sentence of life imprisonment is soon commuted to house arrest in his own plush villa, where he continues working on his *Discourses* (1638) on the new physics. The book is smuggled out of Italy and published in Holland in 1638.

Thus Galileo triumphs in the end.

Or does he?

Frau Hintze's theme today is scientific ethics. She outlines the positions of Andrea Sarti and his former teacher Galileo. Andrea is the pure scientist who believes that the state should not interfere with scientific research. On hearing the news of Galileo's recantation, an outraged and disillusioned Andrea had told Galileo that his "hands are stained." Before his confrontation with the Inquisition, Galileo had held similar views. But now he is a pragmatist. He replies: "Better stained than empty."

As the two men part, Andrea says bitterly: "Pity the land that has no heroes." To which Galileo rejoins: "Pity the land that *needs* heroes."

Frau Hintze turns to Scene 14, which portrays the 33-year-old Andrea's 1637 visit to Galileo, by then 73. The elderly stargazer tells his erstwhile prize pupil that he has continued to work on his heliocentric theory; his scientific treatise, the *Discourses*, is near completion. An overjoyed Andrea agrees to smuggle the document to Holland, and now congratulates Galileo on his crafty survival strategy. But Galileo rejects the assessment, ashamedly and passionately:

> I surrendered my knowledge to the powers-that-be, to use it, no not *use* it, *abuse* it, as it suits their ends. I have betrayed my profession.

The historical Galileo held that science and theology pursued truth in different realms of knowledge; he granted the Church's authority in its own domain. Brecht's Galileo sounds oddly like an M-L professor preaching the gospel of dialectical materialism—less a conscience-stricken son of the Church than a bold heretic who hated Rome and wanted to show that it served the educated and wealthy classes via Brechtian dialectical battles of truth vs. dogma, heresy vs. faith, reason vs. revelation, science vs. religion.[4] Brecht's Galileo has betrayed his profession by betraying the People, who would have been served if he had stood up against the centuries of superstition, dogma, and orthodoxy that have oppressed them. (Was this a self-indictment? I wonder, thinking of Brecht's own

Galileo-like denial of his communist beliefs before the House Un-American Activities Committee on October 30, 1947—and of his unannounced flight to Paris and safety the next day.)

Frau Hintze writes on the chalkboard:

Purpose of science:
a. Old Ethic: Serve truth?
b. New Ethic: Serve the *Volk*? Serve the State?

According to the "old ethic" of Andrea, Frau Hintze explains, impartial, value-free "science" was all-important. Andrea believes that "science is objective," and that the scientist needn't concern himself with the outcome or the beneficiaries/victims of his scientific results. Before the recantation, Andrea had wanted to elevate Galileo into a hero, a genius dedicated to science alone. But Galileo warns that "pure" science is impossible anymore; a "new ethic" has appeared on the forked road of the horizon: Science will be either dedicated to helping Humanity or coopted to strengthen the State. Brecht's Galileo holds that the scientist, like a good Marxist, must work for the welfare of Humanity. (The historical Galileo hoped to convince the Church about Copernicanism, believing that the revelation to a Christian astronomer of the heliocentric cosmos was an opportunity to celebrate the majesty and greater glory of God.)

Frau Hintze quotes from Scene 14, in which the confrontation between Galileo and Andrea culminates:

Andrea: Science knows only one commandment.
Galileo: I believe that the only goal of science consists in easing the hardships of human existence. When scientists get intimidated by dictators and thereby content themselves with the thought that they are piling up knowledge for knowledge's sake, science becomes a cripple and your new machines become only new instruments of torment.

Who is right? Frau Hintze asks. Andrea or Galileo? The pure scientist? Or the socially conscious scientist? Should scientists pursue knowledge into areas that endanger Humanity?

"If Galileo had died," says Ulrike, who is sitting next to me, "the world would never have received his *Dialogues*."

"But do the ends justify the means?" replies Frau Hintze.

"Sometimes it makes more sense to survive and fight in your own way," observes Claudia.

"It's easy to look at a decision of life or death from the outside," says Dirk. "Galileo wrote a great work [the *Discourses*]. The end redeemed the means."

"Galileo's recantation was understandable," says Claudia. "And it allowed him to triumph in the end."

"Galileo was a pragmatist," observes Dirk. "Only the bravest dissenter can withstand the pressure of the state." Given the choice of dying as a martyr or surviving as a cynic, he says, Galileo chose to live. And wouldn't most of us? Dirk quotes a relevant passage from Scene 9: "In the face of obstacles, the shortest line between two points may be a crooked one."

Not a word about the DDR? Nothing about the crookedness of the SED and pressures of the Communist state? Is the Earth, after all, the center of the solar system?

The class seems to believe: "Better stained than empty" hands. Better to lay low—and live to march some Monday night with candles. Until the day you have a chance to triumph. Is this a class of "pragmatists"?

Or are these students—who in 1989 were barely in their teens—too young to have experienced the orthodoxies of the "scientific-technical revolution"? Or to cast doubt on their "wonderful years"?

Frau Hintze nods at the students' answers. But Brecht himself, she notes, assessed Galileo more harshly. Frau Hintze reads a passage from a 1956 Brecht essay ("Building Up a Part"), which discusses the misuse of science by the American nuclear physicists who built the atom bomb. Brecht calls Galileo's recantation the "original sin of modern natural science," suggesting that the atom bomb was the ultimate consequence of Galileo's failure to hold out against the Inquisition. Galileo's weakness thus ushered in the nuclear age: he established the precedent for the scientist's subservience to the state, allowing it to coopt science for its non-humanistic ends.

Frau Hintze pauses to let Brecht's warning lesson sink in. Then she mentions two other, more current examples of science misused by the state. First, the highly sophisticated American war technology employed in the January 1991 invasion of Iraq; second, genetic engineering.

"Should we permit pure science to develop these technologies?" she asks. "On the principle of possible usefulness? Is it moral to do science for purely scientific reasons?"

"Maybe gene experimentation is all right," says Helmut, "since it's being used to combat disease."

"I think that the scientist bears responsibility for the uses to which his work is put," says Heiner. "He shouldn't work for a government that will use his research to hurt people."

Frau Hintze nods in apparent agreement.

"We should be discussing all this in our Ethics class," says Ulrike. She mentions the example of Carl von Weizsäcker—a Third Reich nuclear physicist (and brother of former President Richard von Weizsäcker) who worked halfheartedly for the Nazis, in order to thwart or delay the development of a German atomic bomb. Science is too highly developed and human beings are too underdeveloped, Weizsäcker had noted. How, asks Ulrike, can any wise decisions about the use of great power, scientific or otherwise, be made without human capacities for insight and judgment developing to their fullest? We accumulate knowledge without growing in wisdom.

"So—should scientists be permitted to pursue knowledge without restrictions, even if it endangers Humanity?" asks Frau Hintze.

As if to underline the urgency of the question, the school bell rings. The class disperses for a five-minute break.

During the interim, Ulrike shares her book with me. We point out lines in the play to each other. She calls attention to Galileo's half-humorous, richly ironic, Brechtian warning in Scene 14, on giving Andrea his secret *Discourses* to sneak out of Italy: "Be careful when you go through Germany if you're smuggling the truth under your cloak!" Ulrike smiles at me. Then I turn to Scene 4: "Truth is the child of Time, not Authority." (As Pope John Paul II would belatedly confirm in the 1980s, when he rescinded, after 350 years, Galileo's excommunication from the Church.)

Ulrike riffles through her dog-eared copy of the play, as we trade our delight in some of *Galileo*'s other famous touchstones:

Scene 8: "Only so much truth prevails as we make prevail."

And the line that I have always felt to be the most powerful—and haunting—in the play:

Scene 9: "Whoever doesn't know the truth is only an idiot. But whoever knows it and calls it a lie is a criminal!"

III

Eleven A.M. "Should scientists pursue knowledge into areas that endanger Humanity?"

Frau Hintze's raised voice quiets the social chatter in the back of the classroom. She pauses. Then she smiles.

"Herr Rodden, what do you think?"

Might we discuss examples even closer to home? I ask. Rather than the American scientists of 1945 or the genetic researchers, what about instances from DDR history? Might we consider scientific ethics as applied to scientific socialism?

Murmurs of disquiet flutter through the room.

"But Brecht isn't a DDR author," one pupil says. "He's a German author."

With considerable diffidence, concerned to avoid any tone of smugness or self-righteousness, I tell the class that I don't mean to deny the relevance of *Galileo* to the United States, only to connect it to its German—indeed also DDR—history.

"Brecht *does* seem like a DDR author to me," says Christoph.

Could Brecht have been advancing a veiled criticism of the DDR? I ask. Or a veiled criticism of—indeed guilty (if unconscious) confession about—himself? And why? Perhaps for his knowing the truth about Stalin's purges, the show trials, and June 17—and still, in criminal fashion, branding the truth a lie?

I decide to challenge the class: In the Marxist spirit of urging historical concreteness, should we also talk about racial hygiene and not just genetic engineering? About the DDR government's attempts to deny or downplay that Germans living in the east were also responsible for the Final Solution? And the DDR government's cover-up of the facts about the concentration camps on eastern German soil during 1945–50? Shouldn't we talk first about World War II and the Cold War rather than the war in Iraq?

"The DDR government never denied that Germans in the DDR shared responsibility for the Holocaust!" insists Dirk. "And we never had death camps!"

I mention my trip to Buchenwald last week—and the news, hushed up in the DDR for decades, about its use during the SBZ and early DDR days as a Stalinist internment camp—in which at least 30,000 people were imprisoned and 10,000 died. Here another line from *Galileo* is evocative: One monk-astronomer objects that publicity about Galileo's discoveries should be avoided. "We must be silent from the highest of motives—the inward peace of less fortunate souls." These unfortunates would, he says, be shocked to learn that the earth is not the center of the cosmos but just a stone spinning about the sun in a remote corner of the universe.

Throwing caution to the wind, I toss out a speculation for the class to consider:

Might indeed another twentieth-century example pertaining to nuclear physics and the DDR's own confrontation with a great scientist apply?

The class does not respond. Frau Hintze looks expectant and alert.

Does Galileo's recantation scene possibly pertain to Robert Havemann? Havemann the physical chemist and prominent dissident, the man who had explicitly warned that the SED's repression of dissidents reminded him of the Inquisition's treatment of Galileo?

The class stares blankly; nobody knows who Havemann was.

One girl says that she's heard of him, but she doesn't know exactly what he did. She remembers that Havemann was in the news recently: (Gregor) Gysi had been Havemann's lawyer, and *Stasi* documents just released by Havemann's widow showed that Gysi had reported their confidential lawyer-client conversations to the *Stasi*.

Has anyone heard of a work called *Dialektik ohne Dogma*, published in 1964? I continue. I don't mean that Brecht had Havemann's example in mind—that would be anachronistic, if for no other reason than that Havemann was a loyal Party man until the early 1960s; but the later Havemann strikes me as the model of Galileo as Brecht wished Galileo—and perhaps himself?—might have been. The robes of SED dogma couldn't smother or silence Havemann. The Havemann of the 1960s and '70s became the figure that Brecht's truly socialist self—as opposed to Brecht the cunning careerist—insisted that Galileo should have been: courageous, humane, responsible. A man deeply concerned with the ethical and political consequences of his scientific research.

The class talks about Brecht. Frau Hintze acknowledges that Brecht was planning to stage *Galileo* when he died in August 1956—after the shock of Khrushchev's Secret Speech about Stalin's crimes.

Does everybody here know about Khrushchev's Secret Speech? I ask. A couple of students look doubtful. I explain that the February 1956 speech constituted the first official acknowledgment in the communist world of Stalin's monstrous crimes—though the speech referred only to Party executions, not to mass murder in the millions. But Brecht certainly knew, at least roughly, about the scale of Stalin's crimes. Might Brecht, who was rewriting the play for the 1956 production and still ambivalent about the June 17 uprising, have expanded *Galileo*'s target range to include the evils of Stalinism?

Now the hardest questions come up—and the students do not flinch as we bring them up, one by one. What did DDR citizens know about the regime and the

Stasi—and when did they know it? Did the older generation know the truth? If not, were they idiots? And if they did know the truth, is Brecht right that they—and he himself—are criminals?

"They weren't criminals," says Claudia. "They didn't *lie*; they said nothing."

Lies of omission? I ask. Did East Germans carry the truth under their coats?

Frau Hintze says she'll have to think about all this; she's never approached the play from this "critical" angle before.

"These are different interpretations," says Frau Hintze. "But I still think that we must demand that the scientist serve the *Volk* and society. The scientist must accept responsibility for what he says and does."

"And what about the teacher?" comes a voice from the corner of the room.

"We only learn to discuss these themes 'scientifically'—in an abstract way," protests Ulrike. "Until now, I never would have thought to raise these questions about DDR history. Why not?"

"It was the fault of our teachers," Christoph says. He avoids Frau Hintze's glance.

Frau Hintze listens. She pauses. She says that she regrets much of her pedagogy and her specific views before 1989. And she admits that she thinks "in patterns deeply set during the DDR era." Her openness stuns me: to say all this in front of her 12th-grade class requires moral courage!

For a brief moment, stillness reigns; her words reverberate in the air.

Frau Hintze starts again. She acknowledges that she was a "loyal Party member." She joined the SED in 1985—"for job security."

Again she stops. Then she says quietly:

"Does *Galileo* evoke any more thoughts about the DDR?" Her glance scans the room. "Herr Rodden?"

I borrow Ursula's text. Turning to Scene 11, I read aloud: "I can't see myself as a refugee. I value my comfort." Those are Galileo's words, I remind the class, as he declines the help offered by an admirer to flee Florence for Venice and safety.

How many DDR citizens felt the same? I go on. Were DDR attitudes toward the government like the churchmen who go to Galileo's studio and refuse to look into his telescope, lest they should have to believe their own eyes? And if they had seen what was going on all around them, what would have happened then? Then they would have had the choice that confronted Robert Havemann and the other dissidents: to fight (as Havemann did) or to flee.

The class listens intently.

What have DDR citizens learned from all this? I ask. Is this history over? What, for instance, does the popularity of the PDS in last week's elections signify? And the apparent relationship of Gysi—still PDS chairman—to Havemann?

I speak about my recent visit to the Goethe Gymnasium in Weimar, where the 11th-grade pupils—some of them friends of Frau Hintze's pupils—held a mock election a few days before the October 16 national vote. The PDS received about 70 percent of the pupils' votes; not a single student voted for the CDU or FDP. (In the actual election, the PDS captured 15 percent of the Weimar vote, the CDU 42.8, the FDP 4.8, and the SPD 28.8; the PDS won only 4.4 percent of the vote nationwide, however. Of 88 seats in Thuringia's state parliament, the CDU received 42, the SPD 29, and the PDS 17.)

The PDS is a lightning rod of controversy, especially in Weimar, which is governed by the CDU yet has a sizable PDS following; from all sides of the room come responses, both for and against the PDS. The PDS vote by the Goethe pupils—which most pupils in the Schiller Gymnasium have heard about—was fully justified, says Jürgen. The PDS is a genuinely new party, not the "successor" to the SED, he says, and is the only voice expressing the discontent of easterners with the course of reunification.

The PDS is the only way for easterners to register a protest against Bonn, adds Claudia. Besides, she says with a laugh, the PDS campaign ads were smarter and better, e.g., the picture of a young couple kissing and saying to each other, "PDS, right?" The PDS is "the party of youth," she says.

Anti-PDS pupils in Frau Hintze's class have a different set of explanations for the PDS's successes. Even schoolchildren—like their elders—have *Ostalgie* for the DDR days, Ute says. The PDS, says Beate, is an anti-western party that represents everything western as bad. Students don't know any history, or they just forget the DDR's history, says Anne.

The PDS is the third-strongest party in the east, very much a regional party that focuses on easterners' problems and anxieties. Frau Hintze reminds the class that the party is stronger in the northeast; in Mecklenburg-Vorpommern, the PDS garnered 23 percent of the vote.

Is life better in eastern Germany than it was five years ago? I ask.

"I'm going to Ireland for the summer," says Ulrike.

"Yes, you couldn't have done that in the DDR," Frau Hintze says.

"In the DDR days, we had more equality; today we have more freedom," Ulrike says. "In the DDR, we had the POS; today we have the *Hauptschule* for the dumb children and *Gymnasium* for the smarter and wealthier children."

Which is more important, equality or freedom? I ask.

"I don't even think I had equality back then," Ulrike replies. "You weren't treated equally if you refused to join the Pioneers.

"I used to go to church in the late 1980s," Ulrike continues. "Now I seldom go. I don't have the same relationship to the priests. They think differently now. They always seem to have money on their minds now! They think in capitalist terms."

"The PDS has replaced the church as the voice of opposition," Frau Hintze elaborates. "It's ironic. Whereas the church replaced even the dissident SED voices as the expression of protest during the 1980s, the reconstituted SED—the PDS—has taken over that dissenting role in the 1990s. But with one big difference: church protests always had a Christian content; PDS protests are exclusively secular. And yet, a broad similarity remains, what the Church would call 'the social gospel.'"

And on that ecumenical note, the lunch bell rings; the class slowly files out. Several pupils stop to chat briefly about Havemann, Khrushchev's speech, and the recent election. A few pupils, Ulrike among them, remain a long while after class to talk further with Frau Hintze and me. One of them remarks on the differences between the DDR for him as a 13-year-old and for the generation of Frau Hintze.

"You don't understand," he tells me. "For most of children, the DDR was a good place. Your parents had time for you. A trinket was valued. You had a feeling of community with your neighbors. Today, our parents have no time, and in this consumer society, no possession is valued. A 13-year-old doesn't care about freedom of travel, freedom of speech, and so on. He cares about whether his parents are home. He cares about whether he has playmates and activities that occupy him meaningfully. My years in the DDR were good years."

Perhaps even, I imagine: Wonderful Years.

The conversation with the other students turns to the DDR. All of them say that they want "to learn more about DDR history." We discuss a rumor that I heard in the Goethe Gymnasium last week that Galileo's famous rejoinder to Andrea in Scene 14—"Pity the land that *needs* heroes"—had been dropped in some DDR school editions. Frau Hintze denies it. But no DDR edition is handy for us to check.

True or not, the story is plausible to me: Because the DDR had so stressed heroes and heroic deeds, Brecht's cynical idealism—that everyone could be a hero and therefore a nation required no public heroes—was most uncomfortable to DDR authorities. DDR pedagogy inculcated youth to be heroic anti-fascists. The songs and slogans of the Pioneers, as well as the ninth-grade trips to Buchenwald for the *Jugendweihe*, were explicitly designed for that purpose. To follow in the footsteps of "anti-fascist heroes" such as Ernst Thälmann was the young communist's highest calling.

IV

12:30 p.m. Frau Hintze and I return to the now-empty faculty lounge. She sits pensively, looking down. Suddenly she lifts her eyes and meets my glance.

"Scales have fallen from my eyes," Frau Hintze says quietly. She falls silent. She sighs deeply, as if letting go of a burden, and her countenance brightens.

"We—I—can still keep learning," she says, her voice rising. "We must keep learning."

Frau Hintze proceeds to tell me a little about her life. Married but with no children, she says that her pupils have long become part of her family. It is obvious that she is an excellent, caring teacher, both respected and loved by them.

"It's easier for you in the West," Frau Hintze says. "You've been educated to think critically. I haven't. And it's still a great difficulty for me.

"When I teach the play again, I'd like to do some of the things that you suggest. But I don't know much about Havemann myself. And such an approach as you suggest feels very unfamiliar—threatening even, though exciting."

Why?

Her answers are various. She was never educated toward "critical thinking." Her studies and her continuing education seminars never suggested such an approach. She feared losing her job if she said anything too controversial.

"We weren't criminals or idiots. Just human beings—with vulnerabilities and weaknesses. Just ordinary people who never lost hope that they could one day improve things." Frau Hintze reminds me that such a faith in ordinariness was precisely one of Brecht's key points. "He was challenging the notion that little people are helpless, and that only the extraordinary people—the heroes—can change things." Frau Hintze pauses. Then she draws the connection. Holding to a faith in ordinariness is precisely "why October 1989 finally arrived."

"And there were many good things even before that," Frau Hintze continues. "In my own life too—for example, the teachers in this school. You seem to think that it was just a 'Red' school. That's not so. The former director, it's true, was not a critical thinker. He was loyal to the system and a careerist. He was really an old Stalinist."

But October 1989 proved that people like him were the exception, Frau Hintze says.

Frau Hintze repeats the phrase "critical thinking" several times. It seems to be a term of high approbation for her, somehow related to the strongest virtues of "western": a bold questioning of hierarchy and of received answers, a searching inventory of one's responsibilities in the face of unjust authority, a healthy scrutiny of oneself.

"Truth," I murmur, "is the child of Time, not Authority."

Frau Hintze smiles. She nods her head.

"I had no *Auseinandersetzung* [freewheeling debate] in my studies, only M-L. We were fed teachers' opinions and the verdicts of authorities. I learned to cite authorities—a Party document, a state official, a Marxist touchstone—as proof and defense of all positions. And so I never really took seriously any *oppositional* viewpoint. It wasn't an occasion for thinking about my own viewpoint. It was 'incorrect.' It was just 'oppositional,' and an energetic standard response would neutralize its power.

"Only one opinion on a topic reigned in the DDR," Frau Hintze says. "And I didn't take into account other opinions. Not really. There were never any other opinions to take seriously into account.

"Everything was walled in—quite literally. You've heard the phrase? It's true: The Wall was in our heads.

"And one doesn't unlearn all this quickly. At least not at my age! Until you spoke in class, I never thought about non-Marxist ways of teaching Brecht—even though, I grant you, it's been five years since the *Wende*. I could give lip service to the statement, 'There are a variety of interpretations possible,' but I never really conceived of any serious opinion outside the Marxist *Weltanschauung*.

"You have to understand all this historically," Frau Hintze continues. She is "a product of the DDR." During and after her studies at the Dresden College of Pedagogy (1960–64), she says, she never encountered anyone who thought "critically."

"Even after Prague, I never met a critical thinker. I never learned how to do that, I never encountered anybody who was doing it. We were directed in our course of studies in college to think a certain way. And I learned that particular way of thinking. This is probably very hard for you to understand, because it is just as natural for you to think critically as it was for me to think dialectically."

What about the younger, post-reunification generation?

"The pupils here still aren't being educated to think critically," Frau Hintze says. "Because their teachers don't know how to do it. And because 'thinking' is very hard to do at all in the midst of the confusion and turmoil and upheaval of this transition from the DDR to the BRD. Too many teachers still teach ideologically: they begin with the ready-made answer. And they emphasize rote textbook learning, rather than foster independence of mind and the awareness of diverse viewpoints. The kids go by others' cues and escape into distractions and sloganeering, rather than do the hard work of 'thinking'—whether 'critically' or 'dialectically.'

"And they still feel self-constrained and are biased against critical thinking, which really starts with what the Party called 'self-criticism.' But 'self-criticism' for us was really an apologia to the Party for individualistic excesses."

Self-criticism, says Frau Hintze, was what one hoped to avoid: it was a public act of repentance for one's hubris or disloyalty—an acknowledgment of having been a bad Marxist. She continues: "The idea of your western self-criticism—that one includes oneself in all criticism, or even begins with oneself and one's own side—is very unfamiliar and threatening to us.

"I didn't see any role models. Christa Wolf and Anna Seghers remained silent about most injustices." Wolf's silence was derived from her emulation of and reverence for Seghers, Frau Hintze says.

"In the early 1980s, just two or three years after I arrived here, a stricter syllabus was introduced. I was a new, young teacher. The Schiller EOS was the only EOS in Weimar. It had the best-trained faculty; positions at the school were coveted.

"In 1985, I joined the Party. It was a pragmatic decision. The Schiller EOS was one of the best schools in the state. It was an important school for producing university candidates, and the director wanted more Party members, above all in my subjects, German and history. The director told us that, if there were any transfers, Party members would have the best chance of remaining at the school. So I joined.

"Everybody had been saying for years that an EOS history teacher like me should be in the Party. I had a tough time fending off the pressure to join. And teaching history was so hard—especially 11th grade, which dealt with the worker's movement since 1848, and 12th grade, which covered the history of the SED. At times I hated it. That had to do with my family: my parents were skeptical about the Party and DDR. My father had a position in church administration; before the war, he was a civil servant. When he joined the church and began working for it, he naturally gravitated toward the opposition voices and was constantly among people who were suspected by the regime of activities hostile to the state.

"I was never really a supporter of the regime, but I conformed. I was a careerist like most of my friends and colleagues—we constituted 85 percent of the Party.

"We had absolutely no *Freiraum* in history. Or even German. We could never have taught Brecht in the way you suggested!"

What about events that were contested between East German and West German historians? Did you ever have any doubts about the Party line?

"Strangely enough, no. For instance, the Nazi-Soviet Pact in 1939 was skipped in my studies. And in later years, I don't remember ever discussing it, even once, with a colleague. I never knew about it. And not just that event. When *Sputnik* was banned in 1988, I was shocked. Until the ban, I never knew much about Stalin. When all the news about his regime of terror came out, I couldn't believe it. I never knew about all that."

"You see, I 'knew'—and I didn't know. I had heard various things over the years, but I had never discussed Stalin—he was effectively screened out of my course of studies and the history curriculum of the school. There was a wall around him. I never knew that he murdered millions of people."

Even though you could watch West German TV?

"We didn't watch it much until the 1980s. But you're right: I may have heard things about Stalin from West German TV. But I had a *Feindbild*—I attributed any negative reports to the Cold War and screened them out. We had Schnitzler and *The Black Channel* [which propagandized for the DDR via critiques of West German events], but Matthias Walden did the same thing for RIAS [Radio in the American Sector]. He was a propagandist too.

"I used to smile at Schnitzler—I never really believed him. I had a certain built-in defense mechanism toward him—I was never a Schnitzler true believer.

"Who was telling the truth—Schnitzler or Matthias Walden? I didn't know. And, as I say, I didn't inquire too deeply. In the end, I simply assumed that much of what both sides were saying was false, but that our side was less so.

"And that was a blind spot of mine. Pupils would occasionally ask in history class: But did the *Volk* know about the Holocaust? I would say: grandparents in the Third Reich could have known if they chose to see.

"*Should* they have known? I took a hard line on that: Who wanted to know, did know. But who really *wanted* to know? The very knowledge made you complicit—or put you in great danger. And who would take the risks? For most people, it all depended on the people with whom you were in close contact, and whether they were being directly victimized or not.

"Who wanted to know, did know: I always said that about the Nazi years. That's what I believed—and, for the most part, still believe."

Frau Hintze pauses. Her eyes are pools of tears. The unspoken question—or self-accusation?—hovers in the air.

"And what about us?" Frau Hintze finally asks. "Us"—she means citizens of the DDR. She does not imply that the crimes of the Nazis and the SED dictatorship are equivalent. Her question simply exemplifies, she says, western "critical thinking."

"I gathered that there were some 'excesses' of Party zeal [in Stalin's USSR], attributable to the difficult post-revolutionary [post-1917] conditions and, later, the war. I knew that Khrushchev spoke about a 'cult of personality' around Stalin, but I had never participated in that cult, and I didn't think it was anything more than hero-worship. I was a 14-year-old girl in 1956, very unpolitical. Khrushchev's speech, Poland, Hungary—they all swept by me. In the 1970s and '80s, I heard the name Solzhenitsyn. But I knew nothing about his work. It simply never filtered down to me."

And if you—as an EOS history teacher—didn't know any of this history, then certainly the general population of the DDR would have had little likelihood of knowing, of developing the informed skepticism of "critical thinkers."

"Right. The Wall was in their heads too."

What about the Wall itself? Certainly that event was—and remained—inescapable.

"Yes, but I was studying in Dresden at the time. We were far from Berlin. I never really reacted strongly to the erection of the Wall. The West was already inaccessible to us—you couldn't go there unless you had special reasons. And I never thought of emigrating. I couldn't have taught school in West Germany—DDR teaching credentials weren't recognized *drüben*. And though I had been to Cologne and West Berlin a few times in the 1950s, all my relatives were in the DDR. And they were aging and needed me to help care for them. I had a strong *Heimatgefühl* [feeling of home]. The Wall didn't change anything for us—just made us turn further inward.

"In 1988, I read *One Day in the Life of Ivan Denisovich*. Then I read Sholokhov's *New Country Under Way*, which showed how necessary it had been to collectivize agriculture in the 1930s.

"Nobody in the DDR ever mentioned that Stalin murdered 30 or 40 million people." Frau Hintze pauses. "But I did know it—vaguely.

"The truth was kept at a distance from us. The government kept it from us and didn't cultivate, or even allow, critical thinking.

"And so that is the question: In a society like the DDR, how *do* you get to the truth?"

The truth is difficult, Frau Hintze acknowledges, and poses difficulties once it is ascertained. Difficult to discern, difficult to express if discerned, difficult to share publicly if capable of expression.

"Take Stalin's mass murder," Frau Hintze says. "We in the DDR simply never thought to ask about it. If you did ask, you would receive only a confused, ambiguous answer, anyway. And if you kept on asking: that would be dangerous. You had to be ready to go to jail. You had to be prepared to part forever from your family. You had to be ready to lose your career and your friends."

Frau Hintze looks out the window. Then she turns and faces me.

"You had to be a hero. I was never a hero. I couldn't be a hero. I just didn't have it in me.

"But I had a limit," she continues. "I wouldn't inform. I never did—and never would have—worked for the *Stasi*. That was a line I wouldn't cross, and I have little sympathy today for those who did."

Her voice is steady. She looks me direct in the face.

"Should I be ashamed that I'm not a hero? Well, I'm not ashamed."

The voice remains low and even. The statement betrays neither defiance nor defensiveness.

Again and again the lines run through my head: "Pity the land that has no heroes. . . . Pity the land that *needs* heroes." Which is it, really?

Frau Hintze continues: "Although I now judge all the lying and deception to have been wrong, I just wasn't strong enough to pursue the truth. In hindsight, I couldn't have done things much differently. I wish that I had developed a mode of critical thinking, but I hadn't.

"Havemann, Biermann, Reiner Kunze—how I can teach them? I haven't yet really confronted them myself.

"But I am ashamed in another sense—not of myself, but rather of the nation that I lived in, a nation that effectively dictated that the only truly decent human beings

were those with the courage to be heroes. It was a nation that, by cutting us off
from the truth, made cowards of us all."

VI

Three P.M. As Frau Hintze escorts me to the bus stop, we talk of her career in the
Schiller Gymnasium. She mentions the names of some of the pupils that I met
during my last visit—a few of whom, like Frau Losart and Frau Gammlich, are
now teachers themselves. As we shake hands, Frau Hintze says that her first name
is Bärbel.

Waiting for the bus, I look at the faces of the children dashing by me.

DDR or no DDR: "Who has the Youth, has the Future."

Do they—do we—need heroes?

Perhaps it is my own weaknesses—or only the relative immaturity of the Andrea
in me—but I conclude that we all still do. It would be soothing and self-satisfying
to think that we do not. But the assumption of Galileo—and Brecht—that creation
of a special few heroes excludes the possibility of heroism for the rest of us, that
public heroism elevates those special few at the expense of the vast majority—
may be misconceived.

Maybe indeed just the reverse is the case.

Might not heroes show us what we're *all* capable of? And blaze a trail for the
rest of us to follow, in our own way, to become heroes in our own right?

Might not some part in all of us be destined to be a stargazer, looking upward
to the heroic possibilities of which humans are capable? And isn't the refusal to
do so a self-fulfilling prophecy?

In a utopian world, there might be no need for heroes. Or it would be so much
less arduous to be "heroic" that the word would lose its connotation of aristocratic
excellence.

But we don't live in utopias: we live in a human, all-too-human world of shortcomings and failings, a sometimes Orwellian world of untruths.

Might not heroes show us all the farther shore of human potential?

"Truth only prevails if we make it prevail. . . ."

Perhaps we should pity the land that does not acknowledge and celebrate its
heroes, indeed that feels compelled to repress or destroy their memory. Yes, for
heroes may point us toward that day when all of us might come closer to fulfilling
our own heroic potentials—and show us how to do so. For in the Good Society,
heroism will not be achieved by being or doing or having more than most other
people, but by reaching one's own farthest shore. In the Good Society, everybody
can be a hero—in his or her own way.

The DDR had its heroes, such as Robert Havemann. But very few East Germans
knew about him, during his lifetime or afterwards.

Or know about him even today.

13

Berlin, 1994

No Difficulties with the Truth? The Last Testament
of Philosopher-Dissident Wolfgang Harich

> Microscopic forms of cardiac hemorrhages have become very frequent in recent
> years. . . . It's a typical modern disease. I think its causes are of a moral order. The
> great majority of us are required to live a life of constant, systematic duplicity. Your
> health is bound to be affected if, day after day, you say the opposite of what you
> feel. . . . I found it painful to listen to you when you told us how you were re-educated
> and became mature in prison. It was like listening to a horse describing how it broke
> itself in.
>
> Pasternak, *Dr. Zhivago*

I

Friedenstrasse 8.

"Peace Street."

As we drive up to the home of Wolfgang Harich, 72, one of the leading intellectual controversialists in postwar Germany—indeed a one-man battlefield where
DDR history and identity have fought themselves out—I remark to my friend Ulrike on the ironies of his address. It seemed to evoke what Harich wished for
himself, after decades of struggle to regain his good name: to rest in peace. And
that he not, as he once said, "go dishonored to the grave."[1]

Ulrike, 35, a western Berlin linguist, is interested in hearing more about Harich's
history. The DDR itself is like a dream to her, she says—let alone such distant
events such as Harich's arrest and trial for sedition in 1956/57. She doesn't remember ever paying much attention to the DDR; East Berlin was just a few streets
yet a world away. She does not know much about DDR history, but as a Berliner,
she says, she has always felt some special bond to "the east." She too is eager to
meet Wolfgang Harich, the man whose comprehensive reform proposals constituted the only Party attempt at internal restructuring of the DDR before its collapse
in 1989/90.

I talk about Harich's reputation as a young man—what I've heard of it from
acquaintances, such as Monika Hüchel, wife of the poet Peter Hüchel and a
former colleague of Harich at the *Tägliche Rundschau*. Harich was "quite a
ladies' man," she noted, very much a bon vivant, glittering in his wit and
repartee amid the rubble in postwar Berlin. Brilliant, gossipy, impulsive, prin-
cipled, rational, visionary, high-minded, refractory, moralizing, self-righteous:
Harich, son of the distinguished literary critic Walther Harich—who died when

Harich was a small boy—came from a well-to-do German bourgeois family and seemed in the late 1940s a throwback to an earlier era of broadly cultivated European intellectuals.

I had long hoped to meet Wolfgang Harich—ever since I had read the 1956 *Spiegel* cover story about him[2]—in which the editor of the *Deutsche Rundschau* had called him "an intellectual phenomenon," "a pure intellect on two feet," and "a genius, an intellectual *Wunderkind*." The story also quoted two West Berlin professors as judging him to "stand a full storey above the rest of the young eastern intelligentsia." The *Spiegel* editors themselves described the 32-year-old Harich as a born intellectual revolutionary, "probably, despite his youth, the only intellectual of the Soviet occupation zone in a position to place in question the current foundations and the doctrine of ice-hard Stalinism." "He was one of the few with the courage to present his ideas openly," wrote the editors, "without leaving Ulbricht's power center [the DDR] and speaking from a safe western port."[3]

Had Harich retained his extravagant intellectual gifts? Ulrike asks me. As scholars in our mid-30s, Ulrike and I were both astonished by how much Harich had achieved at a young age; we silently measured ourselves against him—and were humbled. But I found it hard to answer her question. Much of Harich's literary criticism is polemical: attacks on postmodernism, "bourgeois experimentation," and the like. Much of his political and social writing, however provocative, is offbeat to the point of the bizarre. He occupies an odd place in the postwar German intellectual history: very little has been written about Harich in the decades since his trial; indeed, until the fall of the Wall, virtually nothing.

Was Harich "naïve"? Ulrike wonders aloud. Certainly, she says, he must have known that, in October 1956, even to talk "openly" in the DDR—"Ulbricht's power center"—about removing Ulbricht as Party head invited charges of conspiracy to overthrow the dictator. In the end, Ulrike and I agree, Harich really didn't do anything except talk and talk—whatever his ultimate intentions, he was arrested before he got far enough to *do* anything else. And that's largely why Harich felt he was guiltless: all he ever did was talk. And many observers have claimed that it was nothing more than that—"just talk." But Harich had always had his enemies.[4] Besides, even after-dinner conversations about replacing the SED leader— and Harich went far beyond supper-time chats—were dangerous. Because such loose "talk" wasn't just talk to Ulbricht: it was treason. And because, in the DDR of the mid-1950s, the Party was the state, and because the Party leader dominated the Party, Ulbricht's view prevailed.

Harich obviously had Faustian ambitions to be not just a man of reflection but a man of action[5]; he supported a version of the "convergence theory" of the 1950s, holding out the hope that a reformed SED and the West German SPD would obtain power in the two Germanies and move toward a democratic, socialist, reunified Germany. In the wake of Khrushchev's Secret Speech, Harich and his small circle around Aufbau Verlag felt that a new beginning in the DDR and toward German reunification was possible. Harich wanted free elections, the admission of legal opposition groups, and the dissolution of the *Stasi*—and called for them openly. I had always marveled that a young philosophy professor could have had such utopian aspirations—or delusions?—that he trusted that, in a totalitarian state and with the failed revolutions of Poland and Hungary smoldering around him in the fall of 1956, he and a small group of like-minded intellectuals might translate their ideas into reality. I looked forward to finding out what had become of this gifted young communist professor who had believed that intellectual-academic freedom was more than just a word—and who paid for that mistake with the best years of his life.

Questions raced through my mind. Had Harich been a mere philosopher with his head in the clouds? Or were his 1956 plans practicable? From his writings of the mid-1980s on Nietzsche, I knew that Harich still possessed the quixotic courage—or the rash temerity—to present his ideas openly and in public. But was he still the intellectual-verbal "phenomenon" who had, by the age of 25, established himself as early postwar Berlin's most important theater critic, and before the age of 30 as, arguably, the DDR's leading young intellectual? Or had eight years in prison and decades of seeking to overcome what he has repeatedly called his *Rufmord* (reputation-murder) disfigured and exhausted him?

II

With a finely manicured, snow-white beard vaguely reminiscent of Santa Claus— or Karl Marx—a small, frail man shuffles to the door to greet Ulrike and me on this crisp fall day in mid-October. His wife Anne won't be joining us this afternoon, Herr Harich informs us. She has heard his life story "a thousand times" and "couldn't bear to sit through it again." But her absence, he adds merrily, leaves the delicious pastries to be divided among the three of us.

Before conversing, Herr Harich insists that we sample the cakes and tea; he was—as he was reputed to be—very charming. I could well imagine the stories about his many girlfriends and liaisons in earlier days. His urbanity somehow also made plausible the rumor (vehemently and publicly denied by him for years) about his reaction on learning of Brecht's affair with his first wife, Isot, a minor member of Brecht's Berliner Ensemble. Harich himself, a playboy in his youth, was complimented, it is said—and winked at the arrangement.

I glance around at the books in Herr Harich's living room bookcase and on his reading chair: All of them deal with the DDR past, the *Wende*, and the battles raging about *Stasi* revelations and the history of the SED. How difficult it must be for him to accept the BRD of the 1990s! It *is* a unified Germany—*Deutschland einig Vaterland*—but not at all the socialist Germany of which Johannes Becher and Harich dreamed in the 1950s. In fact, the volumes about the past lining Harich's bookcases made me wonder whether Harich ever truly emerged from that traumatic decade of dizzying highs and abysmal lows, whether his struggle with Germany's checkered past—and with his own tragic personal past—is over, indeed in some ways has even fully begun.

The handsome beard catches my eye; yes, his flowing white mane is an arresting feature, dominating the head; but the brightly lit face, indeed the shiny forehead, seem almost polished for combat. And the eyes gleam, very alert, even darting— as if the eyes are a radar system for a man who has emerged from an intricately complicated world, a world ruled by so much intrigue and distrust that vigilance is imperative: things are never as they seem. Lies and betrayal are facts of life; words are puny and ephemeral. How hard it must be for an idealist like Wolfgang Harich to admit that!

Before his release in December 1964 from Bautzen, the notorious Saxony jail for political prisoners, Harich had spent more than seven of his eight years' imprisonment in solitary confinement. And he had suffered in Bautzen: severe bouts of depression and dizziness and, in July 1960, a heart attack; before the age of 40, his hair had already turned white.[6]

As we make small talk, I reflect on Harich's bizarre career after his release. Forbidden to write about philosophy again, he had nonetheless already recommenced his scholarly career. He was permitted to research cultural and literary history in Bautzen, and in early 1964, during what would become his last year in prison, he began re-reading an author about whom his father had written a highly acclaimed book in 1925: Jean Paul Friedrich Richter (1763–1825), a.k.a. Jean Paul, the Rousseau disciple, educationist, and German Jacobin.

Jean Paul: another dreamer and man of action, another Romantic and revolutionary. Influenced by the critical approaches of Lukács and Franz Mehring, Wolfgang Harich thus took up his father's legacy and became a Jean Paul scholar too. Indeed his two books on Jean Paul—dealing with his epistemology and his poetic vision, respectively—are probably Harich's finest scholarship. What an oddly appropriate leap into the utopian might-have-been, sitting in gruesome Bautzen, immersing himself in Jean Paul's psychological fiction.

But was Harich himself a revolutionary? Or a counterrevolutionary? All through the 1960s and '70s, Harich repeatedly reaffirmed that he had been guilty of "counterrevolutionary action" against the SED dictatorship. With the grim vehemence of his pronouncements, he became virtually a neo-Stalinist, declaring his full support for the measures taken against him and other dissidents in 1957.

Indeed, Harich seemed to have undergone something like the Stockholm Syndrome during his prison years. In 1975, he undertook a quixotic campaign for a state communism in the service of environmental protection. In the face of the dire warnings about the "limits to growth" issued by the Club of Rome in the early 1970s, he published *Communism without Growth: Babeuf and the Club of Rome* with Rowohlt Verlag. The book argued that only a neo-Stalinist state with dictatorial authority to enforce environmental standards could avert an ecological catastrophe. Harich's last day in the headlines (before the *Wende*) was in 1979, when he emigrated to Austria. He moved to West Germany in 1980 and became active in Green Party politics. But he soon grew disillusioned with western capitalism. In 1981, he returned to the still *besseres Deutschland*.

And so here he was again, back in the Berlin of his glory days, residing in the *Friedenstrasse*. Ulrike and I have come to talk with Herr Harich about the great moment in his life still mired in lies, betrayal, and confusion—a life that already seems to me not only to represent a cautionary story about the byzantine world of DDR cultural politics, but also to hold some larger lesson about the tragic fate of the intellectual under what might be called "surreal-existing socialism."

III

Harich's arrest and subsequent show trial—those watershed months in 1956/57 discussed briefly in chapter 2—have spawned controversies between Harich and his onetime friends and colleagues, also convicted and jailed. Harich's most notable campaign has been his decades-long feud with his former mentor at the Aufbau Verlag, the recently deceased Walter Janka, whose memoir *Difficulties with the Truth* became a surprise bestseller in Germany upon its publication in October 1989. Some of what Harich told Ulrike and me is also contained in his political memoir, a feisty, indignant reply to Janka entitled *No Difficulties with the Truth* (1993). In our interview, Harich expounded and elaborated on the book significantly, bringing his thoughts up to date from October 1992, when he had finished writing it.

The outcomes of the two trials of March and July 1957, respectively, were known to Ulrike and me. Arrested for "counterrevolutionary activities" judged "hostile to the state"—among them his meetings with the West German SPD, his authorship of a document designed to remove Ulbricht as SED chief, and his close connections with Lukács and with Budapest's dissident Petofi circle—Harich was sentenced to 10 years' imprisonment in March 1957; three other defendants (including his then-girlfriend Irene Giersch) received lesser sentences. Harich then turned state's evidence and became a witness in the July trial against other prominent co-conspirators. It resulted in Janka receiving a 5-year sentence; Gustav Just, deputy editor at *Sonntag*, a leading DDR weekly, was sentenced to 4 years; two other colleagues received shorter sentences.

Aside from these facts about what the press dubbed "the Harich Group," however, the two principal defendants—Harich and Janka—have indeed disputed almost everything else about the events of 1956/57. Our interview focused on these disputes—and on the historical issues and intricate interpersonal conflicts arising from them. Time and again, I realized that Harich had spent much of his formidable intellect and the better part of four decades obsessing about these conflicts: they represented the fateful collision of the intellectual's ivory tower with the Stalinist locomotive of history.

But first: Who was Walter Janka? Born in 1914 in Chemnitz, Janka was the son of a toolmaker and machinist. Like Erich Honecker, he joined the KJVD as a youngster. Trained as a typesetter, 19-year-old Walter was arrested in 1933 by the Nazis after his brother, a KPD Reichstag deputy, was murdered by the SA. A KPD member himself, Janka spent 18 months in Bautzen (at that time a Nazi jail) and Sachsenhausen before communist friends bought his release. He went to Czechoslovakia, then slipped back into East Prussia, worked underground for the KPD, and in 1936 went to Spain to fight with the Thälmann Brigade. He was wounded three times and became a war hero—and, at 23, the youngest battalion commander on the Loyalist side. Indeed he was also a Stalin loyalist—a vocal defender of the Moscow show trials.

Janka spent the war years in Mexico. There he befriended leading radical emigré intellectuals such as Anna Seghers, Heinrich Mann, Ludwig Renn, Lion Feuchtwanger, and Egon Erwin Kisch. He helped found the journal *Freies Deutschland*

and directed the publishing house *el libro libre* (The Free Book), publishing (among other books) Seghers' *The Seventh Cross* in 1942.

Returning to Germany in 1947, Janka worked in the press office of the newly founded SED and as a general director of DEFA. In 1951, at the age of 37, he became the director of Aufbau Verlag, which he would soon turn into the premier house in all of Germany. Under Janka, Aufbau became legendary for its literary excellence, its risk-taking and openness, and its intellectual vitality. Janka's roster of authors included not only his old friends Seghers, Kisch, Feuchtwanger, Renn, Arnold Zweig, and Heinrich Mann, but also Brecht, Becher, Lukács, Bloch, Martin Andersen Nexø, Oskar Maria Graf, Gerhart Hauptmann, Victor Klemperer, Nelly Sachs, Friedrich Wolf, and Bodo Uhse, among many others. But his success was cut short by the events of 1956/57, which transformed him from a cultural star into a political criminal. Janka became one of those working-class leftist tragedies having the rare and dubious distinction of being jailed by both the Nazis and by his fellow communists.

Janka died in March 1993, at the age of 79, maintaining as he had for 36 years that he never had any conspiratorial conversations or ambitions. In *Difficulties with the Truth* and in subsequent books and interviews, he claimed that his one-time friends, some of whom sat in the courtroom day after day, watching him get framed—Anna Seghers, Lili and Johannes Becher, Helene Weigel, and others— found it too difficult to tell the truth publicly and thereby save him. And above all, he maintained, Wolfgang Harich found it too difficult. Harich's false testimony, Janka said, doomed him to 3 years in Bautzen again, which had now become the most horrific DDR jail for political criminals.[7]

And so the onetime friends and close colleagues, Janka and Harich, had become hated enemies. The face-off was archetypal. Janka vs. Harich: the worldly older man vs. the young genius, the practical man vs. the classically educated intellectual, the tough working-class war hero vs. the bourgeois academic utopian. Professing "contempt" for Harich, Janka refused to meet him ever again after the trials. Janka told the press that he "feared losing control" if ever he even set foot in the same room with the "scoundrel" Harich.[8]

These two embittered old communists had been "the heroes of yore" to young DDR intellectuals, said one former Aufbau colleague, the writer Rolf Schneider. He called the Harich-Janka jousting "a depressing drama of mutual slaughter."[9]

IV

It is impossible to give the reader a sense of this "depressing drama"—and a glimpse into Harich's mind—without touching on the minutiae in the events of 1956 that obsessed him. So let us briefly address the four main issues and their bizarre, inconclusive aftermath—issues that divided Janka and Harich across more than three decades:

1. Was there indeed an intellectuals' conspiracy, centered at Aufbau Verlag, to overthrow Ulbricht?

2. If so, was there ever any real threat that Ulbricht would be toppled, or any chance that the Party would be transformed?

3. Did Harich, as he testified, write his allegedly conspiratorial "Platform on the Special German Way to Socialism" at Janka's urging?

4. Did Harich's confession and testimony serve as key evidence that sent Janka and other defendants to prison?

Harich met with Janka and several other colleagues in Janka's house in Klein-machnov, near Berlin, on November 21, 1956. Harich and other visitors have maintained that the conversation was "conspiratorial," including ideas about overthrowing Ulbricht and reconstituting the Party; Janka claimed that it was just a social gathering at which politics was discussed. Harich traveled to Hamburg to talk with *Spiegel* editor Rudolf Augstein on November 26. Judging that Harich's fruitless meetings with the Soviet ambassador and with Ulbricht[10] constituted a veiled official warning not to proceed any further with such independent actions, Augstein implored Harich to seek asylum in West Germany and not return to the DDR.[11] Harich disagreed about the danger; he was arrested on his return to East Berlin on November 29. It was 10 days before his 33rd birthday. He would not see freedom again until the age of 41.

"The difficulty for the [SED] leadership was now, How do we avoid creating a heroic myth? How do we get him to submit?" Harich later wrote. Ulbricht's solution, Harich said, was to define Harich's efforts as counter-revolutionary, making him an enemy of the state—not just a Party dissident—aiming to overthrow socialism.

During the first interrogation, Harich said, he realized that lying was futile. The SSD knew everything. At their request, he wrote a 72-page summary of his activities, including numerous conversations with Janka (and others) about the overthrow of Ulbricht and the reunification of Germany.

"I conceded it all," Harich told us. "I was already sentenced to 10 years, so I cooperated with the state and wrote everything down, as they demanded. If I didn't, they told me that I'd face a death sentence. There's nothing so bad about the document. Of course, you must see it in light of the language of a ritual of humiliation. . . . And I'm no hero after all."

Not a word about Harich's aspirations for reunification would be mentioned in the trial. Nor was Harich permitted to breathe a word of his contact with the Soviet ambassador.[12]

"I was ordered: 'Keep the Russians out of this—not a syllable about Russians!' " Harich said to us. Brecht too, who had just died in August 1956, was to remain inviolate.

"Brecht had been an inspiration for my ideas," Harich explained to Ulrike and me. "I had heard him say numerous times—at least once in the presence of Stephan Hermlin and Peter Hacks—that the Party had to be razed from top to bottom. I told my interrogators this. They answered: 'Brecht belongs now to History. You understand? Not a word about Brecht either.' '*De mortuis nil nisi bene*,' I said to them. They didn't know what that meant. I told them: 'One speaks only good of the dead.' 'Very wise,' they said. 'Remember that. Brecht belongs to us. Brecht has nothing to do with this story.' "

Brecht was to "go down into history as the most loyal friend and follower of Walter Ulbricht," Harich said. Brecht was to appear a disciple of Ulbricht—which was why Ulbricht delivered the eulogy at Brecht's funeral a few months earlier, a speech that Helene Weigel had said would have made even the cynical Brecht wince.

"But I wrote down Brecht's role in my confession. 'Dammit!' the *Stasi* man screamed at me. 'Why do you keep coming back to Brecht?!' 'Because you've bound me to the full truth,' I said. 'Well,' he said. 'In this document, all right—but not a word of this will be breathed at the trial itself. *Nil nisi bene,* eh? And nothing about Russians or about reunification. No Brecht, no Pushkin [the Russian ambassador whom Harich informed about his ideas], no 'third way.' "

"So now Ulbricht had what he wanted," Harich continued. "He was proud that not a single significant representative of DDR culture had to be pursued and prosecuted," Harich said. "Unlike Hungary, only intellectuals of the second- and third-rank had stepped out of line—Janka, Just, [*Sonntag* editor Heinz] Zöger, and me. The really important figures—Brecht, Zweig, Seghers—had all stood behind him. That was Ulbricht's viewpoint."[13]

And the move helped contain the intellectuals' protest within a small circle and stymie the development of anything like the mass uprisings of Poland or Hungary. That was why Ulbricht risked an international scandal and launched a full-blown show trial in the post-Stalinist era, thereby exposing himself to (and enduring) a barrage of international criticism: he calculated that only a public warning would be sufficient deterrent to crush the intelligentsia's unrest. As *Der Spiegel* wrote after Harich's arrest: "The strike against Harich and his friends had the expected effect. It was not a strike for drumming a message into the masses, but rather a warning to the intellectuals. The news had no effect on the general population, because to most people an editor of a philosophy journal [*Deutsche Zeitschrift für Philosophie*] means nothing. But the intelligentsia understood very well what it all meant."[14]

At his March 1957 trial, Harich thanked the *Stasi* for their vigilance in arresting him and the DDR Supreme Court for its lenience. Otherwise, he said, he would have been facing the hangman. In our interview, he repeatedly dismissed these public remarks as the standard "ritual of humiliation" in Stalinist trials. And he stressed that he had been threatened with "a death sentence" if he did not follow explicitly the instructions of the SSD about what to say at the trial.

But Harich had given another explanation in *No Difficulties with the Truth*: "Irony is seldom understood!" Harich claimed there that his confession was "Swiftian satire,"[15] his only means available to ridicule the show trial and, at the same time, tell the public that he had been under surveillance for weeks before his arrest, that it had all been a carefully planned operation by Ulbricht. "In no other way," he wrote, "could I have made it understood that the observation of the group lay far in the past and accused the apparatus for its 'mercy.' " In the July 1957 trial, Harich told us, he merely acknowledged the truth about the conspiratorial conversations that he and Janka had conducted—which other witnesses confirmed in secret protocols.

But others have had a much darker view of Harich's courtroom behavior, and until the collapse of the DDR in 1989/90, their views constituted the near-unquestioned public consensus. British DDR scholar David Childs spoke for them when he remarked in 1995 about Harich's testimony against Janka in the July trial: "On that occasion, the bronzed and fit-looking Harich was given several hours of the court's time to destroy Janka with detailed lies."[16]

V

All this had been disputed, fiercely yet largely by word of mouth—the charges and counter-charges never reached print in the DDR and rarely in the West—until the fall of 1989. But with the explosion of the DDR, the official version of the most notorious trial in DDR history exploded too—detonated by Janka's autobiography, *Difficulties with the Truth*, which topped the best-seller lists of the DDR within a month after the protests against the Honecker regime began.

Through an accident of timing, *Difficulties with the Truth* thus helped ignite the Revolution of the Candles. On October 5, 1989, as the world press trumpeted that trains were carrying 5,000 DDR political refugees from Hungary across East Germany toward asylum in the BRD, three chapters of Janka's book appeared in Hamburg, published by Rowohlt Verlag, the leading West German literary house.

The book aroused little response. On October 28, however, with Honecker having just resigned and the *Wende* now in full swing, Ulrich Mühe read portions of the book in a special performance in the German Theater in East Berlin. Suddenly, Janka's memoir was seized upon by the protest movement as a key document of witness against the SED regime; in a show of *glasnost*, the Culture Ministry ordered that the book be published immediately.

By early November, DDR dissidents were treating the Janka trial as a buzzword for 40 years of *Stasi* spying and Party lies. Janka was lionized as a tragic victim of the SED's machinations; Ulbricht's show trials were portrayed as emblematic of the corruption of the Party and of its passive intellectuals. Janka was honored by the dissolving SED, and then by the PDS, as a man of principle and a heroic opponent of state tyranny.[17]

Janka not only protested his innocence of any crimes against the state and charged his onetime friends with betrayal; he also accused Harich of eagerly turning SSD informant and condemning, on false charges, Janka and other defendants to prison terms. Janka claimed that Harich volunteered himself as the "crown witness" in 1957 and probably was even an NKVD agent. These claims became the focus of Harich's disputes with Janka during 1989–93. Denying the charges, Harich claimed that the Aufbau offices had been a "real witches' cauldron of the spirit of opposition, a Petofi Club in the form of internal editors' debates. . . ." Protesting his *Rufmord* by Janka and refusing to "go dishonored to my grave," Harich finally decided to sue for libel.[18] Among the claims of Janka:

1. Harich's wife Isot Kilian, a bit player in Brecht's Berliner Ensemble, had an affair with Brecht, which made Harich feel "more flattered than in-

jured." Harich's reply: the affair had led to a temporary break between him and Brecht.[19]

2. Harich testified in an interrogation before Janka's July 1957 trial, responding to a question on whether Janka knew of his illegal meetings in West Berlin with the SPD, "I think he surmised it." Harich's reply: Janka had no way of knowing about the meetings.

3. Harich was probably an NKVD agent.[20] Harich's reply: His acquaintanceship with Soviet occupation officials had extended merely to contact with a few Russians who had audited his Humboldt lectures and occasionally sought his opinion about Soviet-German affairs.[21]

Before these issues got to trial, however, Janka published *Spüren eines Lebens* (*Traces of a Life*) and *Der Prozess gegen Walter Janka und andere* (*The Trial Against Walter Janka and Others*) in 1990, wherein he dropped all mention of the Brecht-Isot affair. Janka also altered his report of Harich's testimony at the trial: "I don't know whether he knew." Of the NKVD connection, Janka wrote only that Harich spoke about Russian "officers" that "advised" him. Harich's new suit focused on the latter two issues.

In April 1991, the Berlin *Land* court took up Harich's case. The 67-year-old Harich sued Janka, 76, successfully, for "false claims damaging to my honor." SSD documents—unknown before 1991—had shown that at least two other defendants also wrote reports at the behest of the SSD, which spoke of an "illegal group" that would have led to the overthrow of Ulbricht and "weakening of the socialist camp." The Party representative in the Aufbau Verlag had written the SSD: "My opinion is that, if Janka had said to Harich: 'No, this business won't lead to anything, it's hostile to the state,' then the Harich Group would never have come about. Janka was the backbone of the Harich Group."[22] Settling out of court without a full-scale trial, Janka's lawyer agreed to a statement that acknowledged Janka's pronouncements about Harich were insufficiently grounded and he must withdraw them.

VI

It was a sweet, if belated, triumph for Wolfgang Harich.

Or was it just a paper victory? Harich was charged to pay 80 percent of the court costs (later reduced to half); no trial ever took place, and so Harich's lawyer never formally presented much of Harich's evidence.

As a result, the German press paid little attention to the news. Practically speaking, therefore, nothing much had changed: Janka was still publishing with the leading German houses. He was still a favorite of PDS luminaries such as Stefan Heym and Gregor Gysi (whose father Klaus had succeeded Janka as head of Aufbau Verlag in 1957). And Harich still felt himself an outcast branded as the "traitor" and "crown witness" who had snitched 35 years earlier on his friends.

"*Rufmord*," Harich repeated to Ulrike and me. "Despite the settlement, I was still regarded as naïve, a gossip, a dreamer, a crazy utopian. And Janka was now the *Gallionsfigur* [showpiece] of the PDS." The PDS leaders, Harich repeated, were all on Janka's side—which had delayed Harich's own readmittance to the Party until December 1992.[23]

"Janka remained a great hero of the DDR, a character of utter nobility. And yet, Janka's much-praised toughness, his supposed heroism, whereby no confession could be squeezed out of him, all depended on his expecting that he was going to be freed soon afterward. Since his Spanish civil war days, he had been a *Duzfreund* of Erich Mielke. And during the interrogations, Mielke had personal conversations with him.

"Janka has been built up into a great hero in Germany. But national unity never meant anything to him.

"He is no hero. He is actually a most sinister figure."

Harich pauses. The word "sinister" (*finster*) echoes in the room.

Harich has his own conspiracy theory about the arrests and trials of 1956/57, which, he says, he only began developing in 1992/93. His theory, parts of which he published in *No Difficulties with the Truth*, is that Janka himself was a secret agent—an agent provocateur under assignment from Ulbricht to secure Ulbricht's power, stifle all dissent, and eliminate any Ulbricht rivals.[24]

The key event, Harich now believed, was the meeting in Janka's home on November 21, 1956. Paul Merker, a former Politbüro member and probably the most popular politician in DDR opposition circles, attended. He had lost his Politbüro seat and Party membership in August 1950; he had since been rehabilitated, though not yet readmitted to the Party. Janka had been admired by many people for staying in touch with his old friend Merker during his fall from grace. Harich had formerly assumed that Janka did this despite Party disapproval. Now, he says, he believes that Janka spied on Merker for Ulbricht; and that the November 21 meeting was set up to suck Merker into the conspiracy of the Harich Group—and thereby, at minimum, soil Merker's reputation and forever eliminate him as a potential Party leader. Harich's belief in all this is strengthened by his discovery that Janka had also invited to the November 21 meeting a Leipzig professor, Walter Markov, who had been charged with "Titoism" in 1951 and expelled from the Party. Markov had not shown up at Kleinmachnov, citing personal reasons. But if he had done so, Harich says, his very presence would have lent the meeting a conspiratorial air.[25]

"I wasn't the most important person in the events of 1956," Harich stressed to Ulrike and me. "Certainly not. The most dangerous to Ulbricht was Paul Merker. As a former *Politbüro* member, he was highest in the hierarchy of threat." Merker could have been a great danger to Ulbricht, Harich maintains. The former Politbüro member could reasonably have been placed at the head of a de-Stalinized SED, or a joint SED-SPD regime, much easier than any other DDR leader. For he had never betrayed the SPD, since he had not been in Germany when the SPD was suppressed by the KPD in 1946. Ulbricht's scheme was designed to break the East German opposition, especially opponents from the right-wing of the Party, whose most significant figure was Merker.

"Merker is really the most important man in the whole story," Harich said. "Ulbricht was our enemy—we wanted to overthrow him," Harich said, "and Janka convinced us that Merker was our man." Merker instead of Ulbricht, the German

Gomulka instead of the German (Matyas) Rakosi: That was the topic of conversation in Janka's home, Harich said.[26] Merker demurred, Harich said; the idea that he might be an alternative to Ulbricht was mainly Janka's. Merker, like Harich, reported all this at the July 1957 trial.

"At the [July 1957] trial, Janka accused Merker of lying," Harich said. "But Merker had told the truth. Janka lied. Under assignment from Ulbricht, he acted as an *agent provocateur* and set a trap for Merker. It's increasingly difficult for me to imagine anything else."

Harich then went on to discuss his version of how Janka and Ulbricht worked to cut down Lukács in stature. First, Janka recast himself as a close friend of Lukács by making a big deal out of his alleged attempt to drive to Budapest in October 1956 and, with Becher's approval, whisk Lukács from the hands of the Russians. (Ulbricht apparently nixed the plan.) Then, 14 months after Janka's release in December 1960, says Harich, Lukács wrote Janka about wanting to get in touch with "his old editor, Harich." But Janka "attacked and defamed me to Lukács. He said I had played a terrible role [in the events of 1956] and that I was a human failure," Harich said. And that same summer of 1962, in Harich's version, Janka allegedly smeared the reputations of others, among them Lili Becher, Anna Seghers, and Helene Weigel.

"Aside from Merker," Harich continued, "Lukács was the biggest threat to Ulbricht. "Along with Bloch, he was the leading intellectual influence in the DDR—and the Hungarian uprising showed that he stood opposed to everything that Ulbricht represented. Only with some distance was it worth naming me as an exponent of national communism. And if Becher hadn't been so sick—and so willing to follow Party commands—he would also have been a victim, because he was the most prominent representative of this direction [reunification] and because he was envied for his privileges." Harich's importance in DDR cultural life in the 1950s, he explained, lay in his close relationships to Lukács and Becher.

Based on Janka's relationship to Merker and on the circumstances of the meeting in Janka's home in November 1956, Harich charges that Janka was in league with Ulbricht to trap Merker and the Harich Group. According to Harich, Ulbricht and Janka had three goals:

1. To defame and isolate Merker.
2. To permanently cut Harich off from opposition circles—through slander, ridicule, and distortion.
3. To blacken Lukács' relations with the DDR intellectual avant garde and make certain that he never returned to East Germany.

Harich says that all three goals were accomplished. Merker was not jailed, but he was brought in as a witness in the 1957 trials and thus suffered disgrace by association—his own *Rufmord*. Harich himself was permanently isolated—even opposition figures such as Biermann and Havemann developed hostile attitudes toward him. And Lukács never set foot in the DDR after 1956.[27]

In return for these services to Ulbricht, Harich says, Janka got off with a light sentence and was granted the honor of the hero's defiant pose in the courtroom.

Janka cut a deal with his old comrade Erich Mielke, Harich believes. In Harich's view, that explains why Janka, whose testimony at first had been similar to others in the Harich Group, suddenly changed his testimony after the first week of interrogation, i.e., after Mielke visited him in prison—and began to insist that he was *not* guilty. It also explains why Janka received an early release (after little more than two years in jail), why he was admitted back into the SED in 1972, and why he received the SED's Distinguished Service to the Fatherland Award in May 1989.

But if Harich is right, that Janka had set a trap for them all at Ulbricht's behest, why didn't Ulbricht save his loyal henchman from a second trip to Bautzen? An early release and a heroic profile at the trial hardly seem sufficient compensation for two years in jail! And for a shattered career! Harich does not suggest that Ulbricht double-crossed Janka. And yet, Janka suffered greatly: he did not gain readmittance to the Party until 1972; he lived in near-poverty for years (merely assisting on some DEFA documentaries, for which he was never credited); he never regained his Aufbau job nor worked in publishing again.

But Janka's biographer, Michael Rohrwasser, has a theory about the SED award that puts Janka in a dimmer light, even if it does not necessarily support Harich's conspiracy theory. Rohrwasser says that the award was probably given to Janka so that the SED wouldn't have to formally rehabilitate him—which would have meant reopening the files on the 1957 cases. As such, it amounted to a kind of bribe—hush money for Janka's willingness to bury the past. But that could have been the acquiescence of Janka the Obedient Party Man. It doesn't automatically mean that Janka was in cahoots with Ulbricht in 1956/57, only that Janka—like Harich—agreed not to embarrass the Party after his release.

Of course, Harich is fair to ask what the Party meant by Janka's "distinguished service": one is hard-pressed to name anything between 1957 and 1989. But if the Fatherland Award were a payoff for old services or hush money to keep silent about them, why did the Party wait so long to bestow it? And did Janka himself double-cross the Party? After all, he had already by April 1989—a month before he received the Fatherland Award—submitted *Difficulties with the Truth* to Ro-wohlt. Rohrwasser believes that Janka's arrangement with Rowohlt and the DDR may have allowed for him to submit his memoir to a western publisher, rather than cause a ruckus in East Berlin intellectual circles by having it rejected from a DDR publisher. Under such circumstances, though the memoir would have made its way unofficially to the DDR, it would never have had the chance to become the basis for a public discussion of the events of 1956/57 and of the corruptions of DDR legal history.[28] Janka's simple explanation was that the award honored his services to the Party before 1956 and served as an implicit apology for the events of 1956/57. It was simply a "recognition that came 30 years too late."[29]

Harich has every detail and every charge and counter-charge at his grasp; but my head swirls as I try to grasp it all. Somehow his dizzying story seems a microcosm of the spying and distrust that the culture of DDR politics bred. Each answer seems to raise more questions than it settles, as if names and dates and citations are simply rushing into a black hole of History.

VII

A knock at the door interrupts our conversation: a special-delivery messenger brings to Herr Harich copies of his new book from a small eastern German publisher (Kiro). Harich immediately bestows me with a gift copy of *Nietzsche und seine Brüder: Eine Streitschrift* (*Nietzsche and His Brothers: A Controversy*). The title—originally a line from a famous early postwar essay on Nietzsche by Thomas Mann—alludes to a 1988 conference in Wuppertal (titled "Nietzsche's Brothers") sponsored by the West German KPD, in which prominent West German Communists criticized Harich for his hostility to Nietzsche and advised that the time had come for the SED to readmit Nietzsche to DDR cultural life. Harich's title thus constituted an accusation: German communists had become Nietzsche's "brothers" themselves.

Harich, as we have already seen, strongly opposed Nietzsche's rehabilitation throughout the 1980s.[30] He was angered and hurt that he was not invited to the Wuppertal conference, especially because he had briefly joined the West German KPD during his year in the BRD in 1979/80 and knew personally some of the Wuppertal speakers.

Already in 1985, Harich had written "urgently" to DDR Prime Minister Willi Stoph that the projected publication of selected Nietzsche works had to be stopped. Harich did not pull punches with Stoph: "Nietzsche is the most reactionary, misanthropic figure that ever existed in the entire history of world culture from antiquity to the present day." At the time, a Nietzsche conference at the University of Halle was being planned, and the director of the Goethe-Schiller Archive (who was in charge of Nietzsche's papers) was considering publishing several Nietzsche volumes. As we saw in chapter 10, Harich succeeded, if only temporarily, in halting readmittance of Nietzsche to East German intellectual life.

Harich demurs about his success in opposing the "Nietzsche renaissance," a term that he bandies as a catch-all for problems ranging from genocide in Bosnia and Rwanda to the rise of German neo-Nazism. The "intellectual mafia" of the DDR were already planning to bring Nietzsche back—a big 150th anniversary celebration in October 1994 would have happened in the DDR too, Harich says.

We argue politely for a few minutes about Nietzsche. Harich repeats his claims from *Nietzsche and His Brothers.*[31] Nietzsche's "affirmation of slavery" and "his glorification of power/violence" mark him as "plainly the most negative essence of the history of world culture, from antiquity to the present." No more than Hitler's birthday (April 20) should Nietzsche's birthday (October 15) be celebrated. Hitler was a Nietzsche "pupil" and developed his grandiose ideas of war and genocide "through Nietzsche"; Nietzsche too is "partly responsible" for the concentration camps. It is a "travesty" that Nietzsche wrote in the German language, and it would be "appropriate" to raze the grave of Nietzsche—"the Urfascist from Röcken"—and thereby assure that it will never again become a pilgrimage site.

The vitriolic personal tone of Harich's scorn for Nietzsche stayed with me, and later, after reading an interview between Harich and an acquaintance from *Nietzsche and His Brothers*, I was struck by the relevance of a Harich remark to our immediate conversation. Speaking of the DDR cultural Establishment's dismissive reaction to Harich's 1987 attack on Nietzsche in *Sinn und Form*, the interviewer concluded, paraphrasing Harich's own claims: "The goal was to make you morally unredeemable, a bad character, to stigmatize you as a denunciant and therefore a social and political pariah. And it worked."

Harich agreed: "The murder of my good name is repeated again and again. . . . [Even though] since my release, I've behaved in a reserved and loyal fashion."

Harich's conspiracy theory thus extended its branches beyond the events of 1956/57 to Nietzsche. And even outward: Harich also said in *Nietzsche and His Brothers* that the absence of any DDR commemoration for Jean Paul in 1975 or 1988—even though no previous anniversary of Jean Paul had ever been observed in the DDR—was intended as a deliberate slight to Harich himself. And he wrote in *No Difficulties with the Truth*—in open contempt for a 1990 newspaper profile on him headlined "No Difficulties with Megalomania"[32]—that the release of Stefan Heym's novel, *Collin*—which includes a character that is arguably a satirical portrait of Harich—was timed to coincide with Harich's leaving the DDR in 1979. *Collinere*, Harich notes, means "to smear" in Latin; Heym was apparently in league with Janka to smear Harich.[33]

Isn't that all just a tad paranoiac? I wondered.

But Harich had anticipated me in *No Difficulties with the Truth*:

"It's no wonder that, after eight years of prison and subsequent isolation through systematic slander, that one begins to think paranoically. . . . [But] where [paranoia] appears, there really is an underground spring [of water/truth]."[34]

His alleged "paranoia" had real roots, Harich insisted, even if the flower of his conclusions might be rank.

"*Rufmord*," Harich repeats to us. He pauses. "Yes, I also want to re-establish my honor!" He pauses again. "But please! This is not just about me! It's also about the great communists who are no longer alive: Anna Seghers, Helene Weigel, Paul Merker, Becher. And last but not least, Lukács—the only Marxist philosopher of world stature.

"Nothing is more important [to me] than the poems and plays of Brecht, the thought of Lukács, Becher's Fatherland lyrics, the novels of Seghers. . . . And also I am thankful for the personal character of the great communists. And in the case of Becher, Seghers, and Merker—at minimum—the myth of Janka stands in the way of their ever getting their due."[35]

And even when they did receive "their due," it was sometimes in the form of a cruel joke, Harich says. For instance, in 1969, Merker was given an honorary burial and a special grave, located in a prominent place in the Cemetery of the Socialists in Berlin-Friedrichsfelde. It was as if he had never been ousted from the Politbüro. A street was also named after him in Eichwalde, where he had last lived. And in the 1980s, the Party even devoted a postage stamp to him in the series on "working class elders." As with Brecht, the Party had decided: Merker belongs to us.[36]

"Merker is one of East Germany's most tragic figures, one of the most tragic in the history of the worker's movement," Harich says. "It's high time to do justice to history and to restore his good name accurately."

VIII

Restoring good names—or directing History to judge which reputations warrant blackening—was much on Harich's mind throughout 1993. For instance, claiming to be free himself of the irrational vindictiveness of Janka, Harich told the press that he held it to be a matter of honor that, rather than testify against the DDR judge who sentenced him to 10 years in prison—the only surviving judge from the 1957 show trials—he accepted three contempt of court citations (and a fine of DM 1,800).[37]

But was I the only person to wonder if there might be something from the 1957 trial that Harich didn't want to have opened up? Precisely what he accused Janka of trying to avoid by accepting the DDR Distinguished Service Award in May 1989?

Or was it indeed, as Harich implied, his high-mindedness? Harich ascribed his refusal to his convictions and conscience: the case had outrun the proper statute of limitations, the judge was too old and frail to stand trial, and post-reunification Germany has no right to pass judgment on events in DDR legal history.

Again Harich returns to his relationship with Janka.

"It was awful that Janka, a man of experience, had misled a young man like me into those politically criminal activities," Harich said. Harich pauses. He makes a few comments about the false trust that one develops toward an agent provocateur; he says that he has known several—or at least suspected several—people of being *Stasi* informants.

"An IM or a *Stasi* man is a wonderful person!" Harich says, chuckling. There is an odd lightness in his manner, a twinkle in his eye, a lilt in his voice. He notices my confusion; he continues.

"An agent performs services of all kinds! Look at that painting—it's an eighteenth-century landscape. A valuable painting. I might hesitate about hanging it on the wall, not at all sure about how to nail it. But an IM might go to the trouble of doing all that for me. Or even intercede with pretty girls in whom I might have an interest! An IM is a *very* accommodating person."

Now I have caught the irony in his tone. Herr Harich goes on:

"The IM provides such services so that he can get close to me, can remain in my presence. But after all, I'm never entirely *sure* that he is an IM, am I? I merely have a suspicion. But that suspicion makes me careful. I am on my guard with him: I speak only the Party line in his presence, no criticism whatsoever. Everything is pleasant: he is helping me, I am obviously helping him. Such was the way of life here!"

He pauses. He asks me if I have any questions for him. I produce a September 26, 1994, article from *Focus*, titled "The Collaboration of Comrade H.," which charges Harich himself with having been an IM. What does he say to it?

His monologue is interrupted; he suddenly falls silent. He blinks quickly, then shifts in his chair and looks away, toward the bookcases. I go on to ask Harich about a *Stasi* document, recently released and cited by *Focus*, that alleges Harich's cooperation with the *Stasi* to discredit Rudolf Bahro, author of *Die Alternative* (*The Alternative*), a "third way" critique of East European communism. Bahro had been sentenced to a seven-year jail term (though soon released) for writing his book, had recently been released in 1978, and was living in West Berlin that year. The September profile on Harich in *Focus* is followed by a three-page story of Harich's cooperation to spread disinformation about Bahro and "Freedom and Socialism," a West German defense committee formed to help Bahro; a longer story, complete with extensive excerpts from the relevant *Stasi* documents on Harich, had appeared in the September *europäische ideen*, edited by Andreas Mytze. *Focus* claimed that this was the first report to confirm what many observers had long suspected: Harich's *Stasi* collaboration. A follow-up *Focus* story about Harich's alleged collaboration opens: "History hurts."[38]

"I can't do anything about him [Mytze]," Herr Harich answers. I notice that his voice is becoming strained. "Mytze just doesn't believe me. That's his problem. But I want to tell you—apart from everything else—that I consider it a cruelty and a travesty for a West German group to try to involve a man who had served eight years in jail for state treason. I didn't speak to the *Stasi*—at least as far as I knew. But I did take the news directly to my contact at the [SED] Central Committee—I feared that, if I didn't, the authorities would come after me again. After all, they had warned me that people would regard me as an opponent of the regime—and attempt to use me for their ends against the DDR."

Harich repeated to us what he said in September 1994 to *europäische ideen*: the true identities of his conversational partners had not been known to him. "I believed until then that I had spoken with a contact from the Central Committee of the SED." But Andreas Mytze of *europäische ideen* had told *Focus* that he "regarded such a stupidity as impossible" to credit.[39]

Harich said his motive for reporting to SED officials his connection to the Bahro defense committee was that he felt himself "a victim of a provocation" and felt, "in light of my punishment from 1956" that he had to bring the news to the Central Committee or face another possible round of punishment.

Whatever the truth—Harich later charged the Gauck Commission with a violation of his rights by its release of confidential data[40]—even Harich's admission of cooperation with the SED Central Committee's skullduggery against Bahro constituted an embarrassing revelation. It was especially humiliating for Harich because it came on the heels of Harich's chairing the *Alternative Enquetekommission*, a.k.a., the Alternative Commission on the Investigation of DDR and BRD History. Harich had campaigned successfully for an "alternative," PDS-sponsored review of DDR history—with Harich himself in charge. Fearing that Bonn would seek to undermine the PDS in its report on the role of the SED in DDR history, the "Alternative Commission" would serve as an alternative to the official BRD commission, which was set up with Rainer Eppelmann, now a CDU representative in the *Bundestag*, as chairman.[41] But Harich's triumphant return to the spotlight would soon be spoiled by the revelations of his own personal past: within weeks, DDR history would return again to haunt him.[42]

On May 29, 1994, Harich chaired a much-publicized meeting in Brecht's old theater, the Berliner Ensemble. Honecker had just died that day, and Harich announced the news from the stage with great fanfare.[43] Observers said that, in hindsight, it was as if Harich had indeed returned to the 1950s: It was a final, belated moment in the sun.

The meeting itself was to begin an inquiry into espionage in the DDR and BRD. Top spies were the featured guests: former Generals Markus Wolf and Werner Grossmann of the *MfS* were paired off against their West German counterparts. Plans to host a similar meeting between agents and victims of the secret police units, with Harich himself included as one of the victims, were canceled over disagreements about the list of invitees.

We sensed Harich's embarrassment over the appearance of hypocritical inconsistency between his public positions and his private life. He had won against Janka, at least in the court of History—only now to overreach himself by organizing this alternative commission on German history, with himself as its presiding spirit. So History had suddenly turned on him: the limelight was now glaring. And it was as if a chorus of critical voices were shouting from all directions:

How could a man like Harich put himself forth as the investigator of the German secret services' abuses when he himself had contributed to them? How could Harich proclaim himself a victim when he had served the victimizers?

Clio knows no favorites. Just as the documentary record seemed to vindicate him in the case of his dispute with Janka, now History had dealt Harich himself a cruel blow. History hurts!

"We must stop," Herr Harich tells me abruptly. His heart is weak, he explains. He says he does not feel well—and has already spoken for three hours.

"You do believe me, don't you?" Herr Harich asks, in a subdued tone, as a black line seems to sweep down the bright forehead and across the beautiful white beard like a shooting star.

Is it fear? Is it dread? Is it hope?

"Yes," Ulrike says slowly, as we move toward the door. She pauses. "I do believe you."

Herr Harich turns to look at me. A long, awkward silence ensues. He waits for me to respond.

"I believe that you are sincere," I answer hesitantly, standing in the doorway. "But I really must think it all over."

We shake hands.

"'Til we meet again," Herr Harich says. He smiles wanly and waves goodbye.

IX

As we leave the *Friedenstrasse* and drive back to western Berlin, Ulrike and I talk about our encounter with Wolfgang Harich. We mourn the dark world that enveloped him. We return to our earlier question: Had Harich retained his gifts? We muse on how his virtuosity and brilliance seemed to have been slanted into conspiratorial speculation. I felt that "Traces of A Life" could have been the title for his own memoir: Though there were vestiges of the nobility of spirit and soaring intellect about which I had read and heard so much, Harich was obviously a spent man, a shell of the young intellectual he had once been: virtually an image of the former DDR itself. Indeed his labyrinthine saga seemed finally a cautionary story of how a climate of fear, intrigue, desperation, paranoia, and revenge lays waste to even the most splendid gifts.

Harich's "bourgeois" asides fascinate us: How lavishly he had praised Goethe, Schiller, and Heine. His Lukácian admiration for the great middle-class realists of the classical era. How proud he was to have associated closely with Lukács and Bloch. His respect for *Bildung*: the mark of his bourgeois family heritage. His dismissive remark of a Humboldt colleague: "an uncultured idiot." Indeed his contrast of the Stalinist university with the utopian publishing house was revealing: He distinguished between Humboldt's stagnant philosophy department (with Party-line colleagues such as Kurt Hager) and the exciting intellectual atmosphere of Aufbau Verlag, where famous authors were always coming and going, that "Elysium of intellectual breadth, deep reflection, and productive tolerance, where I could always be led back to myself again," as he wrote in *No Difficulties with the Truth*. Wolfgang Harich was an out-of-the-closet elitist in a world of rigidly egalitarian, Marxist pieties.

Another passing remark of Harich comes to mind: "The SED was always aware of my strong urge to influence politics." Ever eager to proselytize, heedless of the boundaries of friends' (or "the Friends' ") sensibilities, he proceeded to the bitter end with his visionary abstractions. Though he has retained an inner warmth, and certainly his charm, amid a political world of fear and manipulation and deception and hypocrisy, he is driven by his idealistic schemes. As Rolf Schneider once noted, Harich's lifelong quest for political influence and an ideological home set him on an inner/outer emigration through every political faction of the radical Left: KPD, SED, Green, KPD (West German), and finally PDS.

Why did you tell Harich that you believe him? I ask Ulrike.

She says that she's not sure; she admits that she has no firm convictions about the history of the Harich-Janka dispute, about which she knew next to nothing until today. She sighs.

"I told him, 'I believe in you,' because I felt that he needed to hear that from someone," she finally answers. "I believe that he is a decent human being, apart from how he remembers or narrates his life story."

She is right about one thing, at least, which I had not expected: Harich's strong need for us *to like him*.

But I had difficulties with the truth of some of his claims.

And so, I do believe, did Wolfgang Harich.

Ulrike and I forswear any attempts to disentangle Harich's story further. Our forceful personal encounter with Harich feels more compelling.

Had Janka triumphed in the end? Ulrike asks. It would have seemed so. Janka became a national figure with the publication of *Difficulties with the Truth*, he published his next two books (and two other books posthumously)[44] with major publishing houses, he was friendly with the chief figures in DDR culture and politics, he established close relations both with opposition spokesmen such as Havemann and Biermann and with SED and PDS leaders, he was even under consideration in early 1990 to become the president of the DDR. The negative outcome of the 1991 suit seemed little to have changed his reputation among opinion-makers.

And Harich? Harich, by contrast, became ever more regarded as a dilettante and a traitor, even a buffoon and a cuckold. He became less and less visible, he published all his books after the 1970s (when he could get them accepted at all) with small publishing houses, he could not even gain them reviews in the press. Rejected by or suspect among even the dissidents, he stood alone, an outcast among the outcasts, "the solitary egomaniac."[45] He was widely regarded as (in his own words) a *"Spinner"* (crackpot)—despite the fact that his platform of 1956 anticipated many of the reforms of the 1980s dissidents, indeed even set the stage for them.[46]

Even after Harich won his legal suit against Janka, "They"—the PDS leaders—needed a "resolute man" from the early DDR days in order to establish that the DDR communist tradition had its noble side too, Harich says. And so, he claims, the equation followed: If Janka must be an incorruptible, steadfast, white knight and seem "presidential," then Harich—whatever the facts—must remain a cowardly blackguard and megalomaniac. An archetypal face-off indeed.

The injustice and anguish that Harich felt about all this were gripping. The underlying theme of much of his conversation was: Everyone listens and believes Janka, and nobody believes, or even listens to, me. His enumeration at the close of *No Difficulties with the Truth* of 18 friends—those who stood by him, or at least listened to him, across almost four decades since his fall from eminence—rings sad and even pathetic and desperate: Here are loyal few, it seems to say, who do not have contempt for me, who are willing despite rumors and *Rufmord* to remain in touch with me. "I've always met with friendship," Harich closes his memoir gratefully. That incongruous claim seems the least credible of all.[47]

"I'll never forget one remark," Ulrike says in a hushed voice, noting Harich's observation that *No Difficulties with the Truth* appeared a few weeks before Janka's death. " 'He never replied to my book. He died.' " Ulrike is quoting Harich. "How can somebody say such a thing?! As if Janka had died in order to evade and thereby annoy him!"

But in the world of their intrigues and legal battles for support and vindication, Ulrike continues somberly, these former friends ultimately came to exist for each other only as disputants. Janka's significance became simply that of an enormous barrier; it consisted only in his relation to Harich's efforts to clear his name, to win a hearing for his victimage, to influence events as he once did as a young man. And Janka's death was a point of no return for Harich. Since he had castigated Janka for having attacked the deceased Lukács, Weigel, and Seghers, how could Harich assault the dead Janka? It was as if a duelist had merely laid down his sword and walked away, declaring victory. By dying, Janka had, according to Harich's own standard of honor, ended their rivalry—and remained on top. And honor was all. Like a hero of classical tragedy, Harich had almost a Roman sense of honor.

In the end, Harich just wanted to be vindicated by History. For a Marxist intellectual, there is no afterlife except posterity, no Judgment Day except the court of History. And the court seemed to have decided in Janka's favor.

Caught in the crossfire of influence, disinformation, and betrayal, both Harich and Janka tried to tell their stories to whomever would listen. Monika Hüchel, wife of the poet and *Sinn und Form* editor Peter Hüchel, knew both men and stayed in close touch with Janka after his release from Bautzen; she told me that, like Harich, he too would relate the story of the 1956 arrest and trial "ceaselessly and ad nauseam."

"Janka became a one-note symphony!" Frau Hüchel said to me in September 1994. "He became so hopelessly boring—I heard the details about Harich and Ulbricht so many times from him that I could narrate the story for hours myself!"

But Janka did succeed in getting his version widely circulated in the media, taken up by major publishers, and largely accepted by opinion-makers. If he and Harich were virtual opposites, Janka seems also to have been the stronger personality, the more resourceful intriguer, the better seller of his character. And having gained superiority in the battle to win public opinion to his side, Janka rejected all of Harich's attempts to speak with him; as a wily debater, Janka realized that the front-runner never appears on the same stage as the challenger, if winning is all that counts. And in their calculus of power and reputation, it *was* all that counted; no human relationship was left between them. So Janka could only lose by having a conversation—public or private—with Harich. He knew that Harich ultimately did not want a reconciliation, so much as for his own version of events to receive more attention.

TRUST IS GOOD, BUT CONTROL IS BETTER!

The excruciating agony of never letting the past become past. The disabling refusal of (Nietzschean) forgetting.

The Harich-Janka "drama of mutual slaughter": not just the story of a DDR odd couple but the self-detonating psychodrama of the DDR itself.

"Dishonored to the Grave?" *Der Spiegel* had headlined a 1991 story about Harich's fight to resuscitate his reputation. The headline was derived from Harich's own rhetorical question to *Spiegel*'s editors: "Should I let this business be dragged out so long that I go dishonored to my grave?"[48]

Do we now drop the question mark?

The time for a response to the question is nigh, because unexpectedly, our own interview with Harich turned into his last testament: the last detailed public statement that Wolfgang Harich would give before his untimely death. On March 15, 1995—364 days after his nemesis Walter Janka—Wolfgang Harich passed away— after suffering a heart attack—at the age of 72.

Ever faithful to his contradictions, personal as well as dialectical, even Harich's birthdate was cause for dispute in the end. At least one classmate and one well-known historian claim that he was born in 1921, not 1923. The 1956 *Spiegel* title story and a standard western reference work on the SBZ from the early postwar era both state Harich's year of birth as 1921.[49] But why would he falsify his birth year? "Vanity," the classmate told one newspaper, explaining that Harich set the clock back because "he is a political diva."[50]

Peace of mind had eluded Wolfgang Harich, even in his final days.

"A Nonconformist in an Eternal Duel," one newspaper memorialized him: "The tragedy of his life was that he made suggestions that were never accepted." And yet for all that, he may well have been, as another eulogist noted, the DDR's "most original deviant."[51]

Epilogue

Education for Tolerance, Education for National Identity:
The Unusable German Past?

I

Now we're "the happiest people on earth!" exclaimed West Berlin mayor Walter Momper during the euphoria of November 1989.[1] But as this newest of "new Germanies" proceeds past the new millennium, it seems that the normally phlegmatic national temper has once again reverted to type. Almost everyone acknowledges that the task of creating a truly united Germany has been—and will continue to be—far more difficult than former Chancellor Kohl's rosy vision first promised.

Fostering a new Fatherland has been no easy task—as German educators too have discovered. Beyond all the practical issues of fully integrating the two systems have stood larger and even harder questions.

To what extent should German education be directed toward a greater tolerance of non-Germans, especially given their significantly increased numbers since 1989?[2] How explicitly "ideological" should the emerging German educational system be? Should one role of reunified Germany's education system also be to promote a deeper sense of patriotism for the New Germany? To what extent should the western German system change along with its eastern counterpart?

Particularly for eastern German educators, the most unexpected and frightening development in the immediate aftermath of reunification was the increase of xenophobia, dramatically manifested in *Ausländerhass* and anti-foreigner violence. Although the entire nation harbors no more than 50,000 active neo-Nazis,[3] right-wing political parties have exploited the continuing high unemployment rates and perceptions of "second-class" status among easterners. Polls show that only one-third of eastern Germans consider Germany's western-style democracy "defensible";[4] right-wing parties have attracted up to 13 percent of the vote—and up to a third of all voters under 30—in various eastern state elections since 1990.[5]

Indeed the right-wing message—keep the New Germany "clean" of foreigners (*ausländerfrei*), prevent racial mixing, intimidate "un-German" elements—has had particular appeal for German youth. In many depressed regions in the east, almost half of male youths between 18 and 25 sympathize with elements of this message, expressing various degrees of support for sentiments such as "keeping Germany clean and preventing racial mixing." Educators and parents whom I interviewed in 1999 and 2000 believe that these figures may still be on the rise. It is well known that more than 95 percent of violent right-wing extremists are under 18. Surveys show that eastern Germans harbor "significantly more reservations toward foreigners than do westerners."[6] One result is that foreigners are almost 30 times more likely to be attacked by neo-Nazis in Mecklenburg-Vorpommern than in neighboring Lower Saxony, and 20 times more likely in Brandenburg than in Bavaria.[7]

Indeed, many German educators lament that the nation's schools have become breeding grounds of intolerance and violence. According to one criminological study, two-thirds of teachers reported sharp conflicts between Germans and foreigners in school; an Allensbach poll reported that 56 percent of teachers said that they feel "powerless" before their students. A Bochum study found that 80 percent of secondary school students had voiced threats or "hate tirades" against their teachers; one-seventh of Bochum teachers were physically assaulted by students. In a nationwide study in 1998, the Munich Institute for Youth Research reported that 67 percent of German students (ages 6–19) have witnessed "violent acts," with an astounding one-third claiming to have been victims themselves. These figures constitute "a significantly higher percentage of violent acts than in American schools," the Munich Institute noted. The Institute's report concluded that German youth violence was equally worrisome in both west and east: "Brutal violence has become an everyday occurrence in almost every German school."[8]

The Orwellian dimension of official DDR jargon has been a prominent leitmotif of the present study and, not surprisingly, the German language of the post-reunification era has developed an Orwellian vocabulary that has given voice to the xenophobia. As we saw in chapter 4, within a year after German unification German slang had become rife with anti-social neologisms. Indeed, one result was that the Society for the German Language—a watchdog group devoted to exposing German Newspeak—inaugurated an "Unword of the Year" prize in 1991. The award aims to "call attention to thoughtless, often inhumane, and cynical language use."[9] The first winner was *ausländerfrei*. Top honors went to *ethnische Säuberung* (ethnic cleansing) and *Überfremdung* (becoming over-foreign) in the next two years, with other political euphemisms referring to the eastern states (*Anschlussländer*, annexed states) and to Germans' outrage with mass immigration (*multikriminelle Gesellschaft*, multi-criminal society) and *integrationsunfähig* (unable to integrate) in close contention. The neologisms continued to have anti-foreigner or anti-immigration overtones: e.g., 1997's *Wohlstandsmüll* (affluent rubbish, i.e., native and especially immigrant scroungers who milk the system); and 1998's *Osterweiterung* (expanding eastward, i.e., poorer eastern European countries entering the EU).

The unwords reflect Germany's national anxiety over the upheavals that have come in the wake of reunification, as well as popular resistance to top-down, government-sponsored initiatives in "re-education." Indeed, although the German government carefully avoids mentioning that particular "unword"—*Umerziehung* (re-education)—because of its negative associations acquired during the Allies' occupation, German educators have in fact launched a wide range of re-education activities in the schools.

To stem the youth violence and tendencies toward nationalism and racism, educators have developed diverse programs, such as promoting contacts between schools and refugee hostels, arranging for German students to tutor immigrants in

German, coordinating student volunteer activities with immigrant welfare agencies, and sponsoring friendly sport competitions with immigrant teams. Since the early 1990s, social workers have organized weekend seminars that bring together neo-Nazi and Turkish youths, aiming to foster mutual perspective-taking, "foreigner identification," and good will between Germans and foreigners "through music, dance, graffiti—whatever works," as one organizer stated.[10] Germany has also strongly supported the "Education for Tolerance" initiative administered by UNESCO and endorsed by most EU nations.[11] This initiative approaches intolerance as a worldwide problem and defines tolerance not as mere toleration, but rather as acceptance, affirmation, and charity;[12] UNESCO and the EU have shown special concern for mounting racism in Europe, including proposing an annual European "Day of Tolerance."[13]

Education for Tolerance is, in effect, peace education for the new millennium. A hard-headed European version of the "politics of meaning" once promoted by the Clinton administration in Washington, it manifests a post–Cold War educational sensibility focused not upon the old politics of international nuclear disarmament but rather on the cultural issues of interracial respect, interpersonal harmony, and inner peace.[14] The European Union's version of the Education for Tolerance initiative includes recommendations for increases in international teacher and student exchange programs, closer contacts with schools in eastern Europe, professional development courses in "diversity appreciation" for teachers, and intercultural projects sponsored by companies active in work-study apprentice programs of German schools.[15] Prompted by the civil war in the former Yugoslavia, the 18th European Conference of Educators took a decisive turn at their March 1994 meeting in Madrid, which was attended by 57 state and national education ministers from eastern as well as western Europe. At this and subsequent educators' conferences, educational leaders began to develop common, pan-European strategies to meet the rise of racism and nationalism, and to revise social science curricula to stress tolerance, human rights, and a "European historical consciousness."[16]

German educators in particular have pursued curricular innovations based on these proposals. Since the early 1990s, some German *Länder* have had special "intercultural courses" in schools, courses which range from exercises to promote reflection on acts of (verbal and physical) violence in daily life (e.g., hypothetical letter-writing to victims) to week-long, school-sponsored study of and participation in cultural celebrations of other nationalities and races.[17] They have also considered regular contracts to hire visiting foreign teachers.[18] One of the most publicized measures in the east, where old DDR Education for Hate gave way in the 1990s to anti-foreigner hate speech and hate crimes, is the Action Program against Aggression and Violence, an annual DM 12.5 million initiative launched in 1991 to "re-educate" German skinheads.[19] Later, university student unions in Germany joined the leading European student organization to declare 1995 "the Year of Tolerance," with emphasis on world citizenship, environmental awareness, global consciousness, acceptance of diverse lifestyles, and nonviolent approaches to conflict resolution.[20] German university student unions have been the most active members in UNESCO's Education for Tolerance programs since that time.

II

And so, both eastern and western German educators have united in their determination to fight intolerance. Many of them believe that, whatever legislation is passed to forbid violence and racism, only a revolution in German pedagogy—toward character education rather than the traditional German concentration on knowledge acquisition and skills training—will eliminate racial stereotypes, dissolve centuries of bigotry, and instill intercultural understanding. As has long been the case in the United States, "diversity" and "sensitivity" have recently become buzzwords in German and European educational circles. The old slogans of DDR Education towards Socialist Patriotism have evolved into programs that promote a non-socialist form of internationalism.

With a population consisting of more than 7.5 million foreigners—the largest figure of any European country—Germany is now a multicultural society in fact, and, after years of controversy, also officially. The 1999 revision of German citizenship laws, which had long been based on blood rather than length of residence, may soon mean that many resident foreigners will one day become official citizens. (Currently, less than 2 percent of foreign residents are citizens.)[21] Still, German educators realize that the American present is Germany's near future. And they anticipate that the outcries on American campuses about institutionalized white racism, the dominance of western civilization, and the biases of the western-oriented literary canon—objections triggered by the changing demographics of American higher education and the lure of identity politics—will soon be heard in German education too.

Indeed scattered doubts have already been sounded, not only by minorities but also by traditionalist German educators. Few educators oppose racial awareness programs aimed at neo-Nazi youth, and few foreigners, naturalized or resident, have called for institutional or curricular changes in German education. Still, Education for Tolerance reflects a deep discontent with German society and education alike. Not surprisingly, some academically oriented and conservative educators have begun voicing questions similar to those heard on U.S. college campuses about multiculturalism. They are worried that Education for Tolerance represents a sectarian, divisive ideological movement rather than a truly inclusivist educational program. Pluralism necessitates tolerance, but tolerance imposed become intolerance. A healthy tolerance consists of mutual respect for opposing convictions—but not all convictions are worthy of respect.

Educators ask: How to distinguish the worthy ones, especially given the background of modern German history. The very task of such decision making entails dangers of authoritarianism. And yet, as in the case of free speech for extremists, tolerance can be abused. When is the virtue of tolerance exaggerated into a vice? Is Education for Tolerance liable to be become a dubious, leftist intolerance against rightist intolerance, a form of tolerance as tyranny? Could it become a new form of propagandistic "re-education"? Even a new, politically correct Education for *In*tolerance—or Hatred?[22] Are diversity seminars and ethnic sensitivity classes an effective means—and the proper locus—for combating prejudice? And what of those teachers and students who resist what they perceive as fundamentalist liberalism, a variant on the Leninist orthodoxy of "Trust is good, but control is better"? Reconcile yourself—or be re-educated?

American educators have been confronting the same issues for more than two decades, and German educators might learn from our experience. Yet because previous German attempts at *weltanschauliche Erziehung* led to totalitarian dictatorships—"character education" was precisely the pedagogy of both the SED and the Nazis—even many Germans sympathetic to the intent of the Education for Tolerance initiatives worry more than we do about a shift from scholastic and vocational education to social engineering.[23] Fearful of the power of ideological appeals, Germans are much readier to take authoritarian precautions against totalitarian threats, i.e., to ban extremist political parties, prohibit incendiary music, and adopt regulations comparable to our campus speech codes. Most German educators would probably agree with one Berlin commentator that "education is the deciding factor for promoting democratic institutions in society and for society." But they would also second the reservation of the *Süddeutsche Zeitung*: School "cannot be the repair workshop of society."[24]

It is understandable that German educators would affirm this latter contention too. But such a view also has much to do with Germany's self-image—i.e., with the perennial so-called German Question, at the heart of which lie obsessive, ceaseless questions about the German national identity.

Can education for a "European historical consciousness" succeed without education for a healthy German consciousness? Is Germany's good-neighborly ardor for integration within "Europe"—an enthusiasm ("Euromania") that has waned in recent years—simply a flight from its own identity and history, as many critics charge? Are the Germans themselves asylum seekers pursuing refuge in the abstraction "European"?

And those questions culminate in an even more pressing pair: Can Education for Tolerance succeed without Education for National Identity? Finally, even *if* the latter were a desirable goal, is Germany's checkered history "usable" for creating a healthy national identity in the twenty-first century?

III

Education has traditionally contributed to forming a sense of national identity. But in postwar West Germany, education did not pursue—or at least did not fulfill—this role. Nor did the DDR ever succeed in molding a separate national identity, despite its strenuous efforts to present itself as the anti-fascist, "better," Germany and inculcate Education for Socialist Patriotism—often through Education for Hate. Germany's burden of deep historical shame renders problematic the future tasks of German education in its national life. Polls show that Germans, western as well as eastern, have by far the least national pride of all major countries.

Successful nations become "imagined communities," in Cornell anthropologist Benedict Anderson's phrase, whose members feel solidarity with others whom they have never met, a feeling maintained and transmitted through the educational system. But the DDR, and to a lesser extent, the old BRD were *imaginary* communities. The challenge for educators is whether the emerging educational system can help to shape a new, stable German identity.

Particularly in the east, educational reconstruction in the New Germany has taken place against a background of identity confusion. The collapse of the DDR left millions feeling disenfranchised and bereft in an identity vacuum in the new BRD: the "losers," whether they were unemployed, underemployed, or ostracized as *Stasi* informants or Party hacks. Right-wing youth from these families have been particularly susceptible to cries such as "Germany for the Germans!" They proclaim their "right to be German"; they insist that they "just don't want to have to feel shame about being German." Progressive educators worry that alienated youth focus so strongly on nationality as a source of identity. The current German identity crisis is a further reminder not only that German unification has left millions of easterners feeling like second-class Germans, but also that the idea of "Europe" still stirs emotional sentiments far too lukewarm to serve as a firm foundation for Germans' identity, let alone for citizens of nations less supportive of the European Union (e.g., the British).[25]

Do then the Germans, even in the age of the European Union, require a specifically *German* identity?

As many commentators have noted, Germany has been in desperate search of an identity since at least 1945. And it was an unfortunate, burdensome coincidence that, just as a new stage in the quest began with reunification, the issues of a multicultural German society and widespread anxiety about a new, expanded, German-dominated EU entered to hamper the restless search even further. As a result of these complications, some observers worry that the identity of the New Germany will turn out to be much more uncertain than was that of the old BRD and DDR. These were largely unicultural societies whose identities were not just bleached but bolstered by being mirror images of the two world superpowers.

Of course, tensions between eastern and western Germans themselves also severely encumber the ongoing post-reunification task of national identity-formation.[26] Simply to distinguish themselves from western Germans, many eastern Germans have embraced an anti-western identity, or what Jens Reich has called a *Trotzidendität* (identity of defiance).[27] Allensbach polls since the mid-1990s have testified to the large-scale disaffection between eastern and western Germans, with large majorities in both regions reporting that they "felt like citizens of different Germanies with opposing interests."[28] A 1999 poll by the EMNID Institute also found that only 16 percent of eastern Germans feel solidarity with western Germans.[29]

These identity crises reflect deep doubts about the identity of the German nation itself. And these crises of identity are, above all, a long-standing German youth problem, from which western and eastern youth both suffer. Poll results since the 1980s have demonstrated repeatedly that many German youth lack any national feeling. In 1987, only 65 percent of young West Germans (ages 14–29) considered themselves "members of one German people," in contrast to 90 percent of those over 60. Fifteen percent of West Germans over 60 considered the DDR "a foreign state"; among those under 30, the figure was 50 percent. In 1993, polls showed that, among young western Germans (ages 14–27), 48 percent "did not feel any national pride"; the figure was 31 percent for eastern Germans.[30] Subsequent polls in 1999 confirmed these findings.[31]

Thus the identity crisis reflects not only a geographical but also a generational gap. Unlike their elders, those Germans under 50—and especially those under 30, born after the Wall's erection—possess no shared past, no common historical memory.[32] A Cologne Institute for Mass Communications survey reported that nearly 20 percent of teens 14–17 claimed to have "no idea what Auschwitz is or was," and 18 percent of those who admitted having heard of the camp thought "reports about what happened there exaggerated."[33] Polls in the mid-1990s revealed that wide differences persist between westerners and easterners in feeling "safely protected" by the police (43 vs. 13 percent), by the BRD legal system (54 vs. 16 percent), and in opinions about whether "economic justice" prevails under BRD capitalism (48 vs. 19 percent).[34]

Conservative western German intellectuals have long maintained that no healthy German identity can develop without a new patriotism.[35] Liberal-left intellectuals, especially in the west, have sought to promote an identity founded not on traditional notions of pride in and defense of *Heimat*, but rather on what Jürgen Habermas has called *Verfassungspatriotismus* (constitutional patriotism), an expression of devotion not to one's country but to western democratic principles.[36]

Until the eve of reunification, some liberal-Left West German intellectuals argued that a new, postmodern era of collective consciousness was on the European horizon. They felt that West Germany represented the model of the future EU member, given that West Germany had always regarded its status as temporary (with even its capital officially regarded as provisional in the West German constitution). In 1986, in a characterization that received wide notice, political scientist Karl Dietrich Bracher termed Germany a "post-national democracy among nation-states."[37] Precisely because West Germany was not a nation-state and "lacked" a traditional sense of patriotism and national identity, it was already a "Europeanized" nation, and thereby particularly well-suited to herald "the supranational integration of western Europe."[38] Thus, what seemed a want became a windfall: the idea of post-national identity posited Germany as once again the leader of Europe, and once again the beneficiary—rather than victim—of the *Sonderweg*.

IV

A post-national Germany is a post-historical Germany. And the idea of *Verfassungspatriotismus* constitutes an indirect attempt to get Germans out from under and beyond the ever-lengthening shadow of their modern history: a Europeanized Germany might finally lay to rest all doubts—including self-doubts—about another power grab at a Germanized Europe.

Historians are quick to talk of the "death of the past": the waning influence of the past in our lives. But the past—and above all the past of 1933–45—is not dead in Germany. In no other nation is history so alive, and for no other nation has history proved so central to its identity or lack thereof—because no other nation bears such a burden of the past, a past so difficult with which to "come to terms" or "master" (*Vergangenheitsbewältigung*).[39]

A West German book of the 1980s dealing with the problem of German identity was fittingly titled *The Wound Named Germany*.[40] And it has seemed as if every postwar effort to close the wound by charting a new history simply leaves the wound festering—or jabs another finger into it. For the German heart, after all, has two wounds. The second was symbolized by the 1992 logo of *Tag der Einheit*: a torn and bloody heart stitched back together. But the suturing of East and West has not healed the first and deeper wound: Auschwitz.

How can Germany build a healthy, post-Holocaust identity? Might the only way for it to heal be to abandon history entirely? Or is it possible to turn the page of history without tearing it out? The German past is not dead, but it may well be unusable.

Once again, the DDR concepts of *Tradition* and *Erbe* (heritage) are pertinent here. It may be that Germany itself—and not just eastern Germany—possesses a past but not a usable past, a *Tradition* but no *Erbe*, i.e., no capacity to draw on past events as a resource for sustaining the present and constructing a healthy future. ("Who has the Youth"—yes, but who also has the Past—"has the future.") If this be the case, then Germans might well muse, along with "Nietzsche as Educator," on the "Advantage and Disadvantage of History for Life."

Let us, therefore, pause here and devote this issue extended consideration.

While the last four decades in the West arguably provided the old *Bundesrepublik* with a usable past founded on democratic ideals, that hesitant new start has undergone severe strains in the transition to a new Germany and New Europe—and, in any case, the East did not share that postwar liberal western heritage. Indeed, eastern Germany in particular seems almost completely devoid of a usable past. That lack in 1945 was one reason why the DDR turned into a state more Stalinist than other Soviet satellites: the crushing defeat of Nazism had already wiped out traditional nationalist Germany history; East Germany was a palimpsest over which Stalin wrote. Today, with even the meager socialist *Erbe* of the DDR also thoroughly discredited, yet another part of eastern Germans' heritage has been scraped away, leaving a newly blank slate on which remnants of their long-repressed Nazi past are resurfacing. Without even a legacy of dissident socialist leaders—such as Hungary's Imre Nagy or Czechoslovakia's Havel and Dubček—to sustain them, eastern Germans are now reunited not only with the West, but with their long-repressed Nazi past, a past that the DDR always denied had much to do with them, except as heroes and victims.

A culture with no usable past "swallow[s] whole" the heritage of others.[41] Germany's heritage—from Frederick to Bismarck, from Leibniz to Nietzsche—is of little use to present-day Germans. Indeed, even Goethe and Schiller seem utterly, merely "historical" in comparison with the ever-burning contemporaneity of the Nazi era. And to the extent that pre-Nazi German history *is* remembered, it too is problematized. For, long before one can use that past, one collides with the questions: "But where did it lead?" "To what did it lend itself?" And those questions prove fatal. For Frederick, Bismarck, Nietzsche, and much of everything else is then read back through the lens of the Holocaust—and darkened.[42]

Genuine engagement with the possibility of a permanently stained German *Erbe* was always repressed in the DDR, even in the Nietzsche "debate" of 1986–88, since responsibility for Auschwitz was laid at the feet of the capitalists—with the communists and the USSR as chief victims. But the confrontation with the past did erupt, dramatically, during precisely these same years in the West, in the course of the *Historikerstreit* (historians' conflict). This followed closely upon the 1985 Bitburg controversy, coincided with West Germans politicians' debates over plans for two German historical museums (in Bonn and West Berlin), and fatefully ended on the eve of the fall of the Wall.[43] The historian Heinrich August Winkler presciently saw the *Historikerstreit* as a muted "call for German reunification."[44] And once reunification became a political reality, the German question was again poised to be posed. And sure enough, it soon detonated more explosive public conflicts about the Nazi years and its legacy: the Botho Strauss tempest of 1993,[45] the Goldhagen controversy of 1994,[46] the protracted disputes about the Berlin Holocaust memorial during 1996–99,[47] and the Walser-Bubis debate of 1998/99—the latter dubbed "the new *Historikerstreit*" in the press.[48]

Significant as these more recent conflicts have been, none of them have constituted a real advance on the issues as formulated by West Germany's leading historians during the *Historikerstreit*, which dominated West German cultural and academic discourse for months, established the broad ideological lines of these subsequent disputes, and stands today as the defining and most intellectually substantive postwar debate about the Nazi legacy and German national identity. Because its basic themes recurred in the four aforementioned Holocaust-related controversies of the mid- and late 1990s, the *Historikerstreit* bears revisiting here. As its continuing relevance demonstrates: the past is not passed.

The *Historikerstreit* centered on a single issue: Was the Holocaust unique? If it was, after all, comparable to other mass pogroms, perhaps even a (more horrific) response to the Gulag Archipelago, then it need not be seen as a singular evil that is nearly impossible to integrate into the nation's heritage.[49] If the Holocaust was unique, however, then Germany is somehow a forever darkened land, and its search for identity through history will always be frustrated, its past never mastered, never overcome, never usable.[50]

Comparative genocide is a grisly business. Although the viewpoints of the conservative participants (Ernst Nolte, Michael Stürmer, Andreas Hillgruber, Joachim Fest, Klaus Hildebrant)[51] in the *Historikerstreit* won few adherents outside the Right,[52] their arguments reopened—and salted—the German wound. Nolte set off the controversy in 1986 by calling for the "normalization" of Germany in historians' scholarship, a move that would entail letting Auschwitz take its place in history and recede from haunting the present. But Stürmer's emphasis on national identity transformed the conflict into something far more than an academic exercise. Stürmer, who subsequently became an advisor to Chancellor Kohl, referred to the "guilt obsession" that had left Germans a people without a history, "the sons of nothingness."[53] "In a land without history," he wrote, "whoever furbishes the national memory, coins the concepts, and interprets the past will win the future."[54] It was the role of intellectuals, he said, to assume what he saw as these necessary, patriotic tasks of nation-building:[55] "Germans must find their identity in a divided Germany, which is no longer grounded in the nation state," added Stürmer, "but is also not possible without the nation."[56] Now that Germany is united, the task of reinventing an alternative identity to the two postwar choices—"guilty German" or "vassal" in an occupied state—is rendered easier from the conservatives' viewpoint.[57]

But the German liberal-Left (Jürgen Habermas, Hans-Ulrich Wehler, Jürgen Kocka, Hans Mommsen) worried that conservative calls for national identity were reassertions of German nationalism. The philosopher Habermas, who led the attack on the conservative historians and remained at the center of the *Historikerstreit* (one liberal-Left critic derisively termed it the "Habermas Controversy"),[58] charged them with promoting "a revisionist history in the service of buoying up a conventional national historical identity."[59] Habermas castigated the "relativization" of the Third Reich's horrors via historical comparison: the conservatives "compared" in order to exculpate.[60] Habermas held that the new desire for a positive German history was not an expression of German national identity or democratic patriotism but an updated German *nationalism* suitable for the Cold War NATO alliance.[61]

Had the search for the usable past become a quarry for the abusable past? A "usable past"—for what? The German past of this century was "usable" only for remembering crimes, maintained Habermas, not for reviving national feeling. Instead of veiled apologetics, Germany needed to embrace a "post-conventional" national identity in order to become a full-fledged democracy.[62]

The *Historikerstreit* prefigured and partly conditioned later historical debates about the Holocaust in the 1990s; like its successors, it gave voice to the agonized soul-searching over national identity that has constituted a major public issue in reunited Germany. But the latter struggle has been different in two crucial respects: it extends far beyond the intelligentsia and features the eastern Germans' history and identity as a key frame of reference.[63] No eastern German intellectual, historian, or publication has played a prominent role in Germany's post-reunification debates about the past—yet. But whenever the question erupts again—as is inevitable—as to whether the Holocaust was indirectly a response to Stalinism and the Gulag,[64] a distinctively new debate seems likely to break out.[65] This debate will include eastern Germans (many of them only beginning to "cope with" their own Stalinist pasts)[66] and may not be restricted to historians and intellectuals.[67] For nothing was ever decided in the *Historikerstreit*—or in the controversies that have followed. The verdict on Auschwitz and modern Germany is still open; the repressed questions still remain—and eternally return.[68]

Where to "search" for a wellspring of German identity? The Right looks to national historical and cultural traditions.[69] The liberal-Left points to the constitution and democratic institutions. Other observers propose German economic strength (which Habermas has excoriated as *"D-Mark Nationalismus"*). West Germany searched primarily in the latter two areas before 1989, thinking of itself as a democratic, "Europeanized" Germany and a model of capitalist success. With the German political past "unusable," it turned its attention to its present and future—its fledgling federal and republican institutions, its healthy economy and stable currency, its responsible membership in the European Community and European

Union.[70] In the wake of reunification, however, an enlarged, more powerful Germany has had to face the national question—which means engaging the past. No longer can west nor east shift the blame for the political past to the other side and claim to be *das bessere Deutschland*; nor do professions of fealty to the European Union suffice. The problematics of a historical, cultural, and political identity—the confrontation with the Wound—must be addressed.

How valid is Stürmer's claim that "no people can in the long run live without historical identity?"[71] *Can* one educate for identity? *Can* one use the past to create national identity?

Or should historians—and educators—stay out of the "identity business"?[72]

V

Leading German educators and philosophers—among them Herder, Fichte, and Wilhelm von Humboldt—held that education made citizens. Herder and Fichte believed that the state's mission was to create a national consciousness through *Nationalerziehung* (national education); Humboldt maintained that character formation was the key goal of education. All of them stressed the importance of historical consciousness to such a task, and took the guiding motto of western historiography from antiquity through the nineteenth century as their own: *Historia vitae magistra.* "History is the teacher of life."

Is it time, once again, to "re-educate" via history for national identity? Should German history explicitly recover its didactic or pedagogical function?

Both Nazi and DDR educators had certainly believed so—and so today do many Christian Democrats and other politically conservative Germans. As one conservative observer puts it, the day has come for Germany "to step out of the shadow of the Hitler years and re-establish a positive national identity, rather than a negative one based on anti-Nazism and anti-imperialism, i.e., on a program of eternal atonement to prove that the *Bundesrepublik* is a reformed Germany that has nothing in common with the Third Reich."[73] While *Verfassungspatriotismus* constitutes a crucial component of any future German identity, many conservatives regard it as the basis of a self-loathing *Betroffenheitskultur* (culture of contrition), "insufficient and worrisome insofar as it contains a not-so-subtle message that Germany is a diseased nation" in which national feeling can only lead to nationalism.[74]

Liberals such as Günter Grass disagree, contending that modern German history justifies fears about a slippery slope into a reactionary politics. Other liberal critics believe that historians should resist calls for nation-building; they have castigated the conservatives for writing revisionist "Bitburg history."[75] Some observers agree, stating, as one of them has put it, "Germany has not suffered from too little, but from too much 're-education.'"[76] On this view, the rounds of postwar re-education—Soviet, American, British, French—have contributed to the lack of national identity. Having been Americanized and western-Europeanized and Russified, the nation has, arguably, little Germanic ballast still to draw on. But despite attempts to fold the German Question into a European Question, the problem of creating a modern *Germany* remains.

Understandably, the word "re-education" provokes strong reactions among Germans. And yet, however much Germans—especially easterners—cringe at the word, "re-education" remains a long-term task that the New Germany faces. Not a re-education that replaces the ideology of DDR Marxism-Leninism with some new set of capitalist—let alone nationalist and imperialist—values, but rather an education for identity that emerges from the whole of the past and "re-imagines" Germans not simply as postmodern Europeans but as a community within a community of nations. Education for Identity must also be Education for Community. Germans must relearn to celebrate, not merely tolerate, their own differences. They can only be fully at peace with their neighbors if they learn to be at peace with themselves.

The task of education—or re-education—is proving arduous and complex. Germans are learning that the Germany of the new millennium is a multicultural society, and they are unlearning a subtle xenophobia that has implicitly assumed that ethnic Germans alone warrant citizenship in their country. This re-education has entailed, among other changes, accepting somewhat liberalized criteria for gaining German citizenship—although the German public has balked at granting dual citizenship to foreign residents. Still, the new emphasis on residence rather than ancestry as the key criterion for citizenship at least acknowledges a post-reunification reality: Germany has become a multicultural, indeed immigrant, country.[77] And it is in that sense alone that Germany should recognize itself as a "post-national nation." After the asylum laws became more restrictive in 1993, the naturalization laws had to become more open in 1999. And perhaps this turn toward openness presages a new self-understanding: that Germans will re-imagine their concept of national identity beyond notions of race and evolve beyond "their centuries-old concept of an ethnically homogeneous, if regionally differentiated, German *Kulturnation*."[78] Education for Tolerance is in this spirit of a post-national ethnically diverse identity, for it constitutes an inclusivist approach to citizenship that fully embraces long-resident non-Germans.

But the legal changes constitute only a start; ultimately Education for National Identity must be a willing, not a forced embrace. All this will be especially difficult to achieve in the east; German polls of the mid-1990s have showed that two-thirds of westerners, but less than one-fifth of easterners, have had a foreigner as a friend.[79] My own informal surveys in the late 1990s confirm the continued currency of this data.[80]

Nor can Germany abandon or simply "get beyond" its history; it must "cope with" it without jettisoning or forgetting it. Such a task will also mean that the Nazi period and Holocaust (and now, for eastern Germans, the DDR and *Stasi* pasts) must be contextualized without being downplayed or relativized. No single period should stand as the whole of German history. To contextualize is not—and should not be—to radically historicize. German historians must walk the fine, unmarked line between contextualizing to understand and historicizing to whitewash. The present will remain haunted so long as the past remains uniformly black. As Leon Botsein urges, "pre-Nazi, especially pre-1918, German history must be restored to the New Germany and not remain an unusable past."[81] Rising to what some German historians call the "challenge of normality,"[82] the challenge of remembering the past yet re-imagining the present and future will be formidable—especially as Germany struggles toward a fully integrated multicultural society.[83]

And yet, however difficult, some such act of national, communitarian re-imagination is essential.[84] Despite the fact that government officials and media commentators still refer to the "old" and "new" federal states—and however much western German politicians have treated the eastern states as if they were merely *Anschlussländer*—the Germany of the twenty-first century is not "simply an enlarged, dyspeptic version of the old Federal Republic."[85] It is becoming something genuinely different from anything that has preceded it.

And if *that* search can be pursued with integrity and compassion, perhaps this young and restless nation, now that the twain of East and West have met and become one, may yet turn out to be that imaginary land of which German utopians have always dreamed: "*das bessere Deutschland.*"

VI

And last but not least: Are there lessons—or unlessons—in the last half-century of eastern German education for Americans? What can we learn—or unlearn—about the recent fate of communist education in Eastern Europe?

A spate of books, with titles such as *The Challenge of Communist Education*, were published between Sputnik in the 1950s and the European disarmament debates of the 1980s, most of them expressing worry about the weaknesses of American education in the sciences and engineering.[86] Today, however, as we look back on that period and its recent aftermath, a different, more subtle challenge of communist education poses itself: the challenge of how western education is to respond to the collapse of communist education.

Yes: What can we learn—or unlearn—about the recent fate of communist education? And as a man of the liberal-Left, I must also ask: why aren't our own radical intellectuals asking that question more often?

For the state of the American educational system has been a topic of intense debate during the last decade. And Marxist-informed critical theory and cultural criticism are in the very vanguard of radical movements in American pedagogical revisionism, educational reform, and literary-cultural theory. But many of us in the American academy continue on, obliviously, as if the events in Eastern Europe never happened.

Yet they did—and in a time of soul-searching and upheaval in American education too, they pose insistent and fundamental questions to those educators and concerned citizens who will listen. And who will re-imagine a different way.

What *is* the primary purpose of education, anyway? Human excellence? Personal fulfillment? Private pleasure? Character building? Knowledge acquisition? Work-force suitability? Cultural stability? Social welfare? National success?

Should education make methods and skill learning its top priorities, as communist pedagogues such as Anton Makarenko insisted? Or should its top priorities be knowledge and truth-seeking, as Plato urged in the *Meno* and *Symposium*? Should education promote the Good Society, as Locke insisted? Or, as Augustine and Luther thought, should the otherworldly aims of achieving holiness and glorifying God constitute the ultimate purpose of education? Should education possess an end external to itself, as socialists from Marx to Marcuse have argued? Or should it be, as Schiller conceived *Bildung*, an end in itself?

And what about the specific role of the state and educational authorities in educational policy? Should education have a strong civic and nation-building function, as Rousseau and Fichte believed? Or should it primarily cultivate the good man and woman, rather than the good citizen? Should its central focus be the child or the curriculum? Should the student have a strong voice in determining his or her education? What about parents? Or is the decision best left to the educators themselves? Should the state be the educator, or is education better left in private hands? And who educates the educators?

The DDR's choices were clear: The goal of education was to form the "socialist personality." The schools served the State. The curriculum shaped the child. The collective took precedence over the individual. All students deserved—and almost all DDR children received—the same basic education. Skills, character building, and civic training mattered most. And so, the new socialist *Mensch* would exhibit an atheistic, scientific, materialist world outlook, evincing socialist patriotism that entailed hostility to western "imperialism." Youth would possess a collectivist orientation to labor, whereby students gained exposure to the real world of socialist production and worker collectivism. And so on.

The DDR Ministry of Education was secure in its answers. Are we in ours? Should we be?

The little Red schoolhouse was a microcosm of the DDR. Indeed, the foundation of every state is the education of its youth: the classroom is the nation in embryo. All educational curricula reflect—and refract—the values of the society in which they have been developed. Acting upon this knowledge, Soviet-influenced East German leaders set about inculcating the collectivist values that would lay the foundation for the worker's paradise they planned to build out of the ruins of the Third Reich.

But what is the threshold for this kind of *Weltanschauung*-engineering? True, all nations' educational systems invariably reflect and promote their own cultural beliefs at the expense of "universal" values. But how far do you go in "reeducating" people away from their tradition and toward your own? Is this liberal—or illiberal—education? Does it matter? Should educators instill their own moral values in the children under their care? How overtly or covertly? Or should educators pass on the "best" values of a society? But can a society agree on those values? How should minority viewpoints be represented? What kinds of differences should be tolerated—or celebrated?

VII

All these questions lead us inescapably to a single, key one: *Is* there a difference between "education" and "propaganda"? The SED, like the Nazis, frankly called their schooling "propagandistic." We in the United States vehemently reject such a characterization of our own educational system. If there is a difference between the two, where does pedagogy end and indoctrination begin?

The SED did not preoccupy itself with such distinctions.

But they matter.

The SED gained "agreement"—what the Nazis had termed *Gleichschaltung*—at the price of free speech. And so postwar education in the DDR mirrored its immediate predecessor as anti-Nazi re-education turned into a lock-step pro-Soviet propaganda campaign that ultimately denied the virtues of all other ways of living.

In the end, DDR education sought to "produce" nothing less than a higher human being, the "new socialist *Mensch*" who would "build socialism," i.e., the utopia known as *das bessere Deutschland*.

Yet—the DDR utopia failed. Spectacularly, miserably, hypocritically—it failed. Where it professed to achieve a uniform school system and equal educational opportunity for all, it produced a Party-based educational elite. Where it boasted of inculcating a radically democratic *Weltanschauung*, it enshrined Leninist democratic centralism as official DDR doctrine. Where it claimed to teach respect for all nations and races, it bred ideological intolerance and even hatred toward non- and anti-communists. And the final results were clear and disastrous: the DDR became the only nation in the postwar world to lose population steadily throughout its existence. And one chief reason was education: e.g., as we have elsewhere noted, East Germans reporting to West German refugee camps cited "unsatisfactory or insufficient education of children" as their number one reason for fleeing the DDR.

The DDR failed to develop an educational system that could sustain a regime claiming to have "History" on its side. In trying to mold "socialist personalities," DDR educators drastically overestimated the plasticity of human personality. Human beings are more resilient to social engineering than DDR ideologists realized—and than George Orwell feared.

None of this, of course, is by itself proof that "capitalist re-education" succeeded in postwar West Germany—or will succeed in stitching the two Germanies back together again. Still, History's indictment of DDR education is overwhelming.

But need the failure of DDR education mean that we abandon the utopian experiment itself? Need it mean rejecting state-directed efforts to change our schools and universities into life-transforming sites of passage?

If eastern Germans are not just doomed "marxed *Menschen*," uniquely victimized by their embrace of two totalitarian ideologies, if the history of DDR education and its aftermath possesses significance beyond its own case, then a study of pre- and post-*Wende* education in eastern Germany is indeed more than just the monograph of a single institution or region. It serves also as a cautionary reminder for the conduct of educational policy to other nations, including the United States. And the notable point is this: Education that becomes political "re-education"—an attempt to "make over" human beings according to the requirements of an ideology—undermines the freedom and dignity of the individual. And that, in turn, ultimately undermines both the ideology and the state that champions such a policy.

This is a lesson about the formation of public culture that is hard to learn unless one has direct contact with it—and perhaps indeed with its most egregious excesses. DDR education proved a spectacular example of such excesses, an instance of "illiberal education" at its most extreme. Indeed, virtually the entire twentieth-century history of education in eastern Germany points to the dangers of building a nation on ideology, or on any abstract principle—"nationalism," "fascism," "socialism," "the polytechnical human being." (And the lesson also applies to the West, i.e., any extreme formulation of the abstract principle of "capitalism" or "individualism.")

A corollary lesson—or unlesson—is also clear. When culture and education divorce themselves from the concrete aspects of daily living and embrace ideology, they "produce" creatures like "the socialist *Mensch*" or the "polytechnical *Mensch*"—and, in the process, lose touch with what it means to be human. Because the DDR had no real past—indeed no national identity at all—it tried to fill the vacuum with Party-line ideology, with disastrous results.

The lesson is a sobering one. When education moves away from the intellectual and chiefly toward the political, from a vision of schools as the locus of learning and cultural transmission to one of schools as agents of social change—then miseducation is the result. When the goal is no longer to have more outstanding teachers, but simply "more working-class teachers," as in the DDR—or more "minority teachers," as in many U.S. school districts—membership in a group takes precedence over educational excellence. To question ideological orthodoxy is not "revisionist" or bourgeois or anti-communist or elitist—or racist and sexist. It is simply to acknowledge that—whatever the state and citizenry determine its additional goals to be—the primary aims of education should include the creation, preservation, and transmission of knowledge and its application to life in the pursuit of wisdom.

Learn something from that ignominious failure, the DDR educational system? The suggestion seems dubious, if not laughable.[87]

Nevertheless: Perhaps the ongoing repainting of the little Red schoolhouse can serve as a usable past for the West—if only by negative example. Perhaps it can indeed teach us some valuable unlessons—before it is too late.

Notes

Abbreviations Used for Newspapers and Popular Periodicals Cited in Notes

AM	*Atlantic Monthly*	NL	*New Leader*
BG	*Boston Globe*	NR	*National Review*
BS	*Baltimore Sun*	NS	*New Statesman*
BW	*Business Week*	NY	*New Yorker*
CC	*Christian Century*	NYT	*New York Times*
CHE	*Chronicle of Higher Education*	NZZ	*Neue Zürcher Zeitung*
		RLR	*Reuters Library Report*
CST	*Chicago Sun-Times*	SI	*Sports Illustrated*
CT	*Chicago Tribune*	SLPD	*St. Louis Post-Dispatch*
DM	*Der Monat*	ST	*Sunday Times* (London)
DMN	*Dallas Morning News*	SZ	*Süddeutsche Zeitung*
DP	*Deutsche Presse*	taz	*Berliner Tageszeitung*
DS	*Der Spiegel*	TC	*Twentieth Century*
DSd	*Der Standard*	TES	*Times Educational Supplement*
DSt	*Der Stern*		
DT	*Daily Telegraph* (UK)	TG	*The Guardian*
DW	*Die Woche*	THES	*Times Higher Education Supplement*
DZ	*Die Zeit*		
FAZ	*Frankfurter Allgemeine Zeitung*	TI	*The Independent*
		TNR	*The New Republic*
FM	*Focus Magazin*	TS	*Toronto Star*
FR	*Frankfurter Rundschau*	TWIG	*The Week in Germany*
FT	*Financial Times*	USDSB	*U.S. Department of State Bulletin*
HC	*Houston Chronicle*		
IHT	*International Herald Tribune*	USN&WR	*U.S. News and World Report*
JP	*Jerusalem Post*	WSJ	*Wall Street Journal*
LAT	*Los Angeles Times*	WP	*Washington Post*
ND	*Neues Deutschland*	WT	*World Today*

Prologue. Unlessons, Far and Near

1. Schneider, *The German Comedy*, 12.

2. Most studies are translations of official DDR publications or UNESCO-sponsored colloquia, published variously by the DDR Ministry of Education, by the UNESCO Commission of the DDR, or by Panorama (the DDR public relations agency). For a representative list of these items, see Rust, *Education in East and West Germany*. For two short works focusing on DDR polytechnical education, see Klein, *Education*, and Moore-Rinvolucci, *Education in East Germany*. For relevant English-language scholarship on DDR education, see works by Fishman and by Wegner. Although he covers only the period 1945–55, an outstanding German-language work dealing with SBZ/DDR education is Füssl, *Die Umerziehung der Deutschen.*

3. See Grothe, *To Win the Minds of Men*.

4. During the 1970s and '80s, more than a million copies of *Animal Farm* and *1984* were sold in West Germany. On the German reception of Orwell, see Rodden, *Politics of Literary Reputation*, 288–303. See also Klaus Höpcke's article on *1984* in *Einheit* (January 1984).

5. Helmut Findeisen, editor of *Zeitschrift für Anglistik und Amerikanistik* (Leipzig), personal conversation, October 20, 1991.

6. Heinz Osterle, quoted in Rodden, *Politics of Literary Reputation*, 290.

7. As historian Golo Mann wrote in his review of *1984* in the *Frankfurter Rundschau*: "Especially for Germans, *1984* is like a fantastic nightmare. . . . [P]erhaps more than any other nation, we can feel the merciless probability of Orwell's utopia" (quoted in Meyers, *George Orwell*, 12).

8. See Rodden, "Varieties of Literary Experience."

9. Indeed, Professor Wolfgang Strauss of the University of Jena informs me that he has procured *Stasi* files from the 1950s that document this fact. A young man received a two-and-a-half year jail sentence for getting *1984* from West German relatives and then circulating it among a few friends. Writes Professor Strauss: "That was the entirety of his 'crime.' When I have taught *1984*, I always end by reading excerpts from this *Stasi* file aloud. . . . My students are always very moved, since they—thank God!—are too young to have experienced that era" (personal correspondence, December 17, 1995).

10. Peter Grothe also notes that, throughout the 1950s, East Berlin readers would travel to West Berlin libraries and borrow *1984*. He claims that the novel was among the books most frequently on loan in West Berlin before the erection of the Berlin Wall (Grothe, *To Win the Minds of Men*, 207).

11. Quoted in Grothe, *To Win the Minds of Men*, 164. See also Conant, "The Citadel of Learning," passim.

12. For an insightful analysis into how disillusion with liberal democracy led Weimar intellectuals to embrace a politics of both the radical Left and the radical Right, see Jerry Müller, *The Other God That Failed*. On the consequences of a collapse of faith in a proletariat or nation, see Niethammer et al., *Die Volkseigene Erfahrung*.

13. From Louis Fürnberg's "Our Song" (1946).

14. Mieskes, *Die Pädagogik der DDR, Band II*, 308. See also "Bewachte Bewächer." I was also reminded that Vladimir Ilych Ulyanov and Eric Arthur Blair not only died on the same day (January 21) but each also borrowed his nom de guerre from local rivers (the Lena is a tributary in west central Russia; the Orwell flows through Surrey, outside London). The anniverary of Lenin's death was widely commemorated in the DDR. Until the 1970s, annual DDR school memorials honored him in special red "Lenin corners" of classrooms, which were outfitted with communist altars and Bolshevik accessories.

"Who has the Youth, has the Future"

The Banana Revolution?

1. The artist is Thomas Baumgärtner. "Art of the Banana," *Austin [TX] American-Statesman*, May 22, 1993.

2. *DSt*, November 5, 1992.

3. See Roschenlocher, "Der Untergang der Banane."

4. In later years, *Der Stern* joked that Adenauer had elevated the banana to "the Mother Teresa of fruits" (October 10, 1992). Adenauer insisted on tariff-free bananas in exchange for accepting the preferential trade arrangements that the other EEC countries wrangled for their former colonies (e.g., Italy for Somalia, France for Indochina, Holland for Surinam, the Netherlands for the Antilles). Germany itself had no colonies, having lost them after its defeat in World War I.

5. But finally, in 1998, after five years of strenuous opposition to the EU's Com-

mon Agriculture Policy (CAP) provisions for bananas, Germany reversed itself and supported the EU. A summit meeting between Helmut Kohl and French President Jacques Chirac, held in historic Weimar, led to a *rapprochement*: Kohl agreed to bend on bananas if Chirac would support some preferences for Bavarian farmers. Social Democrat Gerhard Schröder has largely continued to cooperate with the EU and its CAP.

Nonetheless, despite the agreement among the politicos, many Germans (and all banana importers) are still screaming holy warfare and would prefer to continue to crusade for their golden fruit.

Ironically, the EU's position so outraged American banana exporters that the U.S. appealed to the World Trade Organization (WTO), claiming discrimination against American bananas. In December 1999, the WTO ruled in favor of the Americans for the third time—with no possible remaining appeal from the EU. (The German government officially supports the EU position, but numerous German politicians have sided with ordinary Germans and expressed sympathy with the Amercians' stand.)

See "Bananenstreit spaltet USA and Europa," *SZ*, November 29, 1999. "WTO Backs US in Banana Row," *Toronto Star*, December 23, 1999.

6. *NYT*, February 18, 1993, 3.

7. Quoted in *DSt*, October 10, 1992.

8. "Art of the Banana." The new import regulations aimed chiefly to assist banana growers in European tropical islands (e.g., France's Martinique and Guadeloupe, Spain's Canary Islands) and in former European colonies in Africa, the Caribbean, and the Pacific. But Germany, which lost all its colonies after World War I, complained that Germans prefer large, bright yellow, Latin American "Dollar Bananas"—so named because of their size and rich color—to the more expensive, smaller, paler "Eurobananas" from the EU overseas territories and former European colonies.

9. And the dire predictions soon bore fruit: The new tariff boosted banana prices 60 percent (from $7.50 in mid-1993 to $11.25 in 1995 for a 20-kilo box). With German banana imports from Latin America down 50 percent, 170,000 jobs in Latin America vanished in 1994/95. When the banana-exporting countries of Latin America threatened to block future world trade deals if Brussels did not reverse its policies, the EC responded in 1997 with token concessions that have increased Latin American access to the European market only marginally. "Seldom have European politicians and bureaucrats more clearly demonstrated," editorialized *Der Spiegel*, "how little they really care about a free world market and about their repeated professions of help for the Third World." As noted earlier, Germany agreed in 1998 to this EU compromise in exchange for French concessions on EU monetary policy—thereby effectively ending the official German fight against Eurobananas and for Dollar bananas. *DS*, January 10, 1994, 75–76.

10. In the 1970s, DDR prosperity enabled Erich Honecker to provide bananas to DDR citizens on special occasions. As the deputy chief prosecutor assigned to investigate Honecker for treason reported in February 1990, Honecker loved to play "Santa Claus of the nation" and "bless the people" with bananas every December. He maintained a special account of DM 100 million for such acts of public generosity, which became a DDR tradition (*DSt*, October 10, 1992). In his short 1992 memoir about his tenure in office, *Erich Honecker and Dramatic Events*, the former SED chief defended his balance of priorities as follows: "DDR citizens may not have always had bananas under socialism, but they could rely on employment and security." Quoted in *Economist*, April 14, 1990.

11. Gleye, *Behind the Wall*, 197.

12. *Der Stern* (October 10, 1992) reported that, according to a survey of sex shop sales in eastern Germany, a banana-shaped vibrator and a banana-flavored condom known as the "Wild Banana" led all other brands. Prostitutes in the Beate

Uhse Shops springing up throughout eastern Germany were also greeting patrons with a (non-edible) toy known as the "Banana Frolic."

13. *BG*, March 20, 1990. *RLR* March 21, 1990. But the Social Democrats have arguably suffered far greater long-term damage from their insensitive "banana politics" in 1990. Shortly after reunification, when eastern and western Germans were fiercely debating their political differences, Bundestag representative Otto Schily appeared on the floor of the Bundestag waving a banana. Schily, who was to become Minister of the Interior in the Schröder government, was demonstrating by this gesture what he considered the main reason that East Germans had wanted unification: bananas = West German prosperity. Eastern Germans took offense at the insult—and Schily apologized.

But eastern Germans have not forgotten—and the gesture has complicated Schily's relationship with easterners and cast doubt on Schröder's respect for the region.

14. On the social dislocations caused by reunification and the problems faced in the economic recovery, see chapter 4 of the present study, especially the section titled "The Unfinished Revolution."

15. *The Reuter European Community Report*, October 3, 1996.

16. By December 1989, the ephemeral moment was already over. The image of the ingenuous East German was being replaced by that of the gullible *Ossi*. Smart-aleck West Berliners began referring to eastern Germans as "*Bananen*." Under the headline "Gabriela's First Banana," *Titanic*, the West German satirical magazine, depicted an East German girl excitedly peeling and peeling—a cucumber. Even the DDR media yielded to self-mockery. One spot on DRR, the East German state TV station, showed an adult consumer grinning idiotically, clutching a pickle, and exclaiming: "My first banana!" Rodden, "Going Bananas." *TS*, October 29, 1993, A21. Rinke reports that a popular Chemnitz cabaret group developed a sketch on a similar self-parodic theme. The act featured a biology teacher lecturing on a new, strange species, "das *Ossi*." The creature is toothless and can only eat bananas. See Rinke, "From Motzki to Trotzki," 242.

Education and Youth—and Re-Education

17. Liebknecht, *Kleine politische Schriften*, 146. On the phrase's origins and applications, see Linton, "Who Has the Youth, Has the Future."

18. Timm, 34.

19. Klier, *Lug Vaterland*, 22.

20. For another encounter with the use of vorher" and "drüben," see Kinzer, "East Germany," *NYT*, February 18, 1993.

Schooling Society and Taming Minds

21. "Bericht des Zentralkomitees der SED an den X. Parteitag der SED," Dresden, 1981. Quoted in *Das Bildungswesen in der DDR*, 5.

22. Quoted in Dornberg, *The New Germans*. See also Helwig et al., *Schule in der DDR*, chapter 1.

23. Quoted in Duncan Smith, *Walls and Mirrors*, 173.

24. For reminiscences about such visits to her *Kinderhort*, see Klier, *Lug Vaterland*.

25. Quoted in *Das Bildungswesen in der DDR*, 5.

26. Hechinger, *The Big Red Schoolhouse*.

27. *Das Bildungswesen in der DDR*, 12.

28. Liebknecht, *Kleine politische Schriften*, 146.

29. Wyden, *Wall*, 45.

30. Dr. Goebbels expressed similarly the same corollary. As he wrote in *HJ Marschiert* (*Hitler Youth on the March*):

The older generation says, "Who has the youth, has the future." We say, "Who has the future, has the youth." That is why our young people follow Hitler and his ideology, which is the embodiment of the dreams and hopes of youth. Don't let the older generation influence you. We will win. YOUTH IS ALWAYS RIGHT!

Or as Hitler himself put it in a celebrated 1929 speech in the Lustgarten in Berlin: "Youth has its own State!"

Born Unfree

31. See Armin Mitter and Stefan Wolle, eds., *Die Ohnmacht der Allmächtigen*; and Armin Mitter and Stefan Wolle, *Untergang auf Raten*.

32. Quoted in Mieskes, *Die Pädagogik der DDR*, vol. 1, 131.

Chapter 1. From Brown to Red: The Fall and Rise of an Educational System, 1945–51

Sunrise in the East

1. In Berlin, 48 percent of all buildings were destroyed and 16.7 percent were badly damaged (Podewin, *Walter Ulbricht*, 169). According to contemporary estimates, 54 to 60 percent of Germany's buildings were in ruins at the end of World War II. In many eastern cities like Dresden, however, the damage was much greater. See Muhlen, *Return of Germany*, 18, 28, and Wendt, *Bonner Berichte aus Mittel- und Ostdeutschland*, 5. Overall, however, as Füssl says, the damage to schools in the SBZ was much less than one might have expected: only 3.7 percent of schools were totally destroyed and only 4.3 percent partially destroyed (*Die Umerziehung der Deutschen*, 332).

2. Uhlig, *Monumenta Paedagogica, Band II*, 155–78.

3. Uhlig, *Monumenta Paedagogica, Band XIV*, 34. See also Füssl, *Die Umerziehung der Deutschen*, 333. By January 1947, 4.3 million of the 11.6 refugees had settled in the SBZ.

4. Uhlig, *Monumenta Paedagogica, Band II*, 156–57.

5. These conditions did not improve rapidly: writing from Berlin about the winter semester of 1947—two years later—a visiting British student reported a professor's survey of 100 "representative students":

- 79 had no warmth in their rooms
- 83 had no bulb for their reading lamps
- 4 lived in refugee camps
- 78 had unsuitable or insufficient paper for their work
- 22 had no warm socks of any sort
- 74 possessed fewer than 10 books
- 29 had no comb

The visitor added that most students had only one set of clothes; no mending materials were obtainable, and buttons and shoelaces were irreplaceable. In bad weather, many students could not travel to class, given inadequate clothing and footwear. "Letter from Germany," 242.

6. One 1947 report found that a total of 40 percent of university students in the SBZ suffered malnutrition or various illnesses related to the war. Müller, *Stürmt die Festung Wissenschaft*, 89.

7. Uhlig, *Monumenta Paedagogica, Band II*, 21, 123. Three-quarters of university faculty—a percentage comparable to the case in the schools—were judged to be "compromised" by their past and released. For example, 170 out of 222 at

Leipzig were fired on political grounds. The University of Halle lost 125 out of 165 faculty members; of the 40 remaining professors, 16 were older than 70 and 13 were older than 60 (Müller, *Stürmt die Festung Wissenschaft*, 63).

8. Uhlig, *Monumenta Paedagogica, Band XIV*, 135–54. Klein, *Education* 12. Many dismissed teachers fled to the West, where they eventually qualified to teach.

9. Uhlig, *Monumenta Paedagogica, Band XIV*, 321.

10. Baske and Engelbert, *Dokumente zur Bildungspolitik*, 134–78. Many of the *Neulehrer* were young former soldiers (officers were ineligible for teaching positions), who saw teaching as their only job opportunity in the collapsed economy of the SBZ. They were also attracted by SMAD's promise to give them coveted proletarian "worker cards" under the rationing system, and to admit them at a future date to university study. Both commitments by SMAD were selectively observed. Wendt, *Bonner Berichte aus Mittel- und Ostdeutschland*, 6.

11. Füssl, *Die Umerziehung der Deutschen*, 335.

12. See Stern, *Walter Ulbricht*, 31–47; Podewin, *Walter Ulbricht*, 9–166.

13. Podewin, *Walter Ulbricht*, 134.

14. Sandford, *From Hitler to Ulbricht*, 3, 23.

15. The idea of *Stunde Null*—especially in West Germany but also in the DDR—was sometimes invoked to suggest a sharp discontinuity with the Third Reich and imply that no Nazi legacy remained in the postwar era—and just as often attacked by both East and West Germans, for the same reason.

16. Uhlig, *Monumenta Paedagogica, Band XIV*, 231.

17. Füssl, *Die Umerziehung der Deutschen*, 335.

18. McCauley, *The German Democratic Republic Since 1945*, 14.

From Brown to Blue?

19. This furthermost eastern region of 39,000 square miles, which lies east of the Oder and Neisse Rivers, consists of East Prussia, Pomerania, and Silesia—all of which were included within Germany's 1937 borders. After the war, the USSR annexed the northern half of East Prussia; Poland was granted administrative control of (though not, technically speaking, title to) the other states; the Poles proceeded to expel, forcibly, 11,000,000 Germans from their homeland. Until Helmut Kohl's formal renunciation in 1991 of any claim to what many Germans still called "the lost lands" in "Polish Germany," the eastern boundary between Germany and Poland remained disputed by the BRD. (The DDR formally recognized the claim of its "socialist brotherlands" to the eastern territories in 1951.)

20. The western Allies abandoned deindustrialization immediately and, by 1950, demilitarization; they never pursued denazification aggressively or consistently. Until the remilitarization of the DDR around mid-century, however, the Soviets pursued all four war aims thoroughly—albeit their own questionable interpretation of them. Thus, SMAD did not limit its reconstruction of Germany to education or denazification. The other "D's" were also systematically pursued, e.g., de-industrialization. On Soviet dismantling, see Naimark, *The Russians*, 178–83.

21. The word "re-education" originated in American psychiatry in the 1930s and described the effort to convert, or rather "re-convert," people from one belief system to another: it was a technique of "brainwashing" people back to their original ideology (e.g., from fanatical religious fundamentalism back to respectable middle-class thinking, or from a newfound capitalistic back to a communistic *Weltanschauung*). Some critical West German historians have referred to Allied occupation as the *Charakterwäsche* (character-washing) of Germany, but the German language has no word precisely corresponding to "re-education." The usual translation is *Umerziehung*, a word that traditionally refers explicitly to schooling or rearing. For linguistic reasons and because SMAD mandated sweep-

ing educational reforms, the familiar German word *Umerziehung* was used in the SBZ. Both words were used in the western zones. Our English word became especially common for referring to the western Allies' psychological approach to German political re-orientation (e.g., via international student exchanges, western-oriented magazines, American films and cartoons). Bungenstab, *Umerziehung zur Demokratie?*, 13. Pronay and Wilson, 1–10, 22–23.

22. Re-education was more than traditional German *Umerziehung*: Allied re-education, especially in the SBZ, went far beyond curricular change and educational reform. It embraced the whole process of revaluing the values of the Germans, as expressed in art, culture, and the media. From the Allies' standpoint, it was a program of moral reconstruction. The aspiration was to foster a new Fatherland committed to popular democracy, including the freedoms of speech, press, and religion. The importation of the foreign word "re-education," however, testifies to the foreignness of the experience for Germans. It suggests the alien character of—and the self-alienation wrought by—"the most ambitious propaganda project of the first half of the twentieth century," in the words of a West German historian. Or as an American occupation official wrote in a confidential 1946 memo to his superiors:

There is no word that the Germans, even most friendly Germans, detest so much and one which is liable to call forth such powerful reactions as this word "re-education." (Pronay and Wilson, 84)

"The Final Solution to 'the German problem,' " one historian has characterized *Umerziehung*. Indeed, the word was pure Orwellian Newspeak to many Germans, who regarded "re-education" as a stark re-deployment of propaganda techniques that would have made Goebbels himself proud. Whatever one's judgment about Allied methods and goals, re-education was breathtaking in its dimensions: never before or since—at least not until the collapse of the DDR in 1989/90—had a power undertaken the wholesale ideological and psychological transformation of a comparably advanced, successful counterpart (Bungenstab, *Umerziehung zur Demokratie?* 9, 163–64; Pronay and Wilson, 1–37).

23. Bungenstab, *Umerziehung zur Demokratie?*, 74.

24. Quoted by Pronay and Wilson, 27.

25. The phrase is associated with Max Horkheimer and Theodor Adorno's famous 1950 study of that title, which discussed the character structure of Germans.

26. Hearndon, *Education in the Two Germanies*, 46.

27. Füssl, *Die Umerziehung der Deutschen*, 347.

28. Hearndon, *Education in the Two Germanies*, 35–38. Others argue that re-education in the western zones was a qualified success. See Bungenstab, *Umerziehung zur Demokratie?*, 45–98. See also Traxler, "The Re-Education of German Youth"; Pronay and Wilson, *The Political Re-Education of Germany and Her Allies After World War II*; and Vollnhals, ed., *Entnazifizierung*.

29. Quoted in Uhlig, *Monumenta Paedagogica, Band II*, 268.

30. See Klier, *Lug Vaterland*, 24–39, 67–76.

31. Quoted in Leonhard, *Die Revolution*, 334.

32. Füssl, *Die Umerziehung der Deutschen*, 335.

33. Quoted in Baske and Engelbert, *Dokumente zur Bildungspolitik*, 57.

34. Quoted in Klein, *Education*, 14.

35. See Ackermann, "Gibt es einen besonderen deutschen weg?" See also Naimark, *The Russians*, 303.

36. The 1946 elections fully confirmed the KPD's fears about free elections: the SED received only 48 percent of the vote in the SBZ; in Berlin, where the parties were not yet united, it received a mere 19.8 percent versus 48.7 percent for the SPD. The Berlin elections *did* expose the weakness of the KPD, but Ulbricht at-

tributed its losses in Berlin (not without cause) to powerful anti-communist propaganda by the western Allies and their German supporters.

37. Fearing that the tide in East Europe was turning against them, they pushed a Left program of "working class unity." Under the illusion that they could serve as an equal partner in the coalition, SPD leaders acceded. Ackermann's concept of a "special German road to socialism"—which was temporarily adopted by the KPD for tactical reasons—also quelled many SPD doubts about the communist commitment to a parliamentary system.

38. Quoted in Krisch, *The German Democratic Republic*, 207.

39. Quoted in Baske and Engelbert, *Dokumente zur Bildungspolitik*, 281.

40. See, for instance, Blackburn, *Education*.

41. Quoted in Baske and Engelbert, *Dokumente zur Bildungs-Politik*.

42. Blue was also the color of the Protestant churches, and in its early days the FDJ was tolerant of, even receptive toward, Christians. In 1945, 90 percent of families in the SBZ were Lutheran. Johannes Becher and Hanns Eisler, writers of the DDR national anthem, had previously teamed up in 1947 to write the FDJ hymn, "The Song of the Blue Flag":

> In the blue sky shines the sun
> and it illumines you, Germany.
> Leftward, leftward sing the marchers
> We German youth.
> Let us build a new *Heimat*
> let us firmly stand together.
> Blue flags high in the blue sky
> wave over Germany.

(Quoted in *Leben, Singen, Kämpfen*, 111.)

43. Helwig et al., *Schule in der DDR*, 69.

44. Uhlig, *Monumenta Paedagogica, Band XIV*, 210.

45. The 1946 Act did, however, permit the churches to give voluntary religious instruction in the schools, a concession that was rescinded in 1959.

46. See Hubertus Kunert, *Deutsche Reformpädagogik und Faschismus*. Moreover, radical as the clauses of the Act were, it did contain elements of compromise. The uniform school pertained only to grades 1–8: it was a uniform *elementary* school. Special courses of study also streamed talented students into higher grades; this measure, however, soon proved unacceptable to SED hard-liners committed to a strictly egalitarian educational system.

47. Uhlig, *Monumenta Paedagogica, Band II*, 165.

48. Quoted in Uhlig, *Monumenta Paedagogica, Band XIV*, 261.

49. Speech of the SMAD head in Thuringia on October 15, 1945. Quoted in *Das kulturelle Erbe*, 73.

50. See M. G. Lange, *Wissenschaft im totalitären Staat*, 1–19.

51. Müller, *Stürmt die Festung Wissenschaft*, 36–37.

52. Müller, *Stürmt die Festung Wissenschaft*, 97. Uhlig, *Monumenta Paedagogica, Band XIV*, 136. Klier, *Lug Vaterland*, 23.

53. Müller, *Stürmt die Festung Wissenschaft*, 53. Hearndon, *Education in the Two Germanies*, 44. Richert, "*Sozialistische Universität*," 10–26.

54. In constructing its intellectual pedigree, the SED made particular reference to the proposals of sixteenth-century educator Comenius, the resolutions of the first general teachers' assembly in 1848, the speeches of Clara Zetkin and the SPD reformers at the turn of the century, the pre-war *Reformpädagogik* movement of progressives like Kerschensteiner, the League of Radical School Reformers led by Paul Ostreich, and the Jena Plan that experimented with a uniform state school in Thuringia during 1922–24. See Mieskes, *Die Pädagogik der DDR, vol. 2*, 222–47.

55. Uhlig, *Monumenta Paedagogica, Band II*, 213. Speaking of *die neue schule*, the mayor added (213):

The democratic uniform school has become a reality. It is the true German *Volksschule*. No longer are there good schools for the rich and well-connected and substandard schools for the poor and workers. There is only one school for all the people, only one great German *Volksschule*.

The Democratic Experiment is zu Ende

56. Uhlig, *Monumenta Paedagogica, Band II*, 218. Hearndon, *Education in the Two Germanies*, 32. Not until the 1960s, after the founding of special schools for the gifted, did an educational elite emerge in the DDR. By the mid-1950s, 53 percent of DDR university students were drawn from the working class; in the BRD, the figure was only 7.5 percent as late as 1970. Hearndon, *Education in the Two Germanies*, 21.

57. Mieskes, *Die Pädagogik der DDR, vol. 2*, 225.

58. Füssl, *Die Umerziehung der Deutschen*, 347.

59. For instance, the 1947 "Rules for Admission for Applicants" to SBZ universities specified for the first time that former NSDAP members could comprise no more than 10 percent of the students in any subject area; and no more than 5 percent of all students could be former officers. Whereas university admissions criteria in December 1945 gave no preferential treatment to workers and peasants, in 1949 they were explicitly preferred, along with "victims of fascism" and "children of intellectuals who are helping reconstruction."

60. Muhlen, a German-educated political scientist who fled Nazi Germany and resettled in the United States, reported after his postwar visits to the SBZ/DDR that approximately one-third of university students consisted of "worker and peasant students" who were "delegated by the party to the universities and forced to study there." Muhlen's articles and books, all of which were sharply critical of the DDR, certainly reflected the Cold War climate. Nonetheless, his reports on DDR education and youth policy have largely been confirmed by recent scholars and intellectuals such as Karl-Heinz Füssl and Freya Klier. See Muhlen, "German Youth in a Vacuum," 5.

61. See Uhlig, *Monumenta Paedagogica, Band XIV*, 356, 111.

62. Müller, *Stürmt die Festung Wissenschaft*, 50–51, 90.

63. Muhlen, "East Germany's Planned Men," 65.

64. See McElvoy, *Saddled Cow*.

65. See Muhlen, "The New Nazis," 2–3. The paranoia among DDR educators during these years was often extreme. "If we have a bottle marked 'cyanide,' " declared East Berlin's Municipal Education Director, "everybody believes us, and nobody wants to first taste and make sure it's really cyanide, or he would be dead. But as concerns the products of western thought, everybody wants to taste them first, and after a person has done so, it's too late; he is lost." Quoted in Muhlen, *Return of Germany*, 186–87.

66. Muhlen, *Return of Germany*, 54–57; and Klier, *Lug Vaterland*, 84.

67. Max E. Lange, *Totalitäre Erziehung*, 121. On the Zwickau pupils, see also *NYT*, October 14, 1951; November 7, 1951.

68. Muhlen, "East Germany's Planned Men," 68–69. *NYT*, January 22, 1951; January 29, 1951; January 30, 1951; and January 31, 1951. On Flade's illnesses in prison, see *NYT*, July 3, 1957.

69. Mulhen, *Return of Germany*, 129–32. *NYT*, October 31, 1950; November 2, 1950; December 21, 1950; January 21, 1951.

70. Muhlen, *Return of Germany*, 23–30. On the case of Arno Esch, a University

of Rostock student sentenced to death in July 1950 by the Soviet Military Tribunal in Schwerin, see Kopke and Wiese, eds. *Mein Vaterland ist die Freiheit*. Esch was falsely accused of having worked as a western intelligence agent. Five other members of the "Esch Group" of Liberal (LDPD) students were sentenced to death on similar charges; four sentences were "commuted" to 25 years' hard labor. Esch was executed in Moscow on July 24, 1951, at the age of 23.

71. Harich, *Keine Schwierigkeiten mit der Wahrheit*, 31. Muhlen, "The New Nazis," 7; and Muhlen, *Return of Germany*, 82–83. For similar stories, see Klier, *Lug Vaterland*, 83–86. The NKVD carried out the re-education of former Nazis and others in former concentration camps such as Sachsenhausen and Buchenwald until 1950. In addition, SMAD established nine new concentration camps of its own. More than former NSDAP members were incarcerated: Anyone hostile to or even potentially critical of Stalinism was often sent there, including anti-fascist conservatives, Catholics, and even socialists. By 1950, when the camps were dissolved—an act of reconciliation by the newly founded DDR—the number of prisoners that had been sent to the camps totaled 200,000. But only 37,500 were released; 96,000 had died in the camps, 41,000 were shipped to the USSR, and the rest were transferred to DDR prisons or forced-labor camps. Hearndon, *Education in the Two Germanies*, 22. Muhlen, *Return*, 80. Füssl notes that, in 1946–47, 5,000 youths from Brandenburg alone were interned "under subhuman conditions" in Siberian camps (*Die Umerziehung der Deutschen*, 360). All of these figures are imprecise. As Naimark notes, wide discrepancies exist in the figures from MVD (Soviet) vs. American intelligence and West German sources: for example, in the number of German internees (119,743 vs. 240,000) and deaths (41,907 vs. 95,643). Naimark, *The Russians*, 377–78.

72. Füssl, *Die Umerziehung der Deutschen*, 28.

73. By 1947, *Neulehrer* comprised already half of the SBZ teaching staff, and when the DDR was founded in October 1949, there were 65,207 teachers, 45,244—or almost 70 percent—of whom were *Neulehrer* (Füssl, *Die Umerziehung der Deutschen*, 341; Childs, *GDR*, 169). *Neulehrer* for *die neue schule*. Theoretically, it made good sense. In many cases, however, the only qualifications that the *Neulehrer* possessed were strong anti-Nazi convictions. Given the low academic standards, it is hardly surprising that "*Neulehrer*" became a code word among eastern Germans for "not a real teacher." Granted, Hitler had perverted the world's finest schools, the majority of *Zonis* agreed, by degrading a system that had once maintained uncompromising academic standards into a machine churning out mindless warriors. But the *Neulehrer* were turning the vocation of teacher into a laughing stock and destroying respect for learning, claimed many critics. Rumors spread about the stupidity of the *Neulehrer*. One story that made the rounds in Chemnitz became legendary. A *Neulehrer* was allegedly instructing children to spell *Blume* (flower) with an "h" because the noun derived from the infinitive *blühen* (to flower). (The mistake is a small one, but it reminds the American of the flap in 1992 in our media over Vice President Dan Quayle's spelling of "potato" with an "e" at the end.) Writing in 1946 in *die neue schule*, a pedagogical magazine for teachers, an official from the Ministry for People's Education claimed that such stories came from bitter Nazi teachers who sought to get their jobs back:

> Most Nazi teachers laughed sneeringly or hissed maliciously [about the *Neulehrer*]. . . . They prophesied a catastrophe for the schools and students. They found ready ears in the population and thus became hopeful about their quick reinstatement.

This, of course, was not to be; unlike the western Allies, SMAD and the SED simply pushed ahead with their educational reforms. By the 1960s, the title *Neu-*

lehrer—like *Neubauer* (new farmer) and *Volkspolizist* (People's Policeman)—had become an honorific salute to the elder generation. The raised status of the word had variously to do with respect for the founding fathers and mothers, nostalgia for the "heroic" days of early postwar reconstruction, the repression or flight of critical voices, the increasing acceptance within the populace of SED policies, and the improved quality of the *Neulehrer* in later years. Uhlig, *Monumenta Paedagogica, Band XIV*, 138, 142, 152.

74. Wendt, *Bonner Berichte aus Mittel- und Ostdeutschland*, 13. In 1950, only 7,000 *Neulehrer* were trained, leaving a gap of 3,000 missing teachers. To meet the urgent need, Ulbricht personally ordered that the positions be immediately filled with untrained teachers. Wendt, *Bonner Berichte aus Mittel- und Ostdeutschland*, 13–14. See also Klier, *Lug Vaterland*, 23; Mieskes, *Die Pädagogik der DDR, vol. 2*, 277; and Naimark, *The Russians*, 457.

75. Wendt, *Bonner Berichte aus Mittel- und Ostdeutschland*, 13. Many of these teachers had first become teachers, if not for idealistic reasons, then for the special benefits. Teachers earned better salaries than most other SBZ workers. More importantly during the early years of widespread hunger, they received the so-called *Pajoks*—monthly packages of meat, sugar, butter, potatoes, coffee, and Russian cigarettes. Teachers were also granted admission to certain cultural clubs where— along with professors, journalists, artists, and politicians—they could receive meals without surrendering their ration tickets. In hindsight, this practice was the beginning of the SED two-tier system for Party members and the general populace: a general policy of preferential treatment accorded to the DDR's purportedly most valuable workers.

76. Füssl, *Die Umerziehung der Deutschen*, 342. But the campaign to storm "the little Red schoolhouse"—to win the village schools—met with mixed success. For instance, as Naimark notes, only 3 percent of *Neulehrer* were from the farming populations; 55 percent were recruited from the working class. Naimark, *The Russians*, 455. Nonetheless, the tightening ideological straitjacket produced noticeable results. Wendt notes that the Fourth Pedagogical Congress in August 1949, which condemned the German tradition of *Reformpädagogik* and mandated Soviet pedagogy, had a shock effect on SBZ/DDR teachers. Now teachers were to become communist functionaries. By 1950, 48 percent of teachers were Young Pioneer leaders; 55 percent had been pressured into joining the Society for German-Soviet Friendship. Even formerly eager Marxist-Leninist teachers found the new expectations excessive: 40 percent of teacher emigrants were former SED members. It was typical of the extreme nature of the "political schooling" that all faculty— even kindergarten teachers—had to propagandize for the regime. Teachers were summoned to regular after-school "work meetings." Here is the list of themes for March 1946 for kindergarten teacher-training:

- How to teach the Nuremberg Trials
- The Nazis and their "men behind the scenes" as the most evil enemies of the German people
- War guilt
- The path to Germany's resurrection and freedom: the democratic renewal of Germany
- The current methods of influencing young people and our democratic school
- The special political tasks of the woman

(Quoted in Uhlig, *Monumenta Paedagogica, Band XIV*, 238.)

77. See Adler and Paterson, "Red Fascism"; Atwood and Freidin, "The Nazis March Again"; Grace, "Islands of Democratic Ferment in Germany"; Muhlen, "The

New Nazis"; and Jean Edward Smith, "The Red Prussianism of the German Democratic Republic."

78. Muhlen, *Return of Germany*, 78.

79. Indeed, many of the main ideological tenets of DDR Stalinism at mid-century drew on the common legacy of communism and fascism—on their celebration of work and *Volksgemeinschaft* (community feeling), their elevation of the state above the individual and collectivism over bourgeois democracy, their totalitarian control of political and cultural life, their lionization of an individual or Party as infallible, their use of censorship and police terror against opponents—and, equally importantly, their indoctrination of youth. The rhetoric of what could be called "DDR Red Fascism" during the Stalin era wove multiple strands of Bolshevism and Nazism together, thereby forming its own distinctive, German pattern. DDR Stalinism made use of the Marxist-Leninist dogmas of the class war, the social ownership of the means of production, and the coming victory of the proletariat and the classless society; and it exploited Nazi appeals involving leader worship, the mystique of power, nationalism, and racism (i.e., DDR anti-Semitism). The last point—about DDR anti-Semitism—merits elaboration. The DDR never imprisoned or exterminated Jews, as had the Nazis, nor even permitted hundreds of high-ranking Nazis to return to prominent positions in public life, as did the BRD. Nevertheless, during Stalin's last years, when anti-Americanism reached a crescendo and a campaign against "rootless cosmopolitans" and "Zionists" resulted in plans for yet another round of mass purges, the DDR too identified "world Jewry" with "American finance capitalism." The Germans' familiar hatred of the Jews was called up in the service of anti-western hate propaganda.

80. Füssl, *Die Umerziehung der Deutschen*, 32.

81. On the Nazi schools, see Kneller, *The Educational Philosophy of National Socialism*.

82. Füssl notes that the first efforts in the communist campaign to promote ideologically correct music and dancing began years earlier. A December 1945 memo from a KPD functionary described the value of KPD-sponsored "dance lessons" to youth and reconstruction policy:

German youth in our cities and villages passionately like to dance . . . This dancing can be a lever to win the mass of youth . . . Dancing can stimulate the productive energies of the youth, which can then be directed toward work. Thus the Party can use both leisure and work to its advantage.

(Quoted in Füssl, *Die Umerziehung der Deutschen*, 352–53.)

83. Quoted in Blackburn, *Education in the Third Reich*, 34. See Muhlen, *Return of Germany*, 90. See also Lilge, *The Abuse of Learning*; and Paul, "German Youth Under the Occupation."

84. Khrushchev reported this remark in his "Secret Speech" at the Twentieth Party Congress of the CPSU in February 1956. Quoted in Chakravarty, ed., *The Stalin Question*, 53.

85. Mieskes, *Die Pädagogik der DDR*, vol. 1, 45–48. Muhlen, *Return of Germany*, 87. Party membership fell from 1,774,000 in 1949 to 1,100,00 in 1952. See also Glaessner and Rudolph, *Macht durch Wissen*.

86. Quoted in Klier, *Lug Vaterland*, 77.

87. The following 1947 letter from the Minister of People's Education in Thuringia, which dismissed the student government president-elect of the University of Jena for rejecting Leninist and bloc party methods, was a harbinger of later trends. Bernhard Reichenbach, an LDPD candidate, had been elected by his fellow students; but he was not approved by the SED.

Dear Herr Reichenbach:

... you still haven't learned to respect the worthy practices of bloc politics.
... You still want to have ballots counted in the elections ... , [thereby] setting candidates against one another.
... [there is] a method common to all parliaments and boards. One unites in
previous meetings about the distribution of votes, and then votes, in order to
achieve unanimity everywhere.

(Quoted in Baske and Engelbert, *Dokumente zur Bildungspolitik*, 12.)

88. Timm, 18.

89. Mieskes, *Die Pädagogik der DDR*, vol. 2, 26. These changes were also reflected in East German school curricula. Until 1947/48, promoting an anti-fascist
democratic program for the "Completion of the Bourgeois Revolution," the SED
supported the great classics of humanism. Works such as Lessing's *Nathan the
Wise* and Schiller's *William Tell* served as the "backbone of a progressive syllabus." Beginning in 1949/50, the "bourgeois" heritage was downgraded in favor of
German socialist and Russian works. Bungenstab, *Umerziehung zur Demokratie?*
57–84.

90. And one small change accompanied another: As if to encapsulate the entire
series of events that had just unfolded, the pedagogical journal *die neue schule*
also underwent an unobtrusive revision: it was uppercased in 1952, becoming *Die
neue Schule*.

91. Bungenstab, *Umerziehung zur Demokratie?* 234–44.

92. Mieskes, *Die Pädagogik der DDR*, vol. 1, 112.

93. The amount of time in the history syllabus devoted to the October Revolution serves as a barometer of the march toward "sovietization." In 1947 the
October Revolution received 4 hours; by 1950 it was receiving 16 hours. Hearndon, *Education in the Two Germanies*, 46.

94. Mieskes, *Die Pädagogik der DDR*, vol. 2, 344.

95. See also Klier, *Lug Vaterland*, 43–60.

96. Muhlen, *Return of Germany*, 43.

97. See Pike, "Planned/Culture," *Politics of Culture*, 487–96.

98. See Bowen, *Anton Makarenko*, chapters 1 and 2.

99. Bowen, *Anton Makarenko*, chapters 1 and 2.

100. Bowen, *Anton Makarenko*, chapters 1 and 2; Mieskes, *Die Pädagogik der
DDR*, vol. 1, 211–31. See also Anweiler and Baske, *Die Sowjetische Bildungspolitik*.

101. Among the books published in the largest editions in the DDR were works
on educational pedagogy, often poorly translated from the Russian and nearly unreadable. Chief among these translations was Makarenko's *Collected Works*,
printed in an astounding edition of 860,000 copies; 565,000 copies were printed
of his occasional lectures. These were the biggest editions ever published for educational books in German, before or since. (To get some idea of the scale of these
numbers, imagine that 30 million copies of John Dewey's treatises on pedagogy
were printed—and in a prose style far worse than Dewey's.) Starting in the 1950s,
Makarenko's *Complete Works* were published in the DDR, where he had a greater
impact than anywhere except the USSR. Makarenko's writings were distributed to
teachers and often used as the basis for training *Neulehrer*. Given the rapid turnover of *Neulehrer*, the high volume of the editions is perhaps understandable.
(Though it is also understandable, if these apparently execrable translations were
actually used in teacher training courses, that frustrated *Neulehrer* were soon led
to resign.) See Mieskes, *Die Pädagogik der DDR*, vol. 1, 150. See also Hillig, *Makarenko in Duetschland*; Anweiler and Baske, *Die Sowjetische Bildungspolitik*;
Bowen, *Anton Makarenko*; and *A. S. Makarenko*.

102. But before his mates in the "Karl Liebknecht" mine could catch their

breath and express their admiration for Hennecke's heroic personal exploit, word got around that in 1947 Hennecke had attended the SED's political academy in Meerane—and had written his thesis on "Stakhanov, a Soviet Example to the German Worker." Hennecke's "feat" had been carefully planned by the Saxony SED. As one DDR refugee later wrote: "Hennecke had been fed, trained, and fostered like a champion boxer for the great day." Brandt, *The East German Rising*, 30. After his achievement, Hennecke received the "National Prize, First Class" (which came with a $30,000 award) and became a top bureaucrat in the Ministry of Heavy Industry. He was elevated to membership in the SED Central Committee in 1954 and retained his seat until his death in 1975.

103. The result, as Stefan Brant notes (83), was patriotic doggerel like the following by Hans Marchwitza, which inadvertently echoed the propaganda from the Goebbels machine:

> We swing the hammers;
> The mines, the plants revive again.
> Courageously we swing the hammers;
> We produce fivefold and ten.

Such propaganda sometimes produced effects opposite from its intentions. Far from being a hero to his fellow workers, Hennecke came to be regarded contemptuously by many of them as a Soviet stooge and buffoon. Elaborate Hennecke jokes flourished. *Life* summarized a few of them in its April 1950 issue:

Name the greatest Hennecke worker in history, East Germans began to ask each other. Answer: Adolf Hitler, who completed the Thousand Year Reich in 12 years. Why did Hennecke suddenly turn up in the British zone? Answer: He began his usual shift in a Saxony mine and dug so furiously that he emerged on the other side of Germany. Had Hennecke really left his pregnant wife? Yes, he divorced her for failing to deliver a child in three months. Had poor Hennecke really passed away? Yes, he drowned in his own sweat. Yes, impatient to get to work, he refused to wait for the mine elevator and jumped into the empty pit shaft. And so on.

To the SED, however, Hennecke jokes were no joking matter. A 1949 decree made the "spreading of false assertions about economic conditions" a penal offense punishable by up to 10 years in prison. Jokes about Hennecke fell under this provision. In Leipzig, the SED offered a prize of a bicycle to children who turned in the names of 10 persons who joked about the Hennecke movement. Hanser, "Speedy Adolf," 11.

104. Naimark, *The Russians*, 200.

105. Muhlen, *Return of Germany*, 145.

106. For these and other examples, see Stefan Brant, *The East German Rising*, 26–27. See also Hanser, "Speedy Adolf."

107. As one disgruntled agronomy professor reportedly declared at a Party meeting: "A cow is a cow, no matter whether the case involves a single farmer's or an agricultural cooperative's cow." Richert, "*Sozialistische Universität*," 97.

108. Wrote the editors of *Pädagogik* in 1950: "The system [of pedagogy] formulated here is the result of the experience of successful teachers of our epoch, especially the best teachers in the Soviet schools. They have critically evaluated the tradition and heritage of classical pedagogy." Quoted in Mieskes, *Die Pädagogik der DDR, vol. 1*, 45.

109. On the Weimar Manifesto, see Mieskes, *Die Pädagogik der DDR, vol. 1*, 117. For the specifics within these traditions, see Uhlig, *Monumenta Paedagogica, Band XIV*, 93–123.

110. Baske and Engelbert, *Dokumente zur Bildungspolitik*, 46.
111. Baske and Engelbert, *Dokumente zur Bildungspolitik*, 25, 23.
112. The most notable victim was Georg Wrazidlo, who went from Buchenwald under the Nazis to Sachsenhausen under the Soviets. A decorated soldier, Wrazidlo had joined the "June 20" officers' plot to assassinate Hitler in 1944. When it failed, he was shipped to Buchenwald and scheduled for execution. Liberated by the Americans in 1945, Wrazidlo settled in the American sector of Berlin, commuting to the Russian sector for medical school at the University of Berlin. Honored by the Soviets as a "Victim of Fascism," Wrazidlo was elected, with SMAD's approval, as the first head of the Berlin University student government. In March 1947, the NKVD arrested Wrazidlo. He was sentenced to 25 years for "covert fascist activities." Originally jailed on charges of drug possession (he was carrying his medical bag at the time of arrest), he was also "guilty" of accepting a jeep ride on Unter den Linden from a young American captain. He was not released until 1956, at the age of 40. Tent, *The Free University of Berlin*, 34–66 passim and 459.
113. [Leisegang], "Die Philosophie," 253.
114. One SED philosophy professor reported in 1947:

Recently one of my students asked me, full of indignation and wonder, whether I didn't engage in propaganda. But his original astonishment was more like indifference when compared to the feeling he had when I answered him: "Of course it's propaganda, and I would regard it as a crude violation of my duties if I didn't engage in propaganda."

(Quoted in Müller, *Stürmt die Festung Wissenschaft*, 62.)

115. Klier, *Lug Vaterland*, 34–37. In one place, however, the SED did meet with conspicuous success: the ABF, the pre-university institute for farmers and peasants. Here the future students were selected not only by economic class, but also according to labor accomplishments and political attitude. Often they were ideologically "reliable" workers whom the Party simply delegated to become students. The ABF was used to build a communist intelligentsia in the DDR, equipped with the correct class consciousness and true to the Party line. As a consequence, the first enthusiastically pro-Soviet professors emerged from the ABF.
116. For instance, only 30 (of 130) Leipzig professors and docents joined the SED during 1946/47. At the technical college in Dresden, they numbered only 8 (of 42 faculty); at the Freiberg Mining Academy, only 1 (of 17). Naimark, *The Russians*, 445.
117. On the resistance of the SBZ academics to "Stalinized science," see Naimark, *The Russians*, 235.
118. [Leisegang], "Die Philosophie," 21–27.
119. [Leisegang], "Die Philosophie," 222–36.
120. Müller, *Stürmt die Festung Wissenschaft*, 158.
121. The questions centered on Engels. SMAD knew that no German would risk criticism of Lenin—any more than a Soviet citizen dared. And allegiance to Marx did not necessarily prove unconditional loyalty to the USSR: both Titoism and the varieties of dissident western Marxism evinced that. One could be a Marxist and yet not Marxist-*Leninist* (a.k.a. an "orthodox" Marxist or Stalinist).
No, a professor's position on Engels disclosed his knowledge and stance on Marxism-Leninism, SMAD believed. SMAD's questions about Engels constituted examples par excellence of Stalinist "political correctness." Some excerpts:

1. Are you familiar with Engels' fundamental division of philosophical systems into materialism and idealism? Do you know that Engels held that Hume's position tottered between these two positions and was "agnos-

ticism," and that he considered Kantianism a deformed version of agnosticism?

4. Do you consider Engels' claim correct that the real unity of the world consists in its materiality? If not, what is your point of view on this question?

5. Do you consider Engels' claim correct that "material without movement is unthinkable, and likewise movement without material"?

10. Do you consider Engels correct that things in themselves [*Dinge an sich*] transform themselves into things for us [*Dinge für uns*]?

14. Do you accept an objective law of social historical development? If yes, how do you handle this law? If not, how do you explain the historical process? What role in history do you attribute to character and personality?

(Quoted in M. G. Lange, *Wissenschaft im totalitären Staat*, 259–60; see also Baske and Englebert, *Dokumente zur Bildungspolitik*, 13–14.)

122. When Walter Wolf submitted his dissertation in philosophy to the University of Jena in 1947, it was turned down flatly. Not even SMAD officials could force Jena's faculty to change their minds. (Wolf had, among other errors, confused "Ontology" and "Ornithology.") At SMAD's suggestion, the dissertation was finally sent to Moscow for evaluation—only to return with a negative vote. Subsequent interventions by the SED finally led to success. Müller, *Stürmt die Festung Wissenschaft*, 42–43.

123. [Leisegang], "Die Philosophie," 55.

124. Leisegang, "Die Philosophie," 248–55. As a result of the harassment and lack of academic freedom, 13 leading "uncompromised" philosophy professors of world stature left East Germany between 1945–50, including Eduard Spranger, Hans Georg Gadamer, Thedor Litt, and Rudolf Schottländer. Hans Leisegang also switched from the University of Jena to the Free University of Berlin. See also M. G. Lange, *Wissenschaft im totalitären Staat*, 48–54, 258–62. The official goal was the creation, in the phrase of A. Zdhanov, the Soviet cultural czar, of a "philosophical front." Most of the emigrants were replaced by reliable SED functionaries. Many of them had not even written a dissertation, prompting one West German critic to dub them "philosophers of the new type." Kaltenbach, *Berichte aus Mittel- und Ostdeutschland*, 71. Wendt, *Bonner Berichte aus Mittel- und Ostdeutschland*, 71, 13. More distinguished philosophers, some of them leading Marxists, fled in later years (e.g., Ernst Bloch and Hans Mayer), along with hundreds of faculty in other disciplines. Combined with the rigorous *Entnazifizierung*, the result of the professors' flight was a constant shortage of qualified faculty. In August 1949, 30 percent of the professorships in Saxony were unfilled; 33 percent of professors were more than 65 years old. Between 1946 and 1951, the percentage of full professors in DDR universities dropped from 58 to 24 percent. To meet the faculty shortages, high school teachers received university lectureships and advanced students were accelerated into junior faculty positions. Müller, *Stürmt die Festung Wissenschaft*, 65, 153, 289–91.

125. Müller, *Stürmt die Festung Wissenschaft*, 36–37; Klier, *Lug Vaterland*, 82–83.

126. Many of the students, such as Georg Wrazidlo, resurfaced in concentration camps; others re-emerged in prison, sentenced to terms ranging up to 25 years. Student opposition to the SED terror campaign led student leaders to appeal to the western Allies for help. In December 1948, near the height of the Berlin crisis—during the months of the Berlin Blockade—numerous courageous former students of the University of Berlin founded, with American technical and financial assistance, the Free University of Berlin.

127. Sample questions from the Universities of Leipzig and Berlin in 1951:

1. Using the example of West Germany, explain the essential and characteristics of imperalism.
2. What does Marxist-Leninist theory teach about the national question that
is applicable to the battle of the German *Volk* for its reunification?
3. What special characteristics does the revived [West] German imperialism
possess?
4. What significance did Lenin's and Stalin's battle against the Trotskyite
conciliators have for the final triumph of the Bolsheviks?
5. On what is the party-minded character of philosophy based? What is the
difference between bourgeois and proletarian partisanship?
6. Why is Marxist dialectics the single scientific method and therefore the
foundation for [your] course of studies? Why is historical materialism the
first and only scientific theory of social development?

(Quoted in Müller, *Stürmt die Festung Wissenschaft*, 242–43.)
128. Muhlen, "The New Nazis," 5.
129. In 1949, 50 percent of students at the University of Halle belonged to the
FDJ. This was about typical for the DDR at the time. The percentage rose steeply
as the 1950s progressed. Overall FDJ membership skyrocketed from 415,000 in
1948 to 1,200,000 in June 1950. Müller, *Stürmt die Festung Wissenschaft*, 173.
130. See "Youth in East Germany."
131. The interviews were strictly political. For example, students applying to
study German and philosophy at the University of Berlin, were asked the following questions:

1. What do you think of the special course of studies for workers and peasants?
2. What tasks do factory boards have in a democracy?
3. Explain the difference between a trust and a People's Firm.

(Quoted in Müller, *Stürmt die Festung Wissenschaft*, 84.)
132. Baske and Engelbert, *Dokumente zur Bildungspolitik*, 61.

Chapter 2. Marooned in the Workers' Paradise: Cold War Catechetics, 1951–61

Of Carnivals and Graveyards

1. For contemporary news accounts of the two-week festival, see *Der Spiegel*'s
coverage: "Zu einem Fest der Familie" (August 1, 1951); "Es muss etwas passieren" (August 15, 1951); and "Glanzäugig und blaublusig" (August 22, 1951).
See also *NYT*, August 11, 1951, and August 12, 1951; *WT*, July 1951; *USDSB*,
September 24, 1951; *TC*, October 1951; and *Collier's*, November 10, 1951. On the
larger political issues, see Clews, "The Berlin Youth Festival"; Ward, "Crucial Battle for the World's Youth"; Atwood and Freidin, "The Nazis March Again"; Balluseck, "Die guten und die bösen Deutschen"; "The Two Berlins"; and JCC, "The
Berlin Youth Festival." On Honecker's role at the festival, see Lippmann, *Honecker*, 133–35.
2. Drew Middleton, "The Youth Festival," *NYT*, August 12, 1951, 4.
3. But the USSR's socialist brotherlands apparently had not yet mastered their
lessons, at least as far as the cultural contests of the 1951 World Festival were
concerned. From Olympic-style team competitions in People's Dancing to People's
Chorus Singing, the Soviets won more than 95 percent of the prizes, including 22
of 23 first-place awards. (Bulgaria alone managed to "learn to triumph," garnering
first-place in the Young Pioneer Chorus category.) *NYT*, August 19, 1951, 23.
4. *Leben, Singen, Kämpfen*, 45.

5. *NYT*, August 14, 1951, 22.

6. Much has been written on the background and details of the uprising in East Berlin and elsewhere in the DDR on June 16–17, 1953. For contemporary eyewitness news accounts, see issues of *Der Spiegel* dated June 25, 1953, and July 1, 1953, and *Der Monat's* reports under the title "Der Aufstand im Juni," in October and November 1953. See also Bäring, *Uprising in East Germany*; Stefan Brant, *The East German Rising*; Herrnstadt, *Das Herrnstadt-Dokument*; Hagen, *DDR-Juni '53*; Hildebrandt, *Der 17. Juni*; Spittmann and Fricke, *17. Juni 1953*; and Degen, *"Wir wollen keine Sklaven sein."* See also *NYT*, June 16, 1953; June 17, 1953; and June 18, 1953; "Seventeenth of June"; *The Reporter*, September 1, 1953, and February 16, 1954; Lewis, "Soviet Germany"; Lasky, "Berlin Notebook"; Goldstein, "The East German Revolt"; *PN*, "East Germany"; Croan and Friedrich, "The East German Regime"; and Muhlen, "The People Speak" and "East Germany: The Date Is Still June 17." On the response of the universities to the rebellion, see Huschner, "Der 17. und 1953"; Croan and Friedrich, "The East German Regime," 45–53. On the impact of June 17 in the schools, see the observations of Max E. Lange, former editor of *Pädagogik*, in *Totalitäre Erziehung*, 416–22; and Uhlig, *Monumenta Paedagogica, Band XIV*, 164, 189. A comprehensive list of slogans used during the uprising can be found in Hagen, *DDR-Juni '53*; 59–62, and Degen, "Wir wollen keine Sklaven sein," 20. See also Stern, *Walter Ulbricht*, 144.

7. Ulbricht, dubbed by his detractors as "the little Lenin," later commented on this slogan, failing to grasp—deliberately or with comic obtuseness?—that it called for his ouster. "I'll definitely shave it off," he announced, "as soon as the peace-loving people of western Germany have triumphed and a peace-loving, democratic Germany has been forged" (Stern, *Walter Ulbricht*, 64).

8. Quoted in Lewis, "Soviet Germany," 883. Three days later, *Freiheit*, the Party organ in Halle, declared:

> You've all seen these provocateurs, these hoodlums, these Western numb-skulls with colorful striped socks and unwashed necks, these work-shy riffraff. . . . We have to clip the wings of this fascist pack. You can't negotiate with provocateurs. You've got to muzzle them.

A few days later, Grotewohl himself lashed out in similar terms, making clear that it was Americanized Berliners, or Americans behind the scenes, who were the main culprits: "These western provocateurs with their colorful striped socks, their cowboy pants and their Texas shirts wanted to trigger a great political provocation. . . ." Quoted in "Der Aufstand im Juni," November 1953, 60–61.

9. Estimates vary. Some western historians place the death total as low as 30 to 50, others judge it in the hundreds. The DDR claimed that only 22 died and 357 were injured, but most historians consider these figures much too low.

10. In fact, to more knowledgeable East Germans, der 17. Juni also suggested a much darker parallel than 1905: "Kronstadt"—a forbidden word in the Soviet Union and Eastern Europe, even into the Gorbachev era. The June 17 revolt in the DDR was the greatest uprising in the history of communism since the Russian sailors at Kronstadt rebelled against the Bolsheviks in 1920—and were similarly crushed by the Red Army. In the decades to follow, June 17 would lead to similar heroic, yet doomed, revolts in Hungary, Czechoslovakia, and Poland.

And, from the vantage point of those later uprisings and the perspective of five postwar decades, we can now see that June 17 was the day when the decline and fall of the Soviet empire began. As the *New Republic* prophesied on June 22:

> Although it would be foolish to predict in what way, or when the house will come down, it now seems certain that some day the whole structure will

collapse, in a way that will have been set off, however indirectly, by the East German revolt.

Or as Karl Marx wrote in June 1848, after the failure of the Paris workers' uprising:

The workers were indeed crushed, but they are not defeated. Defeated are the opposition, as History shall one day teach.

11. Aware of the impending famine—and aiming to score propaganda points, as well as assure East Berliners that the West had not abandoned them—the local mayor of Kreuzberg, in West Berlin, began to issue American food parcels on July 14. By August, more than 1 million East Germans had crossed into West Berlin to pick up the parcels.

12. Brant, *The East German Rising*, 128.

13. Brant, *The East German Rising*, 128; Grothe, *To Win the Minds of Men*, 185. On the relative quiet in the universities, see Huschner, "Der 17. und 1953."

14. Huschner, "Der 17. und 1953," 687–90.

15. Huschner, "Der 17. und 1953," 690–91.

16. Muhlen, "East Germany," 14.

17. Only the conclusion of Brecht's letter, however, was printed in *Neues Deutschland*: "I feel at this moment the need to express to you [Ulbricht] my solidarity with the Socialist Unity Party of Germany." (Quoted in "Der Aufstand im Juni," November 1953, 59.) This damaged his reputation in the West, making it seem as if the great proletarian champion had kowtowed to the regime. Critics have speculated that Brecht, who died in 1956 and never again went on record about June 17, may have been expressing his remorse for his part in the June 17 aftermath in a posthumously published poem, "Evil Morning":

> The silver birch tree, a well-known local beauty,
> Looks an old hag today; the lake
> Like a puddle of dish-water—don't stir!
> The fuchsia under the snapdragon cheap and flashy.
> Why?
> Last night in a dream I saw fingers pointed at me
> As at a leper. They were worn to the bone,
> And they were broken.
>
> Ignorant ones! I cried
> Full of guilt.

The poem bears the date: "Summer 1953."

18. These are official figures, pertaining only to those refugees who registered with West German reception camps. Many DDR emigrants made their own way to the West. For example, the number of unofficial DDR emigrants in 1954 was estimated at 51,000 (McCauley, *The German Democratic Republic Since 1945*, 69).

19. McCauley, *The German Democratic Republic Since 1945*, 47.

20. Cited in Wyden, *Wall*, 45.

Stalinizing the Schools

21. This was Stalin's quip when he was informed, in 1935, that the Pope would welcome his easing of persecution against USSR religious believers as a generous act of conciliation.

22. Baske and Engelbert, *Dokumente zur Bildungspolitik*, 61. On this period, see also Birke, *Nation ohne Haus*.

23. *NYT*, June 30, 1951, 4.

24. The speech on the first day of school in September 1952 by the Minister for People's Education, Elfriede Zaisser, which was piped into East German classrooms, set the tone for the school year. Pupils were told that this was "the year of 'building socialism' " and that they could contribute by patrolling school buildings to monitor enemy invasions, develop close contact with the People's Police, catch truants, volunteer for public reconstruction projects, work on the collective farms, collect scrap metal, and resist any impulse to read western gangster literature. *NYT*, September 2, 1952.

25. Klier, *Lug Vaterland*, 89.

26. Kurt Hager, SED propaganda chief, in a 1952 speech to Halle students. Quoted in *Stürmt die Festung Wissenschaft*, 249. For an analysis of the cult of Stalin as a great economist and linguist, see M. G. Lange, *Wissenschaft im totalitären Staat*, 24–35. On the cult, see also Spittmann and Helwig, *DDR Lesebuch*.

27. *Lehrbuch für den Geschichtsunterricht. 8. Klasse*, 49, 78.

28. *Lehrbuch für den Geschichtsunterricht. 10. Schuljahr* (1956 [1953]).

29. Stalin died of pneumonia after an illness of several weeks. He was mourned throughout the DDR in March 1953—and his life memorialized thereafter. Schools closed. In the Stalinallee, black-garbed commanders of the People's Police laid wreaths at a new shrine, an 11-foot statue of the "faithful Father of the German *Volk*." Government officials forbade all sporting events, dancing, and "gatherings which do not express the deep bereavement of the German *Volk*." All transportation in East Germany was ordered halted for five minutes during the March 9 funeral in Moscow. By the end of the month, in order "to familiarize citizens with our unforgettable Stalin," the SED had inaugurated a year-long education program for all Party members, "Study the Life and Work of Comrade Stalin!" It featured selections of Stalin's own works. A few months later, Ulbricht announced that Fürstenburg an der Oder—the site of the Ost steel mill, the main project of the First Five-Year Plan—was being renamed "Stalinstadt." It would be redesigned to become "the first socialist city" in Germany, e.g., without churches or religious icons. Within three years, of course, the Party would be trying hard to forget the "unforgettable" Stalin—though not until 1961 would Stalinstadt be quietly renamed Eisenhüttenstadt (iron works city). Baske and Engelbert, *Dokumente zur Bildungspolitik*, 102. See also Spittmann and Helwig, *DDR Lesebuch*.

30. Mieskes, *Die Pädagogik der DDR, vol. 2*, 334.

31. Möbus, *Unterwerfung durch Erziehung*, 122.

32. Möbus, *Unterwerfung durch Erziehung*, 199.

33. Grothe, *To Win the Minds of Men*, 185, 187. On the Education toward Hate programs, see also Enders, "Erziehung zum Hass"; Uhlig, *Monumenta Paedagogica, Band XIV*, 146–47, 157, 190; and Max E. Lange, *Totalitäre Erziehung*, 68. On socialist patriotism during this period, see also Lange, 145, 156.

34. On the "Hate the West" campaign, see Grothe, *To Win the Minds of Men*, 57–63. See also Möbus, *Unterwerfung durch Erziehung*, 132–40, 173–82.

35. Uhlig, *Monumenta Paedagogica, Band XIV*, 157, 159. See also Balluseck, "Die guten und die bösen Deutschen."

36. The Pioneer slogans for 1951/52 exemplified a similar escalation. Notice that most of them involve children appealing to adults by mouthing SED slogans— no doubt some of which they hardly understood.

- Teach and Battle for the Honor of the Family of Our Socialist Fatherland!

- Parents! Help Teachers and Your Children to Promote Socialism, to Become Fighters for Peace and to Become Well-Rounded Educated People!

- Parents! Strengthen Our New School in the Struggle for the Unity of Germany and in the Defense of Our Democratic Achievements!

- Parents! Educate Your Children to Become Sincere Patriots Who Are Able and Ready to Defend the Homeland!

(Quoted in Möbus, *Unterwerfung durch Erziehung*, 151.)

37. Mieskes, *Die Pädagogik der DDR*, vol. *1*, 451.

38. Mieskes, *Die Pädagogik der DDR*, vol. *1*, 449.

39. Möbus, *Unterwerfung durch Erziehung*, 261. See also Busch, *Familienerziehung in der sozialistischen Pädagogik der DDR*.

40. Busch, 341.

41. Muhlen, "East Germany's Planned Men," 62.

42. For a full discussion of how the DDR's own homegrown personality cults and its hate pedagogy were transmitted through textbooks, curricula, and songs, see my *Textbook Reds: Ideology and National Self-Legitimation in East German Schoolbooks* (Penn State UP, 2002).

43. Quoted in "Wir sehen die rote Fahne."

44. Mieskes, *Die Pädagogik der DDR*, vol. *2*, 128.

45. Möbus, *Unterwerfung durch Erziehung*, 349. *Leben, Singen, Kämpfen*, 20–30.

46. Quoted in Brant, *The East German Rising*, 44.

47. *Leben, Singen, Kämpfen*, 97.

48. *Leben, Singen, Kämpfen*, 74, 102–103.

49. Harold B. Erickson, "East German Youth Decide for Themselves," 77.

50. Füssl, *Die Umerziehung der Deutschen*, 362.

51. Marx's phrase "rounded personalities" derived from his criticism that, under capitalism, the masses are educated only to become partial people, not whole persons—i.e., only sufficiently to enable them to fulfill limited functions in the production process, thereby making them little more than extensions of the machines they operate. Ironically, however, as Hearndon has pointed out, the embrace of Soviet pedagogy and its emphasis on technical skills rather than *Allgemeinbildung* (general education) meant doing just what Marx had deplored about capitalism. Hearndon, 21.

52. The slogans of the Ministry of People's Education nicely reflected this change from "sovietization" to Stalinization. The motto for the 1950/51 school year had been: "We teach and learn for peace." For 1951/52 it was suitably revised: "We teach, learn, and fight for peace." See Uhlig, *Monumenta Padagogica, Band XIV*, 72–73, and Mieskes, *Die Pädagogik der DDR*, vol. *2*, 279.

53. Mieskes, *Die Pädagogik der DDR*, vol. *1*, 143.

54. Möbus, *Unterwerfung durch Erziehung*, 25–26. See also Mieskes, *Die Pädagogik der DDR*, vol. *2*, 333. On "sovietization" in DDR education, see Müller, *Stürmt die Festung Wissenschaft*, 35–61.

55. Mieskes, *Die Pädagogik der DDR*, vol. *1*, 123.

56. Mieskes, *Die Pädagogik der DDR*, vol. *1*, 46. By the end of 1952, the failure rate fell to 7.29 percent; by 1955, it was down to 2.25 percent. *Monumenta Padagogica, vol. 6* (1945–55), 71.

57. Klier, *Lug Vaterland*, 99.

58. By the 1970s, however, the term had returned to a position of respectability.

59. Mieskes, *Die Pädagogik der DDR*, vol. *1*, 312.

60. Special incentives were also given to youths, in order to induce them to become *Vopos*, which by 1953 numbered 145,000. By no means were all *Vopos* thoroughgoing communists; many of them joined the service for financial reasons. The lowest-rank *Vopo* received 400 marks per month, which was more than a

university professor. An *Unterleutnant* earned up to 1,200 marks per month, which was more than the manager of a factory—and some of these lieutenants were only 19 years old. "Seventeenth of June," 33–51.

61. Klier recalls how she felt about much of the military training in her early elementary school years in the 1950s. She didn't even perceive it as militaristic:

It all seemed like playground games, it offered a welcome change from sitting in school. We weren't even aware of the military aspect of these games, because militaristic thinking and behavior had been part and parcel of our life since childhood. Without a thought, we clubbed puppets, hung them by cords over the stream, and were pleased when we were judged best in the class at it. No enemy ever stood before our eyes—we faced no bloodthirsty hounds, but were rather surrounded by a peaceful student collective.

(Klier, *Lug Vaterland*, 113–14.)
62. Muhlen, *Return of Germany*, 185.
63. Muhlen, *Return of Germany*, 184.
64. Grothe, *To Win the Minds of Men*, 175.
65. The first remark was by Gerhard Harig, State Secretary for Higher Education. (Quoted in Muhlen, "East Germany," 16.) The second quotation is in Vogt, 34. See also Schultz, *Der Funktionär*.
66. The basic texts for this course in 1951 including the following:

1. Marx and Engels, *The Communist Manifesto*
2. Marx, Excerpt from *Das Kapital*
3. Engels, *Utopian and Scientific Socialism, Feuerbach and the Course of Classical German Philosophy*, and *The Origin of the Family, Private Property and the State*
4. Lenin, *Imperialism as the Highest Stage of Capitalism* and *State and Revolution*
5. Stalin, *Collected Works*, vols. 1 and 2, *Questions of Leninism, History of the Communist Party of the CPSU*
6. Plekhanov, *Contributions to the History of Materialism, The Role of the Personality in History*
7. Alfred Norden, *Lessons of German History*
8. Walter Ulbricht, *Handbook for State and Economic Reconstruction*

(Alfred Norden was head of agitprop and in charge of DDR media policy in the 1960s.) Cited in Müller, *Stürmt die Festung Wissenschaft*, 239. See also Baske and Engelbert, *Dokumente zur Bildungspolitik*, 102.
67. This was a current events course. Topics for 1952 included the Korean War, colonial rebellions, German unity and western peacemongers, and the decay of the West under monopolistic capitalism. Muhlen, "East Germany's Planned Men," 65. On the regimentation of the new curriculum, see M. G. Lange, *Wissenschaft im totalitären Staat*, 258–59.
68. Müller, *Stürmt die Festung Wissenschaft*, 236–37, 330–31. See also Moss, "Reforms in the East German Universities."
69. Müller, *Stürmt die Festung Wissenschaft*, 230–31, 236–37. The "10-month" year was eventually recognized by the SED as an excessive burden and abandoned in the late 1950s. See also M. G. Lange, *Wissenschaft im totalitären Staat*, 266–74; "University Reforms in the Soviet Zone of Germany"; Moss, "Reforms in the East German Universities"; and Peck, "Universities Behind the Iron Curtain."
70. Uhlig, *Monumenta Paedagogica, Band XIV*, 196.
71. For instance, working-class students received bigger scholarships than bour-

geois children, even when their parents earned twice as much or more than the middle-class parents. Klier, *Lug Vaterland*, 120.

72. Klier, *Lug Vaterland*, 96.

73. *NYT*, February 6, 1955.

74. Brant, *The East German Rising*, 181; *NYT*, October 1, 1955, 3.

75. *NYT*, March 2, 1963; March 27, 1953; April 18, 1953; April 25, 1953; May 6, 1953. The attempts to quash Protestant and Catholic youth groups had, however, begun years earlier. On such efforts by the Saxony KPD and FDJ in mid-1946, see Füssl, *Die Umerziehung der Deutschen*, 353–57.

76. *NYT*, March 24, 1953; April 22, 1953. See also Grothe, *To Win the Minds of Men*, 218–19; and Nitsche, *Zwischen Kreuz und Sowjetstern*.

According to Ehrhart Neubert, the waves of arrests of *Junge Gemeinde* members ultimately included more than 70 theologians and youth leaders. An estimated 3,000 school pupils and 2,000 university students who did not disavow membership in the *Junge Gemeinde* were summarily expelled. Neubert, a Lutheran minister in the DDR, is Joachim Gauck's assistant overseeing the *Stasi* archives as its director of the Department of Education and Research. See his chapter in *Das Schwarzbuch des Kommunismus*, ed. Stephane Courtois, 855.

77. The secular confirmation rite included the following public exchanges between an SED educator and the students:

E: Are you prepared to devote all your powers to the building-up of a happy, beautiful life and to economic scientific and cultural progress?
S: Yes, we do so vow!
E: Are you prepared to devote all your powers, together with all patriots, to fight for unified, peace-loving, democratic, and independent Germany?
S: Yes, we do so vow!
E: Are you prepared to devote all your powers, together with all peace-loving people, to fight for peace and defend it to the death?
S: Yes, we do so vow!
E: We have heard your pledge. You have taken upon yourself a lofty mission. We, the community of all workers promise you support, protection, and help. With united strength, forward to victory!

Then an orchestra burst into the finale of a symphony such as Wagner's *Die Meistersänger*. One by one, blue-shirted boys and girls in blue skirts approached the red-draped table of Party officials, and received their Marxist-Leninist "bible," *Weltall, Erde, Mensch* (*Cosmos, Earth, Human Being*), an atheistic manual explaining the great questions of life according to the dialectical materialist faith. See Sullivan, "In East Germany."

78. *NYT*, March 7, 1955, 12.

79. Uhlig, *Monumenta Paedagogica, Band XIV*, 234.

80. Grothe, *To Win the Minds of Men*, 219.

81. *NYT*, September 18, 1955, 6.

82. Müller, *Stürmt die Festung Wissenschaft*, 321.

Ulbricht über allen

83. Quoted in Stern, *Walter Ulbricht*, 164.

84. Quoted in Chakravarty, ed., *The Stalin Question*, 3, 4, 9, 11, 34. Compare these remarks with Khrushchev's testimonial on the occasion of Stalin's seventieth birthday in December 1949:

Comrade Stalin's name is the banner of all victories of the Soviet people, the banner of struggle for the workers of the entire world against capitalist slavery and national oppression for peace and socialism. . . . All the peoples of our country, with unusual warmth and feeling of filial love, call the great Stalin their dear father, our great leader and their brilliant teacher. . . . Glory to our dear father, our wise teacher, to the brilliant leader of the party of the Soviet people and of the workers of the entire world, Comrade Stalin!

(Quoted in Chakravarty, ed., *The Stalin Question*, 77, 78, 82.) On the impact of the speech, see Medvedev, *Khrushchev*, 83–103.

85. Nor did some of them ever do so, at least not officially. Molotov, Kaganovich, Malenkov, Voroshilov, and Mikoyan never publicly supported Khrushchev's denunciation of Stalin. For Khruschev's diatribe was not only directed against Stalin, but also against these Politburo rivals. By taking the initiative in exposing Stalin's crimes, Khrushchev was attacking these close colleagues of Stalin too. Whereas they had served as Stalin's advisors during the 1930s and '40s and thereby bore much responsibility for the mass exterminations, Khrushchev was far less tainted, having spent the same period as party leader in the Ukraine, distant from Stalin's machinations. The above-mentioned colleagues were strong enough, however, to slow criticism of the Stalin cult, at least until the early 1960s. Worried about the fallout within the CPSU of his speech, Khrushchev himself was back-pedaling by June 1956, feeling forced to remind Party members that Stalin was "a great Marxist-Leninist" and "a great revolutionary," and that the CPSU "would not allow Stalin's name to be surrendered to the enemies of communism." Quoted in Medvedev, *Khrushchev*, 90, 96.

86. McCauley, *The German Democratic Republic Since 1945*, 79; Podewin, *Walter Ulbricht*, 282–91.

87. Stern, *Walter Ulbricht*, 153–54; Podewin, *Walter Ulbricht*, 284–87.

88. McCauley, *The German Democratic Republic Since 1945*, 79–80.

89. At SMAD's urging, Ackermann had formulated his thesis of the "special German road to socialism" in 1946, when he was head of SED agitprop. During the Stalin-Tito split of 1948, Ackermann was forced to engage in self-criticism; he repented, repudiated his 1946 article, and survived as an official in the Foreign Ministry, rising again until he became, briefly in 1953, Foreign Minister of the GDR. Purged in the wake of the June 17 uprising, he was once again required to recant his views on a German "special road." In *Neues Deutschland* he wrote: "The theory of a special German road to socialism has proven itself unconditionally false and dangerous. . . . After mature consideration, that is the only conclusion I have reached." (Quoted in *DS*, December 19, 1956, 19.) By 1956 he was again rehabilitated, but thereafter held only subordinate government offices.

90. Quoted in Stern, *Walter Ulbricht*, 155.

91. On these professors' specific critiques of SED policy, see Richert, "*Sozialistische Universität*," 157–61.

92. Zudeick, *Der Hintern des Teufels*, 154–55. See also Zipes, "Ernst Bloch and the Obscenity of Hope."

93. Zipes, "Ernst Bloch and the Obscenity of Hope," 219–24. See also Schmidt, *Ernest Bloch*.

94. Zipes, *Ernest Bloch*, 222.

95. Quoted in Bahr, *Ernst Bloch*, 70.

96. Bahr, *Ernst Bloch*, 251.

97. *DS*, April 8, 1991, 165; December 19, 1956, 17. The second statement was by Rudolf Pechel, editor of *Neue Zeit*, the CDU organ of the SBZ.

98. Harich, *Keine Schwierigkeiten mit der Wahrheit*, 34.

99. Harich, *Keine Schwierigkeiten mit der Wahrheit*, 92. On Harich, Bloch, and DDR students, see also Kaltenbach, *Berichte aus Mittel- und Ostdeutschland*, 16–17, 65–68.

100. Kaltenbach, *Berichte*, 21–22. On the evolution of Lukács' political thought, see Kadarkay, *Georg Lukács;* and Löwy, *Georg Lukács*.

101. Heitzer, *GDR*, 109.
102. *NYT*, November 18, 1956.
103. Richert, *"Sozialistische Universität,"* 134, 136–37.
104. Stern, *Walter Ulbricht*, 159. *NYT*, December 1, 1956.
105. "Die rechten Bahnen."
106. *NYT*, November 27, 1956.
107. "Die politische Plattform Harichs und seiner Freunde," *SBZ-Archiv* 5/6 (December 25, 1956), 72–73.
108. Later condemned by the SED leadership as "revisionism," these ideas had nothing to do with the revisionism associated with Eduard Bernstein, leader of the Social Democrats before World War I.
109. Gomulka and Harich, of course, overlooked the fact that Lenin abruptly stopped that call as soon as the Bolsheviks consolidated power. From then on, and especially during the Stalin era, the Party apparatus rather than the workers would decide about factory production and personnel. Amid their outrage with Stalin, the reformers also forgot that Stalin was Lenin's heir in most respects, and Lenin had always held that the party should lead the workers, and never be led by them.
110. Wendt, *Bonner Berichte aus Mittel- und Ostdeutschland*, 67.
111. *DS*, December 19, 1956, 17.
112. Walter Janka, *Schwierigkeiten mit der Wahrheit*, 338–39. Two other Humboldt colleagues received jail terms of four and two years, respectively. Other prominent intellectuals who were accused of having connections with the "Harich group"—most notably, Walter Janka, publisher of Aufbau Verlag—were sentenced in July 1957 to jail terms. On Harich's views of these events and on his later history, see chapter 13 of the current volume, "No Difficulties with the Truth? The Last Testament of Philosopher-Dissident Wolfgang Harich."
113. *DS*, October 9, 1967, 45. The cup, however, would be drunk by his followers, rather than by Bloch himself. In an open letter to the Party of January 22, 1957, Bloch denied all the charges against him, even claiming that he had demanded before witnesses at the university that the Soviet army intervene in Hungary. Defenders of Bloch later claimed that he sought to protect his students and followers under arrest at this time; but the letter apparently came too late and did neither them, nor him, much good. Zudeick, *Der Hintern des Teufels*, 234–35. See also "Wie Sokrates." For other views on the role of DDR intellectuals in the events of 1956/57, see also Croan and Friedrich, "The East German Regime"; and Heider and Thons, *SED und Intellektuelle in der DDR der fünfziger Jahre*.
114. Leonhard, 5. I quote here from the unabridged German edition; the English translation is titled *Child of the Revolution*.
115. Alfred Kantorowicz, *Im 2. Drittel unseres Jahrhunderts*, 158–59. This statement was first delivered over West Berlin radio in August 1957. A few weeks later, in October, Kantorowicz published his "Message to My Students," a reply to letters he had received from DDR students about the broadcast. This exchange also merits quoting, for it captured the predicament of both the elder and younger generation of GDR intellectuals. Kantorowicz began by quoting a student letter:

Was it unavoidably necessary for you—a communist and Spanish Civil War veteran—to leave? You, a man who through his actions demonstrated the force of his convictions? You enjoyed the reverence of the student youth; your escape has torn one of the few threads that still connected us to this state and to its idea, which no longer is our idea. We have been uncertain—simultaneously pulled between two worlds; we have been momentarily excited (not least through your own writings), we have been time and time again disappointed and undermined. And now you have taken, through this step, the final measure of faith that we held in this system of rule by functionaries.

We don't want to conceal our opinions from you. You now carry a difficult responsibility, for through your [August] explanation, you have plunged the youth into a still deeper confusion. What direction should we now head in?

We're not interested in the [DDR] newspaper slanders about the "renegade" Kantorowicz; we are asking this "renegade" to work for our spiritual liberation from his place of asylum. Don't forget! Your word has gained even more weight! And we are waiting for your word!

Kantorowicz replied:

I fled from a tyranny, not from socialism. . . . But you wait to no avail for an answer from me to your questions; I don't know the answers myself. . . . We all face the terrifying question: Are these degenerations that we see, without exception, across the whole expanse of socialist power, just accidents? And if that's the case, what's the link in the chain from Marx to Stalin? . . . Or, is there something decisive in the foundations that is wrong? . . . I plead with you: Hold on! . . . I will, until I receive a call from a West German university, work as a freelance writer and earn my living by my work, and be in nobody's service except my own conscience. . . . You'll hear from me. Carry on till the end.

Kantorowicz, *Im 2. Drittel*, 163–66.

116. *DS*, December 19, 1956, 23.

117. See Heider, *Politik, Kultur, Kulturbund*. The revisionist historian Kuczynski and two of the unorthodox agronomists, Behrens and Benary, soon issued their apologias. But not all intellectuals were willing to bend. In the next four years, many of them fled west. They included writers such as Uwe Johnson, Gerhard Zwerenz, and Heiner Kiphardt; and professors such as the agronomist Viewig. (According to Richert, 752 university professors and college teachers fled the GDR between 1954–61. Baylin puts the figure at 770 faculty and 14,825 students. Cate estimates the totals for 1948–60 as 16,000 teachers and 700 university professors and staff. Richert, "*Sozialistische Universität*," 199. Baylin, 137; Cate, *The Ides of August*, 129.) Bloch was vacationing in West Germany when the Wall went up in August 1961, and decided not to return to Leipzig. The SED leadership among his former colleagues bid him farewell with a fulsome tirade: "Deserter, Renegade, Traitor, Deceiver, dangerous Criminal . . . '*Pack schlagt sich, Pack verträgt sich!*' 'Beware the fickle mob—it kills, it rewards!' " Quoted in Zudeick, *Der Hintern des Teufels*, 247.

118. Richert, "*Sozialistische Universität*," 137. *NYT*, January 12, 1957.

119. *NYT*, December 13, 1956, 8.

120. *NYT*, December 3, 1956, 4. See also Stern, *Walter Ulbricht*, 159.

121. *NYT*, December 2, 1956, 19. See also Richert, "*Sozialistische Universität*," 136–42.

122. Richert, "*Sozialistische Universität*," 141. *NYT*, December 31, 1956, 3.

123. Richert, "*Sozialistische Universität*," 169.

124. "Edel aus dem Grabstein," 74. Ulbricht's deputies thus did what was "required." Ulbricht's exchange with Alfred Neumann, SED Central Committee member who reported to Ulbricht on the results of applying the "good kick in the groin" to the Humboldt University "hotheads," exemplifies their view of Party "democracy." As Ulbricht's first biographer, Carola Stern (123), reports it:

"Just what you predicted" [said Neumann]. "They held out for about two days, but after that, they were so worn out that they went quietly off to bed. We had to get down to brass tacks with only three or four unreasonable fellows."

Smiling, Ulbricht responded: "It's a completely democratic method. . . . I believe now we and the students know where we stand."

125. *NYT*, March 20, 1957; April 4, 1957; April 21, 1957. On music restrictions during this period, see *Stürmt die Festung Wissenschaft*, 337.

126. Among the rehabilitated were Anton Ackermann and Hans Jedretzsky, but not Wilhelm Zaisser or Rudolf Herrnstadt. None of the rehabilitated Party members, however, ever recaptured their former eminence.

127. Stern, *Walter Ulbricht*, 150.

128. By 1958, public criticism of Ulbricht could, once again, land individuals in jail. As the accuser against Schirdewan put it, "[I]n attacking Ulbricht, the imperialist enemy was attacking the Party." In 1958, a dentist earned a one-year jail sentence for referring to Ulbricht as "der Spitzbart," and a teacher got six months for telling a student, "I am not omniscient like Walter Ulbricht." Both men were convicted of defaming the state. Later, one Party slogan ran, "Ulbricht—das sind wir alle" ("We are all Ulbricht"). Stern, *Walter Ulbricht*, 199, 202–05. On Ulbricht's glorification, see also Podewin, *Walter Ulbricht*, 298–307.

129. A sharper political wind in the DDR typically blew East Germans westward, and this occasion was no different. Approximately 1,300 students fled the DDR in 1957, including an astounding 27 percent of the graduates of the nation's top-ranked institution, Humboldt University; many of the refugee high school and university students enrolled in a variety of one-year refresher courses in the BRD, which prepared them to enter BRD universities and technical colleges. Several hundred professors and lecturers also went west (among them Kantorowicz, who had refused to sign an SED manifesto criticizing the Hungarian rebels and even dared propose Lukács for the Nobel Prize). Two distinct groups sought refuge: the remnants of the bourgeois professors and students; and the humanistic socialists, like Kantorowicz, who admired Bloch and rejected Ulbricht's neo-Stalinism. *NYT*, January 18, 1958.

130. Steele, *Inside East Germany*, 113. See also Meuschel, *Legitimation und Parteiherrschaft*; and Birke, *Nation ohne Haus*.

131. "Building socialism" included Ulbricht's industrialization campaign and his offensive against the churches: All teachers were now required to promote atheism in their lessons and to give classes in the *Jugendweihe*—which led, predictably, to yet another mass exodus of experienced faculty. One consequence of re-emphasizing industrial development at the expense of consumer satisfaction was that not until the fall of April 1958 did food rationing finally end. The DDR was the last country in East Europe to end rationing, a fact attributable less to poor economic performance than to its skewed economic priorities.

132. Uhlig, *Monumenta Paedagogica, Band XIV*, 345.

133. In the mid-1950s, it was estimated that one-quarter of *Abitur* graduates were migrating to the West, whereupon they took a six-month preparatory course and entered university. Hearndon, 129. On the institution of the polytechnical system, see Mende, *Die polytechnische Erziehung*; and Baylis, *The Technical Intelligentsia*.

134. The SED educators' 1959 slogan became: "One should work, learn, and live socialistically!" The order revealed the Party's priorities.

135. Quoted in Wendt, *Bonner Berichte aus Mittel- und Ostdeutschland*, 67; Podewin, *Walter Ulbricht*, 295.

136. Mieskes, *Die Pädagogik der DDR, vol. 1*, 117.

137. By the spring of 1958, 5,779 Christian teachers had pledged their loyalty to the regime. *Monumenta Paedagogica*, vol. 6, 84. Announced a delegation of Christian teachers at the April 1958 SED teachers' conference: "In light of the danger of atomic stockpiling by the West German government, especially for the youth of West Germany, and of [Bonn's] misuse of Christianity to promote a new

war, we declare explicitly: socialism is peace, it is the new world of social justice and higher morality. We educators will therefore ensure that the youth entrusted to us become active citizens of our socialist state and models of the socialist future for our entire people." *DS*, April 15, 1958.

138. Richert, *"Sozialistische Universität,"* 176. See also *NYT*, May 18, 1957, 1.

139. Richert, *"Sozialistische Universität,"* 187.

140. Klier, *Lug Vaterland*, 123.

141. *NYT*, February 9, 1955; and February 21, 1955.

142. Quoted in Klier, *Lug Vaterland*, 143. Lending support to Mayer's impressions was the estimate of a West German scholar that, within the DDR student body of the late 1950s, 5 percent were opponents or supporters of the regime, 10 percent were opportunists or private resisters, and 70 percent were "indifferent"— either worried joiners or casual cooperators. Richert, *"Sozialistische Universität,"* 247. On Mayer's *Republikflucht*, see "Immer etwas seltsam."

143. Baske and Engelbert, *Dokumente zur Bildungspolitik*, 176.

144. Uhlig, *Monumenta Padagogica, Band VI* (1945–55), 91.

145. McCauley, *The German Democratic Republic Since 1945*, 89; Childs, *GDR*, 59.

146. Steele, *Inside East Germany*, 115. Mieskes, *Die Pädagogik der DDR, vol. 2*, 222.

147. Prittie, "The Protestant Church."

148. By 1958, government grants were also down to 40 percent of what they were in 1950. If it could not coopt them, the regime hoped that financial need would ultimately kill the churches.

149. Baske and Engelbert, *Dokumente zur Bildungspolitik*, 122. See also Prittie, "The Protestant Church."

150. Richert, *"Sozialistische Universität,"* 99. See also Bodenman, "Education."

151. Cate, *The Ides of August*, 20.

152. Gelb, *The Berlin Wall*, 66.

153. Quoted in Gelb, *The Berlin Wall*, 161. See also Medvedev, *Khrushchev*, 183.

154. Bailey, "Disappearing Satellite," 12.

Chapter 3. After the Wall: Pride before the Fall, 1961–89

The Fenced-In Playground

1. On the background and details of the erection of the Berlin Wall, see the following: Jürgen Ruhle, ed., *13. August 1961—die Mauer von Berlin*; Manfried Hammer et al., eds., *Das Mauerbuch*; Hans Werner Richter, ed., *Die Mauer-oder der 13. August*. See also: Gelb, *The Berlin Wall*; William Heaps, *The Wall of Shame; Ulbricht's Wall*; Cate, *The Ides of August*; Wyden, *Wall*; Honore Catudal, *Kennedy and the Berlin Wall Crisis*; Schick, *The Berlin Crisis, 1958–62*; Ronald A. Francisco and Richard L. Merritt, eds., *Berlin Between Two Worlds*; Sabra Holbrook, *Capital Without a Country*; Windsor, *City on Leave*; Glenn D. Camp, Jr., ed., *Berlin in the East-West Struggle, 1958–61*; and Dulles, *The Wall: A Tragedy in Three Acts*. For news accounts, see "Berlin Divided" and "Bewachte Bewacher." A comprehensive bibliography is *Die Berliner Mauer*, compiled by Michael Haupt.

2. See Carr, "Stone Walls," 20–21.

3. Khrushchev is quoted in Gelb, *The Berlin Wall*, 75.

4. *Geschichte 10* (1968), 21.

5. *NYT*, August 27, 1961, 8.

6. *NYT*, August 21, 1961.

7. For English-language accounts of the 1972 Munich Olympics, and on the German *Sportmacht* generally, see the following:

Richard D. Mandell, *The Olympics of 1972*, and Heinz Maegerlin et al., *Olympia 1972*. See also Hoberman, "The Transformation of East German Sport"; Vinokur, "Sport as an Instrument for National Integration"; Arnd Kruger, "Sieg Heil to the Most Glorious Era of German Sport"; McIntyre, "Sport in the German Democratic Republic"; and Strenk, "Diplomats in Track Suits." For news accounts, see Baker, "The Communist Assembly Line"; "A Century of Olympolitics"; and "Factory of Champions." See also the Olympic coverage in Der Spiegel, September 30, 1964; October 21, 1964; July 31, 1972; August 7, 1972; August 14, 1972; August 21, 1972; August 28, 1972; September 4, 1972; June 21, 1976; July 5, 1976; and August 6, 1988.

8. "Des ist," 29.

9. See Astor and Dunaway, "It's Up Against the World," 37. And in the Olympiads to follow, the DDR *Sportmacht* would grow ever stronger. The athletic gap between the two Germanies would stretch into a chasm, until at the 1980 Winter Olympics at Lake Placid, New York—on the soil of the leader of the class enemy, the heartland of the so-called KA—the DDR would top the medal standings, defeating the Amis and even the formerly invincible Soviet Union.

TO LEARN FROM THE SOVIET UNION / MEANS LEARNING TO TRIUMPH!

Indeed the DDR's combined medal haul from the summer and winter Olympiads best indicates its rise to *Sportmacht* status: 30 in 1968, 80 in 1972, 109 in 1976, and 149 in 1980. The DDR usually placed among the top two teams in both the summer and winter Olympiads thereafter. By 1984, the DDR National Olympic Committee had been elevated to virtual ministerial status; the DDR sports movement was adopted as a model by developing socialist nations such as Cuba and Guinea, and now even the USSR was, somewhat grudgingly, seeking assistance from its star student—a far cry from the supremacy of all things Soviet at the 1951 World Festival of Youth and Students in Berlin.

10. Maegerlein, Koch, and Morlock, *Olympia 1972 München*, 133.

11. Maegerlein, Koch, and Morlock, *Olympia 1972 München*, 133.

12. As late as 1969—before Iraq and Egypt broke the silence—not a single noncommunist nation had granted the DDR official recognition. By the 1976 Olympics, the number had risen to 120, including, finally, the United States in 1975. The biggest breakthrough came in 1972/73, especially after the signing of a BRD-DDR treaty of cooperation (the Basic Treaty) affecting trade and travel in December 1972; 70 nations recognized the DDR in 1972/73, and the DDR and BRD both entered the UN as independent nations in September 1973.

13. "A Century of Olympolitics," 30.

14. By 1972, DDR functionaries occupied 156 posts in world sports organizations; the BRD had only 90. This achievement was also a story of struggle. In 1950, the newborn DDR was welcome in only one international association: chess. In 1951, they gained entry into table tennis, skiing, and volleyball; in 1952 came acceptance from eight more major athletic associations, including swimming and boxing. And in the next two decades, admission to 64 more international associations would follow.

15. *Encounter*, 23. Or as Radio DDR II remarked in a February 25, 1980 broadcast on the DDR school system after their Olympians' first-place finish at Lake Placid:

There are connections which seem at first glance peripheral, but on closer examination they reveal something essential. Take today. As the Olympics Games are ending, the DDR team stands first in the national rankings. Today— exactly 15 years ago—our Parliament voted for the Law on the Uniform Socialistic Educational System, by which for the first time all state and social educational goals were directed toward a great goal: to educate all children to become socialistic personalities. . . . A uniform socialist educational system and sports success go together. The principle of equal, comprehensive, and uniform educational and developmental opportunities for everyone has passed the test.

Willi Knecht, *Wege nach Olympia*, 39–40.

16. Nor was this close attention to athletic development reserved solely for the elite. *Sports Illustrated* estimated that, by the 1970s, an incredible 5 percent of the DDR population—more than 300,000 citizens—were serving as full- or part-time coaches and officials.

17. On the life of a DDR sports school student, see chapter 9 of the present study, "Of Sport, State, and Stasi: Socialism with an Un-Beautiful Face."

18. One example of the loyalty of athletes to the state was that they were often selected to help stand guard at the Wall. Students at the elite German College for Physical Culture and Sport in Leipzig were organized into a reserve force called the Walter Ulbricht Regiment; this was their special *K-Stellung*.

19. *DS*, July 31, 1972, 44.

20. *DS*, August 31, 1972, 45.

21. *DS*, August 6, 1972, 22.

22. "Bei uns ist immer Olympia," July 31, 1972, 79.

23. *SI*, August 12, 1976, 45.

24. Professor Wolfgang Strauss of the University of Jena recalls that, after the 1972 games, he watched a documentary of the Olympiad produced by West German television. The program was titled "Greetings, Comrade!" and reported on the behavior of the DDR's representatives at the Munich Games. Professor Strauss writes:

I was astounded to see how many people I saw who worked at the University of Leipzig [where he taught]. It was then clear to me that, in every single case, only 500 percent SED members [or IMs (*Stasi* informants)] had been chosen to visit Munich.

Personal correspondence, December 17, 1995.

25. *DS*, August 13, 1972, 21.

26. "Bei uns ist immer Olympia," July 31, 1972, 68.

27. His rhetoric was echoed by DDR athletes, who sometimes even used international awards ceremonies to preach "peace" against "warmonger" Bonn. As distance runner Friedrich Janke declared, after setting a new world record in 1958:

I am delighted about my victory in this beautiful facility. However, we must ensure that this facility will continue to exist and that we will acquire more of its kind. . . . A nuclear free zone in Central Europe would be the first step to ending such a terrible threat. We must fight the [nuclear] threat. . . . I do not know quite how, but I would imagine that for the cost of one atomic weapon, one could construct quite a few such sports arenas.

(Quoted in Strenk, "Diplomats in Track Suits," 354.) Other athletes became Party trophies, as had the miner Adolph Hennecke, with their performances to bolster the Party's legitimacy. For instance, the most popular sportsman in the DDR—the cyclist Gustav Adolf ("Tave") Schnur, a two-time Olympic medal winner and a victor in numerous European and international cycling championships—served in the 1950s and '60s as a member of the Central Committee of the FDJ and as a member of the *Volkskammer*.

28. *DS*, August 13, 1972, 55. *The Politics of Sport*, 77. Honecker is quoted in "The Playing Fields of Potsdam," *Encounter*, May 1988, 65.

29. West Germany was, however, also practicing a version of "Diplomacy through Sports" at Munich. Bonn sought recognition that the "New Germany" of 1972 bore no resemblance to the last Germany that staged the Games: Hitler's Reich in 1936. Their successful staging of the Games was overshadowed, however, by a tragedy. On Day 11 (September 5), five Arab members of the Black September terrorist group snuck into the Olympic Village and seized half the Israeli Olympians as hostages, demanding concessions from the Israeli government. In the next 24 hours, as a billion viewers watched in horror, 12 Israelis (and the five Arabs) died in a shootout between terrorists and Israeli commandoes.

30. By the 1980s, however, many intellectuals and some educators—even numerous workers—had become cynical about the DDR's sport machine. One senior educator informed me in 1995 that West German victories were often greeted with furious applause by DDR audiences—albeit only when East Germans were sitting among friends before their TVs, of course.

31. But the Miracle Factory continued to hum until the very end. When the DDR appeared for the last time as a team—at the European Track and Field Championships in Yugoslavia in September 1990, just days before Germany's October 3 reunification—its athletes swept the field, winning 34 medals. The second-place USSR garnered only 22—and West Germany won a mere 7.

32. The athletes knew none of the hardships of the DDR populace; bananas were always available for them. They jumped the queue for scarce items like cars, telephones, and washing machines—and customs officials looked the other way when they returned from abroad with western contraband.

The SED granted all this because, by the 1980s, the "playground" stars were paying off for the state in financial terms. Not just in the abstract sense of international prestige, or even in terms of lucrative contracts with western nations, but quite directly, i.e., via millions of D-marks in western advertising and sports promotions involving DDR athletes.

33. For instance, by the mid-1980s, the chocolate firm Ferrero was sponsoring DDR swimmers, the rowers raced for Commodore Computers, Kodak supported DDR track, and the bobsled team wore BMW helmets, because "they are the safest," explained *Neues Deutschland*. DDR fans would sit in stadia advertising products that no ordinary East German citizen could purchase: Agfa, Buderus, Bauhaus. The schizophrenia would deepen as the fans listened with mounting disbelief to the SED speeches. As Erich Honecker rhapsodized at the Seventh Youth Spartakiad in Leipzig in July 1983: "May the sports festival . . . be a mighty manifestation for socialism and peace, a display of the passionate commitment our young people and athletes feel toward our socialist homeland. . . ." Meanwhile, ice-skating star Katarina Witt was doing sports fashion promotions for West German firms and a number of DDR runners appeared in Adidas ads during the 1980s. The athletes received a percentage of the ad revenue. *Junge Welt* reported that the DDR earned DM 130 million from western ads in 1988; the real figure, when one adds proceeds from TV coverage of the European World Championships and the World Cup, was several times higher. Already by 1968, Olympic medal winners were receiving up to 50,000 mark "bonuses"—up to $10,000—from "Santa Claus" or "the Black Man," as the athletes termed the anonymous gift-givers who would discreetly deliver their rewards. More was paid if new records were set. These direct payoffs for international performance increased substantially in later years. A host of national awards—e.g., the Fatherland Service Award, Banner of Labor, and the Friedrich Jahn Medal—included monetary awards or even annual pension bonuses. By June 1988, DDR communism would seem to have come full circle from the ideas of Marx and Thälmann, from the aggressive anti-capitalist World Festival of Youth and Students in 1951: The Leipzig press diffidently reported that several West Berlin firms were underwriting the track and field events of the DDR Olympic trials. Asked by *Der Spiegel* to explain, DDR sports functionaries admitted that the trend toward

commercialism wasn't "pure," but that under "real existing socialism" one is realistic and makes compromises. See "Neues Weltbild."

34. One measure of the latter: After the Wall fell, Olympic champions and SED darlings Katarina Witt, Roland Matthes, and Kornelia Ender all had their homes and cars vandalized by DDR citizens outraged by the star athletes' privileges and their cozy relationship with the Party.

Rearing the Technical Elite

35. "Du, unsere Liebe," 54–56.

36. Quoted in Ryback, *Rock Around the Bloc*, 52. Speaking to the Soviet Central Committee in December 1962, Khrushchev himself condemned the Twist: "A feeling of distaste is aroused by some of the so-called modern dances brought into our country from the West. . . . [T]he so-called fashionable modern dances are something unseemly, mad, and the devil knows what!" (Quoted in Ryback, *Rock Around the Bloc*, 52.)

37. *NYT*, June 3, 1963. "Erst kommst du," 92. "Jetzt dürfen auch die Uniformierten," 12.

38. "Jetzt dürfen auch die Uniformierten," *DS*, July 22, 1964, 12.

39. "Hirn und Herz," *DS*, April 12, 1965, 46; "Gesunde Naivitat," 12.

40. On the haircuts, see "Mitkommen bitte," A4; and "Für Frieden und Fransen," 38.

41. Biermann favorites were scathingly direct, strumming indictments like "Fredi Rohmeisl of Buckow," who gets beaten up by Party thugs just because "he was madly dancing apart."

Or take the unsubtle "The Party's Feet."

> Once there was a man
> whose foot stepped
> whose naked foot stepped
> into a heap of shit.
>
> He was truly sickened
> by this one foot
> he would not go a step further
> with this foot.
>
> But no water was there
> to wash his foot
> to wash this foot
> there was no water.
>
> So the man took his axe
> and hacked off his foot
> in haste he hacked it off
> with the axe.
>
> But so great was his hurry
> that he had the clean foot
> he had the wrong foot
> hacked off in his hurry.
>
> Then he became enraged
> and resolved now
> to hack off the other foot too
> with his axe.
>
> The feet lay there
> the feet got cold

the man sat on his ass before them
deathly pale

The Party has hacked off
many such feet
many such good feet
has the Party hacked off.

But in contrast to
the above-mentioned man
the Party sometimes grows
the feet back on.

By 1965, Biermann had become the rogue troubadour, the Dylan and François Villon of the DDR, publishing his first book of poems and songs *Die Drahtharfe* (*The Wire Harp*) to acclaim in West Berlin. Calling the book "perverse," and Biermann himself a subversive ideological *Grenzgänger*, the SED banned him from publishing or recording in the DDR. That same year he was put under temporary house arrest and expelled from the SED; in 1966, the SED also forbade him live performances. See Biermann, *Nachlass I*, 25–27, 79–81.

42. *Dokumente zur Kunst-, Literatur- und Kulturpolitik der SED*, 1078. See also *DS*, December 22, 1965, 29.

43. Quoted in Ryback, *Rock Around the Bloc*, 89.

44. "Spur der Steine," 51.

45. *NYT*, January 13, 1966. Ulbricht's remarks are quoted in "The Cultural Commissars," *Newsweek*, January 17, 1966, 47; and "Gift von Affen," 167. *DS*, December 22, 1965, 29, 51. See also the SED documents collected in Agde, *Kahlschlag*.

46. *DS*, May 1, 1967, 168. Indeed, when she criticized the SED's muzzling of Biermann during a 1966 performance in East Berlin, Baez had demonstrated her own "incapacity" in that regard to SED officials.

47. McCauley, *The German Democratic Republic Since 1945*, 119. One of the last public, if indirect, student expressions of nonconformity ended in 1967, when the annual student roast at Dresden's Technical University, complete with jazz band—"Goodbye to Electronics"—fell victim to SED orthodoxy. As *Spiegel* told it, the university rector, a top SED politician, threatened to expel 250 students who planned to perform. Rather than submit their program to the SED censor, student leaders cancelled the roast.

In the refractory youth climate of 1967, the rector feared a replay of the controversial roasts of earlier years. For instance, in 1962, just 10 months after the erection of the Wall, one student had imitated his pedantic engineering professor before a stunned, delighted student audience with the following lecture:

The Chinese are a smart people. In their thousand-year history, they have created so much and enriched science. Only in the political realm did they ever have any difficulties. When they couldn't cope, they built a wall. And a government very recently in Europe also couldn't manage its political problems. And guess what it did?

Although he had already passed his final exams, the jokester was summarily expelled: His fate anticipated the 1967 crackdown at the Technical University. See "Gelbe Gefahr."

48. Baske, *Bildungspolitik in der DDR*, 388.

49. DDR education was widely credited, by the 1970s, with having launched the DDR's economic and athletic successes. Outsiders assumed, not implausibly, that the economic upturn of the DDR and its other achievements owed largely to polytechnic education, which the DDR touted relentlessly; thus the excellent rep-

utation of DDR education abroad was only strengthened by the veil surrounding it. All western studies of DDR education were limited to official documents; foreign educators were seldom allowed to visit DDR schools—or, if they gained permission, to see much of interest. Nevertheless, official DDR statistics of the 1960s certainly supported the western perception that DDR schooling was superior. For example, in 1970, one quarter of DDR children under three were attending day nurseries; the BRD had few such nurseries; 64.5 percent of DDR children were attending kindergarten; only a third of BRD children were doing so; 75 percent of DDR youth were receiving more than eight years of schooling; only half of BRD youth did; the DDR teacher/student ratio was 19.8 to 1; the BRD ratio was 29.6 to 1; 63 per 10,000 DDR citizens received post-secondary education; the BRD figure was 45. The DDR had already enacted legislation for universal 10-year education in 1959; by 1970, the BRD had yet to do so.

"At minimum," maintained West German educationist Willi Voelmy in 1969, "BRD educators should accept that polytechnics in East Germany have presently reached a level that represents a distant goal envisioned by West German educators." East German children, wrote Voelmy in his *Polytechnics in the Ten-Year POS of the DDR since 1964*, were ahead of their West German coevals, especially in creative initiative and independence.

For years, West Germans had casually assumed that they were superior to the East Germans in schooling—as in everything else. But by 1970, according to a poll commissioned by Der Spiegel, West Germans had accepted Voelmy's verdict. Asked which state had the "better" educational system, 35 percent of BRD citizens chose the DDR, 34 percent answered that the systems were equally good, and only 24 percent chose the BRD.

Der Spiegel concluded: "The younger the DDR children, the stronger their advantages compared to their BRD coevals." The price, West German educators noted, was conformity or ideological commitment to communism. But amid the kudos for DDR educational achievements in the early 1970s, they briefly wondered if the price might indeed be worth paying.

See Voelmy, *Polytechnischer Unterricht*, and "Bürger in Krippen."

50. Klier, *Lug Vaterland*, 120.

51. Baske, *Bildungspolitik in der DDR*, 387–88.

52. On Libermanism in the DDR, see Baylis, *The Technical Intelligentsia*, 235–37; and "Kampf der Eliten."

53. *DS*, October 12, 1969, 76. On NOS policy up to 1967, see also Glaessner and Rudolph, *Macht durch Wissen*, 98–111; after 1967, 138–43.

54. Childs, *GDR*, 111. The exodus resulted in an overall drop of the DDR population from 19,066,000 in 1948 to 17,079,000 in 1961.

55. McCauley, *The German Democratic Republic Since 1945*, 111.

56. Klier, *Lug Vaterland*, 134.

57. Klier, *Lug Vaterland*, 131.

58. Asked in 1964 by the editors of *Der Spiegel* about the possibility of Ulbricht himself becoming a genuine Party reformer, Alfred Kantorowicz replied: "To expect Ulbricht to initiate de-Stalinization? That's as if you had entrusted Himmler with denazification." "Das Tauwetter is nicht aufzuhalten," 56.

59. Havemann began one lecture by quoting Brecht's "In Praise of Doubt":

> There are the Unhesitating Ones, who never doubt.
> Their digestion is untroubled, their judgment unerring.
> They don't believe the facts, they only believe themselves. . . .
> Their patience with themselves
> Is limitless. They listen to arguments
> With the ears of spies. . . .

60. Quoted in Heinz Brandt, *Ein Traum*, 287.

61. Quoted in Heinz Brandt, *Ein Traum*, 312. *Forum* refused to publish the reply; it was finally printed in *Die Zeit* (May 7, 1965).

62. Havemann, *Berliner Schriften*, 59.

63. Havemann, "Der Marxismus leidet an Sklerose," 37–49.

64. In *Dialektik ohne Dogma*, for instance, Havemann wrote:

In political-economic terms, the DDR is fundamentally the opposite of the Nazi ideology. Capitalism has ceased to exist. . . .

[But] a number of domestic conditions and appearances in the DDR produce at minimum a continuance, indeed a new edition of fascist forms of behavior and thinking. There is again "the" Party, a boring and controlled press, a far too powerful secret police, a parliament with no opposition party, an official cultural politics, a state-ordained *Weltanschauung*, and suppression by the State of all deviations from the ruling "ideology."

(Quoted in *DS*, December 12, 1965, 202.)

65. By the early 1970s, more than 200 Stasi agents guarded Havemann's house in Grünheide, near Berlin, permitting only the local pastor to visit the celebrated atheist. His *Hausverbot* restricted his travel to trips to East Berlin. Nevertheless, Havemann refused to emigrate and even managed to smuggle out and publish many articles and books in the West; westerners speculated that he was not jailed, as were most other outspoken dissidents, out of deference to the Russians, who still expressed gratitude and respect toward Havemann for his assistance in developing their atomic research program in the 1940s and '50s.

66. Heinz Brandt, *Ein Traum*, 312–13.

67. Quoted in Heinz Brandt, *Ein Traum*, 290.

68. See "Wie Sokrates," "Strich durch den Namen," and "Faule Eier." *DS*, September 28, 1970, 172. On Havemann's reputation among the current generation of DDR pupils, see chapter 12 of the present study, "Difficulties with the Truth: Coping with the DDR's Past in the New Eastern Classroom."

69. *DS*, September 28, 1970, 172.

70. "Faule Eier," *DS*, September 28, 1970, 170.

71. "Zeit der Bedrängnis," 29.

72. Heinz Brandt, *Ein Traum*, 286–87.

73. On the integration of Marxism-Leninism into DDR schools via textbooks and curricula, see my sociological study, *Textbook Reds: Ideology and National Self-Legitimation in East German Schoolbooks*, especially chapter 1, "Ideology as Core Curriculum."

74. Klier, *Lug Vaterland*, 125.

75. *DS*, March 16, 1970, 38.

76. "Note Eins," 139. "Faule Eier," 170.

77. *DS*, March 10, 1969, 41.

78. "Gesunde Kräfte," 33.

79. "Zur Zeit unterwegs," 40.

80. On the long-term consequences of Prague 1968 on at least one DDR educator, however, see chapter 7 of the present study, "Of Laughter and Forgetting: A Faculty-Student Conflict of Generations."

81. "Gesunde Kräfte," 32.

82. Invited to testify at his sons' trial, Havemann was refused admittance when he arrived, supposedly because the courtroom was full. Peering inside as the trial was beginning, the professor pointed to a row of seats completely empty. He was informed that the seats were reserved for a "delegation of businessmen." The courtroom door was then closed; when the guilty verdict was announced, his sons were led away. They were granted no contact with their father, who had waited

five hours outside. He had not been permitted to communicate with them for months.

Havemann said to the court usher: "When I was sentenced to death during the Nazi period, the court permitted my parents to attend the proceeding. They also received permission to speak to me for a half-hour afterwards."

The usher replied: "Yes, but you see, we don't live in the Nazi period any longer." See Havemann, *An Alienated Man*, 202–203.

83. *NYT*, October 26, 1968; October 30, 1968. *DS*, November 4, 1968, 71–72.

84. "Let's Sing Together," *DS*, vol. 42 (1969), 129–30. *NYT*, October 22, 1968.

85. *NYT*, October 27, 1968. For documents on the SED youth policy of the 1960s, see Dubel, *Dokumente zur Jugendpolitik der SED*. For the specifics of Ulbricht's new policy, see Heyen, *Jugend in der DDR*.

86. Klier, *Lug Vaterland*, 129.

87. *NYT*, September 18, 1968; November 24, 1968.

88. "Gesunde Ehe," 41.

89. *NYT*, August 12, 1968.

90. The different estimates voiced by Gerhard Zwerenz, one of the Harich circle who escaped to the west in 1956, reflected the general rise in Ulbricht's standing. In 1958, Zwerenz wrote of Ulbricht in his "Gallows Song of Today":

> You are a little man
> a doorman
> a grey whistling mouse
> who gnaws on the rope
> The rope
> from which a guillotine hangs.

By 1966, however, Zwerenz was writing that Ulbricht was "the single Marxist among German Party leaders," the embodiment of "the German revolutionary tradition" and "a politician of more than national importance." See *DS*, vol. 20 (1971) 36. See also Podewin, *Walter Ulbricht*, 298–307, 387–96, 482.

91. On Ulbricht's 1921 encounter with Lenin in Moscow, see Podewin, *Walter Ulbricht*, 59. See Podewin also on Ulbricht's "feeling of infallibility" (447), conflicts with Breshnev and the Kremlin (423–29, 445–49, 482), and intention to demote Honecker from his "Crown Prince" status (482, 490).

92. McCauley, *The German Democratic Republic Since 1945*, 213. See also Podewin, *Walter Ulbricht*, 488.

The Herr und Frau Honecker Era

93. Not a single foreign dignitary attended Ulbricht's funeral on August 6. Ulbricht had already vanished into unpersonhood. Der Spitzbart had preened himself to become another Lenin; but as Marx predicted, History does indeed repeat itself: the first time as tragedy, the second time as farce.

94. *DS*, August 6, 1973, 47. See also Podewin, *Walter Ulbricht*, 487–88.

95. For contemporary press accounts of the 1973 World Festival, see the following:

DS, July 7, 1973; July 23, 1973; August 6, 1973; and August 13, 1973. *NYT*, July 17, 1973, 14; July 29, 1973, 10; July 13, 1973, 3; July 22, 1973, 13; August 3, 1973, 7; and August 6, 1973, 2. See also Shelby Tucker, "Peace Loving Plodders," *NR*, September 14, 1973, 1000–1001, 1013; and "Youthfest in Berlin."

96. *DS*, August 6, 1973, 47.

97. No DDR youth crossed to West Berlin during this Festival, but the Wall doubtless helped SED leaders risk a measure of openness on their home turf to the outer world. That represented another major change since 1951. Numerous West Germans, including playwright Peter Weiss, singer Hans Werner Henze, and *Juso* head Wolfgang Roth, were given official time to speak. When Roth's speech,

which criticized the SED and called for freedom of travel and the free exchange of ideas, was drowned out by the rhythmic shouting and whistles of true Blueshirts, *Neues Deutschland* took the extraordinary step of printing Roth's speech the following day, unabridged and without alteration—even including his calls for multilateral disarmament and the abolition of military service for young men.

98. *NYT*, August 11, 1973, 51.

99. Especially favored by the SED were The Pudhys, the Beatles of the DDR, who remained five "likeable boys" and exemplary socialists, even after the Fab Four descended into unwholesomeness. "We aren't the partying types," bandleader Peter Meyer said. "We prefer drinking milk and cola over alcohol." The Pudhys became the DDR's most popular group, selling more than 16 million records during the 1970s and '80s—one for every DDR citizen. For upstanding conduct becoming young revolutionaries, the Party rewarded the abstemious Pudhys lavishly: state honors, television and film contracts, East bloc tours, even western tours—eventually, in 1981, even to the U.S.

The Pudhys would prove more exemplary—and less wholesome—than DDR fans had realized. Stasi records released in August 1993 showed that Peter Meyer worked as a Stasi informant or IM (*Inoffizieler Mitarbeiter*, unofficial employee) for 16 years (1973–89). As chairman of the *Sektion Rockmusik*, Meyer had regular meetings with Stasi officials who, according to his file, praised the quality of his information on DDR avant garde artists and radio and TV personalities.

The Klaus-Renft-Combo, on the other hand, became the Rolling Stones of the DDR. Loud, foul-mouthed, long-haired and bearded, dressed in rags and often drunk or hung-over, the Klaus-Renft "bad boys" attracted thousands repelled by the goody-goody Puhdys. So long as Klaus-Renft supported SED politics—e.g., via solidarity songs such as "Chilean Metal" and "That's How Neruda Died Too"—the SED supported Klaus-Renft. But with numbers like "Doubts," which attacked the DDR's compulsory draft, and "The Rock Ballad of Little Otto," which criticized the Wall and expressed sympathy for DDR draft resisters, Klaus-Renft infuriated the SED. In September 1975, the Party retaliated and ordered the band disbanded.

100. Ryback, *Rock Around the Bloc*, 135.

101. *DS*, May 22, 1971, 49.

102. Childs, *GDR*, 211. See also Ludz, *Die DDR zwischen Ost und West*. On the Honecker-Stoph rivalry, see Lippman, *Honecker*, 190–91. On Honecker's manuevering to oust Ulbricht, see Podewin, *Walter Ulbricht*, 423–72.

103. Ludwig Harig, "Erich und sein Strohhut," *FR*, June 20, 1981, ZB 2.

104. Andert and Herzberg, *Der Sturz*, 108–15. In his autobiography, *Aus meinem Leben* (1981), Honecker acknowledged how his father, a KPD miner, and others in the mining town of Neunkirchen, which was 20 percent communist during World War I, influenced him. His father explained to him "why the rich are rich and the poor are poor."

This gave me a clear conception of the world. I undertook to devote my life to the struggle for a world of peace and socialism. I have stuck to this life's work to this day. . . . I can never recall a moment in my life when I had the slightest doubt about our cause.

Oddly, a British publisher, rather than a DDR house, issued Honecker's autobiography and held the world rights. Honecker wrote his autobiography for the "Leaders of the World" series of Pergamon Press, at the request of its editors. Pergamon claimed that the SED had not subsidized the book, nor had Honecker received an advance; the costs were purportedly born entirely by Pergamon. BBC World Broadcasts, July 7, 1980; September 4, 1980.

105. See Lippmann, *Honecker*, 49–204. Beginning in 1946, Lippmann worked closely with Honecker in the FDJ; during 1949–53, he served as secretary of the

Central Committee of the FDJ, until his 1955 defection. Robert Bialek was head of the Saxony FDJ (1946–48), but fell out of favor with SED leaders. He fled to West Berlin in 1953 after the June uprising. In April 1956, he was kidnapped. Apparently he died mysteriously in Bautzen in 1956 after being tortured and receiving an overdose of narcotics. On Honecker's relation to Bialek, see Lippmann, *Honecker*, esp. 58, 75, 78, 107–108; and Herms, *Heinz Lippmann*, 63, 156, 177, 213.

106. Lippmann, *Honecker*, 129. On Honecker's role in the Berlin Wall's erection and on Honecker as the "continuation" of Ulbricht, see Lippmann, *Honecker*, 188–89, 218. See also Ludz, *The Changing Party Elite in East Germany*.

107. Friedhelm Kemna, "Mehr als Erichs Frau," *Die Welt*, December 5, 1979, 6.

108. For Frau Honecker's positions on the formation of "well-rounded socialist personalities," on the relation between education and the scientific-technical revolution, on the role of Marxism-Leninism in school curricula, and on the pedagogics of hatred toward imperialism, see her addresses to the SED and teacher's congresses, especially: Baske and Englebert, *Dokumente zur Bildungspolitik*, 435–38; and Baske, *Bildungspolitik in der DDR*, 190–91, 210–11, 300–301, 358, 397, 442.

109. See Andert and Herzberg, *Der Sturz*, 177–94.

110. Edith belonged to the far left wing of the Social Democrats. Her politics were really quite similar to Honecker's. She too preferred the KPD, she said; apparently she joined the postwar SPD in a (failed) attempt to guide it toward unification with the SPD of the western zones of Germany. On Edith Baumann's background, see Lippmann, *Honecker*, 52, 147.

111. Lippmann, *Honecker*, 152–54. On Margot's ambivalence toward the role of First Lady, see Andert and Herzberg, *Der Sturz*, 301–302.

Honecker's 1981 autobiography, *Aus meinem Leben*, draws a veil over his life with Edith Baumann, and DDR news organs never even mentioned that Margot was Honecker's second wife.

Although Ulbricht had not yet, in 1951, handed down his Ten Commandments of Communist Morality, Honecker's playboy style displeased him and did not accord with the neo-Victorianism of the late Stalinist era. On hearing that Margot was pregnant, the puritanical Spitzbart allegedly intervened. Fearing a scandal, Ulbricht reportedly insisted—over Edith's objections—that Honecker's duty to the Party was to divorce Edith and marry Margot.

Edith was vice-chairman of the FDJ Central Council when she married Honecker in 1949. She was already a member of the Sekretariat of the SED Central Committee in 1950, possibly the most powerful woman in the SED at mid-century. Although she retained her Central Committee seat and became a candidate member for the Politburo in 1958, Edith never advanced to the Politburo. A friend and political ally of Otto Schon, a sometime Ulbricht opponent, she and Schon were ousted from the Sekretariat in 1953 after the events of June 17. Thus did the personal and the political intertwine: At Ulbricht's behest, Edith the left-wing Social Democrat lost Erich; Margot, the better comrade for Honecker, advanced.

And comrades they remained, in an apparently loveless marriage of convenience. The Honeckers' personal lives remained shrouded in mystery for decades; for years, it was not even publicly known if the couple lived together in Wandlitz; when Margot traveled in the West, she always listed her address as "SED Central Committee." By 1970, unfounded rumors circulated that Erich and Margot had divorced; both of them reportedly had several affairs during the 1960s and '70s. The couple remained ideologically compatible, but Margot never entered the Politburo, perhaps on account of personal differences with her husband. Although their marriage continued for reasons of state and Party, Margot was seldom seen with her husband at leading state functions.

See Lippmann, *Honecker*, 126–62. On Ulbricht's own decade-long affair with

Rosa Michel, which resulted in an illegitimate child but not marriage, see Pode-win, *Walter Ulbricht*, 112. See also Andert and Herzberg, *Der Sturz*, 234–43.

112. *The Listener*, February 12, 1973, 5. See also Baylis, *The Technical Intelligentsia*, 256 ff.; Grunert and Siegert, *Die DDR*; and Glaessner and Rudolph, *Macht durch Wissen*, 175–328.

113. Russ, ed. *Dokumente zur Kunst-, Literatur- und Kulturpolitik der SED*, 287. See also Ruther, *Greif zur Feder*.

114. Quoted in *DS, vol. 20* (1971), 30.

115. Ibid., 30.

116. Baske, *Bildungspolitik in der DDR*, 378.

117. Heitzer, *GDR*, 202.

118. See Barm, *Totale Abgrenzung*; Steele, *Inside East Germany*; and Wallace, *The GDR under Honecker*, 1971–81. Curiously, none of this seemed to hurt relations with the BRD. Indeed, just a week before the June exchange of diplomatic representatives between the two Germanies, Bonn decided that it would not observe the 21st anniversary of the June 17 uprising, which had been heretofore commemorated as the Day of Unity, symbolizing hopes for reunification. The events of 1953 now seemed a relic of the Cold War: a poll had shown that 33 percent of West Germans did not even know what June 17 signified.

119. Klier, *Lug Vaterland*, 123–28.

120. Klier, *Lug Vaterland*, 156.

121. Quoted in Klier, *Lug Vaterland*, 156.

122. Despite SED Ostspeak, however, the percentage of working-class students in higher education continued to decline. In 1974, only 35 percent of students had fathers who were skilled or unskilled workers; by 1985 it was down to 18 percent. (In the sciences, less than 1 percent of students had fathers who were unskilled workers.) By contrast, 34 percent of students had fathers with a university degree in 1974; in 1985 it had risen to 59 percent. Klier, *Lug Vaterland*, 116.

123. According to testimony in May 1991 from Hans-Joachim Hoffmann, then-Minister of Culture of the DDR, the decision was secretly reached by Honecker and Stasi chief Erich Mielke alone; neither Hoffmann's ministry nor even other Politburo members were consulted. Keller and Kirchner, *Biermann und Kein Ende*, 130.

124. The sole exception was Biermann's impromptu concert at the World Festival of Youth and Students in August 1973, when visitors who recognized him on the street implored him to perform. Eager to make a good impression on the foreign guests, SED authorities did not interfere. So for two hours Wolf sang (without guitar) old numbers and new songs, such as "Commandante Che Guevara," which he had submitted to Festival authorities. SED organizers had rejected it as unsuitable for the Festival's program. One can see why from the second stanza:

> You [Che] never became a Party big shot
> Never a top dog who hankers after money
> Who, though desk-bound, acts as if he's a hero
> Bedecked with medals and possessed of rare spirit.

Rossellini, *Wolf Biermann*, 80.

125. Indeed the Stasi did. But even Biermann was shocked by the devotion of his SSD retinue. His Stasi file, which he obtained in 1991, ran to 40,000 pages; between 70 and 200 agents had been assigned to him at any one time. They had bugged his house, sabotaged his car, and tried to lure his wife into an affair with Stasi agents (and did help break up his marriage).

But there were amusing, if sometimes macabre, bits. Among the Stasi's preoccupations were the lyrics to all Biermann numbers they could transcribe from their bugs. Or mistranscribe. Biermann found their version of "The Stasi Ballad" in his file, only to notice that his line, "The Stasi is my Eckermann"—alluding to Goethe's Boswell—had been mistranscribed: *Die Stasi ist mein Henkermann* (executioner). On the "Stasi Ballad," see Biermann, *Nachlass I*, 445–48.

126. *Chausee Street 131* was a CBS re-release in 1975; it was originally released by Wagenbach in 1969. The title alludes to Biermann's home address in East Berlin. Rossellini, *Wolf Biermann*, 81.

127. On the Cologne concert and its immediate aftermath, see Keller and Kirchner, *Biermann und Kein Ende*, 94–126.

128. On Biermann's youth and background, see Rossellini, *Wolf Biermann*, 12–20.

129. Indeed, despite direct personal evidence of what he later came to call "the Stalinist syphilis," Biermann himself was interrogated by the Stasi shortly after June 17. He was accused of being a western "agent"; instead of imprisoning him, however, the Stasi wanted him to spy on his *Gymnasium* classmates. By the end of the interrogation, the Stasi had relented, but swore him to silence about having been interrogated. Rossellini, *Wolf Biermann*, 16.

130. *WP*, December 3, 1989, 10. Reflecting on his outspokenness and comparing himself to his coevals, Biermann observed in 1990: "It was my good bad luck that my father died in Auschwitz and not in Stalingrad. My childhood behavior patterns are thus different, because I never had to compensate for anything. And I never had to prove anything to the new powers-that-be. I spoke in an arrogant tone about my political heritage. And that was also the reason why my songs never contained any 'slave language.' I battled naïvely, without a helmet, and I spoke always, even in rhyming, in boldface. I was not spared the consequences." Quoted in Keller and Kirchner, *Biermann und Kein Ende*, 7.

131. The characterization was Biermann's own. Rossellini, *Wolf Biermann*, 28.

132. Not all intellectuals protested. Among the most vocal exceptions was Wolfgang Harich, who had already made his sharp right turn into neo-Stalinism. The original circumstances of the SED ban against Biermann performances in the 1960s, Harich argued, had to do as much with Biermann's "insolent obstinacy and vain egocentricity" as with Ulbricht's "rigidity." Biermann was "smug and narcissistic," and he cultivated his western fame, "clutching his martyr's crown long after the thorns had turned to rubber." Harich also suspected that Biermann had little desire to return to the DDR. Biermann probably instead preferred "to exchange the crown of thorns of the Oppressed One for a crown of thorns of the Exiled One." Quoted in Keller and Kirchner, *Biermann und Kein Ende*, 160–62.

133. Rossellini, *Wolf Biermann*, 87. *DS*, November 22, 1976, 30–34.

134. Western estimates were that the flights included 270 musicians, thespians, and entertainers; 20 writers; and 15 sculptors and painters. In a 1986 interview, Biermann claimed Swiss socialists had told him that Honecker confided to them "that my expatriation was a mistake." But Honecker considered his "mistake" not an excess of severity toward Biermann. On the contrary, Biermann reported, Honecker said:

We should never have exiled the pig [Biermann]. That was our mistake. We should have simply put him behind bars, which we also thought about doing. That would have been less costly for us politically.

Keller and Kirchner, *Biermann und Kein Ende*, 169–70. See also Jäger, *Kultur und Politik in der DDR*.

135. Ryback, *Rock Around the Bloc*, 140. See also Ludz, *Die DDR zwischen Ost und West*.

136. Ryback, *Rock Around the Bloc*, 205.

137. December 11, 1980. See also Ryback, *Rock Around the Bloc*, 192–93.

138. As in Rosa Extra's "I don't wanna work / I don't wanna fill the quota / I don't wanna be a bourgeois jerk."

139. Ryback, *Rock Around the Bloc*, 138–39, 192–93, 204–207.

140. DDR citizens who reached 65 were called, half-jokingly, "grenzmündig" (old enough to cross the border), since retirees were free to travel abroad. (Because they were no longer productive workers, the regime was little-worried about losing senior citizens. If they didn't come back, the government declared them *republik-flüchtig* and cut off their pensions.) A new joke now went around about "our Erich": "Erich turned 65 on Thursday, and on Friday moved to the West."

141. Nawrocki, "Ein Fest für Honecker" and "Von zentralen Zielen weit entfernt."

142. "The Dramatic Death of Pastor Brusewitz," *CC* 93 (November 3, 1976), 949.

143. *DS*, August 30, 1976, 36. Thirty DDR youth protested publicly the official SED story about Brusewitz's death. Three of them were arrested; two were sentenced to jail terms of several years. *DS*, April 3, 1978, 36. See also Goeckel, *The Lutheran Church and the East German State*, 239.

144. Lenin's statement derived from Mephistopheles' line in the "Schoolroom Scene" in Faust I, which served as the epigraph to Part I of the present study: "Gray, dear friend, is all Theory / And green is the golden tree of Life."

The Revolution of the Candles

145. Goeckel, *The Lutheran Church and the East German State*, 16–19.

146. Each of these commitments would, in the next decade, be arbitrarily disregarded or broken by state authorities. For example, despite SED professions of religious liberty—a right guaranteed in the 1968 DDR constitution—official discrimination against Christians continued. Armed forces officers had to sign declarations that they were not Christians; Christian doctors and teachers were told that they could not reach senior positions; pastors' children, while no longer barred altogether from higher education, were still disadvantaged in the admissions process. For more on Schönherr's policies and on the historic March 1978 meeting, see Goeckel, *The Lutheran Church and the East German State*, 238–39, 276–77.

147. *NYT*, October 9, 1984. Goeckel, *The Lutheran Church and the East German State*, 241–46. See also Braun, *Volk und Kirche in der Dämmerung*.

148. Ironically, the celebration followed within months of a smash hit rock-opera that swept the West, and was by 1981 well-known in the DDR: Pink Floyd's *The Wall*. Thrashing to the ominously martial beat of the opera's eerie, Orwellian themes, hundreds of thousands of DDR youth could chant along:

> We don't need no education
> We don't need no thought control
> No dark sarcasm in the classroom
> Teachers leave the kids alone
> Hey! Teachers! Leave those kids alone
> All in all it's just another brick in the wall.
> All in all you're just another brick in the wall.

149. Two of the Baltic republics, Estonia and Latvia—which remained part of the Soviet Union until its collapse in 1991—are also Protestant. But the national outrage at reports of Stalin's 1940 annexation of the republics, along with Moscow's loosening grip on its empire, played a more important role than the churches in the republics' protest movements and return to independence. See Goeckel, *The Lutheran Church and the East German State*, 288.

150. In May 1979, apparently on grounds of poor health, Havemann was released from house arrest, which had been imposed on him after his outspoken

defense of Wolf Biermann in November 1976. He died of lung cancer in January 1982. In 1992, however, his widow Katja gained possession of her husband's *Stasi* file—and, like Biermann, was stunned. According to Frau Havemann, *Stasi* documents showed that her husband was "not adequately treated" and that Havemann's personal doctor had worked for the *Stasi* and prescribed inactivity in order to minimize Havemann's contact with the western press. Reports in 1994 also surfaced that Gregor Gysi, formerly Havemann's lawyer and now chair of the PDS, had regularly reported his conversations with Havemann to the *Stasi*.

151. See Goeckel, *The Lutheran Church and the East German State*, 256–73; and Childs, *Honecker's Germany*, 66–82. See also Allen, *Germany East*.

152. The design chosen to accompany this biblical phrase was ingenious: a statue of a man beating a sword. Technically, the emblem alluded to the Soviet-donated monument that stood in front of UN headquarters in New York, thereby draping Bonhoeffer's message in Marxist-Leninist imagery.

153. See Mushaben, "Swords into Ploughshares."

154. The year 1983 witnessed an unprecedented attempt by the SED to associate these two great "sons of the DDR," and to reconcile socialism and Christianity. The larger goal was now to integrate German religious history into the DDR's socialist history, thus giving a historical dimension to the Party's embrace of "the church in socialism."

The Luther Year congresses were organized under the church motto *"Vertrauen wagen!"* (Dare to trust!). Honecker congratulated the Party repeatedly during 1983 for "daring to trust" the churches—but he actually maintained a good deal of old-fashioned Leninist control.

Honecker himself headed the 104-member "Luther Year" committee, and the SED members quite openly enlisted the father of the Protestant Reformation in the DDR campaign for historical legitimacy. Because Luther had not only believed in God but also bitterly opposed the Peasants' War of 1525, which pitted the serfs against the aristocracy, the claim to him as part of the progressive heritage of the Workers' and Peasants' State posed special problems. (As did the anti-Semitic Luther of the 1540s, who branded Jews as ritual murderers who should be driven out and whose synagogues should be burned—lines that the Nazis had gleefully exploited as part of their own drive to present him as a German nationalist hero.)

Heretofore, SED ideologues had attacked Luther as a *Fürstenknecht* (princes' lackey), praising him only for his contribution to the German language via his translation of the Bible. Now, however, Party spokesmen concluded that Luther's sympathy for the poor, his fight against illiteracy, and his concept of a "just war" marked him as a "progressive" for his time; his unfortunate linking of "throne and altar" resulted from his tragically limited bourgeois background.

The Luther campaign anticipated and set the stage for similar reclamation attempts of Händel, Heinrich Schütz, and Bach during their own commemorations in 1984/85; all three of them were composers whose music featured religious themes. Socialist economics had failed to outdo the BRD; now the DDR would turn to history. See Goeckel, *The Lutheran Church and the East German State*, 249.

155. Quoted in *TI*, September 2, 1990.

156. Kurt Hager, "Jedes Land wählt seine Lösung," *DS*, April 9, 1987, 142.

157. *ND*, June 28, 1987.

158. Switching to his pidgin Szenesprache, Honecker also met with BRD pop singer Udo Lindenberg, one of the first western stars to sing in German. Lindenberg's 1981 single, "Sonderzug nach Pankow" ("Special Train to Pankow"), had poked fun at "Honi," mellowing Honecker's reputation for a new generation of West Germans. By now, the nickname had become, at least in the West, a quasi-official term of endearment and exasperation. Lindenberg's humorous lyrics, set to the tune of Glenn Miller's "Chattanooga Choo Choo," suggested that "mein Erich" was a closet rocker and begged permission to perform in the DDR:

> Deep in your heart, Erich, dear, I know
> You too are a rocker.
> You don your leather jacket
> And lock the door to the Klo [toilet]
> And tune in to western radio. . . .
> Hey, Honi,
> I'll sing for little money,
> Ach, Erich, are you such a stubborn mate
> Why don't you let me sing
> In the Workers' and Peasants' State?

With his black fedora and tight black leather pants, suggestive gyrations, and hilarious lyrics, Lindenberg had captivated East German youth. "Special Train to Pankow" finally melted "Honi's" heart too; in 1983 Honecker officially invited Lindenberg and his Panic Band to perform a televised concert in East Berlin. But a spring 1987 return visit was suddenly canceled after the release of a less agreeable number, "Mr. General Secretary," which portrayed "Honi" in black leather and demanded that he dismantle the Wall.

The reconciliation in September was facilitated by an exchange of gifts a few months earlier between "Udo and Honi," as the western press called the odd couple. In June, just days after the clashes between the police and fans at the Wall, the rock star sent "his Erich" a black leather jacket, urging him to go out in it to meet East German youth; "Honi" thanked him and reciprocated by sending Udo an old-fashioned horn, similar to those used in the KJVD "Red Front Fighter" bands of his youth.

159. *DS*, November 20, 1989, 45–46. Nawrocki, "Die Jugend dem Sozialismus opfern," 2.

160. Still, there was no stopping the rock craze. On July 19, 1988, the regime relented to the insatiable demand for western music and sponsored the first performance by an American superstar: Bruce Springsteen. Apparently without Springsteen's knowledge—Springsteen disavowed any political side-taking during his performance—the concert was scheduled by SED authorities to mark the ninth anniversary of Nicaragua's Sandinista revolution.

But never mind the SED machinations: The fans came to hear Springsteen. Before 160,000 enraptured youth at a cycling stadium in Berlin-Weissensee, The Boss belted out hit after hit, without pause and without rest. The crowd's delirious response to the refrain of "Born in the U.S.A." prefigured the intensity of hatred toward the regime that would erupt a year later. But the refrain also resonated, as if suspended in time, as if it captured an eternal moment of ecstasy and hope in the hearts of DDR youth. A western observer later wrote:

> As Springsteen intoned the song's passionate refrain, amidst the blue-shirted ranks of communist youth members, small hand-painted American flags flashed in the crowd, and tens of thousands of young people raised clenched fists and thundered as one, "Born in the U.S.A.! I was born in the U.S.A.!"

(Quoted in Ryback, *Rock Around the Bloc*, 111).

161. *ND*, January 20, 1989.

162. Frau Honecker's fierce communist convictions and eye-catching pastel-tinted hair earned her these nicknames. (Some DDR Bürger preferred "the blue-haired witch"; the western press called her the "Iron lady.") Easily the most powerful woman in the DDR by the mid-1970s, she exuded the aggression that her outwardly meek husband lacked. Once admired for her beauty, confidence, and flair, she was, by the 1980s, perceived as a combination of Margaret Thatcher and

Imelda Marcos: merciless and with an extravagant style. She was thus a far more hated and controversial figure than her husband among the DDR populace.

Moreover, after 26 years as education minister, Frau Honecker's draconian school policies had reached into every family. Her two most heavily criticized policies were forced adoptions (a form of state kidnapping that placed the children of jailed dissidents in the homes of loyal SED members) and DDR youth reformatories (which led to the physical and mental abuse of *asozial* and antinomian youth).

163. Sample questions:

1. Why was the erection of the Wall another defeat for German imperialism?
2. Why was it fortunate for the world, for Europe, and for the German Volk that the DDR was founded?
3. Why are we today already richer than the wealthy BRD?

164. *ND*, June 14, 1989.

165. *ND*, June 14, 1989. See also Albert Hinze, "Im Profil: Margot Honecker," June 22, 1989, 4.

166. One West German study reported that 76.6 percent of emigrants in 1989 were under 40; 51.4 percent were single men between 18 and 30. *The German Revolution of 1989*, 155.

167. *NYT*, May 14, 1989; *WP*, July 16, 1989.

168. Karl Heinz Baum, "Die Zeit überholte ihn, und er verstand es nicht," *FR*, October 19, 1989, 3.

169. On the events in Plauen, see chapter 6 of the present study, "From Schoolmarm to Revolutionary: Annaliese Saupe, Old 'New Teacher' and Local Heroine."

170. I am indebted to Frau Annaliese Saupe of Plauen for sharing her extensive personal archive of slogans and memorabilia of the DDR protests, which she donated in 1991 to the National History Museum in Bonn. I also cite examples of puns and jokes from Arn Strohmeyer, *Visafrei bis Hawaii* (Frankfurt a.M., 1990) and Ewald Lang, *Wendehals und Stasi-Laus* (Munich: Wilhelm Heyne, 1990). See also Ruddeklau, *Störenfried*; Zwahr, *Ende einer Selbstzerstörung*; and Keithly, *The Collapse of East German Communism*.

171. Evidently Erich Mielke, Minister of State Security and an old Honecker friend, joined the conspiracy to overthrow him. Mielke had procured compromising data from West German archives on Honecker's days as a Nazi prisoner. Acting like a German J. Edgar Hoover, Mielke apparently gave Honecker an ultimatum: resign or face publication of the embarrassing facts. *The German Revolution of 1989*, 172. See also *Deutschland Archiv* 1 (1991), 5–7.

172. *NYT*, November 4, 1989.

173. Without a doubt, student participation in public protests increased in late 1989. One report stated that, in the last four months of 1989, DDR students participated in an average of four demonstrations each, with 20 percent of students involved in more than five. Many of these participants, however, doubtless became involved after early November, when the risk of retaliation had disappeared. *The German Revolution of 1989*, 96.

174. *NYT*, November 11, 1989.

175. Wandlitz, protected by its own special wall (painted forest green), was the home of the elite of the elite. It was occupied by 23 families who enjoyed the best of the West: swimming pools, saunas, banned western films, paid staffs of maids, and meats and wines unavailable in the DDR, all meticulously kept up by groundskeeping staff of 88.

No wonder the Politburo was indignant about the ruckus in the streets. Contrary to the troublemakers' carping, the DDR was indeed a workers' paradise!

176. But Big Brother's belated valentine from the Ministry of Love went unrequited. Instead, in October 1993, after a surreal 20-month trial, Mielke received a six-year jail sentence—not for any of his actions as *Stasi* chief but for a murder charge dating back 62 years. The self-appointed four-star general—Mielke used to wear 250 medals emblazoned on his uniform, as if to illustrate Biermann's stanza about the party big-shots in "Commandante Che Guevara"—was convicted on the basis of Nazi documents that investigators discovered in his own office—documents that he himself had discovered and saved, so proud was he of them. The 1993 decision was controversial; the only evidence against Mielke were the Nazi documents, which Mielke claimed were trumped-up. He had been convicted in absentia by a Nazi court in 1935 of killing two policemen in August 1931.

177. Rossellini, *Wolf Biermann*, 142.

178. For Biermann's songs, see Biermann, *Klartexte*, 124–25, *Alle Lieder*, 439–41, 412–14.

179. Vera Gaserow, "Asyl für einen Mühseligen und Beladenen," *taz*, February 3, 1990, 5.

Chapter 4. After the Wall II: The Fall and Rise of an Educational System

Trabulations, or Lurching Toward Unity

1. The Trabi returned to its starring role in a 1992 sequel, another post-communist western titled *Das war der Wilde Osten* (*That was the Wild East*), which also played to packed houses in eastern Germany.

2. The following jokes are drawn from Strohmeyer, *Visafrei*, and Lang, *Wendehals*, respectively.

3. See Rodden, "Lurching Toward Educational Reform: East Germany's Trabulations," *America*, October 26, 1991, 285–89.

4. *WP*, February 24, 1990. The six pupils expelled from the school on grounds of opposing the DDR's military parade on October 7 were also "rehabilitated."

5. *NYT*, December 21, 1989.

6. *NYT*, December 21, 1989.

7. Like so many other prominent figures, dissidents and Party *Bonzen* alike, however, Modrow too was soon touched by scandal. Accused by lower Party officials of giving orders to falsify the May 1989 election results in Dresden, Modrow went on trial in March 1992. Modrow was convicted, but punished only with a reprimand.

8. *NYT*, September 29, 1990.

9. *NYT*, January 16, 1990.

10. The nightmare stories of hundreds of victimized educators gained publicity too. One such case was that of Helmut Warmbier, former M-L professor at the Karl-Marx University in Leipzig, who had been jailed on political grounds in the 1970s and then "re-educated" as an auto mechanic. "Rehabilitated" in the spring of 1990, he returned to the University to coordinate its new program of General Studies.

Some of the revelations about Stasi procedures had their comical side. For instance, files showed that the Stasi preferred to link spies' cover names with their course of study: i.e., "Caries" for a dental student, "Concrete" for an engineering student, "Bach" for a music student, "Runner" for a sports student. *DS*, vol. 12 (1990), 82–87 *Nature*, April 12, 1990, 605. *DS*, vol. 6 (1990), 74.

11. *NYT*, February 12, 1990.

12. *DS*, February 20, 1990, 155. One student told *Der Spiegel*: "We've squandered years just copying [by hand]." Another said: "It's just as it was 150 years ago—we copy everything down."

13. Quoted in *DS*, May 21, 1990, 49.

14. Quoted in *DS*, May 21, 1990, 47–50.

15. *DS*, August 20, 1990, 45–6.

16. *DS*, July 23, 1990, 141. *Time*, April 23, 1990.

17. *Nature*, June 21, 1990, 653.

18. Childs, *Germany in the Twentieth Century*.

19. This is a reference to Goebbels' famous 1943 speech in Berlin, in which he thundered to 100,000 faithful Nazi Party members: "Do you want total war?"

20. The joke alludes to Luther's celebrated explanation of free will: "The human being thinks, but God directs."

21. Rodden, "Lurching."

22. One official reported that the German Gymnastics and Sports Union—the DDR sports bureaucracy—would be cut from 12,000 staff to 1,500. *NYT,* February 12, 1991.

23. *DS*, July 23, 1990, 137. *Nature*, April 12, 1990, 605.

24. *Nature*, April 12, 1990, 605.

25. *Time*, July 9, 1990.

26. For comparison, see the report on the situation at Rostock University, *Spektrum der Wissenschaft*, November 1990, 42–43. For other institutions, see *DS*, September 3, 1990, 148–53.

27. *Neues Deutschland* is quoted in *RLR*, December 18, 1990. *NYT*, December 30, 1990.

28. *RLR*, April 29, 1991; *LAT*, April 30, 1991; UPI, April 30, 1991.

Ossification, or Purging through Merging

29. In May 1993, Reich ran as the the Alliance 90/Green candidate for BRD president, receiving a disappointing 5 percent of the electoral college vote. Nevertheless, Reich did win a few backers: e.g., the Young Socialists and Young Liberals—the youth wings of the SPD and Free Democratic Party—announced their support for him, as did the German Jewish community.

30. These jokes are taken from *Der Besserwessi* (Berlin, 1990).

31. *Der Besserwessi*, 6, 23, 34, 50.

32. Other newly popular terms of doublespeak included *Personalentsorgung* (personnel disposal, a.k.a. job firing), and *Warteschleife* (holding pattern), used to describe the period before a scheduled layoff took effect. During this employment twilight zone, workers were officially on *Kurzarbeit Null* (short hours/zero), which meant that their hours had been "reduced" to nothing. Such workers were not included in eastern unemployment statistics; they were officially "underemployed." They were usually still required to show up to work to draw their wages. Bonn soft-pedaled high unemployment and social upheaval in the east, preferring to stress the region's progress toward *schlanke Produktion* (lean production).

Easterners were quick to note with derision that Bonn's architects of *Abwicklung* avoided more direct, colloquial terms such as *Auflösung* (dissolution, closing down) or *Kündigung* (firing, laying off).

Indeed the word *Abwicklung* received such bad press in the east that, in mid-1991, the *Abwicklung* department of the Treuhandanstalt, which was in charge of selling off old DDR state firms, decided a change was needed. The department initiated a public campaign—complete with DM 1,000 reward—to rename the department with a "more fortunate term." A more pleasant euphemism was indeed found among the 1,600 entries: "Department of Rekonstruktion."

And so, down the Orwellian memory hole went *Abwicklung* too: it was officially *abgewickelt*. On these and other Orwellianisms, see *SZ*, December 19, 1992; *TWIG*, December 20, 1991; February 7, 1992; February 14, 1992.

33. As Dieter Simon, professor of European Legal History in Frankfurt and chair of the German Scientific Council board assigned to evaluate eastern universities,

put it ironically: "Our much criticized system of scholarship and education in the west seems to improve day by day as we learn more about the shortcomings of the system in the east." Simon admitted that the western German professoriat had its flaws, but insisted that "the problem pales by comparison with a system wherein membership in the SED was a main criterion for selection." *Nature*, April 4, 1991, 366.

34. Quoted in *DS*, April 29, 1991, 74.

35. *DS*, September 30, 1991, 112.

36. Rodden, "Lurching."

37. *DS*, September 30, 1991, 110.

38. And even in these cases, lawsuits instigated against the schools in 1992/93 frequently resulted in the reinstatement of dismissed teachers. Throughout the east, all dismissed teachers and professors went on dormant employment status, which meant that they were no longer engaged in teaching but were entitled to 70 percent of their former salaries for the next six months.

39. *DS*, September 30, 1991, 111–12. Saxony's criteria for dismissal were, therefore, much broader than those in other *Länder*. In addition to the standard criteria already mentioned, teachers who had held the following positions also received *blaue Briefe: Bezirk* (district) or *Kreis* (local) SED functionaries, top functionaries in DDR bloc parties, members of the FDJ central board, and SED *Volkskammer* representatives.

40. The pressures took their toll on Rehm. Another dissident thrust into high office after the Revolution of 1989, she was a woman of high integrity ill-suited to the rough-and-tumble of bureaucratic politics. She resigned due to ill health in February 1993—another victim of the *Wendekrankheit*. Other states also witnessed controversies over the political past that affected educational policy at the highest, as well as the lowest, levels. In SPD-ruled Brandenburg, for instance, Premier Manfred Stolpe became embroiled in accusations of *Stasi* activity. When he refused to step down, Marianne Birthler, Minister of Education in Brandenburg, resigned in protest against the "double standard" for top politicans and classroom teachers. Stolpe, a senior legal advisor for the Lutheran Church during DDR days, claimed that he had simply "cooperated" with the *Stasi* in order to promote reform from within the system; Birthler, having reluctantly fired hundreds of teachers who had made similar claims, judged Stolpe's arguments specious and hypocritical. Birthler's resignation was another loss for eastern educational reconstruction. A civil rights activist in New Forum in 1989 and a leading figure in the Alliance 90 party in 1990, she had painstakingly worked out an "80 percent model" to save hundreds of Brandenburg teaching positions, whereby teachers accepted shorter hours for less pay so that more could remain employed. Unlike Rehm, however, Birthler remained in politics as a member of the Alliance 90/Green Party executive committee. On Rehm, see *DS*, September 30, 1991, 114; *SZ*, February 17 and 18, 1993. On Birthler, see *FT*, October 15, 1992.

41. *DS*, July 15, 1991, 50.

42. But when such retrained former East Germans were hired in the east, they—like those who went east to teach—received the standard western salary plus a bonus. ("Bush money," resentful easterners dubbed it, perceiving that Bonn regarded the east as African "bush" country.) This meant that western teachers were earning more than three times the salaries of their eastern colleagues (roughly $2,000 per month vs. $655 per month).Thus westerns did indeed seem to many easterners like viceroys in the "Wild East." Inevitably, the situation provoked western defensiveness and superciliousness and eastern anger and resentment.

43. *DS*, September 3, 1990, 148.

44. *THES*, September 27, 1991, 10.

45. *CHE*, January 16, 1991, A41.

46. *DS*, March 18, 1991, 86.

47. *Spektrum der Wissenschaft*, November 1990, 42–43.

48. Peter Marcuse, "Purging the Professoriat: Fear and Loathing in the Former East Germany," *Lingua Franca*, December 1991, 32–36.

49. Niermann and Möllemann quoted in *CHE*, November 7, 1990, A40. Fritzsch quoted in *DS*, July 23, 1990.

50. *IHT*, April 1, 1992.

51. *CHE*, November 7, 1990, A40.

52. In mid-1991, and in subsequent reports, investigators concluded that DDR sports physicians and scientists had secretly engaged in inhumane practices, including committing politically "difficult" citizens to sanitoria and the systematic doping of an entire generation of athletes with steroids. According to State Plan 14.25—a perfect example of science in disservice to the state—DDR biologists sought to perfect a type of steroid hormone that could evade international detection. Ph.D. candidates wrote their theses on methods of doping athletes while avoiding discovery; the theses were classified and never published.

53. *DS*, July 1, 1991, 40–41.

54. *Science*, March 1, 1991.

55. *Science*, March 1, 1991.

56. *Science*, March 1, 1991.

57. See also chapter 8 of the present study, "Dialectical Dilemmas in the Universities: West Side Story, East Side Story."

58. *DS*, December 31, 1990, 24.

59. For instance, Heinrich August Winkler, a Freiburg historian appointed in 1991 as director of the Humboldt Institute for Historical Science, took a hard line against retaining DDR-era professors. Long accustomed to packed auditoria of 250–600 students for his lectures and expecting a grand reception in Berlin, he found himself orating to a spacious Humboldt lecture hall housing only 12 students. *Die Zeit*, February 14, 1992, 14.

60. *SZ*, November 14, 1992.

61. *Nature*, July 19, 1991, 262; *DS*, January 21, 1991, 72–77.

62. *THES*, July 3, 1991; July 5, 1991; December 25, 1992. Nevertheless, Fink continued to proclaim his innocence, claiming that he provided information unknowingly, and more than 3,000 Humboldt students jammed a meeting to support him, interpreting his ouster as a western attempt to purge the east of all uncooperative elements. Prominent eastern intellectuals such as Stefan Heym also defended Fink and condemned the "western campaigns of character assassination." UPI, December 23, 1991. The exposure of Fink as a *Stasi* informant was one of several prominent public cases that spawned a new usage for a recently imported word from English: *outen* (to "out"). Formerly pertaining, as in the Anglophone world, only to the practice of revealing homosexual orientation without a person's consent, it was now expanded to include the unwilling disclosure of *Stasi* collaboration. On Fink, see also *DS*, vol. 4 (1991), 72–77; *RLR*, November 28, 1991; *CT*, April 26, 1992; *SZ*, November 3, 1992, and November 14, 1992.

63. Erichsen, quoted in *Nature*, June 6, 1991, 432; *TI*, November 4, 1992.

64. "Stop the World! I want to get on!" ran one such ad from the Saxony-Anthalt Ministry of Culture. Except in technical and business fields, however, eastern university enrollments continued to sink, not rise—even in medicine and law. At the Technical University in Magdeburg and the Martin Luther University in Halle, for instance, enrollments were down 10 percent in 1992. *SZ*, October 12, 1992.

65. DDR higher education employed 30,000 faculty for 130,000 students, a teacher/student ratio of 1 to 4.5. (The school ratio was 1 to 11. The old BRD rate was, as in the United States, 1 to 20 or higher at both levels.)

In 1991, western German universities had 1.5 million students in facilities designed in the 1960s for an expected student population of 850,000. This overcrowding was contributing, in turn, to lengthening the western German student's undergraduate course to an average of seven years, with most graduates being in their late 20s by the time of completion—the oldest in the world. Overcrowding and the excessive matriculation period led many vocal western German educators to focus on their own immediate financial needs and view the higher education crisis in the east as, to a large extent, a matter demanding the exercise of political and fiscal responsibility.

66. Rodden, "Lurching."

67. In a June 1991 meeting of the 24 leading industrial nations to discuss Eastern European aid, Germany promised more than 25 percent of the total, including 55 percent of trade and investment guarantees. Once signs of the recession became unmistakable, criticism raged throughout the east that Germany was overextending itself and neglecting its responsibilities at home.

68. *BW*, October 28, 1991, 51.

69. *Social Studies*, January/February 1991, 9.

70. *Economist*, September 14, 1991, 15. Eastern Germans themselves developed punning, self-mocking neologisms that reflected their fears of devolution, not only as in *Verrostung* (rusting out), but also *Verzonung* (becoming the Zone, i.e., the SBZ). The latter was a self-deprecating term of black humor reflecting the anxiety that the post-reunification east would degenerate into an atavistic condition much like the reparation-torn SBZ. *SZ*, November 11, 1991.

71. *SZ*, December 14, 1991.

72. *NYT*, December 9, 1992.

73. Since German citizenship rights are based on blood rather than residency, however, it is difficult for foreigners to gain citizenship. Only 20,000 (out of 8 million) foreigners gained citizenship in 1990. *NYT*, November 30, 1992.

74. *NYT*, March 19, 1992.

75. *SZ*, May 16, 1991.

76. Although the eastern depression seemed to bottom out in 1992—the region's economy grew by 6.4 percent in 1992—the recovery was emerging from a very low base. Worse, unemployment was still rising, reaching nearly 40 percent when those on temporary work programs and mandatory early retirements were included; by year's end, more than 8 million eastern Germans were jobless, up a third from 1991. Indeed even the notion of eastern growth was deceptive, since it was being fueled not by private investment or rising industrial production, but rather by public works projects sponsored by Bonn. Productivity stood at little more than a third of western standards. (Wages were 65 percent of western rates.) Two German economic research bureaus announced that, despite more than $200 billion in transfers from Bonn since 1990, the eastern economy remained in "deep crisis." Moreover, western Germany's economy declined even further from its 1991 performance, expanding only .8 percent and suffering a 4 percent inflation rate.

77. During 1991/92, the German press published reports that asylum seekers were cheating the generous German social welfare system by applying for aid in more than one locality. Several German cities required that registered asylum seekers appear on a specific day to verify their identities; 3 to 25 percent of registrants did not show. A Munich official estimated that 80 to 90 percent of asylum seekers were not political refugees escaping persecution but economic migrants wanting a more comfortable life. That a million eastern emigrants to the west—or, given the election results of 1990, arguably half the eastern population—had wanted (and continued to want) the same thing seemed to carry no weight with frustrated Germans, especially young Germans. *NYT*, March 19, 1992.

78. *WSJ*, December 4, 1991, 1.

79. *NYT*, November 2, 1992.

80. *TES*, December 9, 1991, 11.

81. *DSd*, November 25, 1991; *SZ*, May 18, 1993.

82. The description and lyrics of the fascist music scene are taken from the

following: *SZ*, December 8, 1992, May 25, 1992, November 15, 1992; *NYT*, February 8, 1994, *ST*, December 13, 1992; U.S. Newswire, December 2, 1992; *TI*, December 7, 1992; *CT*, November 24, 1992.

83. The word "Oi"—a Cockney greeting meaning "Hey!"—has an additional meaning on the German right-wing scene: It alludes impishly to the English fascist name for the Nazi fitness slogan "Strength through Joy." An early German LP of neo-Nazi rock was titled "Strength through Oi."

84. On the Cologne study, see *TES*, October 16, 1992; *WSJ*, December 4, 1991.

85. *NYT*, February 8, 1994. The article is based upon research by the staff of *Searchlight*, a London-based anti-fascist magazine that reports on neo-Nazi activities worldwide and collects the lyrics of most European and American skinhead bands.

86. *NYT*, February 8, 1994.

87. *NYT*, February 8, 1994.

88. *SZ*, December 8, 1992.

89. *THES*, October 25, 1991, 11.

90. *TES*, August 16, 1991, 9.

91. *NYT*, November 2, 1992.

92. *SZ*, May 18, 1993.

93. *SZ*, December 8, 1992.

94. *SZ*, December 8, 1992.

95. *USN&WR*, December 14, 1992, 33.

96. *DS*, October 26, 1992.

97. *NYT*, March 19, 1992.

98. *USN&WR*, December 14, 1992, 33.

99. *NYT*, October 21, 1993.

100. *LAT*, December 5, 1992.

The Unfinished Revolution

101. *TS*, March 14, 1993; *TWIG*, March 5, 1993; *DMN*, March 4, 1993; *LAT*, March 2, 1993; *TG*, February 4, 1993.

102. *SZ*, December 22, 1993; December 18, 1993; October 20, 1993; February 26, 1993; *CST*, December 18, 1993; *ST*, December 12, 1993. *CT*; December 24, 1993.

103. *NYT*, August 7, 1993.

104. *DW*, May 19, 1993.

105. *NYT*, March 8, 1993; *NYT*, February 9, 1994, March 15, 1994, and April 27, 1994; *SLPD*, October 17, 1993.

106. *NYT*, March 8, 1993, August 7, 1993, and September 15, 1993.

107. *FT*, May 4, 1994; *NYT*, March 10, 1993, March 15, 1993, and June 8, 1994.

108. The agreement provided, for instance, that the east receive DM 33.6 billion in 1995, with Bonn providing DM 30.7 billion and the *Länder* paying the remainder. Bonn's share would be financed through a new 7.5 percent income tax surcharge, which would remain in effect at least five years. *NYT*, March 16, 1993.

109. Indeed the neologisms and Newspeak continued to proliferate. Feeling like an occupied country that had lost its rights, some irate eastern Germans even began referring to the five new federal states as the *Anschlussländer* (the annexed states). The implied comparison between the actions of Bonn's politicians and Hitler's henchmen was clear.

Other *Ossis* attacked easterners who were succeeding in the new system; one term was OM (*ostdeutscher Mitläufer*, eastern German fellow traveler), which referred to eastern "collaborators" with the *Wessis*. It was a pun on the IM, i.e., on the *Stasi* collaborator.

110. Whether deliberately or not, the Kohl government did, in effect, acknowl-

edge the special role of eastern youth affairs in German life by its cabinet appointments: aside from Minister Günther Rexrodt (and before him, in the same office, Günther Krause, a former professor of computer science), the other eastern members of Kohl's cabinet were all in education and youth affairs: Angela Merkel was Women and Youth Affairs Minister; Rainer Ortleb, the only eastern FDP cabinet officer, was Education Minister; and Paul Krueger was Research and Technology Minister. Merkel, 38, who was also deputy party leader of the CDU, was the youngest member of the cabinet. Daughter of a Protestant pastor, she had worked as a chemistry researcher in the East Berlin Academy of Sciences. Her rise was spectacular, and it was certainly helped by her lack of either an SED membership or a *Stasi* IM file. She had joined the CDU only in 1990 and worked that year as Lothar de Maziere's deputy; she gained election to the *Bundestag* in December 1990. On Merkel, see *SZ*, July 30, 1991, September 1, 1991, October 2, 1992, and March 2, 1993.

111. Rust and Rust, *Unification*, 211.

112. *DW*, August 12, 1993.

113. *NYT*, November 25, 1994.

114. *SZ*, December 3/4, 1994, 13; *DW*, July 28, 1994.

115. *NYT*, October 14, 1994; *DW*, July 28, 1994.

116. Syllabuses of the Thuringia Education Ministry. Courtesy of Frau Angelika Ehspanner, principal of the Goethe Gymnasium, Weimar.

117. *WP*, October 18, 1993.

118. *SZ*, January 19, 1995. In December 1994, the Federal Court in Kassel ruled in favor of the Saxony school adminstration's decision to fire a DDR-era party secretary; a similar May ruling held that all teachers of *Wehrerziehung* were "unfit to teach the young in the democratic era." *Süddeutsche Zeitung*, December 20, 1994; Reuter German News Service, May 16, 1994.

119. *WP*, October 18, 1993.

120. By the close of 1994, signs of change were in the air. For instance, in October 1994, Thuringia gave tenure to 23 teachers—all of them principals and school directors; half of the remaining 26,000 later received tenure. The state also fired more than 15,000 teachers during 1990–95. This has included conducting more than 1,000 legal battles to prevent dismissed teachers from regaining their positions.

121. *SZ*, December 3/4, 1994, 13.

122. *NYT*, May 22, 1993; *TWIG*, October 14, 1994.

123. *SZ*, December 3/4, 1994, 13.

124. *SZ*, December 3/4, 1994, 13. But the spiritual vaccuum left by the collapse of communism had some unexpected consequences. One survey showed that 10 percent of eastern youth were "preoccupied" with the occult, and that up to 80 percent "flirt" with it.

125. *NYT*, August 27, 1994, Y2.

126. *SZ*, June 8, 1993; *NYT*, June 11, 1994; *SZ*, June 8, 1993.

127. *NZZ*, December 11, 1993.

128. *DW*, May 19, 1993; *SZ*, September 29, 1993.

129. *NYT*, October 21, 1993, and November 25, 1993; *TG*, January 31, 1995; *IHT*, November 24, 1993; *LAT*, November 23, 1993.

130. Federal education officials attributed the 1994 decision to the October election; the Kohl government worried that the book might embarrass the government and be abused by right-wing groups aiming to turn Hitler into a comic-book hero. In December 1994, however, Bonn reversed itself and decided to distribute 20,000 copies of *Hitler: the Comic Book* to the schools. *The Guardian*, January 31, 1995.

131. *NYT*, May 10, 1993.

132. *NYT*, June 4, 1993.

133. *NYT*, October 31, 1993, and November 2, 1993.

134. *SZ*, November 30, 1992; *IHT*, February 12, 1993.

135. *NYT*, February 8, 1994, and June 22, 1993.

136. *NYT*, May 3, 1994, March 26, 1994, and March 27, 1994.

137. *NYT*, May 14, 1994.

138. *SZ*, April 30, 1993. See also: Schramm, ed., *Hochschule im Bruch*, esp. 120–59.

139. *Science*, June 18, 1993.

140. *Science*, June 18, 1993.

141. *SZ*, March 17, 1993, P14. For Mecklenburg, see *SZ*, January 29, 1993; for Potsdam, see *SZ*, January 2, 1993. Saxony was still the toughest *Land* in educational reconstruction on former SED members and *Stasi* informers. Higher Education Minister Hans Joachim Meyer reported that 1,500 higher education faculty were laid off; only 457 of 1,230 from before October 1989 were still employed; the technical colleges had been more rigorous than the universities, where half of the old professors had managed to hold on to their jobs. Three quarters of all new hires were from eastern Germany. *SZ*, January 30, 1993.

142. *NZZ*, November 16, 1994. See also *DS*, April 19, 1993.

143. *TWIG*, December 3, 1993.

144. In late November 1994, the Berlin City Council ruled that most college students could take no more than nine semesters to earn a degree; students in engineering and the natural sciences were permitted 10 semesters for their degrees. Of the nation's 1.25 million students in higher education institutions, 15 percent (142,689) had already studied more than 19 semesters. *DW*, May 6, 1993, November 4, 1994.

145. The figures are as follows:

1991/92: east to west: 4,800; west to east: 2,000
1992/93: east to west: 4,200; west to east: 4,200
1993/94: east to west: 3,800; west to east: 6,000
1994/95: east to west: 5,000; west to east: 5,000

Die Woche, November 4, 1994; *DS*, vol. 42 (1994), 77. See also *Süddeutsche Zeitung*, April 24, 1993; and *DS*, vol. 1 (1993), 47–49.

146. *SZ*, April 24, 1993. Western students rarely had access to their professors; one study showed that the typical student had only six interactions outside class per year to discuss scholarly or occupational issues—and only one meeting involving personal issues. *DW*, November 4, 1994. On the situation in Jena, see *SZ*, November 13, 1993, and April 24, 1993. On the use of the word "*Wossi*," see *ES*, June 16, 1993; and *TWIG*, June 4, 1993.

147. *SZ*, January 30, 1993; *TG*, April 5, 1993; *SZ*, November 27, 1992.

148. One research group published a list of 10,000 classified, never-published DDR dissertations on subjects ranging from *Stasi* spying to blood doping of athletes at the Leipzig College of Physical Culture and Sport. An astonishing total of 12.5 percent of DDR dissertations had been classified for "restricted use." *SZ*, August 2, 1993, July 17, 1993.

149. *NYT*, December 16, 1994. Nonetheless, a new coinage emerged to account for the revelations. As we have already noted, "*outen*"—"to out" (taken from the English)—now applied to revealing not only another's homosexuality but also another's collaboration with the *Stasi*.

150. *DS*, April 19, 1993, 88.

151. *DS*, April 19, 1993, 89.

152. *SZ*, September 24, 1994. Political discontent was reserved for such gestures as the protest at Leipzig University against awarding Steffen Heitmann, former Justice Minister of Saxony and Kohl's hand-picked candidate for president,

whose conservative remarks about women's roles and German family values violated post-reunification standards of political correctness.

153. *NYT*, November 6, 1994. Thirty percent of young Germans go on to institutions of higher education; 40 percent of them drop out within two or three years. A third of them study for more than seven years, completing their courses well after the age of 28, the average age at which most German students leave university.

154. UPI, November 25, 1994.

155. *NYT*, June 18, 1994. On new German slang, neologisms, and Orwellian euphemisms in 1993/93, see *SZ*, December 22, 1994; Reuters German News Service, December 21, 1994; and *TWIG*, November 4, 1994, and October 28, 1994.

156. For the responses of one Weimar *Gymnasium* class to the election results, see chapter 12 of the present study, "Difficulties with the Truth: Coping with the DDR's Past in the New Eastern Classroom."

157. *NYT*, October 19, 1994, November 16, 1994.

158. *SZ*, June 1, 1994. *FM*, June 6, 1994.

Chapter 10. Zarathustra as Educator? To the Nietzsche Archives

1. See, for instance, the special issue of *Zeitschrift für Didaktik der Philosophie*, vol. 6 (1984), devoted to teaching Nietzsche in *Gymnasium* and university courses such as "Introduction to Philosophy" and "Introduction to Ethics." In 1983, one *Gymnasium* teacher assigned Nietzsche's work in a 13th grade course titled "Philosophical Aspects of War and Peace." Most of his students were strong supporters of the European peace movement, but Nietzsche "provoked the students to a remarkable militancy." The teacher concluded: "Nietzsche mobilizes thinking—however double-edged his sword may be. . . . Nietzsche is and remains a provocation to thinking, whom we philosophy teachers should present—not in the sense of a duel, but of a promise: Nietzsche helps one think freely." (169–70)

2. Kaufmann, *Nietzsche*, 345.

3. On Nietzsche's classroom duties and manner, see the chapter titled "Nietzsche als Erzieher" in Ross, *Der ängstliche Adler*, 345–69.

4. For an overview of the response to Nietzsche among Wilhelmine-era German educators, see Cancik, "Der Einfluss Friedrich Nietzsches." Many of the leading educators of the day visited the Archive and even befriended—and, sometimes, became disenchanted with—Elisabeth Forster-Nietzsche. For instance, Ellen Key frequented and lectured at the Archive in the early 1900s. Ludwig Gurlitt was a leading member of the Society for German Education, which held its annual meeting in Weimar. He became acquainted with Elisabeth in 1904, corresponded with her regularly, and was the only philologist invited to speak in the Nietzsche Archive on the gala occasion of her 65th birthday in 1921 (p. 69). Walter Benjamin is an especially interesting example of a young intellectual interested in the pedagogical dimension of Nietzsche's work. A student of Wyneken, Benjamin was a great admirer of Nietzsche's "aristocratic radicalism." Before his Marxist turn, the 20-year-old Jewish banker's son, who had recently graduated from an experimental Berlin "reform school" that combined *Gymnasium* and *Realschule*, even wrote a treatise against the reform movement in 1912. Benjamin urged educators to resist modernizing and "industrializing" the school, and instead to revive the aristocratic spirit of Greece, as Nietzsche urged. In 1914, Benjamin presented similar ideas in a lecture at the Nietzsche Archive, titled "The Life of Students." His enthusiasm for Elisabeth and the Archive cooled in the 1920s, however, especially after her embrace of fascism and the scattered reports of her fabrications of Nietzsche's letters. In his hostile pamphlet, *Nietzsche and the Archive of his Sister* (1932), Benjamin attacked Elisabeth for betraying Nietzsche (56–58).

5. Aschheim, *The Nietzsche Legacy*, 114.

6. See Thomas, *Nietzsche in German Politics and Society*, 102–103.

7. In SED eyes, Nietzsche was not only the hated Nazi idol, but also the champion of the Good European—a threatening cosmopolitan intellectual—and "*der Kosmopolitismus*" was an early postwar code word in SED jargon for "western," "anti-socialist," and therefore "subversive."

8. See Penzo, "Zur Frage der 'Entnazifizierung' Friedrich Nietzsches."

9. The phrase is Thomas Mann's, applied to Wagner. See *Thomas Mann: Reflections*, 121.

10. Walter Kaufmann's portrait of a liberal, humanistic Nietzsche effectively started the process of "denazification" in the Anglophone world, but no comparably significant revaluation occurred in the BRD. The following passage in a BRD history of philosophy text of the 1950s typified the attitude toward Nietzsche for much of the postwar era:

> It's time that our flirtation with the nonsense, the insanity, and the so-called depth of Nietzsche's world of thought came to an end. Nietzsche has already caused enough trouble. Germany ruined culture, he said. It would be more correct to say: Nietzsche ruined philosophy. A young person who has his first contact with philosophy through Nietzsche's work will never learn to think clearly, critically, soberly, and above all plainly. Rather, he will begin to lapse into one-sidedness and a subjectivity, make aphorisms, and fire off edicts.

(Quoted in Janssen, "Behandlung von Friedrich Nietzsches 'Also sprach Zarathustra' im Unterricht," 467.) Educators' misgivings about Nietzsche's work persisted into the 1980s. In the 1984 special issue of *Zeitschrift für Didaktik der Philosophie*, one *Gymnasium* teacher admitted that her inclusion of Nietzsche in a 12th grade course "may be received by some with astonishment" (p. 156). Two other *Gymnasium* teachers related the reservations of colleagues about their decision to teach Nietzsche: If we teach Nietzsche, the colleagues objected, "isn't relativism, nihilism, and even cynicism just around the corner?" (p. 151). Still another teacher declared: "A spectre is haunting the German *Gymnasium*, years ago and now once again: Nietzsche" (p. 167).

11. Weimar: *Bilder einer traditionsreichen Stadt* (Berlin: Aufbau, 1990).

12. Zwerenz, "Ein Partisan dichtet sich selbst," 3.

13. *DS*, November 13, 1981, 24.

14. The Archive was officially closed by SMAD in December 1945. In October 1949, the Archive was turned into a work room of the Goethe and Schiller Archives, whose director had already assumed administrative control of the Nietzsche papers. For a report on the Archive by its administrator from the Goethe-Schiller Archive during the last years of the SED, see Hahn, "Das Nietzsche-Archiv."

15. See Lukács, *Die Zerstörung der Vernunft*. For an overview of Nietzsche's reception in Eastern Europe and among German socialists, see Behler's articles, "Nietzsche in der marxistischen Kritik Osteuropas" and "Zur fruhen sozialistischen Rezeption Nietzsches in Deutschland." One large difference, however, distinguished pre-war and postwar views of Nietzsche among orthodox Marxists. During the 1930s and '40s, Nietzsche was identified with fascism and Nazism. After 1950, in response to western attempts to "denazify" his work, Nietzsche was linked in the DDR to western imperialism—which signified a return to the theme of Mehring's criticism. The postwar work of Lukács bridged the gap and linked all three views. Lukács argued both that Nietzsche was a spiritual ally of Hitler and that the postwar West's humanistic reinterpretation of Nietzsche represented "the deepest nadir that we have ever reached, evidence of the downward slide of American imperialism."

16. Gunther and Wallraf, eds., *Geschichte der Stadt Weimar*, 470–71.

17. Nor are the cases of Heidegger and Nietzsche really comparable. Heidegger lived through the Nazi period and wrote many letters explicitly supporting Nazi doctrine. Whereas Heidegger was the Nazis' handpicked rector of Freiburg University in 1933, allegations about Nietzsche's "Nazism" are speculative and unsupportable.

18. See Pepperle, "Revision des marxistischen Nietzsche-Bildes?" 934–69.

19. See Harich, "Revision des marxistischen Nietzsche-Bildes?" 1018–53. Harich's final allusion was all-too-fitting. At the SED's insistence, Brecht turned the 1938 play into a Stalinist tract in 1951, and changed its title to *The Condemnation of Lucullus*. (The new play still did not please the DDR cultural censors, who ordered cancellation of the 1951 production after a few performances; soon thereafter it had a successful run in West Berlin.) Intellectuals other than Harich also had harsh words for Nietzsche in the 1970s and '80s. But their condemnations were generally reserved for western attempts to rehabilitate Nietzsche. See, for example, Heller, "Nietzsche," and Malorny, "Tendenzen der Nietzsche-Rezeption in der BRD."

20. "Meinungen zu einem Streit," *Sinn und Form*, 40 (1988), 179–220. In addition to the aforementioned participants in the Nietzsche debate, the contributors included: sociology Dozent Hans-Georg Eckhardt; the writer Rudolf Schottländer; Aufbau editor Stephan Richter; Gerd Irrliltz, professor of the history of philosophy at Humboldt University; Klaus Kandler, instructor at the Academy of Fine Arts; and poet Thomas Böhme.

21. The result was the 22-volume *Complete Works* and the 16-volume *Letters*, which began appearing in 1967 and 1975, respectively. These works were simultaneously published by Adelphi in Italy, by Gallimard in France, and by de Gruyter in West Germany. Neither work ever appeared in the DDR.

22. Harich, "Revision des marxistischen Nietzsche-Bildes?" 1045. Harich meant what he said. It was not the first time he had stepped in to stem the Nietzsche "infection" in the DDR, which had been been building for more than a decade. The story of Nietzsche's underground life in the DDR is fascinating and complex. Since 1976, a secret circle of DDR authors, including the poet Rolf Schilling, had met every year in Röcken to pay homage to Nietzsche's memory and discuss his work. Their activities remained unknown until 1989. But several years earlier, apparently with initial SED approval, two Halle philosophy professors prepared a carefully selected edition of *The Untimely Meditations* and *The Joyful Wisdom*. They also organized a small Nietzsche colloquium, whose proceedings were to be published. In addition, Karl-Heinz Hahn, director of the Goethe-Schiller Archive, worked with Montinari on an expensive limited edition of the *Ecce Homo* manuscript, primarily designed for export to the West. At the last minute, Buhr and Harich—who had returned from the West in 1981 after two years of voluntary exile—stepped in and scotched all these publishing plans. Only a few copies of *Ecce Homo* ever reached DDR bookstores. Still, rumors flew that Harich had seen a copy in one bookstore, raised his voice and cane, and demanded its removal. It was removed. Later, in 1988, Harich supposedly threatened Erich Honecker that he would depart again for the West if the SED lifted the Nietzsche ban. For further details, see: Schwik, "Eine Andacht für den Antichrist," and Corino, "Abwertung aller Werte." See also the interview conducted by A. James McAdams with Kurt Hager, who discusses his correspondence with Harich on the topic of the Nietzsche Archive (July 11, 1991). GDR Oral History Project, Hoover Institute, Stanford University.

23. That Colli and Montinari were members of the Italian Communist Party—and that their Nietzsche editions were partly underwritten by the Italian CP—makes clear that the East German misgivings about Nietzsche had always less to do with his connection to fascism per se and more to do with his links to German militarism and Nazism.

Ironically, however, in certain ways Italy is much "closer" to Nietzsche than is Germany. Fascists like Mussolini and Gabriele D'Annunzio were early admirers of Nietzsche; Hitler and most other NSDAP leaders probably never read a line of him. But there is no trace of guilt about Nietzsche felt by Italians, probably because Nietzsche was never exalted as Italy's national philosopher. Likewise, despite fascist interpretations of Nietzsche in Vichy France, the French have always been able to see Nietzsche apart from his fascist reception history. Already in 1945, Parisian intellectuals founded the Society for Nietzsche Studies; French intellectuals of the Left ranging from Sartre and Camus to Georges Bataille, Jean Granier, Maurice Blanchot, Michel Foucault, Jacques Derrida, Sarah Kofman, and Gilles Deleuze have written hundreds of admiring pages about Nietzsche.

24. For a controversial West German view of Nietzsche and Marx as rival antagonists, see Ernst Nolte, *Nietzsche und der Nietzscheanismus*. Nolte sees Nietzsche and Marx as two great intellectual gladiators who finally confronted each other posthumously, at the turn of the century, in the faceoff between their followers on the Right and Left, the champions of Nietzcheanism and Marxism.

25. On Nietzsche and the alternative Left, see the following: Werner Ross, "Nietzsche taucht aus der Versenkung auf"; Magris, " 'Ich bin der Einsamkeit als Mensch' " and Augstein, "Widerkehr eines Philosophen." Augstein's 1981 article ran as *Der Spiegel*'s cover story. The *Spiegel* cover depicts Hitler rising from the head of Nietzsche-Zeus—and pulling a trigger aimed at the philosopher's head as he emerges.

26. See Stephen A. Erickson, "Nietzsche and Post-Modernity," *Philosophy Today*, Spring 1990.

27. Quoted in Frank Christian Stärke, *Krise ohne Ende*, 269.

28. Quoted in Heimer and Schmidt, eds., *Erbe und Tradition*, 122.

29. Quoted in Augstein, "Widerkehr eines Philosophen."

30. Ross, *Der ängstliche Adler*, 8.

Chapter 11. Bridge over Broken Glass? A Journey to Germany's Sole Jewish High School

1. On Mendelssohn and the *Freischule*, see Lowenstein, *The Berlin Jewish Community*, 50–53, 64–65.

2. See Ostow, *Jews in Contemporary East Germany*.

3. See Gay, *The Jews in Germany*, 264–66.

4. On the changes in Germany's Jewish community since reunification, see Gilman and Remmler, *Reemerging Jewish Culture in Germany*.

Chapter 12. Difficulties with the Truth: Coping with the DDR's Past in the New Eastern Classroom

1. See the introduction to this volume, "Who Has the Youth, Has the Future," especially the section titled "Schooling Society and Taming Minds."

2. The Nietzsche window was removed in 1960 by an orthodox SED principal. On the 1994 ceremony to reinstall it, see chapter 10 of the present study, "Zarathustra as Educator? To the Nietzsche Archives."

3. *FM*, September 26, 1994, 50–53.

4. For a story of a Dresden class and its encounter with Brecht's *Galileo*, see *DS*, April 19, 1991, 103–107.

Chapter 13. No Difficulties with the Truth? The Last Testament of Philosopher-Dissident Wolfgang Harich

1. *DS*, March 25, 1991, 100.

2. For Harich's early history, see "Ulbricht über allen" in chapter 2 of the present study.

3. *DS*, December 19, 1956, 13, 17, 19.

4. Typical of the attitude held toward Harich by his enemies was the characterization in *Neue Zeit* (October 10, 1947) that he was "a smug, precocious shyster who substitutes refined demagogy for what he lacks in profundity." Quoted in Pike, 379.

5. In *Durch die Erde ein Riss* (403), Erich Loest claimed that Harich wanted to be First Secretary of a newly reconstituted SED (and that Walter Janka sought to be Minister President). Along with Harich, Gustav Just (and others) have disputed Loest. "Not a word of it is true," wrote Just in *Zeuge in eigener Sache* (149).

6. Harich, *Keine Schwierigkeiten mit der Wahrheit*, 99–101.

7. On Janka's biography and the history of Aufbau Verlag, see (in addition to the books cited in this chapter): *SZ*, March 18, 1994; *DSd*, August 9, 1991; and *SZ*, November 2, 1989. On Harich's admiring memories of Janka as a publisher, see Harich, *Keine Schwierigkeiten mit der Wahrheit*, 31–32.

8. *DS*, March 25, 1991, 98.

9. *DS*, March 25, 1991, 97.

10. See "Ulbricht über allen" in chapter 2 of the present study.

11. Harich, *Keine Schwierigkeiten mit der Wahrheit*, 80.

12. For Harich's report of the *Stasi* interrogations in 1956/57, see Harich, *Keine Schwierigkeiten mit der Wahrheit*, 92–100. For excerpts from Janka's interrogation protokols, see *Der Prozess gegen Walter Janka und andere*.

13. Or as Ulbricht announced on January 30, 1957 to the Central Committee:

It shows the strength of our Party and our Worker and Farmers' Power that the western agents found nobody for their counterrevolutionary purposes other than a Wolfgang Harich and a small group.

(Quoted in *Der Prozess gegen Walter Janka und andere*, inside front flap.)

14. *DS*, December 19, 1956, 24.

15. *SZ*, January 20, 1990. Harich's claim that his confession was "Swiftian satire" is not entirely far-fetched. Nikolai Bukharin's confession at his Moscow purge trial in March 1938 is sometimes interpreted similarly. In their study containing the English translation of the trial, Robert C. Tucker and Stephen Cohen have suggested that Bukharin used his courtroom confession to send an Aesopian message to the outside world. See *The Great Purge Trial*, ed. Robert C. Tucker and Stephen Cohen (New York, 1965).

16. March 22, 1995. For Janka's version of the events of 1956/57, see *Der Prozess gegen Walter Janka und andere*, passim; and Janka, *Schwierigkeiten mit der Wahrheit*, 276–80, 295–300, 337–70, 387–95.

17. On March 30, 1990—during the dying months of the DDR—the Supreme Court of East Germany lifted the 1957 sentences of "state treason" imposed on all members of the Harich Group. It also announced that Harich, Janka and the others would receive compensation for the years of unlawful detention.

18. *DS*, June 4, 1990, 98; and *DS*, March 25, 1991, 100. Information about the suit is taken from: *DS*, June 4, 1990, 85–98; and *DS*, March 25, 1991, 97–107; *SZ*, April 23, 1991. On Harich's protestations of "*Rufmord*," see *DS*, April 15, 1991, 13.

19. An oft-quoted statement of Brecht's doubtlessly fueled speculations such as Janka's. Brecht allegedly told Harich: "Divorce her now. You can marry her again in about two years' time." Hayman, *Brecht: A Biography*, 375. See also Völker, *Bertolt Brecht*, 388.

20. Just voiced the same suspicion about Harich in his memoir *Zeuge in eigener Sache* (*Witness of My Own*). Moreover, speaking of the July 1957 trial, Just mocks Harich's "phenomenal memory" and says that his testimony had "the character of a denunciation." "In this sense, Harich played an nasty role. . . ." Just implies the "crown witness" charge against Harich was well-deserved, since "no witness—-

except for Harich"—testified against him, Janka, and the other defendants. Just also recalls that Janka spoke with "pained, justified anger" and "rejected the entire proceeding as unjustified, stressed he had only been concerned with the welfare of the Party and socialism in his entire 30 years of Party membership" (165–67).

21. Harich, *Keine Schwierigkeiten mit der Wahrheit*, 38–41.

22. *DS*, March 25, 1991, 107.

23. On Harich's formal rehabilitation and readmittance, see *SZ*, December 12, 1992.

24. Harich, *Keine Schwierigkeiten mit der Wahrheit*, 178–230 passim.

25. For Harich's views of Merker and Markov, respectively, see also Harich, *Keine Schwierigkeiten mit der Wahrheit*, 55–61, 178, 196, 206, 216.

26. See also Harich, *Keine Schwierigkeiten mit der Wahrheit*, 55.

27. Harich, *Keine Schwierigkeiten mit der Wahrheit*, 95.

28. On Rohrwasser's views, see *SZ*, April 23, 1991.

29. *SZ*, November 2, 1989.

30. For a fuller discussion of Harich's role in the 1986/87 "Nietzsche debate" within the SED, see chapter 10 of the present study, "Zarathustra as Educator? To the Nietzsche Archives."

31. Harich, *Nietzsche und seine Brüder*; see esp. 67, 91, 113, 149–62, 183, 189, 191, 204–205.

32. *SZ*, January 20, 1990.

33. See also Harich, *Keine Schwierigkeiten mit der Wahrheit*, 204.

34. Harich, *Keine Schwierigkeiten mit der Wahrheit*, 236.

35. In *No Difficulties with the Truth*, Harich repeatedly protests Janka's unjustly positive reputation. Janka is "constantly presented as a resolute character, as the unbowed, upright man, from whom no confession could be extracted." "Against Merker until the end of his life, and against me to this day, he is a reputation-murderer [*Rufmörder*] on contract [from Ulbricht] in the pose of a pillar in bronze" (85, 94).

36. See also Harich, *Keine Schwierigkeiten mit der Wahrheit*, 206.

37. On the outcome of these legal proceedings, see *NZZ*, December 20, 1993, and December 18, 1993; *DP*, December 18, 1993; *DW*, January 13, 1994.

38. *FM*, February 13, 1995.

39. *FM*, September 26, 1994.

40. *FM*, February 13, 1995.

41. On the official commission's findings, see *FM*, November 21, 1994.

42. And not just Harich: Gustav Just was also hurt by the return of the repressed. Just had to resign as deputy of the Brandenburg SPD in March 1992 after *Stasi* documents revealed that he volunteered to take part, as a 20-year-old soldier, in an execution by firing squad of six Ukrainian Jews in July 1941. *WP*, March 10, 1992; *AFP*, March 10, 1992.

43. Ironically, Harich had already delivered a verdict on Honecker that coincided with the view of the Committee for Solidarity with Erich Honecker, a group of old SED members (dubbed "The Fan Club" by the media) that supported his rehabilitation. "Leave Honecker alone," Harich told the press in July 1992, as Honecker prepared to fly to asylum in Chile. "This man should be able to finish his days in peace and dignity, in the country of his choice." *APF*, July 10, 1992.

44. Janka, . . . *bis zur Verhaftung* (1993) and *Die Unterwerfung* (1994).

45. *SZ*, January 20, 1990. This was especially the case after the publication of Erich Loest's *Durch die Erde ein Riss* (1979). Loest was active in DDR opposition circles and spent six years in Bautzen. He claimed in his book that Harich was a privileged favorite of the Bautzen prison authorities. For Harich's defense, see Harich, *Keine Schwierigkeiten mit der Wahrheit*, 233–35.

46. Harich insists that his 1956 reform platform was not just a "pie-in-the-sky" notion of a utopian intellectual. "As I look back, our position was similar to the

later DDR opponents in the period of Gorbachev," wrote Harich in *No Difficulties with the Truth*. Indeed, many of the proposals that Harich advanced elsewhere in Eastern Europe in the 1980s, albeit in different form, with the coming of Gorbachev in 1985. But whereas Harich saw his proposals as fulfilling the Left's dream of a united, socialist Germany, Ulbricht saw it as counterrevolution. Harich said that he was merely being faithful to the German Marxist line on German reunification for more than a century; he often cited Marx's prediction and hope of 1848 that "all Germany will be declared a single indivisible republic." In *No Difficulties with the Truth*, he addresses at length his commitment to the Marxist legacy of a Greater Germany; though he acknowledges that Marx and Engels had become opponents of a Greater Germany under Bismarck by 1867, Bebel, Wilhelm Liebknecht, and other nineteenth-century SPD leaders supported the idea, as did the pre–World War I SPD and the KPD under Thälmann and Pieck. "But there was one big difference: the national question." By the 1980s, DDR reformers took two German states as established realities, Harich says. Unlike the Harich Group, for whom the war years were still close in memory, the reformers of the late 1980s wanted a better DDR, a better socialist state—and so they did not think much about, let alone campaign directly for—reunification. Until after the Wall's collapse, it lay for most of them in the realm of the unimaginable. Whereas the reverse lay in the realm of the near-unimaginable for the Harich Group. "The thought of an improved DDR—as a socialist alternative to the DDR that we would maintain for the long run—was distant," he wrote. "Even Ulbricht didn't really believe in an eventuality such as that." Harich, *Keine Schwierigkeiten mit der Wahrheit*, 171. See also Harich's posthumously published autobiographical fragment, *Ahnenpass: Versuch einer Autobiographie*, ed. Thomas Grim (Berlin, 1999). Part One is a personal memoir written in 1972 and covers Harich's life up to that year. Part Two consists of an interview that Harich gave to the filmmaker Thomas Grim in 1989, shortly after the fall of the Berlin Wall.

47. Harich, *Keine Schwierigkeiten mit der Wahrheit*, 244, 251–53.

48. *DS*, March 25, 1991, 100.

49. See, for instance, *DS*, December 19, 1956, 9.

50. *SZ*, December 14, 1993. See also the Harich birthday commemoration on December 9, 1993.

51. *SZ*, March 18, 1995. Whatever the truth of that contention, one conclusion was beyond dispute: "Our intellectual life," ruminated Rolf Schneider, "will be much duller without him." *DW*, March 24, 1995. But it was not to be without him for long. In 1996, several Harich admirers formed the "Wolfgang Harich Society" and petitioned Harich's widow, Marianne, to see his unpublished manuscripts and journals. She refused all interested parties any access to Harich's papers. Harich's admirers voiced fears that Marianne Harich planned to bowdlerize and "demarxify" his papers, and they compared this possible "new case of manipulation"—irony of ironies!—to the example of Nietzsche and his sister Elisabeth. *DW*, March 27, 1996.

Epilogue

1. *NYT*, November 11, 1989.

2. One cannot forget the terrifying events of the early 1990s, which witnessed an explosion of neo-Nazi activity partly triggered by an influx of foreigners in greater numbers than the immigrant flow into the rest of the European Union combined.

3. Rightist attacks exceeded 650 in 1997, more than half of which were aimed at foreigners. The German government classifies about 50,000 people as far-right sympathizers, of which 7,600 are considered capable of violent acts. Nearly half of the far-rightists live in eastern Germany, where most of the attacks on foreigners

have occurred even though foreigners comprise barely more than 1 percent of the local population. G. Pascal Zachary, "Letter from Magedeburg," *Washington Quarterly*, vol. 22, no. 2 (1999), 152.

4. The figure is from a 1998 Allensbach Institute for Demography survey. "Protest in Braun," *Die Woche*, April 30, 1998.

5. Running on an anti-foreigner and anti-Euro platform, Gerhard Frey's German People's Union (DVU) captured 12.9 percent of the vote in Saxony-Anhalt's state elections in April 1998. This included more than 30 percent of the youth vote, making it the most popular party among electors under 30. Frey freely confessed that he had targeted two age groups: those aged 18–29 and over 60. The DVU's success makes it the first far-Right party to enter a state parliament in the east. As one headline in the mainstream press uneasily put it: "Rechtsextrem ist 'in' im Osten," *SZ*, August 26, 1998.

6. For instance, easterners and westerners approved these assertions by different margins: "Foreigners deprive us of jobs" (48 vs. 28 percent); "Too many foreigners live in Germany" (65 to 53 percent). "Ostdeutsche laut Umfrage anfälliger für Fremdenhass-Parolen," *AP Worldstrem*, March 21, 1998. Thirty-two percent of PDS voters in the east also agreed that "too many foreigners live in Germany." PDS leaders were shocked to discover during the 1998 election season that the most popular slogan was "German jobs for Germans!" See "Protest in Braun."

7. "Rechtsextrem ist 'in' im Osten."

8. On the Bochum study, see "Faustrecht macht Schule," *Focus Magazin*, March 21, 1998, 72–84. Nor is the reported violence by the Munich Institute merely rough play. The Institute defined "violence" as "hard bodily violence," including beating, tripping and punching, and bodily injury. This study was confirmed by a report by the Munich Institute for School Pedagogy, which concluded that Bavarian youth demonstrated a "generally aggressive attitude," "intolerance," "no sense of justice," and "a pleasure in exercising power over others." "Faustrecht macht Schule," *Focus Magazin*, March 21, 1998, 72–84.

9. But some observers argue that the awards juries are administered by a "left-wing Thought Police." "Unwörtler lassen nicht spassen," *Frankfurter Allgemeine*, February 3, 1999.

10. *TES*, September 11, 1992. See also *THES*, July 3, 1992, 10.

11. At the first Education for Tolerance conference sponsored by UNESCO in June 1992, Rita Süssmuth, then president of the Bundestag, was one of the featured speakers. *RLR*, June 23, 1992.

12. On specific initiatives in the schools, see *SZ*, June 26, 1993. See also *DP*, April 11, 1995, which discusses the participation of 260 schools in a pilot project to incorporate "tolerance education" into German literature classes. See also Wilhelm Heitmeyer's 1995 study *Die bedrängte Toleranz*.

13. "UNESCO-Seminar zu Menschenrechten in Nürnberg eröffnet," *AP Worldstream*, August 20, 1998. Educators were instrumental in getting 1997 named as the "European Year Against Racism." But, as many commentators noted, the initiative seemed to do little to stem the rise of racist attitudes in the EU.

14. See Barbara Hasler, "Erziehung zur Toleranz," *Tages-Anzeiger*, May 27, 1998.

15. On the latter, see *SZ*, October 7, 1994.

16. *NZZ*, March 30, 1994.

17. *SZ*, June 28, 1993.

18. *SZ*, June 24, 1993. See also *AP Worldstream*, August 20, 1999 and *NZZ*, July 1, 1999.

19. *HC*, December 25, 1993. Its activities include sponsoring minority speakers in BRD schools, multicultural street fairs, and inter-ethnic hikes and soccer games.

20. *NZZ*, April 11, 1994. See also *DSd*, June 25, 1992 and September 15, 1990. The UNESCO-sponsored "Year of Tolerance" in 1995 culminated in the Paris Dec-

laration of Principles on Tolerance, issued in November 1995. See *SZ*, January 15, 1996.

21. With the exception of Switzerland, Germany is the only European country still to base its nationality law largely on who your ancestors were, rather on where you were born or live. Since 1913 and until mid-1999, the principle of "Jus Sanguinis," which deemed "Germanness" to reside in the genes, allowed Germany to grant citizenship only to those who could prove their German ethnicity.

This nationality law created much unfairness: after the end of the Cold War, thousands of ethnic Germans scattered through Russia and eastern Europe since the late Middle Ages—and barely able to string together two words of German— were able to gain the citizenship denied to children born in Germany to foreign parents, chiefly immigrant "guest-workers" who began to pour into West Germany in the 1960s during the country's postwar economic boom. For decades, Turks and other ethnic minorities born, living, and paying taxes in Germany were not allowed to vote or hold public office there. This discrimination undoubtedly hampered immigrants' integration into German society. By 1999, for example, only one Turk held a seat in the German parliament (though the Turkish population in Germany numbers 2.2 million), since holders of public office need citizenship, which was difficult to obtain. Indeed, many immigrants—and even first-generation residents—lost interest in integrating into German culture.

Although the nationality law had clearly become outdated, attempts in the early 1990s to reform it repeatedly foundered, largely because of most Germans' fear of being swamped by aliens. In 1991, the Kohl government made a gesture toward fairness, allowing foreigners resident in Germany for 15 years, as well as children born in Germany of foreign parents, to opt for German citizenship—but only if they renounced their original citizenship.

Finally, in mid-1999, Germany consigned the ancient "Blood Law" of the Second Reich to the dustbin of history, granting foreigners who have lived in Germany for 8 years—rather than the former 15 years—eligibility for citizenship. An estimated four million immigrants, including "guest-workers" and their families, can now claim German passports under the amended nationality law, which the Bundestag adopted by a massive majority. No longer will "Germanness" reside only in the genes. Chancellor Schröder calls the new citizenship law a millennial event for Germany, saying that the "Berlin Republic" he is inaugurating will be "at once more German, in the good sense of the term, and more welcoming toward foreigners." (But the new law is actually a pale shadow of its sponsors' original intentions to extend double citizenship to long-term foreign residents.)

22. The phrase *politische Korrektheit* has already entered the German language and appears frequently in educational contexts.

23. Commenting on the "fanatics" who insist that German women in solidarity with Turkish residents wear the veil, an editorial in the *SZ* (November 11, 1993) declared:

> One doesn't know who to fear more: the old order's conservatives or the politically correct thinkers, . . . who are praying for a new *Götterdämmerung*. . . . Both the conservatives and the politically correct ones are still wallowing in the swamp of the German past, even if their late birth has excluded their active participation in it.

24. See *SZ*, December 12, 1992; June 26, 1993; November 11, 1993.

25. On the general difficulties of creating a European political identity, see Anthony D. Smith, *National Identity*, 8–25, 71–177. Also see Smith's "National Identity and the Idea of European Unity." Smith notes that national identification is the chief form of collective identification in the modern world, and he doubts whether the idea of the nation can be superseded by "Europe" or any continental

allegiance. Indeed he warns that efforts to create a European identity may be leading to a racist "Euro-nationalism," a new form of ethnic exclusion that may ease discrimination against Eastern Europeans at the price of exacerbating violence against blacks, Asians, and other non-Europeans. He also notes, however, that substantial progress toward such an identity will not be achieved until education changes from *national* systems of education—featuring national history and national literature—to a pan-European system.

26. These tensions have much to do with the ongoing economic disparity between the eastern and western regions. For example, in 1999 a white-collar employee still earned 40 percent more in Stuttgart than in Rostock for the same work. The appeals of neo-Nazi groups resonate in no small part because of such differences, not to mention that the unemployment rate among eastern youth exceeded 20 percent throughout the late 1990s, and in some cities approached 50 percent. By contrast, the western jobless rate was under 10 percent. Easterners are also outraged by the "conquistadorial lack of feeling" and "absence of solidarity" among westerners. Will Birgit, "Neue Bundesbürger ticken anders," *Lebensmittel Zeitung*, July 9, 1999, 37.

Meanwhile, the 65 million westerners resent paying a bailout that approaches DM 2 trillion since reunification. They consider easterners ungrateful, too dependent on the government (because too tied to the caretaking of their socialist past), and hopeless at adapting to the realities of the global market. Some easterners agree. For instance, Joachim Gauck has criticized his fellow easterners for "deficient democratic consciousness," a "fear of freedom," and "loss of good citizenship sense." But many easterners consider themselves far more "German" than westerners: e.g., August 1999 surveys, during the 250th anniversary celebrations of Goethe's birth, found that 50 percent of easterners have read Goethe's *Faust*, as opposed to only 19 percent of westerners. "Ostdeutsche Fremdenhassparolen," *AP Worldstream* August 23, 1999. Hans-Joachim Maaz, head of the Psychotherapeutic Clinic in Halle, has summarized German reunification to date in a fitting metaphor: "A bad marriage between a crass, big-mouthed western man and a depressive eastern woman." "Sehnsucht nach der Mauer," *Focus Magazin*, July 19, 1999, 44–46.

27. Cynical jokes among *Ossis* about their post-reunification fate under the Wessis have been a leitmotif of this book—and they show no sign of dying out. (Question: What do you get when you cross an *Ossi* with a *Wessi*? Answer: An arrogant, jobless laggard.)

A sign of the "Trotzidentität" is the revival of a specifically DDR identity. Throughout the east since the mid-1990s, *Ostalgie* parties have been celebrated by *Ossis* in FDJ uniforms decked out with NVA insignias, medals, and flags. In a September 1998 poll, 80 percent of easterners said they felt "like second-class citizens." This also accounts for the success of the PDS in presenting itself to easterners as "their" party, a regional party championing eastern interests. (Support for the PDS has remained stubbornly about 20 percent in the east, as opposed to less than 1 percent in the west.)

28. Cited in Heinrich August Winkler, "Rebuilding," 117. See also Le Gloannec, "On German Identity," 142. In a 1982 poll, 68 percent of West Germans supported eventual reunification, on the conditions that it would not entail a change in the political system or lower their standard of living. The second condition, to date, has not been met. Despite the euphoria of 1989, West Germans never wanted reunification if it meant shouldering additional major burdens. Cited in Mommsen, "History and National Identity," 569.

Telling evidence of this gulf is that the Education for Tolerance initiatives have even encompassed attempts to bring youth together from east and west Berlin. One project begun in the mid-1990s, titled "Action against Hatred of Aliens," has regularly brought together ninth graders from eastern and western Berlin. The director has observed: "Stereotypes and prejudices are extremely crude." In the eyes of the west Berliners, easterners are right-wingers and hostile to foreigners, wear weird clothes, and listen to strange music; east Berlin students consider "Wessis" arrogant, condescending, drug-addicted, and boastful. "Acceptance on both sides has dropped significantly" since 1990, a sociological study has confirmed. Amazingly, 17.5 percent of western Berlin youth and 9 percent of eastern Berlin youth "want the Wall back." "Sehnsucht nach der Mauer," *Focus Magazin*, July 19, 1999, 44–46.

29. Other survey research concluded that "the mental divides between the East and the West are deeper than ever." "Sehnsucht nach der Mauer," *Focus Magazin*, July 19, 1999, 44–46. Pollsters confirm these dismal findings. A 1999 survey by the Allensbach Institute found that 37 percent of easterners believe the former East Germany remains a place apart from the 11 states that constitute the former West Germany—compared with 30 percent the year before. "Die Zwei Seelen des Ostdeutschen," *SZ*, April 13, 1995. Another 1999 poll found that while only 17 percent of easterners favor a return of the old communist regime, more than 60 percent do not consider themselves citizens of a united Germany. Jack Ewing, "Why East is Still East, and West is Still West," *Business Week*, November 8, 1999.

30. Cited in Heinrich August Winkler, 112–13, 119–20.

31. Indeed, results were even worse when the same question was phrased positively. In a 1999 poll by the Ipsos Institute for Market Research, only 13 percent of Germans confessed to patriotic feelings. Michael Berger, "Patriotismus des Konsumenten," *Die Woche*, October 15, 1999.

32. A June 1999 poll conducted by the Leipzig Institute for Market Research found that 85 percent of eastern Germans believed that it will require a minimum of 15 years before "Germany is really united"; one-third set the minimum at 25 years, with young easterners especially pessimistic. Will Birgit, "Neue Bundesbürger ticken anders," *Lebensmittel Zeitung*, July 9, 1999, 37. Moreover, whereas in 1990 most easterners and westerners looked to the future with "almost euphoric joy" (79 and 70 percent respectively), in 1996 only 55 percent even expected a "positive" future. An October 1999 poll showed that 37 percent of easterners felt "angst about the future." The "top theme"—to establish a more secure future, cited both by easterners and westerners (79 percent)—was an educational priority: "career training." "Mehr Lust am Leben," *Focus Magazin*, June 28, 1999, 80–83.

33. Roger Boyes, "Postwar Generation Seeks Release from Shackles of Nazi Guilt," *The Times* (London), November 10, 1998.

34. Poll results of this Allensbach survey were published in "Die Zwei Seelen des Ostdeutschen," *SZ*, April 13, 1995.

35. In surveys by the Allensbach Institute, the response "I don't know of any best qualities of Germans" increased from 4 percent in 1952 to 18–22 percent in the 1970s and 80s. In a 1987 poll, 11 advanced industrial nations, West Germany "came in last in national pride—and showed the largest gap between parents' and children's values." Chancellor Kohl once referred to the "Gnade der späten Geburt" providentially bestowed on his generation, who bore no personal guilt for Nazi crimes and could thus move on to build a New Germany. But the polls suggest that younger generations of Germans do not seem to have recognized their fate as a similar "blessing of late birth." Elisabeth Noelle-Neumann, "Do the Germans Have a 'National Character'?" *Encounter*, March 1987, 68.

36. Political scientist Dolf Sternberger coined the word *Verfassungspatriotismus* in 1982. See Sternberger, *Staatsfreundschaft*, 9–34.

37. Quoted in Heinrich August Winkler, "Rebuilding," 107.

38. Heinrich August Winkler, 107.

39. Other nations seem, more or less, to pass through their histories; but History itself seems to pass through Germans—viscerally and repeatedly.

40. See Walwei-Weigelmann, *Die Wunde Namens Deutschland*.

41. I am indebted in this paragraph to the excellent essay by Neil Postman, "My German Problem," esp. 47, 49.

42. Or as Michel Friedman, a Frankfurt lawyer and member of the Central Council of Jews in Germany, put it during the course of comments about the 1998 Bubis-Walser debate: "If you want to remember Goethe, you have to remember Hitler." Paul Geitner, "German Holocaust Debate Seeks New Language," *The Jerusalem Post*, December 15, 1998. But such an assertion sounds like just another brand of the "fascism cudgel" to many Germans. They acknowledge that the Holocaust is a dreadful chapter in Germany history. But is it—should it be—a measure of all things German? As many younger Germans—and Jews—believe, perhaps the controversies will dissolve only when the last survivor of the Third Reich has died.

43. For detailed discussion of the *Historikerstreit*, see Geiss, *Die Habermas-Kontroverse*; Charles S. Maier, *The Unmasterable Past*; Evans, *In Hitler's Shadow*; and Baldwin, *Reworking the Past*.

44. Quoted in Rabinach, "German Historians Debate the Nazi Past," 197.

45. In 1993 Botho Strauss, Germany's leading playwright, sent shock waves through intellectual and political circles with an essay in *Der Spiegel* tilted "The Swelling Song of the Billy Goat"—the goat being the symbol of the New Right in France and Germany. Strauss explained neo-Nazism as the inevitable reactionary consequence of a deformed, self-loathing generation, which has created a politically correct version of German history indicting the Bonn republic as a permanently abnormal nation. Strauss lamented that Germany had exchanged a sense of nationhood for rampant consumerism. Those who are "prepared to sacrifice blood"—such as the neo-Nazis, said Strauss—"we no longer understand, and, in our liberal-libertarian self-delusion, view as false and damnable." Strauss' essay later appeared as the lead contribution in a 1995 New Right manifesto, *The Self-Confident Nation*.

46. Every effort to commemorate a traumatic event in the modern German past seems to call forth a reaction that erupts into a major debate. After the 50th anniversary commemoration of the end of World War II in 1995, and the national attention accorded Steven Spielberg's film *Schindler's List*, came 15 minutes in the spotlight for Daniel Goldhagen, a young American Jewish sociologist, who in mid-1995 published the German edition of his book *Hitler's Willing Executioners*.

Goldhagen asked this question: How wide and deep was anti-Semitism within the German populace of the Third Reich? Based on case studies such as that of the Hamburg police battalion 101, Goldhagen charged that an "eliminationist anti-Semitism" prevailed among Germans—and had done so for many decades before Hitler's election. But Goldhagen never demonstrated that his case studies were representative. Nor did he engage in comparative history between Germany and other nations with a modern history of anti-Semitic sentiment (e.g., France and Russia).

The *denouement* was odd. In 1997, on receiving a book prize in Germany, Goldhagen lavishly praised postwar Germany as a "normal" country, indeed a "model" for other nations. For Goldhagen knew of no other country that treated "so openly and systematically the inglorious chapters of its past," which rendered it exemplary. Markus Franz, "Preis für den Beobachter der willigen Vollstrecker," *taz*, March 11, 1997.

47. Unlike many of the other public disputes about German history, the Holocaust memorial debate centrally involved German legislators, since it involved disbursing billions of marks to erect some commemoration to Holocaust victims. This decade-long battle over how and whether to build a memorial near the Brandenburg Gate went through many twists and turns. Finally, a modified version of the original plan gained support and was approved by the Bundestag in June 1999 over the objections of such legislators as Berlin's CDU mayor, Eberhard Diepgen.

48. See "Streit mit Walser ist neuer Historikerstreit," *SZ*, December 11, 1998; and Stephan Reinicke, "Markiert der Streit um Walsers Rede ein neues Kapitel deutscher Geschichtspolitik?" *taz*, November 28, 1998.

Martin Walser, one of Germany's leading writers and a former Left-liberal turned neoconservative, took up the issue of Auschwitz in a Frankfurt speech accepting the prestigious German Booksellers Literary Prize. Auschwitz, declared Walser, should not become a "tool of intimidation, a moral cudgel, or just a compulsory exercise."

Walser's attack was directed against the abstract, anti-fascist rhetoric of the "memory industry," as conservatives refer to the liberals' reminders about Auschwitz. Walser proposed a departure from public gestures altogether, "a reduction to the sphere of the individual," indeed a "kind of ontologizing of the individual citizen's conscience," since "the political realm seems to be an ineffective terrain for authentic remembering." He senses already a historicizing, a "media-izing," a "de-dramatizing of the German past" under the Social Democrats—hence a "normalization" of a new kind. The "politics of memory" will become more universal, concerned more with Turks, Kurds, and Bosnians than with Jews and other victims of the Holocaust. (Walser also criticized plans for the Holocaust memorial in Berlin as "the monumentalization of disgrace.")

As Walser's critics noted, his position runs the risk of confusing conscience and memory. For by saying that when one no longer has personal memory (conscience), then public remembrance (memory) is just an empty gesture, Walser comes close to sanctioned reducing public memory to "how people feel."

Ignatz Bubis, chairman of the Central Council of Jews in Germany, accused Walser of "spreading intellectual nationalism" and of "latent anti-Semitism" and "spiritual arson" likely to lend support to the far Right.

Days later, former Hamburg mayor Klaus von Dohnanyi—whose father was a Resistance hero murdered by the Nazis—defended Walser and lambasted Bubis. Whereupon former President Richard von Weizsäcker chided both Walser and Dohnanyi and called for moderation. In turn, von Weizsäcker was criticized by numerous conservatives as well as Marcel Reich-Ranicki. Surprisingly, however, liberal Günter Grass—with the added authority of a recently awarded Nobel Prize in his cap—defended Walser against what he agreed was the "fascism cudgel." See "Grass verteidigt Walser," *FAZ*, October 8, 1999.

Months later, after a personal exchange with Walser, Bubis issued a partial retraction of his accusations. Ironically, it was the last public statement of Bubis before his death in August 1999.

49. Or as Evans puts it: "For if the Germans did not commit a crime that stood out from all others in its horrors, then they have no more to be ashamed of than any other nation, and so it becomes possible for them to tread the international stage unburdened by a degree of guilt that no other nation can share." *In Hitler's Shadow*; quoted in *LAT*, November 8, 1989, 5. That burden sometimes appears to amount, as Susan Eisenhower, daughter of Dwight D. Eisenhower, put it in an interview, to an "ethnic original sin." *NYT*, June 5, 1994.

50. Some historians want to leave the Nazi period as tradition, not *Erbe*: but part of the task of memory entails acknowledging that it is *both*.

51. Nolte was professor of history at Free University of Berlin; Stürmer taught at Erlangen; Hillgruber at Cologne; and Joachim Fest was a Hitler biographer and a *FAZ* editor. François Furet and Ernst Nolte, *Feindliche Nähe: Kommunismus and Faschismus im 20. Jahrhundert* (Berlin, 1998).

52. The major exception was the liberal-Left historian Imanuel Geiss, who in *Die Habermas-Kontroverse* condemned Habermas for truncating and distorting the conversatives' quotations, poisoning the climate of German academe, and transforming a scholarly debate into a Right/Left intellectual civil war.

53. Quoted in Rabinach, "German Historians Debate the Nazi Past," 194. Chan-

cellor Schröder shares these sentiments. As he said in February 1999, in a much-quoted interview in *Die Zeit*: "People who don't have their own memories—my generation and younger—should be able to live without a guilt complex" about the Nazi years. Schröder was a toddler during World War II; his father was a Wehrmacht soldier killed in action in Romania.

54. Indeed Stürmer believed that the future of Germany lay in wresting control of the "interpretation monopoly" over history wielded by the Left. But as Habermas warned, "Historical scholarship degenerates easily into historians' politics"—and Habermas himself was not above this tendency. "Die Leere der Geschichte," *SZ*, March 12, 1997.

55. Quoted in Rabinach, "German Historians Debate the Nazi Past," 194. Just as Gorbachev had called upon Soviet scholars to fill in the "blank spots of our history," Stürmer was in effect calling on fellow German scholars to tone down the luminous dark brown spots of their history. But to some ears such pleas have Orwellian overtones: they smack of ideologues exploiting the mutability of the past to paper over the memory holes of history.

56. Quoted in Rabinach, "German Historians Debate the Nazi Past," 195.

57. Mushaben, "A Search for Identity," 400. Stürmer's position has more supporters among German intellectuals today than it did in the 1980s. The German intellectual landscape shifted rightward in the 1990s, with writers such as Strauss and Walser joined by Hans Magnus Enzensberger, political scientist Hans-Peter Schwarz, Brigitte Seebacher-Brandt (widow of Willy Brandt), and the historian Michael Wolffsohn all expressing various degrees of patriotic sentiment and/or contempt for the perceived domination of the left-wing "68 generation" over German intellectual life. Among the leading members of this leftish group are Günter Grass, Jürgen Habermas, and the historian Hans-Ulrich Wehler, who are accused of wielding a "fascism cudgel" and enforcing a moralistic, "politically correct" version of history that stresses the uniqueness of Nazi crimes so as to suppress German national pride.

58. Imanuel Geiss, *Die Habermas-Kontroverse*.

59. Quoted in Rabinach, "German Historians Debate the Nazi Past," 194.

60. Rabinach, "German Historians Debate the Nazi Past," 194. The Israeli historian Saul Friedlander calls this "the symmetric version of the past," whereby crimes of the Third Reich are compared to a series of other horrors, from the Gulag to the killing fields of Cambodia, in a chain of equivalences that reduces the scale of the Nazi terror. Quoted in Wood, "The Holocaust," 360.

61. Habermas referred to the conservatives' "identificatory grab at national history." Quoted in Wood, "The Holocaust," 375.

62. Rabinach, "German Historians Debate the Nazi Past," 196. Habermas, "Apologetic Tendencies in German Historiography." Habermas' concept "post-conventional identity" remained abstract and was not elaborated in detail. Chancellor Schröder broadly endorses these sentiments, though he sees them as the condition for Germany becoming a "normal" nation. His age plays a decisive role in his outlook: For the first time in the history of the *Bundesrepublik*, a chancellor has come to office with no personal experience of World War II. In his inaugural address to the Bundestag, Schröder said Germany now possesses "the self-confidence of a nation that has come of age, that feels neither superior nor inferior to anyone." Although Schröder is the first German leader to have no memory of the war (Helmut Kohl was not a soldier, but he was in the Hitler Youth), Schröder's family was touched by the war; his father died in action in Romania.

63. Unlike the *Historikerstreit* or the Goldhagen controversy, the Walser-Bubis debate did not center on fundamental historical and philosophical questions, i.e., on the Nazi past or comparative evil, but rather on allegedly misunderstood formulations and personal sensitivities. See E. Gujer, "Kein Schlussstrich unter Deutschlands Geschichte," *NZZ*, December 5, 1998.

The Walser-Bubis debate was also different because most of the participants weren't intellectuals or historians, and so had no particular competence in German history. Rather, they were prominent citizens who were viscerally engaged in a personal way by the issues—not just Walser and Bubis, but also the other major participants: Dohnanyi, von Weizsäcker, Augstein, and Reich-Ranicki, all of whom had either fought in the war or lost family members in it.

Moreover, this time the conservatives were not figures who could be suspected of secretly harboring reactionary impulses. Bubis' assault on Walser was directed at the liberal thinker who had courageously first addressed the issues of German national guilt (in his essay "We Guilty Germans") in the 1960s, the writer who had become the conscience of West German literature and the model of German self-introspection. And Dohnanyi's credentials were equally unassailable, given his own distinguished political career and his father's murder in a concentration camp. So Bubis was not attacking right-wing thugs, but rather two of the liberal beacons of Germany. See "Schuldkultur oder Schamkultur," *NZZ*, December 12, 1998; and Detlev Claussen, "Deutschland, ein Wintermärchen," *Tages-Anzeiger*, December 21, 1998.

64. In *Livre noir du communisme (The Black Book of Communism)*, published in German translation in 1998, Stephane Courtois accused the Western intellectual establishment of using a double standard to measure degrees of totalitarian evil, demonizing the Nazis but refusing to judge—and even remaining silent about— the crimes of communists around the world. Courtois charged the European Left with complicity in those crimes.

Courtois also claimed that European communists were responsible for "manipulating" the German public into having a permanent "guilty conscience" for Nazi crimes—which conveniently took the focus off communism's still greater crimes. *The Black Book* should have been written in Germany, Courtois added, because Germans have a fuller perspective to understand totalitarianism, given that they were both the victimizers and victims of both Nazism and Stalinism.

65. Such a debate would amount to a comprehensive East-West *Identitätsstreit*, a combination of the *Historikerstreit* and the so-called *Literaturstreit* of 1990/91. The latter, which to some extent was a prosecution trial conducted by leading western intellectuals, centered on criticism of Christa Wolf, Heiner Müller, and the question of the relationship of leading DDR "state authors" to the *Stasi* and the SED. It was triggered by publication of Wolf's *Was bleibt?* (1990), a memoir portraying her own suffering under *Stasi* surveillance in 1979, and of the revelations about Müller's contacts with the *Stasi*. For an overview of the *Literaturstreit*, see Anz, *Es geht nicht um Christa Wolf.*

And such a debate could have broken out in 1998, even before the Walser-Bubis debate erupted, with the publication of Courtois' *The Black Book of Communism* in German translation. Courtois is a former Maoist and passionate renegade turned hostile (if not identifiably conservative) toward the Left. He made comments comparing "race genocide" and "class genocide" that echoed those of Nolte a decade earlier.

So why did Courtois' book arouse little controversy in Germany—even though a special added chapter for the German edition was devoted to crimes in the DDR's past? Why did the book not trigger the new German *Historikerstreit*?

The main reason is simply that Courtois is French and these issues bear a closer relationship to the postwar politics of the French Left. By contrast, the German Left—unlike Sartre, Merleau-Ponty, Althusser, Foucault, and other leading French intellectuals—had long since distanced itself from Stalinism and/or communism. (The French CP is also the only major communist party in Europe still under its original name, i.e., never to have undergone any discrediting or renewal.) Moreover, unlike in Germany, Stalinism is still frequently equated in France with wartime anti-fascism (and thereby legitimated or relativized).

66. Oddly, the discussions about *The Black Book* featured few prominent DDR figures (except for Wolfgang Berghofer, former mayor of Dresden [1986–90] and Joachim Gauck, the author of the DDR chapter in *The Black Book*). The discussions were dominated by western German historians such as Hans Ulrich Wehler and Hans Mommsen.

67. No eastern Germans played notable roles in any of the post-reunification debates, though a few did register their opinions. For instance, the writer Monika Maron rushed to Walser's defense and asserted that he did not go far enough: "I, for my part, neither think nor feel that young Germans must carry the shame of their nation," she wrote in *Die Zeit*. "For me, young Germans are as little incriminated as young Danes or young Frenchmen. How can we convince other countries of our normality if we ourselves deny that claim? . . . Now that I defend Walser, I am also trembling a little bit. Why? Where do I live that I am afraid even to say what I think?" Quoted in Roger Cohen, "Germany Searches for 'Normality,' " *New York Times*, November 29, 1998.

68. How should today's Germans, those who had no involvement in the crimes of the Nazis, address them? Here is one answer:

> What should our second generation . . . do with the knowledge of the horrors of the extermination of the Jews? We should not believe we can comprehend the incomprehensible, we may not compare the incomparable, we may not inquire because to inquire is to make the horrors an object of discussion, even if the horrors themselves are not questioned, instead of accepting them as something in the face of which we can only fall silent in revulsion, shame, and guilt. Should we only fall silent in revulsion, shame, and guilt? To what purpose? . . . That some few would be convicted and punished while we of the second generation were silenced by revulsion, shame, and guilt—was that all there was to it now?

That is how Michael Berg, a character in *Der Vorleser* [*The Reader*], a novel published in 1996 by Bernhard Schlink, sees it.

69. Rabinach, "German Historians Debate the Nazi Past," 195.

70. Harold James argues provocatively that the absence of durable national institutions—an absence due to wars and changes of political systems—has generated and frustrated the search for German identity. James considers these distinctive features of Germany's history the real character of its *Sonderweg*. As a result, the Germans have relied primarily on economic success for their identity and political legitimation. But when the economy grows weak—as in the 1930s—both identity and government totter. Economic upheaval always produces political instability, but as the German recession of 1991–94 proved, this may be a special problem in Germany. See James, *A German Identity*.

71. Rabinach, "German Historians Debate the Nazi Past," 198.

72. The phrase is used by Charles S. Maier in *The Unmasterable Past*.

73. Quoted in Charles S. Maier, *The Unmasterable Past*.

74. As Christian Meier, the chairman of the German Historical Association, put it in December 1986: "With all due sympathy for a postnational identity, can it suffice when we live among nations?" Meier questioned whether Habermas' notions of constitutional patriotism and post-conventional identity were sufficient for inspiring collective loyalty and a strong consciousness of community. Quoted in Charles S. Maier, *The Unmasterable Past*, 55.

75. Charles S. Maier, *The Unmasterable Past*, 12–34. Maier defines "Bitburg history" as the "multiple muddying of moral categories and historical agents" (13).

76. Lothar Kettenacker, *TI*, May 1, 1992. Kennenacker is a staff member of the German Historical Institute in London. The thought echoes Nietzsche's warning against an excess of historical memory in "On the Advantage and Disadvantage of

History for Life," that "we are suffering from a destructive historical fever. ..."
Quoted in Charles S. Maier, *The Unmasterable Past*, 161.

77. See Le Gloannec, "On German Identity," 144–45.

78. See Fulbrook, "Aspects of Society and Identity," 232.

79. Cited in Heinrich August Winkler, "Rebuilding," 120–21.

80. In an opinion poll conducted recently by German research organization EMNID, 72 percent of respondents agreed that an austerity budget was necessary. A majority of the public apparently agree that the government needs to cut generous welfare provisions, which have now become a burden to German society, and prepare the country for competing in the global market.

81. *TNR*, April 3, 1989. Or as Robert B. Goldmann, the European representative of B'nai B'rith's Anti-Defamation League, put it: "There is as little justification for Jews and [Germany's] neighbors to remember only what happened until 1945 as for Germans to recall only what has happened since." *NL*, November 2–16, 1992, 12.

82. Heinrich August Winkler, "Rebuilding," 110.

83. Chancellor Schröder has repeatedly asserted that Germany is now a "normal" country. As he said in his first address to the Bundestag in November 1998:

> We are proud of this country, its landscape and culture, the creativity and will to achieve of its people. We are proud of the older generation that rebuilt the country after the war and gave it its place in a European peace. We are proud of the people in the eastern part of Germany, who threw of the communist yoke and brought down the Wall. That is the self-confidence of a nation that has come of age, that feels neither superior nor inferior to anyone.

But the outcry over Walser's address, just days after Schröder's remarks, would soon prove the Chancellor wrong—or at least premature. (Because Schröder came to power near the eruption of the Walser-Bubis debate, many observers associated the two events.) However much Schröder might attempt to deny it, the Walser-Bubis debate "reveals just how torn the German identity remains today," as one young German journalist stated. It also summarizes the Germans' ongoing historical dilemma, as she added:

> On the one hand, Germans are raised with a strong awareness of history, of who they are, and most notably of what they have done to Jews. On the other hand—and this applies particularly to the young—they want to be defined by who they are today, not by the atrocities that some of their forefathers committed. Germans feel that if they talk about guilt and shame, they are written off as ponderous and unable to enjoy life. But if they step beyond their past for just a moment, they may be reproached for being superficial and insensitive, or even neo-Nazis.

Uta Harnischfeger, "Historical dilemma sparks strong reactions," *Financial Times*, June 1, 1999.

84. "When reality collides with ideology," Schröder likes to say, "reality wins."

85. Fulbrook, "Aspects of Society and Identity," 211.

86. See Margarete S. Klein, *Challenge of Communist Education*.

87. See also Hamm, "Von der DDR lernen?"

Glossary

The following list includes German-language terms frequently used in the main text, with the exception of those items already noted in the List of Abbreviations.

Abgrenzung. Delimitation, demarcation. Term for Honecker policy of carefully circumscribed relations with BRD.

Abitur. German school-leaving examination, which qualifies a student for university admission.

Abwicklung. "Wrapping up" or "winding down." Euphemism used for the dismantling of DDR institutions and the laying off of thousands of eastern German employees.

Antifa. Short for *Antifascist*, i.e., an opponent of fascism.

antifaschistischer Schutzwall. Anti-fascist Wall of Protection. Official DDR government term for the Berlin Wall.

Asylanten. Asylum seekers.

Ausländerfeindlichkeit. Hostility toward foreigners.

Besserwessi. A smart-aleck or know-it-all *Wessi*.

Blueshirts. The FDJ.

Brüderländer. Brother lands. A communist term for the international fraternity of socialist nations.

Bundestag. The lower house of the (West) German legislature.

Bundi. Western German. Early postwar-era nickname.

Bürger. Citizen.

das bessere Deutschland. "The better Germany." Term often applied both to the German socialist tradition and to the DDR.

Demo. Short for demonstration or protest march.

Demosprüche. Protest slogans.

DIAMAT. Dialectical Materialism. Shorthand term, along with M-L, for required university courses in Marxism, as well as for Marxist philosophy itself.

Dorfschule. Village school.

drüben. "Over there." Used both in West Germany and the DDR to refer to "the other Germany."

Entnazifizierung. Denazification.

Erbe. Heritage. DDR term for that part of the German past admissible to progressive DDR historiography.

Erdkunde. Geography.

Erziehung zum Hass. DDR school program in military training. Generally used to describe proper attitude of socialist patriots toward imperialists and warmongers.

Fachschule. Technical school or college that trains for white-collar jobs.

Feindbild. Enemy image.

freigekauft. Bought free. Refers to BRD policy of ransoming DDR political prisoners.

Freundschaft! Friendship! A communist greeting.

Geschichte. History.

Giftschrank. "Poison shelf." Colloquial, populist expression for books officially on the DDR's proscribed or limited access list.

Gleichschaltung. Forced coordination. Nazi term for lock-step conformity demanded of all Third Reich institutions.

Grenzgänger. Border crossers.

Grepos. Short for *Grenzpolizei*, the DDR border police. Chiefly used by West German media.

Gymnasium. German academic school.

Hauptschule. General education (West) German school.

Heimat. Homeland. A German term with patriotic overtones.

Heimatkunde. Local and regional studies. A DDR school subject (known in the early postwar era as *Deutschkunde*).

Historikerstreit. Historians' debate. The 1986–87 controversy among West German historians about the status and uniqueness of the Holocaust.

Hoffnungsträger. Carrier of hope.

Immer bereit! Always prepared! A slogan of the communist youth organizations.

Jugendgesetz. Youth Law. The highlights of DDR youth legislation were the three youth acts incorporated into the national constitution in 1946, 1964, and 1974.

Jugendweihe. Youth consecration ceremony. A communist confirmation rite administered to youth at the age of 14. Inaugurated in pre-war Germany under the auspices of the SPD, it had been voluntary until the 1950s.

Junge Gemeinden. Youth Congregations. The Lutheran youth organizations of the DDR.

Kader, K-Stellungen. Cadre, cadre positions. The latter term was chiefly used by the West German media.

Komsomol. The Soviet mass youth organization.

Kristallnacht. Night of the Broken Glass. The pogrom inflicted upon the German Jews on November 9, 1938.

Land, Länder. State(s).

Nachholbedarf. Backlog demand. "Need to catch up."

die neue schule. "The new school." The uniform, democratic school of the DDR, a term chiefly employed by early postwar DDR educators.

Neues Deutschland. New Germany. Formerly the official SED newspaper; associated since 1990 with the PDS.

Neulehrer, Neulehrerin. New Teacher. Mainly used to refer to teachers of antifascist convictions hired in the early postwar era of the DDR.

Oberschule. Generic name for DDR and pre-war German high school.

Ossis. Eastern Germans. Term used since 1989/90.

Planmensch. Planned human being, a.k.a. the "new socialist man." Chiefly used by West German media.

Realschule. Technically oriented German school.

Reformpädagogik. Reform pedagogy. The liberal-radical tradition of German education, much indebted to educators and politicians in the pre-war SPD.

Republikflucht. Flight from the Republic. Escape from the DDR; an official term of reprobation.

die Schandmauer. Wall of Outrage. Cold War term of West German media for Berlin Wall.

Seilschaft. "Climbing rope." Term of disapprobation used in the post-reunification era to describe the effective PDS network of helping old communists who "hang together."

Scheindemokratie. Pseudo-democracy. Ulbricht's liberal, pre-1948 policy of strategic cooperation with, and cooptation of, the eastern SPD.

der Spitzbart. "The Goatee." Mocking sobriquet applied to Walter Ulbricht.

Sportmacht. Athletic power.

Sportwunder. Athletic miracle. Refers to DDR's Olympic successes.

Stabü, Staatsbürgerkunde. Citizenship studies, or civics. DDR school subject.

Stacheldrahtsonntag. Barbed-Wire Sunday. Day of erection of Berlin Wall.

Stasi. Short for *Staatssicherheitsdienst*, State Security Service; i.e., the secret police. Also known as MfS and SSD.

Stunde Null. "Zero hour." Refers to the year 1945 and often used to imply or claim not only a new beginning in postwar Germany, but also a break or discontinuity with the Nazi or authoritarian past.

Trabi. Short for *Trabant*, the DDR state-produced automobile.

Überprüfung. Audit, investigation. Term for formal screening conducted of all DDR teachers.

Übersiedlerstrom. Immigration flow. The term was officially used to denote the migration of ethnic Germans from the DDR into West Germany.

Umerziehung. Re-education. German-language term (used more frequently in the SBZ than western Germany) for Allied program of anti-fascist, democratic renewal.

Unterrichtshilfen. "Lesson aids." Term used by Volk und Wissen for its teaching guides.

Verfassungspatriotismus. Constitutional patriotism.

Vergangenheitsbewältigung. Coping with the past. German short-hand term for the national challenge of coming to terms with the legacy of the Holocaust.

Volkskammer. People's Chamber. The DDR parliament.

Vopos. Short for *Volkspolizei*, the People's Police of the DDR. Chiefly used in West Germany and in DDR slang.

Wehrerziehung. Wehrkunde. Defense education, military studies. DDR school subject.

weltanschauliche Erziehung. Education for a world outlook. The Marxist-Leninist philosophy of education.

Wende. The "turn." Used in the DDR and eastern Germany to refer to the change from SED rule to parliamentary democracy during 1989/90.

Wendehals. "Wryneck," or turncoat, quick-change artist. Applied to SED loyalists who recast themselves as reformers after October 1989.

Wendekrankheit. "Turn sickness." Refers to adjustment trauma undergone by eastern Germans during post-reunification era.

Wessis. Western Germans. Term used since 1989/90.

wissenschaftlicher Assistent. University instructor, junior faculty member.

Wirtschaftswunder. Economic miracle. Refers to economic boom in West Germany during the 1950s.

Zoni. Eastern German. Early postwar-era nickname.

Bibliography

This bibliography includes all books, memoirs, monographs, and journal articles cited in the text and notes of this book, along with the most significant reviews and periodical articles. It also includes numerous other items that have exerted influence on my thinking during the writing process.

DDR textbooks and other curricular materials have been variously obtained from the archival collection at the International Textbook Institute at Braunschweig, from the DDR Ministry of Education records at the Bundesarchiv Potsdam, from the Thuringia Ministry of Education and the Goethe Gymnasium in Weimar, from the FDJ and Institut für Jugendforschung records at the Stiftung Archiv der Parteien und Massenorganizationen der DDR im Bundesarchiv (SAPMO) in Berlin, from a special collection of DDR textbooks at the University of Wisconsin at Madison, and from the textbook collections at the University of Kentucky at Lexington and the University of Texas at Austin.

Ackermann, Anton. "Gibt es einen besonderen deutschen Weg zum Sozialismus?" *Einheit*, vol. 1, no. 1 (1946).

Adler, Les K. and Thomas G. Paterson, "Red Fascism: The Merger of Nazi Germany and Soviet Russia in the American Image of Totalarianism, 1930s–1950s," *American Historical Review*, 1970, 1046–1064.

Agde, Günter. *Kahlschlag: das 11. Plenum des ZK der SED 1965: Studien und Dokumente*. Berlin, 1991.

"Aktion Ochsenkopf." *Der Spiegel*, September 6, 1991, 23.

Albrecht, Sylvia, Manfred Jendryschik, and Klaus Walther, eds. *Menschen in diesem Land: Porträts*. Halle (Saale), 1974.

Allen, Bruce. *Germany East: Dissent and Opposition*. Montreal, 1991.

Andert, Reinhold, and Wolfgang Herzberg. *Der Sturz: Erich Honecker im Kreuzverhör*. [East] Berlin, 1990.

Anweiler, Oskar, and Siegfried Baske, eds. *Die sowjetische Bildungspolitik, 1917–60*. [West] Berlin, 1979.

Anz, Thomas, ed. *Es geht nicht um Christa Wolf*. Munich, 1991.

Arnold, Heinz Ludwig, and Frauke Meyer Gosau. *Die Abwicklung der DDR*. Göttingen, 1992.

Aschheim, Steven E. *The Nietzsche Legacy in Germany, 1890–1990*. Berkeley, 1992.

A. S. Makarenko: Das deutschsprachige Schriftum bis 1962. [West] Berlin, 1963.

Astor, Gerald, and Jason Dunaway. "It's Up Against the World this Summer for America's Athletes." *Esquire*, August 1972.

Atwood, William, and Seymour Freidin. "The Nazis March Again: This Time for Stalin." *Collier's*, vol. 126 (November 25, 1950).

Augstein, Rudolf. "Wiederkehr eines Philosophen: Täter Hitler, Denker Nietzsche." *Der Spiegel*, vol. 24 (1981), 156–84.

Bachmann, Bert. *Der Wandel der Politischen Kultur in der ehemaligen DDR.* Berlin, 1993.

Bahr, Erhard. *Ernst Bloch.* [West] Berlin, 1974.

Bailey, George. "Disappearing Satellite." *The Reporter*, March 16, 1961.

Baker, Lynn. "The Communist Assembly Line for Olympic Champions." *National Review*, May 16, 1980, 584–87.

Baldwin, Peter, ed. *Reworking the Past: Hitler, the Holocaust, and the Historians' Debate.* Boston, 1990.

Balluseck, Lothar von. *Die guten und die bösen Deutschen: das Freund-Feind-Bild im Schriftum der DDR.* Bonn, 1972.

Bambach, Jürgen. "The Transformation of East German Education: A Comparison between the Federal States of Berlin and Brandenburg." *European Education*, vol. 25, no. 2 (summer 1993), 58–65.

Baring, Arnulf. *Der 17 Juni 1953.* Stuttgart, 1983.

———. *Uprising in East Germany: June 17, 1953.* Ithaca, 1972.

Barm, Werner. *Totale Abgrenzung: Zehn Jahre unter Ulbricht, Honecker und Stoph an der innerdeutschen Grenze.* Stuttgart, 1971.

Bartel, Walter. *Unser Präsident Wilhelm Pieck: Erzählungen aus seinem Leben.* [East] Berlin, 1954.

Baske, Siegfried. *Bildungspolitik in der DDR, 1963–76.* [West] Berlin, 1979.

Baske, Siegfried, and Martha Engelbert, ed. *Dokumente zur Bildungspolitik in der sowjetischen Besatzungszone.* Bonn/Berlin, 1966.

Bauer, Edda, ed. *Rilke-Studien: Zu Werk und Wirkungsgeschichte.* [East] Berlin, 1976.

Bäumler, Alfred. *Nietzsche, der Philosoph und Politiker.* Leipzig, 1931.

Baylis, Thomas A. *The Technical Intelligentsia and the East German Elite: Legitimacy and Social Change in Mature Communism.* Berkeley, 1974.

Becker, Jorg J. R. Becker. "Textbooks and the Political System in the Federal Republic of Germany, 1945–75." *School Review*, vol. 86, no. 2 (February 1978), 251–70.

Behler, Ernst. "Nietzsche in der marxistischen Kritik Osteuropas." *Nietzsche-Studien*, vols. 10/11 (1981/82), 92–93.

———. "Zur frühen sozialistischen Rezeption Nietzsches in Deutschland." *Nietzsche-Studien*, vol. 13 (1984), 503–520.

"Bei uns ist immer Olympia." *Der Spiegel*, July 31, 1972, 68–80; August 6, 1972, 78–91; August 13, 1972, 82–94.

"Berlin Divided." *Economist*, August 19, 1961.

"Bewachte Bewacher." *Der Spiegel*, August 30, 1961, 17.

Biermann, Wolf. *Klartexte im Getümmel: 13 Jahre im Westen*, ed. Hannes Stein. Köln, 1990.

———. *Nachlass I.* Koln, 1977.

———. *Preussischer Ikarus: Lieder/Balladen/Gedichte/Prosa.* Koln, 1978.

———. *Wolf Biermann: Poems and Ballads*, trans. Steve Gooch. London, 1977.

Birke, Adolf M. *Nation ohne Haus: Deutschland, 1945–1961.* Berlin, 1989.

Blackburn, Gilmer W. *Education in the Third Reich: Race and History in Nazi Textbooks.* Albany, 1985.

Block, Robert. "Racists Forge Links Across the World." *The Independent*, December 7, 1992.

Bode, Dirk. *Polytechnischer Unterricht in der DDR.* Frankfurt am Main, 1978.

Bodenman, Paul S. "Education in the Soviet Zone of Germany." *School Life,* vol. 41, no. 3 (December 1958), 14–17.

Bortfeldt, Heinrich. *Von der SED zur PDS: Wandlung zur Demokratie?* Bonn, 1992.

Bothig, Peter, and Klaus Michael. *Machtspiele: Literatur und Staatssicherheit im Fokus Prenzlauer Berg.* Leipzig, 1993.

Bourke, John. "A Letter from Germany." *German Life and Letters,* July 1947, 72–76.

Bowen, James. *Anton Makarenko and the Years of Experiment.* Madison, 1962.

Brandt, Heinz. *Ein Traum, der nicht entführbar ist: Mein Weg zwischen Ost und West.* Munich, 1967.

Brant, Stefan. *The East German Rising.* London, 1955.

Braun, Johannes. *Volk und Kirche in der Dämmerung: ein Einblick in die vier Jahrzehnte des Sozialismus in der DDR.* Leipzig, 1992.

Bridge, Adrian. "One Germany." *The Independent,* October 3, 1990, 18.

Brinton, Crane. *Nietzsche.* Cambridge [Mass.], 1941.

Brokerhoff, Karl Heinz. *Mit Liedern und Granaten.* Bonn, 1972.

Bryson, Phillip J., and Manfred Melzer. *End of the East German Economy: From Honecker to Reunification.* New York, 1991.

Buch, Günther. *Namen und Daten wichtiger Personen der DDR.* [West] Berlin, 1982.

Bungenstab, Karl-Ernst. *Umerziehung zur Demokratie? Re-education-Politik im Bildungswesen der US-Zone, 1945–49.* Düsseldorf, 1970.

"Bürger in Krippen." *Der Spiegel,* November 17, 1969, 55–57.

Busch, Friedrich W. *Familienerziehung in der sozialistischen Pädagogik der DDR.* Düsseldorf, 1972.

Cancik, Hubert. "Der Einfluss Friedrich Nietzsches auf die Berliner Schulkritiker der wilhelminischen Ära." *Der altsprachliche Unterricht,* vol. 30 (1987), 55–73.

———. "Der Nietzsche-Kult in Weimar: Ein Beitrag zur Religionsgeschichte der wilhelminischen Ära." *Nietzsche-Studien,* vol. 16 (1987).

Carr, G. A. "The Involvement of Politics in Sports Relationships of East and West Germany, 1945–72." *Journal of Sport History,* vol. 7, no. 1 (spring 1980), 40–51.

Carr, William G. "Stone Walls a Person Make." *PTA Magazine,* June 1962, 20–21.

Cate, Curtis. *The Ides of August: The Berlin Wall Crisis, 1961.* New York, 1978.

"A Century of Olympolitics." *Economist,* August 26, 1972, 30–31.

Chakrabarty, Banbehari, ed. *The Stalin Question.* Calcutta, 1979.

Chalupsky, Jutta, and Renate Rothmann. *Freier Markt auf nackter Haut: Wessi-Report aus Leipzig: Vom Top-Manager bis zum Puff-Besitzer.* Berlin, 1991.

Childs, David. "East Germany: Towards the Twentieth Anniversary." *World Today,* October 1969, 440–50.

———. *GDR, Moscow's German Ally.* 2nd ed. London, 1988.

———. *Germany in the Twentieth Century.* London, 1991.

———, ed. *Honecker's Germany.* London, 1985.

Childs, David, Thomas A. Baylis, and Marilyn Rueschemeer, eds. *East Germany in Comparative Perspective.* London, 1989.

"Christians in East Germany." *Times Educational Supplement,* December 12, 1952, 1001.

Claussen, Horst, and Norbert Oellers. *Beschädigtes Erbe: Beiträge zur Klassiker-rezeption in finsterer Zeit.* Bonn, 1984.

Cless, Olaf. *Die DDR-Forschung in der Bundesrepublik in den siebziger Jahren: ein Beitrag zu Rezeptionsgeschichte Bundesrepublik-DDR*. Marburg, 1978.

Clews, John. "The Berlin Youth Festival." *Twentieth Century*, October 1951, 289–97.

Cohn, Michael. *The Jews in Germany, 1945–93*. New York, 1994.

Conant, James Bryan. "The Citadel of Learning." *Yale Review*, May 1955, 48–61.

Corino, Karl. "Abwertung aller Werte." *Süddeutsche Zeitung*, September 22, 1990, 49.

Croan, Melvin, and Carl J. Friedrich. "The East German Regime and Soviet Policy in Germany." *Journal of Politics*, vol. 20 (1958), 44–63.

"The Cultural Commissars." *Newsweek*, January 17, 1966, 47.

Darnton, Robert. *Berlin Journal: 1989–1990*. New York, 1991.

Das Bildungswesen in der DDR. Bonn, 1985.

"Das Tauwetter ist nicht aufzuhalten." *Der Spiegel*, March 25, 1964, 55–58.

DDR Zeittafel, 1945–87. [East] Berlin, 1989.

Degen, Hans-J. *"Wir wollen keine Sklaven sein . . .": der Aufstand des 17. Juni 1953*. [West] Berlin, 1979.

Dennis, Mike. *Social and Economic Modernization in Eastern Germany from Honecker to Kohl*. London, 1993.

"Der Aufstand im Juni." *Der Monat*, September 1953, 596–624; October 1953, 45–66.

"Des ist, wie wenn's d'Mauer dabeihätten." *Der Spiegel*, vol. 37 (1992), 26–32.

"Die politische Plattform Harichs und seiner Freunde." *SBZ-Archiv*, vol. 5/6 (March 25, 1957), 72–74.

"Die rechten Bahnen." *Der Spiegel*, November 7, 1956, 12–14.

Diefendorf, Jeffry M. "Teaching History in the Polytechnical Schools of the German Democratic Republic." *History Teacher*, vol. 15, no. 3 (1982), 347–62.

Dornberg, John. *The New Germans: Thirty Years After*. New York, 1976.

———. *The Other Germany*. New York, 1968.

———. *Schizophrenic Germany*. New York, 1961.

Dorst, Werner. *Erziehung, Bildung, und Unterricht in der Deutschen Demokratischen Schule*. [East] Berlin, 1953.

"Du, unsere Liebe." *Der Spiegel*, October 12, 1969, 54–81.

Dubel, Siegfried. *Dokumente zur Jugendpolitik der SED*. Munich, 1966.

Duff, Michael F., and Willard Mittelman. "Nietzsche's Attitudes Toward the Jews." *Journal of the History of Ideas* (1984), 301–317.

Dulles, Eleanor Lansing. *The Wall: A Tragedy in Three Acts*. Columbia, S.C., 1972.

"Edel aus dem Grabstein." *Der Spiegel*, vol. 40 (1964), 68–81.

Education in the GDR: How It Works and What It has Achieved. [East] Berlin, 1984.

Eigler, Friederike Ursula, and Peter Pfeiffer. *Cultural Transformations in the New Germany: American and German Perspectives*. Columbia, S.C., 1993.

Eisenmann, Peter, and Gerhard Hirscher. *Bilanz der Zweiten Deutschen Diktatur*. München, 1993.

———. *Die Deutsche Identität und Europa*. München, 1991.

"Elections in East Germany." *America*, October 30, 1954, 115–16.

"Elisabeths Wille zur Macht." *Neue Deutsche Hefte*, January-June 1957, 248–49.

Ellwein, Thomas. *"Die deutsche Universität": Vom Mittelalter bis zur Gegenwart*. Königstein, 1985.

Enders, Ulrike. "Erziehung zum Hass." *Kirche im Sozialismus*, vol. 2 (1987), 52–55.

Engelmann, Roger, and Paul Erker. *Annäherung und Abgrenzung: Aspekte Deutsch-Deutscher Beziehungen, 1956–1969*. München, 1993.

Erbe, Günter. *Die verfemte Moderne: die Auseinandersetzung mit dem "Modernismus" in Kulturpolitik, Literaturwissenschaft und Literatur der DDR*. Opladen, 1993.

Erickson, Harold B. "East German Youth Decide for Themselves." *California Journal of Secondary Education*, vol. 31, no. 2 (February 1956), 75–78.

"Erst kommst du." *Der Spiegel*, March 27, 1963, 92.

"Es muss etwas passieren." *Der Spiegel*, August 15, 1951, 5.

Etzold, A. "Der Platzkampf der Eliten." *Die Zeit*, February 14, 1992, 14.

Evans, Richard J. *In Hitler's Shadow: West German Historians and the Attempt to Escape from the Nazi Past*. New York, 1989.

"Factory of Champions." *New York Times*, July 3, 1988.

"Faule Eier." *Der Spiegel*, September 28, 1970, 172.

Feldman, K. F. "Walter Ulbricht." *Contemporary Review*, vol. 195 (June 1959), 341–43.

Fischer, Horst. *Schalck-Imperium: ausgewählte Dokumente*. Bochum, 1993.

Fischer, Ruth. "Communism in Germany." *World Review*, January 1948, 22–26.

———. *Stalin and German Communism*. Cambridge, Mass., 1948.

Fishman, Sterling. "After the Wall: A Case Study of Educational Change in Eastern Germany." *Teachers College Record*, vol. 94, no. 4 (summer 1993), 744–61.

Fishman, Sterling. " 'The Berlin Wall' in the History of Education." *History of Education Quarterly*, vol. 22, no. 3 (1982), 363–70.

Fishman, Sterling. *Estranged Twins: Education and Society in the Two Germanies*. New York, 1987.

"Flight of the Intelligentsia." *Time*, September 10, 1956, 79–80.

"Freundschaft siegt." *Der Spiegel*, June 8, 1950, 13.

Fricke, Karl Wilhelm. *MfS Intern: Macht, Strukturen, Auflösung der DDR-Staatssicherheit: Analyse und Dokumentation*. Bielefeld, 1991.

Friedrich, Walter. "Changes in Attitudes of Youth in the GDR." *European Education*, vol. 23, no. 1 (spring 1991), 6–30.

"Frühling auf dem Eis." *Der Spiegel*, vol. 13 (1964), 40.

Führ, Christoph. *On the Education System in the Five New Länder of the Federal Republic of Germany*. Bonn, 1992.

Fulbrook, Mary. "Aspects of Society and Identity in the New Germany." *Daedalus*, January 1994, 211–34.

———. *Two Germanies, 1945–1990: Problems of Interpretation*. Basingstoke, Hampshire, 1992.

Fuller, Christian. "Der rigorose Blick zurück." *Süddeutsche Zeitung*, November 14, 1992.

"Für Frieden und Fransen." *Der Spiegel*, October 12, 1965, 38.

Füssl, Karl-Heinz. *Die Umerziehung der Deutschen*. Berlin, 1995.

Garton Ash, Timothy. *In Europe's Name: Germany and the Divided Continent*. London, 1993.

Gauly, Thomas M. *Die Last der Geschichte: Kontroversen zur deutschen Identität*. Köln, 1988.

Gay, Ruth. *The Jews in Germany*. New York, 1988.

Gedwin, Jeffrey. *Hidden Hand: Gorbachev and the Collapse of East Germany.* Washington, D.C., 1992.

Geerts, Rudi. *Hier lacht das Volk: Witze aus der alten und neuen DDR.* Hamburg, 1990.

Geiss, Imanuel. *Die Habermas-Kontroverse: Ein deutscher Streit.* Berlin, 1988.

Gelb, Norman. *The Berlin Wall: Kennedy, Khrushchev, and a Showdown in the Heart of Europe.* New York, 1986.

"Gelbe Gefahr." *Der Spiegel,* July 3, 1967.

Genet, "Letter from Berlin." *New Yorker,* August 1947.

German Democratic Republic. [East] Berlin, 1986.

Geschichte 10. Berlin, 1968.

Gesetz über das einheitliche sozialistische Bildungssystem der DDR. [East] Berlin, 1971.

"Gesunde Ehe." *Der Spiegel,* March 10, 1969, 41–44.

"Gesunde Kräfte." *Der Spiegel,* September 1, 1968, 32–33.

"Gesunde Naivität." *Der Spiegel,* July 22, 1964, 12.

"Gift von Affen." *Der Spiegel,* June 6, 1967, 19.

Gilbert, Doug. *The Miracle Machine.* New York, 1980.

Gilman, Sandor, and Karen Remmler, eds. *Reemerging Jewish Culture in Germany: Life and Literature since 1989.* New York, 1994.

Glaessner, Gert-Joachim. *Der Lange Weg zur Einheit: Studien zum Transformationsprozess in Ostdeutschland.* Berlin, 1993.

———. *Der schwierige Weg zur Demokratie: Von Ende der DDR zur Deutschen Einheit.* Opladen, 1991.

———. *Die andere deutsche Republik: Gesellschaft und Politik in der DDR.* Opladen, 1989.

Glaessner, Gert-Joachim, and Ian Wallace, eds. *The German Revolution of 1989: Causes and Consequences.* Oxford, 1992.

Glaessner, Gert-Joachim, and Irmhild Rudolph. *Macht durch Wissen: Zum Zusammenhang von Bildungspolitik, Bildungssystem und Kaderqualifizierung in der DDR.* Opladen, 1978.

"Glanzäugig und blaublusig." *Der Spiegel,* August 22, 1951, 10.

Gleye, Paul. *Behind the Wall: An American in East Germany, 1988–89.* Carbondale, 1991.

Goeckel, Robert F. *The Lutheran Church and the East German State: Political Conflict and Change under Ulbricht and Honecker.* Ithaca, 1990.

Goldstein, Thomas. "The East German Revolt." *New Republic,* March 20, 1953, 9.

Görtemaker, Manfred. *Unifying Germany: 1989–1990.* Prague, 1994.

Grace, Alonzo G. "Islands of Democratic Ferment in Germany." *American Scholar,* vol. 19 (summer 1950), 341–52.

Gransow, Völker, and Konrad Hugo Jarausch. *Die Deutsche Vereinigung: Dokumente zu Bürgerbewegung, Annäherung und Beitritt.* Köln, 1991.

Grothe, Peter. *To Win the Minds of Men: The Story of the Communist Propaganda War in East Germany.* Palo Alto, 1958.

Grunert, Horst, and Ernst P. Siegert. *Die DDR: Staat, Gesellschaft, Wirtschaft.* Frankfurt am Main, 1978.

Günther, Gitita, and Lothar Wallraf. *Geschichte der Stadt Weimar.* Weimar, 1977.

Gysi, Gregor, Uwe-Jens Heuer, and Michael Schumann. *Zweigeteilt: über den Umgang mit der SED-Vergangenheit.* Hamburg, 1992.

Haase, Baldur. *Orwells DDR*. Offenburg, 1997.

Habermas, Jürgen. "Apologetic Tendencies in German Historiography." *Die Zeit*, July 11, 1986.

———. *The New Conservatism: Cultural Criticism and the Historians' Debate*, ed. Sherry Weber Nicolson. Cambridge, Mass., 1989.

———. "Nachwort." In *Erkenntnistheoretische Schriften von Friedrich Nietzsche*. Frankfurt am Main, 1968.

———. *Vergangenheit als Zukunft*. Zurich, 1991.

Hagen, Manfred. *DDR—Juni '53*. Stuttgart, 1992.

Hahn, H. J. *Education and Society in Germany*. New York, 1998.

Hahn, K. H. "Das Nietzsche-Archiv." *Nietzsche-Studien*, vol. 18 (1989), 1–18.

Hamalainen, Pekka Kalevi. *Uniting Germany: Actions and Reactions*. Aldershot, 1994.

Hamm, Bernd. "Von der DDR lernen?" In *Das Ende eines Experiments: Umbruch in der DDR und deutsche Einheit*, ed. Rolf Reissig and Gert-Joachim Glaessner, 240–42. Berlin, 1991.

Hanhardt, Arthur Monroe. *German Democratic Republic*. Baltimore, 1968.

Hannig, Waltraud. "The GDR—A Country of Books and Readers." *Contemporary Review*, vol. 244 (1984), 43–44.

Hanser, Richard. "Speedy Adolf." *Life*, May 26, 1949, 2, 4, 6, 8, 11–12.

Harich, Wolfgang. *Kleine Schwierigkeiten mit der Wahrheit*. Berlin, 1992.

———. *Nietzsche und seine Brüder: Eine Streitschrift*. Schwedt, 1994.

———. "Revision des marxistischen Nietzsche-Bildes?" *Sinn und Form*, vol. 39 (1987), 1018–1053.

Haritonow, Alexander. *Sowjetische Hochschulpolitik in Sachsen, 1945–1949*. Berlin, 1995.

Havemann, Robert. *An Alienated Man*. Trans. Derek Masters. London, 1973.

———. *Berliner Schriften*. [West] Berlin, 1976.

———. "Der Marxismus leidet an Sklerose." *Der Spiegel*, December 16, 1964, 37–49.

———. *Dialektik ohne Dogma*. Hamburg, 1964.

———. "Tauwetter ist ein gefährliches Klima." *Der Spiegel*, March 16, 1970, 38.

Hayman, Ronald. *Brecht: A Biography*. New York, 1983.

———. *Nietzsche: A Critical Life*. New York, 1980.

Hearndon, Arthur. *Education in the Two Germanies*. Boulder, 1974.

Hechinger, Fred M. "The Battle for German Youth." *Harper's*, March 1948, 180–88.

———. *The Big Red Schoolhouse*. New York, 1959.

Heider, Magdalena. *Politik, Kultur, Kulturbund: zur Gründungs- und Frühgeschichte des Kulturbundes zur Demokratischen Erneuerung Deutschlands 1945–1954 in der SBZ/DDR*. Koln, 1993.

Heider, Magdalena, and Kerstin Thons. *SED und Intellektuelle in der DDR der fünfziger Jahre: Kulturbund, Protokolle*. Koln, 1990.

Heimer, Helmut, and Walter Schmidt, eds. *Erbe und Tradition: Geschichtsdebatte in der DDR*. [West] Berlin, 1986.

Hein, Christoph. *Die Fünfte Grundrechenart: Aufsätze und Reden*. Frankfurt, 1990.

Heinemann, Karl-Heinz. *Arbeit und Technik in der Erziehung; Studien zum polytechnischen Unterricht in der DDR*. Köln, 1973.

Heitmeyer, Wilhelm. *Die bedrängte Toleranz: ethnische-kulturelle Konflikte, religiöse Differenzen und die Gefahren politischer Gewalt*. Frankfurt, 1996.

Heitzer, Heinz. *GDR: An historical outline*. [East] Berlin, 1979.

Heller, Peter. "Nietzsche." *Nietzsche-Studien*, vol. 7 (1978), 27–58.

Helwig, Gisela., ed. *Jugend und Familie in der DDR*. Köln, 1964.

Helwig, Gisela, et al. *Schule in der DDR*. Köln, 1988.

Henke, Klaus-Dietmar. "Misszelle: Zu Nutzung und Auswertung der Unterlagen des Staatssicherheitsdienstes der ehemaligen DDR." *Vierteljahrshefte für Zeitgeschichte*, vol. 41, no. 4 (1993), 575–87.

Herms, Michael. *Heinz Lippmann: Porträt eines Stellvertreters*. Berlin, 1996.

"Herr Ulbricht's Happy Birthday." *Economist*, June 29, 1968, 32–33.

"Herr Ulbricht's Students Revolt." *Economist*, July 6, 1957, 43–44.

Herzberg, Wolfgang. *Überleben heisst Erinnern: Lebensgeschichten deutscher Juden*. Berlin, 1990.

Heuwagon, Marianne. "Zwangsadoptionen in der DDR." *Süddeutsche Zeitung*, June 6, 1991.

Heydemann, Günther. *Geschichtswissenschaft im geteilten Deutschland*. Frankfurt am Main, 1980.

Heyen, Rolf. *Jugend in der DDR: Auf dem Weg zur sozialistischen Leistungsgesellschaft*. Bad Honnef, 1972.

Hildebrand, Robert F. "Teacher Union Blitz in the Former East Germany." *European Journal of Education*, vol. 28, no. 1 (1993), 99–104.

Hildebrandt, Rainer. *Der 17. Juni*. [West] Berlin, 1983.

———. *The Explosion: The Uprising Behind the Iron Curtain*. New York, 1955.

Hillig, Götz, ed. *Makarenko in Deutschland, 1927–67*. Braunschweig, 1968.

Hoberman, John. "The Transformation of East German Sport." *Journal of Sports History*, vol. 17, no. 1 (spring 1990), 62–68.

Hochhuth, Rolf. *Wessis in Weimar: Szenen aus einem besetzten Land*. Berlin, 1993.

Hohendorf, Gerd, Barbara Musick, and Gerhard Schreiter. *Monumenta Paedagogica. Band 15. Lehrer im antifaschistischen Widerstandskampf der Völker*. [East] Berlin, 1974.

Hollingdale, R. J. *Nietzsche: The Man and His Philosophy*. Baton Rouge, 1973.

Honecker, Margot. "Unsere Jugend zu guten Kommunisten erziehen." *Neues Deutschland*, May 21, 1976, 3.

———. *Zur Bildungspolitik und Pädagogik in der DDR*. [East] Berlin, 1986.

Huschner, Anke. "Der 17. und 1953 an Universitäten und Hochschulen der DDR." *Beiträge zur Geschichte der Arbeiterbewegung*, vol. 33, no. 5 (1991), 681–92.

Iggers, George. *The German Conception of History: The National Tradition of Historical Thought from Herder to the Present*. Middleton, Conn., 1983.

"Immer etwas seltsam." *Der Spiegel*, September 4, 1963.

"Interview with an East German Teacher about the Effects of German Unification on Schools in the 'New Federal State.'" *Social Education*, vol. 57, no. 5 (September 1993), 249–50.

Introducing the GDR. [East] Berlin, 1978.

Jäger, Manfred. *Kultur und Politik in der DDR: ein historischer Abriss*. Koln, 1982.

James, Harold. *A German Identity, 1770–1990*. London, 1989.

Janka, Walter. . . . *bis zur Verhaftung. Erinnerungen eines deutschen Verlegers*. Berlin, 1993.

———. *Die Unterwerfung: eine Kriminalgeschichte aus der Nachkriegszeit*. Munich, 1994.

———. *Schwierigkeiten mit der Wahrheit.* Hamburg, 1989.

———. *Spuren eines Lebens.* Berlin, 1991.

Janssen, Peter Heinrich. "Behandlung von Friedrich Nietzsches 'Also sprach Zarathustra' im Unterricht." *Die pädagogische Provinz*, vol. 13 (1959).

Janz, Curt Paul. *Friedrich Nietzsche: Biographie.* Munich, 1978.

Jarausch, Konrad Hugo. *The Rush to German Unity.* New York, 1994.

JCC. "The Berlin Youth Festival: Its Role in the Peace Campaign." *World Today*, July 1951, 306–315.

"Jetzt dürfen auch die Uniformierten." *Der Spiegel*, July 22, 1964, 12.

Joas, Hans, and Martin Kohli. *Der Zusammenbruch der DDR: soziologische Analysen.* Frankfurt am Main, 1993.

Jones, W. Treharne. "If the Wall Came Tumbling Down." *World Review*, vol. 201 (1976), 289–99.

Jöppke, Christian. *East German Dissidents and the Revolution of 1989: Socialist Movement in a Leninist Regime.* Bassingstoke, Hampshire, 1995.

Just, Gustav. *Zeuge in eigener Sache: Die fünfziger Jahre in der DDR.* Frankfurt am Main, 1990.

Kadarkay, Arpad. *Georg Lukács: Life, Thought, and Politics.* Cambridge, Mass., 1991.

Kaltenbach, Bernd. *Berichte aus Mittel- und Ostdeutschland: Die Fachrichtung Philosophie an den Universitäten der Sowjetzone, 1945–58.* Bonn, 1959.

"Kampf der Eliten." *Der Spiegel*, January 1, 1968.

Kantorowicz, Alfred. *Deutschland-Ost und Deutschland-West: Kulturpolit.* Münsterdorf, 1971.

———. *Im 2. Drittel unseres Jahrhunderts: Illusionen, Irrtümer, Einsichten, Voraussichten.* Köln, 1967.

Karau, Gisela. *Stasiprotokolle: Gespräche mit ehemaligen Mitarbeitern des Ministeriums für Staatssicherheit der DDR.* Frankfurt am Main, 1992.

Kashyap, Subhash C. *The Unknown Nietzsche: His Socio-Political Thought and Legacy.* Dehli, 1970.

Kaufmann, Walter. *Nietzsche: Philosopher, Psychologist, Antichrist.* Princeton, 1950.

Keithly, David M. *The Collapse of East German Communism: The Year the Wall Came Down, 1989.* New York, 1992.

Keller, Dietmar, and Matthias Kirchner, eds. *Biermann und Kein Ende: Eine Dokumentation zur DDR-Kulturpolitik.* Berlin, 1991.

"Klassenkampf im Stadion." *Der Spiegel*, vol. 28 (1976), 108–109.

Klein, Helmut. *Education in a Socialist Country: The GDR's Education Policy.* [East] Berlin, 1976.

———. *Learning for Living: Education in the GDR.* [East] Berlin, 1980.

Klein, Margrete Siebert. *Challenge of Communist Education: A Look at the German Democratic Republic.* New York, 1980.

Klier, Freya. *Lug Vaterland: Erziehung in der DDR.* Munich, 1990.

"Knall, Schuss, bumms, raus, weg." *Der Spiegel*, vol. 36 (1972), 24–38.

Knecht, Willi. *Wege nach Olympia.* [West] Berlin, 1980.

Kneller, George Frederick. *The Educational Philosophy of National Socialism.* New Haven, 1941.

Koch, Hans. *Grundlagen Sozialistischer Kulturpolitik in der Deutschen Demokratischen Republik.* Berlin, 1983.

Kocka, Jürgen. *Historische DDR-Forschung: Aufsätze und Studien.* Berlin, 1993.

Kocka, Jürgen, and Martin Sabrow. *Die DDR als Geschichte: Fragen, Hypothesen, Perspektiven.* Berlin, 1994.

Kohn, Michael. *The Jews in Germany, 1945–1993: The Building of a Minority.* Westport, Conn., 1994.

Konrad, Low, von, ed. *Ursachen und Verlauf der Deutschen Revolution 1989.* Berlin, 1991.

Köpke, Horst, and Friedrich-Franz Wiese, eds. *Mein Vaterland ist die Freiheit: Das Schicksal des Studenten Arno Esch.* Rostock, 1990.

Kösing, Alfred. *Theoretische Probleme der Entwicklung der sozialistischen Nation in der DDR.* Berlin, 1975.

Krisch, Henry. *The German Democratic Republic: The Search for Identity.* Boulder, 1985.

———. *German Politics under Soviet Occupation.* New York, 1974.

Krüger, Arnd. "Sieg Heil to the Most Glorious Era of German Sport: Continuity and Change in the Modern German Sports Movement." *International Journal of the History of Sport,* vol. 4, no. 1 (May 1987), 5–19.

Krüger, Hans-Peter. *Demission der Helden: Kritiken von Innen, 1983–1992.* Berlin, 1992.

Kuhrt, Eberhard, and Henning von Löwis. *Griff nach der deutschen Geschichte: Erbeaneignung und Traditionspflege in der DDR.* Paderborn, 1988.

Kultur und Kulturträger in der DDR: Analysen. Berlin, 1993.

Kunert, Günter. *Der Sturz vom Sockel: Feststellungen und Widersprüche.* München, 1992.

Kunert, Hubertus. *Deutsche Reformpädagogik und Faschismus.* Hannover, 1973.

Kunze, Reiner. *The Wonderful Years.* Trans. Joachim Neugroschel. New York, 1977.

Lange, M. G. *Wissenschaft im totalitären Staat: Die Wissenschaft der Sowjetischen Besatzungszone auf dem Weg zum "Stalinismus".* Stuttgart, 1955.

Lange, Max E. *Totalitäre Erziehung.* Frankfurt am Main, 1954.

Langenbücher, Wolfgang R., Ralf Rytlewski, and Bernd Weyergraf. *Kulturpolitisches Wörterbuch Bundesrepublik Deutschland/Deutsche Demokratische Republik im Vergleich.* Stuttgart, 1983.

Lasky, Melvin J. "Berlin Notebook: 2 Putsches That Failed." *The Reporter,* December 30, 1954, 20–21.

———. "The Oozing Mire of Lies." *The Spectator,* September 13, 1957, 329–30.

"The Last Cold Warrior." *Time,* August 13, 1973, 39–40.

Leben, Singen, Kämpfen: Liederbuch der deutschen Jugend. [East] Berlin, 1954.

Leben und Alltag in der DDR. Dresden, 1982.

Le Gloannec, Anne-Marie. "On German Identity." *Daedalus,* January 1994, 129–48.

[Leisegang, Hans]. "Die Philosophie in der Sowjetzone." vol. 2, no. 1 (June 1950), 248–55.

Legters, Lyman H., ed. *German Democratic Republic: A Developed Socialist Society.* Boulder, Colorado, 1978.

Lehrbuch für den Geschichtsunterricht. 5. Schuljahr. Berlin, 1951.

Lehrbuch für den Geschichtsunterricht. 6. Schuljahr. Berlin, 1954.

Lehrbuch für den Geschichtsunterricht. 8. Schuljahr. Berlin, 1953.

Lehrbuch für den Geschichtsunterricht. 10. Schuljahr. Berlin, 1956 [1953].

Leiser, Ernst. "The Students Strike Back at Stalin." *Saturday Evening Post*, February 18, 1950, 36–37, 67–73.

Leonhard, Wolfgang. *Child of the Revolution*. Chicago, 1967.

"Let's Sing Together." *Der Spiegel*, no. 42 (1969), 129–30.

"Letter from East Berlin." *New Yorker*, vol. 29 (February 13, 1954), 84–94.

"Letter from Germany." *German Life and Letters*, April 1948, 242–47.

Lewis, Geoffrey W. "Soviet Germany: The Unruly Satellite." *Department of State Bulletin*, December 28, 1953, 883–91.

Liebknecht, Wilhelm. *Kleine politische Schriften*. Frankfurt am Main, 1976.

———. *Speeches of Wilhelm Liebknecht*. New York, 1928.

Lilge, Frederic. *The Abuse of Learning: The Failure of the German University*. New York, 1948.

Lindner, Bernd, and Ralph Grüneberger. *Demonteur: Biographien des Leipziger Herbst*. Bielefeld, 1992.

Linton, Derek. *"Who Has the Youth, Has the Future": The Campaign to Save Young Workers in Imperial Germany*. Cambridge, Mass., 1991.

Lippmann, Heinz. *Honecker: Porträt eines Nachfolgers*. Köln, 1971.

Lipschitz, Leslie, and Donogh McDonald, eds. *German Unification: Economic Issues*. Washington, D.C., 1990.

Love, Nancy S. *Marx, Nietzsche, and Modernity*. New York, 1986.

Lowenstein, Steven M. *The Berlin Jewish Community: Enlightenment, Family, and Crisis, 1770–1830*. New York, 1994.

Löwith, Karl. *Sämtliche Schriften: Nietzsche. Band 6*. Stuttgart, 1987.

Löwy, Michael. *Georg Lukács: From Romanticism to Bolshevism*. London, 1976.

Lubbe, Peter. *Dokumente zur Kunst-, Literatur- und Kulturpolitik der SED 1975–1980*. Stuttgart, 1984.

Ludz, Peter C. *The Changing Party Elite in East Germany*. Cambridge, Mass., 1972.

———. *Die DDR zwischen Ost und West: Politische Analyse 1961 bis 1976*. Munich, 1977.

Lukács, Georg. *Die Zerstörung der Vernunft. Der Weg des Irrationalismus von Schelling zu Hitler*. Berlin, 1954.

Maaz, Hans Joachim. *Das gestürzte Volk: die unglückliche Einheit*. Berlin, 1991.

———. *Der Gefühlsstau: Ein Psychogramm der DDR*. Berlin, 1990.

———. *Die Entrüstung*. Berlin, 1993.

Maegerlein, Heinz, Thilo Koch, and Martin Morlock. *Olympia 1972 München*. Munich, 1973.

Magnus, B. "Nietzsche and Postmodern Criticism." In *Nietzsche-Studien. Band 18*, 1989, 301–316.

Magris, Claudio. " 'Ich bin der Einsamkeit als Mensch.' " *Süddeutsche Zeitung am Wochenende*, January 3–4, 1981, 45.

Maier, Charles S. *The Unmasterable Past: History, Holocaust, and German National Identity*. Cambridge, Mass., 1988.

Maier, Helmut, and Walter Schmidt, eds. *Erbe und Tradition: Geschichtsdebatte in der DDR*. Köln, 1989.

Maier, Joseph B, Judith Marchus, and Zoltan Tarr, eds. *German Jewry: Its History and Sociology*. New Brunswick, 1989.

Malorny, Heinz. "Tendenzen der Nietzsche-Rezeption in der BRD." *Deutsche Zeitschrift für Philosophie*, vol. 27 (1979), 1493–1500.

Malzahn, Manfred. *Germany, 1945–1949: A Sourcebook*. London, 1991.

Marcuse, Peter. *Missing Marx: A Personal and Political Journal of a Year in East Germany, 1989–90*. New York, 1991.

Markovits, Andrei, and Simon Reich. *From Bundesrepublik to Deutschland: German Politics after Unification*. Ann Arbor, 1993.

Markovits, Inga. *Die Abwicklung: ein Tagebuch zum Ende der DDR-Justiz*. München, 1993.

Mattox, Gale A., and John H. Vaughan, eds. *Germany through American Eyes: Foreign Policy and Domestic Issues*. Boulder, 1989.

Mayer, Hans. *Der Turm von Babel: Erinnerung an eine Deutsche Demokratische Republik*. Frankfurt am Main, 1991.

————. *Ein Deutscher auf Widerruf: Erinnerungen. Band I und II*. Frankfurt am Main, 1982.

McAdams, A. James. *East Germany and Detente: Building Authority After the Wall*. New York, 1985.

————. *Germany Divided: From the Wall to Unification*. Princeton, 1993.

McCardle, Arthur W., and A. Bruce Boenau, eds. *East Germany, a new German Nation Under Socialism?* Lanham, Md., 1984.

McCauley, Martin. *The German Democratic Republic Since 1945*. London, 1983.

McElvoy, Anne. *Saddled Cow: East Germany's Life and Legacy*. London, 1992.

McFalls, Laurence H. *Communism's Collapse, Democracy's Demise: The Cultural Context and Consequence of the East German Revolution*. New Hampshire, 1995.

McIntyre, Ben. *Forgotten Fatherland*. London, 1992.

McIntyre, Thomas D. "Sport in the German Democratic Republic and the People's Republic of China." *Journal of Physical Education, Dance, and Culture*, vol. 56 (January 1985), 108–111.

Meador, Daniel John. *Impressions of Law in East Germany: Legal Education and Legal Systems in the German Democratic Republic*. Charlottesville, 1986.

Medvedev, Roy. *Khrushchev*. Oxford, 1982.

Mende, Klaus-Dieter. *Die polytechnische Erziehung im Schulsystem der DDR*. Bad Harzburg, 1972.

————. *Schulreform und Gesellschaft in der Deutschen Demokratischen Republik, 1945–65*. Stuttgart, 1970.

Merritt, Richard L., and Anna J. Merritt, *Living with the Wall: West Berlin, 1961–85*. Durham, 1985.

Meuschel, Sigrid. *Legitimation und Parteiherrschaft: zum Paradox von Stabilität und Revolution in der DDR, 1945–1989*. Frankfurt am Main, 1992.

Meyer, C. H., "Margot Honecker." *Süddeutsche Zeitung*, July 31, 1992.

Meyer, Gerd. *Die DDR-Machtelite in der Ära Honecker*. Tübingen, 1991.

Meyers, Jeffrey, ed. *George Orwell: The Critical Heritage*. London, 1975.

Mieskes, Hans. *Die Pädagogik der DDR in Theorie, Forschung, und Praxis. Band I und II*. Oberursel, 1971.

Mintrop, Heinrich, and Hans N. Weiler. "The Relationship between Educational Policy and Practice: The Reconstruction of the College Preparatory Gymnasium in East Germany." *Harvard Educational Revue*, vol. 64, no. 3 (fall 1994), 247–77.

"Mitkommen bitte." *Der Spiegel*, vol. 46 (1965), A4.

Mitter, Armin, and Stefan Wolle. *Untergang auf Raten: unbekannte Kapitel der DDR-Geschichte*. München, 1993.

————, eds. *Ich Liebe euch Doch Alle!: Befehle und Lagerberichte des MfS January-November 1989*. Berlin, 1990.

Möbus, Gerhard. *Unterwerfung durch Erziehung: Zur politischen Pädagogik im sowjetisch besetzten Deutschland*. Mainz, 1965.

Moldenhauer, Gebhard. "2 × Deutschland, 2 × politische Bildung." *Schulpraxis*, vol. 6 (1989), 35–37.

Mommsen, Hans. "History and National Identity: The Case of Germany." *German Studies Review*, vol. 6 (1983).

Monumenta Paedagogica. Dokumente zur Geschichte des Schulwesens in der deutschen demokratischen Republik. Band 6. [East] Berlin, 1970.

Moore-Rinvolucri, Mina J. *Education in East Germany*. Hamdon, Conn., 1973.

Moreau, Patrick, Jürgen Lang, and Viola Neu. *Was will die PDS?* Frankfurt, 1994.

Morgan, Edward P. "Echoes of the Hitler Jugend in Germany." November 27, 1949, 13.

Morshäuser, Bodo. *Warten auf den Führer*. Frankfurt am Main, 1993.

Moss, Walter E. "Reforms in the East German Universities." *German Life and Letters*, October 1954, 56–58.

Müller, Marianne. *Stürmt die Festung Wissenschaft*. [West] Berlin, 1953.

Muhlen, Norbert. "East Germany: The Date Is Still June 17." *The Reporter*, February 16, 1954, 14–18.

————. "East Germany's Planned Men." *American Mercury*, vol. 75 (August 1952), 60–69.

————. "German Youth in a Vaccuum." *Commentary*, vol. 9 (May 1950).

————. *Return of Germany, a Tale of Two Countries*. Chicago, 1953.

————. "Some Student Problems in East Germany." *World Today*, vol. 13, no. 11, November 1957, 481–89.

Muller, Jerry. *The Other God that Failed: Hans Freyer and the Deradicalization of German Conservatism*. Princeton, 1987.

Müller-Michaels, Harro. "The Teacher is not Always Right: Teaching Literature in the Two German States." *European Education*, vol. 23, no. 1 (spring 1991), 59–65.

Muschter, Gabriele, and Rudiger Thomas. *Jenseits der Staatskultur: Traditionen autonomer Kunst in der DDR*. München, 1992.

Mushaben, Joyce Marie. "A Search for Identity: The 'German Question' in Atlantic Alliance Relations." *World Politics*, vol. 50, no. 3 (April 1988).

————. "Swords into Ploughshares: The Church, the State, and the East German Peace Movement." *Studies in Comparative Communism*, vol. 17 (summer 1984), 123–35.

"Music of Hate." *New York Times*, February 8, 1994, 23.

Musiolek, Berndt, Jürgen Eichler, and Carola Wuttke. *Parteien und Politische Bewegungen im letzten Jahr der DDR: Oktober 1989 bis April 1990*. Berlin, 1991.

Naimark, Norman M. *The Russians in Germany: A History of the Soviet Zone of Occupation, 1945–49*. Cambridge, Mass., 1995.

Nawrocki, Joachim. "Die Jugend dem Sozialismus opfern." *Die Zeit*, June 23, 1989, p. 2.

————. "Ein Fest für Honecker." *Die Zeit*, August 19, 1977, 4.

Nener, Gerhart. *Allgemeinbildung. Lehrplanwerk. Unterricht*. [East] Berlin, 1972.

Nettl, J. P. *The Eastern Zone and Soviet Policy in Germany, 1945–50*. London, 1951.

"Neues Weltbild." *Der Spiegel*, vol. 32 (1988), 132.

Neumann, Thomas. *Die Massnahme: eine Herrschaftsgeschichte der SED*. Reinbek bei Hamburg, 1991.

Niermann, Johannes. *Sozialistische Pädagogik in der DDR: Eine wissenschafts-theoretische Untersuchung*. Heidelberg, 1972.

Niethammer, Lutz, Alexander von Plato, and Dorothee Wierling, eds. *Die volkseigene Erfahrung: Eine Archäologie des Lebens in der Industriepassung der DDR*. Berlin, 1991.

Nitsche, Hellmuth. *Zwischen Kreuz und Sowjetstern: Zeugnisse des Kirchenkampfes in der DDR, 1945–81*. Aschaffenburg, 1983.

"Note Eins." *Der Spiegel*, April 14, 1968, 139.

Oehler, Richard. *Friedrich Nietzsche und die deutsche Zukunft*. Leipzig, 1935.

"Olympia im Vatikan." *Der Spiegel*, October 7, 1968, 27–28.

Opp, Karl Dieter, Peter Voss, and Christiane Gern. *Die volkseigene Revolution*. Stuttgart, 1993.

Ostrow, Robin. *Jews in Contemporary East Germany: The Children of Moses in the Land of Marx*. New York, 1989.

Padgett, Stephen, ed. *Parties and Party Systems in the New Germany*. Aldershot, 1993.

Paul, Leslie. "German Youth Under the Occupation." *World Review*, January 1948, 38–41.

Peck, Reginald. "Universities Behind the Iron Curtain." *The Spectator*, May 23, 1952, 666–67.

Penzo, Giorgio. "Zur Frage der 'Entnazifizierung' Friedrich Nietzsches." *Vierteljahrschrift für Zeitgeschichte*, vol. 34 (1986), 105–116.

Pepperle, Heinz. "Revision des marxistischen Nietzsche-Bildes?" *Sinn und Form*, vol. 38 (1986), 934–69.

Peters, H. F. *Zarathustra's Sister: The Case of Elisabeth and Friedrich Nietzsche*. New York, 1977.

Pfahl-Traughber, Armin. *Rechtsextremismus: eine kritische Bestandsaufnahme nach der Wiedervereinigung*. Bonn, 1993.

"Pflaumenköpfe raus." *Der Spiegel*, May 25, 1950, 5–6.

Phillips, David. "Transitions and Traditions: Educational Developments in the New Germany in their Historical Context." *Oxford Studies in Comparative Education*, vol. 2, no. 1 (1992), 121–36.

Pike, David. *The Politics of Culture in Soviet-Occupied Germany, 1945–1949*. Stanford, 1992.

Pleschinski, Hans. *Ostsucht: Eine Jugend im deutsch-deutschen Grenzland*. München, 1993.

PN. "East Germany: A Survey of Soviet Policy, 1945–50." *World Today*, July 1950, 297–308.

Podewin, Norbert. *Walter Ulbricht: eine neue Biographie*. Berlin, 1995.

"Politik bis unters Zeltdach." *Der Spiegel*, August 21, 1972, 38–46.

Pritchard, Rosalind M. O. *The End of Elitism? The Democratisation of the West German University System*. New York, 1990.

Prittie, Terence. "The Protestant Church in East Germany." *The New Statesman*, May 1958, 7–8.

"The Professional Classes in East Germany." *The Listener*, December 25, 1958, 1063–1065.

Pronay, Nicholas, and Keith Wilson, eds. *The Political Re-Education of Germany and Her Allies After World War II*. London, 1985.

Protzman, Ferdinand. "In Europe, Howls of Protest Over Price of Bananas." *New York Times*, February 18, 1993.

Rabinach, Anson. "German Historians Debate the Nazi Past." *Dissent*, vol. 35 (spring 1988), 192–201.

Rauschenbach, Brigitte, ed. *Erinnern, Wiederholen, Durcharbeiten: zur Psychoanalyse Deutscher Wenden*. Berlin, 1992.

"Rebellion in the Rain." *Time*, June 29, 1953, 20–23.

Reifenrath, Bruno H. "Die Nietzsche-Rezeption der nationalsozialistischen Pädagogik." *Vierteljahrschrift für wissenschaftliche Pädagogik*, vol. 56 (1980), 245–69.

Reissig, Rolf, and Gert-Joachim Glaessner. *Das Ende eines Experiments: Umbruch in der DDR und deutsche Einheit*. Berlin, 1991.

Richert, Ernst. *Agitation und Propaganda: Das System der publizistischen Massenführung in der Sowjetzone*. Frankfurt am Main, 1958.

———. *Das zweite Deutschland*. Gütersloh, 1966.

———. *"Sozialistische Universität": Die Hochschulpolitik der SED*. [West] Berlin, 1967.

Richter, Edelbert. *Erlangte Einheit, verfehlte Identität: auf der Suche nach den Grundlagen für eine neue deutsche Politik*. Berlin, 1991.

Riesenberger, Dieter. *Geschichte und Geschichtsunterricht in der DDR*. Göttingen, 1973.

Rinke, Andrea. "From Motzki to Trotzki: Representations of East and West German Cultural Identities on German Television After Reunification." In *The New Germany: Literature and Society after Unification*, ed. Osman Durrani, Colin Good, and Kevin Hilliard. Sheffield [UK], 1995.

Riordan, James. *Sport, Politics and Communism*. Manchester, 1991.

Ritter, Gerhard. "Prospects of a New Germany." *Contemporary Review*, vol. 176 (1949), 205–210.

Rodden, John. *The Politics of Literary Reputation: The Making and Claiming of 'St. George' Orwell*. New York, 1989.

———. "Varieties of Literary Experience: The Prophecies of *1984*." *Zeitschrift für Anglistik und Amerikanistik*, vol. 38 (1990), 209–23.

Roschenlocher, Thomas. "Der Untergang der Banane." In *Begrenzt Glücklich, Kindheit in der DDR*, ed. Wilhelm Solms. Marburg, 1992, 7–11.

Ross, Werner. *Der ängstliche Adler: Friedrich Nietzsches Leben*. Darmstadt, 1980.

———. "Nietzsche taucht aus der Versenkung auf." *Rheinischer Merkur/Christ und Welt*, September 19, 1980.

Rossellini, Jay. *Wolf Biermann*. Munich, 1992.

Rüddenklau, Wolfgang. *Störenfried: DDR-Opposition 1986–1989: mit Texten aus den Umweltblättern*. Berlin, 1992.

Rudder, Helmut de. "Transforming Higher Education in East Germany." *Review of Higher Education*, vol. 16, no. 4 (summer 1993), 391–417.

Russ, Gisela, ed. *Dokumente zur Kunst-, Literatur- und Kulturpolitik der SED, 1971–74*. Stuttgart, 1976.

Rust, Val Dean. *Education in East and West Germany: A Bibliography*. New York, 1984.

Rust, Val, and Diane Rust. *The Unification of German Education*. New York, 1995.

Ruther, Günther. *Greif zur Feder, Kumpel: Schriftsteller, Literatur und Politik in der DDR 1949–1990.* Düsseldorf, 1991.

———. *Zwischen Anpassung und Kritik: Literatur im real existierenden Sozialismus der DDR.* Melle, 1989.

Ryback, Anthony. *Rock Around the Bloc.* New York, 1990.

Sandford, Gregory W. *From Hitler to Ulbricht: The Communist Reconstruction of East Germany, 1945–46.* Princeton, 1983.

SBZ-Biographie: ein biographisches Nachschlagebuch über die Sowjetische Besatzungszone Deutschlands. Bonn, 1964.

SBZ von 1955 bis 1958: die Sowjetische Besatzungszone Deutschlands in den Jahren 1955–1958. Bonn, 1966.

Schäfer, Peter. "United States History at the Universities in the Former German Democratic Republic." *History Teacher,* vol. 25, no. 3 (May 1992), 339–44.

Schalk, Hans. "Der historische Stoff—entscheidende Grundlage für Bildung und Erziehung im Geschichtsunterricht." *Geschichtsunterricht und Staatsbürgerkunde,* vol. 7 (1965), 568–76.

Schedlinski, Rainer. *Die Arroganz der Ohnmacht: Aufsätze und Zeitungsbeiträge 1989 und 1990.* Berlin, 1991.

Schick, Jack M. *The Berlin Crisis, 1958–62.* Philadelphia, 1971.

Schiller, Bill. "West Berliners Resent High Cost of Integration." *Toronto Star,* October 29, 1993, A21.

Schiller, Dieter, and Helmut Bock. *Dialog über Tradition und Erbe.* [East] Berlin, 1976.

Schilling-Werra, Georg J. *Im Osten wird es hell: Tatsachenroman um den Volksaufstand in der DDR am 17. Juni.1953.* Graz, 1983.

Schlenker, Wolfram. *Das 'Kulturelles Erbe' in der DDR: Gesellschaftliche Entwicklung und Kulturpolitik, 1945–1965.* Stuttgart, 1977.

Schlesak, Dieter. *Stehendes Ich in laufender Zeit.* Leipzig, 1994.

Schmidt, Burghart. *Ernst Bloch.* Stuttgart, 1985.

Schmidt, Gerlind. *Hochschulen in der DDR. Eine Untersuchung zum Verhältnis von Bildungs- und Beschäftigungssystem.* Cologne/Vienna, 1982.

———. *Die polytechnische Bildung in der Sowjetunion und in der DDR; didaktische Konzeptionen und Lösungsversuche.* [West] Berlin, 1973.

Schneider, Eberhard. *Die DDR: Geschichte, Politik, Wirtschaft, Gesellschaft.* Stuttgart, 1977.

Schneider, Peter. *Vom Ende der Gewissheit.* Berlin, 1994.

———. *The German Comedy.* New York, 1991.

Schneider, Rolf. *Frühling im Herbst: Notizen vom Untergang der DDR.* Göttingen, 1991.

Schöneburg, Karl-Heinz. *Errichtung des Arbeiter-und-Bauernstaates der DDR, 1945–1949.* [West] Berlin, 1983.

Schröder, Klaus, and Peter Erler. *Geschichte und Transformation des SED- Staates: Beiträge und Analysen.* Berlin, 1994.

Schubbe, Elimar, ed. *Dokumente zur Kunst-, Literatur- und Kulturpolitik der SED.* Stuttgart, 1972.

Schultz, Joachim. *Der Funktionär in der Einheitspartei: Kaderpolitik und Bürokratisierung in der SED.* Stuttgart, 1956.

Schulze, Winfried. *Deutsche Geschichtswissenschaft nach 1945.* München, 1989.

Schütz, Wilhelm Wolfgang. *Bewährung im Widerstand.* Stuttgart, 1956.

Schwik, Heimo. "Eine Andacht für den Antichrist." *Rheinischer Merkur/Christ und Welt*, August 31, 1990, 21.

"Schwierigkeiten mit dem Grössenwahn." *Süddeutsche Zeitung*, January 20, 1990, 9.

S.E.S., "New Policy Trends in East Germany." *World Today*, vol. 12, no. 5 (May 1956), 173–81.

"The Seventeenth of June." *New Yorker*, vol. 29 (August 29, 1953), 33–51.

Shears, David. *Ugly Frontier*. New York, 1970.

Shingleton, Bradley A., Marina J. Gibbon, and Kathryn S. Mach, eds. *Dimensions of German Unification: Economic, Social, and Legal Analyses*. Boulder, 1995.

Shirley, Dennis. *The Politics of Progressive Education: The Odenwaldschule in Nazi Germany*. Cambridge, Mass., 1992.

Siebert, Horst. *"Bildung"spraxis in Deutschland: BRD und DDR im Vergleich*. Düsseldorf, 1970.

Sievert, Christel, and Herbert Mühlstadt, ed. *Zu Fragen der Erziehung im Geschichtsunterricht*, [East] Berlin, 1955.

Sippel, Heinrich. *Staatssicherheit und Rechtsextremismus*. Bochum, 1994.

"Skinheads' Records Alarm Germans." *Chicago Tribune*, November 24, 1992, 2.

Smith, Anthony D. *National Identity*. London, 1991.

"National Identity and the Idea of European Unity." *International Affairs*, vol. 68 (1992), 55–76.

Smith, Duncan. *Walls and Mirrors: Western Representations of Really Existing German Socialism in the German Democratic Republic*. Lanham, Md., 1988.

Smith, Jean Edward. *Germany Beyond the Wall: People, Politics, . . . and Prosperity*. Boston, 1969.

———. "The Red Prussianism of the German Democratic Republic." *Political Science Quarterly*, vol. 82, no. 3 (September 1967).

Spittmann, Ilse, and Karl Wilhelm Fricke. *17. Juni 1953*. Köln, 1982.

Spittmann, Ilse, and Gisela Helwig. *DDR Lesebuch: Stalinisierung, 1949–1955*. Köln, 1991.

"Spur der Steine." *Der Spiegel*, vol. 52 (1965), 50–51.

"Stalin Still a Hero to German Pupils." *New York Times*, July 15, 1956, 8.

Stärke, Frank Christian. *Krise ohne Ende: Parteiendemokratie vor neuen Herausforderungen*. Köln, 1993.

Stärke, Manfred. "Stationen der marxistischen Rilke-Rezeption." *Rilke-Studien: Zu Werk und Wirkungsgeschichte*, ed. Edda Bauer. East Berlin, 1974.

Steele, Jonathan. *Inside East Germany: The State That Came in From the Cold*. New York, 1977.

Stern, Carola. *Walter Ulbricht: A Political Biography*. New York, 1965.

Sternberger, Dolf. *Staatsfreundschaft*. Frankfurt, 1947.

Strenk, Andrew. "Diplomats in Track Suits: Linkages Between Sports and Foreign Policy in the German Democratic Republic." In *Sport and International Relations*, ed. Benjamin Lowe, David B. Kanin, and Andrew Strenk. Champaign, 1978.

"Strich durch den Namen." *Der Spiegel*, vol. 15 (1966).

Stürmer, Michael. *Dissonanzen des Fortschritts: Essays über Geschichte und Politik in Deutschland*. München, 1986.

Sullivan, Walter. "In East Germany." *New York Times*, March 29, 1955.

Sutterlin, James S., and David Klein. *Berlin: From Symbol of Confrontation to Keystone of Stability*. New York, 1989.

Sweet, Denis M. "Friedrich Nietzsche in the GDR: A Problematic Reception." In *Studies in GDR Culture and Society 4: Selected Papers from the Ninth New Hampshire Symposium on the German Democratic Republic*, ed. Marjorie Gerber, 227–43. Lanham, Md., 1984.

Tagliabue, John. "Evolution in Europe." *New York Times*, September 29, 1990, 7.

Tent, James F. *The Free University of Berlin: A Political History*. Bloomington, 1988.

Thomas, Hinton. *Nietzsche in German Politics and Society, 1890–1918*. London, 1983.

Treichel, Hans. "Probleme bei der Behandlung hervorragender Persönlichkeiten der Geschichte." *Geschichtsunterricht und Staatsbürgerkunde*, vol. 7 (1963), 600–617.

Trilling, Lionel. *The Liberal Imagination*. New York, 1950.

Trittin, Jürgen. *Gefahr aus der Mitte: Die Republik rutscht nach rechts*. Göttingen, 1993.

"The Two Berlins." *Commonweal*, August 24, 1951, 467.

Uhlig, Gottfried. *Monumenta Paedagogica. Band II. Der Beginn der Antifaschistisch-Demokratischen Schulreform, 1945–46*. [East] Berlin, 1965.

———. *Monumenta Paedagogica. Band XIV. Zur Entwicklung des Volksbildungswesens in der Deutschen Demokratischen Republik in den Jahren 1949–56*. [East] Berlin, 1974.

Ulbricht, Walter. "Whither Germany?" *Speeches and Essays on the National Question*. Dresden, 1966.

Ulbricht, Walter, Willi Stoph, and Erich Honecker. *German Democratic Republic at the Beginning of Its Third Decade*. Dresden, 1969.

Ulbricht's Wall: Facts, Figures, Dates. Bonn/Berlin, 1965.

"University Reforms in the Soviet Zone of Germany." *Department of State Bulletin*, December 3, 1951, 907–908.

Van der Vat, Dan. *Freedom Was Never Like This: A Winter's Journey in East Germany*. London, 1991.

Vinokur, Martin Barry. "Sport as an Instrument for National Integration in East Germany." In *More Than a Game: Sports and Politics*, ed. Martin Barry Virokur, Westport, 1988.

Voelmy, Willi. *Polytechnischer Unterricht in der zehnklassigen allgemeinbildenden Oberschule der DDR seit 1964*. Frankfurt am Main, 1968.

Vogt, Hartmut. *DDR; Theorie und Praxis der Lehrplanrevision in der Deutschen Demokratischen Republik*. München, 1972.

Vogt, Hartmut, et al. *Schule und Betrieb in der DDR*. Köln, 1970.

Völker, Klaus. *Bertolt Brecht: Eine Biographie*. Munich, 1976.

Vollnhals, Clemens, ed. *Entnazifizierung: Politische Säuberung und Rehabilitierung in den vier Besatzungszonen, 1945–49*. Munich, 1991.

Wallace, Ian. *East Germany: The German Democratic Republic*. Oxford, 1987.

———. *The GDR under Honecker, 1971–81*. Dundee, 1981.

"Walter Ulbricht—das sind wir alle." *Der Spiegel*, April 1960, 30–32.

Walwei-Weigelmann, Hedwig. *Die Wunde Namens Deutschland: ein Lesebuch zur deutschen Teilung*. Freiburg, 1981.

Wann bricht schon mal ein Staat zusammen!: die Debatte über die Stasi-Akten und die DDR-Geschichte auf dem 39. Deutschen Historikertag. München, 1993.

Ward, Barbara. "The Crucial Battle for the World's Youth." *New York Times*, November 3, 1951, 13–14, 71–73.

Watson, Alan. *The Germans: Who Are They Now?* London, 1992.

Weber, Hermann. *Aufbau und Fall einer Diktatur: kritische Beiträge zur Geschichte der DDR.* Koln, 1991.

———. *DDR: Grundriss der Geschichte.* Hannover, 1991.

———. *Die DDR 1945–1990.* München, 1993.

Weber, Jürgen, and Thomas Ammer. *Der SED-Staat: Neues über eine Vergangene Diktatur.* München, 1994.

Wegner, Gregory P. "Germany's Past Contested: The Soviet-American Conflict in Berlin over History Curriculum Reform, 1945–48." *History of Education Quarterly,* vol. 30 (spring 1990), 1–16.

———. "Ideological Change and Curriculum Transition: Teaching About the Legacy of the Third Reich in East German Secondary Schools." *Education Today,* vol. 44 (1994), 14–21.

———. "In the Shadow of Buchenwald: The *Jugendstunde* and the Legitimation of Anti-Fascist Heroes for East German Youth." *German Studies Review* vol. 19 (1996), 127–46.

———. "The Legacy of Nazism and the History Curriculum in the Secondary Schools." *History Teacher,* vol. 25, no. 4 (August 1992), 471–87.

Weidenfeld, Werner, ed. *Die Identität der Deutschen.* Munich, 1983.

Wendt, Emil. *Bonner Berichte aus Mittel- und Ostdeutschland: Die Entwicklung in der Sowjetische Besatzungszone seit 1945.* Berlin/Bonn, 1959.

Wer ist Wer in der SBZ? Ein Biographisches Handbuch. [West] Berlin, 1958.

"Wie Sokrates." *Der Spiegel,* vol. 12 (1964), 33–34.

Wilhelm, Jutta. *Jugend in der DDR: der Weg zur "sozialistischen Persönlichkeit".* [West] Berlin, 1983.

"Will East Germany Blow Again?" *Saturday Evening Post,* June 1, 1957, 28–31, 79–83.

Williams, Raymond. "What Happened at Munich." *The Listener,* vol. 88 (September 14, 1972), 321–22.

Williams, Rhys W., Stephen Parker, and Colin Riordan, eds. *German Writers and the Cold War 1945–61.* Manchester, 1992.

Windsor, Philip. *City on Leave: A History of Berlin, 1945–62.* New York, 1963.

Winkler, Heinrich August. "Rebuilding of a Nation: The Germans Before and After Reunification." *Daedalus,* January 1994, 107–127.

Winkler, Karl. *Made in GDR: Jugendszenen aus Ost-Berlin.* [West] Berlin, 1983.

"Wir sehen die rote Fahne." *Der Spiegel,* November 22, 1950, 6–7.

Wollkopf, Rosawith. "Die Gremien des Nietzsche-Archivs und ihre Beziehungen zum Faschismus." *Im Vorfeld der Literatur,* ed. Karl-Heinz Hahn. Weimar, 1991.

———. "Das Nietzsche-Archiv im Spiegel der Beziehungen Elisabeth Forster-Nietzsches zu Harry Graf Kessler." *Jahrbuch der Deutschen Schillergesellschaft,* ed. Wilfried Barner, Walter Müller-Seidel, and Ulbricht Ott, 125–70. Weimar, 1990.

Wood, Nancy. "The Holocaust: Historical Memories and Contemporary Identities." *Media, Culture, and Society,* vol. 13 (1991), 360–76.

Woods, Roger, ed. *Opposition in the GDR under Honecker, 1971–85.* New York, 1986.

Worst, Anne. *Das Ende eines Geheimdienstes, oder, Wie lebendig ist die Stasi?.* Berlin, 1991.

Wyden, Peter. *Wall: The Inside Story of Divided Berlin.* New York, 1989.

Yack, Bernard. *The Longing for Total Revolution: Philosophic Sources of Social Discontent from Rousseau to Marx and Nietzsche*. Princeton, 1986.

"Youth in East Germany." *Survey*, vol. 87 (October 1951), 417.

"Youthfest in Berlin." *Time*, August 13, 1973, 39.

"Zeit der Bedrängnis." *Der Spiegel*, January 3, 1966, 29.

Zimmerman, Hartmut, Horst Ulrich, and Michael Fehlauer. *DDR Handbuch*. Köln, 1985.

Zimmerman, Hartmut, and Gert-Joachim Glaessner. *Die DDR in der Ära Honecker: Politik, Kultur, Gesellschaft*. Opladen, 1988.

Zipes, Jack. "Ernst Bloch and the Obscenity of Hope." *New German Critique*, vol. 45 (fall 1988), 3–8.

"Zu einem Fest der Familie." *Der Spiegel*, August 1, 1951, 5.

Zudeick, Peter. *Der Hintern des Teufels: Ernst Bloch, Leben und Werk*. Buhl-Moos, 1985.

"Zur Zeit unterwegs." *Der Spiegel*, September 16, 1968, 40–41.

Zwahr, Hartmut. *Ende einer Selbstzerstörung: Leipzig und die Revolution in der DDR*. Göttingen, 1993.

Zwerenz, Gerhard. "Ein Partisan dichtet sich selbst." *Frankfurter Rundschau*, September 16, 1985, 3.

Index